ADVENTURES OF NIMON
Volume One

Raymond Hoche-Mong

MONTARA, CALIFORNIA

Raymond Hoche-Mong
835 George Street, POB 370937
Montara, CA 94037-0937

Publisher's Note: I have tried to recreate events, locales and conversations from my memories of them. In order to maintain their anonymity in some instances I have changed the names of individuals and places, I may have changed some identifying characteristics and details such as physical properties, occupations and places of residence.

Book Layout © 2014 BookDesignTemplates.com

Editing by Christine Myers, ladymyerswordsmithing.com

Cover Design by Debbie Brady

Cover Formatting by Eileen Swift

Adventures of Nimon: Volume 1/ Raymond Hoche-Mong. -- 1st ed.
ISBN 978-1530252398

CONTENTS

Photographs

To Emily Darden, and to Dominique and Michel

who have been patient with me.

Acknowledgments

Several people have given me encouragement and also have shared information to help me write this autobiography. I will mention a few but will have to leave out a number of names because listing them would convert this book into an enormous volume.

I began writing it in 1995 as a letter to my children but then my daughter, the English and Medievalist scholar, suggested that a book would be more appropriate. Since that comment, my daughter has been invaluable in helping me manage my thoughts. I am grateful for her support.

Someone sent me a quote stating that if I wanted to be a writer I needed to marry an English major. I did. I married Emily, she has become over the years my best critic and editor of all my writings both professional and personal.

Because I have not kept a journal or notes but relied only on recollections, I am grateful to all who have contributed details; especially the many who have helped me remember facts, incidents, the names of people, project details, and sundry other necessary historical bits and pieces. I will mention a few and hope that those not included will forgive me because they are not forgotten.

I am happy to note Dr. Rebecca Jernigan, a friend of many years and an avid fan. Dr. Stuart White a colleague during our graduate academic years and still a person I turn to when I need to discuss important issues. Drs. Denis Slavich and Ronald Brooks, and also Robert Jackson, who have given me support and crucial details on issues that were related to my work on projects. In addition, I cannot omit Barry and Margaret Pugh from the list; both have been stalwart supporters for many years.

In addition, I am indebted for the information and direction shared with me by Glenn Plymate, Charles Sands, Umberto Bozzo, the Reverend John Schively, the Right Reverend William E. Sanders, the late Reverend Therrel Holt, the late Right Reverend and Lord Peter Walker, the late Reverend and Attorney Donald Mackenzie Williamson, the late Colonel Lawson Wynn (USAF Retired), and the late Ralph Finch (retired mayor of McCaysville,

GA), Newell (Do) Anderson — my last living college classmate. What is notable in this acknowledgement is the number of dear friends who have terminated their travels around the Sun!

A note of gratitude for Nancy Key for her generous hospitality to share her house and to allow me to work without interruption.

Eileen Swift has applied her graphic design talents to the formatting of the cover and I also appreciate the attention to details and creative enthusiasm she has imparted beyond being an invaluable friend.

Readers of sections of the books such as Emily Oppegard, Dr. Kate Hodgson, James and Ellen Ellingsworth, and James Harrington have been most helpful in sharing suggestions, photographs, anecdotes, and various tid bits for enriching the book.

My editor Christine Myers has been helpful in many ways, especially in searching for a publisher, tending to details that turn a story into a book, and for being the reliable administrator, something that I cannot possibly want to do. Christine has the patience of an angel and the good judgment of a genius.

This autobiography could not have been written without the wisdom, the astuteness, the editorial management, and the love and support of Emily my "tractor", associate, world traveling partner, and wife.

Finally, any errors are my responsibility and any interpretation of facts is simply the result of my perspective; we each have our own way of accepting reality.

I have shared many tasty meals and expansive conversations with Raymond. He engages both with élan. Nourishing body and mind; taking time to break—or make—bread, RHM draws out tales that reveal a companion's underlying passion and often the chance to share the works created to express it. RHM seeks the ebb and flow of creative process, with its potential for deep, connecting recognition. For Raymond, this is an everyday act, an art of living, connecting people to one another, to themselves, back to the places within from which so much originates.

Emily Oppegard, Artist

The Purpose Intended

Writing an autobiography, even in its simplest form, is difficult and challenging for me. It is also an exercise, I believe, in both egocentricity and integrity.

Who will care to read it and why? Where does one begin? At birth? Before birth? When one becomes aware that time is sufficiently important because less and less of it remains as one grows older? Then what does one include and what is excluded?

It is obvious also that one does not know firsthand all the facts, all the details, all the nuances that accompany one's life because some parts depend on hearsay, some parts are interpolated from various facts and bits of oral history, some are selectively shared to complete a picture that is fragmented, and some are simply remodeled to attain a level of coherency that otherwise would be unavailable. I shall share what I presume to know.

I must admit that my sources never furnish me with unmitigated factual information because oral history is often clothed in myth. Myth, however, is not a lie but an event that has become important enough to carry its own symbolic value and hence has adopted many layers of value giving it embellishment.

I have not kept a diary. I do not have access to letters, notes, autobiographies, and certainly not access to relatives. After going to school I lost contact with most, if not all of them. I'm certain that I have no living relatives who would know me. Moreover, I have been separated from family for many years as a consequence of the Second World War, a war that killed or scattered my family to the seven continents of the globe. If a few relatives exist, I do not know where they are. I'm certain that here and there a few folks remain who might claim a link with me, but because I have been independent, unconnected, and away from where family members used to call home, it would be difficult for anyone to contribute to this autobiography.

A few who read this work may have a different interpretation of some of my actions; they may even attempt to analyze my motives. So be it. I am the only one who is able to say anything about my motives. No one can be inside my brain and interpret them. They are my motives and mine alone. Hence it is my life as I see it, understand it, enjoyed it (more often than not), and lived it.

This autobiography is written in response to many questions, some asked explicitly and others implicitly. It is also written to address some of the questions that have been asked and whose answers have been ignored over the past several decades.

I am convinced that history has its importance and one should explore one's own portion of it. Some parts of my story were kept from common knowledge because of a promise I made as a youngster to my mother, around 1947, and have honored since then. Indeed, now I see that the promise made by a young man was not only silly but truly infantile. For what it was worth, I kept it. The result of this promise may be disconcerting to many who know me, and a few people may question my judgment for keeping quiet. Nevertheless, I kept the promise. But I have since learned that promises are a bane that haunts humanity. Why? Because we agree to make a promise never really knowing what the future is going to be, the mitigating consequences that might surface, and who we are going to be as we mature. If time does not stop at a particular moment why do we expect the flow of life, of circumstance, of occasions to be arrested?

In May 1995 my mother died. By her death, I was released from the promise. It has always been my understanding that upon her death I could reveal the core of the secret. If it has taken long to write all this it is because it is difficult to gather all the facts and place them in a coherent fabric — at least as coherently as I am able to do it.

Brian Lamb, the one-time host of C-SPAN's "Booknote," often asked the guest author the following denuding questions: "Why did you write the book?" and "Who do you think will read it?"

Most authors are taken aback by these queries. Why does one write a book and who is the expected readership? In my case I hope to tell the story of someone who has led an interesting life and who hopes to give the world a little more than he has received. A major historical personage I have not been, but neither have I been just a mere cog in the workings of humanity. As I have oftentimes suggested, no one is unimportant, no one is insignificant, and no one needs to be condemned to the shadows of life. Each human being is valuable and hence the life of that human being is worth noting because it also offers certain contributing qualities, qualities that may help others to live a more profound life.

I am the product of being a child of World War Two. That war has left in me indelible marks that have affected me throughout my life. For example: loud blasting noises rattle me to the core; I cannot buy groceries without purchasing more than I need because my reasoning is that I may not be able to find the items another day; I am almost anxious when I cross borders, when I see border guards, when my passport document is examined; much as I like to be in Germany, I am always cautious when I walk the streets, enter shops, or undertake any transactions. War is not forgotten; it is always present in the mind of a war child. I am that child, a child without a real home because I am not French, not Egyptian, not English, not Italian, and not quite American. I cannot attend a school reunion because I have no school. I cannot see members of my family because I cannot locate them. A war child is an orphan and it is high time that adults recognize what war does to their children.

I intend to explain that I have tried to reinvent myself by keeping what I judged to be good from my parents and tossing out what I thought to be less than admirable, that I have tried to acquire from society, friends, mentors, and others certain qualities that would enhance my person, and to share some insights.

Each one of us living on this earth has the opportunity to redesign him/herself. The task is tedious, complex, and ongoing but the result ends up being much better than what we started with. Thus to read what is being offered in this autobiography may be valuable to many people; it may suggest that no life is irrelevant.

As for the second question posed by Lamb, I'm not certain that I can answer it. In the larger content of society, I'm not a known entity. In comparison to most people I'm an unknown, except perhaps among colleagues, friends (and I only have a few), and people I've touched through projects, speeches, and technical papers. But no, I'm not a known entity hence I'm not at all certain who will read this autobiography. Nevertheless, each one of us who has lived has a story to tell and to share; to share because no human being is irrelevant, no life is without a quality that makes it important, and no person who has trod on this planet has not left an imprint. Why are you reading this autobiography?

No parent is perfect. No parent attends a school to learn the task of parenthood. Of course there are "parenting" courses given by many institutions. But parenting, when all is said and done, is learned on-the-job by trial and error. And so mistakes are made because the job is difficult and we are not perfect. The same is true for children; it is an on-the-job learning process for them, too.

As offspring of imperfect parents we learn (at least some do) to be selective in shaping our stance, who we want to be, who we think we can be. Like the painter and his palette full of pigments, who incorporates some colors and rejects others or mixes a few of them to obtain a new shade, we engage in a selection process that is undeniably a painstaking one but in the end produces a work of art. The result is perhaps not quite as clearly defined in a human being; nevertheless it is a better product than the original specimen, one would hope.

Life is a process of selecting how best to become a citizen of this planet. The quest for most of us, if not the goal, is to leave this earth a little better than when we entered it. This autobiography is a testimony to that purpose, despite, or perhaps in part because, I am a child of the most violent wars that ever mankind produced.

I am certain there is much I have left out. Writing an autobiography is a tedious endeavor but I shall do the best I can. Because I don't view history as a chronicle of consecutive facts, which to me is a boring proposition, I tend to dramatize the process by rounding the corners, by polishing the facts, and by presenting a crystal with several facets, each of which reflects a bit of the overall perspective. Life is not a technical assembly book where each step leads directly to the next. Life is a drama where each scene contributes to the next emerging scene and then on to the conclusion. Each scene is viewed differently by the audience, each action is perceived personally, and each movement is interpreted through one's own history; the author and playwright are set aside. The viewer or reader molds the topic as he or she wishes. Like a play, life is also a process. One scene follows another and the next is anticipated. The termination is still the same.

Follow your star
(Dante Alighieri)

I

PART ONE

The Act of Gathering

On my sixth birthday my grandfather, Joseph, thought that it was high time this young boy, Raymond, learned something about the birds, the bees, and the wonders of mating. My grandfather was an extraordinary person. He was my mother's father, a physician, a pharmacist, and a most adorable human being. Now who was this boy Raymond?

It was at noon on Sunday 8 May 1932, that I first yelled to the world that I was alive and ready to make my mark. The years passed quickly and much was said to me about those early years by my parents and members of my family. My own memory is not very clear about those first years. As a young boy I recollect living in Cairo and in Alexandria and playing in the garden of our house with boys and girls from the neighborhood but the details are not very distinct. Yet even now I vividly recall seeing the shutters of our house in Alexandria being removed, tied together and then thrown into the sea for cleaning. During those early years I don't remember attending any organized or school. I do remember being taught to read and also listening to poetry and fiction when either my mother or father, both great readers, introduced me to books or read to me. Books, very early in my childhood, were important to me because they offered ways to learn about many events, people, interesting places in the world, and the histories of different cultures.

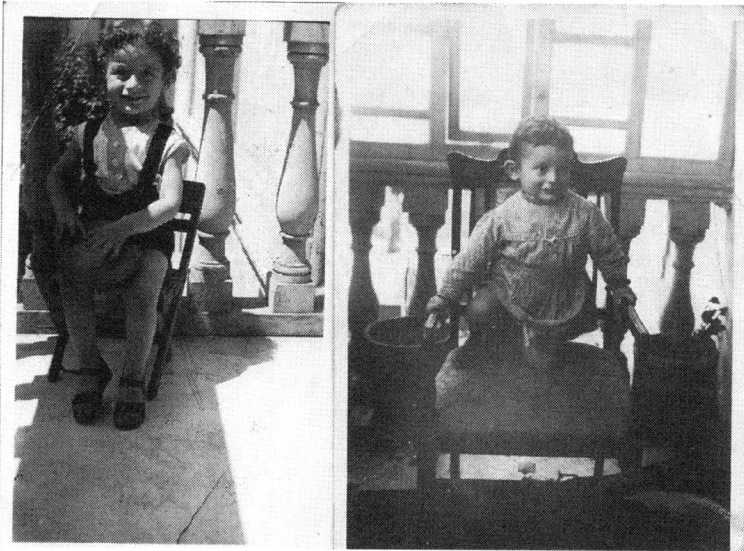

Author at three years & at 20 months

Indelibly etched in my brain is the birth of my younger brother Sylvain. His entrance into our family was a momentous occasion, but he died soon and I cannot say that I remember him clearly. He was tiny and not too noisy or active. He became ill with meningitis and that is all that I can recall.

Another important memory is a gift given to me by my mother's father. As mentioned earlier, on my sixth birthday my grandfather, Joseph, thought that it was high time this young boy, Raymond, learned something about the birds, the bees, and the wonders of mating. Grandpère gave me a brown and white Turkish male pigeon with a crest on its head and a beautiful white female columbine dove.

I was ecstatic and hugged my grandfather several times. I was filled with joy to have my beautiful pigeons. It seems that with the pair in my arms I ran around the house several times until I was stopped and reminded that the birds were not going to be too happy to be subjected to the noise I was making and the behavior I was imparting to them.

The pigeons were going to become my teachers, and sure enough they did teach me a great deal about caring for others, about responsibility, about recognizing that I was not the center of my universe, and that I could express love in many ways to many creatures.

When my pigeons were settled in individual cages that had access to freedom when I opened the enclosing catch, I could monitor their behavior and learn about how they managed their existence as pairs of birds. One morning after breakfast I opened the cages and released the pigeons. Twenty pairs of pigeons fluttered into the warm, clear, humid, Cairo blue sky.

Of course I had a lot of help from Grandpère with the cages and the general setup for the pigeons. It wasn't long after I had the pigeons that the columbine produced two eggs, and not long after that I heard the chirping of the little young pigeons craving food from their parents.

Pigeons are fun to raise; I learned much from watching them. The male cares for the female and is quite attentive to the needs of his mate. Pigeons try to be good parents who feed and tend their young, and always return to their nests, no matter how far they are from them. Monogamy is always their mode of operation; hence they live all their lives with the same mate. Mine showed that they were implicitly monogamous as long as I had them.

My grandfather added another pair of columbine pigeons, which soon enough produced a new pair of offspring that mated with some of the offspring of the original pigeons and on and on it went. Pigeons are great multipliers and in a few months I had several pairs of beautiful pigeons, all offspring of my original Turkish and columbine pair and of the new white African columbine pair.

With a white flag attached to a two-meter pole, and by watching other pigeon owners in the local park, soon I learned to manage the flight of pigeons, to guide them to that tree or that roof or that ledge. After some practice and training for both the pigeons and their keeper, when a neighboring flight would be aloft, I was able to direct my flight right through the other flight and not lose a single pair.

Tending to pigeons was a fine hobby for a young lad. "Sex" was no longer a nasty word to be avoided but became a constructive element for understanding animal — and later in life human — behavior. I enjoyed the hobby and still remember my excitement surfacing when I discovered that a new pair of pigeons had been born overnight.

No, we never ate the pigeons, but I did have to give them away when it was time for me to leave for school — but that is another story. I could write volumes about tending pigeons, the behavior of the birds, even the street variety, but my task is not ornithology but to write an autobiography. I shall do it forthwith.

The Shaded Truth

I hope that this insight is accepted with grace and with much understanding. It has not been easy to evade questions on the subject that has been shrouded in a secret and I've always tried to avoid long discussions of the issue. I did try to glue together two traditions and a generous portion of history that fortunately supported the story employed to answer queries on the subject. I knew that ultimately the truth had to be told but the time for telling it had to be chosen when it could no longer affect my mother's wishes or put me in a more tenuous position with her.

I am aware that my mother was not the only one affected by this untold story and that several persons who are connected to me have also been influenced. My children, my friends, my colleagues, and others not specifically identified here, however, were considered always even when it was obvious that their involvement was counter to their and my will. But I had foolishly accepted — though not entirely — to participate in this lie, this management of truth.

I had also agreed to bind myself with the silence of a promise. Promises are the shackles that inhibit our liberty to abide by our honor to be good neighbors, good citizens, good offspring, and good persons. Had I not made the promise, I could have argued with my mother that its purpose was no longer relevant to her life — nor to mine.

The promise, however, became a tool for her to hold me tightly to a frozen moment in my youth. The lesson has currency in many situations in life. A promise is made at a certain age, at a certain moment, for a certain occasion and then we grow older, we grow out of the relationship, we enter new situations, we change from one age to another, from one perspective to another, perhaps even from immaturity to a higher level broaching the semblance of maturity. The alternative then is to keep our word! To keep our word is an exercise in building trust, to become a person whose word is sterling. When that happens, when trust surfaces, promises become unnecessary. That, however, is a difficult transition to achieve.

And so, now I can share the important facts that for many years have been kept secret.

Underpinning

I have always maintained that my origin was rooted in the French culture. I have often visited France, have concentrated some of my interests in France, and have maintained my fluency in French. I have been heard to complain about the French in general terms: their ethics or lack of ethics, their attitudes, their political mentality, their mode of operation on the world's scene, especially their crass mercantilism, their cooking, and their self-importance.

I have also been proud to be linked to the French culture. I have loved their sense of art in whatever they do. To be French is to be passionate. To be French is to be proud. It is to be loved or hated by others, but never ignored. To be French is to bear the responsibility of complexity and ambiguity. As I have often said, I am French in origin by accident of parental connection. It is inescapable that I carry French attitudes toward life, some of which I consciously reject, but many that I dearly cherish.

In me you will also find a strong connection with the culture found in northern Italy. That is so because my family originated from the frontier section of Europe that joins Italy and France. This is the region of the Mont Blanc, a lovely portion of God's acreage. Connected to it is the Aosta Valley, a region often disputed and often claimed by both France and Italy, depending on the political circumstances. As for me, I was born in Cairo, Egypt. I am also an American naturalized citizen by choice and not by accident. One might then say that I am a French-Afro-American human being who was educated in England and in the United States of America.

The question then to be answered is: who am I? Once I shed the coating that has prevented me from stating the whole truth because of a promise, I will still remain the same person. You, the reader, may change your attitude towards me. You may feel cheated because many of the blank gaps were filled in to shade the truth, but the truth may appear to be less of an embellishment of reality than one may surmise. You may realize that the names you bear (even for Dominique and Michel) are less enigmatic now than before you read this document. Nevertheless, I offer no apology for opening the door to reveal what is no longer a secret, a secret that I found deplorable long ago. Thus, who is Raymond Hoche-Mong?

That I have reinvented myself and continue to do so is a fact of life, as I understand it. So let me share a few photons to shed light on the issue of who I am, just a few, because there are too many aspects to a person's life and identity that cannot be revealed in an autobiography. Since some of you have known me for many years, you may know more than you realize about me. Those few selected photons will give you the means to interpolate much of the whole. Be mindful that I am not about to write a confession. I will continue to maintain some degree of privacy both to safeguard my motives and to avoid standing naked before you.

My father was William (Guillaume) Hoche. He was born in Les Houches, a small hamlet in Haute Savoie, near Chamonix. This region links France and Italy, and is not far from the Swiss border and the city of Geneva, which lies approximately 95 kilometers northeast of Chamonix. It is also across the border from Italy and not too far from the Franco-Italian city of Aosta, to which we are much closer in temperament and language than to the Swiss. In fact most of the family, including me, possessed dual citizenship — French and Italian. The people in Aosta and in the region speak more French than they do Italian. The famous 11.6-kilometer Tunnel du Mont Blanc carved through the Alps connects Chamonix in France and Entrèves in Italy. The Italian-French border crosses the tunnel midway.

I am told that the name for the village "Houches" is a way the local villagers in their French-Italian dialect pronounced the word "hoche" but who can tell how it was pronounced centuries ago? The story I received was that the regional government adopted this pronunciation in making the signs identifying the village after World War II. When Italy invaded the village in 1941, the name became "hocco."

In 1943 the Vichy government, those collaborators with the Nazi Germans, changed the name to "houcé." The compromise came about in 1947 with the current name Les Houches, an adaptation of the original, ancient "hoche."

At any rate this is the story I was given when I met the mayor of the village (a retired history professor) in 1959. The village of Les Houches lies approximately eight kilometers west of Chamonix and fortunately off the main Autoroute to Geneva in the northeast. Les Houches is at an elevation of 1,200 meters and looks directly at the Mont Blanc's northern face, the peak of which rises above 4,800 meters and is covered in snow year-round.

Obviously, you can recognize that the name reflects the identity of the major inhabitants of the village, the Hoche family of which a certain famous military man is a descendent: General Lazare Hoche born in 1765, son of Louis Hoche and Anne Merlière, of Chamonix and Versailles respectively. Louis was a prominent horse trainer. The family predates the general by several centuries.

Albert Hoche was a friend and associate of the philosopher and mathematician Pascal, a leader of the Jansenism Movement in France.

Guillaume (William) Hoche was Ambassador of France to the court of Elizabeth I of England for several years and died and was buried in Bury St. Edmond's the year of the Queen's death.

Thus the family of Hoche reaches back into history a long way. A genealogist would have a pleasurable time searching for the roots, branches, and leaves of this, the historic Hoche family. The City Library of Lyons has several sources for additional information on the Hoche family.

Recently I was informed that there are no Hoches left in Les Houches. After a short visit to the town in 1988 I was told at the Hotel de Ville (City

Hall) in Chamonix, where the regional records are kept, that there was no one by the name of Hoche in the town. There are some gravestones of members of the family, but none that I knew. I do know that World War II destroyed the family or scattered them all over the globe; many were either killed or lost. I had an uncle living in London until a few years ago by the name of Samuel Hoche, but he died in 1981.

My father died a couple of weeks after his birthday in October 1951 in Paris as a passenger in an automobile crash. I had maintained contact with him until his death and saw him for the last time a few months earlier.

I found my uncle Samuel by accident in 1973. He lived in London and was an investment analyst. I spoke with him the last time in 1980. There were three brothers: Maurice, William, and the youngest, Samuel, who were children of Moise and Rebecca Hoche.

Moise was on the faculty at the Ecole Polytechniques de Lyon where he taught philosophy and mathematics and was a fighter against the rise of Communism in Europe. He left the University in 1917 and volunteered to fight with the White Russians against the growing menace of Lenin and his supporters. He died in Russia and the date is unknown to me. His wife, my paternal grandmother, I was told died at the beginning of WW II in Lyon after returning from a visit to Cairo. I was too young to remember much of her except for having a mental image of sitting on her lap at age five or six when we visited France on holiday from Egypt, prior to the war, or when she visited us in Cairo. The mental image, however, may be more manufactured by hearsay than reality.

Maurice and William followed partially in their father's footsteps, except for service against the Bolshevik in Russia. Maurice taught mathematics at the Sorbonne and operated a dairy farm as a gentleman farmer near La Roche, located approximately 70 kilometers from Les Houches. He was killed during WWII. I have not been able to connect with his family but I suspect that they are living near Paris.

The middle brother, my father William, became a linguist and went into teaching French and other languages, and was sent on assignment to Cairo, Egypt to teach at the College Français. My mother, Marie, a secondary school teacher, received an offer to teach French at Les Cours Maintenon, also in Cairo, where I was born on a Sunday morning in 1932 and where a younger brother, Sylvain, was born in 1936, but died four months later of meningitis.

To trace the genealogy of this family would be an enormous endeavor, one that over-reaches my passion for history. Suffice it to say that the taproot of the family is buried in France with some smaller roots buried in Northern Italy, in the region of Aosta. When one lives through two major world conflicts such as World War I and World War II, families are torn apart and it takes generations for new connections to be created, if at all. And when the dynamics of a Diaspora come into play, the family is scattered even more and the tearing apart of the fabric becomes more pronounced and more final. I have a maternal uncle and an aunt living in Brazil but I have never had personal communication with them. My mother may have.

Hence for me to rely on genetic bonds to recreate the dispersed family is not only foolishness but also a wasteful effort. It is nonsense to say that someone who lives in Brazil and with whom I have no real social bond, just a blood bond, is kin to me. Indeed we are all kin to each other on this earthly globe through the process of evolution but that does not mean we are then one closely-knit family. I have a general and sufficient, I dare say, idea about my origin and for me that is enough.

Many members of my family have made contributions to the world, which ones in particular are irrelevant to me. And some members have not added one iota to benefit the human fabric, and that is just as irrelevant to me. It is my present generation that matters. Am I contributing to the benefit of the world? Are my offspring, Dominique and Michel, making worthwhile contributions to the human fabric? I question whether or not, in the grand scheme of creation (if there is one), I have made a difference. Am I a contributor to life, a creative addition, or a parasitic nuisance?

I suspect that the scattering of families will increase as conflicts are generated, as human displacement increases around the globe, and as the search for work in a global economy forces or lures folks away from their native habitats. Rootlessness will increase because the size of Planet Earth has become less of an obstacle for moving from one place to another.

The United States is a good example as it is a nation of immigrants. Soon enough the world will become a planet of immigrants. Historically, of course, from mankind's roots in Olduvai Gorge, Ngorongoro, Tanzania, Africa, we are all immigrants.

In the process the family will suffer, as it always has, because its elements will be sown into the winds of necessities to implant themselves in various parts of the globe. The scattered family will supersede the gathered family. Perhaps communication by way of the Internet will minimize the separation between family members as it is doing for me between acquaintances and offspring.

It is obvious that there are probably other members of the Hoche family living in places unknown to me — and the spelling of the name may have incurred variations. Because I have distanced myself from the French core of the family, if there was one left after WWII, it is difficult for me to make connections at this time. And if I did find a connection what would I do with it? It has been too long and too many elements of history have come into play to make such connections relevant, except maybe for reconstructing the family lineage as an historical task — a difficult and nearly impossible effort at best. I am not a lover of puzzles and do not care to expend much energy on the subject. Others are invited to do the reconstruction.

Of course my curiosity has not died. It would be most interesting to see from whence I came, but that would only be as an intellectual curiosity with little, for me, of pragmatic value.

I am always surprised and envious to see my wife Emily associate with her family and her childhood friends. Nashville is where she finds her roots — and the friends of her family. A search for my family has never produced any adequate result to compensate for the energy expended. So much has come in between, so much history has evolved between "the family" and me that social bonds have taken greater meaning than those of genetic associations.

I tried to look for connections in Haute Savoie, in Cairo, in Aosta, in Paris, in Grenoble, even in Geneva but time has transformed me into a stranger. It is a climb on a highly polished surface; I have no place to hang on. There are no family hooks to prevent me from sliding down the sheer face. Wars and the mobility of modern people make a search fruitless. This is not a condemnation of the times but merely a value judgment recognizing that gone are the days of the romantic picture of the tribe living out life for centuries in the small villages.

The maternal side of the family emerged from Livorno, in Tuscany on the Tyrrhenian Sea, and from the region of Aosta, located at the foot of the Alps. Mostly a family of physicians, teachers, and pharmacists, the family, as I was informed, was mainly made up of professionals. I never knew my maternal grandmother Angèle because she died when I was just two years old. She was headmistress of the Lycée Français du Caire. Although Italian by birth, but educated in France, she too had been sent by the French Government to promote French language and culture in the colonies and protectorates of which Egypt was one.

My maternal grandfather, Joseph, was a physician who could not stand the sight of blood, hence after receiving his medical board certification, he studied further to become a chemist-pharmacist. He was interested in the research and the development of antidote medicines for tropical and river Nile diseases.

Working on assignment of the renowned hospital in Montpellier, France, and with several grants funded by the British, my grandfather did research in Cairo and also opened a pharmacy to serve both as a place for his laboratory and to collaborate with other researchers on similar pursuits. This was still the time when apothecaries fashioned and mixed their own medications to treat medical problems.

Both France and Britain functioned as guardians of the Middle East and Egypt was an important protectorate. The cooperation between Britain and France predated the European Union and was not quite altruistic but provided many returns from several sources. One of these sources was the Suez Canal, which was a major revenue producer, as was the presence of oil in the region, and by the decade of the 1930s it was necessary for the British and the French to keep the region safe from German Nazi and Italian Fascist hands. One must remember that Somalia and Eritrea were under Mussolini's Italian boot in the mid-1930s, and Il Duce was an ally of Hitler. In that atmosphere, Egypt enjoyed and absorbed much of the culture of the British and the French — as well as the Greeks, the Maltese, the escaped Armenians, the escaped Yugoslavs, and the expatriate Italians who fled from Mussolini. Both France and Britain paid a great deal of attention to Egypt, especially to the education, health, security, and economy of its indigenous and foreign residents.

My grandfather Joseph died in Cairo soon after the abdication of the Egyptian King Farouk in 1952. The last time I saw him was in 1949 when I made a short visit to Cairo after my Matriculation examinations and before I moved to the New World, via Canada. I loved my grandfather Joseph and I learned a great many things from him. We often discussed chemistry and cooking, especially the preparation of "fruits de mer," seafood. By the time I started university, I knew so much more organic chemistry than other students that I was allowed to skip the sophomore courses.

My mother was one of six siblings, four boys and two girls. The eldest was Maurice, and then came Mathieu, Marie (my mother), Robert, Adèle, and Marcel.

My favorite was Mathieu who emigrated from Egypt to America and lived in Los Angeles. He was married to Camille and had a daughter, Francis, seven years younger than I.

Maurice was a professor of mathematics at the Grande Ecole de Science in Paris. Mathieu told me that Maurice was a member of the French underground resistance and was killed just before the liberation of Paris when a car jumped the curb and hit him. I have no idea where his wife and only son are. I suspect that they still live in France but I have been unable to locate them.

The other siblings are in Brazil. As I indicated earlier, I have had no communication with any of them since the late forties. Mother did communicate with some of them but was always in a fit or angry with one or the other. Mother and Adèle often had bouts followed by silence. I took the easy road and maintained regular communication with my uncle Mathieu and Camille.

Francis was studying genetics, married a French-Algerian biochemist who immigrated to America, and both taught and lived for a while in Indiana. I lost contact with them around 1970 when I was occupied with my second round of graduate school. Yet I remember a special occasion while I was in seminary in the early 1960s when Francis (Fannie) visited San Francisco for a few days and I escorted her about town and to dinner. It was a lovely and special time for me.

With a few elements of history clarified, the question again comes up: Who am I? How did the name "Hoche-Mong" surface? It is not a complicated issue but it does include a promise to my mother who divorced my father in 1945. It was a conflict between two people that was not surprising to me. In many ways I was devastated by the divorce, but would have been more devastated had it not occurred. I am not sure that I understood what divorce meant; I am not certain that I understand now, even having experienced it. Regrettably, it seems that selfishness is impossible to cure and it is, in my opinion, the root cause of divorce.

Europe in centuries past indicted people who proceeded with divorce as social criminals of sorts. Because divorce was so unacceptable, extramarital affairs were not frowned upon but merely regarded as matters of course. Movie stars were divorced, but that was seen as part of the aura and immorality that came with fame and fortune. After all, the rich and famous possessed their own social code, which the rest of the human race was not entitled to share.

Anyway, what was happening in America where divorces appeared to be more common than in Europe was viewed as strange and possible only because the culture was corrupt and flaunted tradition. America was thought by Europeans to have no moral code to guide the rich nation.

Divorce was not acceptable in Europe. In fact I don't remember many of my fellow classmates mentioning divorce or alluding that divorce happened or could happen in their family. I remember one classmate who always spoke of his mother but never mentioned his father — and would not even acknowledge his existence. A few of the Arab students, such as those from Saudi Arabia or the Trucial States spoke of fathers with several wives, but divorce was taken as a special option available only to Moslems. My naiveté was obvious.

As a European, at least as one from a French family, the whole idea of parents divorcing was totally repugnant to me. How could parents do that? I don't know if I sided with one or the other parent but it was obvious to me a few years later that my mother had placed me in her camp. I was told to forget the divorce and not speak about it because time would heal any scar that might develop.

The School and War Years

World War II was declared in Europe on 3 September 1939. At that time we lived in an old house with a flat roof where we could sit on warm days and look over a good portion of the city. I was playing on the roof of our house when Kassem, our young Nubian house attendant, came to announce the news to me. I was seven years old.

War was not a strange word to me. I had heard much talk about Mussolini's Abyssinian campaign (Somalia and Eritrea). I had heard about the devastation of parts of Czechoslovakia, and the overnight invasion of Poland. I had both Czech and Polish neighbors who were very concerned and worried about both the situation and their families. There were other mentions of conflicts, especially civil, particularly the current Spanish Civil War, which began in 1936 and was still actively producing somber news. War was part of my childhood memory in Cairo. I don't recall a time when war was not part of conversation.

The Cairo I knew and was familiar with in those early days of my youth was a pleasant and lovely place. We lived for a while at Giza, not too far from the Nile River, and a short distance from the Giza Sporting Club — a haven for foreigners, especially English expatriates. I used to ride my bicycle, a racing Raleigh with curved handlebars, to the Club for their famous Sporting Club egg salad sandwich on a long hotdog-type bun. The egg salad had a flavor that haunts me to this day and I've often tried to duplicate it, but never quite achieved the taste of the original flavor. I've come close, very close, to producing the Sporting Club taste, but still something is missing. It could be the Egyptian eggs, the local handmade mayonnaise, the onions, or the flour for the buns. The sandwich was always brimming with egg salad which oozed from the sliced side and moved one to lick it lest it fall onto the plate or, horribly, onto the ground.

I knew a lot of people at the Club. It was a place where Europeans gathered to discuss subjects of consequence and visit with each other to exchange simple greetings. Many of the members knew me and I could hop from table to table. Quite often I would be given ice cream or the famous egg sandwich and more.

Because of their teaching positions, my parents were the recipients of free memberships. They, however, seldom frequented the Club, preferring to meet at Groppi's Cafes (there were several Groppi's Cafes in Cairo, and they were superb cafes and restaurants fashioned after the French or Italian variety) where an ongoing literary group met regularly to discuss topics in French and only in French.

At the Club, the language used was mostly French for me, but English was quite common although I spoke none of it. Sometimes I'd play tennis, paddle a tennis ball against the training wall, obtain a ride from a member in a sailboat and sail the Nile for a few hours, or just read a book I'd brought with me.

Sitting outside was a pleasure in Cairo because the weather was mostly mild year round. It was hot in the summer but never insufferably hot; I cannot remember ever complaining about the heat. In winter when it rained, the downpour never lasted more than a few minutes and it was never a deluge. Neither air conditioning nor heating was ever needed.

My first experience with air conditioning was when the new Metro cinema house advertised artificial "acclimatization," a term that was new to many people. Metro Goldwyn Mayer, the American film studio, had invested much to bring to Cairo the latest technology in a fine theater to show their productions. I don't recall the name of the first film shown when it opened, but I do remember seeing, when I returned to Cairo in 1949, *Mrs. Miniver* starring the team of Greer Garson and Walter Pigeon, recounting the story of the Dunkirk retreat. The film brought back many somber memories of the early days of WWII, especially the efforts exerted to save the soldiers who had managed to escape the Wehrmacht onslaught. I had been in the Cambridge area during the Dunkirk retreat. All English-speaking films shown at the Metro cinema had French subtitles. Films were shown at ten in the morning, then three, six, and nine because in Cairo one reserved a seat for a particular showing.

A few months after the Metro was built, Fox Studios of America constructed a lavishly appointed cinema. The films shown were produced either by J. Arthur Rank Studios of England or Fox Studios. When I returned in 1949, I saw at the Fox Sir Lawrence Olivier's *Hamlet* for the first time. Olivier's *Hamlet* is a classic, and since then I think that I have viewed six performances of it.

Unfortunately when I visited the Fox cinema in 1979 I discovered an Islamic group had burned it to the ground in 1950. The Metro cinema, however, had been spared. When I returned to Cairo in 1979, I treated myself to a second performance of *Dr. Zhivago* made and directed by David Lean in 1965 starring my classmate Omar Sharif (Michel Chalhoub).

There were many movie houses in Cairo, and Egypt had a good domestic film industry, one that exported films to several countries in the Arabic and non-Arabic speaking world. One of the many other attractive features of Cairo was the open-air cinema with seating under the stars. A section was reserved for diners who would partake of a serious meal while watching the latest French, British, Italian, or American picture show.

I would often go to the cinema with a neighbor friend, Ralph Balarciano. Ralph was a talented young artist who could draw, freehand, lively scenes of swashbuckling heroes saving maidens in distress. I was sad the day we said goodbye when I went to England and he headed for Rhodesia, now Zimbabwe. As expected, I lost track of Ralph a few years later.

It was a joyful time with very few cares for a boy of my age. A bicycle, a book, and a friend were all that was necessary, plus the beauty of the Nile River, flowing majestically along the banks carrying *feluccas*, the traditional boat that sailed quietly carrying passengers and cargo.

Cycling was one of my passions and allowed me to escape from home and the overbearing control that my mother tried to exert over me. I would ride to the Pyramids, to Maadi, to Helwan, and to Heliopolis. Local cycling was also fun because Cairo had no hills and traffic was accustomed to bicycles, donkey-drawn chariots, horse-drawn carriages, and camel and mule caravans hauling goods on the streets, avenues, and boulevards of the capital city. Bike theft was unheard of, and I could prop my bicycle outside a shop, a cinema, or some establishment such as Tsepas the pastry shop and never worry that it would be stolen.

Across the river from the Club one could see several houseboats where families lived and enjoyed the quiet river flowing by. Houseboats were common residences for many families, both the poor and the wealthy, although each selected different locations dictated by proximity to their social standard. We knew several families who lived on some quite handsome houseboats, boats that floated but could not move unless towed. Often these boats were anchored to the banks and connected to city utilities. Spacious decks were designed to accommodate families living a leisurely existence while on board. Kitchens, sleeping quarters, dining rooms, and servant sections were carefully configured to provide comfort, quiet, and space.

At night the houseboats seen from across the Nile appeared to be magically lit, like jewels afloat in the darkness. I always enjoyed visiting a family living on a houseboat; it was a happy occasion because it was so unlike where we lived. No apartment or house had the charm for me that a houseboat had.

Mother would not live on a houseboat, and she did not care much for a house either; her style of living leaned towards an apartment. I disliked apartments. I yearned for open space, a garden, and a place that was mostly my own. My father was interested in a house, and had moved us to a couple, and had mentioned renting or buying a houseboat. My mother found both unacceptable. Apart from nursing a few African Violets in shallow pots near windows, gardening was not a preferred hobby for my mother; in fact she hated the idea of tending a patch. She was an ingrained apartment dweller, which often caused some harsh arguments with my father. Apartments are an abomination; even townhouses and condominiums are abhorrent to me.

As a young boy growing up in Cairo there was a delicious sense of freedom that permitted me to wander about the city without fear or concern. Whether I walked down the Clot Bay Street, which in later years I learned was the prostitution quarter, to Bab el Luk, the center of commerce, or to Midan Ismalia (now Tahrir Square), the center of downtown Cairo, I was never touched by any anxiety that something dangerous would happen to me. Quite often I would see amputees, deformed human beings with leprosy or what I was informed was leprosy (which today would be a dubious diagnosis), and others who showed countless maladies, yet the streets were safe for a little boy to explore. My mother always feared that something would happen to me, but really nothing ever did.

I was annoyed in a movie house one afternoon by a fat man who unzipped his pants, but I changed seats and called the usher who promptly threw the slob out of the theater. I cannot recall one occasion when I was concerned for my safety, and I cannot recall a friend who was concerned either.

At first we lived in Giza, then in the center of Cairo on Emad el Din Street, the street that had the Metropolitan Electric Railroad (Metro) to Heliopolis. I liked riding the Metro, especially if I could stand next to the driver and watch the track slip under the train. The Metro was made in Belgium by the firm of Baron Empain Compagnie Electrique. Heliopolis was approximately 30 kilometers from downtown Cairo and the ride for me will never be erased from my memory. There was nothing in Heliopolis that interested me, but the ride on the Metro was exciting. I knew that I was the driver. I controlled the speed. The real driver was merely my copilot; I was in command of this projectile as it raced on smooth steel tracks. The Metro was my toy for the ride.

On another occasion I took the Tramway (tram) to the zoological garden accompanied by my friend Ralph. I knew several of the conductors on the tram run to the zoo because I often escaped to that extraordinary garden to see my friends the tigers.

On this occasion, probably one of my last visits to the zoo, I boarded a tram and the conductor who knew me let me manipulate the two controls of the vehicle. I had been shown how they worked and had acquired the simple procedure on other trips. The conductor greeted me then invited me to control the tram. There was one crank that controlled the rheostat and a turning wheel attached to a pulley chain that controlled the brakes. The difficult task was stopping at the correct spot at stations for passengers to enter and exit, and to watch that the track was correctly connected and not diverted to a different routing for another vehicle heading to a different destination.

There were only two such questionable shifts of track; hence the process was not complicated. I took over the controls as the conductor smoked a cigarette and chatted with the passengers. Because there was no windscreen, the wind hit my face and at times tears streamed down my cheeks, but it was good fun. Ralph could not believe that I was in charge of the vehicle and that I knew what to do. It seems to me that I was just eight years old and this was surely going to be my last trip, as you will see later.

Upon our return home (on the return trip I did not know the conductor and hence I did not operate the controls) Ralph repeated the story of my maneuvering the tram and each time he embellished it a bit more. Admittedly I enjoyed the fame and Ralph's adornment of the episode.

As I started saying it was to the zoological garden that I was going. The Cairo Zoological Garden was created to show the many varieties of animals present in Africa and to compare them with some other species that did not reside on the so-called "dark continent." The zoo had been designed by the British following the rule that expansive space provides the best atmosphere for animals and limits the sense of incarceration that often pushes caged animals to pace back and forth in their limited environment. Cages were large and connected to open areas where trees, ponds, rocks, sand areas, and canyons represented quite well the terrain that made up the real veldt or the jungle. It was a wonderful place for me to escape for a day. At the zoo I would head directly to the tiger cages and review my pets. Mustapha, the huge Bengal male had that tiger musk smell about him. Often he stared at me as if to beg for release from his confinement. If I could, I would have. Lenin, the Siberian was a bit smaller but longer than Mustapha. I liked Mustapha for his allure and comportment but I loved Lenin for his sleek beauty and gentle eyes. How I wished I could have either tiger.

After the tigers I would wander to the hippopotamus pond to see the sayed-eshtas. Those huge mouths would open wide as I popped a carrot as far as I could throw it. Of course, in that enormous mouth one little carrot was almost a negligible taste. I would then throw a whole bunch that contained two dozen carrots purchased for three millims. After the hippos I would go visit my old friends the elephants, giant African creatures with ears in the shape of the continent that was their domain. Elephants are almost human in their behavior. They may be big and heavy, but they behave like we do — often gentle but at times with terrible tempers when things are not going their way. With his sensitive trunk an elephant is able to pick up a single peanut from a person's palm.

Egyptian bread packed with Tamiya (falafel) and salad doused with tahini, all washed down with a Tsepas soda, made for a good lunch. A piece of chocolate packed by Kassem, our cook, was often found in my knapsack for sweetness after lunch. Then off to see other residents of the zoological garden, perhaps the so-called carnivorous plants, the birds, or the gentle giraffes with their soft brown eyes and long necks. A platform was available to allow one to give a carrot or an apple to them.

A day at the zoo alone or with my father was memorable. Our conversation was always exciting and informative. I looked forward to the time when we could share a day together at the zoo or at the Pyramids. Mother sometimes would find the freedom from teaching to accompany me on an outing but these usually were primarily to see one or two things and then settle in a cafe for several hours. When she came along I usually slipped a book in my knapsack to help me pass the time when at the cafe. Also, a trip to Tsepas's Patisserie was an exciting time for me. This meant that I could enjoy a good pastry and a glass of milk while reading one of my favorite books by Alexandre Dumas.

Of course I had friends in Cairo, Ralph Balarciano was one, but otherwise I was able to amuse myself quite well when alone. A few of my friends were girls and they were always willing to go on adventures with me. One was Nicole, a French neighbor when we lived in Zamalek. She would accompany me to the zoo or for a bike ride along the river or for a visit to the Cairo Historical Museum, which was always fascinating for us.

Mario, an Italian boy, was often ready for an adventure that would lead us to discover a new site. We played with marbles, tossed a ball, or he helped me with my British-made Meccano set to build something exciting like a locomotive, a truck, or a crane. The Meccano set was one that I could expand as I needed, and it was one that came with me to school in Trumpington.

I would spend hours constructing some piece of machinery or a vehicle that would then entertain me for several days if not weeks. I suspect that I learned more about designing, engineering, and construction from the Meccano set than I did later at university. I had such a good experience with my Meccano set that I gave a more modern set, rather than an American Erector set, to my son some forty years later, a set that he also enjoyed for many years, and which is currently stored for some future generation.

Then there was my first visit to the grand Cairo Opera House. It was just before any talk of war was in the air. My mother told me that I was going to the opera to hear *Aïda*, which had been written by Giuseppe Verdi to celebrate the opening of the Suez Canal. *Aida* had its inaugural performance in 1871 at the grand Cairo Opera House, a splendid building with exquisite acoustics. All dressed up in suit and tie, I went to the performance with two French young ladies, Martine Marteau and Annie Guyot. Both Martine and Annie were sixteen, hence much older than I. I was treated as their escort and protector. Cash had been given to me for the refreshments at the interval, and I took on the role of gallant gentleman. The music was extraordinary and to this day I can hum the "Triumphal March." The tenor was Beniamino Gigli and I can still recall his voice. I can also visualize again the stage with its actual live elephants, horses, and camels, and hear the famous trumpet fanfare of the March.

After the Opera we meandered to the Continental Hotel, which was across the square, and regaled ourselves with Profiterole dessert. The afternoon performance topped with the luscious dessert and accompanied by both

Martine and Annie made for a memorable experience. I wonder what has happened to those attractive ladies?

Because I did not go to regular school, both my parents took the responsibility to give me the necessary education. Whenever I'm eating tangerines I am inevitably reminded of Mother teaching me the multiplication tables or helping me memorize poetry. She would spend time helping me memorize poetry so that someday my French could be enriched with pertinent quotations from premier poets. French is the language that is indelibly ingrained in me. I learned my multiplication tables in French and I learned to resolve arithmetic calculations in French. To this day I do not know my tables in English but must revert to French. I have the same problem with addition and subtraction; orally I can only do them in French.

As for poetry, the French poets were the main focus of my attention. I did memorize some passages from Dante in Italian but on the whole attention was focused on French poetry and literature. Saint Exupery's *Le Petit Prince*, *Vol de Nuit* and other works were read by me only in French, as were the many books by Alexandre Dumas, La Fontaine, and Victor Hugo. I still have some trouble listening to the musical *Les Miserables* in English and in lyric form. Indeed I neither object to the lyric version nor the English version of Hugo's work, it is simply that it rings strangely to me to hear Jean Valjean or Javert sing, and sing in English. As I write this I can repeat "Les Conquérants" word for word after more than sixty years since I memorized it:

> Comme un vol de gerfauts hors du charnier natal,
> Fatigués de porter leurs misères hautaines,
> De Palos de Moguer, routiers et capitaines
> Partaient, ivres d'un rêve heroïque et brutal.

> Ils allaient conquérir le fabuleux métal
> Que Cipango mûrit dans ses mines lointaines,
> Et les vents alizés inclinaient leurs antennes
> Aux bords mystérieux du monde occidental.

> Chaque soir, espèrant des lendemains épiques,

L'azure phosphorescent de la mer des Tropiques
Enchantait leur sommeil d'un mirage doré;

Ou penchés à l'avant des blanches caravelles,
Ils regardaient monter en un ciel ignoré
Du fond de L'Ocean des étoiles nouvelles.

"Like a flock of falcons out of their nests,
Tired of enduring their enormous miseries,
From Palos and Moguer, sailor and captains
Left, drunk with a heroic and brutal dream.

They would conquer the fabulous metal
That Cipango held in its distant mines,
Trade winds bowed their ship's masts
As they sailed by the mysterious edge of the occident.

Every evening, hoping epic tomorrows
The phosphorescent azure of the tropics' sea
Enchanted their sleep with a golden mirage;

Or leaning on the bow of their blanched caravels
They saw in an unheeded sky reflection
Of new stars on the bottom of the ocean."

This magnificent sonnet by José-Maria de Heredia, a Cuban who became French (1842-1905), was elected to the French Academy. He wrote 118 sonnets retracing the history of the world and one of them, "Les Conquérants," depicts the voyage by ship from Spain to Japan wherein the sailors hope to make their fortune.

For the poetry, each verse was preceded and succeeded by a piece of tangerine (mandarin orange). To my amazement I acquired a great deal of knowledge through the medium of the tangerine — and ice cream, chocolate, pastry, etc. Mother would run me through this learning process either while walking or while sitting in a cafe, preferably at Groppi's. My ultimate reward was a dish of ice cream called Trois Petits Cochons (three little pigs). It is amazing how much learning bribes can make possible! Of course, animal psychologists have long used this process of giving mice or primates rewards for achievements.

To some extent my father also participated in this process but his emphasis was more on etymology, word usage, and concept, mostly philosophical. He would take me on long walks through Cairo and we would discuss some word that he chose, some concept on peace, the rights of human beings, and often some aspect of the political scene in Egypt, France, or the Soviet Union, and a European country. The rise of Hitler in Germany was a puzzling concept for him, especially since he spoke German and knew the high level of intellectual climate in that country. He would say, shaking his head: "Comment peuvent-ils accepter cela? (How can they accept this as okay?)" On the walks with my father we would discuss the origin of words, and why this word or that word had this or that root. We also talked about history and how the affairs of past cultures affected what developed in our time. My father was not a fan of Bonaparte and often mentioned that many of the problems that currently existed in Europe were the result of poor political determinations by the Corsican. Father and Mother disagreed on the issue of Napoleon. From my father the rewards were either pastry or a good sandwich or full meal at some local Egyptian restaurant; he would introduce me to new and exotic dishes or foods.

At a very early age I remember being interested in food and cooking. Cooking was especially of concern to me because I liked to eat and when both parents were away I took charge of the kitchen. When that kitchen invasion was in effect, Kassem would delight in helping me create concoctions or borrow from available recipes, which were always adjusted to suit my taste. I would watch both my parents prepare food and work diligently with our cook Kassem to learn some of the special techniques he used in the kitchen.

Improvisation was part of my learning in the kitchen; if a dish didn't work out as anticipated no harm was done. Kassem reminded me one day that "only scrambled eggs could not be reversed!" As a seven year-old I could make an omelet, lamb stew, potato pancakes, Tamiya (falafel), tahini and homousaya (tahini with garbanzo peas also known as chick peas), cucumbers in sour cream, chicken soup with rice, and several types of sandwiches. I found the kitchen was a place where I had fun; the product of any labor was always rewarding to the palate. Kassem also taught me to manage myself in the kitchen so that I cleaned up after myself. "Start with hot soapy water in the sink," he would advise me before I started preparing anything. I follow his advice still whenever I'm cooking.

World War II Comes to Me

It was a good time to be in Cairo. World War II, however, brought a harsh disjunction to life there. The date of 3 September 1939 has been etched in my memory. The news of the declaration of war was chilling, shocking, and paralyzing. All work in Cairo was suspended. The city was quiet and few people were seen in the streets and although public transportation functioned, the trams and buses were nearly empty of passengers. It was gruesome.

Kassem had told me about the news of the declaration of war, and for safety reasons advised that I had better go to my room. I turned on the radio and heard the news from the French Broadcasting Station relayed from Lebanon. Father came into my room to announce that war was beginning. He hugged me.

Just before war started we had moved into an apartment because the British Army needed our house. Compensation for the house was quite generous as my father informed me years later when we discussed the early days of the war and the family. A few weeks after the initial military campaigns by the Germans into Poland that had given the world a more distinct view of what could be expected from Hitler's forces, I heard my father and mother discussing the options open to us foreigners. The prevailing mood in Egypt was that Germany would send liberators to free Egypt from the oppressive control of the British, and, to an equal degree, from the French.

Cairo was in reality an international city populated by a large expatriate community originating from Italy, Czechoslovakia, Poland, Turkey, Britain, France, Germany, Malta, Greece, and many other countries. There were so many non-Egyptians living in Egypt that a Judicial Court for Foreigners had been established. Egyptians used a different judicial system and a different court. My uncle Mathieu was an attorney who practiced law in the Court for Foreigners. If my recollection is sound, Egyptian law was a diluted form of the Islamic Shari'ah but without the violence, oppressive restrictions on females, and juries being replaced by magistrates. Foreigners were under a common law system similar to the one used in Britain.

Soon several friends and neighbors came over to our apartment and joined the discussion that lasted well into the night. I do not remember when the discussion ended because I went to sleep. I awakened in the morning, however, to see that some of the folks from the previous night were still talking and things, attitudes, and conversations were not as they had been days before the Declaration of War.

The living room had a smell of cigarette smoke, stale coffee, and uneaten sandwiches. When I went to the balcony, I could see that the atmosphere in the street was tense. Because I did not attend school as other kids my own age did, but was taught by Mr. Roberto Orvieto, an Italian tutor who came to our home, I could sense the adult tension much more readily than if I had been in school and had been involved in playing with other kids.

Mr. Orvieto, an Italian citizen, was concerned that he might be sent to a detention camp for the duration of the War. That he was against Mussolini and the whole Fascist political movement did not count for much when the war started. German residents, many who had escaped Hitler's rise to power in 1930 and who were against the Nazi political mentality, had already been gathered and sent to detention camps, and soon Italians would follow.

Both the British and the French military commands in Egypt were careful to isolate any citizens of an Axis country (the name given to the enemy of the Allies) from the social fabric to reduce the potential infiltration of the Fifth Column (spies working for the Axis regimes). The father of Mario, my young Italian friend, had already been sent to a detention camp, and he was a third generation resident of Egypt. Fortunately the detention program did not personally affect us because our dual citizenships of French and Italian could be covered with just the French papers.

On one side the British and French forces were working to reduce the possibility of German infiltration in Egypt and the Middle East; on the other side, the Egyptians were openly favoring a German invitation to their country in the hope that they would be liberated from the colonial presence. The news received was that King Farouk was courting the Germans to come to Egypt and seize the Suez Canal in the process. Life had become somber and laughter was a scarce commodity. Noisy Cairo was hushed and at night the city was dark. It was a frightening time for me because everybody was talking about death, casualties, and the oppressed nations under the mighty German Boot.

In the spring of 1940, just when the annual Khamsin windy season was in full bloom with darkened reddish skies and whistling winds blowing sand, which penetrated every orifice in the apartment, my father took me aside for a talk. He had the look that normally indicated displeasure and anxiety, yet he placed his hand affectionately under my chin. He announced to me that I was to be sent away to school in England and then perhaps to Canada. He informed me that Mother was against this move, but she had accepted the reasonableness of the option reluctantly. I was told that I would leave soon after my birthday on 8 May 1940, my eighth year anniversary.

England was far away and the English spoke a strange language, one that was not among the ones I knew. I spoke French, Arabic, Italian, and a smattering of Greek, but no English. Why was I going, and going alone? Later my father informed me that I would not be going to Canada but would remain in England. I was advised that I would begin my education at Victoria College, a preparatory school for foreign children and children from the British Colonies. I would be taught English, the expected operative language of the future — that is, he added, if we all did not end up speaking German. French, my father explained, would always be my language and I was not to dismiss it as irrelevant. I was to keep French alive and maintain it to the highest quality.

He and my mother were to remain in Cairo, now their home because France was in a precarious position in the gun sight of the German Wehrmacht. All this was very strange and confusing to me, but it was also quite exciting. I would be going on a trip to England. I had visited France and Italy as a younger child but never England.

The move to send me to England was one that literally offered inconceivable changes to my life. Canada was no longer the destination for evacuees because the German submarines — U-boats — were sinking too many passenger ships in the North Atlantic.

In jest I have often said that Adolph Hitler's war had been good for me. This was said lightly but there is some truth to it. Had there not been a major conflict in Europe and in the world between the Axis (Germany, Japan, and Italy) and the Allies, or United Nations (Britain, USSR, and, France, etc.), I would not have been sent to England for my education, I would not be speaking English today, and in fact my life would have been remarkably different, and perhaps not for the better.

Because World War II separated me from my parents and permitted me to function as an individual, I evolved as a more responsible young adult, even at the age of eight. Some would claim that I lost my youth during the war. Perhaps I did. I was, however, forced by circumstances to mature too soon. Consequently, my position is that my youth was different from those kids who remained home and attached to their parents. Certainly family ties were torn asunder by the war, by any war, but my personal development moved in interesting, rewarding, and self-determining directions.

Most of all I learned that one must grow up without blaming one's parents for whatever shortcomings are encountered. My parents did the best they could. Their marriage may have been more readily affected by the trends surfacing from the world's conflict but that is moot. In the commotion caused by the international struggle they may have seen that the marriage was doomed and that neither economics nor raising a child could save it.

Mother had great difficulty in accepting part of the blame or that she was partly instrumental in creating the cause for the divorce. I can say in candor that Mother should never have gotten married, as she was not one to share with another person, even a husband. Mother was determined to have her way, unwilling to accept advice, and extremely possessive. I was her possession and she equated that possessiveness with love. Father was willing to let go of what he loved. He was curious, creative, searching, and a dedicated scholar. Both parents loved me but Mother wanted to suffocate me with her possessiveness, and father moved to let me fly away to a far off land — for my own good.

It was many years later that I understood the difference in attitude because in a sense I too have difficulty accepting someone else's direction but I believe that I know the difference between possessiveness and love. As a young boy, it was well beyond my understanding. I accepted Mother's position, her restrictions, and her demands without questioning them. I'm certain that my father felt that I betrayed him because I would often take Mother's side. Admittedly it was only after I'd gotten married and had my own children that I began to see her in a different light, a light that showed the blemishes clearly — and much of that was seen as I compared her with my wife Trudy, who was so terribly un-possessive that she ignored the children, except for the minimum of control.

The contrast was an eye opener to me. I saw what harm my mother could do and I also saw what harm the opposite could do to our children. Mother wanted me to exist in a kind of hermetic box with tight boundaries and Trudy offered no boundaries, no control, and no interest in laying out rules. It was an amazing revelation to me. I accepted my boarding school limits as useful for me to live a life that could be expanded when I could prove that I was responsible enough to extend the limits of those boundaries. Indeed as a young boy in school I was not a model of behavior. I fought discipline as best I could. I broke rules — some accidentally and many on purpose, and for causes that were mine and only mine to justify. Petit Nimon was not an angel.

Living in boarding school I learned quickly that I was responsible for my own comportment. The odds of my pegging someone else for my shortcomings were nil. Neither my classmates nor my teachers would have let me get by with bad behavior. Much of the attitude in school depended on honor, trust, neatness, and congeniality. In many respects the golden rule applied as the operative mode in school.

My new independent life as a young adult had its genesis on 15 May 1940, a few days after my eighth birthday. I was added to the cargo manifest of a Royal Air Force (RAF) aircraft flying from Cairo's Payne Field to the RAF base in Duxford, East Anglia, a few miles from Cambridge, England. This was my first airplane ride and a most memorable ride it was.

We departed Cairo in the early afternoon to allow us to overfly Europe at night, after a refueling stop in Malta. If memory is not failing me, it was a converted Avro 683 Lancaster bomber. It was both a freight carrier and a fully armed reconnaissance aircraft. Apart from a crew of six, I was the only passenger aboard. I was bundled midway in the fuselage over the wings. Inside the aircraft during the flight, it was cold, drafty, and noisy. It was scary but exciting. Before heading to the Cairo airport in an RAF lorry I had said goodbye to my parents. My mother had cried and was only restrained by my uncle Mathieu when she tried to stop me from boarding the lorry. My father told me to decide immediately that I was to become responsible for my own wellbeing. I was in charge of myself.

"Tu seras maître de ta personne," he told me. He then added, "Tu n'es plus petit Nimon, mais grand Raymond." My nickname *Nimon* was the product of my inability as a young boy to say the name Raymond; it stuck as a nickname.

It was exciting. It was nevertheless still frightening. Off to the airport I was taken.

After passing the inspection kiosk, the security and passport attendants, I was escorted across the tarmac to the military green aircraft and directed to climb into the aircraft. Inside it was dark, dank, and hot. A uniformed person helped me don a backpack parachute and to sit on it. Restraining belts were slipped around my waist and shoulders. I was given a box with sandwiches and juices. Then I received several instructions that I did not understand. I spoke no English and it appeared that I was the only passenger for the flight. Several sentences were spoken to me, but it seemed to me that the word "rather" was used often. What did it mean? Anyway, after my unintelligible briefing I repeated the word I had often heard: "rather." The briefer smiled and patted me on the head and departed. He was not flying in this airplane. Much was being done to get the aircraft ready and people were going back and forth inside the fuselage and to the cockpit. The front crew was already seated in the cockpit and was busy doing many things, none of which I understood although I could hear words.

I'm not sure that I knew how and why I was a passenger, the only passenger, on this military aircraft. I felt as if I was a package to be delivered to someone far away. Most children that I knew who were being sent away were traveling in groups and usually went on ships by way of South Africa. French children were usually disembarked in Madagascar, a French colony. British children either went to England or across the southern Atlantic to America and then to Canada. Shipping passengers across the north Atlantic had ended because of the German submarine attacks which had resulted in enormous casualties. That I was to overfly Europe was puzzling to me but I was happy not to have to endure a long sea voyage. Moreover, I was going to enjoy, I hoped, my first flight in an airplane.

The entry door located behind the trailing edge of the left wing was closed by a crew member. A uniformed man came out of the cockpit and checked that I was tied properly. He said a few words, gave me a piece of chocolate, patted me on the head and smiled broadly. Very soon thereafter, I heard the backfiring and roar of the firing of the first engine. There were four engines I discovered by the sound of the growls. The whole airplane vibrated. Then we started moving and bouncing.

After several minutes of movement we stopped and I heard the pitch of the engines heighten for a few moments. The noise was deafening and the vibrations accentuated. The engine pitch was reduced slightly and we moved a little, and then we seemed to turn right. All of a sudden the engine pitch increased to such a heightened level that the plane shook and rattled; we began to roll, first slowly then faster until the fuselage leveled and was no longer pitching at an angle towards the back. No sooner had this leveling occurred, than I no longer felt the vibrations.

It was noisier but much smoother. The sound of the wind increased and soon the floor was level and no longer pitched backwards. Now we seemed to tilt to the right and after a few moments we tilted to the left, then we leveled again. I suspected that we were turning onto the course that would take us across the Mediterranean Sea. We droned on for several hours. I released the pressure of my restraining harness by unbuckling it and soon I was drifting into sleep. It was well past my bedtime.

Awakened by a hand patting my head and a voice scolding me I was retightened in my safety harness and told something incomprehensible in English. This was the same man who had given me a piece of chocolate before departure. I responded with the word "rather." The man took a few steps towards the cockpit and turned around saying something else which was just as incomprehensible as the first utterance. I responded with another "rather."

He stared at me. There was a puzzled look and then he said, "Vous ne parlez pas Anglais. Vous parlez que Français."

"Oui, oui" I responded, then added "rather." He burst into laughter! He proceeded to instruct me in French and also informed me that soon we would be arriving in Malta where I must go to the toilet in preparation for the remainder of the trip. He added that we would be in Malta for about an hour to refuel and refresh our sandwiches. We would also be given some hot food for dinner. From then on the man spoke to me in French and I was scolded no more. His name was Squadron Leader Edward (Ted) Beadle; he was the senior officer on board. Squadron Leader (Sqn Ldr) Beadle would play a major role in my evolving life.

It was dark in Malta when we arrived. When I got off the plane a man in uniform checked my passport and said a few words to me in English to which I responded in French and also in Italian. He then continued in Italian and directed me to the dining hall. After a quick hot dinner, tea, and a visit to the toilet we were off again. This time I was permitted to sit in a jump seat in the cockpit right behind the two pilots. This was a much better arrangement. Sqn Ldr Beadle told me about the instruments, showed me the four throttles, tilted the steering wheel (called the yoke), left then right and back and forth. The plane followed by turning first one way then another and by climbing and descending. When he returned to the course he gave a geography lesson.

I could see much of what was on our route across the Bay of Lion and across southern France. Lights were visible in France during this period known as the "quiet war." The quiet was not to last too long, but long enough for us to reach England and our destination. Several hours later, flying over Paris, the Eiffel tower was pointed out to me. Paris was really the "city of lights," the jewel of Europe. We encountered no German interference although I was informed that we had expected some German fighters.

Just when dawn was beginning to show its light, the white cliffs of Dover appeared on the horizon. England was in front of us and the journey across Europe from Cairo was a success. We were safely in protected territory. Soon we landed at Duxford and my passport and entry papers were checked. My luggage was transferred to a small lorry and I was whisked off to Victoria College (a middle and high school) located in the small village of Trumpington, in the shadow of Cambridge University.

I was to be a resident of the school in Trumpington until I matriculated in 1947. As for Sqn Ldr Beadle I was to see him a few more times and then there would be no sight of him for two years. He informed me that he was on his way to Africa and would return when a reassignment came his way. The next time I saw him he was in the uniform of Air Commodore (Air Cdr.; in American terms, the equivalent of Brigadier General) and wearing one star on his collar. I would see him a few years later in Lydda, Palestine.

Victoria College (VC) was where I completed the last year of my primary and the remaining years of my secondary education. The school was sponsored by the British Council for the Education of offspring of those who lived in the British colonies and protectorates. Many of my classmates were from the Trucial States (Emirates), Saudi Arabia, Egypt, Trans-Jordan (now Jordan), Palestine (now Israel), South Africa, Rhodesia (now Zimbabwe), Australia, Canada, and other members of the Colonial Empire or of its allies.

There were students of other nationalities that were neither colonials nor protectorate members but students who had escaped from the German occupation, such as Polish, and Americans who had resided in Greece and had escaped the Italian invasion before being caught in the vise of the Axis power.

It was a most interesting school with an excellent faculty made up of a mixture of several nationalities. Most teachers were English as were many students.

A few words about two boys at VC. First the lad Hussein, future king of Jordan and a great international humanitarian and aircraft pilot of some renown. Hussein was the grandson of the king of Transjordan in the mid-forties. When Hussein's grandfather died, because his father was not capable of ruling, Hussein was crowned king and ruled Jordan for many decades. Hussein was an amiable lad and a good student who was never aloof or distant from other students. He was liked by all. After Victoria College he went to Harrow School, and then to the Royal Military Academy Sandhurst to complete his education and learn flying. He ascended the Jordanian throne in 1952 and died in 1999.

As for Nicolas Hilton, wealth showed on him. He was a poor student and a little unpleasant to be around. Hollywood had matched him with the young actress Elizabeth Taylor, also a rather unpleasant person, and both were more interested in showing off their wealth than in socializing with the students of VC. Elizabeth was one month older than I and on my sixteenth birthday she attended a reception at the school given by one of my favorite teachers and his wife. At that party, Elizabeth planted a kiss on my lips. Conrad Nicholson Hilton Jr., known as Nicky, married Elizabeth soon after that event and I believe died a few years later.

When I arrived at VC in the summer of 1940 I spoke and understood absolutely no English. It was difficult. Michel Chalhoub (who stayed only two years before moving to Lebanon), Victor Farhi, and a few other students were helpful in getting me settled for they spoke French.

To not speak English was embarrassing and off-putting because it placed me outside all activities. Moreover, because I had no experience of how to function in a school environment, I had much to learn. True that although a few weeks before classes were to begin I was immersed in conversational

English, the beginning period in an English school was nevertheless very difficult. For a few weeks, I was or felt like a dummy.

Yet not once did I think of abandoning the situation by running away — and I had no place to go. Writing home took weeks for mail to reach its destination and what could I say? Telephoning was out of the question because telephones were still not a ready and available means of communication. I often felt alone and even forsaken. Crying was often a way to fall asleep at bedtime.

My room was shared with two pleasant boys, both of whom had lost their families when the Wehrmacht invaded their Poland or Sudetenland. But as in all things in life this phase soon passed. My memory tells me that when classes started in September, I was able to manage adequately in English.

Much as I had a lot of support from my classmates, still there were one or two who chose to pester me. One in particular was a bully to me and to many others, and was determined to make my life as miserable as possible. As an eight-year-old, I was not big or hefty, but rather small and thin. Walter Shafferman was several inches taller than I and a few pounds heavier. Walter, a most unpleasant boy, was from St. Helier, the capital city of the island of Jersey. He would come behind me and push me to make me walk faster. He would mimic my accent. He would grab my curly hair and pull. At lunch or dinner he would try to spill water on my food but was never successful.

Other classmates tried to protect me, to talk him out of being such an obnoxious creature, and to keep him away from the smaller guys but that was in vain. Shafferman was a dedicated louse. Needless to say, I was getting tired of his antics and my life was complicated enough: The adjustment was difficult, the new language was a chore, and the times were in themselves worrisome. Asking the teachers for help in this matter with Shafferman was not too productive because he never acted like a hoodlum when teachers were nearby. I was informed that the school knew about his behavior but nothing could be done about it until he was caught in the act, and that was impossible.

The Shafferman issue, the cause of my own personal discomfort, is anecdotal. Shafferman continued to be annoying and to bully others and me. He had added Chalhoub and Farhi to his list of victims. One day the end arrived with an opportunity that I could not resist.

In the library we had small tables for each student to study independently, where a student could spread out without overtaking another student's area. The chairs were made of bent wood and were very light, strong, and comfortable. Each table had two inkwells, one filled with black and the other with blue ink because on some assignments the teacher specifically requested one color or the other — and I never did know the reason.

Working on a précis for Mr. Loughton, my English teacher, I was nearly to the end of my final text when Shafferman came over and tipped the inkwell on my final page, then gave a belly laugh. The library was silent. I jerked up before the ink could reach my shirt, picked up my chair, and in one smooth stroke hit Shafferman directly on the side of his head. The chair broke in many pieces and Shafferman crumbled in a pile to the floor; his eyes rolled up to the top of their sockets and then closed.

Shafferman lay on the floor immobile. My classmates applauded. Even the attending professor and librarian were clapping. Shafferman was out cold on the floor. Finally it occurred to me that perhaps I had killed him. The same thought registered with the librarian who soon came running to Shafferman's side. He was alive but had a deep gash on his cranium. The nurse was called and stood near Shafferman to see what he would do now that he was awakening. I reached down to help him up but he jerked back his arm in an apparent reaction that indicated a fear that I would hit him again. I had made my point. Shafferman neither said a word nor did anything to me or to Chalhoub or Farhi again. Avoidance became his operative behavior; he would quickly elude me when I was in proximity. We never spoke a word. In the process I had gained a certain stature of respect among my peers.

Meanwhile, the rout of the British Expeditionary Force at Dunkirk had given us all in East Anglia a frightening sense that the Germans were invincible and that soon they would be in England. The great air Battle of Britain, although won by the RAF, had left the forces in East Anglia, the main region of England for airbases, wondering if another German attempt could be resisted. The Luftwaffe and the Wehrmacht were obviously invincible and stood ready to pounce on England at the first sign of weakness. Many children slated to be shipped over to Canada or the United States by boat were diverted to Scotland or Northern Ireland (Ireland did not participate or offer any help by claiming that it was neutral although it refueled German navy ships).

The German submarines, the U-Boats wolf packs, were devastating Allied shipping. Supplies from Canada and the United States were not reaching the British Isles. East Anglia was a haven for the British forces that had escaped from Dunkirk.

***

At the school several soldiers were housed and tents were erected in the front garden for the evacuees until the military could reintroduce them back into their appropriate units. The soldiers took their meals in the refectory with us so we had ample opportunity to talk with them about the miserable time they had in France and the might of the Wehrmacht and its several Panzer divisions of fast, agile, and invincible tanks. Those were frightening times in England.

I soon learned that the German Afrika Korp had landed in North Africa and was moving rapidly under General Rommel's command towards Egypt. Little news had reached me from my parents, except for a telegram a few weeks after my arrival. Communication with Egypt was impossible. Would we be speaking German soon, now that I had managed some English? Soon another great event would rear its head: The Battle of Britain — 10 July to 31 October 1940.

Victoria College followed precisely and to the letter the English system of education and it was only after I came to America, attended university and had children in secondary school that I discovered what was amiss with the English system. It offered no room for creativity or options to develop one's opinions based on facts. The system adhered to a policy that students had empty heads much in need of being filled to the brim. A student's opinion was only permitted in informal conversation with a teacher, never in a response to a query when in course.

Because I had never been to elementary school and had been taught by a tutor, I was neither very passive nor was I trained to suppress my opinion and my own reasoning. At times that got me into trouble, but all learning, in whatever form, can be troublesome. I took the approach that if I couched my commentaries in diplomacy — and that is almost counter to what I normally do — it would be accepted, and it was. Many of the teachers recognized that the system was deficient and allowed some leeway for its manipulation. It was wartime, the academic community was busy with resolving security and intelligence problems and all issues concerning pedagogy had to wait for the end of the war, if then.

There was, however, a good faculty at VC. I got along well with most members of the faculty but that did not mean life in school was without hitches. To fit into a predetermined box was not easy for me; I was and still am a bit libertarian in my approach to rules, codes, and laws. My tendency is to push the limit whenever I can to enlarge the envelope, to allow for more options, more freedom, and more self-expression, but all within the rules of the game.

That mode of operation has served me well in many organizations such as preparatory school, the United States Air Force, the Church, and industry. People create organizations and people can be forced to change, perhaps slowly, but change will surface even in the most conservative mentality. Nothing produced by human beings is indelible, eternal, or so sacred that it cannot be changed, altered, improved, or trashed. VC was no different — it was forced to change and it did, as we shall see.

The daily schedule was followed to the letter. The routine was unchanging. Awakened at 6:45 in the morning, I was to shower in tepid water, not cold and not hot but tepid. At 7:15 it was a breakfast of eggs, bread that was good, dark, thickly cut and painted with margarine, and some jam. For the mid-morning break, we were given an apple or pear and a cup of tea with milk and sugar. Lunch at noon was often roast lamb or chicken (rarely beef and never pork) with sweet potatoes (mashed, baked, or allumette fried —

French style). I don't remember having real potatoes until after the War. For vegetables we were given daily sliced fresh onions, sliced turnips, and sliced cucumbers. On occasion we had beans, carrots, celery (cooked or raw), radishes, and every so often green peppers. Variations of other vegetables were limited and not available until the war was over in Europe.

When classes were ended at 15:00, we were given a large cup of tea with milk and sugar and a sandwich with some good English cheese. We were then to go to the study room to do our assigned homework. The study room was next to the library where we went if some research had to be done. The library was well stocked with the necessary books for research and also with a good selection of novels in four or five languages, and we could check books out for a seven-day period with one option for renewal.

Dinner was served at 19:30 and consisted of a thick soup, usually made with white beans, barley or lentils and a piece of cured pork; for the Moslem boys mutton was substituted. Preferring mutton, I would opt for the latter. Added after the soup were again sliced onions, cheese, and a fruit.

Because soon after my arrival I was diagnosed with anemia, the physician prescribed a six-ounce bottle of stout ale to be consumed with my dinner. This went on for five years and I was undoubtedly the envy of my classmates, even of the Islamic boys who are forbidden from imbibing alcohol. My anemia has been cured ever since but my taste for ale continues to this day.

Bedtime was enforced at nine o'clock. This allowed me about thirty minutes for personal reading, which I did in French, Italian, or English.

* * *

Raising silk worms brought me one of the joys that I remember in England during those terrible years of the war. A neighbor who was a farmer and a dairyman gave me a few silk worms to nurture. Because he had several mulberry trees on his property, feeding the worms was not a problem at all; silk worms eat only mulberry leaves.

The worms were most interesting because they metamorphosed into moths after a long period of self-isolation in a cocoon made of silk. Once out of the cocoon and in the body of white moths, no food was consumed at all, and after copulation the females deposited hundreds of pin-head-sized round flat eggs. When the eggs were produced, both male and female moths expired.

Months later, the eggs hatched into tiny worms less than one eighth of a centimeter long. I kept the eggs in a cigar box and when the little silk worms emerged, I would transfer them to a shoebox. The shoebox had strings crossing from side to side to permit the cocoons to be attached when it was time for the metamorphosing stage to change the worms into pretty white moths. I think that I kept the silk worms for several years and collected a rather large number that I kept in the library.

Raising silk worms taught me much about the delicate process of life and its complexity. From egg to worm to moth to death is but a very short time. Just unraveling the strand of silk from a cocoon is a sufficient sign to show that the process of creation is not simple: the strand of silk is continuous, even in texture, and several meters long. The caterpillar worm spins the silk thread without interruption for several days while enveloping the body at the same time. It is an amazing feat of endurance, architecture, dedication, purpose, and preservation. After several attempts I was able to find the beginning of the silk strand and carefully, very carefully, unravel the thread all the way to the internal cavity where the worm resided. If you wait until the moth self-liberates from the cocoon, a hole is cut and the continuous thread is then severed. A silk thread severed can be knotted, hence no harm is done except being able to have one continuous thread, which is a reward, but one must do that operation without harming the moth.

I enjoyed the raising of silk worms as much as I did tending pigeons in Cairo. Watching the life cycle of creatures is both educational and humbling. I learned much about the enigma of existence, the delicate balance that keeps life and death in equilibrium. The responsibility for nurturing pigeons and silk worms is demanding and made me recognize how devastating inattention to the task may produce havoc.

Early spring was a favorite time for me because the snow geese would fly into the Fens to begin the activity of laying eggs and raising the young chicks. Snow geese are all white, regal, and extraordinary, especially in flight. Flights of snow geese are small, of less than fifteen pairs, they are quiet, and magnificent flyers keeping their formation in a V, with each taking turns at being the lead bird. In early spring when I would first spot them in the sky over East Anglia, I would head for the open Fens on my bike to see them land.

I think that much of my love for flying stems from watching these magnificent birds in the air. Without shame I admit being envious of the snow geese and their ability to manage the air at great heights, navigate over long distances without error, and produce an aesthetically enticing tableau. Geese could walk, swim, and fly. Would that I could fly like a snow goose!

Our social lives were well scheduled. Apart from sporting events with other regional schools, we also had dances and teas. I was taught the customary dances of the times that included the waltz, the foxtrot, and the tango. There was a girls' school not too far from ours in Trumpington, which often invited VC students to various events.

At that school, St. Magdalene's, we often were invited for proper teas following the custom of the refined class of England. Because we were young our invitations were prepared as "high tea" to replace dinner for that evening. There was a girl named Nicole in whom I had some interest. She was quite special and for a few years we would take walks, enjoy each other's conversations, and exchange books.

When an invitation from St. Magdalene's arrived, I was always one of the first to sign my acceptance form. It was at St. Magdalene's that I was taught the "correct" English method for making tea. Indeed, the headmistress showed us all how to heat the teapot, count the spoons of loose tea for each drinker, with the reminder that the teapot also required a measure of tea, and how tea is poured in cups; sugar and milk are added before tea is poured into the cup. We were taught how to balance the cup and saucer and stir delicately with the spoon, then placing it on the saucer's ledge, being careful not to have it fall off. The cup and saucer occupied the left hand, and the right hand was free to manage the savories or sweets. We were slowly becoming "gentlemen" able to cope correctly in the company of "ladies."

I found those invitations to be fun and pleasurable. Many boys, however, found them to be painful and even horrid and that was why the school did not mandate that all students participate in these occasions. After tea was served, if a dance was to follow, the boys signed a small booklet that the girls made available to reserve certain dances with them. I was not a good dancer hence I preferred to limit my choice to Nicole who knew that I was slightly clumsy on the dance floor. My clumsiness on the dance floor has never left me; in fact, I've come to dislike dancing so much that I avoid it whenever possible.

VC had an interesting faculty that was predominantly made up of men and women who could not serve in the military because of age or certain physical impediments. Many but not all teachers were English, some had served in the colonies, several were "British," meaning that they were from the possessions and hence were not entitled to English citizenship. This distinction was not considered discriminatory but merely a fact that was welcome, especially when British-ness allowed citizens to enjoy the privileges that Britain shared with its colonies. For example, a bright student from Malta or the Trucial States (now the Emirates) could participate in the educational process in England.

The faculty teaching at VC was a mix of several nationalities that included some who were neither English nor British but French, who had escaped from France in anticipation of the German occupation. Many French citizens had foreseen the weakness of France and had decided to leave, not unlike the decision made by Le Grand Charles, General De Gaulle who escaped France and established his command of the Free French Forces (FFF) in London early in 1940, just after France, under pressure from Britain and its Prime Minister Winston Churchill, had declared war on the Nazi regime.

* * *

"Who will hang me today?"

My French teacher Raoul Parme was of Maltese origin, but had lived in France, especially in Corsica, all his life until just before the German occupation, which he had anticipated. A Sorbonne graduate, he gave me a love and respect for "good" French. Mr. Parme taught me to love literature and poetry

ADVENTURES OF NIMON · 49

— and geography. Often after class at tea in the afternoon, he would challenge us with the game of "hanging." We had to find a difficult geographic place, and let him ask questions to identify the place's name. For each incorrect answer a pencil stroke was used to draw a scaffold. Mr. Parme always won. He could identify the most insignificant geographical location on the planet. We tried hard to stump him but were never successful. This game gave us the opportunity to learn not only geography, but also the names both in French and in English.

Mr. Parme was a delight even though he had a serious demeanor. Correct spelling was of paramount importance and the way to learn spelling was through good grammar and repeated exercise of dictation. He taught us every day, five days a week. As he entered the classroom, he would immediately ask us to get a clean sheet of paper and pen. He would dictate one or two paragraphs from some book or article. When that was completed we exchanged papers with the student sitting at the next desk and we would correct each other's dictation. Mr. Parme would write the original text on the blackboard. We would report the number of errors and which word most students had missed, then he analyzed with us why this or that word had been misspelled.

Grammar for Mr. Parme was a dynamic tool for aiding communication; this was long before communicating was such an august discipline. He always bemoaned the fact that only ten percent of the French people wrote their language correctly. To this day I am always very concerned when I write in French, to the point that I use a computer program approved by the Academie Française to recheck both grammar and syntax. George Bernard Shaw said in his play *Pygmalion* that in French it didn't matter what one said as long as one pronounced it correctly. Mr. Parme added, in jest, that it didn't matter what you wrote in French as long as it was grammatically correct!

At first mathematics was a problem for me because I was careless with my arithmetic calculations. The various parts of mathematics were not taught separately at VC. In other words, arithmetic, algebra, and geometry were all part of mathematics and were studied as one and not as separate forms to be studied in different years.

From the very beginning math was all that made up mathematics. That approach was good for me because I was weak in plain old arithmetic. I understood the principles but was careless with the arithmetic operations.

For math, my professor was Vice-Dean Kenneth Griffith, a Welshman and a graduate of Oxford. He insisted that we understand what a math problem asked before we attempted to resolve it. Math was more than calculations; someday there would be an instrument that would do the calculations for man, he assured us. The task ahead was not calculation but comprehension. Arithmetic was for me an impossible task but I could resolve a problem rapidly and correctly, if only I did not have to arrive at a correct numerical answer.

One day during the first session of my second year, Mr. Griffith called me into his office. Being called into the Vice-Dean's office always meant that a reprimand was expected. When I entered his office he pointed to the blackboard and asked me to solve the problem on the board.

Mr. Griffith said to me: "Sir, I want you to solve that problem without calculating the final result. I want you to break that problem into its parts and indicate how you would construct a calculating tool to resolve it. Write each step clearly."

I proceeded to attack the problem that was about water filling a leaking reservoir and I had to consider in the calculation the evaporation factor of the liquid occurring during the filling. In a few minutes I had broken the parts down, stated them one by one, and offered the means to obtain an answer. I recall that there were about eleven or twelve steps, and all of them were identified in their order of priority. When I completed the task, I turned to him. He had been following every step of my work.

"Sir," he said, "your work has correctly identified not only the parts but has systematized the steps to reach the correct solution of the problem. You are reading the advanced mathematics curriculum and should be. Now I do not want you to give me an arithmetic answer to any problem I give you either for homework or on an examination."

I was puzzled. "Mr. Griffith, are you telling me never to give you a final arithmetic solution?"

Drawing on his pipe and exhaling a cloud of smoke he replied, "Exactly, but I also want an estimate of what the answer might be and in proper units."

It was a strange request but I loved it because arithmetic was always my Waterloo, where I made my mistakes. Today the calculator does exactly what Mr. Griffith had suggested. I resolve the problem and the calculator performs my calculations. A lesson well taught and received which, had it not been given to me, might have altered my educational path drastically. Indeed, in later years, the calculator would become a soteriological tool for me. I must add that during one holiday, Mr. Griffith gave me an old Pascal mechanical calculator that I used regularly until I finished with VC.

A few weeks after my arrival at VC, my Scout leader Mr. Linsteson, who was also my physics teacher, gave me an Alsatian puppy to keep me company. I named the dog Trick because he was able to roll over on command with just one lesson. The dog was good company and a delight to train. I taught it to eat out of a bowl that did not lie on the ground. The dog would be given bones by the kitchen staff and often a stew was specially prepared for the dog from meats that were left over.

Trick was a fine, smart, affectionate dog with the admirable quality of following me no matter where I went. When I purchased a bicycle, a Raleigh racing model, Trick would run behind me for great distances. One day, the school carpenter adapted a large basket to fit snugly where a back seat would have been attached. The basket was large enough for Trick to jump into. At first I had to learn how to balance the movement of the dog when it was in the basket, but soon, I think that Trick learned to sit in the basket and remain still so as not to tip the bike too much — perhaps tipping the bike affected his sense of balance in his inner ear. At any rate, we traveled great distances on the bike.

In January 1950, I had to give Trick a pill to bring about his death because I could not take him to Canada; quarantine was for six months for dogs and cats. Trick died quickly and without pain. He was buried in the school's garden near an apple tree; unfortunately, the school and its surrounding land have since been cleared of any buildings, garden, and sport field.

* * *

Soon after I enrolled at VC the great air combat against the possible invasion of England started. The dates framing this great air battle are 10 July to 31 October 1940. Many of the fighter aircraft were stationed in proximity to Cambridge. We could see and hear the Spitfires and Hurricanes taking off and a few hours later landing, and soon taking off again; the action was almost round the clock. All of us students and teachers worried that if the fighters were defeated England would become part of the German conquest. Many of the students had escaped German occupation and no one wanted to be subjected to that again.

The months that framed the Battle of Britain felt extensively long to all of us in school, and it must have been exhausting to the pilots and their support crews. At last when the Germans were defeated by the force of the RAF and terminated their onslaught on the Island nation, we all in East Anglia were able to relax for a short time, at least until the bombing began, first of London, then of the surrounding area, especially of the airfields near Trumpington. My thoughts in passing were that I had left Cairo for the safety of England and here it was that I was in the very midst of a German concentrated attack — when Cairo was quietly enjoying a warm summer!

The students at VC were of a special breed. After he left school, Michel Chalhoub became known as Omar Sharif, the renowned actor. Victor Farhi was a surgeon who worked with Doctors Without Borders and who died during one of the Congolese wars. Hussein of Jordan became king and ruled the small country for several decades and avoided several assassination attempts on his life. King Hussein was a fine pilot who flew his long-range Boeing 727 on his last flight from America to Jordan. He was diagnosed with cancer and died a few days later. Ahmed Marborak was a nephew of King Ibn Saud of Arabia and a civil engineer who supervised the land planning of the Jubail Industrial Complex, on the coast of the Gulf of Arabia (Persian). Several other school colleagues have entered positions of some note, but I cannot recall them after so many years without correspondence or notes.

There are a few classmates who have made lasting impressions on me. Arendt Dormitian was a quiet, friendly, and considerate student who had the strangest habit of touching lightly every object before him. With the tips of his fingers he would gently caress walls, tables, chairs, automobile surfaces, any object that was near him. Students thought him a little off, especially because he was academically a mediocre student. I found him interesting and kind.

Arendt owned a sport bicycle and often we would go for long rides into the pathways of the Fens in East Anglia. The Fens or Fenland is a naturally marshy region in Cambridgeshire. Our conversation always focused on the human senses, and how human beings encountered the world around them. Later in life I considered our conversations to be philosophical in nature but then as two boys talking we were exploring our capacity to make sense of the environment that surrounded us. Arendt spoke to me of the use of the fifth sense, the sense of touch that most human beings, except perhaps the blind, never fully employ. Our conversation often lasted hours.

One day he asked me to follow him on my bike to a farm not far away from the school but on the south side of the Camb River and behind the Cambridge University Library. He would not tell me why he was taking me there. At the farm we pedaled to a shack that he opened with his key. It was a workshop. Behind a large sheet of plywood that he removed promptly, stood a superb two-meter tall sculpture of polished wood. It was his work and he had been at it for several months. Arendt called it the "Angel of Liberation" to remember the families that had perished during the Turkish genocide of the Armenians who resided in Turkey. The sculpture represented a being with arms open and extended forward, eyes that were fixed on the viewer yet looked beyond the viewer, and a hint of a smile on the lips. It was beautiful.

"Touch it please," he invited me. I did and loved the touch. "You are using your sense of touch. A sculpture must be caressed," he advised me. I did as he advised. It felt so good, so pleasing, and so deliciously intimate.

I asked Arendt if he had shown this sculpture to others at school. "No," he said as he pulled the plywood forward to hide it. "Only the farmer here and his wife know about it," he replied. "They gave me the piece of oak from a tree they cut years ago."

He walked towards the door, then turned around and informed me that he was starting a new sculpture. "Someday you'll see it when it is finished."

He stopped and put his hand on my shoulder, "Please don't tell anyone about what you saw here or about me."

I've never spoken to anyone at school about Arendt's creation. Moreover, I've lost track of Arendt Dormitian but I've often wondered if his sculptures are exhibited under a new name. In several exhibits I've seen works that mimic Arendt's but the sculptor's name was never recognizable.

Another classmate, Ronald Basilisk, had electrified his book closet. VC provided each student with a small closet to store books in a location near where classes were held. Ronald had electrified his closet so that it was bright with lights energized by a motorcycle battery that he recharged with an old bicycle light generator. He had built a bike stand by placing two concrete blocks close together to hold the back wheel off the ground, thus when the battery was low he would connect it to the light generator and pedal to charge it.

Ronald was amazingly good with electricity, so much so that often the maintenance people would come to ask specific questions about a problem they encountered in the school's grid. As a student, Ronald was one of the best, especially in math and literature. In addition he was a scout, and a good one and both of us served in the same troop.

Ronald's family had been displaced at the end of the 19th century from Sofia, Bulgaria when the Ottoman forces overran the country. The Basilisks settled in Tiranë, Albania, but in 1938 the Fascist Italians under Mussolini invaded the country. Ronald's family escaped to France and from there to England. On the way to France traveling over the Alps, his mother died, as did his older sister. Mr. Basilisk cared for the young boy with the help of an aunt, the mother's sister. Arriving in England in 1938, Ronald's father settled in Sussex taking a job as a metal worker in a defense plant. In later years, I heard through the grapevine that Ronald had become an electrical engineer.

* * *

Barney "Pappy" Campbell was a Squadron Leader in the RAF but not part of the faculty of VC; he was a senior instructor in aviation for the Royal Air Force (RAF). Pappy was not at all connected with VC but his influence on me was enormous. Barney was based at Waterbeach Royal Air Force Base, a premier flight and combat training complex.

If one took the footpaths and other shortcuts available to a cyclist, Waterbeach was approximately seven miles from Trumpington. When time allowed it, I often biked to Waterbeach to watch airplanes land and take off. There were several models of aircraft on the apron for me to admire, from the wooden Mosquitoes, to the Tiger and Gypsy Moths, to the Spitfires; there were also a few that I could not identify. A few aircraft had no national insignia; later when I became more acquainted with the personnel, I learned that a few aircraft were of American, Polish, French, and Czech origin acquired to demonstrate to new pilots their different characteristics.

As a young lad who took his first airplane ride when he was eight years old and developed a fascination for flying which has continued for more than seventy years, I made many visits to Waterbeach Royal Air Force Base. I would hang on the metal fence and look at the airplanes, following what the pilots did, and watching takeoffs and landings. Often I stood by the fence for several hours just looking at what was taking place on this busy and stirring air base. The only time I did not go to the Base was when it was raining.

Every so often a guard, a mechanic, or a pilot would come over to chat with me. I learned that Waterbeach was a flight training school specializing in teaching the fundamentals of flight and flying to boys who were still in their late teens. Also taught at Waterbeach were the techniques required of fighter pilots when encountering enemy fighters. I could at certain times see proper maneuvering of two or several aircraft above the field and towards the Fens. Few of the pilots were much older than nineteen or twenty, and these men were to become members of the flying squadrons that defeated the German aces. Pappy had trained a large number of these good brave pilots at Waterbeach Air Base.

After several visits to the air base I was lucky to be introduced to Pappy by one of his subordinates. He asked me what I was planning to do around the military compound. My reply was "Nothing, just looking."

"Are you a spy?" he growled.

"Of course I am not," I quivered.

"Then you are loitering around the Royal perimeter." I didn't know what that word meant.

"Well," he said, "if you do not want to be arrested for spying or for loitering, then start picking up nuts and bolts and anything that should not be on the ground, and could be struck by airplane propellers or embedded in a tire. Run along and start working now."

I had a job. A little while later a young man came with a bucket for me to put my collection of items in. When he gave me the bucket he also gave me a letter and a hand-made badge to pin on my coat. It was an aluminum round disc with the outline of a spitfire etched and blued on it. The letter affirmed that by order of Pappy Campbell I was allowed on the air base to do my job for "the defense and protection of the King, Britain, and its Empire."

Pappy became a mentor to me. He taught me to fly first in a 1936 de Havilland DH-82 Tiger Moth (modified to have the exhaust pipe on the right side — and all of us who flew it had a burn mark on our right arm, a badge of pride), and later other aircraft.

Pappy examined me and authorized the request for a "youngster temporary pre-aged flying permit" from the Air Ministry. When I was eligible for a permit, I was six months shy of the legal age of 16. The temporary permit was granted. I was a pilot. Pappy was as proud as a peacock when I received my permit, although he had instructed many RAF young men and some women. How he was able to get me through the RAF system, with fuel rationing, security, and the pressure of the war was beyond my understanding. He would never explain to me how he managed to accomplish that feat through the strict bureaucracy of the English system. Anyway, he had made a pilot out of me in December 1947. He had also produced a safe aircraft driver.

There was an outward gruff appearance in Pappy, but the fact that his pilots called him by his nickname to his face was proof that there was also a gentle side to him. Pappy was married to Gladys and they had a boy who was killed at Dunkirk at the start of the hostilities in 1940. Pappy and Gladys were family to me for most of my years in school. In 1948, Pappy retired from the RAF and bought a small farm in Wales. I kept a steady correspondence with them until both of them died; she in June 1956 and he in July 1956 — death came to them a month apart.

Spending time with them during my years in school and the war gave me a certain anchor that precluded any hint of loneliness. The years of my schooling were difficult years for me. Because of the many airfields around the Fens, East Anglia was not spared from Luftwaffe's nightly bombing. It was only by good fortune and the work of able British fighters that neither Cambridge nor Ely lost any historical buildings.

Pappy would fly over the Fens after the bombings to inspect the damage and to report to the authorities if any major structures had been destroyed, especially if the canal pumps had been hit. He was beyond the age when the RAF required him to fly missions, but it was known that he would sneak and hitch a ride on occasion with a bombing flight.

At other times he would check out a pilot in a fighter and take him over the Channel, where an encounter with a Luftwaffe fighter was a possibility. Pappy always returned, sometimes with a strike, but nothing was ever said about any encounter, although rumors were rampant and anecdotes aplenty. It was understood that credit for any strike would go to the student pilot; Pappy did not need any more credits.

* * *

Scouting was a major activity for boys in England even during the war. George VI was a scout and often spoke about the benefit of scouting as a good way for building social responsibility, good citizenship, and the path to leadership. VC had a scout troop with an excellent record of social support in the Cambridge area, especially during the difficult years of the bombing, the retreat from Dunkirk, and aid to the elderly for grocery shopping, hospital escort, and other assistance that was needed in times of stress and civil unrest.

Being a scout was a source of great pride for me because it made me part of a respected group and it opened up new avenues for leadership and ways to identify talents that I did not know I had. I found that I could easily plot a course through the woods and find my way just by using a compass, and at times a simple sextant. Reading maps was almost second nature for me and I could teach others to read maps as well.

The fact that I was not too happy with overnight camping did not disturb me but it did instill in me a lifelong dislike for camping for no reason other than braving the elements, courting insects, and enduring the annoyance of encountering large amounts of dirt in food, clothing, and on one's body. But there were some rewards in the enjoyment of campfire foods. Somehow it became my duty to manage the food situation (and be awarded the Chef's badge) for the twenty or so scouts in my troop.

Mr. Langsdale, who replaced Mr. Linsteson when he left to serve in the British Intelligence service, was an able scoutmaster, and he soon discovered that I could make a fine stew when I was tested for my cooking badge. Thus began my career as a chef of sorts for large crowds. I was allowed to obtain the necessary ingredients from the school and I was given freedom to select the menu of my choice. Cooking was not a problem for me and furthermore, it allowed me to cook what I wanted to eat and in the way I wanted it prepared.

My tenure as a scout spanned a period of five years and I rose to the level of King's Scout. I suppose that the discipline, the cooperative activities, the training, and the camaraderie contributed to a great degree in forming who I am and how I handle a hierarchical milieu, such as the US Air Force, Church, and Bechtel Corporation.

Perhaps under this empirical experience, I learned to make a large organization work for me rather than having me become a pawn subservient to it. Any large organization is forced to move ahead only when one, two, or three people within it exert the necessary pressure to alter its course, change its traditional position, and propose a new operative paradigm. Mr. Langsdale was a fine scout leader but he was restricted by the tight rules of the Scouts and often they were in conflict with good sense for a particular occasion such as joining a Girl Guide group on a day outing.

Holidays were fun, warm, and a time for conversation, story telling, and eating. At the Campbells, I had a standing invitation to their house for the holidays or for any other occasion. Often on weekends I would go to the house and do my homework and help around the house. The Campbells were Anglicans (Church of England) and they often attended services at Ely Cathedral. On rare occasions they attended services at Old St. Edward's, Cambridge where his son had served as an acolyte.

When I was baptized and received the laying-of-hands, upon my return from the Middle East the Campbells presented me with the Church of England Book of Common Prayer (I have since lost it). Pappy knew Ted Beadle, my godfather and the pilot who first brought me to England; they had both served together somewhere although Pappy was much older. When I announced that Ted would be my godfather, Pappy and Gladys were delighted. I don't know why I never asked them to join in as godparents too. It is possible that I did not know that one could have three godparents.

At any rate, Ted was in Palestine. It was only upon my return from Palestine that Pappy and Gladys told me that Ted was a widower; his wife Jane had been killed by a mob in Nuremburg during Kristallnacht which took place all over Germany, but especially in Nuremburg on 9-10 November 1938 as a cleansing effort to rid the nation of Jews. When the supporters of the Nazi regime stormed the streets and destroyed the property of the Jewish community and killed many Jews and foreigners, Ted's wife was caught by a mob of crazed German supporters of the Nazi Party and killed. Ted neither mentioned that incident to me nor alluded that he had had a wife; I knew that he had no children.

The routine of attending classes filled most of my day, except when I could escape to Waterbeach or walk around Cambridge University and its many colleges. It was known by the faculty that my head was in airplanes but as long as I produced good grades nothing was ever said about my "hobby."

Sports were not my passion, although I did well in running track, cycling, and tennis. I was poor at football (soccer) but a fair cricket player — the sport of gentlemen. Cricket was fun, quiet, and with reduced activity, a game I could enjoy and still do as an observer. At cricket I could do much quiet thinking unless I was at bat or pitching, and I was good at either.

Academically, the school offered me an opportunity to sharpen my intellect quite a bit — often with great conflict ensuing. I was a good student when justice prevailed, but the English system at the time was quite unjust when it dealt with the less academically fortunate. When that situation occurred I toyed with the system and fortunately once defeated it.

The English system was centered on grades, "marks" as they were called, and the student with the highest grades was given special privileges and regarded with much respect. The poor student had relatively no status and few teachers had the time to examine the cause of the poor grades.

If a student had a First in some subject he was looked upon as being special and warranting some extra attention. The student at the bottom of the heap was tantamount to flotsam and jetsam. This was how Arendt Dormitian was regarded; with the exception of a few no one knew that he was an artist, a fine sculptor, and that a little attention might have revealed much of his personality and his talents.

Let me explain the situation in some detail. But I also wish to admit that I am unable to tolerate laws, codes, traditions, systems, policies, and standard operating procedures that do not make sense and hence are incoherent in my estimation. No, I am not a rebel. Laws are necessary to maintain order in society. But people are important, more important than any law, and so if a law is unjust then it must be changed — and that is never an easy process. When bad laws are kept everybody loses. Human beings live rather short lives, too short to tolerate idiotic laws, systems, policies, and traditions that enhance the egos of a few people in control. No one should be enslaved or ridiculed by policies that make no sense.

Truly, I am neither the savior of the world nor Don Quixote looking for windmills. Quite often I was frightened by the possible consequences of my actions but I had to do them. A bad situation cannot be allowed to remain unchallenged. Here is an example that I attacked as a young boy enrolled at VC: Students were seated in class according to the monthly grade standing. Marks were the predominant identifier of character for students. It was an unjust system and I fought it with every bit of wit at my disposal. Students with poor grades were seated in the front row; and those students with good grades were in the back row. The rationale was that the lower-graded students needed to be closer to the teacher because more attention would be given to them. That never was the case. The poor students got even less atten-tion from the teacher because they were thought to be slow-witted, intellectually inferior, lazy, or goof-offs.

Arendt, a fine sculptor but a mediocre student in academics was an ex-ample of the foolishness of this policy. Thus with posted grades and the obvious seating order, the lower-graded students were immediately identi-fied. Most teachers followed this policy, except Griffith and Parme who would not post grades.

With the posting of grades the poor students were embarrassed, identi-fied, and probably demoralized because they were stigmatized as being either slow learners, if learners at all, or just plain "bad" students. In rebellion to this imbecilic situation, I would work for good grades one month, and use every opportunity the next month to have poor grades. It mattered not to me because I still did my work, my parents could not receive my reported grades, and I could manage to turn in material that would be judged as bad. My grades would then fluctuate from month to month, and my seating position would reflect that fluctuation.

Soon enough, I was called to the Dean's office on a Saturday morning, the day for reprimands, for receiving the stick, for being placed in the "black book" or for being notified that one was expelled from Victoria College — a fate worse than death. I was petrified but I was not apologetic for my actions. Where would I go if expelled? My heart was beating hard and my tummy was in pain.

At the door to his office, Dean Price motioned me to come in. He had a short square body, dark hair parted in the middle, and his head was a large cube pivoting on a stout neck. I stood in front of him awaiting his judgment and condemnation. I was ready for the worst. Perhaps, the thought came to me, if I were to be expelled, I would be accepted at the King's School in Ely.

With a stern but low voice he spoke, "Sir, your marks are intriguing." He stared. "One month you are first or second of the class, the next you are twelfth of thirteen students, very nearly at the bottom." He touched his chin, " . . . and the next you are second. This pattern has been reviewed by the faculty and was found to be a repeated pattern." I said nothing but stood very still with my eyes fixed on his.

"What is the cause of these variations?"

I kept my silence.

"Speak up boy and answer my question."

How does one explain rebellious behavior, especially when the architect of this structure was facing me — and he had all the power at his disposal?

"Speak up young man, and at this very instant."

I stared at him and took a deep breath, "Sir, I have my reasons — some of which may or may not be acceptable to the school."

He got up from behind the giant oak desk and walked towards me. He came close and I could smell his pipe tobacco. He took the top of my right ear and pulled it hard.

"I will hear your reasons and immediately. Do you wish to be expelled?"

"No, Dean," I replied quickly.

"Tell me boy and tell me now," his voice a little higher and his grip a little tighter.

"I will sir, if you let go my ear." He did. He went to the window to look at the garden.

"Tell me now. I'm waiting and you don't want to add rudeness to the list of discrepancies."

I had to give him my reasons but I must do it in a way that would be understood so that the system could be corrected, my standing in school not jeopardized, and my butt rescued.

"Sir, it seems to me that Victoria College is practicing an unfair policy by posting the monthly marks of the students and then arranging the seating of students to reflect the marks they received," I had opened Pandora's box. I had started to state my case and my heart was about to jump out of my chest.

I continued, "By seating students according to their marks and by posting the marks on the board, the school is saying that some students need to be embarrassed for them to improve. That, Sir, is unfair, unjust, and an insult to the weaker and less brilliant students."

He turned and looked me straight in the eyes. He approached me. "Young man, are you making your point by playing the school's academic reputation and yours against each other?"

"Sir, I'm simply stating that grades are not all that important and that they can be manipulated easily when the system is terribly unjust," I explained. "This was the only way that I could bring this before you and the teachers and I know that I could be expelled for being a rebel."

I took a deep breath and added, "I apologize but I am not sorry."

He stared at me breathing harder and biting his pipe stem. He paced back and forth in the study — pacing from my position then on to the window and back several times. He stopped and stared at me for the longest time. I was beginning to feel warmth in my cheeks and becoming more uncomfortable, even nauseated. My legs were feeling weak and my head was pounding.

Dean Price stopped pacing. He approached me with his eyes fixed on me. Then he said in a slow, deliberate, and clear voice, "You will do well to be no less than second of your class for the rest of the year." He came closer to me. His eyes were still fixed on me but they had softened a bit.

Then he added, "For my part I will change the system immediately. I like your spunk and your courage." He moved back a few steps and added, "Is it a bargain?"

A moment of silence ensued, and then I repeated as a question, "Immediately?"

He nodded and smiled for the first time. I was no longer warm but a bit cold. Finding my voice I replied, "Yes, Dean, I accept the bargain — and the challenge."

I moved a few steps towards the door but he stopped me by saying, "You are not dismissed yet."

Was there another infraction, one that I had created inadvertently? I stood at attention. What was there to discuss, I thought?

Dean Price continued, "You almost declared war on the school by your tactics. You are one courageous human specimen but courage has its price. And the price must be paid."

He walked away from me and moved towards his desk. Then he commanded, "Put both hands on the desk, feet apart, and look straight ahead — set your eyes on King George."

He reached for the stick, a thin bamboo that had a silver handle. He moved behind but stood to my right and without pausing he struck me three times on my bottom. It hurt but not too much. I did not cry. "This is the price you have to pay for your rebellious behavior. Go now."

I left the office. Outside Victor and Michel greeted me and asked me what had been the problem? Had I received the stick? Would I be expelled? Guiding them away from the office and into the garden, I explained what had happened and why — leaving out the comment on courage.

On Monday following the reprimand given the previous Saturday, at the first class of the day, the teacher came into the room and looked at the class for a long moment, then informed us that from now on we could sit anywhere we liked, but had to keep the same seat for the duration of the year. Then he added as he approached my desk and looked me straight in the eyes, "Grades will no longer be posted on the door or on the information board."

He paused a moment, fiddled with the cover on my inkwell then added, "Your individual grades will be put in sealed envelopes and placed in your postboxes."

He stood near me a moment longer then went to the blackboard and started the lesson. The system was changed immediately. That evening I found a note in my postbox from the Dean and Mrs. Price inviting me to lunch on Sunday at their home. All's well that ends well, goes the saying. I did keep my bargain and my grades no longer fluctuated from month to month.

I also learned a lesson that has guided me all these years. Challenges can be made when systems or conditions need to be changed but the consequences of such actions against them often cannot be avoided, and should not. Active disobedience has a purpose but there are consequences that have to be borne when that course is taken.

* * *

My attendance in church was sparse but when I went I enjoyed the whole event. While at VC I found myself attending worship services at Ely Cathedral quite often and even volunteering for the boys' choir. I had a fair voice, I could follow a tune, but I could not read music. I just added amplitude to the choir. It was fun and I loved the liturgy of the Church of England, and have ever since. There is more to that side of the story and a great deal more will be shared later.

* * *

My subsequent years at VC were mostly uneventful except for flying. Flying offered additional fun to my life. Because I did not have to pay for my flying lessons, my parents were not informed. I just did not wish to receive word from Mother that I had to stop this foolishness because it was dangerous, that she loved me, that she would never forgive herself if something happened to me, and that she would go through a slow death every time she thought about me flying.

Some things are best not said. In fact that approach has much value in dealing with society, I soon learned. Of course the fact that I am writing this personal history goes counter to what I've followed for many years. Nevertheless, there are some things that I will not say, some people that I will not name, some occasions, incidents, and relationships that I will not divulge. Privacy is still a commodity that I wish not to share too much. After all this is not a confession.

The war was still raging and the bombing didn't stop until late in 1944. The invasion of Normandy had been successful and all of the students and teachers found time to rejoice. The folks of Cambridgeshire were more than happy that the Allied Forces had landed in Continental Europe. We could foresee the termination of the war in Europe and the defeat of the Nazi regime.

As I mentioned earlier, East Anglia was the target of many bombing runs by the Luftwaffe because of the many military aerodromes. Our chemistry laboratory, as it was called, but really our science building, was destroyed by a V-1 bomb. It was never rebuilt. The football field had two bomb holes that were promptly filled in. School buildings had several windows that needed replacing regularly throughout the war.

I remember spending several nights in shelters during air raids. It was not uncommon that we would eat, read, sleep, or discuss the war while in the shelter. I think that eight hours was the longest, without interruption, that I spent in our shelter. Even today I still cringe when I hear a noon siren blowing or the explosion of a firecracker. These are noises that immediately drag me back to the war years, to the rush to get out of a warm bed and into our shelter, and to the long hours when darkness was barely dissipated by the flickering flame of a candle. I remember well the war years but dwelling on their frightening effect is not a recurring pastime for me.

A few VC graduates who had gone to fight were killed in battle on German soil. We always remembered them at assemblies. Then also several dignitaries visited our school since we were so close to Cambridge University. Whenever an important person visited the University, it was quite likely that he would pay us a call during afternoon tea.

Archbishop William Temple spent a few days with us just before he died in 1942. I didn't quite know who he was until the time of his introduction and I was very pleased that he patted me on the head. He was such a superb man and a great contributor to both society and the Church.

One day in 1943 we were informed that Mr. Winston Churchill, the Prime Minister, was coming for a visit. He arrived and greeted us all. He looked much like the picture we saw often in newspapers, a cigar in his mouth and a scowl on his face. He spoke to several of us but did not pat my head although he did say a few words in French to me.

In 1946 the young Princess Elizabeth also visited us but she did not speak or try to confer with any students. Elizabeth just toured the school and spoke to a few adults.

Life continued and I received more than an education. I received the wherewithal to become a productive adult with the advantage of being able to be responsible for one's person, one's action, and one's thinking. I cherished the opportunities that were offered, especially the few meetings with important people of that generation. There were several visitors who came to the school and I wish I had been old enough to appreciate their visits more or to remember whom each was. Statesmen, scholars, scientists, military leaders, and a score of other prominent people came on occasion to visit our school and to chat with the students and teachers but I cannot recall many of them. I was too young to appreciate what I witnessed.

Because I was living in East Anglia during my growing years, I considered Trumpington more my home than Cairo. I was happy to complete my secondary education at Victoria College. I suspect that had Europe not been ravaged by war, a superior academic institution would have been found for me; but I have few grievances. VC was adequate and prepared me sufficiently well for university.

It is not the school that should receive all the credit, but how a student handles the school, its policies, and its educational program, especially those opportunities that reside outside the compound of the institution. The school is merely a tool, a dictionary, and a source book. It can be used fully or ignored completely. Teachers are just like lighthouses shedding light to remind a ship's crew that there are dangerous rocks nearby. The student, like the ship's master, must plot his/her course away from the rocks. The student must navigate towards a goal.

VC gave me an opportunity to fend for myself. I asked myself what road I wanted to take, the low road or the high road. And if I accidentally found myself on the low road what was I going to do to find a better course? One takes what material is available and fashions it into who we become. Parents share with us some material. Schools share with us some material. Universities share with us some material. And society shares with us some more material. We take from all the sources and either make the most of what we have received or make the least of it — and lose out in the process. That we must take what material is received from whatever source and reinvent ourselves "at all times and in all places" is what enriches life and empowers us to live a productive, contributing, valuable, and graceful life.

There were many points ahead on the horizon and I was searching for the right one to guide me. It had to include flying. University would have to wait a few years because I was not ready to buckle down and study in that environment or choose a discipline. Nevertheless, I had to decide what my next step would be. It seemed to me that while I was relatively free in East Anglia to roam to various places, I still needed to see what was "out there." I had not had the opportunity to visit the Continent because of the War, which was now over.

My next step took me across the Channel to the mainland of the Continent of Europe and to an adventure that included new lessons. I had no funds but my father who was now living in France gave me one hundred English pounds (I suspected a schism with my mother). For additional funds I would have to earn them by working odd jobs if I wanted to spend several months in Europe, traveling and absorbing the history. Europe was a place that drew me; I could not escape the attracting force that beckoned. I had to visit Europe. Standing on a bluff in the south of England, although I could not see France, I could visualize what it looked like and what all of Europe looked like.

Continental Exploration

France was calling her prodigal son. I had been to France as a small child with my parents but the memory was long buried in my subconscious and inaccessible for the time being. It was time for me to see what was on the other side of the English Channel. It was time to visit la Belle France.

After matriculating from VC in April 1948, I spent some additional time in Ely with the Olivers, communicants of the Cathedral, who offered me lodging and kept my belongings while I traveled to the Continent.

The day of my departure arrived and a train to Folkstone was on time. The ferry to Calais was waiting. I dreaded the crossing because I am very prone to seasickness. From some good fortune I did not get woozy as we sailed to the coast. The sight of France was wonderful and my first cup of café au lait and a croque-monsieur were superb. It was a little unsettling to me to hear every person speaking French; my experience before that occasion when I first set foot on foreign soil was that people around me spoke several languages but here French were the common words I heard!

When I took a short walk in Calais as I waited for the train to take me to Paris I could see much of the destruction from the war. Buildings had missing walls and stones and rubble were still piled on the sidewalks. Shops and restaurants were doing business but the display windows were boarded. The signature of the war was still very present. On the Continent I spent approximately eight months visiting sites that I had read or heard about and acquainting myself with the remnants of the war.

When I arrived on the European mainland I saw that it was very much disfigured by the ravages of war. If London and several English cities were in shambles from the bombing by the Luftwaffe, the Continent was marked here and there by wrecked buildings, piles of bricks and concrete, and streets that were adorned with hideously mangled tramway and train rails. The Allied bombing had demolished much of north and northeast France, Belgium, the Netherlands, and Germany. Central and southern France and northern Italy were in less of a shambles from the fierce battles between the Allied military and the defeated Axis forces.

Germany was impossible to describe other than as one big pile of rubble. Few buildings were left standing as whole structures were demolished and none remained without the markings of war. Many Germans were still living in makeshift structures on the site of destroyed buildings. Cologne, Frankfurt, and Nuremberg were left with mountains of broken stones, concrete, and wrenched iron rebars.

Because of the demarcation sectors imposed by the American, British, and French forces, I could visit only certain places, hence I visited Hesse-Darmstadt and Hesse-Castel in the southwest of Germany, now known as Hesse, on my way towards the Alps, and could not locate one building that was still left standing. The walls that remained vertical were without support and often a breeze or the rumbling vibrations of a passing heavy vehicle would send them crashing to the ground or into each other and a series of crashes ensued like houses of cards. The cacophony itself was enough to scare the wits out of any person in the vicinity. The destruction that I saw was a reminder that thirteen years of Nazi rule had metamorphosed Germany from a beautiful country into a heap of rubble.

What was more distressing was the human misery that was still quite evident in the streets. People huddled in makeshift lean-tos constructed of cardboard, particleboard, metal sidings, and other odds and ends. Children were asking pedestrians for coins or whatever they could obtain to allow them to purchase food. I saw very few dogs, cats or pigeons in the streets and assumed that they had been consumed as food. In the evening the streets were dark and very scary. Bars that were open could not be less inviting to honest people. Human misery was clearly depicted by the tragedy that enveloped the people of Germany. Had they anticipated the end of the war and how it would be for the Germans?

My lodging in Hesse was without a window; a gaping hole by a mortar shell replaced what had once been a window. My plans were to stay in that Pension for a week to fan out and see what was left of Hesse-Darmstadt when the owners advised me to leave, as they were too, because the Soviet Army was moving to occupy the region. My hosts were extremely uneasy to be under Soviet authority and preferred to leave and abandon their family house rather than remain.

Ownership of property, family houses, and personal effects were of no value to anyone; life and freedom had become too precious. Materialism was now the domain of black marketeers and not of ordinary citizens. The Soviets were feared more than the Allies, and for good reason; the Soviets moved into territories that were not theirs under agreements drawn and it always took pressure from the British or the Americans to hold them back. The occupation of Hesse-Darmstadt occurred even after the partitioning agreements with the Americans, the British, and the French were designed to stabilize the German territories into four regions. Ultimately Hesse-Darmstadt was freed from Soviet occupation, but I don't know what happened to my hosts.

These were difficult times on the Continent, times when Berlin was being choked by the Soviets and the airlift was being readied to supply the city with food and necessary commodities after Stalin closed all routes into the territory. These were sad times that were often punctuated by gay, funny, and enriching events, at least in the western sector. Germans, in the western sectors, were hopeful that life would regain some semblance of sanity and that the tyranny experienced under the rule of the Third Reich would be history. Few mentioned Adolph Hitler or his henchmen. It had been an insane time for their nation, Germans admitted. A few Germans still blamed the Jews for the disaster that was wrought on their country. A large number, however, admitted that their political ignorance and laissez-faire attitude was the root cause of Hitler's rise to power.

The German oompah-pah spirit was not destroyed by the war, as I experienced. Restaurants were serving food in West Germany and in West Berlin. Sausage, beer, bread, and other staples were available for just a few coins. People sang, danced, and participated in the cleaning, rebuilding, and redesigning of the region.

It was interesting to note that non-Germans did not see Germans as enemies but as victims of a scoundrel government, which had invaded their country. Plumbers and mechanics were using old flags with Swastikas as drip cloths, blankets for pets, and rags.

Berliners could not understand how they had been swept into the Nazi Party or into the belief that the government would resolve their economic difficulties. Most saw the thirteen years of Nazism as a horrid period of suspended disbelief where reality had been stolen from them. Germany, the intellectual jewel of Europe, had been seduced to self-destruction by a group of rogue unethical manipulators! Self-debasement is the worst crime that humans can generate for themselves.

Odd jobs were easy to obtain because labor was scarce and much work had to be done cleaning, storing food, collecting stray farm animals, fixing leaking roofs, and clearing brush off roads. After four years, Europe was still in the reconstruction mode, and would be for several more years. In this period, I was able to find several odd jobs to keep me in change and more. Farms were the favorite for jobs because farmers were usually hospitable, the food was good, accommodations were comfortable, and the work was not difficult. Tending chickens, feeding horses, milking a cow, and cleaning stalls were not too demanding, and I learned a great deal about machinery, repairs, farming, and what people thought about life, politics, religion, and the future.

Routine life was slowly returning in the countryside much more rapidly than in the cities. Farms had to be functioning to keep their dynamic sense of life. Agriculture, cattle, poultry, and everything that feeds the population had to be revived, and quickly. Farmers had the tools and the labor to rebuild their production generators.

It was easy for me to obtain work because I was willing to tackle any task from restarting a diesel engine to repairing a well pump. I learned quickly to guide a plow horse and to produce a fairly straight furrow for planting. Using wood tools and hammering nails or dowels in fences was sweaty work but not impossible for me. A good breakfast, followed by a substantial lunch, produced in me abundant energy for accomplishing tasks. In the evening a rich meal washed down with beer or wine and completed with a dessert added to family conviviality and the laughter. I learned a great deal about human nature and made good friends, some of whom continued to be my friends for more than a decade — until life went on a different course once I left Europe for the New World.

After visiting Germany I decided to return to France and to begin at the very top where William the Conqueror in 1066 took to the Channel and invaded the English Island. This was the last successful invasion of the British Isles. I took a rickety bus from Strasbourg located on the French-German border and now home of the European Union's Parliament. My destination was Cabourg, Normandy.

In Cabourg I purchased an old English Austin car — well, sort of a car. It was small. It had little or no power. It overheated and had one windshield wiper (on the driver's side fortunately), and no heat. It was adequate transportation for me if only I didn't wander too far away from civilization and a mechanic's shop. Bailing wire and a can of lubricating oil did enough to keep it moving.

I used the car for about four months after buying it from a British nurse who was scheduled to return to England. With the steering wheel on the right it was impossible for the nurse to find a buyer on the Continent, and the car was too dilapidated for shipment back across the Channel. I bought it for eight English pounds, and that was when one pound was worth about five US dollars. It was a good purchase and it served me well until I gave it a fitting and glorious end.

I drove the Austin to Caen, and then on to Brittany, to the small town of Lézardrieux, near Paimpol. In Lézardrieux, I found work on a dairy farm where I met a sweet young lady by the name of Nicole. Nicole was pleasant, quite attractive, and good company with a great sense of humor and a taste for adventure. She also worked on the dairy farm; her job was to milk and tend the cows with the help of three older, more experienced girls.

She was from Normandy but had family in the Midi and in Italy. She had relatives in Aosta and was willing to keep me company as I traveled to Haute Savoie, in the Alps, then on to Aosta, Italy where I intended to spend a few days. Nicole told me that she left her family a few years earlier to travel and gain experience by finding work here and there. Her intention was eventually to attend law school in the Netherlands or in England because she wanted to specialize in international law and set a practice in Le Hague.

The voyage to Savoie was going to be long, slow, and require a fair amount of cash. We would be traveling across France on roads that were not especially perfect. After Nicole and I had accumulated enough cash, we set off in our limousine for the high country of the Alps. The Mont Blanc was like a magnet for me. My paternal family had its origin there and I was curious to visit the region, particularly the village of Les Houches. This was, however, high territory, quite high with narrow roads and steep climbs.

Chugging along in my Austin was an adventure and a tour de force. The little car did well for most of the way but unlike "the little train that could, that could..." the Austin reached a spot where it just gave up its last particle of energy. It couldn't go on any more. It stopped and died, and nothing that I could do would coax it to start.

I had become quite adept at getting it started, repairing its broken whatnots, and finding enough life in it to get it going, often resuscitating it from death. This time it was unwilling to make any encouraging sound. The electric starter also decided to die. So it was hand cranking that became the norm at that moment. It still would not express any hope of life.

Pulling a spark plug, I discovered that it had practically no compression left in the cylinders. There it stood as a monument to good engineering and as a reminder that entropy is a real issue in physics. In the closed thermodynamic system of the Austin's state, all available means for generating energy had ceased to exist. The Austin now was merely a pile of junk parked on the edge of a 2,000-meter precipice. The Austin had labored hard to the end of its life. Now we were stranded and it was beginning to snow.

By our estimation, we were about 10 kilometers from the nearest village and my companion, Nicole, who had been my travel companion for six weeks, suggested that we push it over the side. She would take a photograph of the splendid tumble, fire, and ghastly mess.

These were the days before environmental consciousness existed. It was the Old World. Europe was still a repository for rubble and junk, and one more contribution to the junk pile would not change the existing condition very much. It was, of course, irresponsible for me to think that it would not affect the environment but I was not always a model of good sense; I am not now either.

So off it went after we removed our few possessions from inside the car. It was a long fall to the lower ledge, which was at least 1,000 meters straight down. Fortunately, because we had very little fuel, there was no fire and the car disintegrated into pieces as it struck rocks on the way down to the lower ledge, its eternal resting ground. The snow soon covered the pile of junk as it settled.

We walked to the village and soon found a farmer willing to give us, for a few days of work, lodging, food, and cash in return. The farmer told us there was plenty of room and beds in the loft of the warm barn. We settled in the loft for the evening after a good meal. In the morning we were expected to work to earn our keep.

As I recall I never saw the photographs of the tumbling automobile but spent a delicious evening and night with Nicole in the loft. Indeed, this was my first such experience and it was a memorable one. My innocence was dissipated and there was nothing to regret. Nicole had had some experience and was rather tender in helping me attain what it was that I should. The next morning we smiled and spoke very little. We both knew that it had been a fine and extraordinary night. The experience was repeated several times until we left the farm and recalled again that our time together was wonderful and memorable. Today as I think about our encounters I'm still surprised that pregnancy did not occur. The tender experience of lovemaking produced no fruit.

Six days later, after visiting Chamonix and several small villages in vain to see if I could reconnect with any members of my family, we boarded a bus that took us through the tunnel and the rest of the way to Aosta, Italy. I had found some documents mentioning my family in the library of Chamonix but it was obvious that I needed to return at a later date to pursue the search more intensively and with more time devoted to the task. Moreover, the files and the documents needed to be gathered from underground vaults and made accessible to researchers. We departed for Aosta.

The region of Aosta, located in northern Italy and not far from France, is predominantly Francophile in attitude. In that region, still within the influence of France, very little Italian is spoken and French is the operative language. Government administrative functions, church services, restaurant and cafe menus, and hotel reservations are all in French. It was a different country in all ways except for the spoken language that was imported from the north.

Aosta is one of five regions of Italy that has been granted a special status of autonomy and is permitted to establish its own regional legislation based on cultural grounds, geographic location, and on the presence of ethnic minorities — in this case, French citizens who possess full Italian citizenship.

I went to Aosta to identify the roots of my paternal family. Because the family on the paternal side straddled the French-Italian boarder, dual citizenship was the norm. My maternal family, however, came mostly from Liguria, around the city of Genoa, bordering the Ligurian Sea. I thought of heading that far south but because time and money were running short, I just explored Aosta and gorged myself on French-Italian cuisine.

Nicole left me to find her family and I've never heard from her again. I tried to locate her but I did not have much luck because the information she had given me had been incomplete and too general. I think of her at times and I hope that she remembers something of me, also, at times.

There was little evidence that a war had been fought between the Italians and French. As far as I could tell, war had simply passed over this region leaving no trace. I took the opportunity to visit the local passport office to renew my Italian passport, which had been left unattended since my last trip to the Continent with my parents, when I was a child. After the required pictures were taken and the few liras paid, my new passport was issued to me the very next day and the clerk welcomed me back into the bosom of Italy. This had been the fastest bureaucratic interchange that I had ever experienced. For a nation that has trouble keeping a government in office, the system and the economy seem to work in spite of who is running the show.

The historical city of Aosta is a jewel nestled in the long valley of the Alps. I walked to the old fortress walls, which had been incorporated, though not defaced or altered, into the expansion of the town. On one side of the street there were relatively recent buildings and houses, but on the other side, the fortress walls were part and parcel of houses constructed centuries ago.

In the alleys of the old section one could find small restaurants, coffee shops, bookstores, and stores selling handmade lace and other wonderful items that included jewelry, fine small sculptures, and beautiful cameos on local slate. It was a quiet part of the noisy city (no Italian city or town is quiet — ever). Sitting in a café sipping an excellent black coffee, munching on a brioche, and reading a book made for a most pleasant rendezvous with one's self. I had seen a good portion of Western Europe and had been away for a long time. I needed to catch up with myself, reorder my thoughts, plan my next venture, and enjoy a few moments of inner quiet.

It was time for me to head back but I wanted to see Rome, the Eternal City. I took the train via Turin and on to Rome. On the train I met a horse dealer-breeder who had a farm located on the outskirts of the city. By the time we reached Rome, I was offered a job as a jack-of-all-trades on Emilio's farm. I was able to save some money, learn a great deal about horses, and make several visits to the city of Rome and to the Vatican. "A funny thing happened on the way to the Forum," but that anecdote is told a bit later here.

Although I had earned some money, I was running out of energy. The holiday had been enormously instructive but it was time for me to return to England and I considered that the re-crossing of France would once again add more pleasure to my trip. Crossing France would be another opportunity to encounter the unique French mentality, a mentality that was supremely convinced of its superiority over all other cultures. The impossible French attitude was a challenge even for someone like me who was able to speak the language and was French.

The French are a peculiar people. For example, every request made of them is immediately responded to with a "non!" Probably this is the product of a language that employs double negatives as a matter of good grammar. It may also be an approach that demands justification to precede any request. Yet it can be infuriating to English speakers, especially when helpfulness is the norm of a polite society to them. One can get around this superficial negative attitude by maneuvering the conversation carefully to avoid a direct response and a subsequent negative reply. To achieve that takes diplomacy, as demonstrated in the following encounter.

At one point my little Austin had needed some air in one rear tire. I stopped at a repair station and asked for some air to put into the tire.

"Non, monsieur," he said. He told me that he had no air for my type of tire. I looked around and spotted a hand pump propped against one of the walls.

"Could I use this pump?" I asked.

"Non, monsieur," he shook his hand. "Non, non, it is for une bicyclette," he added. I went over to the pump and examined it. "Non, non," he repeated. I looked at him after ascertaining that the pump worked.

"May I try it?" I asked. He got up from his work and sighed in obvious exasperation.

"Non, non," he repeated. "It is not the right pump for a car tire." As he said that he grabbed the pump from my hand and said a few words that I will not repeat and proceeded to tend to the tire. After a few strokes of pumping the tire was well inflated. I thanked him and was about to give him some money. "Non, non," he scolded me. "We must check the pressure!" He did and it was correct. Thus it all started with a negative and ended positively and he refused any money.

I took a bus from Rome to Lyon, and a train from Lyon to Paris. What can be covered in one day took four. From Paris the train to Boulogne-sur-Mer was a whole day trip, then the ship over a rough English Channel to Folkstone, another day trip. On to London then Liverpool street station to catch a train to Cambridge, with a change to Ely, another day trip which brought me back a few days before Christmas 1948. It was time to decide what I was to do for my future.

* * *

My hosts, the Olivers, in Ely were happy to see me. I had kept up with them through postcards and a few letters. They knew the time of my return and prepared the traditional roast beef dinner for me. It was a lovely welcoming party and I was quite taken by their warmth and kindness. Neighbors and other Cathedral parishioners came to bid me welcome and quite a few pints of Green King ale were consumed. It seemed that the party was to welcome my return but I suspected that it was simply an excuse to let off steam with other friends. Several times I was asked to recount parts of my trip and report conditions on the Continent.

A man who lived in the house next door had a prewar Jaguar (red 1936 SS100) that he could no longer drive because when he attempted to depress the clutch the arthritic pain in his leg was augmented. I had often looked at that snazzy automobile with covetous eyes. He offered to sell me the car for a mere £25. I did not have any money; in fact I was almost penniless. With school no longer giving me an allowance, my parents curtailing most financial support to me, and the continental jaunt exhausting all my savings, I was broke. My neighbor offered me a job as a stock clerk in his small electrical manufacturing company. The pay of £20 per month would not only quickly pay for the car, but would replenish my depleted funds. For the Jaguar, I was asked to pay £5 every month. The Olivers asked only £5 per month for room and board.

The offer of the job, the car, and housing were too good for me to refuse and so I accepted. The job taught me a lot about going to work every day, meeting schedules, having the stock available (I was responsible for ordering stock ahead), and responding to supervisors. The firm was well run and a most pleasant place to work. I quickly moved from the stock room to the dynamo (generator) reconditioning shop to repair and overhaul dynamos. Working at the electrical firm was a delightful experience that also paid good wages and provided me with a lifetime British work permit.

The Jaguar I had purchased, however, was a disaster. As the joke goes: candles are still being made because Lucas Electric still makes electrical components! The electrical systems and the ignition harness were the worst mess that I had ever seen. Every other wire caused a short in the system. The two carburetors were designed to work against each other, or so it seemed. Adjustment of the carburetors was good for about twenty miles, and then the float would fill up with fuel and sink, thus flooding the system. This was not a matter of sealing a pinhole in the float; rather it was redesigning the float to prevent fuel from entering at the connection lever, which was open. In addition, the canvas roof was a joke. When it rained outside and the top was closed, it just poured inside — and water drenched the instrument panel, the driver's feet and legs, and the floor mats. With no drainage outlet, water simply sloshed inside the car. The car was a catastrophic design. I sold it three months later to an automobile restorer for exactly £25. No gain, but no loss either in this experience. I was convinced that I would never again own a Jaguar, and I haven't.

I worked at the electrical firm for seven months. It was now time for me to decide what my next step would be. I had restored my funds in a limited way but now I had to give serious thought to the next phase of my life. On one of my London visits, I had obtained applications for residence visas for Brazil, Canada, and Australia. I had also made inquiries of their Air Forces at their respective Consulates and whether each country needed pilots with the 425 hours I had accumulated. The countries contacted were receptive to my inquiries and each offered me a flying slot with their Air Force if I could satisfy their requirements, which were not all that demanding. I decided to start with Canada. Travel was ahead for me again but it would not be like my long, carefree visit to the Continent of Europe.

My stay on the European Continent taught me many things that have since come to my rescue. With only a few Sterling pounds to my name, I managed to travel the Continent for eight months and in the process visited France, Italy, Belgium, the Netherlands, Germany, Austria, Luxembourg, and Switzerland. Finding work in exchange for food, lodging, and a few coins was not too difficult. Pitching hay; brushing, feeding, and exercising horses; stacking firewood; cooking; picking apples, pears, cherries, and flowers; helping with the construction of barns; repairing roofs; and shoring water holding ponds; each was a splendid task that gave me what I needed, cash and experience, and allowed me to meet people of all walks of life and in many places.

I enjoyed meeting people, eating different foods, and seeing new sites — many that I had read about. Working with horses and constructing barns and water holding ponds gave me experience that I used in later years when I tended horses, built swimming pools, and worked on my house. Housing construction in Europe is very much different than in America. Europeans build their houses out of stone, brick, and plaster while the United States mainly builds in wood and sheetrock; if bricks or stones are used they are often used as a veneer, especially in earthquake regions.

I became quite knowledgeable about the European countryside and many of the cities, especially Paris, Berlin, Amsterdam, Brussels, and Lyon. Paris became one of my favorite cities and remains a special place for me. The city is sensibly designed, the Seine River is beautiful, enchanting, and divides the city to produce two sides of the same coin, and each side has its own character, its own magnetism, and its own flavor that sparks one's intellect, one's palate, and one's sense of romance. Yes, Paris is the queen city in my heart.

Each city I visited furnished me with an anecdote, a story, and an occasion that will always remain in my head. For example, outside Rome, I worked for a horse dealer and breeder, and on one occasion I was allowed to borrow a white horse to ride into Rome (traffic was still docile after the war). My reason for this adventure was historical, and Signore Emilio, the owner of the horse farm, approved and gave me permission to ride the white horse into the Eternal City; in fact he offered to meet me with his horse trailer at the Coliseum so I would not have to ride back. Whether that kind gesture was for me or for the horse I leave it to the readers to decide.

Recounting history, I mimicked the Roman emperor Lucius Domitius Aurelianus, who after his victory against the German hordes rode a white horse upon his return to Rome in 274 and was hailed the victor as *restitutor orbis*. Much later in 1925, Benito Mussolini entered Rome on a white horse when he declared himself Il Duce, the Fascist Premier with absolute emergency power in Italy. And here I was a young boy riding into Rome on a white stallion. I did not, however, declare myself either emperor or dictator. Today I wish a photograph had been taken of this brash kid entering Rome on a white stallion, a Lipizzaner no less!

Seeing the European Continent against the background of the destruction of World War II was quite a jolt for me. I had read many books on European history and the bloody battles that were fought for causes that often made little sense. The 30-year war, the 100-year war, the Napoleonic conquests and defeats, the Russo-Swedish conflicts, the Ottoman occupations, the Islamic invasion of Spain and subsequent expulsion, and World War I, all terrible accounts but none as poignant as seeing a land denuded, in rubble, and nearly shorn of its architectural heritage. The people looked aged, tired, afraid, and bankrupt of assets and energy.

Germany was a basket case. Most Germans could not believe what had happened, and it had all occurred in the short time of Adolph Hitler's thirteen-year rule. Often I would hear people say "we Germans had chosen the morally bankrupt route to success." The failure of that choice brought total wreckage burdened by enormous guilty feelings. Oh, yes there were a few hardened folk, as I alluded to earlier, who lamented the demise of Hitler's period, the end of the Nazi era. These people were in the minority and were regarded as living in an ethical vacuum and also to be ethically corrupt. Nevertheless, seeing Germany's ruin and the destruction it had caused for others offered food for a future idea: a united Europe.

The Marshall Plan coupled with the airlift to Berlin were examples that benevolence was not crushed by the war. There still existed some modicum of good in humanity. Yet the margin for benevolence in human beings is thin and frail, and is often overwhelmed by self-righteousness, feelings of self-aggrandizement, and a quest for power produced by unabated greed. The malady that rises from greed and self importance is not limited to Europeans, it is found in all countries and contaminates many leaders, even leaders of the United States Witnessing the results brought about by WWII was a lesson worth learning, and to a young boy it was memorable.

Today when in Europe I'm still looking at the new just as much as I recall the old, the historic. Whether in London or in Nuremberg the recollection has not left me, particularly when I meet people of WWII's generation. People of that period behave differently and even act in peculiar fashion. I am a war child and as such I am able to recognize the attitude effectively displayed by other war children or survivors of the war. For example, our grocery purchases are more abundant, we buy more than we can consume — because, perhaps, we believe that tomorrow will bring the return of penury. This is just one simple example but an indicative one. It gives an insight as to why we are great consumers: tomorrow the shelves may be bare. Any news of impending conflict moves me to restock my pantry, my freezer, and my vegetable cooler. Food becomes the focus of my attention. Although I never suffered moments of hunger during the war, I've known people, close folks, who missed meals because of their bare pantries during night after night of air raids.

Another side effect of the war years is that I am (we are) wary of border controls, passport checkers, and security and police officers, except perhaps for the English staff, but they too are beginning to lose their safe image for me. So many stories have been shared with me about the unethical behavior of border civil servants, these pseudo pillars of the law, that I am often anxious, vigilant, and prudent when I encounter them. Even after the war I can remember being stopped by Austrian control officers telling me that I had to leave my passport with the authorities before I could enter the country — even though I had another valid passport with me. I would not leave my passport and at my insistence was finally, after three hours of discussion, permitted to enter Austria. This procedure has been changed by their need for tourism and the pressures of the emerging European Economic Union.

Perhaps not as restrictive as it used to be but the requirement to scrutinize a passport, a visa, a particular entry-exit document is still prevalent in Russia, Ukraine, Saudi Arabia, Slovakia, and Belorussia. Tin gods are found in many third world countries too and thus I remain apprehensive and distrustful when I cross a border and that reflects much of my experience and conversation with people who lived through WWII. Arriving in Saudi Arabia, usually after midnight, I can be assured that to check the passenger manifest of a Boeing 767 will take at least three to four hours and every document will be analyzed, every piece of literature will be examined, and every personal article will be inspected (all of this long before the incident of the World Trade Center in 2001). Even when entering Canada, the experience was encountered again in 1950, and the result was sixteen days of incarceration because a border officer did not like what he heard. But more on that later in the story.

The Continental experience was an indelible lesson offering both good and bad feelings but mostly good ones. Roaming Europe helped me become an adult and gave me the knowledge needed to manage my affairs, my funds, and my needs. It also reinforced my independence and my self-reliance as a young man. Being away from my mother was propitious. It was such a gift to be independent of parental control that I cherished it all my life and counted myself fortunate that I had been given the opportunity to be as much as possible master of my actions. I've never relinquished that gift no matter the circumstances, the organizations, or the relationships.

The Time of Troubles

While in school I was not only physically separated from my parents but I was mostly out of the loop of family politics. For the short time I visited them in 1942 I noticed that there were several indications that the relationship between my father and my mother was not jolly. Mother was very demanding but in a way that was suffocating to others. My father was also demanding but not possessive. Father's way was usually well thought out, reasonable, and considerate. Mother's was arbitrary and domineering. There was a tendency to be manipulative in my mother's approach with relationships, and especially with father and me. Fortunately I escaped by some stroke of good fortune; he could not.

I am certain that the tension built up or was building up to dangerous levels but the war was a distraction. Yet, one always assumed that her possessiveness was an expression of affection and love, and it may have been, at least I thought so for many years, but I was removed from the immediate environment. Being removed from the center of family affairs I became objective and even tolerant, especially tolerant because I was not affected by any manipulative expression for very long.

Nothing that I say should indicate that what I am stating about my mother is a negative condemnation; it is merely a judgment of mother's actions. Mother cannot defend herself and probably would throw the whole commentary into the trash and call it rubbish, as she did with my dissertation years later. She would not stew over it but would regard it as a non-issue. The world owed her a certain respect that she demanded regardless of the consequences or the damages inflicted on others. I thought for a long time that she was my greatest defender, admirer, and source of love — until she turned around and sued me for the reason that I was trying to protect her health and her assets. That, however, is a story to be told at a later time and a difficult story for me to tell.

Being away at school in 1947 I was informed by my mother in a night cable that there was another woman in my father's life. Mother and Father were divorcing and he was returning to France to seek employment, now that the war was over in Europe. The cable was Mother's, and no, she was not giving me Father's address. Father was a cad and a playboy, a man with little consideration for family responsibilities. Unwilling to defend himself he did not contest the accusations, hence he just changed venue. The court judgment assigned custody of me to Mother's jurisdiction, as was the normal procedure before men demanded more fairness in child custody issues. In the 40s custody of children usually was given to mothers regardless of who was at fault.

A few weeks later I received a telegram from Father giving me his new address in Paris in the Faubourg Saint Germain-en-Laye. In the telegram my father informed me that he had taken a freighter across the Mediterranean Sea to Marseille, then traveled to Paris by train where he was interviewing for a position at one of the universities or colleges. In the meantime he was temporarily lecturing at the College de Paris from which he was drawing a small salary.

By her omission of Father's whereabouts, it was obvious that Mother did not want me to have his address. In fact, in a subsequent missive from Mother she forbade me from communicating with Father because he was a scoundrel of the worst kind. She also wrote a long and disparaging letter to Dr. Price, the Headmaster of VC, about my father and was instructed not to let me communicate with him. Dean Price ignored her instructions and I suspect that he filed her letter without paying much attention to it. Dean Price did, however, inform me that Mother did not want me to correspond with my father but he was not going to enforce any such sanction. The letter from Mother moved Dean Price to become more fatherly and concerned about my wellbeing. He assured me that the financial trust on deposit made at the beginning of the war was sufficient to keep me at VC until I matriculated.

Soon after civilian travel resumed after the war, around 1947, Mother took a ship to Southampton for a short visit with me and to meet some friends and head for a holiday in Norway. I was puzzled about Norway but I counted that to curiosity and adventure. I knew nothing of Olav Cartwold Mong at the time. Olav was a Norwegian/American engineer who had finished an assignment in the Western Desert of Egypt. Mother had met him at some reception and an intimate relationship developed that I was not privileged to know about for several months. Ultimately Olav and Mother married and he offered to adopt me.

I took the train to London and met Mother at the Alliance Française, where she had reserved a room. Mother spoke very little English and so I was able to show off a little of my capability to speak the language. After dinner, she spoke of my father and deprecated his character with every sentence. The intent was to convince me that he was a louse, but I still admired him and enjoyed him whenever I was with him, which had not been often since I was in school. Mother assured me that I would be better off if I dismissed my father from memory. That evening mother had consumed an ample quantity of Scotch whisky and was speaking quite freely. I listened. I also recognized that she had been consuming too much alcohol. Not having lived with her for several years and seeing my mother a bit intoxicated was new and unpleasant to me. I did not care for it. She continued to talk and talk.

My mother apparently never did accept any responsibility for the marriage breakup. I don't fault her, but it would have been more reasonable if she had accepted more, perhaps not all, of the responsibility for it. Integrity requires that one examine all the facets of one's behavior. That done, the process of selecting which action is causing a problem becomes more realistic. Conflict often requires that both sides get exposure to the light of integrity. In the breakup of the marriage she took the role of being the victim and assigned Father the role of the perpetrator.

It was predictable that Mother never objectively and carefully examined the issue that had caused the marriage to disintegrate. She conceded that the relationship between them had not been good for some years, but they could have plodded along that way. Yet, in her eyes my father was neither satisfied nor willing to maintain the status quo in tension. The information given to me by my mother was that Father asked for a separation, which then was transformed into a divorce after several arguments surfaced. Mother accused him of seeing another woman but his denial did not convince her.

The next morning when I met her at breakfast before she boarded a ship to Norway she made me promise that I would never tell anyone that they had divorced. She was adamant that I make that promise. In confusion and sympathy for her I made the promise, a promise that I've regretted making ever since. She also asked that I erase his memory from my own. It was an innocuous promise at the time but one that would cause me great difficulties in the future, especially with my own family after my marriage. I made the promise and thought little of it at the moment. She had convinced me that father was not a good person — but nevertheless I still liked him. I respected my mother's wish to hide the fact of the divorce and to my own detriment and ill ease, but that was how it was handled. In truth at the time I thought that it would not affect anything. Perhaps I was young, perhaps I was intimidated, perhaps I just wanted to get on with the situation and see her leave, sail away to Norway. Mother made me promise as long as she lived I would not indicate that she divorced my father.

My father, when I discussed the issue with him, said that it did not matter to him but that I was still his son. In retrospect I am certain that I did not clearly understand either what the consequences of managing the truth would entail or how much my relationship with Father would suffer. Life was in front of me and I had to tend to it. The details of the conflict between my parents did not cause me great distress at the time. If I made a foolish promise, it was not important to me, but later the burden of keeping it was of enormous importance, especially when it presented me a maze from which extrication was difficult.

In later years I discovered that Father was not the evil person that was described to me but that it had been a total fabrication by my mother. I do not believe that I questioned it because my father was, if anything, charming, bright, handsome, and interesting. Father's return to France was to teach linguistics. He was given a professorship in one of the colleges of the Sorbonne where he taught for many years. I was able to see him when I could travel to France — and that was only on extended school holidays, which were rare.

Travel to the Continent was difficult at first immediately after the war ended, and lodging was miserably poor. My father lived in a small flat with only the minimum of necessities which included his enormous library. But he was employed and the academic system was being rebuilt rapidly. Interestingly, his university office was larger than his apartment and it had a large couch, a small kitchen, and a tiny bathroom: all quite adequate for spending a night or two. I did learn that Father had begun to see a woman.

What I remember most of my father were the long walks and the accompanying talks. How is the Mobius surface relevant to human thinking? Why is "tough" spelt with "gh" and not f? What does the "ç" replace in French grammar? What about the circumflex accent on the "ô"? Why is the velocity of light a constant and how does it affect us? What is meant by "coherence" and does it change with people, with circumstances, and with time? Is there a meaning to life? Why are humans the only creatures cooking their food? How is God understood in your life? Is it necessary to be free? These were a few of the questions that took us miles of walking to explore, yet I never felt exhausted.

Father was a fine cook who had certain specialties that I remember and often duplicate. For example he was the one who taught me how to roast both eggplants and peppers. He taught me how to cut meat like a butcher, how to de-bone fowl, and how to remove the bones from a whole fish. He also taught me how to mix hot mustard using Colman's English powdered mustard. Watching my father in the kitchen of his apartment was seeing a confident and adept person.

When it was time to learn how to ride a bicycle, he would not have me use a training wheel. He put me on the bike, held the back of my seat and ran behind me while I pedaled. Soon, I was riding without his help and did not realize it until he made me ride past a large shop window and asked me to look at the reflection.

In Paris we walked to many important sites, from the library, to the main research departments of the Sorbonne, to the gardens, to many other places that are engraved in my memory. Often we stopped for a bite to eat, some ice cream, or a piece of fresh bread to munch on as we walked further. Walks were always punctuated by questions, tidbits of information exchanged, philosophical queries explored, and other topics shared. Our conversation was always filled with themes that enlightened me.

In the mid-40s divorce was a blight on society — it may still be. In isolation from family events, I went to school. I did what had to be done and lived with it. It was wrong but it was a fact in my life. When mother met and later married Olav C. Mong in 1948, I accepted that. My father, William, was surprised but in a sense relieved. In 1949 William remarried a woman I never met by the name of Violette, and that was that. Violette was also a professor (I believe at another university), but of literature. Father appeared happy and willing to remake his life. We continued to communicate by letter or by telegram on a semi-regular basis.

Because Olav was a naturalized US citizen, he and Mother moved to America and he kindly offered me his name thinking that it would help if I wished to emigrate from Europe to the United States of America. At the time I did not wish to emigrate to the United States of America. In conversation with Father, we agreed that he had no objection to my joining the names of French and Norwegians, if the circumstances deemed necessary — something that had been done extensively during Napoleon's reign. I did not want to obliterate the name Hoche, and thought that a hyphenated name was not only the solution to the problem but was also historically correct. At the time, however, I had no interest in either going to the United States or of adopting Olav's name. It was a kind offer but not one that interested me. But more on the name change and the circumstances that promoted it later. For the eager reader, the hyphenated name "Hoche-Mong" saw first light in 1950 in Canada, but only after some very serious deliberation on my part. The change of name at the time was merely an act of expediency as I alluded earlier, long before it happened.

Regrets do not haunt me. Were I to reconsider the issue of changing my name today, perhaps I would not. The fact remains that not only did I change my name but also I kept the silly promise made to my mother. That promise caused me to be regretful. I should not have made it. Even if Mother had pitched a fit, it would have lasted just a little while then been over. The promise, however, has haunted me for most of my life. It was a miserable commitment to make, and, perhaps, Mother should not have asked me for it. But it was done and I accepted the consequences. That was that.

The unfortunate qualities of life are that a person is given one pass, and only one pass for the duration. There isn't a second opportunity given that would provide some correction to poor decisions. We have one chance to make correct choices. That is unfortunate because I can see how preferable it would be if one could erase the board of old choices and redraw new choices, when experience has given a person better options and a longer view. This is not said as an excuse but as a notice that I should have chucked the promise long, long ago. A promise made at one age, when one is young and naïve should not be carried throughout life as being indelible. Now I view the whole temper of promises as being valid only for a short time, less than a decade at the longest.

Human beings change, society places new pressures on us homo sapiens, and contemporary culture evolves so rapidly and dynamically that a commitment made one day may no longer be applicable the next day or the next decade. Of course this realistic position on promises, that they are outdated and irrelevant, cuts through the fabric of many positions, many issues, and many conditions. What does that imply about witnesses in courts, marriage vows, constitutional commitments, and a gamut of other situations where human beings make vows, pronounce promises, and accept commitments one day that are ineffectual the next?

Decades later with a Jesuit friend and mentor, Dr. James Mara, SJ. we discussed the subject of promises because they had bothered me and were making him miserably unhappy. Jim had been a devoted member of the Society of Jesus for 35 years and was wretchedly treated by the Jesuits. Because Jim had voiced issues, positions, and philosophical ideas that went against the very grain of the Society and of the Roman Catholic Church, and because he still associated with intellectuals of other persuasions, beliefs, and faiths, he was censored and inhibited. His creative spirit had been dampened often. His writings could no longer be published. He was no longer allowed to teach in an academic institution. In the terminal days of his life, he had been parked in a retreat center to hear confessions and not even to conduct a program. His stature in the Society had been slowly diminishing. I had met him when he was still teaching and loved his creative, inquisitive, perceptive mind and approach to scholarship. I had included him in the examining committee for my doctorate.

One day after I had kidnapped him for dinner away from the retreat center, we talked about promises made. He would not leave the Society of Jesus even though he had ostensibly parted company with it. He had seen what the Society and the Roman Catholic Church had done to his friend Dr. Teilhard de Chardin (his colleague at Oxford), what treatment had been given to Dr. Hans Kuhn at Heidelberg University (his colleague in Rome), and the shoddy way several of his contemporaries on many university and seminary faculties had been treated. Jim had had his own writing censured and then denigrated because of his liberal philosophical and theological bent and his criticism of the dogmatic attitude taught by the Roman Catholic Church.

Although Jim was quite devoted to Pope John XXIII and his approaches in Vatican II and had the support of the Society of Jesus' leadership, he was nevertheless ostracized by Rome and censored. John the XXIII's life ended too soon and by his death the process of liberalization was quickly arrested and Jim was once again restricted from voicing his thoughts.

"Why don't you leave the Society and just teach in a secular institution?" I asked him.

"Raymond," he replied, "I made a promise as a young man to the Society and to God that I would be a Jesuit all my life and that I would follow their discipline. I cannot just abandon that promise because it no longer suits me."

"But Jim, you were a very young man and the Society was full of promise for you. Now it has abandoned you, parked you in a dead-end institution, and is censoring your thoughts, as much as they have censored Teilhard's and Küng's, and by the way, also Galileo's and others of the same ilk."

We discussed that Teilhard remained with the Society until his death but that Küng abandoned the Society to continue his work as a teacher and at the same university.

"A promise is a promise and I cannot break the one I made."

We spoke of the fact that a 20-year-old is very much different from a 60-year-old, even becoming a different person forty years later. Yes, that was true and had some value but it was not sufficient to convince Jim to abandon the Society. This was the argument that Küng used when he abandoned the Society. Jim was not taking that path; a promise made was a promise kept. Period. Jim died three weeks later.

The solution to my inquiry about promises did not materialize. I stayed the course for a few more years. The act of choosing inaction was painful, disheartening, but easier than that of action. Postponement was the better part of valor. I remained silent and avoided the issue although it gnawed on me. My children suspected that a problem existed but were polite enough to wait the silence out. For how long, I do not know. How I wish I had not been put in that situation.

Now that my mother is dead, I still find it hard to open up, to be candid, even after all the years of a somewhat "trompe œil" history. I was foolish. I was stupid. To protect my inner being from the public I stuck my head in the sand. I became reserved in my dealings with other people. Others attributed this behavior to dispassionate aloofness. The real culprit was that I was more concerned with acquiescing to my mother's whim than with living an open life. I was a wimp, but it was easier to avoid the issue than to confront it head on.

I think that I've learned a lesson. Both my mother and father are dead. My children knew my mother. They never had the good fortune to know my father, their grandfather. I hardly knew him, and wish I could have known him more and shared more of my life with him; a tragedy perhaps.

We are young for such a short time and as parents we have little opportunity to enjoy and to participate in the development of our children. Life seems to be open before us for a few moments and then all of a sudden it begins to display signs of ending, and we are old, the children are no longer children, and mutual involvement in each other's lives is dissipated by time, busy-ness, affliction, conflict, and all the obstacles that surface from one moment to the next. I can share some aspects of my life with my daughter and son, and they can share some of theirs, but on the whole we are too involved in living to devote enough time to each other. It is a regret that will never abandon me that I was not able to share my love for both my daughter and son fully and constantly and without reservation. My marriage to Trudy did not help at all but it maximized the reserved attitude that I displayed; but that is a story that will be dealt with later.

I suppose that the requirements of the modern world are to blame, but only in part. We lead a fragmented life and much of this life is in separation from family because of employment requirements and a hundred other intrusive commitments.

Enough of this self-analysis and introspection for the moment — my life did continue in a splendid manner.

Naples and Cairo

As I indicated earlier, after making inquiries about Air Forces in Brazil, Canada, and Australia, I chose to start with Canada. I notified my mother that I would be going to Genoa, Italy to catch the passenger ship *Conte Biancamano* of the Navigazione Generale Italiana, sailing to Halifax, Nova Scotia, Canada. My mother asked me if I would find time to go to Cairo to finalize the transfer of some funds from the Banque du Crédit Lyonnais to her account at Manufacturer's Hanover Bank in New York. Because Mother was in New York and I was in Europe and without pending schedule, I could travel to Cairo. That opportunity to revisit Cairo was just what I wanted, especially since my expenses were to be paid. She cabled me 800 US dollars, which was an ample sum of money for such a trip.

In spite of the fact that the timing was questionable in 1949 I wanted to visit Cairo once more. Egypt was in the midst of a developing political revolution with a government that was ineffective, a monarch, King Farouk, who was a despicable international playboy, and, a group of hotheaded young colonels who were plotting a coup. Anyway, with some apprehension I decided to visit Cairo for a couple of weeks.

There were many small ships sailing the Mediterranean to Alexandria from the port of Naples, Italy. I made inquiries in London and found one that offered me a steward's job for the price of a round trip fare plus tips. I took it. The *Pace*, a 5,000-ton ship, would be leaving in a week's time from Naples. After packing my few belongings in three suitcases, saying goodbye to my hosts, and attending Ely one more time (VC was no longer functioning; it had been absorbed into the larger British Council educational system, and the faculty and students had been transferred to other schools), I took the train to London to buy my international train pass to Naples. It would take five days of traveling night and day and that allowed me two spare days before the *Il Pace's* departure.

The train was quite adequate although the trip was long and tedious. With a change of trains to cross the English Channel, once on continental soil, a Franco-Italian rail system took me all the way to Rome. In Rome a locomotive hitched on to the cars heading south to Naples, and off we raced to the Mezzogiorno section of Italy, the departments that lie below the latitude of Rome.

Arriving in Naples on a clear morning with blue sky and the island of Capri visible just beyond the city and Mount Vesuvius rising in the distance, I headed for Piazza Garibaldi and the hotel by the same name. I was given a front room overlooking the piazza and I could smell all the good scents emanating from kitchens, street vendors selling pizza, and fresh brewed coffee from nearby cafés.

Though hungry I still wanted a shower before heading for food. The showers were in the hallway and I commandeered one to remove five days of accumulated body odor laced with cigarette smoke from fellow passengers. Once clean, I gave my dirty laundry to an attendant (it was too dirty for a quick sink washing) and off I went to explore, register at the docks, and see what the *Pace* looked like. After buying a slice of pizza covered with tiny smelt-like fish, tomatoes, green peppers, and wonderful cheeses I washed it down with a triple Italian espresso coffee. My energy restored, I headed for the docks.

Finding *Il Pace* was not easy. I had never traveled by ship and the image in my mind was of a passenger ship like the French liner *Normandie* or the British Cunard liner *Queen Mary*. I looked and searched and all I could see were rusty old tubs in disgraceful condition. I asked a man sitting at a desk if he could direct me to *Il Pace* but all he did was point at a white vessel with more rust than paint covering its side. It looked awfully small.

I walked over to the ship and asked a beefy bearded sailor where I could sign in as a member of the crew. Without uttering a word, he seized my shoulder with his huge hand and guided me to what I thought was the purser's office. After signing in and being welcomed aboard by a man who spoke French to me, Pierro, the hefty bearded sailor, took me to where I would bunk for the crossing. Pierro pointed to a top hammock and spoke for the first time by telling me that it was better for sleeping to be above the other two men below me, who had not reported for duty yet. I was given a duffle bag for my personal possessions and a padlock with a key.

After that I was shown the toilet, the sinks, and the showers. All of them were located in very tight quarters, but I didn't mind that because the crossing would only take five days. Pierro then introduced me to the chief steward of the cabins whose name was Mario and who had been, I was informed, with the *Pace* for three years. It was his home, his domain. We chatted a bit and then he decided to assign me to the first class section because I could speak some Arabic, and was fluent in French and English. I gathered that few Italians made the crossing and practically all instructions were in French or English. After an espresso, a brioche, some instructions from Mario, and a tour of the ship, I was informed that I had to be on board at 7:00 the morning the day the ship was to sail. The *Pace* was scheduled to cast off and sail at 14:00 two days hence.

With a day and a half of no commitments, it was time for me to become a tourist. Nearby I found the staging dock for a small ferryboat that could take me to see the island of Capri, the enchanted island for many romantic novels. Off I went across the harbor to Capri. It was beautiful, lush with flowers, and carved by small streets. White paint was the predominant tone of the island.

After spending several hours walking, eating, and looking I took the ferryboat back to Naples' glorious seafront, known as Santa Lucia. It was lined with beautiful hotels, restaurants, and expensive shops. In the hills overlooking the sea and the harbor, the villas were extraordinary, beautiful, and splendid in architecture. I decided to climb the hill and take a closer look at the villas. After looking and saying "buon pomeriggio" (good afternoon) to several people working in their gardens, I was greeted by a pleasant and attractive lady in her middle-fifties who asked me what I was about. She spoke Italian and I responded in my spotty Italian that I was visiting Naples before embarking on a ship for a short visit to Cairo.

The lady had lived in Cairo before the war but had decided to settle in Naples to write her tenth book. The book would be a romantic novel set in the village of Sorrento. I rediscovered my fluency in Italian. She invited me onto her veranda for a drink, a Campari to cool my throat, and helped me enjoy more the hospitality and view of Santa Lucia.

The lady's name was Ivetta Arletta and she soon informed me that the Germans had killed her husband during the war because he was a sympathizer of the Allies and was accused of being an undercover agent for the Americans. As it turned out after his execution, he had been a member of the underground and opposed Mussolini and his Fascist government.

We talked for several hours and discussed the war years, my education, my love for flying, my pending trip to Cairo, and my soon-to-develop adventure to join the Royal Canadian Air Force. Her butler, a courtly gentleman probably older than God, came after sunset to announce that dinner would be served on the veranda in one hour; did we want an aperitif? She ordered a light wine for us and insisted I stay for dinner. I accepted willingly. The dinner and the wine were lovely.

At around ten in the evening I excused myself to return to my hotel. For me it had been a long day and sleeping on trains is not restful. I was tired. Indicating that I looked tired, she would have her driver take me to Hotel Garibaldi and bring me back to her villa at noon the next day. I was driven to my hotel in a bright red Maserati Quattro Porte. We would go to see Sorrento the next day for a picnic.

Next morning in a café not far from the hotel I had two café lattes, cheese, and three brioches. At noon, the chauffeur arrived again in the red Maserati Quattro Porte with Mrs. Arletta, who insisted I call her Ivetta. We drove to the yacht club and boarded an impressive boat that must have been longer than 50 feet. The yacht was sumptuous and the members of the crew numbering five or six men were all dressed in appropriate uniforms identifying their position and tasks. We motored out of the club mooring space and set sail for Sorrento, the enchanting coastal village mentioned in many songs and depicted in scores of novels.

I asked the first mate who owned the beautiful yacht and was informed that it was Signora Arletta's. She liked sailing and long voyages in comfort and she often sailed the Mediterranean, the Adriatic, and the Aegean seas. I was impressed by her lifestyle. We passed near Castellammare di Stabia and soon we approached the small harbor of Sorrento and docked. After a walk of two hours along the Corniche, we returned to the boat for a late afternoon tea with savories and sweets served under the deck's awning. On the return trip, Ivetta asked me again to dinner. But returning to Ivetta's villa for dinner the driver gave us a tour of the city of Naples including the coast road that hugs the cliffs overlooking the Tyrrhenian Sea to Pozzuoli and Bacoli. After dinner I was taken to the hotel in a small Fiat Topolino, a very compact car. This would be the car that would take me in the morning to the ship so that I would not be embarrassed or teased by the crew. Ivetta insisted that upon my return from Cairo I stay at the villa until I left for Genoa and the crossing to the New World.

At 6:00 in the morning I boarded *Il Pace* and after stowing my belongings I was ready for work. Mario, the chief steward, gave me two black pairs of trousers and three white jackets, my uniform for the trip. Taking me to the storage closet, Mario briefed me, showed me the equipment I would need, the towels, linens, and cleaning cloths that I would use to clean and freshen the cabin under my watch. Because I served the first class section, my shifts would cover around the clock. On the night shift I could sleep but I had to listen to buzzer calls from cabins, in the event that fresh towels were needed, a bed remade, or a bathroom re-stocked. My job was not to be a waiter but a cabin steward in charge of keeping six cabins in top condition. There were a total of twelve cabins in first class.

We sailed out of the harbor on time. All guest luggage had been placed in the correct cabins and I was waiting for my first call to serve. I was informed that good service produced good tips. Once out of the harbor and into the open Tyrrhenian Sea and moving towards the turbulent straights of Messina I became quite nauseated. I ran to the side railing and lost my lunch. Pierro happened to pass by and saw my awful condition. I was seasick. How could I serve my cabins? I thought. This was my first experience with the sea. Crossing the English Channel had never been much of a problem; nausea often gripped me but never to the point of losing my lunch. I had never been airsick, but the sea was not the air.

"Raimondo," he called me, "I fix your sickness, subito," he said in English.

He returned a few minutes later with a cup filled with tart pickled cucumbers, onions, carrots, cauliflowers, and peppers. Pierro put a piece of tart cauliflower in my mouth and insisted I chew and eat it. Just the thought made me sicker but I ate it. He continued to feed me piece after piece of these pickles, then he asked me to drink the pickle juice, a swallow at a time. Soon the sickness diminished. The sea swells looked enormous, and the 5,000-ton *Pace* bobbed up and down, right and left, like a paper boat, yet I was no longer seasick. The pickles had rapidly cured my nausea.

Pierro made me keep a small jar of pickles in my pocket in case "the sickness" returned. When my passengers became slightly ill from the bobbing of the sea, I would offer them pickles. The proof of the cure was in the large tips I received. I offered Pierro part of my tips but he would not accept anything. When I crossed the Atlantic on the 40,000-ton *Conte Biancamano*, I kept the same pickle jar in my possession, but replenished with a fresh batch.

Pierro fetched me to see the coast of Egypt on the horizon and the light of Alexandria at the entrance of the harbor. It was early dawn and *Il Pace* would be docking by eight o' clock that morning. I would catch the train to Cairo at noon for a three-hour ride to the capital. I did not know where I would be staying but I thought the Carlton would be a good place because it was close to places I had to be and was familiar. A taxi or fiacre (horse buggy) would be the best way to go to the hotel from the train station.

Il Pace tied up at 7:30 and passengers began to disembark as soon as we reached the gangplank. Passengers disembarked rapidly and by 11:00, after cleaning, re-stocking the cabins, and briefing a crewmember as my replacement, I was free to leave the ship. The *Pace* was scheduled to depart and return to Naples at three o'clock in the afternoon of the same day. I would re-board it in a fortnight for my return to Naples. I said "ciao" to my dear shipmates, collected my belongings, and caught a fiacre (horse-drawn carriage) to the train station.

I picked up my ticket for the ride in second class and boarded the steam train. It left on time but arrived fifteen minutes early in Cairo, which is approximately only 110 kilometers from Alexandria. The train made very good time and I had a pleasant voyage from the Nile Delta to Cairo, with a short stop in Tanta where I purchased a Tamiya sandwich and a Tsepas lime soda bottle.

Again I hailed a fiacre to the Carlton Hotel after crossing the parts of Cairo I knew best, Emad El Din and Fouad streets, past Tsepas patisserie, Groppi's restaurant, and the Court of Justice for Foreigners. The Carlton Hotel was a small but good hotel on a quiet street in mid-town Cairo. I was able to get a large room on the seventh floor with a view of the city. It was now time to unpack and call my uncle Mathieu. My uncle Mathieu was to fetch me in the morning at nine to help me sort out my mother's financial affairs. He was a solicitor and barrister attorney practicing in Cairo. My uncle (who was also my most favorite uncle) was listed on the American immigration quota to arrive in New York in 1954.

It was off to Groppi's after a shower and clean clothes to order first an Amstel beer to quench my thirst from the long hot voyage and safe arrival on firm land. Groppi's had not changed much; Mohamed, the now older and distinguished "garcon," recognized me.

"Bienvenue Monsieur Raymond," he addressed me in French.

Mohamed had known me for many years ever since I could go by myself to Groppi's for ice cream before heading to England. In 1942, when I returned to Cairo for the summer months, I stopped at this branch of Groppi's almost every day, and Mohamed was always the one who served me. Upon my return from Palestine in 1942 after my Baptism, Mohamed was the first to congratulate me by giving me an extra scoop of ice cream. Mohamed was a dear person who had often helped us at home when we had a party; that was how he earned a little extra cash and my father treated him quite well.

Mohamed and I shook hands warmly. He had aged quite a bit but still stood quite tall and erect in his white robe, red tarbouch on his head, and red cummerbund around his waist. It had been a long time, almost seven years, since we spoke last. I ordered and waited for the Amstel to arrive. After eating the main dish of lamb shank, rice, green beans and courgettes, the profiteroles arrived. Delicious is too mild a word to describe the wonderful taste of Groppi's profiteroles and the thick warm chocolate sauce on it.

After dinner, I gave Mohamed an Egyptian £100 note. He was almost in tears; I stood up and gave him a strong hug. He brought me a cognac on the house. He was a wonderful man, kind and patient with a young boy who must have been a terror as a child. Groppi's was also a café where my father met his colleagues to discuss intellectual subjects as I wandered around the place and pestered Mohamed and others. I was recognized and forgiven. I saw Mohamed three more times before I departed Cairo. The last time was on my last evening before taking the train back to Alexandria and the return voyage to Naples on *Il Pace*.

Cairo: My Birthplace

Cairo had changed since my last visit in 1942; perhaps it was that I was a bit older and saw it less from a child's perspective. Seven years can bring a great deal of change in the perspective one has on a city, especially the city of one's birth. As a child Cairo was my playground; I knew the streets, I knew the alleys, I knew where my friends lived, and I saw the city as my home. Seven years later the city was no longer my home, just the place where I was born.

Politically the city had changed to the point where foreigners were obviously unwelcome. The government was weak and about to fall any day. The King's disastrous and embarrassing reign was visibly terminating. Farouk was no longer loved but despised, abhorred, and hated both as a monarch and as a man. The King had sullied his father's crown, the country, and his family. One could see a coup coming followed either by assassination, deposition, abdication, and/or marshal law. The military was in the shadows waiting for the right moment to make its move. It was common knowledge that a group of colonels under the leadership of a disgruntled general was plotting a change.

The conflict with the new state of Israel was a time bomb waiting for the fuse to be ignited. The Egyptians and the Arab nations were poised to ignite the fuse as soon as a leader emerged from their midst. Weak as the Arab world was, they had been given an unjust hand to play with the establishment of the new State of Israel. With veneer and arbitrary geographic boundaries imposed on them by the British and the French, the Arab world had been forced to accept new borders, different tribes and peoples both largely uneducated and from mainly economically unproductive lands, lands that were not too suitable for cultivation. With the exception of some land in Syria, Lebanon, Iraq, and Egypt the rest was desert or practically arid land.

The enormous store of crude oil found in Arab territories played right into the hands of their own greedy leaders who grabbed the profits and enriched themselves, leaving their less fortunate citizens to bear the brunt of financial poverty. The city was showing its impoverished state like a sullied petticoat under a worn dress. Indeed there were many changes in Cairo and many more to come in Egypt and in the Arab world, all of them earthshaking.

Foreigners had lived side by side in the capital city. Jew, Copt, Roman Catholic, Greek Orthodox, Muslim, and Anglican all rubbed elbows and worked side by side with few irritating issues. Some friction at times surfaced but nothing that could not be healed with discussion, a laugh, a joke, and an apology. On this visit, however, I saw the burned shells of two Jewish synagogues, an historic Coptic church vandalized, and the courtyard of the Anglican Cathedral littered with trash.

The English School in Heliopolis had been closed, Les Cours Maintenon (the excellent French secondary institution) had ceased to operate and its principal, Mme. Louise Develet, had been deported. This was the school where Mother had been on the faculty for many years. When after the war the British Council had accepted an invitation by the Egyptian Ministry of Education to open a branch school in Shubrah, called Victoria College after the one in Trumpington, the Egyptians were delighted. The school opened to great fanfare, but in 1949, a few weeks before my arrival, the name had been changed by order of the Ministry to "Victory" College. No foreign connections, including faculty, would be tolerated or even accepted on the staff. In later years the venue of Victory College was changed to the suburban town of Maadi. There were many changes and not many of these were for the better. In essence the quality and impetus of Victoria College, as supervised by the

British Council, was never reached; Victory College was a poor facsimile of the original.

Poverty was seen everywhere in Cairo. Work had become scarce, factories had been closed because many Europeans had been forced to leave, there was an obvious brain drain and educated people were escaping Egypt in droves, and thus unemployment had spiraled upward. Hospitals were closing because of lack of funding or lack of professional staff. The conflict with Israel was draining what little financial reserves existed. Agriculture was in shambles because either payment for growing was not forthcoming from the government or the "fellahins," the peasants, were abandoning the fields and flocking to Cairo to find work in the military industrial sector making armament supplies. Egypt, the food producer of the Golden Crescent throughout history, was importing basic foodstuff.

During my fortnight visit to Cairo, I absorbed much of the shambled situation that prevailed in the city. Unless one looked below the surface or contrasted the present with the past, one would not notice any qualitative effect. Superficially all appeared normal, except that I saw fewer foreigners and smiling people and more beggars, homeless people, dilapidated automobiles, buildings in disrepair, more burnt churches and synagogues, and potholes in the streets.

Looking for some of my friends and neighbors, I discovered that all had left the country. My Maltese neighbors at Emad El Din Street had left for Malta. My Greek buddies from across the street had moved to England, as had my Indian cycling buddies. Even the Nubian concierge and his family had left Egypt and immigrated to Kenya. Kassem, our cook and helper for many years, had left for Kenya too, one of the Egyptian plumbers in the shop across the street informed me, and he added that he was moving to Morocco.

When I met my uncle Mathieu he told me that he was leaving for Italy at the end of the year to await his visa for America. Cairo was no place for a European to live. An Italian client from the small state of San Marino had put him on retainer to do some research and offered him a house in Rimini. He was liquidating his business office and preparing to leave because the situation in Egypt was expected to get worse before it would get better, if ever. He was right.

My grandfather Joseph was still practicing and had decided to remain even if the situation became almost impossible because he was needed both in the pharmacy and the hospital. I saw him briefly and was happy to see that he was still in possession of all his faculties. I loved him dearly. I spent a whole day with him and it was a joy to be with him and listen to his stories. He died in 1951 at the age of 93 or so I presume. He died just before the abdication of the king but because communication was sparse and I was not in a position to maintain it regularly the details are unknown to me.

The Muslim Brotherhood is still as active as it was in the 1950s. Democratic elections are more a veneer than a reality. Economically, Egypt has improved to a small degree, especially since it made peace with Israel and reduced its military expenditures, but it has a long way to go. Democracy and free general elections have yet to emerge as honest procedures in Egypt. Indeed no Islamic country, even Indonesia, has moved to a totally free elected government. Perhaps it is that free elections and democracy are not attuned to the current theological mode of Islam. Roman Catholicism offers the same obstacles to democracy but where democracy has overcome these obstacles it was only when the Catholic Church's grip on society was weakened or diluted. When will the Islamic theocratic grip weaken in Arab nations and when will leadership emerge that is less greedy and more willing to serve the people? Neither then in 1949 nor today in the 21st century can this question be given a coherent answer.

Anyway, my short visit was productive and interesting. My mother's assignment was completed with the help of my uncle Mathieu. I'm certain that the banking transaction could have been made internally by the respective banks but I was happy to revisit my place of birth — which I then believed would be the last time.

That night my uncle invited me for dinner and promised me that my Aunt Camille would prepare stuffed tomatoes: they were my most favorite and hers were superb. Camille was a wonderful cook and also a dear person to me. She had been married once to an Italian businessman and had a daughter,

Nora, with him. After her divorce, illegal in Italy but possible in Egypt, she had met my uncle when he helped her with several legal issues. Over time Mathieu and Camille had married and soon gave birth to my cousin Francis (or Fanica).

At dinner that night, my grandfather Joseph was invited, and that was a pleasure because I adored him. I had planned to see him but his presence at dinner made it all the more pleasurable to be en famille. The evening, the dinner, the conversations were most rewarding and obviously would become one of the last such occasions for me. Before leaving Cairo, I spent several hours with my grandfather and these I still cherish.

The day before bidding goodbye to Cairo, I went to my favorite Tamiya (falafel) and *foul mudhamis* (beans) restaurant, which I remembered was owned and operated by Bosnian Muslims. The Bosnians were gone and a Sudanese family had taken it over, but the quality was still excellent and *ei-yech baladi* (local bread) was superb.

I took a quick trip to Khan Khalil (the souk) to see if Mr. Emil was still in business. Mr. Emil was a carpet and furniture merchant who was an old friend of my parents. Emil was no longer in what was his store because he had returned to Beirut, Lebanon. Many merchants of Khan al-Khalil had either closed or sold their shops and had escaped from Egypt. Even the renowned restaurant Al Hatti in the souk, owned and operated by an Egyptian family for two or three generations, was closed. A teashop owner nearby informed me that the Al Hatti family had left to settle in Crete. The teashop owner was also planning to escape Egypt but for Bahrain.

With time still available, I walked to see the magnificent Opera House which stood majestically not too far from the exotic Shepheard Hotel; both were splendid monuments of colonial Egypt. Giuseppe Verdi had written *Aïda* especially for the Cairo Opera House — Khedivial Opera House — to celebrate the opening of the Suez Canal in 1871. I had seen my very first opera there and it was a performance of *Aïda*. I would always remember the "Triumphant March" from *Aïda* because the Middle East radio broadcast for the news by the British Broadcasting Corporation (BBC) always played the theme to introduce the readings. For my introduction to the Cairo Opera

House, I heard the tenor Beniamino Gigli sing the lead part. At the time, I was only seven but I still remember how wonderful it was. As for the Shepheard Hotel with its magnificent garden, great entrance, superb lobby, well-appointed lounges, and first class restaurants, it was still one of the finest gathering places in the world.

On my last day in Cairo, I said goodbye to my uncle Mathieu, and to my Aunt Camille, to my cousin Francis, and to my grandfather; I was not sure when I would see them again, if ever. The train to Alexandria was on time and I was able to have one whole day to visit the city before boarding the *Pace*. Alexandria was still almost the fresh city by the Mediterranean with beach after beach for sun worshipers as it had been when I was a boy.

I visited Sporting and Stanley beaches where as a kid I played during the summer months. It was at Stanley Beach that I was thrown by a friend of my parents into a giant wave and nearly drowned. I stuttered for three months after that episode and refused to swim in deep water thereafter. I'm certain that I will never forget that incident; nor will I ever be reconciled with the sea to swim happily in it. Throwing me into a big wave was dumb after I'd been assured that I would be held safely by one of Mother's male colleagues. Never abuse trust, was the lesson that I learned and practiced with my own children. When I assured them for a jump that I would catch them, I made certain that they would be caught immediately.

Alexandria, the glistening city on the Mediterranean, had lost some of its glitter, wealthy appearance, and beauty. Many villas gracing the seafront were in disrepair or boarded up — perhaps even abandoned. The many restaurants near the sea were closed. It was curious that few people were on the beaches. The Corniche vendors who normally sold hot falafel sandwiches were not in sight. The coast seemed deserted and abandoned. In the city center there was some activity, some commerce, and some joviality in the cafés but not as much as I remembered as a boy. It was a case of either I had grown up and became cynical or Egypt had become a shabby, disheveled, and unkempt old place.

The *Pace* was in port ahead of schedule, which made it easy for me to spend the night on board and to save the price of a hotel room. All my buddies from the previous crossing seemed happy to see me again. Pierro would not be on this voyage because he was taking a few weeks' holiday. Mario assigned me to the first class section again but to different rooms. He told me that two rooms in this section were empty for this crossing and that I could have the one he was not occupying. Such unexpected luxury! My jar of pickles was filled and ready to help medicate my seasickness.

That night, with only the crew on board, the captain threw a party. A fine dinner arrived and it was washed down with many bottles of good vintage Italian wine. Italians do not starve themselves, and the wine is always "abundante." Several singers were among the crew and all enjoyed many songs; even the captain soloed and sang a couple of operatic songs.

The next day, we sailed out of the harbor, and the *Pace* passed by the Light of Alexandria and into the open sea. To my surprise and pleasure this crossing went without my incurring seasickness. Spending the night in a stateroom with all the luxuries of a grand hotel was much appreciated. The guests were mostly English and made very few demands as long as I kept the ice bucket filled and bottles of tonic water available. At the end of the voyage my tips doubled what I had received previously. Serving on a ship could easily become a lifetime endeavor, if only I could serve mainly first class passengers.

Upon arriving in Naples and after my goodbyes, the little Fiat Topolino was waiting to take me to Ivetta's villa. Before leaving the port area I stopped at the Italia Line office to inquire about the exact departure of the *Conte Biancamano*. It was scheduled to leave five days hence from Genoa. I bought and paid for my ticket for a shared cabin in second class. Five days were enough to give me three days in Naples, one day for travel, and arrive in time to spend the last night on board and again avoid the price or the search for a hotel room.

Off we went to the Santa Lucia area and to the lovely home of Mrs. Ivetta Arletta. Ivetta was waiting on the terrace and typing rapidly on a typewriter. I did not interrupt her but waited in the living room after depositing my belongings in the guest room. The room had a large balcony that overlooked the bay and beyond to Capri. I took my book and plopped myself in a straight back armchair to read and wait for Ivetta to break from her writing.

At two o'clock Ivetta came into the living room and reached over to welcome and embrace me.

"We will have tea and a few sandwiches and at eight o' clock we are having dinner with friends at the Luna, a restaurant on the waterfront."

She asked me if I was comfortable in the room and if my long voyage to Egypt had been good and worthwhile. I responded positively to all the questions and thanked her for her hospitality and kindness. We talked a bit about her book and how much she had written since I left. She was almost to the last chapter and the draft would be going to the publisher in London in a few days. I was surprised that London would publish it, but she reminded me that the book was written in English. Editing of the English and translations in Italian and French would be made in Britain, but these were the responsibility of the publisher. The subject was an historical account in novel form of the founding of the monastery of Saint Catherine located in the southern portion of the Sinai Peninsula.

Tea soon arrived and we continued to talk about many subjects, including what lay ahead for me when I reached Canada. I admitted that I was not too certain which direction my life would take but that flying was a priority for the moment.

Ivetta asked me about my education and my plans to further it. I assured her that I would not neglect my education and that somewhere along the way university would be included. I was assured a place at one of the colleges in Cambridge but I wanted to try a new outlook, something not in the British system. She agreed that it would be a good idea to investigate other educational systems, but cautioned me to choose well.

Ivetta shared with me her educational history that had started in Italy, moved to England's University of Leeds where she obtained her bachelor's degree in history, and then she attended classes in Greece, Spain, and Egypt, particularly at Cairo's American University. Following her introduction to American education in Cairo, she spent several years in the United States where she met her husband. No children were born out of her marriage and when Mussolini gained power and the war broke out all ideas of having a family were forgotten. Had they had a child he or she would be about my age.

We chatted for several hours until it was time to prepare for dinner. I went back to my room to discover that my luggage had been emptied and the clothes neatly placed in drawers. My one suit had been cleaned and pressed, my shirt pressed too, and a new silk tie had been given to me with a note from Ivetta. I could quite easily get used to this life, I thought.

At 7:00 I was dressed and ready. Ivetta was dressed in a lovely white out-fit. She looked stunning and displayed her 55 years splendidly. I thanked her for the tie and for all the kindnesses extended to me. The dinner was superb and Ivetta's friends were charming, interesting, and cosmopolitan. It was a wonderful evening. We returned to the villa before midnight and I took leave to go to bed. I was quite tired. I believe that Ivetta poured herself a cognac and buried herself in a book.

The next two days were spent doing some touristy things like driving across to the heel of Italy to explore the region around Taranto, Apuglia. We stopped in many small restaurants where we savored the gastronomical offer-ings of the south of Italy. One afternoon we sailed to Capri's yacht club for lunch and then on to a small village on the Isola Di Procida for dinner. Re-turning by the light of a full moon, Naples looked like a jewel shimmering against the darkness of the hills and Mount Vesuvius in the distance.

On my last evening, I offered to take Ivetta to dinner but she refused.

"I will cook tonight," she announced. She asked me to take a long walk, stop somewhere at a café, and read a book. Dinner would be served at seven o'clock.

I walked along the Santa Lucia and enjoyed both the sea breeze and the salt air of the sea. I stopped somewhere and ordered one or two Campari and sodas and read my book. Returning to the villa in time for dinner I could in-hale the wonderful aromas of cooking. It was a superb dinner and the dessert was phenomenal. I don't remember the name of the wine but I do remember that it was red, full-bodied, and dry. After dinner Ivetta informed me that the next day I would be taken to the train station at 10 a.m. to catch the "ràpido" to Genoa which would bypass Rome. She handed me a ticket for first class seating with prepaid lunch. After thanking her and bidding her a goodnight, I went to bed. On the night table by my bed I found several pieces of dark chocolate.

I had awakened early the next morning to pack my luggage but soon a knock on the door announced that coffee was ready for me. At breakfast, Ivetta gave me her home address in Naples, and the address of her apartment in London in the event that I returned to England. I had no address to give her because I did not know where I would end up. We embraced. Again I thanked her for her goodness, warm hospitality, and friendship. I waved goodbye from the car and went to the station. I kept thinking of the good fortune that had come my way in meeting Mrs. Ivetta Arletta. We corresponded for several years and I read one of her books but because they were romantic historical novels they were a bit uninteresting to me. I never saw Ivetta again. While I was in Alaska and busy flying, correspondence soon waned and consequently I lost track of Ivetta. She was a wonderful, kind, lovely, and hospitable person. Her gracefulness was indelibly marked on me; she gave much of herself, and in the giving she obtained pleasure, satisfaction, and recognition. I shall never forget my time with her; I just hope that she noted my deep appreciation for having known her. Emulating her giving, hospitality, and graciousness has been my guide throughout my life: give of yourself without keeping a record.

Onward West to the New World

Sitting comfortably in first class on the Rapido train and eating an exquisite lunch compliments of Ivetta, I tried to sort out what I had been doing and what I would be doing in the next few weeks and months. The Atlantic crossing from Genoa to Halifax would take approximately ten days. I wished that I were able to decide immediately where I would establish myself. Where was I going to sink my roots? The New World was strange, foreign, and worrisome to me. I had no intention to settle where my mother lived — I had been independent for too long.

At the moment, Canada was the best option for me. English and French were spoken; hence I expected that I would find living in this immense country acceptable. Canada was a new country compared to those of Europe and therefore opportunities were to be aplenty for a young man willing to develop a life there. Yet, I was a bit anxious that I would find myself overwhelmed by the new frontier in front of me. The Canadian Air Ministry had been receptive to my inquiry about joining the Royal Canadian Air Force (RCAF), and because of my current British passport and residence permit, I was not considered to be an alien.

I struggled with several ideas and then realized that too many were still floating in the air, like the colored balls in a juggler's act. My funds were limited and I had to continue to be careful and frugal. For the moment my future was evolving and a little out of my direct control. Perhaps I was a juggler who was increasing his risks by juggling his many balls while walking on a tightrope, with no net below to catch him if and when he fell. The ten days on the ship would help me sort out a few things, but many issues were out of my control because there were too many unknowns affecting my decisions. I was confronted with how limited my control was soon upon arrival in Halifax.

The train arrived on time and I took a taxi to the Port of Genoa and to the ship, a ship so unlike the *Pace* of the Naples and Alexandria circuit.

Westward Crossing

The *Conte Biancamano* was a glistening and beautiful white-top superstructure and black-bottom massive vessel on this September of 1950. It was more than a ship; it was an ocean liner, slick, smooth, glossy, and with a slippery look about it. In comparison to the *Pace*, it was enormous while the latter was a tiny boat much in need of an overhaul and several new coats of paint.

The reception office was located in an enclosed section of the dock and contained passport control, ticket examination or purchasing, luggage identification check-in, and cabin attendants to guide passengers to their respective cabins. After showing my British passport with a temporary residence visa for Canada and my boarding ticket, I was quickly escorted to my cabin in the second-class section. My Italian passport was not required for this crossing because the Canadians were more interested in the fact that I was a legal British resident.

My roommate was already in the cabin. He was a stocky young man, perhaps in his mid-twenties. Alfred Torricelli was a pleasant fellow from Albany, New York, who turned out to be a good roommate and fine ship companion. He was returning to the United States from Italy after a three-month visit with his family in the "old country." The Italian branch of his family came from Turin.

For Alfred, this had been his first visit to Europe but now he was happy to be returning to America. He informed me that he would kiss the ground upon arrival in New York. Alfred had missed America and he told me in no uncertain terms that the "U.S. of A. was without any doubt God's country."

I had never encountered such nationalism, not since hearing the English translation of many Nazi speeches. It frightened me a little but then I discounted this attitude to be the response of a homesick boy on his way home after a long absence. But then I noticed that he really felt a very strong emotion for anything American.

Alfred Torricelli's passion for the United States was more a love for his country than a right wing expression of American superiority. He had been to Europe and had enjoyed meeting his Italian family but he was happy, thankful, and proud to be an American. He was aware that America was not perfect and had to improve immensely before it could achieve any perfection. America, especially, needed to improve its treatment of those who were foreigners, blacks, and Latinos. Yet he saw possibilities that could materialize because Americans were a people of heart. There was nothing that America or Americans could not do. America had the propensity for doing great good and likewise for doing great harm. Americans, Alfred noted, were braggarts and fanatics — especially about religion, money, sports, and the mismanagement of their politics. On the overall slate of great powers, Americans had heart, Alfred assured me. He was convinced that, ultimately, American would turn and do the right thing, and for this he paraphrased Winston Churchill's words: America at first will try all the wrong solutions, then will settle down and implement the right one!

Without American power, the War, Alfred assured me, would have been lost. Now the American Marshall Plan, which had been developed to reconstruct Europe after the destruction was another indication that America was a great nation, and that Americans were a benevolent people. He had a point there, I thought; Europeans were most grateful that American aid for reconstruction was given.

At this point, I was confronted with an ambivalent feeling. On one hand I was tired of listening to pronouncements of American greatness, benevolence, and power. On the other hand, the restoration of Europe through American financial aid and the military power, which coupled itself to the British and French forces, did suggest that America was exceptionally kind to both its allies and its enemies.

The bragging heard on the Voice of America was tiresome yet much that was said was true. American assistance had been phenomenal and indispensable during and after the War, and certainly now during the current Cold War. All this evaluation meant that I had to reexamine my judgment of America. I had not met too many Americans, and Alfred was the first one with whom I could discuss their contribution to Europe, their approach to geopolitics, and their government. He was a President Harry Truman supporter and dyed-in-the-wool Eastern Democrat, liberal, and supportive of giving aid to honest needy nations.

As a European, I saw America as a rich uncle who gave support willingly when it was needed but expected much in return; at least that was how it was interpreted on the Continent. After all, why would Americans give so much aid if they did not expect a hefty return for their generosity? The British press that I read never was concerned with America's benevolence. English speaking countries supported each other and that was the reason for the giving. The English had been given aid when aid was direly needed and thus they respected the Americans.

But the French press had another point of view, especially the one that reflected General De Gaulle's attitude. France was a great nation and America was attempting to minimize her greatness by showering Europe with financial help. It seemed that the French could not accept the support that came through the Marshall Plan without some commentary that America was implicitly undermining the greatness of France, and that of Europe, the obvious satellite of France. After all, what was Europe without France and French culture? This was the attitude promoted by the French press.

This point of view, I confess, did affect my judgment of America. I still looked at the world from the perspective of French geopolitics. In its defeat under the German occupation was not France ceding its place to the English speakers of the world? France would never cede its grand role in Europe and in the World to "a nation of shopkeepers," as Napoleon called the English. Decades later I would observe that the mercantile mentality was not English but explicitly French. My conversations with Alfred gave me a new point of view and a new understanding of America. After all, Alfred was, as I admitted, the first American with whom I had a real political conversation. He was not pompous, demanding, pushy, or overwhelming; he was a pleasant and helpful sort who genuinely loved his country and was happy and proud to be an American.

Alfred Torricelli and I went to explore the ship — at least as far as the second-class boundary extended and below; we could not enter the first class area. The ship was big enough and the amenities good enough that avoiding first class was not a big loss. At dinner we met two other travelers. One, Barbara Longley, was returning to Halifax after a period of studying architecture in London and in Rome. She was the daughter of a Canadian solicitor residing in Halifax who also owned a cottage on Butterfly Lake in Hubbards. The other table companion, Jo Levino, was a Brazilian student of political science who was returning from Europe after months observing the procedures of the new West German government in Bonn. He was going to New York to work as an intern at the United Nations.

The four of us made a good group, and because we ate every meal together we became well acquainted with each other. Alfred had graduated from Cornell University, Ithaca, NY in physics. He was headed to the Massachusetts Institute of Technology (MIT), Cambridge, MA to begin a doctoral program in astrophysics. Alfred often spoke to me about the beauty of the study of physics and how it encompassed all the disciplines including philosophy. I listened carefully and somehow recorded his words for the long term. Barbara was hoping to work for an architectural firm in Ottawa and complete her apprentice training so she could obtain her professional license and begin work as an independent architect. It seems that I was the only oddball of the group: I was heading neither for a university nor a career. I was looking for an avenue that would allow me to fly a variety of aircraft for a few years.

"Do you intend to enter aviation or engineering after you fly for the Canadians?" Alfred asked, and so did the others.

My reply was indefinite, vague, and perhaps tentative to them. I did not know what I wanted to do, except obtain an education. The specific field of learning was still fuzzy in my head. I knew nothing about what was offered at university. Engineering was in my head, simply because Olav C. Mong, my mother's new husband (whom I had not met) was one, and the discipline was discussed extensively in many publications that I had encountered in the late 40s, especially as they related to the rebuilding of the world after the war. My father was in linguistic studies; could I make a go at that? My mother had taught French but that was not terribly interesting to me.

Where should I direct myself? I had no idea. Well, I would cross that bridge when the time came. For the moment I zeroed in on my target: flying. But still I worried that I lacked information about a possible career path and that I had no one to help me select a fitting discipline. It was quite obvious to me that flying would not end up being my life's career. I was seeking something more substantial and more intellectually challenging. But I did not know what it would be. A mentor would have been of great help, but none was visible on the immediate horizon.

The next morning the ship set out into the open sea of the Mediterranean. My jar of pickles was ready to serve me. I remembered Pierro of the *Pace* and his wonderful bearded face and kindness. The sea was calm with very few swells. Italy receded into the horizon, and it was sea and sky again like the crossing to Alexandria, except this trip would take me to the New World.

Breakfast on the first morning was interesting. Our table was served fresh fruit, ham and eggs, brioches and pastries, coffee, milk, and a jug of red wine. Red wine for breakfast! Red wine was served at every meal.

After breakfast we went off to walk around the deck. Somehow I was paired off with Barbara Longley. We talked a great deal about her experience studying in London and in Rome. She mentioned that her mother, Dorcas, was American, originally from Boston, and was an attorney, who now did not practice law but taught prisoners subjects on justice, order, and ways to reenter society as productive citizens.

She asked me where I was staying in Halifax and I responded by saying that I hoped that the Air Ministry would offer me an acceptance letter soon so that I would not have to spend too much time in a hotel. I explained that my funds were limited and would stretch only so far. Barbara responded by inviting me to stay with her parents until my situation was clarified. She would cable her parents to clear the way and confirm the invitation. Once more, another kind soul extended hospitality to me. I accepted and thanked her.

Barbara told me that her parents had had a bout with alcoholism but had been dry for several years. Currently they lived in Halifax near her father's office, and on weekends and holidays they would escape to the small village of Hubbards, and paddle a small boat across Butterfly Lake to a cottage on the lakeshore. It was a pleasant way to live and work, I thought, but I was a long way from this type of existence. I would, however, accept an invitation to go to the lake.

The days on board ship were filled with talking, walking, sunbathing, eating and drinking, reading, and staring at the sea. I was anxious to see the New World and wondered how I would react to it. Was I prepared for it? Thinking about the adventure of going to North America was foremost in my mind. On board ship much time was available for solo thinking. One did not exert too much energy while aboard a ship, and the food intake was always greater than what was needed. I tried to exercise and control my eating, much of that was because I was not sure what the Canadians required of a pilot. I knew that perfect eyesight was a requirement. Excess weight was also part of what a physical examination revealed, but where the minimum and maximum limits were established, I did not know. The fact that I was skinny made me feel less anxious about weight requirements. Height was also to be considered and my size was normal for my age; I did not have the towering height of a basketball player.

We were informed at noon over the public address speakers that soon we would be seeing land on both sides of the ship. Gibraltar was just a few miles west of our position. The African and European coasts would be visible simultaneously. As both coasts became discernible, so did a cavorting school of dolphins alongside the ship. A bit later we passed near the rock of Gibraltar, where hawkers in small boats called to the passengers to buy items they were selling. Apart from crafts, jewelry, and sweets, small carpets and clothes were also for sale. Ropes and baskets were used to transfer both the goods and the cash from boat to ship, from seller to buyer. My group did not buy anything but we looked and wondered if the items bought were of any value — we soon learned that many were not, but returning them was impossible. The diversion, however, was exciting.

As we neared the Pillars of Hercules, the Strait of Gibraltar, the swells became more noticeable and the Moroccan boat merchants soon receded behind us. The waters of the Atlantic Ocean were not as calm as those of the Mediterranean Sea. The ocean swells were becoming bigger and the ship was following their rhythmic movement. I was feeling nauseated and smartly ate a few pickles to ward off the motion sickness. The ship began to bob up and down, climb hills and descend valleys. The motion of the ship was soothing and not brisk, in fact it was pleasurable; the sour pickles were doing their task well. During all the attention I gave to warding off seasickness, it also occurred to me that this was my first crossing of the Atlantic. I felt like an explorer reaching out for new lands, trespassing over unknown territories, and waiting eagerly for my first sighting of both new shores and new peoples. It was exciting.

In decades to come I made many crossings of the Atlantic, but they were by air, and some were smooth, some were turbulent, but none were as exhilarating as the first one. Leaving the side of the vessel I ran to the front to see what was ahead firsthand. More ocean, more blue, greater swells, and an unimaginable vastness spreading before my eyes as all vestiges of land disappeared from sight. Petit Nimon was an insignificant speck on the ocean, and I wondered how Christopher Columbus or Amerigo Vespucci felt when they entered the Atlantic Ocean in their tiny wooden ships.

Soon passengers settled into a routine. Clocks were adjusted before going to bed. Cables were delivered at breakfast. Weather forecasts were posted. Entertainment schedules were printed and placed on each table. Laundry was delivered midmorning to the cabins. Four meals were served at exactly the same time every day, or so it seemed to the passengers. Snacks were served all day, as was red wine, coffee, and tea. Stronger drinks were available at the many bars from the time after breakfast to late in the night.

Because I went to bed early, I did not participate in too many late activities. My roommate, Alfred, was most considerate and did not awaken me when he returned to the room after the evening of entertainment was over. My time was spent reading and chatting with Barbara Longley about her studies, Canada, Nova Scotia, and her parents. Barbara was curious about my love of flying and the singular goal I had about becoming an active member of the RCAF. Would I not need a university degree to become a pilot? This question had been posed by many people and I had done my due diligence research on the subject.

Because of the War recruiting young men to serve was difficult — there just were very few available. The militaries of the western nations had consequently reduced the educational requirements. Moreover, because I had been matriculated, I was considered as having completed tantamount to one or one and a half years of university education. The times were propitious for me, or so I thought.

Barbara was a year older than I, a cigarette smoker, and had completed her university education in architecture. Her eyes were fixed on developing a career as an architect, earning a good salary, and finding a compatible husband. She liked me, found me interesting, perhaps a bit irresponsible in that I admitted that I would not make flying my life's goal, and strange in that I was willing, sight unseen, to adopt a new and different culture than the ones I was accustomed to in Europe. Barbara kept reminding me that the New World was quite different from the Old World; she had spent four years in the old one and found it impossible to adapt.

Barbara and I found that we had much to discuss and enjoyed each other's company, although I did not like the cigarettes and the smoke that always enveloped us except when on the breezy deck of the ship. A cable from her parents had arrived making the hospitable invitation to me definite; I could stay with the Longleys for as long as I needed. As I said earlier, another graceful hand had been extended to me.

The morning of the last day, the announcement was made over the public address that in an hour we would see the coast of Nova Scotia. Arrival time was to be at 2:00 p.m. Passengers disembarking in Halifax were to mark their luggage and place the appropriate green tag, which had been given to us upon boarding, on their cabin doors. It was my call and I was all packed and ready for the new phase of this fresh adventure, but I was edgy and restless. Alfred sensed my anxiety and invited me to his home in Albany if events did not turn out well for me.

"America will always welcome you as will I and my family," Alfred assured me.

I was, nevertheless, still anxious. He represented an image of the American, the private citizen, which was refreshing, intimate, considerate, and kind. After giving me his contact information, Alfred reached over and gave me a tight bear hug. Jo, the Brazilian, also came over to bid me goodbye and gave me his home address in Brazil. Barbara simply assured me that she would be waiting for me after the Canadian authorities had cleared all documents.

"Canada here I come," I murmured to myself. I was ready but not quite for what I encountered.

Canada, A Way Stop

Upon arriving in Halifax, my mother and her husband met my ship. I had neither planned for this welcoming committee nor had I expected it. I cleared customs and walked to the passport control stand. It was an open desk with practically no control to keep greeters separated from arriving passengers. All had gone well for me until I reached the visa control desk. The officer looked at my six months visa for Canada stamped on my British passport (having British residency I was entitled to a British — though not an English — passport).

"Why are you in Canada?" the officer asked.

"To decide if I want to settle in the country and to join the Royal Canadian Air Force," I replied.

"Are you eligible for drafting in England and coming to Canada to escape the draft?"

"No, Sir," I answered. "I've inquired of the Air Ministry if the Royal Canadian Air Force (RCAF) would be interested in using a pilot with my qualifications and they replied that they would. I'm to go to Ottawa for an interview as soon as I telephone the contact officer for an appointment."

I added, "Ottawa has already given me an appointment file number. I am expected."

He had a puzzled look on his face. "Where are you residing in Halifax?"

"With Mr. and Mrs. John Longley," and I gave him the address. "Mr. Longley's daughter Barbara has just cleared passport control," I added.

The passport control officer was satisfied or so it seemed. He reviewed my visa and reached for the stamp....

Olav, who was standing within earshot came over just at this inopportune moment and interrupted the proceedings by interjecting that I was probably going to settle in the USA with him and my mother, if I found Canada to be unsuitable! That was it.

It was so far from the truth that it was an absolute fabrication of what my plans specified. Indeed, it was a classic example of someone butting in while his brain was not engaged but his mouth was in full operation. I should have hit Olav but that would have caused more problems.

The Canadians are very sensitive about being used as a back door entrance to the United States. This is a nation that constantly has to contend with an 800-pound gorilla south of its border. More to the point, Canada is a nation that does not want to be intimidated by the United States.

In response to Olav's gratuitous and untrue comment, the officer closed my passport, hailed a security officer, said something that I could not hear, and gave him my passport. The passport officer then ordered me to follow the security man. Another security man took my luggage and joined us and both escorted me to the detention sector. Not a word was spoken to me. I did not look back. I did not acknowledge my mother's presence. I did not even have the opportunity to say anything to Barbara. I was furious. I was appalled by Olav's stupidity. This encounter marked my introduction to Olav Cartwold Mong, engineering graduate of the Massachusetts Institute of Technology!

I did have the good sense to ask the security man if I could give a message to people who were waiting for me at the exit door. He agreed. I wrote a few words on a piece of paper that I had stuck in my pocket and asked the security man to find the Longley family. He assured me that would be done and then he wished me well.

I was incarcerated for 16 days! What an overture to my excitedly anticipated entrance to the "New World."

Fortunately the jail was not really a jail but a holding section for people who had problems with their immigration documents. The senior director of the detention facility was Mrs. Hagen, and she acted more like a grandmother than a warden. She was a wonderfully kind person who took good care of her ward. There was another detainee by the name of Swanson who was incarcerated with me. Having gotten sick while on shore leave from his merchant ship he had missed its departure. Now this sailor had to wait for the return of his ship before he could be released.

There was also a mother and her four-year-old child from Poland who had landed in Canada without the appropriate visas. They were waiting for their visas to be issued and were released within a few days to settle in Victoria, British Columbia where her husband worked.

When the mother and child left, Swanson and I were left to rattle around the detention sector. Swanson knew when his ship was expected to return so he took his stay as a holiday; I knew nothing of what would happen to my status. I had telephoned Ottawa to see if anything could be done to legitimize my status in Canada, but no word came from the Ministry. Barbara Longley had telephoned me to tell me that her father was sorting through the paperwork to find a way to obtain my release. The security man had informed Mr. Longley that I was being held because word had been given to the passport officer that I was attempting to enter the United States through Canada. Barbara had assured her father that I had specifically told her in many conversations that I did not want to go to America, but hoped to remain in Canada as a pilot in the RCAF.

In the detention sector, we had chores to do while we waited for our release. I learned how to use a buffer on parquet floors. Washing windows and dusting were other chores to be done, as were vacuuming and mopping, tasks that I did not mind doing. Swanson was a good companion and a pleasant fellow who told me many stories about his travels, his ships, his family, and his home in Sweden. After attending the Swedish Merchant Marine academy, he had hired on as an engine specialist on an old bucket sailing to India. After that voyage, he decided to obtain advanced papers so that he didn't have to occupy miserable quarters on vessels. He then showed me his First Mate's papers that were one step closer to his obtaining Master's papers and the material that allowed him to prepare for the next and final level. With Master's papers and sufficient time under a good Master, he would be able to command his own ship as Captain, which he hoped to attain in three to five years.

While in detention, he was spending his time studying navigation, the law of the sea, and crew management. Just talking with Swanson gave me a better understanding of navigation, especially celestial navigation. That we did not have access to a sextant was unfortunate, but I obtained enough substantial information that when I did have the instrument in the military I was able to use it quite rapidly.

Mrs. Hagen took good care of me and invited me to stay with her family when I was released from detention. She had three daughters but also had an empty guest room that I could use. She knew John Longley and was aware that he was working to clarify my status with the authorities. Barbara Longley would call every day to check on me, as did John. Mrs. Hagen would bring me parcels of goodies that she would prepare, such as cakes, cookies, chocolates, and books. I would share my treasures with Swanson and the few other detainees, when any arrived. During my sojourn in detention, three or four people were detained for no longer than a couple of days, and usually for misdated visas.

On the fifteenth day of my detention, John Longley came to see me and announced that I would be released the next day and that I could accept Mrs. Hagen's offer of a room because she had a larger house than he did. I was to be released in his care; henceforth he called me "his hostage." My parents had returned to New York and I was happy that I did not have to confront Olav this soon upon my release. My temper was still steaming.

John Longley had done the whole legal procedure *pro bono,* at Barbara's insistence. Mrs. Hagen was asking only 20 dollars a month for rent but I had to participate in house and kitchen chores. It was a wonderful offer, especially with three daughters in the household. Mrs. Hagen was a widow of a few years because her fisherman husband drowned on a commercial fishing trip in 1948 to the Grand Banks area of the Atlantic.

At ten o' clock in the morning of the sixteenth day I was set free from detention. John Longley had communicated with the Ottawa office of the RCAF and had received a letter assuring the immigration officials that I was expected to join the force when the procedures were completed. The RCAF had allowed me six months to get acclimated to as much of the Canadian culture as was possible in that short time.

Halifax and my Hosts

After settling in at the Hagen home I was now free to explore Canada, at least Halifax. Still concerned about what my plan and my lot would be in this new, vast, and somewhat strange country, I began to explore Halifax to get a feel of the citizens and customs of Nova Scotia.

It was a lovely city with a prominent hill overlooking the deep narrow harbor. Across the harbor was Dartmouth, a sister community to Halifax reached by ferry. Halifax was a Canadian city akin to one in Scotland. Kilts and tartans were worn often. Lamb and the variety of fruits from the sea, especially mussels, were the main staple of most residents of the region.

Supplementing the traditional transplanted Scottish food and customs, American-style hamburgers with fries, English fish and chips, and French tarts also could be found. I liked Halifax. It would be an acceptable place to settle.

Nova Scotia was, however, not all of Canada. As a maritime province, it was poorer than the other larger provinces but it was also a magnet for tourism. Yet Nova Scotia reflected the same inferiority complex vis-à-vis the United States, and that bothered me a little. At any rate, I wanted to fly and Canada might offer me good options. Mr. Longley found that I could translate between English and French, and because Canada was becoming a bilingual nation where every document had to be available in both languages, he gave me some tasks and provided me with a work permit, and I was able to earn a little money.

My goal was to fly serious modern aircraft. Air forces were the simplest means by which I could reach that goal.

The British Royal Air Force had been weakened by the war. The British had to rebuild their nation before they could rebuild their air force. It was impossible for me to wait for the time when the RAF was modernized and ready to take a leading position in aviation. Hence I looked elsewhere for opportunities to do serious flying.

I applied to Brazil (mother's youngest brother Marcel had settled there and reports were passable). Brazil was a new nation and had promised to improve its air force, but it was on the verge of becoming a dictatorship under military rule; that was not favorable to me.

I also applied to the Australian Air Force (a girlfriend from England had settled there with her family and spoke well of the place). Australia was building itself to become a growing power in South East Asia. Australia had much that could lure me to settle on its continent: Aviation was a principal mode of transportation for this large territory, and it was taken seriously. On the negative side, there remained the fact that Australia was a racist nation. I did not care for that.

Canada offered some good options because it, too, was large, flying was a necessary means of transportation and defense, and an emerging aviation industry was becoming apparent. Also, the languages employed, French and English, were mine, and apparently racism was only a minor irritant.

Soon after my release from immigration detention, I communicated with the Canadian Air Force. Mother and Olav had settled in New York and they felt that it was acceptable for me to live in the Canadian Maritime Provinces, which were sufficiently near New York for repeated visits. Nova Scotia's proximity to New York was not a plus for me, but then Canada was an immense country. Having learned that far was better than near when family is concerned, I chose to be as far away as possible but I was not always successful. As I have often said earlier and will probably repeat, WW II was destructive to most of the world but for me, it gave me an escape and a bit of soteriological grace by putting me in England, many miles away from family, thus allowing me room to mature on my own. Settling in Canada offered the same advantage even if the separating distances were less — but they could be more.

A couple of weeks later, the RCAF recruiting office at the Air Ministry informed me that my interview would be forthcoming and could take place at the air base in Dartmouth, a town directly across the harbor from Halifax. As soon as the details of the arrangements could be made, the RCAF would contact me and send a car for me.

After moving in with the Hagen family, settling in the guest room, I met Teresa (Tessie), Mary, and Patricia (Patsy). Tessie was the oldest at age 26, Mary age 23, and Patricia age 19. All were attractive girls who were quite friendly, hospitable, and helpful. With the Hagen family I entered a new phase in my adventurous life.

Living with the Hagens was a delight. All the sisters catered to me, I guess because I was the only male. Tessie was working as a paralegal and studying to pass her law exams. Mary was the born housewife engaged to a soldier who was on a United Nations peace monitoring assignment in Cyprus.

Patricia was working as a secretary while deciding if university was one of her options. She was a pretty and vivacious girl of whom I grew very fond. Her stable of interested young men was large and well stocked, but she always had time for me and often would include me in any outing with another boy. Patricia, "Patsy" as she was called, introduced me to my first hamburger and my first genuine hot dog. The Canada-zation of Raymond had begun. This change would eventually by supplanted by the Americanization of Raymond.

Patsy was a lot of fun and I had a crush on her. With her, I experienced my first American long, wet kiss! I was also introduced to the wonderful pastime of "necking" and being taken to "passion pits," the drive-in movies. I was learning a great deal. Much of this new education, of course, served me well in later years.

On weekends, John, Dorcas, and Barbara would head for Hubbards and the cottage on Butterfly Lake. I was always invited to join them, and I did. Hubbards was about an hour's drive from Halifax and the lake crossing to the cottage took about thirty minutes. By 7:00 p.m. we were settled in the cottage and waited with a cup of tea, while the pre-prepared dinner by Dorcas was warmed in the wood-fired oven. In the morning, the enticing aroma of sizzling bacon and brewed coffee coming from the stove awakened me. Breakfast consisted of coffee, eggs, bacon, fried toast, sliced apples, or freshly picked berries. On some mornings fried trout and sliced potatoes replaced the eggs and bacon. For dinner, Dorcas would bake an apple or berry pie or turnovers for dessert. John and I would take the dirty dishes and pans and wash them with soap and heated lake water to get them ready for the next meal.

With no bathing facilities and only an outhouse for a toilet, swimming was a necessary event. The lake was calm, the bottom readily visible because of the clarity of the water, and the sandy grade not too abrupt. I soon lost most of my fear of water and started swimming again, even in water that was above my head. I still avoided seawater, especially when it was not calm. So early in the morning or late at night I would jump in the lake for a restorative swim and a bath. Bathing suits were optional and often omitted.

There were few residents living near or on the shore of the lake. For all practical purposes the lake was the private domain of John and Dorcas Longley. Canoes were the only boats allowed on the lake. John had three canoes, two small ones that seated four people, and one large one for six people. Every passenger was given an oar when in the canoe: no free loaders were allowed. On Hubbards Lake I learned quickly how to handle a canoe and was taught by John how to right a canoe that was capsized. He was a good and patient instructor.

The village of Hubbards had one drugstore with a soda fountain, a restaurant, a gasoline station, a post office, and a bakery. On Saturday evenings Barbara would invite me and we would take one canoe and row to the village to meet other young folks. We would head to the soda fountain for a root beer float (another first for me). For my float I insisted on dollops of chocolate ice cream instead of vanilla and that always made for fun comments from other kids and the soda "jerk" tending the counter. She smoked cigarettes, which I did not, though other kids smoked too. Barbara knew many other young people — all of them weekenders from around Halifax or Dartmouth.

I liked Barbara but may have disappointed her parents because there was nothing between us except friendship. Anyway she was much too old for me at age 22, had completed her bachelor's degree, and was on her way to work as an architect. I was still on the first rung of the ladder of life and too young even to think of attachments. Neither Barbara nor Patsy was able to derail me from aviation. Both were wonderful girls and we kept writing letters regularly until well into the mid-70s, when each married. Patsy married a policeman who served in Halifax and Barbara married a Belgian engineer who settled in Ottawa. While in Halifax in 1995 I tried to locate them but discovered that I could not find anyone who could give me their married names. Both John and Dorcas died in the 70s within months of each other and the last time I saw them was in 1955, when I chose to visit them prior to starting as a freshman student at the University of Tennessee.

Peggy's Cove

John and Dorcas Longley owned another cottage, but this one was located on the coast at the foot of Peggy's Cove lighthouse. Peggy's Cove is a small peninsula jutting out into the Atlantic from the mainland and can receive some strong winds and endure violent storms. Peggy's Cove harbors a small fishing fleet and a few private leisure boats. John owned a small boat that he kept moored near his two-bedroom cottage. Often he would pull the boat up on the large flat rock adjacent to his cottage. Moored on the rock, the boat was less prone to be smashed by the surf and strong winds that often were present at Peggy's Cove.

Commercial fishing boats were moored further up the cove on the lee side of the peninsula but that was too far away for John. Moreover, there was a rental fee that John preferred not to pay. In either case, whether moored in the water or pulled up on the rock, taking the boat out into the bay and out of the cove was a feat that required some experience and dexterity, if not a long dash of courage. Once floating on the bay, the next adventure was being able to return it to the cove, its mooring, or onto the rock. The bay itself was quite safe on good weather days when the ocean was calm. Otherwise, using good sense I avoided the boat and the ocean altogether. Barbara would never venture on the water at Peggy's.

John had purchased the boat from a retired fisherman in Halifax. It was a sturdy longboat of some 18 feet with a small diesel engine, probably made in the 1920s or earlier. It worked well when it worked, but at times it was temperamental if the diesel fuel was contaminated with dirt or water. Much as I disliked working on engines while learning to fly at Waterbeach, I had become quite adept at starting the stubborn diesel engines of airport tugs so when John purchased the boat and wanted to sail it from Halifax to Peggy's Cove, a good twelve-hour journey, I was recruited to help do the trip.

John, Dorcas, and I entered the boat for the long ocean adventure. Dorcas had brought sandwiches, hot tea, fruit, drinking water, and chocolate. We had a spare container of diesel, half a gallon of motor oil, and a few necessary tools. Off we started on a bright Saturday morning at 6:00 a.m. The ocean was calm as we exited the harbor and entered open waters while still hugging the shoreline for navigation. My task was to tend to the diesel engine, feed it oil, and clean the filter bowl.

At noon, because the morning had gone well and the water was still calm, we decided to eat lunch. I was given a crab sandwich and a warm cup of tea. I was hungry, not having had any food since breakfast at 5:00 a.m. During the morning I had not felt hunger because I was anxious about the engine's performance and the journey on the Atlantic, something I had never done, especially on such a huge body of water and in such a small boat — 18 feet a big boat does not make. Sailing off Naples was not a problem because it was a much bigger boat, a ship with a crew made up of professional mariners. None of us on this longboat were professionals.

After lunch it hit me. I vomited over the side all that I had consumed. It was not seasickness, but stomach sickness caused by spoiled food. It was obvious that my time may have come. This was a prelude to my final hour. I knew that death was around the corner. It was awful. I heaved what was left in my stomach over the side. John and Dorcas had eaten the same type of sandwich except that mine had mayonnaise but theirs did not because they were calorie counters. Life returned and I put away my thoughts on death. I recuperated soon enough to finish my tea, which fortunately had no milk.

By mid-afternoon we were all jollier and our confidence was rebuilding. The sun was not too hot because of a cloud cover. It was most pleasant. The stomach conflict had been forgotten and tea was good medicine — except that the bladder was filling up quickly. What to do about relieving myself? John made it easy. He just relieved himself overboard. Soon Dorcas did the same but in a most interesting pose. Because my bladder was full and pressing painfully, I followed suit in front of John, Dorcas, God, and the gulls and was soon relieved of the pressure. We all had a good laugh at the social inconveniences that culture had adopted. The ocean was azure blue. The sky was clear of clouds. Gulls were flying overhead because we were not far off the coast. There was some kelp not far off and Dorcas noted that we might spot an otter or two.

After an hour or so, we heard a loud snarling sound and the diesel engine stopped with a jolt. I checked the fuel and the oil but nothing was amiss. I tried to turn the crank but I could not move it. I grabbed the flywheel to see if I could turn it, but it would not budge. It seemed as if a giant vise had seized the engine or perhaps a bearing had failed. That was a possibility but with plenty of oil in the pan it seemed unlikely. What was the problem?

John was certain that we would have to send a message to the Coast Guard. He had a hand-cranked radio which was vintage mid-1930s or thereabout. I decided, however, to disconnect the driveshaft before sending an emergency message. Four bolts did the job and the shaft was free of the engine. The flywheel for the engine now turned quite readily. I was even able to start the antique engine. The next investigation concerned the driveshaft. I tried to turn it but it would not budge. Something was acting as a powerful brake on the shaft or on the brass screw underwater. The only way to find out was to dive under the boat — not something that I relished at all.

John took off his clothes, and naked as a jaybird slipped into the water. We both heard him work the shaft but it still did not move. He came back to the surface. He wanted my help and two sharp knives. The problem was that kelp had wrapped itself around the propeller and acted as a powerful brake. I took my clothes off, except for my shorts, and dove into the water. It was not too cold. I looked at the propeller where the kelp had managed to entwine itself firmly around it. Cutting the kelp was tantamount to cutting thick leather or denim cloth. After surfacing for air three times we were able to clear the kelp and push it away from the boat. Climbing back into the boat we stopped to catch our breath and rest for a moment. We reconnected the driveshaft to the engine but before starting it I suggested that we paddle the boat out of the kelp area. Forty or fifty feet later I started the diesel and off we continued on our adventure with no more calamities. In the sun, my shorts dried and I was able to get dressed before reaching Peggy's Cove.

Peggy's Cove is a tiny community built around a delicately constructed, tall lighthouse that has its own post office. The lighthouse is still functioning as a sentinel overlooking the entrance to Halifax harbor. Seen by ships that are rounding the rocky eastern shore of Nova Scotia, its light offers a safe route into the harbor.

The community residents are primarily tied to the active fishing industry. The houses are built of stone and blend well with the surrounding rocky cliffs of the cove. Each house has a garden patch and access to the ocean. The Longleys' house was about a hundred meters away from the water line and between it and the water was a flat rock upon which John moored his longboat. A wooden slip-rope winch had been anchored in the upper side of the rock and when used with dexterity John or I managed to haul the boat onto the rock. The trick was to haul the boat so that the shaft and screw remained out of the water and high above the flat rock, then a block of wood could be inserted under the shaft to prevent it from tipping over and damaging the brass screw. The ocean below the rock was never calm. One slip of the mooring rope out of one's hand or off the tie post, and the boat would escape, fall, and crash into the water after undergoing irreparable damage. Fortunately, the longboat never did slip or crash. A local fisherman had instructed John and he in turn taught me how to manage the boat and the mooring. After a few tries, I was able to take the boat out by myself and explore the small bays near Peggy's Cove. I was invited to Peggy's Cove several times while hostage to John and Dorcas but the trip was always in their 1939 Chevrolet convertible and not by boat. Several years later I revisited both Hubbards and Peggy's Cove but that is another anecdote ripening for the telling.

Dartmouth and the RCAF

Six weeks after my release from immigration lockup and after returning from a weekend at Peggy's Cove, I received a letter from the RCAF informing me that a car would fetch me at a certain day and time to go to the airbase in Dartmouth for an interview. I waited for the driver for the ride to the Airbase and was delivered to the proper office. The officer in charge was pleasant and spoke both English and French. We talked for about an hour then went to lunch at the club where I met the senior flight instructor who joined us. After lunch I was given a tour of some of the flight line and aircraft which were mostly C-47s and P-51s, with a couple of Supermarine Spitfires. All the aircraft were vintage WWII leftovers.

After visiting the line we went to the instructor's office where he informed me that I would be notified in a few weeks about the procedures necessary for signing up for a career in the RCAF and the training that I would receive. I asked if the RCAF had any newer aircraft than those I saw. Of course the RCAF had some C-54s, a few B-17s, and a collection of arctic aircraft made by de Havilland. Not a very impressive lot for a wide-eyed kid who wanted to try new and exciting models, not the worn out machines left over from the war. Was the RCAF acquiring jet aircraft and was there a training program for crews? The instructor hesitated for a moment then admitted that a conversion program was in the works. Implementation of such a turbine-dependent program would take years before Canada could acquire aircraft.

"The American Air Force is first in line to acquire new products, and Canada would follow through soon after," he told me. I was disappointed, and it must have shown on my face.

"We do not produce many aircraft in Canada, and those that we do are not designed for the RCAF." Then the instructor offered me a ride back to Halifax.

In the car he mentioned that if I was disappointed, he was also, but the RCAF did not have the funds available to commit to research and development for new airplanes. Jet research was being done in England and in America but nothing like that was currently developing in Canada.

Nevertheless, the instructor added that "the RCAF was a good group and I would climb the ladder quickly because most of the officers were leftovers from the war and soon would be reaching retirement age."

As a shopper I did not find the product offered blindingly appealing.

A few days later I received a letter from Australia which stated that the Royal Australian Air Force was quite receptive to my request but assured me that I would have to work my way up the enlisted ranks for a few years, and then I would be sent to flight training. For the moment, the letter writer stated, Australia had too many qualified pilots left over from the war. After my visit with the RCAF I presumed that the Australians' flight line would be displaying aircraft of the same vintage as the RCAF.

I visited the local Halifax library and looked at the 1949 edition of *Jane's World Aviation*. In the book, which was reporting the current aircraft for Australia's Air Force, I found that the procurement list was no newer than that of Canada. After looking at Brazil's Air Force, I learned that their aircraft were even less modern than Australia's or Canada's. Taking a deep breath, I turned the pages to the UK and found that the RAF was upgrading their fleet as quickly as production permitted. The UK's research and development programs were moving ahead rapidly with invested funds from the United States.

Canada and my Options

I should have done my research in Europe and I should have been more thorough in my search for a new home. Perhaps too, I should have discussed my plans and my goal in greater detail with either my godfather or with Pappy. As an independent young man I, at times, thought that I knew it all. One of my many failings.

I had to decide what to do before I received a letter from the Canadian Air Ministry. Canada was and is a lovely place and a good introduction to what I call the peculiar culture of North America. It is a culture quite different from those found in Europe. I was beginning to conclude that Canada was not for me. Australia and Brazil were also not for me. Should I plan to return to England and start my university education in the hope that when I graduated the RAF would be modernized? I had some thinking to do. The Royal Canadian Air Force did respond by letter and extended open arms to me with an invitation to come to Ottawa. I was not, however, certain that I could function in Canada and in the RCAF.

In my head I revisited some of my reservations about Canada, not because of my dislike for the country but because I wanted to be very careful and not commit myself to an environment that was not to my fullest satisfaction. I was ambivalent about Canada and that ambivalence haunted me. Indeed, French and English were spoken, but so was American, and that accent was more prevalent than any other. Canada was a "trompe œil" for the USA; it appeared to be very much like America, at least as I gathered from speaking with my Canadian friends — but it was also somewhat like France and England, but most of all it was in the shadow of the USA. The 800-pound Gorilla operating south of the border had a great deal of influence on Canada. The Canadian spirit was always looking over its shoulder at what the

USA was about. Moreover, Canada was a surrogate child of England, and a neglected foster child of France. In Canada, I sensed a country possessed with a personality crisis, and I wanted none of that. My heritage and personal life were already confused by a family living in a Diaspora, fragmented because of the war, and troubled by the social objections towards divorce. I did not want to compound my sense of fragmentation. I was looking for an opportunity to fly but I was also determined to live a wholesome life and to put down permanent roots in an environment that was satisfying for the long haul.

As for Brazil, I cared neither for its political framework, nor for its language. I was not interested in adding another language to my collection. In looking at Australia, the main thought was that it was too far from what I considered to be the center of the world, Europe. Anyway, Australia was "down there" with not much of a positive attraction for me — and I was "up here." I decided to seek John Longley's advice. His evaluation would be truthful and he would understand the issue emanating from America's influence on Canada, and the Canadian counter-attitude.

John Longley immediately sensed my disappointment and understood my situation. He suggested that I investigate the US Air Force. He was most sympathetic with my reluctance to remain in Canada. I had a life to lead and after living through a war I had to make a purposeful choice. Returning to Europe was not an option. I remember what he said to me.

"Raymond," he said, "patriotism is no longer an issue in this world. Make your decision on what will be best for you. At the moment no country cares a penny for your future. You have to make your own and I think that the United States might offer you the best future." John was a Canadian who recognized Canada's failings and its limitations.

The United States of America

The next morning John called me to tell me that he had obtained from a colleague in the United States the address of the recruiting department at the Pentagon. That evening I wrote a letter to the US Air Force recruitment officer and included the pertinent information about my flying experience, especially the type of aircraft and hours that I had accumulated. Now I was in a hurry. I did not wish to commit myself to the RCAF simply because I had no other option in my pocket. Four months had elapsed on my Canadian visa and I did not wish to return to England, to find a home in Europe, or to consider Egypt as a location for my future to emerge.

That afternoon, I went to the library to look again at *Jane's World Aviation*. Undoubtedly *Jane's* is the most complete public book on aviation available. I found again the 1949 issue. The United States Air Force (USAF) had the most advanced air Armada in the world and it was developing a supersonic aircraft that had yet to be tested. I was a little excited at the prospect, just a little. Leafing through *Jane's* I looked at the air forces of France, Italy, even the USSR; none matched that of America's air force.

Exactly 15 days after mailing my letter to the Pentagon, I received a reply from a Captain Sebastian Gonzales asking me to meet with the US military attaché who was visiting the American Consulate in Halifax. I was given an identification number and a telephone number to set up an appointment. My luck would have it that the attaché was Colonel David Rohrs, Chief of the Officer's recruitment sector in the Pentagon, and the recipient of my letter of inquiry.

John took me to the consulate the day I was to have my meeting. There was a tea given to welcome the military attaché. As things worked out before my official meeting with the colonel, I was introduced to him during the reception. We chatted informally for a few moments and after his official welcome and general introductions he guided me to his office.

I soon discovered that Colonel Rohrs was a senior pilot and had the wings on his shirt to prove it. To me he was a most cordial, interested, and affable person. He was keen to learn more about my hopes and aspirations; all went well with the interview (he examined my flight records, logbook, and had photo copies made of a few pages). He was certain that the USAF could find a flying place for me if I "really" wanted to be a pilot. There would be, however, some obstacles to address and some formalities to overcome because I was neither a citizen of the USA nor was I a resident. In short, it would be necessary for me to obtain my First Papers of Naturalization, and also to request a waver from Congress, through the help of a local House Representative. I knew none, but Colonel Rohrs would put me in contact with one as soon as I was legally a resident of the USA.

He left me in the office where I was interviewed to discuss the matter of my residency with the Consul General. Soon he returned to inform me that I would be given a visa to enter the USA that would be followed with a permanent residence visa as soon as I signed the notarized papers of commitment for service in the USAF; these papers were not my enlistment contract, just papers stating my intention and willingness to join the USAF when all was in order. In essence, this procedure amounted to an official invitation to immigrate to the USA.

The fact that I was not a US citizen was to become a problem because as a pilot I would need to be commissioned an officer and an officer must be a citizen. It was this requirement that made me apply for a waiver from Congress. It was also necessary for me to obtain a security clearance, pass a rigorous physical examination, profess allegiance to the US Constitution, and agree to do a four-year tour of active duty plus four years of active reserve duty. All these requirements had to be dealt with during the Korean Police Action, commonly known as the Korean War, and at the time of Senator Joseph McCarthy's Senate Inquiries that was on a hunt for Communist infiltrators in all walks of American life.

Col. Rohrs suggested that I immediately apply for permanent residence in the USA and also for my First Papers to begin the process of naturalization (today called a "green card"). The US Air Force could only begin to help me after I was sworn in and when my First Papers were issued. I immediately filed as instructed for my First Papers at the American Consulate in Canada. Everything seemed to be moving rapidly and I felt as if I was caught in a whirlwind that was carrying me into America.

The American Consul General reviewed my papers and informed me that since I was now over 18 years old the process required a formal invitation from a relative in the USA, application to be listed on the immigration quota, or enrollment in the Armed Forces. The latter required that I step over the border into the USA, something that I could not do because I had no visa, and to obtain one would take three months. I had less than two left on my Canadian visa, and hence could not wait. To obtain an invitation required that I ask my parents for it plus an affidavit that they would support me until I joined the Air Force. Moreover, John Longley brought up the notion that if Olav adopted me it would further facilitate the process. That option was not readily to my liking but any other choice would cause me great difficulties.

The invitation to immigrate to the United States required that some bureaucratic obstacles be overcome. The US Air Force was most helpful but only up to a certain level. I was given the necessary papers, shown the way to maneuver the various paths through the system, and who to approach for assistance. Because I was not a member of the USAF I had to go at it alone but nevertheless under the watchful eye of Col. Rohrs.

In the presence of the Consul General, I telephoned Olav and Mother. It was a most confusing conversation with me standing aside while the Consul General, who was most sympathetic to my situation, conducted an animated conversation with both my mother and Olav. Would they, immediately, send a letter with a financial affidavit by Western Union cable to his attention at the consulate, he would personally award me a three-month visa to enter the USA. In addition, the adoption papers by Olav had to be filed in Canada as soon as possible. John Longley joined in the conversation and volunteered to handle the adoption papers and file them as soon as signatures were obtained from Mr. and Mrs. Mong. The whirlwind was becoming more powerful by the day.

When the phone conversation was completed, the Consul General announced that Mr. and Mrs. Mong were taking the train to Halifax to begin the adoption proceedings! I was not sure that I wanted to take that route but the alternatives were returning to Europe, going to Brazil or Australia, staying in Canada or forgetting the whole issue and returning to England. None of these were acceptable to me, so I bit my tongue and agreed to the adoption. When in John's office I called my father in Paris to check again his position. He agreed without hesitating.

John Longley was very helpful in walking me through the legal and emotional step of the adoption; he understood my hesitation and reluctance. John also cabled my father William and obtained by return cable words authorizing the adoption that he quickly filed with the court before my mother arrived to avoid any problems and to not reveal that I was in communication with my father. She never knew.

John asked me how I wanted to be named. I insisted that "Hoche" remain in the name. John agreed. When Olav and Mother arrived the very next day, John moved the proceedings ahead by his influence with the court and it took less than an hour for the adoption to be legal and final. Henceforth, I was to be known legally as "Raymond Hoche-Mong," in spite of Mother's objections. She did not want me to keep the name "Hoche," but that was my name and I insisted. I was convinced that without the hyphen soon enough the Hoche would either become the middle initial H or would be dropped from usage eventually. Because I felt that any other name ascribed to Hoche would be simply a suffix and no more, the hyphen has remained.

The adoption papers were filed with the USA immigration officer in Halifax (there was now no need for a financial affidavit), the consulate filed my request for First Papers and in less than a week I received my permanent visa for residence in the United States of America. Col. Rohrs pushed the Air Force's side quickly and I was issued a date for the "swearing in" event. This rapid development was briskly stopped because of the McCarthy Senate hearings and the Korean Police actions. I needed a Congressional waiver authorizing my commission as an officer. None would come through under the Democratic Congress of 1950, which was intimidated by the Republican members who focused on hunting communists.

Both the McCarthy Senate hearing and investigations plus the security searches conducted by the House on Un-American Activities Committee (HUAC) were obstacles that delayed me from moving directly to the USAF.

Hello America

It was time now to say goodbye to the Hagens, the Longleys, and all the folk who had made my stay in Nova Scotia pleasant and memorable. I had again been fortunate to find myself in good company when I needed help. Help had been provided, hospitality gladly given, and support from bureaucrats willingly supplied. It was time for me to leave Canada for the USA.

To conserve my funds, I took the bus. The Canadian Acadia bus traveled through New Brunswick to the border town of St. Stephen. After clearing customs and immigration at Calais, on the American side, it was "Hello, America." I was now in the United States of America and the date was 23 September 1950.

After the luggage was transferred, I boarded the American Greyhound Bus that took me through Maine, New Hampshire, and into Boston, Massachusetts, then on to New York City. Olav and Mother were waiting at the 42nd Street bus terminal.

Soon after arriving in New York, I telephoned Col. Rohrs, who informed me that my request was with a Congressman from Maryland and would soon be presented to the appropriate sub-committee for a decision. Col. Rohrs still hoped that a Congressional waiver would be forthcoming. I'm not certain that I was given the name of the Representative; I believe that he was Col. Rohrs's own District Congressman. A few days after I learned about the Congressman's involvement on my behalf, I was advised that a delay was imminent because of the problems with the McCarthy investigation and the procedures of the HUAC. Now with the delay becoming a fact for me, I needed to find a job to cover my expenses.

I camped for two weeks with Mother and Olav in their apartment on Amsterdam Avenue and 80th Street, New York City. Because this was my first US address it is engraved in my memory; certain addresses somehow are indelibly recorded in one's brain. Waiting for a decision to be made by Congress was difficult for me. I could not just sit in the apartment and do nothing while waiting for my status to be defined.

I telephoned Alfred Torricelli, my shipmate from the Atlantic crossing. He was delighted to hear from me and wanted to know everything that had happened to me since we parted in Halifax. He invited me to come for a visit to his home in Poughkeepsie, NY for a few days and gave me train directions for the trip. In fact he mailed me train tickets, which I received the very next day. Alfred met me at the train station and drove me to his home to meet his lovely family. On the way to his house I told Alfred what had happened to me and that I was now waiting for Washington to decide my fate. He thought that I could use a job while I waited so he took me to the Social Security office in Poughkeepsie to obtain a number, and to the Draft Board to register, even though I was awaiting word from the USAF. A few days later, because Alfred was on his way to Boston, he offered me a ride to visit the city and also see Cambridge. We walked through Harvard Square, and through MIT where he would be going to graduate school. He then bought me a ticket for the train to New York City and suggested I go to the nearest State Unemployment Office.

Now in possession of a Social Security number, I began to look for a job. I had to find a job and move out of Mother's apartment. Soon after arriving in New York City, I discovered that Olav was attached to a hard alcoholic drink called a "boiler maker," which consisted of a glass of beer and a jigger of bourbon. Olav consumed a fair amount of boilermakers, starting in the morning before going to work. I had to leave.

There is something about drunks and alcoholics that utterly disgusts me. Intentionally losing authority over one's sense of control seems to be a decision that overtly denies one of his or her humanity. I cannot stand the glassy and hazy eyes, the slurred and incoherent speech, or the wobbly stance. I have no patience with that aspect of human misbehavior. It is not that I am against the consumption of alcohol; it is just that when one cannot manage it, then one should ration or avoid it.

Alcoholism may be the result of a disease, but this does not make the behavior it produces excusable. Perhaps I am intolerant of those who are afflicted by alcohol. Perhaps I don't understand how they suffer from alcoholism and how they have an uncontrollable craving for it. This may be one more of my shortcomings. Try as I want to, alcoholics who know that they are alcoholics yet refuse to seek treatment to help them abstain from it are not people whom I want as company.

Even today I cannot tolerate a person who is not alcoholic and yet who knowingly abuses alcohol, especially when he/she is aware of the behavioral changes. Because I like the taste of a drink now and then, a pint of good ale, a well-made martini, a glass of vintage wine, and a shot of single malt whiskey, I cannot abide those whose sole purpose is drinking for the effect it has on self-control. Yes, I may be intolerant, but so be it.

As Alfred suggested, I went to the nearest State Unemployment Office in lower Manhattan. Before noon on the first day of my search, I found a job making toy gun holsters in Manhattan's lower Eastside. The owner of the factory also had a room, which he would rent to me until I was settled. The room cost me $7 per week and the job paid me $32 per week. It was a good beginning and it allowed me to move out of the maternal nest once again.

The owner suggested that I obtain an automobile driver's license with a truck option. On the third day after I started work at the firm he sent me to Long Island to a truck-driving school for training. Two days after attending the training, I passed my driving test and was able to handle an 18-wheeler, hitch the tractor to a trailer, and perform a full 90-degree backing maneuver between two parallel lines to a loading platform. My boss, the owner of the factory, often sent me on weekends, if I was willing, to Boston to deposit a trailer of furniture and return with another trailer full of canned foods. For these expeditions I would be given $100, a good sum for a day and a half of work. In total I drove a truck for five or six weekends, and although it was hard work driving, it was not too unpleasant a task.

Making holsters for toy cowboy guns was fun and easy. I worked all afternoon on a riveter and assembled the holsters from leather I had cut in the morning. At noon, I usually bought a sandwich from a lunch truck and talked to a pretty Puerto Rican girl named Eliza. Eliza was a fine and most attractive girl who had sparkling hazel eyes, long dark hair, and stood approximately five feet three inches. We found a great deal to talk about and enjoyed each other's company.

Eliza worked on the sewing machine with which she added the design stitches that adorned the belts and holsters. She introduced me to an ice cream dessert covered with chocolate on a stick called an Eskimo Pie, which I could purchase for five cents, a nickel. Eliza and I often went to movies or to dinner after work. She was attending night school to finish her high school diploma before entering City College of New York (CCNY) to study accounting and become a certified public accountant.

After working on holsters for four months, in February 1951 I found a better job with Hayden Chemicals (makers of the main ingredient for Bayer Aspirin) in Garfield, New Jersey, first as a wringer operator ($80/week) drying the wet powdered material for aspirin tablets, and then a few weeks later, as a lab technician ($95/week).

When I said goodbye to all my friends at the holster factory I showed them that I had carefully kept the first dollar that I had earned in America and had placed it with the first dollar I had earned in Canada. A small, simple, and quite warm luncheon party hosted by the owner was prepared for me in the employee rest area, and for dessert, several Eskimo Pies were distributed. After leaving the holster factory I never saw Eliza again but we did talk on the telephone several times and she told me that she had earned her high school diploma and had been accepted at CCNY.

After my few weeks in New York City, I moved to East Rutherford, New Jersey and rented a three-room apartment ($60/month including utilities and basement) in a two-family house. I had the upper floor and part of the basement and remained at that location until entering the USAF.

At Hayden my job was to work on two spinning wringers where the powdered chemical was spun-dried before being dumped into 60-pound capacity bags by the worker who was located below me. The work was pleasant but required precision on my part. It also demanded that I work shift schedules, which was not too terribly enjoyable. It had, however, its rewards. For unskilled labor, which was what I was classified as, shift work pays better than regular work. In addition I had the opportunity to meet blue collar workers who, as a lot, worked hard, were conscientious, and were always helpful, courteous, and kind to me.

My shifts consisted of a schedule that covered the hours of 7:00 a.m. to 3:00 p.m. (the day shift), 3:00 p.m. to 11:00 p.m. (the evening shift), and 11:00 p.m. to 7:00 a.m. (the graveyard shift), each to be rotated every seven days after two days off. On holidays we were paid double time, and if there happened to be a need for more than eight hours of work, when a replacement was ill, then we were paid time and a half, but never to work in excess of twelve hours per day.

I enjoyed working with my colleagues, and we all developed a camaraderie that was most satisfying to the point of going to picnics and meeting their families. It was a known fact by the workers that I was in that group only temporarily, but still I was treated as one of their own kind even to the point of being invited to join the Machinist's Union after working six months; I didn't put six months on that job but soon, as noted earlier, moved to a better position.

Through the personnel office at Hayden, I found that a position was open for a Laboratory Technician. I soon applied for the position knowing that I had had enough chemistry to be of some value in a chemical lab. After an interview with the chief chemist, Jim Walt, I was given the job and was invited to begin the following Monday. I worked as a lab tech until I entered the Air Force on 3 July 1951.

A special time for me was when I was either getting off the evening shift or coming on for the graveyard shift at Hayden before working as a lab technician. I would stop at Pete's Coffee Shop, located in Passaic, across the bridge from Hayden in Garfield, and order a cup of coffee and a piece of apple pie. Never have I since eaten a better-made apple pie than the one I ordered at Pete's. Pete, the owner and baker, had lost his left arm at Anzio, Italy, during WWII when a German artillery shell exploded close to his position. He was a decorated soldier and proud to have served in the war against the Nazis (never referring to them as Germans). Even without an arm, he could knead dough and make doughnuts, pies, and crisp Kaiser rolls.

His coffee shop was set up so that the counters encased his kitchen and work area. Customers could see him work and speak with him while he tended to his chores, always working with a smile, a tune, and attention to his customers. I would watch him roll the pie dough onto the rolling pin so that he could transfer it to a pie plate. I learned much about pie making simply by watching him. His dexterity was beyond anything I had yet seen. He would make four or five pies at a time and then start over again, making a total of twenty pies a day. The freshest was when I arrived just before midnight because they were made for the next day. I would be given a hot piece of apple pie that he had slid out of his massive gas-fired brick oven. Delicious. His pieces of pie were not small but large and filled with apple chunks seasoned to perfection.

"Raymond," he would remind me, "a slice of Vermont Sharp Cheddar?" How could I resist? Then Pete would cover the pie with a thick slice of Cheddar cheese, which would immediately begin to melt.

Even when I stopped working shifts and started regular work as a lab tech, I would make a point of stopping three or four times a week for a piece of Pete's pie but I would skip the coffee and substitute a glass of whole milk instead. Stopping at Pete's was a ceremony that I honored before heading for bed. I could walk from Pete's to my apartment in East Rutherford, which was located about two miles across the Passaic River.

Just before leaving for the USAF, I stopped to say goodbye to Pete and give him an envelope with a $50 bill and a thank-you note. He wanted to know where I was going for my basic training. I told him. A few weeks later during the time when all recruits were given a weekend of leave, I was called into the adjutant's office where a package was awaiting me. The writing on the package said: OPEN IMMEDIATELY. I opened it and found an apple pie from Pete. It never left the adjutant's office. I shared the pie with the adjutant and his staff. The First Sergeant had a fresh pot of coffee made and we all delighted in the gift from Pete. The adjutant had received a telephone call from Pete (he knew the number because Pete had phoned earlier in the week to ask if he could send me the pie) that informed him that a special and perishable package was arriving for me. With the adjutant's permission and his telephone, I called Pete and chatted with him for a few minutes and we all told him how much we appreciated his pie. I kept track of Pete until he died about five years later in the Veterans Hospital in Newark, NJ.

While working at Hayden Chemicals and waiting for all the papers to be completed and for the USAF to call me, I had bought for the total sum of $100 a 1939 Pontiac Chief. It did me well and when I left for the USAF I bequeathed it to Olav, who did not have a car. Mother refused to learn to drive. The car served me well for the five months or so that I enjoyed the East Coast. I traveled to Connecticut, Rhode Island, Maryland, Pennsylvania, and upstate New York. My laboratory colleague John Bossman and his fiancé Jane often joined me on these trips or I went in their car, a new 1950 Ford Sedan with twin mufflers, twin carburetors, and rear-wheel fender skirts.

John was a car buff who constantly worked to improve the speed and efficiency of his Ford. John was also a stock-car racing enthusiast who often raced for independent car owners. Because of his interest, I was introduced to stock-car racing but only as a spectator, of course. It was exciting and something I had never seen, especially when it came to the demolition derby at intermissions. John was a good friend and initiated me into many American traditions such as working on cars on Saturdays, going for long drives on Sundays, and other festive events that are identified as things that the "young" do. On occasion I dated Allison, Jane's younger sister or double dated with John and Jane. I also dated Joan, Hayden's technical assistant librarian who later that year enlisted in the Marines.

In the meantime, Col. Rohrs was actively trying to push through a waiver with the help of several Representatives on the Armed Services Committee. He was certain that the skids had been well greased for a waiver. He telephoned me to advise that I should be sworn-in immediately in the Air Force to give support to the waiver process being discussed in the Committee. I agreed and headed to the recruiting office in New York City located on famous Times Square.

After completing the application, I was sent to Newark, NJ to complete the requirements of physical examinations, intelligence evaluations (which included a psychological interview), career orientation, military code of justice briefing, and Air Force standard operating procedures information. I passed all the given tests and absorbed as much of the information as I could.

My head was saturated to the point where I was on the verge of experiencing a headache.

As I was leaving the Air Force Center in Newark, Col. Rohrs met me at the door and offered to give me a ride to my apartment and treat me to dinner. The colonel was concerned that the McCarthy Senate Investigative Committee was going to torpedo my request for a waiver. For the moment no negative indication had surfaced, but McCarthy was hounding the military and attacking them on every occasion where foreigners were given special treatment. Controlling both the Senate Committee and exerting pressure on the HUAC, McCarthy was, in those years, an evil force to contend with. This period was a shameful segment of American history when neither outgoing President Truman could intercede nor the phlegmatic new Republican President, Eisenhower, would do anything. All the branches of the military were pushed to the limit to hunt communist infiltrators in their ranks. If a father had so much as read the "Daily Worker," the socialist paper, the son was considered to be communist and other members of the family were accused as collaborators. Businesses floundered, jobs were lost, careers were terminated, and few were spared from the persecution that the McCarthy hunt initiated.

A Recruit in the USAF

On 3 July 1951 I raised my right hand to swear allegiance to uphold and protect the Constitution of the United States of America. Here was a foreigner in times of great stress for American democracy, American freedom, and American customs, promising to be one of this Nation's protectors, even to the point of forsaking one's life to fulfill that oath. Less than a few hundred miles south of me, in the Nation's capital, was a senator with numerous supporters slowly and methodically gnawing at the very bones of what America stood for: freedom of thought, freedom of speech, and freedom of action.

Eisenhower's election did little to lift the cloud from this miserable period. Fortunately, a few short years later, the Senate censored Senator McCarthy and he died soon after. It was during this questionable period that I entered military service. It was also during these years that I witnessed many solid, patriotic, and contributing Americans be savaged by McCarthy's group. Hollywood actors, writers, and directors, the press, teachers, Nobel scientists, career diplomats, and a score of other outstanding people were reduced to poverty because they could no longer obtain employment after being "black-listed" by McCarthy's Senate Investigations Committee and by the members of the House on Un-American Activities Committee. Indeed, it was a shameful era for the United States. Not until President Johnson's time in 1975 did the HUAC cease to exist. Even Dr. J. Robert Oppenheimer, the theoretical physicist and director of the Manhattan Project was stripped of his security clearance and removed from his directorship. It was a reprehensible time for America!

My very first day in the USAF began with a surprising occurrence: I was given a three-day pass because the day I affirmed my oath was the day before the 4th of July. I always took this act of benevolence as an indication or omen of how my tour in the military would turn out to be. Consequently my time in the Air Force was begun with a leave and proceeded onward in the same vein; indeed this was a propitious beginning for a lad who felt a little over-whelmed by events. The journey for this boy had started with a fervent interest in flying and now he was in the American Air Force, not as a pilot but as an airman third class going to boot camp with young men who were quite unlike himself, who had different and parochial backgrounds, and who in essence spoke a different language than young Raymond.

I was part of a mixed group that included New Yorkers, New Jerseyites, Afro-Americans from Georgia, Brooklyn, and Manhattan, and Hispanics from Puerto Rico, Cuba, and Panama. All of them were American citizens and I was the only exception. Each man spoke a distinctive American dialect. I spoke English-English and my name was hyphenated and I claimed to be French-Italian and was born in Cairo, Egypt, Africa — the continent where black people originated. It was most confusing to my colleagues in arms. I was at every turn of events, at every meeting, obliged to explain why I was different. Ultimately, my associates called me "Frenchy," a name that stayed with me for many years.

In 1951, the United States, in conjunction with other nations and under the banner of the United Nations, became further committed to the Korean Police Action, otherwise known as the Korean War. Ambassador George Keenan, once America's ambassador to the USSR, had produced a study that emphasized a policy of "containment" to protect the free world from Soviet encroachment. Both the United Nations and the United States had adopted this policy. As a result, the goal was to contain North Korea's advancement into South Korea. The purpose of the Police Action was to push back North Korea's force to north of the 38th Parallel. When as neophytes in the military, we said the oath of allegiance, we were all informed by the recruiting welcoming committee that some of us would find ourselves serving in Korea either as combatants or as support personnel — the choice depended on the technical training we would receive after basics were completed.

For basic training I was assigned to Sampson Air Force Base in upstate New York near Geneva and Seneca Lakes. That location was considered to be a resort on the Finger Lakes and certainly much better than the horrid base of Lackland in Texas where the majority of recruits were assigned. Basic training lasts eight weeks and is inescapable. During the eight weeks a recruit is tested, retested, interrogated, interviewed, and finally assigned to a school for training to become a "technically productive" airman.

During my seventh week of basic training the Base Commander called me into his office to tell me that the Pentagon would be telephoning me in a few minutes. The call came and Col. Rohrs informed me that I would not be receiving any waivers. The problem was indubitably the McCarthy Senate hearings and the investigations conducted by the HUAC. Congress was in a state of paralysis. President Truman was so exasperated with Congress that he decided not to seek a second term. Colonel Rohrs offered me two options: I could be released from my commitment, and possibly be liable to a draft call, or I could remain in the enlisted rank and then the Air Force could directly apply all possible pressure towards obtaining my naturalization papers to become a US citizen. I chose the latter option. Now that I was staying in the Air Force the decision by the hierarchy was that I start accelerated courses of training. Ultimately, I was sent to radar technology school in

Biloxi, Mississippi. Before being assigned to radar school, a glitch occurred in the assignment system and I was selected to attend cook's school at the Army's facility in Kentucky! (Fortunately, this glitch was soon repaired and I headed for Biloxi and the USAF's radar and electronic school.)

At six a.m. a few days before I was informed of my training assignment, I was rousted out of bed to meet with the Base Commanding Officer in his office. When I arrived dressed in freshly pressed fatigues, I was immediately escorted inside.

"Airman," the CO said in a loud voice, "you have been mistakenly assigned to cook's school and your Orders have already been cut."

I was stunned but said nothing. How did the cook's school assignment come about, I asked myself?

"Col. Rohrs was notified last night and he's been burning the telephone lines to me and to Air Training Command's Personnel Department to resolve this f——g mess."

I still was unable to say anything. I was struck dumb.

"Airman, as it stands you are under arrest and will not leave this building until this situation is cleared up satisfactorily."

But I had not done anything to be placed under arrest, I thought to myself.

"Sir, what have I done?" I asked in a weak, almost inaudible voice.

"As long as you are under arrest you can go nowhere, and I can keep you for as long as I want to. Go to the outer office and eat the breakfast that was brought for you. You are dismissed."

As I was leaving his office, the CO added, "Your qualifications are excellent and you need not worry too much about this cooking assignment. By the way do you like food preparation?"

"Yes Sir, but...."

"It showed in your testing results! Now go."

I saluted, did an about face, and walked out of the inner sanctum. Later in the day after eating my noon meal in the outer office, the CO called for me.

"Airman, you will leave from Geneva's train station at 0700 tomorrow morning. A car will come for you at 0500. Be ready."

Where was I going? I thought, but said nothing. I saluted, did an about face, and started to walk out, then I did another about face and looked straight at the CO. "Sir, where am I going?"

The CO burst into laughter, "Young man, you are off to Keesler AFB and to Radar Technical School. Good luck." He came over and shook my hand. "You have a good and solid friend in Col. Rohrs."

I left to pack my belongings.

Biloxi, Mississippi

Biloxi was an interesting town especially for me, one who was born in Africa, and had come from Egypt. Six of us arrived by train in Birmingham, Alabama, then transferred to a local train for our final destination where we were met by a blue troop carrier to be given a ride to Keesler Air Force Base, Biloxi, Mississippi. The six of us airmen had traveled from Samson AFB to Keesler AFB to begin radio-radar technology training. Because radar was a new discipline it was part of the radio training instruction sector in the Air Force. This training was to prepare me for the Distant Early Warning (DEW) line that was being constructed along the North American Pacific Rim that included the western Pacific States, western and northern Alaska, and the Polar Canadian coastline. This system was to become the principal tool of the Air Defense Command (ADC), the precursor of the Northern Radar System (NORAD) — fundamentally, a radar monitoring and fighter interception system aimed at precluding Soviet intrusion on the North American continent.

The training was intensive and required total immersion to learn not merely the fundamental physics of the system, including general maintenance of the equipment but also the strategic, tactical, and operational procedures and operations. There was no goofing off now. Of the six recruits who were with me only three remained to finish the training, the others were reassigned because they could not make the grade.

I loved the training because of the complex strategic combat problems. The logic required to resolve solutions had variations, options, analyses, and good methodologies for obtaining coherent solutions. The training included a great amount of technical, electronic, practical, and theoretical work as well as lots of flying once I received my wings. All the training was conducted with great acceleration and enormous pressure, but all under the eye of excellent instructors, many of who were employed by American Telephone and Telegraph (AT&T), Western Electric Corporation (a sub company of AT&T), General Electric Corporation, and Radio Corporation of America and were on loan to the Air Force to conduct the classes.

Not having had much education in electronics, I had to work very hard to obtain good grades. Much as I worked hard, I was motivated to produce the best results because both the instructors and the curriculum were excellent. When it was all completed, I discovered that I was one exhausted young man, very much in need of a rest but I was pleased to be told that I was at the top of the class and had earned a three-day pass with a 100-mile travel limit. I decided to head for New Orleans but stopped in Gulfport instead. But that story comes later.

The coastal town of Biloxi was strictly a segregated community in 1951 where whites and colored (black Afro-American today) were openly separated. I remember getting off the train in Biloxi and seeing, for the first time, a water fountain labeled for whites and a separate fountain labeled for colored. It must have been the same in Birmingham but I did not notice. On Keesler, of course, segregation was not practiced; in fact President Truman with an Executive Order had integrated the USAF from its inception in 1947. It was puzzling to me to see such strict racial separation especially when America had fought a major war against racial discrimination. Racism was not what I thought America was about. I did not like it.

Perhaps this discrimination was present in New York or in Boston but I had not noticed it. I was very much aware that white residents did not live close to colored residents, but neither did Italians live close to Puerto Ricans. I simply assumed that birds of a feather choose to live together without so much as a deliberate and open revulsion of the other individuals. In Biloxi, the mood was different and hateful. Colored and whites seemed to be at war, and mostly incited by the white's attitude of superiority — not unlike the Nazi attitude of racial superiority. I thought that in America the issue to defeat the "master race" and its preclusions was why the war was fought. Was I naive?

The roommate assigned to my room was an Afro-American person from Augusta, Georgia. We got along quite well and enjoyed each other's company. We often went to the Enlisted Airmen's Club for beers and conversation alone or with others. The conversation inevitably returned to racism and the shabby way that colored people were treated in all walks of American society. Even in the northern states where whites and colored were not kept apart, the social structure was such that the separation was part of the very fabric. At the table, although my skin was not colored, I was the real African by birth, but because I looked European or Caucasian I was often served with more courtesy, even in the Club.

The injustice was apparent and was wholly counter to the meaning of what America stood for. I struggled with this problem all the time that I was in Biloxi. One of my instructors, a black man with a fine mind, was not able to obtain a beer in town, unless he went to the colored section where everything was dilapidated, rotting, and awful. It was not so much that the colored could not maintain a decent neighborhood, but that the white municipality refused to spend any funds on colored roads, sidewalks, garbage removal, sanitation, and the infrastructure that sustains a community.

On my day off (we had just one day per week) I would rent a moped from an agent just outside the main gate of Keesler and go exploring the coast, the inner town, and the white and colored neighborhoods. Once I stopped for a sandwich in a colored section and was warned that whites did not come to this restaurant. Was it illegal? No, I was quickly assured. Would I be served? Yes, was the response. I stayed and ate lunch. Upon leaving I was told kindly not to return because they could get into trouble with the police. I left and did not return. When I returned to the base, after telling my story I was advised that such an act of defiance, if seen by whites, would incur retribution on the colored establishment. In fact whites still practiced the lynching of "niggers," burning of houses, mutilation of girls' and boys' genitals, and beatings.

In the 1950s, Americans just lived with racial separation. Congress was furious with President Truman's integration of the military, and especially those who joined the States' Rights Party, called the Dixiecrats, led by Senator Strom Thurman of South Carolina. In a sense, Truman nailed his coffin shut and lost much of his support for a second term, were he to run, which he did not. General Dwight Eisenhower won the election (and reelection for his second term) in part because he was willing to avoid the segregation issue completely, plus the Senator McCarthy and HUAC issues, too.

As I intimated earlier, these were embarrassing times for America, and Ike did not help much to improve the image of America before the world. In fact, Eisenhower was very unhappy with Chief Justice Earl Warren, his appointee to the US Supreme Court, because of the Court's ruling in 1954 supporting desegregation. If anyone could turn me away from the Republican Party, no one could have done it better than Ike, McCarthy, and the 1956 Republican Platform. In fact in 1956, against the advice given to me by Mother and Olav as a guide for my first presidential vote, I voted for Governor Stevenson for President and Senator Kefauver for Vice President, both Democrats. That they lost and Ike was reelected did matter to me because I could not support the unethical posture of the Republican Party.

When I took my well-earned three-day pass I boarded a bus for New Orleans. In Gulfport, midway to New Orleans, the bus stopped and I decided to catch the next one and tour the city in the meantime. It was just noon and I had some time for the side visit. Walking through the town I saw that it had a girls' school. I walked onto the campus and saw that T.S. Elliot's *Murder in the Cathedral* was to be presented in the theater, in the round, that evening. My decision was to spend the night near the school and see the play. I went to the ticket office to purchase a seat and inquire if there was any lodging close by that the school could recommend. Because I was in uniform I was invited to spend the night in the family guest quarters for the price of two dollars that included dinner and breakfast in the student refectory. My room was perfect.

Not having had lunch I sauntered to the student cafeteria for a snack and a Coke. I was invited to join a table by a group of students who wanted to know what I was doing in Gulfport. That bit of information shared, we began to discuss the Korean War, Europe, Africa, Egypt, and education in England.

One of the girls, a smart and pretty lady, whose father was working in Venezuela, invited me to join her and a few others for tea in the afternoon. She also asked me if I wanted a tour of the campus before tea. Her name was Diane and she was a senior, hence in her last year. Diane had been accepted at Stanford and would begin in September 1952.

My overnight visit to Gulfport extended to the whole three days and I never reached New Orleans, but that was just as well. My time with Diane offered a great deal more than a tourist's visit to New Orleans. I dated Diane a couple more times before I finished with my training.

While at Keesler AFB I ordered the first new car I had ever owned. Up to that time, cars that I owned were used and mostly unreliable vehicles. Now, with a little money saved from the minuscule salary received from the Air Force, and practically no expenses other than toiletries, a 10-cent beer now and then, and chocolate, I could indulge myself and reach for a new car. It was an early 1952 Ford straight six cylinder (not a V-8) with air conditioning, grey, blue-tinted sunroof (non-movable), but without a radio. When I went to the dealer and asked for the price with the air conditioner (a/c) he quoted me $1,900 but questioned the wisdom of buying the cooling unit, which cost $400, a fifth of the price of the car. I insisted that the order be placed and paid for the down payment in cash, which surprised the dealer.

Because I knew very little about banks, bank accounts, or checks, I kept my money either in cash or at the post office, which was what I had been accustomed to in Europe. I had never handled a personal check. I had been accustomed to bank drafts, cable drafts, and postal letters of credit, but never personal checks or personal bank accounts. In school, I received an allowance drawn from a trust fund prepared by my parents, and to some extent contributions from my maternal grandfather Joseph. All funds as gifts sent to me while in school had been in the form of postal money orders. Work I performed in Nova Scotia, New York, and New Jersey was paid in cash. The military paid me in cash. It was my belief, therefore, that banks and personal checks were for people who had millions, which obviously excluded me. It was only when I relocated to California a few months later and began to be paid by the Air Force by check that I was introduced to checking accounts and banking, but not until I had first opened a postal savings account in Mill Valley.

To California, Here I Went

My technical radar training was completed in June 1952; I did have to return in August of that year for an additional week of training on a new phase of airborne radar lobe detection. In the weeks in between I took a two-week leave and went to New York to greet my Uncle Mathieu and Camille and my cousin who were arriving to settle in Los Angeles. Before heading for Los Angeles, they were invited to Aiken, SC to visit my mother and Olav who was working on the Savannah River project. Olav had purchased a newer Pontiac and I was recruited to drive to New York, meet the arrival of Mathieu and Camille and then drive them to South Carolina. I stayed in Aiken a week and then headed for New Jersey and New York before returning to Biloxi for my week of training.

Upon graduation from the technical program, I was assigned to the 666 Aircraft, Control & Warning (AC&W) Radar Squadron, San Francisco Bay Area, California. My plan was to go to Flint, Michigan, and receive delivery of my new car, then drive the car off the Ford factory floor to California. But that did not prove possible because the car was not ready for delivery. The Ford Customer Service representative, when I spoke with him by telephone, apologized and offered to pay my way to California. I accepted and decided to take a train west. I boarded the train from Mobile to Atlanta then on to Chicago. In Chicago after changing stations I boarded the express train, the *City of San Francisco*, for a journey of three days to the Bay Area. I had booked a roomette with pull-down bed, shower, and toilet. The trip was a delight and worth the time spent traveling across some extraordinary territory. My California arrival was in mid-July 1951.

Because I had no specific address for my new assigned location except 666 AC&W Radar Squadron, San Francisco Bay Area, California, I assumed that upon arriving in San Francisco there would be someone to meet me at the train station. Wrong. First of all, the train did not travel into San Francisco but terminated in Oakland, in the East Bay. Bus transportation was offered to passengers heading for San Francisco. I did not take the bus and soon missed it because I searched the terminal for an Air Force representative but found no one. Arriving late, 8:30 p.m., in Oakland, I thought it wiser to spend the night in a hotel and search for the 666 AC&W Radar Squadron in the light of morning. There was a small but good hotel near the train station and I booked a room. In the room I searched the telephone pages for the Squadron but found nothing. I called telephone information to see if there was a listed number but none was found. Showering and going to bed was sufficient for this day. Under the morning light I would hunt for my destination.

In the morning, after breakfast I asked the hotel reservation clerk if he could help me. He referred me to Tom, the concierge. Tom could not locate the Squadron, and a telephone search was futile because we did not know which city or which section of the San Francisco Bay area was domicile for my destination. With a stroke of genius, Tom called the Army Presidio Base in San Francisco for information. No sooner had he done this than the Army Sergeant at Presidio informed us that a vehicle and driver would be expedited immediately to fetch me. I could expect the vehicle an hour after the call. He arrived exactly an hour later. I thanked Tom and boarded the vehicle for my first trip to San Francisco by way of the Oakland Bay Bridge.

At the Presidio I was taken directly to the dining (chow) hall to be given lunch. First things first are performed in the military, of course. Incidentally, the young army driver did not know where my squadron was located but was sure that it would be found, and anyway, as long as I was on a military base I would not be declared "Away Without Leave" (AWOL). That was comforting because my leave and travel time were to end at midnight of that day!

After lunch, an airman approached me and asked for my name. After showing him my orders he informed me that he would drive me to the 666 AC&W Radar Squadron, then he welcomed me to the squadron on behalf of the Squadron Commander, Colonel Vincent Gravette.

"Where is the Squadron located?" I asked.

"On top of Mt. Tamalpais, near the old mill town of Mill Valley, in Marin County."

"The Military Orders I had in my possession never indicated the exact address."

"Often they forget that small detail...or do it for security reasons."

"That's silly," I said. "How would an airman ever find the base without a specific address?"

The driver agreed.

Airman Bob drove me across the Golden Gate Bridge and into the town of Mill Valley, then up the mountain to the radar site. What a panoramic view was presented from the peak! The radar domes were clean and white. The base, or radar site, as Bob called it, was immaculate. The housing quarters were first class. I was taken directly to my assigned room and given a door key. Door key? Do we need door keys here, I thought? Then after depositing my duffle bag, washing my hands, and adjusting my blue Class-A uniform, I was taken to the base adjutant's office to sign in and receive the next phase of my assignment. It was approaching 15:00 hours.

First Lieutenant John Miller had been a Master Sergeant who moved through Warrant Officer grade, then was commissioned to officer's rank. He greeted me and apologized for the incomplete address on my orders, which was not an unusual occurrence and was more due to an omission rather than a security precaution. He asked me to sit down. He then informed me that I was going to be on Mt. Tamalpais only for a few days, then I would be heading south to Half Moon Bay (HMB), in San Mateo County. My task was to evaluate the operational capability of the HMB site located in Princeton Harbor atop a bluff. The few days on Mt. Tamalpais would be devoted to a review of the general operational and combat capabilities of all the related sites under the purview of 666 AC&W command site. The 666th was the principal site to which all other Northern California sites reported. I would be leaving in four or five days. I had been issued a key to my room because I did not need to take all my personal items, but could store them in the room.

In HMB I would be staying in a room at the site for a couple of days but I was to find quarters off base. All expenses would be borne by the USAF. With an assigned blue Air Force automobile, I was to leave for Half Moon Bay as soon as I was satisfied that I was prepared for the task and ready. It should not take me more than two or three months to complete the evaluation of the HMB site. After this brief introduction, he announced that my First Papers had been issued (I was given the original) and that now I could start counting the months to full citizenship, which would probably be in January 1954. The Air Force was pushing as hard as it could. My security clearance had already been issued, and my operational identification card would be given to me in a day or two, but before I left for HMB. In the morning Col. Gravette would meet with me to give me a tour of the operational radar facilities and to discuss my assignment in greater detail.

The whole attitude made me uncomfortable because it seemed that I was given special privileges and, certainly, a special assignment. After all I was only an E-2, the same as a corporal: low on the hierarchical ladder of the Air Force. Experience was something I did not have. I may have had book knowledge but none of it had been applied in the field to any real problems. I was a neophyte with no rank, no authority, and no seasoning. Certainly it would not do me much good to be seen by members of the squadron as an airman who received special treatment. It worried me that my evaluation would count for something beyond my reach. Soon enough I would ask why I was given such a special assignment, an assignment that possibly required an airman with a higher grade, more experience, and knowledge of the area under the control of this command. Much as I projected a certain amount of assurance, confidence, poise, and arrogance, I was scared, very scared that it was all above my head, and that I could get into serious trouble.

The next day I went, as ordered, to the Squadron Commander's office. After the welcoming, the cordiality, and the cup of coffee were over, I was asked if all the needed technical material had been made available for my review. When I required, however, additional information, it was to be given to me immediately. I inquired when I would see the procurement list of the operational equipment, the maintenance and operational logs, and reports by the technical representatives (Tech Reps)?

"We're going up to the dome now where you'll find the material you need and speak to the personnel," he replied.

It was about one mile up to the highest peak of Mt. Tamalpais where the radar dome, operational control, and maintenance facility were situated. We stopped at the gate before driving up the hill and Col. Gravette showed his security pass and mine, which he then handed to me. Now I was legal to go anywhere on the site or any other related complex in the DEW line system because my security clearance had arrived by telex during the night.

While the Colonel tended to other tasks in the operational facility, I reviewed the logs, the reports, and the maintenance facility and chatted with the maintenance personnel to learn more. After that session, I was taken to the Operation Control Area (OCA). I discussed the capability of the 6B antenna at HMB and inquired if all maintenance requirements had been made. Was the system functioning up to its fullest level? Was there a hidden hardware problem? All my questions were answered to my satisfaction but it was obvious that HMB's radar facility was not producing the results expected. I left with an option that I could request further assistance from the maintenance team and the tech reps any time. One item that bothered me was that the range of the HMB antenna was too short to make it an effective early warning system. If I could reach that conclusion why didn't others?

With Col. Gravette by my side I entered the transition operation area. It was dark and my eyes needed a few minutes to get accustomed to the lack of light. When the transition was completed for both Gravette and me, we entered the dark operation facility. I was introduced to the Operational Director (OD), Captain Buchanan, the Flight Controller (OpsA), Lt. Horvath, and the Operational Technician (OpsB), Technical Sargent Pete Matthews. Each man explained his task and his responsibility. Then I was led into the radar display rooms where airmen monitored the radarscopes and called in information to the plotting operators who stood behind the large Plexiglas plotting operational area. The Plexiglas plotting surface had a map of the northern coastal Pacific that reached 800 nautical miles out to the west. In other words, incoming aircraft approaching the California coast could be first plotted when they crossed the outer limit of the board and hence the limits of the radar antennae up the coast. Radar sites in British Columbia; Seattle, Washington; Crescent City, California; and Mt. Tamalpais were technically able to locate an incoming oceanic aircraft, friend or foe, that far out. At a normal cruise speed of approximately 500 knots (not a speed that the USSR's bombers could attain), it would offer ADC a little more than an hour to prepare for an interception. This was sufficient time to ward off a Soviet attack.

After visiting the command section, I was led to the Navigation Controller's dais where Staff Sargent Undercoffer worked. He too described his task of checking flight plans, identification maneuvers, and on-time tracking from oceanic flights approaching the northern American and Canadian airspace. All the tasks were familiar to me from my training, but this was the first time I had seen an actual operational contingent at work. I was impressed. Gerry Undercoffer and I became close friends after I returned from my HMB venture. We even developed a small landscaping business to earn some additional income.

It was past noon when Col. Gravette and I entered the fast-food snack line for a quick sandwich and a drink. During the snack, I finally mustered my courage and asked why I was being treated as if I were a visiting congressman on the Armed Forces Appropriation Committee. Col. Gravette looked into my eyes for a long moment. It was a look that gave me chills. Had I overstepped my bounds? I was a lowly enlisted man and he was a full colonel with years of experience and much authority. Then he said with just a wisp of a smile on his face,

"We know that you are officer material, that you graduated with honor from Keesler, and that you are waiting naturalization to enter flight training."

I supposed that I had a puzzled look on my face. "Your file has arrived and Lt. Miller and I have reviewed it. In addition there was a letter of commendation from the Base Commander at Keesler and a letter from Col. Rohrs. Both letters indicate that you are able to perform good investigative research and evaluation."

He paused, then continued, "We have a sticky situation on the peninsula coast, where one of our radar sites is inefficient, thus providing us with a surveillance hole which we have to fill with two additional long-range antennas from here and from Cambria; in some cases we have to readjust Crescent

City's antenna to cover the blank area. This evaluation of HMB will give us proof of two things."

He drank from his coffee cup. I listened. "One, we will evaluate you and your analysis."

Another sip of coffee. "Two, we will find out what can be done with HMB. These sites are expensive and we hate to waste taxpayer's money, and we abhor having holes in our defense coverage."

So I gathered that I was on the spot to produce a reliable evaluation. Were the big brass already considering a specific solution? I did not know but I was sure time would reveal the answer. Would my evaluation have any importance or was it primarily an exercise in futility? Who was I to offer an evaluation?

"Suppose," I said, "I do not measure up to your expectations; what then?"

His smile lit his whole face, "That's our calculated risk." He continued, "You might offer us an alternative solution to this problem."

Then I said in a whisper, "The site at Princeton is almost at sea level and that's not adequate for long-range radar surveillance."

"Yes, we know and I'm glad that you've noticed that problem but what can we do with the site so that it can be useful?" I wasn't given any slack for this task. I was the pawn to be watched by the big players, and I was expendable.

We finished our lunch in silence. As he stood to leave and return to his office, I asked if I could stay until the current shift ended and then return to the base in the crew bus. "Of course," he said and then left me.

I wandered around and inspected various pieces of equipment, talked to maintenance personnel again, chatted with tech-reps from Western Electric Co., a branch of American Telephone and Telegraph (AT&T). Then I entered the OCA and approached the OpsB. I asked him to explain the procedure for checking an in-coming oceanic flight.

"We have one coming in now and he is off-course, he is late, and he seems confused about his identification (ID) maneuver."

The flight was a Northwest Orient (NW) DC-6 coming from Tokyo or so the OpsB presumed.

"Undercoffer," he called on the phone, "what else do you have on this bogey?"

"He is 21 minutes late and 12 degrees off-course, and 250 feet above his assigned altitude. That's NW Flight 203."

"I'm calling for a scramble on 203 because he is beyond the 15 minutes error margin," the OpsB replied. "And 203 has not called in for an ETA change."

Matthews called aloud to the OpsA for a scramble. Lt. Horvath phoned Hamilton AFB's alert hangar for a scramble of two F-89 Scorpions all-weather interceptors.

"Matthews we've got a scramble for 203. Advise for plotting," Horvath called.

"This is where the fun begins," the OpsB smiled. "If 203 is the flight in question, it'll cost the company $7,000 for the scramble."

I moved to the Ops A's position in the hope that I could listen to the conversation with the scrambled lead pilot. Matthews handed me a set of earphones. I listened.

"Nora One, vector 270. Bogey is 92 (nautical) miles."

Mt.Tamalpais's call name was Umbrella. "Umbrella Control, we're 270 degrees and 140 miles at 23 Angels (23,000 feet in altitude)," the scrambled lead pilot stated.

"Affirmative," replied the Ops A.

"Umbrella, bogey is in sight 10 radar miles. Request permission to intercept."

"Granted and give positive ID," replied the FC.

"Umbrella, bogey is a Northwest Orient DC-6: November 124-November Whiskey."

"Roger Nora One, Copy 124 November Whiskey."

Horvath checked with Undercoffer who said, "That's Northwest Orient Flight 203."

Horvath called Nora One, "Begin break off and return to base. Vector 097. What is fuel state?" When the fuel state was given, the scrambled flight was vectored to Hamilton AFB in Novato, California.

"Northwest 203 maneuver recorded," Horvath spoke to the wayward oceanic, "copy arrival late, above assigned altitude, and off-course. If negative vector requested, proceed to San Francisco and contact Approach on 135.6. Good day."

"Negative vector requested Umbrella. Heavy winds out of Alaska. Will make corrections and contact Approach on 135.6. So long!"

Northwest Orient would be billed approximately $7,000 for missing the mark and the captain would be reprimanded unless he had a good reason to justify his deviation.

"Does that give you some idea of the process?" the OpsB asked me.

"Thanks for the show and on demand."

"We aim to please." I went over to the Navigation dais to chat with Undercoffer. "You have a direct line to Flight Service. Does it give you a copy of all oceanic flight plans and how far ahead?" I asked.

"Usually an hour ahead and corrections relayed immediately. They come on the Teletype and I separate the strips and place them on this board."

"What about Northwest, did you get a correction on his ETA?"

"No. We received a call from our radar base in Honolulu warning us that Northwest was late into Honolulu, he was off course, and with a messy maneuver," he replied. "So we expected a problem with him. But it could have been a Soviet aircraft playing tricks and making us think that it was Northwest Orient." He showed me the Teletype set-up, and how he kept track of all the oceanic flight plans as he watched the plotting board.

"Nora One and Two are on the ground," the OpsA called out. The plotters erased the interceptors from the board.

It did not occur to me that one day soon I would be part of the interceptor group and would fly out over the Pacific Ocean to identify an incoming oceanic that was off course and would be controlled by Umbrella, and the call sign assigned to me for the duration of my time in the Air Force would be the marvelous moniker, Sunbonnet.

After poring over every document that was given to me and some additional that I requested, such as operational logs, I decided that it was time for me to head south and tackle the problem without wasting another moment. I was ready to leave for my assignment on the fifth day. The next morning, at the Squadron office, I informed Lt. Miller that I was ready for my assignment. He asked me to wait until Col. Gravette could speak with me. Soon, the Col. called me into his office to give me my final instruction. Lt. Miller followed me and they each wished me a good trip. Lt. Miller handed me a set of Orders, an envelope with $300 in cash, a USAF Credit Card from Texaco, and a set of car keys. Lt. Miller shook my hand and led me to the car. It was a blue Buick, an officer's standard car; enlisted men usually were given a Ford or a Chevrolet.

"That is a Buick," I said.

"Yes, son, take care of it!" and he squeezed my shoulder. I saluted and drove away through the Base gate. The guard almost saluted me.

The drive down the coast to Half Moon Bay by way of Highway 1, over what is known as Devil's Slide, was exhilarating. The Pacific Ocean was blue and calm. In the distance I noticed the peaks of two islands, which later were identified as the Farallon Islands.

Just before HMB, past a small airport, I turned right towards Princeton, the harbor, and on up a small hill to the radar site. Princeton was a fishing town located south of the small airport of HMB, which was sometimes used as an alternate for San Francisco International Airport when the weather in the Bay produced reduced visibility; it is no longer used as an alternate because it cannot accommodate today's larger aircraft. The area reminded me very much of the Italian coast near Genoa.

Soon upon my noon arrival at the radar site in December 1951, I reported to the Commanding Officer, a young First Lieutenant, who thought that I was more of a hindrance and an annoyance than of value. I was given a tiny room in the basement of the antenna building and could feel the vibration of the rotating mechanism, which made rest impossible. As a result of the poor accommodation provided and also because I was authorized to do so, I moved to an apartment in HMB the very next day. There was an apartment in a small house on the same street as the old Methodist church. I was going to be comfortable before I tackled both the assignment and the CO. Now settled in the small apartment, I soon began the work of evaluating the site.

The CO was Lt. Rogers; a man trained as a navigator who was assigned to a non-flying job because he had a health problem, which took him off flying status. HMB was for me still a strange assignment. Anyway, I asked him to give me a thorough tour of the facilities, which he did semi-reluctantly. I was introduced to the maintenance chief, the chief of operations, and the crew chief of the current shift that comprised six men; all working on radar scopes. Information gathered from the radar was immediately telephoned to Umbrella — 666 AC&W's command center. The radar maintenance seemed in good order and Technical Sergeant Bongard, who was maintenance chief, kept good records, which made it easy for me to proceed. The operations crew attended the radar monitors; the farthest distance where anything could be captured with the extended antenna was 18 nautical miles. I asked the operations crew chief if he could ever capture something further out and his reply was negative.

I moved to the height finder and saw that it could capture an inbound oceanic aircraft that was at 28,000 feet but the horizontal antenna had yet to capture the reflection of that aircraft. With the maintenance chief's help we tilted the horizontal antenna to see if we could improve the capturing capability of the inbound aircraft's reflection. I called Umbrella to inquire at what distance the inbound oceanic aircraft was painted (reflected) at 28 angels. The reply was 260 miles.

Over several days with the assistance of both maintenance and operations chiefs we repeated the tests using several inbound aircraft coming towards San Francisco. The results were the same as the first one I witnessed. On the horizontal plane 18 miles was the limit for the antenna. I looked at the antenna and its position relative to the horizontal plane and the horizon. It was obvious that the horizontal radar antenna had the minimum range because it was less than 180 feet above sea level, not a sufficient height to extend its sight beyond the horizon. At that height it barely captured anything further than the 15 nautical miles to the horizon. Could it be raised structurally?

Bongard and I looked at the blueprints to see what could be done to raise the antenna. Lt. Rogers joined us as we reviewed the drawings and discussed various options. Western Electric had connected the entire antenna system and it worked very well as a piece of hardware but the USAF had done the engineering for the location of the site. The site engineering had been accomplished by the Air Force. A local contractor had been engaged to build the facility, boiler-plated from the site in Cambria but without including the specifics of the current terrain. (In later years the Princeton operation when modified became an excellent rocket-tracking station for those launched from Vanderburgh AFB and still later a satellite-tracking site, which it remains).

What if we located an antenna with a reflector atop the costal hills, which offered an elevation between 1,200 to 1,900 feet, a quick gain of 1,000 feet above the current Princeton facility?

Bongard looked at me and smiled. "Why didn't we think of these options?" he asked me.

After discussing the idea with the Western Electric team by telephone I was ready for my report. The conclusion entailed mainly two major issues: 1. Placing a reflector on the coastal hills to extend the distance of the nearly-sea level antenna; 2. Emphasizing the value of the site as a height finder instead of longitudinal distance site. Other suggestions were to be included in the report but these two were the major ones and they would offer the most efficient value for the least cost. Of course in the 1950s the Air Force did not have to obtain authorization from local municipalities to install a reflector on the hill, which anyway was controlled by the US Government.

I had been in HMB for a month now. My notebook was thick and I was ready to write my report and draw my conclusions. Laying all my material out for review, I decided to let it all simmer for a few days as I investigated the coast. The coast was full of open spaces and offered magnificent weather. It was neither hot nor cold. Average temperature for the year was around 55 to 60 degrees Fahrenheit. I should have purchased a piece of property, especially in the village of Montara, but I was unthinking, too young to plan for the future, and poor. Had I not purchased a car, which still was not delivered, I might have been able to swing a deal for property. At any rate, I was on assignment and needed to complete my report. I spent more time asking questions, searching for specific answers, and looking at alternative options for the site.

The effectiveness of the HMB site as an early warning location was marginal but it could be an excellent height calibrator for Pacific oceanic air traffic and could paint incoming lateral flights if the antenna could be placed on the nearby coastal hill to give it at least an additional 1,000 or more feet of elevation. This was the conclusion that kept surfacing. My report was finished two months to the day after my arrival, and indicated that as an early warning site, HMB radar did not produce the needed range unless the added height was incorporated; but as a height calibrator, the site could be a complementary instrument to the 666th, if height equipment could be connected specifically to a dish-tracking antenna. I discussed the report with Lt. Rogers and discovered that he accepted it readily. After saying goodbye to the people at the site, I packed my bag and returned to Mt. Tamalpais.

Back atop Mt. Tamalpais, I officially submitted my report to Col. Gravette. I was assigned to the operating crew called B-666 and started working as a radar operator; this assignment would give me hands-on experience tracking aircraft by radar.

About a month later I was made assistant to the OpsB and worked in that position for a few weeks until I was moved directly to become the OpsB for B-666 crew and assistant Operation Controller on another crew. My grade was raised to airman first class and I was allowed to exert control over many of the flight interceptions. I enjoyed this assignment because it gave me direct access to, and experience with, pilots of interceptors. I remained in that position and was authorized to control most interceptions on my shift until December 1953. I got to know many of the line pilots who flew interceptions from Hamilton AFB, and on several occasions I was allowed to ride in the Radar Officer's (RO) seat behind the pilot on training flights. I flew in F-94s and F-89s, the operative aircraft of the Interceptor Squadron based at Hamilton AFB in Novato, California.

Assignments on Mt. Tamalpais were routine and 8-hour shifts were part of the 24-hour schedule. With two days off between shifts there was plenty of opportunity for exploring the San Francisco Bay area. Soon with the help of Lt. Horvath's brother-in-law, who was a Ford dealer in Oakland, I was able to obtain my long-awaited new car with air conditioning. The car was a 1952 grey sedan with the new six-cylinder in-line overhead valve engine. Ford had been making V-8s and V-6s for a long time, but these were knuckle-breakers when it came to tuning the ignition system. The six with overhead valves was a much easier engine to tune and maintain; it was not as robust or fast as a V-8 but it suited me well. The reason for the delivery delay of my car was because of the unexpected high demand; Ford was behind in its production schedule. I drove it across the USA four times, and when I went to Alaska, after putting it in storage for a few months, I returned to drive it across the Alcan Highway in January 1953 to Fairbanks and then to Anchorage. Before selling it in 1960, I had put 220,000 miles on the same engine. It was a good car that served me well, and I was pleased to have ordered it with air conditioning.

While on Mt. Tamalpais, I was able to save quite a bit of money because my expenses were almost insignificant. The location atop the mountain was ideal for reading, nature exploration, and model making. I made several balsa wood models and gave them to schools, either on the AFB or to the Mill Valley intermediate school. I went often to Muir Woods or Stinson Beach located at the foot of the mountain. The assignment atop Mt. Tamalpais was a bit of a vacation. I enjoyed the work, the attitude of the Air Force personnel, the living conditions, and the location that gave me an unobstructed view of much of the San Francisco Bay area.

The Air Force had the aura of the military but without the rough edges of militarism. It was a technical command, and ADC was the most technical of all the commands. Each one of us was treated well, respected as a knowledgeable individual, and encouraged to expand our knowledge through correspondence courses. A good on-site library was available all the time, a well equipped work-hobby shop was furnished, and easy access to all superiors was possible. We worked our rotating shifts, but were permitted to take on other interests on our off days.

A colleague from San Angelo, TX who worked in the adjutant's office and who was a graduate of Princeton University befriended me. Lynn Steward was awaiting his orders for Officer Candidate School (OCS). We became good friends and enjoyed many laughs, good dinners, and also exchanged many books. We both were avid readers and the small Base library was unable to keep up with our demands. We managed to help the Base library develop an agreement with the Marin County Library to borrow books.

Lynn was an Episcopalian and attended the local Episcopal Parish in Mill Valley regularly. One Saturday when my schedule permitted me a full weekend off, Lynn asked me go to church with him.

"There's a fine Episcopal Parish in Mill Valley that you might find interesting," he stated.

"What is 'Episcopal'?" I asked.

"If you are Anglican in England, then you are Episcopalian in America," he informed me. "In the USA, the Anglican Church is called the Episcopal Church and it is in communion with the See of Canterbury and its Archbishop."

That was news to me, especially since I had not darkened the portals of a church since leaving Ely. I accepted the invitation and at eleven o'clock the next day in November 1952 I found myself seated in a pew in the Church of Our Savior, on Old Mill Street, Mill Valley. The sermon that Sunday was on Christ the King and was given by the rector David Murray Hammond, a delightful man that I see at times when we meet at the annual Grace Cathedral Nave Chaplain's Tea. I told Murray in a recent meeting during the annual tea that I still remember his sermon and his warm reception when I attended Our Savior. While in Mill Valley I attended as often as I could not only the Sunday Eucharist but also several of the programs offered during the week.

Lynn encouraged me to attend a reception at the French Consulate sponsored by the Alliance Française. After much convincing by Lynn, I accepted, but reluctantly because I knew no one in the French community. I went and had a wonderful time.

The Consul General was Pierre Romain who was born in Laos, French Indochina. For some reason, Mr. Romain took a liking to me, and I to him, and he invited me for dinner into his home the next Sunday. The dinner in the Consul's house was simple but delightful. I was introduced to Madame Colette Romain, a strikingly beautiful and tall Eurasian woman who was fluent in French, English, and Mandarin Chinese. I also met the daughter,

Nicole, also showing strong Eurasian features and jet-black hair. Nicole and I became quite good friends and dated a lot. In fact, I believe that I was in love with her and suspected that she was with me, although neither one of us admitted it to the other.

It was obvious that I was quite welcome in the Romains' house and could count on at least one or two dinners a month as their guest. Nicole and I explored the San Francisco Bay area extensively. When we had Thanksgiving dinner at the radar site and I could invite a guest, I brought Nicole with me; she was quite a hit and I was proud to have such a beautiful girl with me. For the Christmas dinner in 1953, after I was made an American citizen and was also commissioned an officer (this was to be my last Christmas on Mt. Tamalpais) I invited the Consul, his wife, and Nicole for the event.

It was a splendid evening with several enlisted men and officers invited to the Romains' residence after dinner for refreshments and French dessert. Toasts were given to France, America, Indochina, and for the guests who were present, especially the few men who were scheduled to leave for Korea. After that party, I said goodbye to the Romain family and especially to Nicole. I was slated to leave for flight proficiency training two days hence and would probably not return in the immediate future to the San Francisco Bay area, at least that was my expectation, which was wrong. Nevertheless, much as I did return to San Francisco and particularly to Hamilton AFB, I never saw the Romain family again because the Consul was reassigned to Australia, and Nicole was enrolled, I believe, in a university in France. Correspondence never did materialize much because I was very busy learning to be an officer and absorbing new techniques of flight. Without the modern conveniences of the Internet, communication was difficult in the 1950s.

While all that was mentioned above was happening, Gerry Undercoffer, the Navigation Controller, had developed a part-time job with Mr. R.V. Smith, in Mill Valley. Smith was a major building contractor in San Francisco who had had a hand in several of the city's administrative buildings. Gerry asked me if I was interested in a part-time job because there was an opening for a general handyman on Smith's home property, which covered several acres. I accepted because I wanted to learn about contracting and also wanted to make a little money before officer's status. I did both and loved it. Gerry and I worked well and complemented each other so flawlessly that Mr. Smith let us do what was necessary without much supervision except when special projects developed. Mr. Smith's property included a large house, several stables for pure Arabian horses and a mean Shetland; cleaning the stables was my weekly responsibility. Gerry was responsible for tending the flowerbeds, the trees, and any gardening chores required.

One day Mr. Smith wanted to know if we were interested in building a swimming pool for his house. He had made the drawings and would bring in a hoe and a truck from his contracting yard. All the necessary material would be supplied but we had to place orders a few days earlier for on-time deliveries to be made. Neither Gerry nor I had ever built a swimming pool but we assumed that Mr. Smith had the know-how to guide us through the project. He did and became for us a superb instructor; we learned a great deal about pouring concrete, placing pipes for natural gas and testing the pressure tolerances, connecting electricity for the pumps and filters, and we finished the pool in two months without problems.

It was a kidney shaped pool with a depth of eight feet on the larger end and three feet on the narrow end. It was faced with white ceramic tiles. The heating and pumping system was installed by another contractor but we built in the plumbing and the electrical conduits for the wiring to be added. On the 4th of July 1952 (the first anniversary of my enlistment in the USAF) I took my first swim when the Smiths had an inaugural party. In addition to the pool, I learned to tend and ride horses, build a stable, do rough gardening, construct stonewalls, and shovel horse manure.

In August 1952, after a short visit to Keesler AFB for special instructions on airborne radar, I had to return for a couple of weeks to HMB for an evaluation of the new height tracking capability of the radar site and the offset antenna on the coastal hill. Biloxi's weather was humid and hot with temperatures in the 100s and humidity in the high 90s. Biloxi was miserably uncomfortable, especially since this was before air conditioning units were installed in buildings. Arriving in HMB was a shock for me after Biloxi. It was that summer that convinced me that the coastal region near Half Moon

Bay would be the place for me to settle and establish my future home. Why this place? I'll tell you:

It was cool (64 degrees Fahrenheit for August and at noon). The Pacific coast, beautiful, slightly windy, enveloped in cool and refreshing fog, was near the city of San Francisco, and without having to cross the Bay over bridges and the traffic that accompanies the travel. The San Mateo County coast was even cooler than Mt. Tamalpais, Mill Valley, or Marin County. I was, however, still too poor to purchase land. It took me 21 years before I could afford to establish my home on the coast by buying a house in Montara (just north of HMB and even foggier). Yet I was able to put down $5,000 for five acres of coastal land in Stinson Beach as an investment that did me well several years later.

Let me inform the readers that my evaluation of the radar site received commendable recognition and the suggestions made in the report were followed almost to the letter.

Sojourn into Fancy Land

My schedule at the radar site had been exhausting; in fact most of the end of 1952 and the first part of 1953 had been work, work, and more work. At the end of one of my shifts I was handed a six-day pass for R&R. A crew friend suggested I grab a hop to Los Angeles; he too had a pass, but his was good only for three days. Jack Barbour was an awfully nice person and the idea of going with him to LA was fun and exciting, especially since I had not been there.

We managed a hop to March AFB in a C-47 and upon arrival we were offered a ride into Santa Monica. I'd heard of Santa Monica and remembered thinking that someday I would see that city by the Pacific Ocean. Soon we were in Santa Monica as registered guests at the Sea Breeze Hotel with a room overlooking the ocean. It was an expensive room but this was my first time in Southern California, paradise country.

After we settled in and had taken a walk along the cliff overlooking the beach, Jack asked me if I wanted to have dinner and listen to a nightclub singer.

"Peggy Lee is singing at the Sun and Sand," he said. "For the price of dinner we can spend the evening listening to her," he added.

"I like her music," I replied.

"Well, I'll introduce you to her. She's my sister-in-law."

"What?" I asked with a clear note of incredulity.

"She really is my sister-in-law," he asserted. I stared at him skeptically.

"She is married to my older brother Dave, a guitarist. He drinks a bit too much and so they are separated for the moment — until he gets sober for good."

We went for dinner at the Sun and Sand. Jack went to the Maître d' and said something that I could not hear. Soon a gentleman came over to us and escorted us to a ringside table in front of the microphone.

"I informed the manager that I was Peggy's brother-law," Jack let me know. A few minutes later the waiter came over and said that dinner was on the house, compliments of the manager. A bottle of wine soon was brought to the table but I declined because I was not of age. Jack, however, was older and of age.

I had always enjoyed Peggy Lee's music. I especially liked her way with the phrasing of lyrics and her rhythm. So I was game for the adventure of the evening. Once settled at the table and after ordering a ginger ale for me, Jack left me and went through a door and out of sight. About fifteen minutes later he returned, sat down, sipped his wine, and then announced that Peggy Lee would join us after her performance that ended at midnight.

At exactly ten o'clock, and right after we finished our splendid dinner, Miss Peggy Lee arrived on stage and began with "It's a Good Day!" She was beautiful. The way she twisted her body and puckered her mouth as she molded each word and note was quite exciting. Her voice and manner of casting her songs was exactly as I had heard her on the radio. She was magnificent. She was a fine musician, a musical instrument in person. She finished her performance with "Lover." The nightclub burst into applause. I was delirious from the pleasure she had given me with her music.

After the applause had terminated she came over to our table. Jack introduced her to me as "Peggy, my lovely sister-in-law," and he kissed her on the cheek. We chatted for a few moments, and then she asked if we wanted to come to her house for a drink and a midnight snack. Jack and I accepted readily. Her car was parked in the lower garage and she would meet us there in half-an-hour.

At her house in Bel Air, Peggy offered me a pure malt scotch whisky and a tray of sandwiches that she fetched from the kitchen. Jack carried a soupière of hot potato-leek soup and three bowls with spoons.

"After a show I'm starved because I cannot eat anything before a performance," Peggy informs us.

"It is just the right supper to greet the early morning and friends," I replied.

When the food was consumed, Miss Lee asked where we were staying. We informed her that we had a room at the Sea Breeze Hotel. Miss Lee insisted that we move immediately to her house because she had two guest rooms.

"I am not working for the next few days, and would be happy to show you some of the important places in LA."

We accepted the offer happily and off we went to the hotel, checked out, paid the bill after insisting that Peggy Lee could not pay for our hotel, and moved to her home in Bel Air. The next day, or rather later that morning, Peggy Lee took us to several places in LA, including the MGM and Disney studio complexes. Miss Lee insisted that I drop the formality and call her by her first name. I did, but with a tinge of shyness at first. We had lunch in Manhattan Beach at a restaurant that overlooked the ocean. After more sightseeing we returned to her house for a real "Swedish dinner" prepared by Peggy.

It was at dinner that I learned that she was born in North Dakota of Swedish parents. Her off-stage name was Norma Egstrom and she invited me to call her by her real name. Her mother had died when she was a little girl and when her father remarried Norma was mistreated by her stepmother. After singing locally when she was fifteen or so for civic gatherings, churches, and the local radio station in Valley City, the radio host Ken Sydness (known as Kennedy), changed her name to Peggy Lee to make it more agreeable to radio listeners. She took music seriously and found a teacher who coached her to develop her voice, helped her become more proficient with music notations, and taught her music composition. Upon graduating from high school she left first for Minneapolis and then for Chicago where Benny Goodman, who discovered her, engaged her to become his lead singer. Goodman also sent her to the Chicago Academy of Music for some serious music education. After attending for two years and working with Benny Goodman, Peggy graduated with honors from the Academy where she had specialized in voice and composition.

The next day Jack had to catch his hop back to Hamilton AFB but I still had three more days of R&R. Peggy and I drove him to March AFB and we arrived just in time to catch a mail flight north. I signed up for a possible space for three days hence and left with Peggy Lee to return to LA. We returned by way of Pasadena, where we had dinner in a small Greek restaurant before heading west to Bel Air. At her house, Peggy dished out ice cream and Courvoisier for us to enjoy in her music studio. Soon she sat at the piano and began to sing several songs, but this time there was no microphone to dilute her wonderful voice. I was thrilled to have this personal concert.

I must admit that Peggy Lee was a fantastically beautiful woman, and I was fortunate to be in her presence. I was treated to "As Time Goes By," laced with a personal expression of "I am in Love," and "I am a Woman," with a special rendition of "Lover," and "Fly Me to the Moon," and many more as I sat sipping cognac in my own auditioning studio with a wonderful and lovely performing artist singing exclusively for me. Never could I forget this day and evening and this special gift, a gift that I would cherish for many years.

My last day was spent mostly relaxing, seeing new things in the LA Basin, and learning from Peggy that her marriage was falling apart because her husband was an alcoholic who would do nothing about his illness. He had tried to get dry several times but each time it failed. She still loved him and respected his musical talents. They had collaborated on several new musical pieces but the relationship could not continue for long. He was too attached to the bottle and nothing would pry him away from drink, which ruined his great gift of music. The chasm between them had broadened. It was sad. I respected her trust and was a bit awed that I could be trusted with her painful story.

When I left on the sixth day we promised to correspond and we did for a while, but such as life is, the correspondence dried up and I saw her no more until after I was married and was vacationing in Las Vegas. She was the featured singer at the Thunderbird Casino. I went backstage to say hello and she recognized me and hugged me tightly. Too many people were around for any solid conversation to develop. She was divorced and was seeing someone else. We said goodbye and she dedicated a song to me when the show was in full swing. I never spoke with her again.

In the late 80s she was the featured singer at the Fairmont Hotel in San Francisco but I did not go backstage to see her. She still had a magnetic and lovely voice but she was unable to stand as a result of a fall. I wanted so much to speak with Peggy but I knew that time had passed us by and both of us were currently on different planes of this universe. History can be remembered but never repeated. I walked out of the Fairmont Hotel with a heavy heart. Miss Norma Egstrom, aka Peggy Lee, crossed into the larger life in 2001. Recently I purchased a CD that contained many of the songs that I had heard in her house.

A New Juncture Surfaces

On the Friday after Thanksgiving 1953 the First Sergeant handed me a registered letter. I opened it and read the letter. The surprise was obviously visible on my face because the First Sergeant was concerned that it might be bad news. But the letter was from the Department of State, United States of America, and the contents informed me that on 4 December 1953 I was to present myself before a particular judge of the Federal Court of San Francisco to be "naturalized" (I love that word) as an American citizen. After shaking hands with the Sergeant I asked if I could see both the CO and Adjutant. Immediately I was ushered into Lt. Miller's office to share the news. He was delighted and offered to stand with me as a witness. Then Miller ushered me into Col. Gravette's office to share the news. Gravette also volunteered to stand as witness by my side. Lt. Miller, who knew that my good friend Gerry Undercoffer would be interested, too, asked one of the clerks to fetch him. When Gerry arrived and was informed he instantly asked if he could stand as a witness. Now I had my "staff" which was made up of a field rank officer, a lower rank officer, and an enlisted rank airman.

On the appointed day I was taken to the Federal Court in a staff car wearing full dress uniform, as were the others. The First Sergeant volunteered to drive the car. With the entire command team away who would be in-charge of the site?

"I've asked the Supply Officer to act as the temporary CO, and I've cabled the Russians to behave today," Col. Gravette announced when in the car.

In the Chambers of the Judge, I was examined, given a lesson in history, asked repeatedly if this was what I wanted to do, and then asked to relinquish my passport. I pulled out my three passports, the British, the Italian, and the French and held them out to the Judge, as one does when holding playing cards. The judge took the middle passport, the Italian one, and gave it to the clerk sitting next to his desk. Called to stand up, the judge asked me to raise my right hand and to repeat after him the Oath of Allegiance.

"Airman Raymond Hoche-Mong, on this day you are to be recognized as a citizen of the United States of America. Welcome to our nation. I hope, and I am certain, that you will be a good citizen, a voting citizen who will always practice compassion, good judgment, and tolerance." The judge reached over and took my hand in both of his.

"I am sure that we will run into each other again, and very soon," the judge added with emphasis and a smile on his face.

"In a moment you'll be given your official papers," he added. A few minutes later a large envelope was handed to me and inside was my Citizenship Certificate. I was now an American citizen, and the ceremony took place in the US Federal Court, located on Sansome Street in San Francisco. I thanked the judge for his good wishes and he said, "Let me give you a little advice: Americans always complain and that's the way it should be. So complain when something is amiss!"

After the ceremony, I was taken to the Allouette French restaurant and treated to a delicious lunch that began with escargots Provençal and ended with a Napoleon and coffee. During the lunch I took a moment to look at my naturalization certificate. It had my picture, the seal of the nation, and a statement that I had been an Italian citizen. Neither the British nor the French citizenships were mentioned and that was fine with me; at any rate, I considered myself a citizen of the world who had now a focused allegiance to the United States of America.

Returning to the radar site, the administrative clerk handed me another registered letter, but this one was from the Department of Defense. It was a large tan envelope that held unfolded pages. Written on the first line was a sentence that began with "By order of the President of the United States of America and in accordance with Article...of the Military Code of Justice, and the authorization of the Congress, you are instructed to..." and it ordered me to present myself to the chambers of Judge...(the same judge, who was also a reserve general in the USAF) on 5 December 1953 to be commissioned a Second Lieutenant in the USAF.

"Raymond, congratulations," and Lt. Miller gave me his 2nd Lieutenant gold bars to wear. Miller and Gravette had been informed the previous day. The same crew escorted me to the Judge's chambers. Because I was overwhelmed by the occasion I cannot recall the words used for the commissioning act. All I recall was that the general, the judge, pinned the gold bars on my uniform and Lt. Miller replaced the enlisted badge on my cap with the Eagle emblem. Gerry Undercoffer turned to me and snapped a most ceremonious salute, to which I responded immediately. In two days I had jumped two major hurdles, hurdles that had seemed so far away as to never be overcome. It was comforting to me to be surrounded by a warm and friendly team of genuine friends.

This time, however, I was not taken to a fancy civilian restaurant but to the field rank section of the Officers Club at Hamilton AFB to be treated again to a wonderful lunch and my first Tanqueray gin martini. Because I was now 21 years old and an officer I was considered an adult. Upon returning to the squadron I was saluted at every opportunity by many of the enlisted personnel, my friends and fellow crewmembers. I was a bit confused and often I saluted before being saluted or worse I forgot to respond. No harm was done, especially when the enlisted person reminded me in words to return the salute. When I went to the radar site at the insistence of the CO, as I entered the darkness past the transition passage all the lights were on and the entire crew stood to salute me and cheered. Both OpsA and OpsB greeted me but Matthews saluted me. After that greeting, the lights were doused and darkness returned. Work and duty could not be interrupted for too long.

I had to move from my room to new quarters in the Bachelor Officers Quarters (BOQ). Several of my floor mates in the enlisted barracks helped me move to the point where I did practically nothing but supervise the process. When I went that evening to rejoin my crew on the 3 to 11 shift, there was again a loud "hooray" for the embryonic officer. After saying goodbye to all my friends, I briefed my replacement in the OpsB position. I took a position on Gerry's dais and out of the operations traffic.

When settled on the dais I picked up the phone and called Col. Rohrs and informed him of the several changes in my status. I was surprised to learn that he was aware of the changes and that he had been in communication with Col. Gravette who had assured him that once calm, I would contact him. We had an extensive conversation and he admitted that he had, and would continue to, monitor my progress in the Air Force. Col Rohrs has been given a new command of a combat flight squadron stationed in Korea and he would be leaving the Pentagon in a few days.

An Embryonic Office in the USAF

My time on Mt. Tamalpais was to be short because I was to leave for Texas as soon as the appropriate orders were cut and given to me. For the next few days, I was out of work and with no specific assignment. I joined my crew as often as I could and sat with Gerry, although I had completed my packing except for a few things that would take a minute or two to add to my bag. I was keeping my laundry to a minimum. On 8 December I was forewarned that my orders would be arriving soon and to be ready for departure. I rejoined my crew and said goodbye to each member. This was my last shift with the 666 AC&W Squadron.

The next morning, 9 December 1953, I was given a set of orders that had arrived by Teletype during the night. I was to depart on 10 December for James T. Connally AFB, Waco, Texas for flight training briefing, review, and retraining. I had to finish packing my belongings, store my car at Hamilton AFB, obtain a complete flight physical, and acquire my pay records. When all this was done Col. Gravette came to see me at the BOQ and we went to the mess hall for lunch and a chat. He handed me a copy of a letter of appreciation he had included in my records and a photograph of my whole crew in front of the C-47 that had taken us to Las Vegas when we won a contest for proficiency and efficiency.

A seat on a courier flight was reserved for me leaving Hamilton AFB for Waco in two days. At Waco, I soon discovered that Texas was not California, not by a long shot. For breakfast at the BOQ refectory, I was given an enormous broiled steak with three eggs, country fried potatoes, baked beans, black coffee, and a glass of canned orange juice. Later I learned that the beans were refried and not baked. Refried beans? Strange dish but it had a passable taste, although a bit on the greasy side. This was a cowboy's breakfast, not a flyer's. The breakfast alone would put me above the weight envelope limit and ground me. Maybe, I thought, this would be my last meal before auguring into the Texas ground on my first flight: "And he died with a full stomach."

My training and check flights were done in accordance with the regulations that covered pilots transferring from other branches of the military. Aside from receiving a lecture every evening on how an officer is to "behave, act, and represent the service," the indoctrination into commissioned rank was painless, if not pointless for a prep-schooler. Stories told to me of cadet training and the idiocies that accompanied that training were fortunately by-passed, and not through my doing, just my good fortune because I was already an officer.

Pappy's meticulous flight training at Waterbeach served me well because I was knowledgeable about the fundamentals of flying. I could recite at the drop of a hat the physics that controlled flight, and because I had experienced flight in rudimentary flying machines, airplanes that had neither brakes nor flaps, I was not ham fisted with the controls.

My daily routine was quite predictable; it was reading, absorbing data, testing, and flight training in aircraft that had been part of my dreams for many years. I had not been acting as pilot for at least three years although I had maintained my physical checks. Expecting to be one rusty pilot, it was surprising that once with a control stick in hand I was quickly back in the mode. As a starting point, I was given the necessary technical training for the F-51 Mustang reciprocal fighter, the hot fighter of WWII. The aircraft in which I was to receive my instruction was manufactured by North American and had been fitted with an instructor's rear seat and controls. When I first set eyes on the F-51 I was awed at the size of its engine, its looks, and the roar of its monstrous engine. Yes, I was frightened a bit — no, a lot! The Mustang was bigger than anything I had operated. Just the instrument panel on the 51 was intimidating to me, especially when I noticed the limit of its airspeed indicator. My mechanic crew chief reminded me to watch for the P-factor, the gyroscopic pull to the left, which needed to be compensated for with full rudder on the opposite side. The chief knew that I had flown British aircraft that have their propeller rotating in the opposite direction.

I spent several hours flying with a wonderful, patient, and demanding in-structor. Then came my time in solo flight, and that in itself was challenging and ultimately helped me build my confidence. Given the operating numbers of a particular flying machine and a little forethought, I was fairly certain that I could manage a safe flight. Aerobatic maneuvers were more demanding for reciprocal engines, but that soon proved doable once fright could be set aside or used as a safety mechanism. My transition logbook was signed and I was assigned to the next aircraft.

Then came the training on aircraft powered by turbine engine, called jets. The F-80 Shooting Star and the F-94 were the first turbine aircraft for my training upgrading. Indeed, there were a lot of airplanes interspersed in these two models to learn to fly in a short time. It was hard, precise work, and monitored at every step. Starting a jet had to be handled quite differently than a reciprocal type. Management of the ratio between fuel and air required some learning. I managed to do well, but I also produced some classic and embarrassing flubs, though nothing considered by my instructors dangerous enough to eliminate me (wash me out) from the program.

My initial training lasted 30 days at Waco; after that I was flown to Bergstrom AFB in Austin to get checked out in the twin turbine F-89D by Northrop, the famous and beautifully designed Scorpion all-weather interceptor. This was the aircraft used at Hamilton for interceptions of oceanic flights.

By mid-March 1954 I was officially rated for these four aircraft types (F-51, F-80, F-94, and F-89). Indeed I was rated for these aircraft types but I was far from being a smooth and confident pilot; in fact I've never been a totally confident pilot. On a clear morning I was called to the flight operations briefing room where several senior members of Training Command were present, including the Chief Pilot for flight instruction. A short ceremony followed and the Chief Pilot pinned shiny silver wings on my uniform and handed me the official certificate stating that I had completed all the requirements to be an aircraft pilot in the USAF. I had reached the point in my dreams where I was finally recognized as an aircraft driver of new and different types.

I was exhausted from the accelerated and intense training, and it was obvious to my supervisors. Issued a three-day pass, I took time to see a movie, enjoy a good meal with wine, read two novels, and catch up on sleep. After returning from my rest, I was handed a new set of orders to head to Mather AFB, Rancho Cordova, CA for 10 days of navigation training and then head for Ontario International Airport, California for training on the four-engine reciprocal Lockheed Super Constellation, the RC-121. The Super was an aircraft about which I knew nothing. I had ridden as a passenger on one that was operated by the Trans World Airline but that was the sum total of my knowledge of this Lockheed beauty.

Life with Four

The day arrived when I stood on the tarmac and had a close look at the Lockheed aircraft. The Super Connie, as it was affectionately called, was a magnificently designed aircraft, with lines that set it apart from any other passenger airplane. Triple rudders immediately identified this aircraft as different from any other. Created for Trans World Airline under the direction of Howard Hughes, the Connie held the speed record for the fastest passenger aircraft until the DC-7 by Douglas and the Boeing 707 came on the flying scene. For the time being, the Connie ruled the skies without challenge.

The Super Connie had three tails because Hughes didn't have a hanger big enough to handle the tall single rudder that it needed in the initial design; hence Lockheed redesigned it with three tails! This addition not only singled it out among all other aircraft, but gave it a certain aesthetic pizzazz.

At this stage of the training, I was not quite certain what direction the USAF was taking me. After the intense training I underwent on interceptors, why was I assigned to a four-engine airplane that was used mainly for long distance passenger service? The answer was soon to be revealed, and it was a pleasant surprise and assignment.

In Ontario I was immediately slotted with a team of three pilots who had extensive experience with multi-engine aircraft. I didn't have any such experience except for the twin F-89. I soon learned that my training would consist again of intense technical book learning and a great many hours of on-the-job training in the aircraft. Two weeks after my arrival at Ontario, I was qualified to shoot instrument approaches to minimum requirements at Ontario, Los Angeles International, Long Beach, and El Toro Marine base. The RC-121 was as much a joy to fly as it was beautiful.

The RC-121 to which I was assigned was reconfigured and modified for early warning reconnaissance, air traffic control applications, and the Loran (Long Distance Radar Navigation) oceanic system. With new and more powerful engines, jet assist pods for rapid takeoffs and accelerations, and long-range fuel tanks, the Super Connie became a hot aircraft — the hotrod of the big birds. Such modifications made the Super Connie the precursor of the modern aircraft warning advance command (AEW & C). In the 1980s, with the introduction of jet-type aircraft, the service became known as the airborne warning and control system (AWCS), also known in common language as the flying command post.

The Super Connie had been given an enlarged cockpit compared to the older regular Connies that were first used for line service with TWA. It had also been given comfortable seats, not only for the pilot and two copilots, but also for the relief pilot-flight engineer (4th Officer), and the navigator/radio operator. The RC-121 was configured for long flights and four men in the cockpit still left ample room for a cubicle with two bunk beds. The Connie had a galley for hot meals, a flight steward compartment, a crew chief/maintenance compartment, five radar screens for five operators plus a spare for monitoring, and OpsB/Controller dais for two officer controllers, and several bunks and toilet facilities in the tail section for off duty rest periods. The crew chief was also the maintenance specialist and flight steward, and radar operators were enlisted men with extensive flight training.

The controllers, the senior 2nd, and 4th pilots had all been trained in global navigation at Mather AFB, Rancho Cordova, CA. My training was in combat operations strategy and radar technology, apart from being a pilot. The pilots had sterling records with the USAF and had logged several thousand hours of flying experience in many types of aircraft. My experience was embarrassingly limited, but each pilot took the time to show me the ropes and literally nursed me into becoming a better pilot.

Brigadier General Howe (Lefty) Parker was the flight commander, and a fine commander he was. A short wiry man, with more than 20,000 hours of active flying in 27 types, he was a superb pilot, a magnificent commander, a patient teacher, and the possessor of a finely tuned sense of humor. Work was tantamount to play for Lefty. That he needed a seat pillow when in the left slot of the RC-121 did not in the least inhibit his capabilities as the senior pilot of this crew.

The flight engineer who was also the 4th Pilot was a whiz with the four engines. He could make those big radial engines hum a fine tune at his command. Coaxing every bit of energy from each radial, the flight engineer would give us the necessary speed or climb whenever we called for it. When turbine assistance was required, the flight engineer turned the Super Connie into an interceptor aircraft but with much longer endurance, which on many occasions embarrassed actual interceptors.

On my first night with my new colleagues, General Parker took us all for dinner to a restaurant in Cucamonga, a town adjacent to Ontario. Over dinner and a bottle of wine I was formally introduced to the flying crew and for the first time I began to see why I had been chosen out of a long list of potential candidates. The HMB evaluation had paid off and identified me as one who is not afraid to tackle a major, but not unsolvable, problem. The fact that I had progressed without too many hitches through the flight training also counted in my favor. Lastly, that I knew something about combat operations strategies, radar, and controlling aircraft flights gave momentum to my being selected.

"I was also curious as to why you had selected the USAF, when you could have stayed in Britain, and would have avoided the many obstacles that you so ably surmounted," the general told me.

Introductions followed after he explained to the attending officers much of what he had learned about me. I was a bit uncomfortable during his prologue, but soon discovered that he had me pegged correctly; he even knew about my relationship with Col. Rohrs, who was no longer in Washington D.C. but commanding a fighter squadron in Korea. The second officer, a major, was Edward Spain from Vermont. The fourth officer, also a major, was James Corona, a graduate from the California Institute of Technology. General Parker was a career pilot who had seen combat in Europe and Southeast Asia and was a graduate of the Naval Academy with a degree in aeronautical engineering. In comparison to the crew's pedigree and as 3rd copilot, I thought of myself as the uneducated flunky who had been lucky. With the first glass of wine poured, General Howe Parker told me, specially, that I was to call him Lefty unless we were in the presence of senior officers not affiliated with our mission.

"The name is Lefty," he instructed me.

For my benefit, Lefty informed me that the RC-121 was the first of its kind and was designed as an airborne early warning and Control (AEW & C) platform to work in conjunction with the partially completed Distant Early Warning (DEW) line erected around the perimeter of the North American Continent. We were given a 12-month assignment to cover the northern polar region, the Pacific Ocean, the North Atlantic Ocean, and parts of Southeast Asia, with additional assignments and time to be added as required. We were all to log "pilot in command" time, even when we were not actively in control of the aircraft. In other words, and Lefty stressed that point, we were on flying duty all the time while in the air. He expected me to spend as many hours as possible actually flying the RC-121 until I reached a level of competency that would recommend me for approval as Senior pilot, as were all the other pilots, except for Lefty who sported Command Pilot wings.

My training began with Lockheed engineers who showed me every portion of the Connie's structure. The technical training included seven manuals that I needed to absorb or be proficient in locating the information I would need when flying. How to switch from one fuel transfer pump to another? How to resolve a power spike and which buzz system to energize to redirect the electrical power flow? How to operate the wing bleeding system or activate the heat on the outer edges to remove ice accumulation? There were thousands of questions and twice that many answers to be found in the manuals quickly in a black-out or when weather turbulence made everything in the aircraft dance around.

After the technical training came the hands-on flying of this aircraft, enormous when compared to the Tiger Moth or the F-89. To make the Connie behave in a taxi mode was work because the high nose wheel configuration urged it to turn too sharply or made me induce it to angle itself to the point where it forced the wheels to slip sideways, and produce a torn tire or a tire pried off the wheel rim. Gentle operation of the tiller was imperative and braking was to be activated lightly and in short bursts of pressure.

Rolling down the runway to attain takeoff speed required a light touch on the rudders when they were activated. Once the nose gear floated off the ground, steering control was essentially done with the rudder until it lifted off the hard surface. In flight, the Connie was a piece of cake. It had sports-car lightness in its controls. The 121 was a very responsive aircraft that could be over-controlled and quickly put into a disastrous attitude with a steep bank angle. Otherwise, the Connie was fun. It could climb rapidly when its four engines produced the required power to make the massive propellers bite into the air. Set at a 14-degree angle of climb, the Connie could almost embarrass a fighter but when the pod turbines were ignited, the embarrassment was definitely made obvious. Moreover, it could continue in that configuration for twice as long as a fighter because it carried much more fuel than the jets, and the radials consumed much less fuel. On several occasions we proved that quality both in time of training and also in actual conflict situations.

After much concentration and coaxing by Lockheed's test pilots and Lefty's patient approach, I was able to maneuver the Connie with a light touch, and perform landings that even surprised me. It took me a few days to learn to fly the aircraft from either left or right seat because I had not attended instructor school; all my flying had been done from the left seat. I was a little ham-handed with my right hand, but Lefty quickly taught me to lighten my hold on the yoke. At the beginning of my tour with the crew, Lefty made me fly from the right seat more often than from the left. Soon I was able to slip into either seat and operate the Connie deftly with either hand. When I proved that I could handle the big Connie smoothly and proficiently, I received an endorsement in my logbook from Lockheed's Chief Pilot, and the information was also entered into my personnel file. By a few weeks short of my 22nd birthday I was qualified and rated as copilot of the RC-121 Super Constellation. A few weeks later I was given my upgrade to Pilot in Command.

After Ontario Airport and when our general training and familiarization were completed, we made an overnight stop at Moffat NAS, near San Jose, to show off the aircraft to the Navy and to install some added rescue equipment for ocean flying. We then flew to Hamilton AFB, our home base, to show off the aircraft to both military and base resident civilians. Once the dog and pony shows were over and after we had an overnight rest, we flew first to Fairbanks and then to our "temporary" home base, which was Elmendorf AFB, Anchorage, Alaska.

It was the end of March 1954 and Fairbanks, just 130 miles below the Arctic Circle, was still enveloped in winter, a late winter I was informed. As I stepped out of the aircraft into the cold icy wind of the northern latitude, I fainted and collapsed to the floor of the step-platform. The cold wind and the increased density of the air shocked my system. I awoke in the hospital with a splitting headache and a bruised hip. Lefty was at my bedside when I opened my eyes.

"You've made quite an entrance here," he smiled.

We chatted for a few minutes and he told me that I would be discharged from the hospital that afternoon and that a staff car would come for me. A bit embarrassed, I thanked Lefty and apologized for the way I had reacted to the northern latitude — and that I did not want to be removed from the crew.

"Son," he said with a stern voice, yet with a kind look in his brown eyes, "I chose you and I don't expect to be proven wrong. You are part of the crew." He departed.

That afternoon I was picked up by a staff driver and taken to the BOQ for a short meeting and further rest. The wind outside was blowing fiercely and the temperature at night dipped to five degrees below zero Fahrenheit. Every time I poked my nose out the door and into the cold, my head would feel like it was on verge of exploding and my lungs were unable to inhale the cold air. How would I manage in the severe northern latitude?

The next day we departed for the short flight to Elmendorf AFB, located in Anchorage. The few days spent in Anchorage allowed me to acclimatize to the cold. After Anchorage I never experienced the physical problems that first hit me when I deplaned in Fairbanks.

After many days of briefings and discussions with several people from the Army, the Navy, the Coast Guard, the Federal Aviation Administration (FAA), and tech reps from Western Electric, we decided that our first flight would take us to Adak, in the Aleutians, then on to Honolulu, Manila, Philippines and Canberra, Australia. Lefty scheduled five days of rest and recu-peration (R&R) in Canberra. This would be my first long flight to remote Adak, an island in the Aleutian chain, then down the Northern Pacific Ocean and crossing the International Date Line, and then to the Southern Pacific across the Equator and again cross the International Dateline to Australia. We would be flying over the world's largest body of open water with refueling landings at Midway, Wake, Honiara, Guadalcanal, Solomon Islands, and onto Canberra.

After deicing the aircraft we took off from Elmendorf AFB at 0500 hours on a snowy, chilly morning with our windshields glazed with frost. I was assigned the takeoff and to fly the first leg of the flight to Adak. At the run up area all engines were checked, systems tested, and the aircraft stayed deiced. I set my instruments, copied my clearance from Air Control and then tower called, and rolled on the runway with this magnificent RC-121 in my hands for our first real mission. As I accelerated, Lefty called speeds and at the proper speed I rotated into the sky and gained altitude rapidly. I remember that at 26,000 feet I was to level off to cruise to Adak.

On my right I could see some red and golden light of the shortened spring breaking through the dawn over the 20, 320-foot Mount McKinley — I was still climbing through the 15,000-foot level. It was an extraordinary sight. On the right was Mt. McKinley, like an ice cream cone, and on the left the spread of the Gulf of Alaska and the last peak of the Chugach mountain chain. This was exactly what I had yearned for, flying into the cold, crisp, fresh dawn and delighting in the new light shining on the world below me.

The flight to Adak was uneventful. I remained in the right seat with the autopilot on and a cup of coffee in my hand. The steward offered me a ham sandwich and an apple. The view was fantastic. It was clear at our altitude with unlimited visibility (CAVU). Below me were clouds and soon both ocean and land disappeared. I was advised that Adak had 1/8 of a mile visi-bility with fog and a 15-knot crosswind from the west, gusting to 20 knots. I was to shoot a Ground Controlled Approach (GCA). This would require my undivided attention, my firm control, and absolute calm. Intersecting the localizer, I turned toward Adak and heard the beeps on the radio indicating that I was exactly on course, but could see nothing, not even the approach lights of the runway.

I switched to the GCA controller and soon I heard his voice giving me precise instructions and asking me not to acknowledge his calls. GCA guided me down the glide slope and onto the runway while my windshield was filled with opaqueness that, were it possible, I could cut with a knife. Soon I heard,

"Thirty seconds to touchdown. Stay on course. To the right one degree. Too much, ease off. Fifteen seconds to touchdown. Begin flare now. Nose up. Mains down in... NOW!"

YURK, YURK! And I was on the runway, and that's all I could see. Lefty flattened the props to reduce their pull and to make them increase their drag and I started applying the brakes. I saw the high speed turn off and took it to leave the runway. A "Follow Me" Jeep met me and led me to the operations apron. The aircraft secured, the crew chief was the first off the airplane to manage the refueling process. Lefty instructed me to make certain that the aircraft was secured, refueled, and restocked with food for the next leg of the mission.

About two hours later we started on the next leg, which was to be a flight with a zigzag course to Midway, Hawaii. The zigzag pattern was to learn how to confuse enemy radar operators by changing course at whim. Lefty was to take that leg. I was to sit in the jump seat and learn how the course was executed.

The Super Constellation was a terrific learning platform because it allowed me to mature as a transoceanic pilot in a large and stable aircraft. Because of the type of missions the Air Force assigned to us, I was able to visit a lot of countries, land on many runways, experience a variety of weather conditions, and, in particular, learn about crew teamwork, management, and interdependence.

The latter attributes have served me well in many situations, with many colleagues, on many projects, and with different groups. I served on the RC-121 for 13 months until the aircraft was turned over to the Navy. It is interesting to ponder the fact that in 1955 the Navy took over the control of the RC-121 fleet (five ultimately entered service) and in the late 1980s the Air Force regained control of the AWAC fleet. At times the logic used by the Pentagon and by the Department of Defense was curious. The Navy, because it was the oceanic power, was given the responsibility of the RC-121. Why did the Navy, in terms of the AWAC, relinquish its oceanic responsibility in the 1980s?

Several of our missions were classified and some were dangerous but on the whole they were enjoyable and relatively out of harm's way. We logged many hours in good and interesting weather conditions and over territories that had never been visited by an aircraft, least of all a bizarre-looking American military aircraft on strange classified missions. Crisscrossing the Pacific Ocean is tantamount to being over water for many long hours to experience different temperatures and weather patterns. Flying from the Arctic, about 60 miles from the North Pole, to Southeast Asia, and on two occasions from Christchurch, New Zealand, to McMurdo, in Antarctica, about 800 miles from the South Pole, offers many challenges, inhospitable locations, and yet opportunities for interesting places for R&R.

One of our missions in the Connie called for a voluntary penetration of the Soviet Union. Each member was individually and privately asked if he accepted an assignment that would require him to be in harm's way and with a mission that would be ultimately denied by the Defense Department and the President. Not one of us refused and this was long before Gary Powers and the fateful U-2 incident where Eisenhower denied knowledge of the flight mission over the USSR. Had we known how the United States would treat Gary Powers perhaps we all would have had second thoughts about the mission. Our crew, however, was certain that we could penetrate the Soviet defense radar without being detected. The mission was accomplished successfully and the penetration was approximately 1,800 miles into Siberia.

Of course, there are details of the Siberian mission that are still classified, but the gist of the flight is that we managed to penetrate the Soviet defense system without being spotted. We did, however, choose to indicate our presence in the Connie when we approached Vladivostok. We revealed our position by entering the Soviet coastal radar lobe in order to have our aircraft profile reflected into their radar as our unique greeting! The Soviet

Air Force scrambled interceptors to catch us but we descended to 200 feet above the ocean surface and thus avoided giving their radar any further reflection of our position; and at such low altitude, interceptors consume fuel too quickly for a long pursuit. The Connie was soon out of the interceptors' range, and also out of Soviet territorial space. The mission was a success and the USA made the point clear that it could penetrate the Soviet defense system.

As I indicated earlier our home base was at Elmendorf Air Force Base, just outside of Anchorage, Alaska. My time at Elmendorf was one of the most memorable I had in the USAF. The base was well operated, and the weather was most interesting, even in the winter. Anchorage is located in what is called the Alaskan Banana Belt, a name that implies that it is not as cold as the rest of Alaska. Protected to the north by the Chugach chain of mountains, and to the south by the waters of the Gulf of Alaska, the winters are milder than in Fairbanks, Nome, or Point Barrow.

The Territory of Alaska

For me Alaska was a wonderful experience. It was in Alaska that I learned to fish, use snow shoes, and learn about the cold wilderness; survive the two-week Arctic Indoctrination program; taste glacier icicles; see and smell a polar bear; meet an Eskimo and share a meal with his family; talk and have dinner with a prostitute and not use her services; see the famous dog-sledding race culminate; eat moose and elk meat; drive a D-9 Caterpillar tractor; and begin to attend church services.

Our C-121 missions often took us over the Pacific for long hours of flying, but when we returned to Elmendorf it was usually in the late evening or nearing midnight. Because we used one of Anchorage's broadcasting radio stations as a navigation beacon, we could tune in to its programs. After several trips, the local broadcasting radio station, which would monitor aircraft communication, was able to listen to our transmissions with Elmendorf air traffic control, and thus knew the exact time of our return. It became a special greeting to us when the station would broadcast "Clair de Lune." Listening to that piece as we approached home after several hours or even days of flying was a most comforting experience. I believe that every member of the crew at some point sent a thank-you note to the station manager.

On one flight to Barrow, Alaska, located above the Arctic Circle and about 1,400 miles from the North Pole, we arrived in mid-December in the early afternoon. It was freezing cold, midnight-dark with a howling wind, and the visibility was only good for a few yards unless guiding lights were set up, as they were on the runway and taxiway. Where no lights were set up, ropes were strung out from the apron area to the door of the Operations building to prevent people from getting lost in the whiteout (no sky, no horizon, and visibility was only a few feet).

On the runway and approach area, navigation lights were positioned every five feet on the sides, and in the middle the lights were three feet apart. It was crisply cold; that is, it was very, very cold. The thermometer indicated that the outside temperature was 40 degrees Fahrenheit below zero, with the added factor of the blowing wind, the chill factor made the cold even more acute and penetrating and certainly well below 40. In the air when we began our descent into Point Barrow the temperature was 80 degrees below zero Fahrenheit. I had been informed that all the outside material — tires, rubber, aluminum, rivets, Plexiglas, etc. — were rated to withstand the cold to 125 degrees below zero. It was cold!

Our C-121 RC had its wheels (gears) stopped on top of a black rubber-like material that prevented the tires from freezing and affixing themselves solidly onto the surface ice. The solid permafrost on the ground was a year-round condition. Many an aircraft had lost chunks of tires as the wheels, warm after landing and taxiing, melted the ice beneath them, then when the water cooled and froze again it would embed the tires in several inches of solid ice. Liberating the tires from such a condition was impossible without damaging the outer casing. Fortunately a way had been found to prevent this from developing. A type of thick grooved rubber-like mat, too heavy to be blown away by either the prop-wash or jet-blast, had been developed to keep the wheels off the frozen ground and it served its purpose well. Of course it took some delicate maneuvering to position all the wheels exactly on the mat, but with the able help of ground point personnel, the operation was accomplished in minimum time.

On that mid-December arrival, it was my task to secure the aircraft for the night. Hot air was supplied inside the aircraft by outside flexible pipes to prevent the electronic equipment and instruments from being destroyed by the cold. An aircraft auxilary power unit (APU) was brought near the aircraft to supply continuous power to the electronic gear to avoid a complete shutdown of the systems. With the manifest in hand, and the large loading door locked, I waited at the main exit for General Parker to finish what he was doing, which was preparing charts for the next day's mission. I waited patiently for Lefty. Wrapped up in my parka, and my mittens over my gloves, I was keeping warm even though I knew that once off the aircraft I would be confronted by the bitter cold and wind. I was ready to leave the Connie.

"General," I called (I still had trouble calling him Lefty), "all is secure."

A moment later Lefty replied that he was coming. He joined me and reminded me that his name was Lefty, and we both exited the aircraft. While standing on the top of the aluminum stairs, we both closed the huge door and tightened the rotating locking device.

"Raymond," Lefty said, "give me the clipboard and I'll sign the manifest here."

"Sure. Here it is," I said, and handed it to him. It was a simple act that required scribbling his name on the dotted lines but as he pulled off his mitten to reveal the wool lined leather glove from his left hand, he momentarily lost his balance. Mitten gloves are held with a cord that makes them dangle about the wearer's neck; the insert gloves are slipped into the leather outer mitten. In that awkward motion of removing his thick mitten, his leather wool glove also came off his hand. With both outer mitten and insert gloves removed, his left hand was exposed to the freezing cold. His balance unsure because of the blowing wind, Lefty, to prevent being pushed by the stiff wind, grabbed the stair rail to steady himself!

It was a senseless mistake. That act done in the bitter cold was sufficient to freeze his hand solidly to the aluminum handrail. Lefty, with his hand firmly frozen to the metal railing, had only a few seconds, maybe less, before frostbite would set in, which could require amputation. Not much time and only one way to dislodge his hand from the railing. Really there was only one way and we both knew it.

"Sir, I propose the obvious solution," I shouted above the howl of the wind.

"Raymond, go ahead," he yelled. Immediately I unzipped my pants and cast a look towards the operations building. Several faces, most of them crew members, were looking at us. Because we had taken so much time securing the aircraft they had been concerned about our safety, not only because visibility was marginal and the cold fierce, but often polar bears roamed across the parking apron in their never ending search for food — the airport was very close to the sea where seals, walruses, and sea lions could be found on the shore, and sometimes as far in to where the garbage lockers where stored.

Would I be able to make my system function? I only had a few remaining seconds left. It is often difficult to urinate when one is pressed to do so on command, and especially when a crew is watching a 2nd Lieutenant pee on the commanding officer's hand, a general no less. Fortunately, I was able to urinate on Lefty's hand and without wetting his parka or his other clothes. It was an act of pee marksmanship, at best, with the howling wind. At worst I was quite embarrassed!

"Thanks Raymond," Parker whispered as he smiled. I took the manifest from him; it could wait until we were inside the operations lobby before receiving the signature. We ran to the operations building because Lefty did not slip his hand back into the gloves.

General Parker's hand was not harmed. The warm urine did the job of dislodging his frozen hand from the aluminum railing, and precluded any frostbite. In the operations building Lefty washed his hand, signed the manifest, thanked me profusely and insisted on the two of us having dinner together. He gave me a hefty bear hug. I was touched and embarrassed. But that was not the end of the incident. One of the crew members, James Corona, the Caltech graduate, wrote an account of what had happened and submitted it to the *Air Force Times* which published it with headlines that stated: Lieutenant Urinates on General. The story also appeared in several non-military papers.

The entire crew disliked hot humid weather (why else would we have chosen duty in Alaska?), hence when we were often sent to Manila, Bangkok, Hat Yai, Djakarta, Port Moresby or Bombay for some reconnaissance assignment on the way to these humid ovens, just as often we found good reason to leave as soon as possible for Tahiti, New Caledonia, Sydney, and Singapore — places where, although still warm were comfortable, and where we found some good options for R&R.

Our crew chief, who was also our maintenance specialist, readily found cause to give us a few days off to perform minor repairs on the aircraft, on items that were not critical but needed massaging. Because we flew into several challenging areas and at high altitude and required clean air with a good volume of oxygen, filters were critical and had to be either replaced or cleaned often — and that took a day or two, of course. Our maintenance sergeant was always able to find some reason why we had to stop for a couple of days in pleasant places; he required a clean environment to perform his maintenance. Lefty never challenged the need to perform any repairs on the Connie. He recognized that a hardworking crew needed time to relax.

On a visit to Seoul, Korea, I ran into Brigadier General Rohrs in the Officers' club. He had received his star only the month before we saw each other. It was a fine reunion. He was a good, dependable officer, a friend, and a man of his word. We went to the dining room and enjoyed a good dinner and a bottle of French wine. He was on his way back to the States to accept a new assignment in the Chief-of-Staff's office. We talked about every aspect of his and my history. He told me about his family, his wife, his two children, and the house he had built in Vermont and where he hoped to retire after his thirty years in the Air Force. I related some of the aspects of my current assignment and my delight in working under General Parker, whom he knew only casually. I admitted that I was the recipient of much good fortune in my short life.

"Return some of that good fortune whenever you can," he advised me.

Off and on in later years Rohrs and I communicated and once, when I was in seminary, we met for an evening in San Francisco. I believe that he died in 1971; at least that is what I learned from the personnel office when my letters were returned unopened. I think that his wife died a few years before him. Rohrs was a most perceptive person who was willing to take risks and envision possibilities for the future. Surely I did not present much of a good first impression the first time he met me, but he was able to see a future where I could make a difference and where the Air Force could make a difference in my life. I hope that I did not let him down. He was a fine man.

Other Issues while in Alaska

Quite often I would use the Armed Forces short wave radio facilities that could link me to stateside telephones on bases to contact my mother and inform her that all was well. She always assumed that I was in Anchorage working usual shifts on some aspect of electronic equipment. After I had flown several thousand miles over land and ocean, Mother still did not find out that I was a pilot on flying status until 1959 (about eleven years after my Private Certificate had been issued in England).

Had I been an obedient son whom she could direct, I would never have been "allowed" to fly or even enter the Air Force. Indeed she was a very difficult person in many ways. At times she was petty, always possessive, regularly manipulative, and on occasions malicious. Mother was not interested in world affairs, politics or even why she was a conservative, racist, and a member of the Republican Party. Mother never questioned her political affiliation or the ethical position of the Grand Old Party (GOP). She opposed my relationship with my father; the fact that I had been adopted was to be kept a secret from many; flying was anathema to her; the priesthood was something that she objected to vehemently; and finally, she never supported the work towards my doctorate. Alas, I could not accept her various positions — even her political orientation — but I reluctantly recognized her political and racial prejudices and simply worked around them.

Mother had good qualities that contributed greatly to my interests. She was a superb knitter and working on crochet was second nature for her. At one time in her youth, she did paint well enough to become the recipient of an International Art Masters award. I am sorry that today I find that I have no record of her art. What happened to her several paintings? The last time she painted was when she taught art classes for a few months in South Carolina, but I have none of her work. Always active with her fingers, she created many objects, sweaters, Christmas decorations, and other artifacts on schedule for any occasion. Mother was talented, creative, and productive. She was also a fine cook, had an excellent possession of French language, and had a flair for colors, perspective, and harmony.

It seems to me from experience that offspring need to retain the good qualities of their parents, accept them as fallible and imperfect human beings, reject what is not of value or acceptable to them, and move on to redesign their lives. Dwelling on the failings of parents is wasteful. None of us is perfect so why should we require perfection from parents?

I took advantage of her artistic qualities and perhaps that was why I focused a great deal of my energy on aesthetics, cooking, and admiring creativity.

As children grow to adulthood, society and peers influence them more than the parents. When offspring are in midlife or older and continue to blame parents for their maladjustment this seems to be the absolute apex of irresponsibility. Even the love we have for parents should be qualified and not blindly given without consideration. Undefined love is valueless and truly insulting, to the giver as well as the receiver.

I loved my mother but there were many serious issues of concern to me that I could not accept. Choosing the best qualities that parents and peers offer and jettisoning the less desirable portions is a better way to produce a whole individual.

Summary Thoughts

I will recapitulate my active service years in the US Air Force (USAF). After serving approximately two years in the San Francisco Bay area atop Mt. Tamalpais, which was part of Hamilton Air Force Base, Novato, California, I was reassigned on temporary duty (TDY) to Alaska. But before shipping to Alaska, I spent several weeks at various USAF bases to receive training, familiarization of aircraft, and to sharpen and upgrade my flying skills. I was assigned to the first AWAC aircraft, the RC-121, a refurbished Super Constellation known fondly as the "pregnant goose" because it carried a large circular antenna over its top and a bulge under the fuselage that enclosed the electronics gear for the radar. The RC-121 was also known as the Super Connie, which stood for Super Constellation; the aircraft was as efficient as it was beautiful, even with the added radar appendages. With a four-pilot crew, two officer controllers, and eleven radar technicians under the command of General Lefty Parker, we covered a lot of Pacific territory as well as other regions.

Both in California and in Alaska, I served in the Air Defense Command (ADC). After my assignment in California was completed, and after extensive training, I went on TDY to Elmendorf Air Force Base (AFB) in Anchorage, Alaska to be on loan to the Alaska Air Command (AAC) for the next two years; the period was actually 19 months in order for me to begin university. The Air Force sent me to obtain my undergraduate degree at the University of Tennessee but I remained on active reserve and flew missions from McGee Tyson AFB, a joint military and civilian airport.

ADC was a technically oriented part of the USAF and was charged with the protection of the United States and Canada and the monitoring of the Distant Early Warning (DEW) line. The DEW line consisted of a series of radar outposts and control centers that were placed along the Pacific and Arctic coasts of North America. I was trained in radar technology strategic defensive operations and was assigned to Combat Operations Group (COG).

COG was responsible for developing all navigation and early warning facilities in the Arctic, Antarctic, Pacific Ocean, and the North Atlantic. In addition, COG was responsible for examining any confrontational intelligence obtained on the Soviet Union and the Peoples Republic of China (PRC). COG's immediate area of responsibility also included the two Koreas, Siberia, and China, but it also maintained great interest in activities occurring in the North Atlantic. The Korean Police action was still a hot issue, although a ceasefire had been instituted through the UN. In spite of the ceasefire, skirmishes occurred daily between the North and the South Koreans, and often involved UN Forces; hence a watchful eye was unceasingly maintained.

No one knew what the USSR or China would do to quell the belligerency of the North Koreans. Of certainty was the fact that China had entered the conflict in the late part of the war and that perhaps it would reenter it again to prop up the weak North Korean military. Several clandestine reconnaissance penetrations into North Korean airspace had indicated that Chinese troops were stationed near the Demilitarized Zone (DMZ). As a reconnaissance tool, the Connie and its crew maintained a strategic vigilance and noted any movements that indicated that all was not quiet and peaceful. Without a doubt, what we did was part of a cat and mouse strategy. Who was the cat and who was the mouse?

My duties gave me opportunities for many hours of flying. This was exactly what I had wanted to do. The Super Connie took me to places I had only read about in geography and adventure books. I suspect that because I was able to see the world as a manageable planet and the sky as a dynamic portion of the universe, which could be interpreted for fine navigation support, my attitude towards God's existence and his Creation were re-examined.

I was awe-struck by the beauty of the world, the firmament, and hence the Universe. No, it was not a cosmological proof of God's existence that was encountered, but rather an appreciation that there was much more to understand. I don't believe that I framed God in my reasoning as a person or even in person-form. Identifying God in literature or in the Prayer Book as "Father" was understood by me only as a symbolic categorization of some super being who may (or may not) recognize humans as worthy of attention. I find it difficult to look at the Earth, glance into Space, and consider the sub particles without some thought about something called God; maybe it is merely another name for $E=mc^2$ or some other descriptive symbol for the mystery. Religion always acted as a barrier to my understanding of God, the Divine, or Providence. On many occasions I know that I was precluded from making horrible decisions by some manner of guidance, but I know little about its origin. Life is neither simple nor void of unknown forces. How we recognize these influences depends on how we see ourselves in the Cosmos.

No, it was not the watchmaker God of deism that I accepted. In a sense I preferred the symbolic title "Almighty" as more appropriate and as the more descriptive address. It would have been gratifying for me to know for certain that God was, indeed, Father and personal. That I could rely on this aged super creature as one would rely on a crutch, a dear uncle, or a mentor would have sweetened my life in times of conflict, uncertainty, and pain.

But it did not quite pan out this way, although I've often felt that "someone," in a strange way, was watching over me. I cannot put my finger on that awareness; nevertheless, it is with me all the time. I don't want to make too much of that enigmatic sense now or ever. I don't fathom it, really I don't. In years to come I would have to struggle with this issue of how God is not only addressed, but how God is grasped, if at all. From my perspective of physics and science in general, I recognize that no aspect of science can fathom the realities that affect even the minuscule particle or source of energy. It is this complex realization that moved me into philosophical exploration to learn what was, for instance, beyond the "singularity" issue.

Flying at night or in the light of the moon made everything on the horizon appear to be more delicate, more fragile, and more spectacular. It also made me realize that I might be insignificant in the grand scheme of the universe. Yet, I could never quite accept that I and everyone else were simply occasions of minor value. In spite of the tension generated by the Korean altercation and the conflicts that existed in other parts of the world, I could not help but realize that there was a beauty in human nature, and in all living creatures that was "divine" in quality. The long hours of flying allowed for profound cosmological, and even ontological, thinking.

In flight over the Pacific, there was always a purple-hued light coming from some source, either from the sun's reflection on the troposphere, from the moon redirecting the light from the sun, or from the brightness of the firmament emitting light from the billions and trillions of stars. I was struck with wonder and amazement at the richness of the skies, the numbers of stars and planets my eyes could see, and the apparent insignificance of my presence, and yet the inner emotional grasping that even I was significant in front of this mysterious beauty.

I began to revisit the Episcopal Church to see if I could obtain any comprehension, to penetrate a little further into the mysteriousness of the universe. By participating in services at the Base Chapel, by being confronted with the words of the Prayer Book, and by beginning to see that the mystery of creation was truly a mystery and not a mere enigma, I was faced with the realization that there was more before my very eyes, before my understanding, than I could come to terms with.

I visited the base chapel when the Episcopal chaplain was presiding at the Eucharist. The other denominations just did not respond to my needs. I did not want doctrine but the freedom to piece together ideas on my own with some guidance; I needed a sounding board. Major Howard Bliss Scholten was the Episcopal chaplain at Elmendorf Air Force Base. I began to attend services quite regularly on Base whenever my schedule allowed it.

On Christmas Eve 1954, there was thick ice fog over the entire region of Anchorage, which included Elmendorf AFB. The approach weather had been a hundred feet above minimum decision height, but with GCA this allowed us to land, thus sparing us a diversion to an alternate airport. The ice crystals caused us to have nearly opaque windshields and but for the blowing air from the heaters and the embedded electrical heating coils in the plastic we would have been blind. We had landed the Super Connie but had the limited visibility to taxi and that required us to trail a "Follow Me" vehicle to our parking place.

After landing and shutting down, I had but a few minutes to make the Christmas Eve Eucharist. Icy fog crystals pricked the portions of my face that where not protected by the parka. I was cold and tired but determined to attend the Midnight Eucharist. I did arrive with a few minutes to spare for the Eucharist and thoroughly enjoyed the celebration. I felt lifted and refreshed, although quite hungry and in need of time to relax. When the service ended it was past midnight — early morning of 25 December 1954.

Chaplain Howard Bliss Scholten, the Episcopal chaplain at Elmendorf, invited me to his house after the service. He soon learned that I had been on duty for nearly 24 hours and had been flying almost as long. After a drink of malt scotch and several canapés smothered with smoked salmon, the chaplain and I began to chat by the fireplace. He was happy to see me participate in the Eucharist when I was on Base, and hoped that I would continue with the good attendance.

"I find the Eucharist to be totally uplifting," I told Scholten. "But I'm not certain that I understand the whole sense of its meaning, its effect, and its historical depth and relevance."

Scholten looked at me and assured me that in time more of the "Eucharistic onion," as he called it, "would be revealed to me when layer upon layer would be peeled by participation and serious study."

We chatted further even when his wife joined us and entered into the conversation. She inquired about my "Christian education" and where I had been baptized. I answered her questions and added that my Christian education was mostly zero except for what my curiosity had moved me to learn from reading at Victoria College or when in Mill Valley. I did admit that I had read a great deal while in England and that when possible I still read a lot, some of which dealt with Christianity and with the other major denominations and religions, even the Eastern religions to which I had been exposed in the course of my travels. After our conversation that night I left for my room and a good night's sleep. He did invite me to Christmas day dinner.

After a good night of rest and some walking, I returned to the Chaplain's house the next day and was met by Mrs. Scholten who greeted me and led me to the sitting room and then left me to tend to dinner. Scholten introduced me to the few guests, who were discussing politics.

After dinner and when the guests left I was asked to remain for a nightcap. Chaplain Scholten resumed the line of conversation but then said something quite startling:

"Raymond, I've watched you for the past several months and wish to ask you a personal question."

I swallowed and said that he could ask anything he wished if it did not touch on my military assignment.

"Have you ever considered serving in Holy Orders?"

I was stunned and quickly replied that I certainly had not. Moreover, I added, I did not know what one did in holy orders. No, I had never considered it.

"Me in holy orders?" I repeated several times. Scholten did not reply.

As I was leaving, Chaplain Scholten reminded me that I was always welcome to visit him, and he hoped that we would resume the conversation soon. We never did. Chaplain Scholten died in 2000, but I saw him a few times before he died because we were both in later years canonically resident in the Diocese of California. Yes, he did remember our conversation on that cold Christmas day and found it humorous that he had been quite correct in his evaluation of me, especially since later I had so much studied the Eucharist, its history, its meaning, and its relevance.

Several years later I did propose, while in Knoxville in 1958, that I was considering Holy Orders to another chaplain, this time to the university chaplain of the University of Tennessee and then informed my mother in a letter. She telephoned me to tell me that when I was in Alaska she had received a note from a chaplain inquiring if I had ever considered the ministry. Chaplains often wrote notes to parents telling them that their offspring were doing well and also keeping out of trouble. Scholten's note to Mother was disturbing. Mother was neither happy about the note nor about the news that I had discussed the priesthood with yet another chaplain. The whole idea of a son in the priesthood was anathema to her. Was that a way to earn a decent living?

In the USAF, my field of operation was global in mission, but with major emphasis on the Pacific Rim and the ocean adjacent to it. Although my home bases were first Hamilton AFB, in Novato, California and then Ent AFB, in Colorado Springs, Colorado, where ADC was headquartered, I was on temporary assignment at Elmendorf in Anchorage, Alaska. This temporary status exempted me from normal and routine resident chores that often required time. Instead, I was often able to do things that I wanted to do. I volunteered to fly supply cargo that included transporting cases of beer to several radar outposts in Alaska.

On three occasions I took a job driving bulldozers with a construction firm improving the highway from Fairbanks to Anchorage. It was very good pay, long hours, and lots of fun operating those construction behemoth Caterpillar D-9s.

In general, my time was put to good use by reading a great many books, working profitably, seeing a lot of Alaska's hinterland, and developing a good and substantial record with the USAF. In June 1955, I was sent back to Ent AFB for re-assignment into the active reserve and admitted into a program called "Operation Bootstrap," which granted me the GI Bill, hence tuition with books, regular USAF salary with flight pay, and privileges to a military base. It was time for me to start a new phase of my personal development. I was beginning to look at academic education as part of that next phase. University education was coming into focus.

East Asia, the Pacific, Europe, and the two icy Poles made for an exciting understanding of the world, the people who inhabit it and their customs. Food was varied and at times strange, even repulsive to me. The Philippines introduced me to stewed dog — neither a dish that I would recommend nor one I relished. In Thailand, I was given roasted monkey! Fortunately, I only discovered that it was monkey after I had consumed a plateful. The shocking moment occurred when the host offered me one forehand while he ate the other. We were to share this "delicacy" because I was the guest and he was the host. I declined with the excuse that I was stuffed from the excellent repast. My host understood and accepted my weak excuse. The monkey's hand had been severed at the wrist and was served on a banana leaf. It appeared too human, too baby-like, too disconcerting. Why had both the monkey's hand and the dog's flesh been so repugnant to me?

I puzzled over this issue of food for many days and weeks. I eat beef, pork, sausage made with mixed meats, chicken, rabbit, birds and fowl. Why don't I eat dog, cat, or monkey? One of the reasons is that I am accustomed to eating herbivores and not carnivores. Is that choice the result of custom or is there a hidden reason for avoiding carnivores? From my limited experience they both appear to taste similar, at least they are not totally alien to the palate, even if they are foreign. I've eaten reindeer, kangaroo, moose, whale, and even bear — of these whale and bear will not ever be repeated.

I found that when whale meat was given to me in Japan as a delicacy I was most disturbed after chewing a couple of bites and being told what it was. Because whale is such a noble animal to me I am truly unable to eat it. Nevertheless, I did find the whale meat tasted good and resembled veal in its delicate texture and flavor. Bear, also a noble animal, is just not to my taste, however.

Eating habits have cultural, historical, and religious dimensions that unequivocally control our choices. Human beings have quite varied diets, and location and race determine the content. I love caviar and many is the person who finds "fish eggs" to be repulsive if a taste for it has not been cultivated. The same goes for liver or other animal organ parts. Steak and kidney pie, a common dish in England, is frowned upon by most Americans, especially American Southerners who also avoid lamb or mutton. Why not enrich our diet with insects? I suppose that it all depends on what we are accustomed to.

On one of our longer visits to the city-state of Singapore, I had a few days of leave and decided to accept an invitation from the owner of a coffee plantation to spend time on the island of Sumatra located across the Strait of Malacca. I was taken by boat to Medan, on the northeast side of the Island of Sumatra, and then by jeep to the plantation near the village of Tebing Tinggi. I was accompanied by Lefty, who knew our host Karl Von Druk, quite well. He was Dutch but had lived on his father's coffee plantation all his life after receiving his education in the Netherlands.

After the death of his father and mother, Karl had assumed the responsibility of managing the plantation. Karl was certain that his days in Sumatra were limited because of the anticipated political upheaval once Indonesia gained its independence. He was going to abandon Sumatra, convinced that Indonesia was unmanageable as a political entity, especially when it became independent.

At any rate, we motored to his plantation and settled in his lovely house on the edge of the sea. The house was a spacious structure made mostly of wood and followed the local design of houses found in a Sumatran village, but it had all the amenities of a modern house, including indoor plumbing. I was given a bedroom facing the Strait of Malacca with my door opening just a few feet away from the white sandy beach and the warm, clean, and blue surf.

After settling in and taking a dip in the sea, I was called for drinks and savories on the veranda. In the course of our conversation I was informed that "George" would be here around dusk, and that he was a friendly and harmless chap. I assumed that George was a dog or perhaps a cat and thought no more about it. After dinner and a brandy, I retired to my room for some reading before falling asleep. Sometime past midnight, I was awakened by something that seemed terribly heavy on my feet. I quickly slipped my feet from under this weight and turned the lights on. Coiled at the foot of my bed was a medium-sized pale brown with dark crossbars boa constrictor!

It was seeking the heat of my body. It stared at me with those round silver eyes. After a few minutes, I suppose that when it recognized that my feet were no longer available to give it warmth and that I was out of the bed, the boa slowly and deliberately slithered off the bed and into the adjoining living room. I firmly closed the door putting a chair to block it from opening in the event that the latch would not hold, read for a few minutes and resumed my sleep after this inopportune interruption. I was surprised that I fell into a deep sleep after that episode and did not dream of snakes.

When I related my experience to Karl, he laughed and apologized for not making us aware of his pet George. This boa had been rescued from the road when a truck almost crushed its head. Karl had nursed it back to good health. George was fed once every six or seven weeks, I was informed, a freshly killed piglet or other small animal that was swallowed whole. The boa constrictor was approximately 10 feet long but would reach a length of 15 to 16 feet in adulthood. For the next few days, although I did see George several times, it never returned to my room. I suspect that it found my room and its occupant unwelcoming.

A New Adventure with a New Aircraft

After our assignment on the Connie was completed and we turned over the RC-121 to the Navy, we were all dispersed and sent to other locations for duty. Lefty Parker was given the command of the F-86D Intercept squadron at Elmendorf, and my good fortune was being sent to training at Nellis AFB, Las Vegas for — guess what — the F-86D. After completing my type training I was re-sent to Elmendorf AFB. This assignment meant that in my entire career in the Air Force I was attached to only two air bases, Hamilton and Ent, Colorado.

Once I was greeted by Lefty, I was told to work for a few days with Major Ernie Wolf, the Senior Check Pilot. That rigorous training checkout accomplished successfully, I was placed on the scheduled duty roster to fly as Wolf's wingman. It was again temporary duty related to Combat Operations rather than on-scramble interceptions. This time I worked with the DEW group section.

A month later a young lieutenant pilot was assigned as my wingman, and I became the senior pilot wearing the rank of First Lieutenant sporting the Senior Crest on my wing. The surprise was that Lefty made certain that his old wings were given to me. I had logged 3,900 hours of pilot-in-command for the Air Force. Thus, I considered flying the North American 86-D all-weather interceptor over the Alaskan skies a reward and not an assignment.

I spent another nine months in Alaska and often my mission took me past Mt. McKinley and on to Kotzebue, just north of the Arctic Circle, for refueling. Other missions took me to Nome, just off the coast of the Bering Straits, the closest point to Siberia. A few missions called for me to patrol the International Date Line (IDL), a geographic line over the Pacific Ocean to separate the end of one day from the beginning of another. The IDL passes between Little Diomede (US Possession) and Big Diomede, called Ostrov Ratmanova by the Russians. My mission would take me past Saint Lawrence Island and just west of Saint Matthew Island, where I would meet an air-tanker, refuel then return to follow the Date Line north and eventually back to Nome, past the interesting village of Mary's Igloo.

Yes, I did visit Mary's Igloo once to see what was in that village. The village was unprepossessing and served mainly as a fishing harbor for pollock fishermen and Eskimo seal trappers. I was informed that at one time, in the 19th century, Mary's Igloo had the best bordello in Western Alaska, which even drew clients from Siberia in the winter when the Bering Strait was frozen and passage could only be made by dog sled.

On a few occasions I was assigned to patrol east of the IDL. Many times I encountered Soviet Migs (Mikoyan) also patrolling on their side of the IDL. One clear morning, I saw a Soviet Mig 17 interceptor approach me, and come quite near, nearer than usual. It did not appear to be an unfriendly act. At any rate, I was not allowed to engage or shoot a Mig unless the Soviet fighter shot at me first. I was tense and my finger was ready to press the armed triggers of either my rockets or my 50 caliber guns.

This encounter appeared to be harmless but I did alert defense control and signaled my wingman. I had seen that particular aircraft on several occasions and simply tipped my wings as a greeting. The Mig responded immediately. It was obvious that the Soviets were also patrolling the Date Line. This time the Mig came closer than we had ever been. The distance between us was perhaps less than 20 feet. Because the USSR did not monitor the international emergency radio frequencies, we could not communicate. Yet the Mig tightened the distance between us, and I was ready to report to my controller and to order my wingman to be ready for a conflict. Then it happened!

In a flash I stopped pumping my adrenaline. I relaxed and laughed. The Mig pilot flashed the cover of the American *Playboy Magazine*. I waved and tipped my wings, and he too waved his hand, then the magazine. He tipped his wings, and peeled off towards Providenija, on the tip of the Poluostrov Peninsula, home base for the Migs. *Playboy Magazine* as a diplomatic tool!

To accumulate more flight hours and experience I would volunteer to fly cargo C-47s (Gooney Birds) to radar outposts to replenish the supplies, especially of beer. These re-supplying ventures took me to several remote sites, and strangely oriented runways. Apart from Kotzebue and Nome, I re-supplied Galena with its sloping runway where landings and takeoffs were only to the southeast, no matter what the wind was, hence landings were made uphill and takeoffs were conversely made downhill.

Barrow was to the north, where I had landed many times in the Connie and had brilliant memories, and Naknek in the south, then across to the beginning of the Alaska Peninsula, to Port Moller.

Once I flew as co-pilot in a C-54 (Skymaster), first to Dutch Harbor and then to Adak, on the Aleutian Islands and was fortunate to have absolutely CAVU weather. In the interior I flew once also as co-pilot in a C-47 to Tanacross, north of the Rangel Mountains and east of the Alaskan Range, near both the Tanana River and the north fork of the Alcan highway. This flight demanded an experienced driver to maneuver through the mountain passes, and find the runway in a hidden clearing in the midst of giant trees, ridges, and sheer granite cliffs. I learned that the C-47 can land on a 2000-foot runway, then take off, clearing a 70-foot rise, but it takes a good pilot with ice water in his veins, lots of brakes, and screaming engines to give the aircraft the necessary catapulting momentum. On that particular flight every rivet on the nacelles was dancing.

While in Alaska, I continued to work, when time permitted, on the D-9 Caterpillar bulldozer on the improvement of the highway between Fairbanks and Anchorage. Lefty required that we not fly more than 36 hours per week; the limit was strictly enforced unless it was for obtaining a new rating. Hence in that context, I obtained a new rating as PIC on the Boeing KC-135, a four-engine jet tanker operated by the refueling wing at Elmendorf AF Base. Because the fueling aircraft usually had long missions, I quickly accumulated approximately forty hours of flying time and Lefty never objected. Nevertheless, I continued to work on the D-9 Earthmover, which gave me an opportunity to save money for university and afforded me a change of activity.

The Alcan Highway and the USAF

Lefty was reassigned in January 1955 and Col. Lawson Wynn was given command of my section with Combat Operations. Wynn was a close friend and golf partner of Lefty. When Col Wynn checked my records he discovered that I had nearly sixty days of accrued leave. He immediately forced me to go on leave and I caught a flight to the East Coast. I took my Ford Six out of storage in Passaic, NJ and began preparing it for the exciting trip across the northern States, into Canada, then to connect with the Alcan Highway heading to Fairbanks and south to Anchorage.

The trip from Passaic to Anchorage via Fairbanks from Minot, North Dakota took 16 days. It was an adventure that I will never forget. On one occasion I had to keep my engine running all night because the heater plugs at the only motel in Whitehorse, Yukon, were all taken. Not keeping the engine at idle all night would have meant a frozen engine packed with congealed oil in the morning.

Temperatures will dip to 40 or 50 degrees below zero Fahrenheit in the winter. Precautions are to be taken if one does not want to become a statistic in the frozen north. When one is driving the Alcan, the Canadian Mounted Police require that drivers carry food for three days, two spare tires, several cans of oil, a 10-gallon can of gasoline, blankets, a kerosene stove, lots of waterproof matches, a small bottle of drinking alcohol, and a first aid kit.

Keeping the engine running all night was no inconvenience; in the morning the Ford engine and cab were warm as toast. An interesting historical fact for the current reader who pays four (or more) dollars/gallon for a US four-quart gallon, the Imperial gasoline gallon (five quarts) cost 18 Canadian cents per gallon. I made the trip without any mishaps and saw some extraordinary sights such as Lake Laberge, Champagne Village, Kluane Lake, Destruction Bay, the Coastal Mountains, the Klondike region, and North Pole Alaska (not the real magnetic North Pole).

The Air Force was good to me and contributed much towards putting me further on the road to maturity and giving me a keen sense of self-discipline and the ability to work and cooperate with my fellow human beings. Many of my superiors were good examples for me. I had several excellent commanders and fine colleagues.

One of my commanders contacted me recently after 47 years. He saw my name in an article in *Aviation Week and Space Technology* and searched for my address and phone number. Needless to say, I was thrilled to hear from Col. Lawson Wynn.

A few years ago, a night phone call brought me back to my time on Mt. Tamalpais when a colleague, Gerald Undercoffer and his wife, Jean greeted me with "Remember me?" I had not seen them since 1956 when I had stopped for a day in Clearfield, Pennsylvania, on my way to Chicago. Both have continued to be on my list for repeated communication. Unfortunately, Gerry died in 2007 and Jean has had a difficult time tending to the business and closing loops.

Recently I reopened the lines of communication with college friends, friends I had not seen for more than 30 or 40 years. Communication was re-established with Newell Anderson, Donald Williamson (who died of leukemia in 2007), Judith Schrim Mack, Bill Senter, Chris Clements, Warren Robertson, and of course Meg Blackman, and others. I've also been in regular communication with the Rt. Rev. William E. Sanders, the good bishop who deaconed me in 1964. Last year Bishop Sanders, after several years as a widow, married Marlin Jones and I was present for the occasion in Nashville.

I hope that more friends of old will reemerge from oblivion. We are allowed to play but once on a team in this arena called Earth and we might as well maintain contact with our teammates for as long as we can and while we can. Death, Alzheimer's, relocation and distance, busyness, and other contributing factors help in separating us from each other, yet the telephone and the internet have come to our rescue, if only we are willing to make the effort to reconnect with our fellow voyagers on this planet. Being alone — and we are alone for the most part — or being constantly surrounded by strangers on Earth is a terrible predicament when we can reconnect with our fellow teammates so easily, and continue to share a common history for as long as we live this short life.

In June 1955 I completed my tour of duty in Alaska and headed to Tennessee. I was now assigned to Active Reserve instead of Active Duty with the reserve rank of Captain, and the permanent grade of Staff Sergeant having declined the offer to commit myself to the Regular Air Force. I enjoyed the USAF but did not consider it as a career, especially one that would require a

20- or 30-year commitment and where advancement would require that I reduce my flying and take on command duties and administrative functions. I would have enjoyed command duties, but the accompanying administrative tasks would not have been to my liking.

A similar reluctance surfaced in later years when I found that I enjoyed the sacramental and teaching functions that came with Holy Orders, but disliked greatly the administrative tasks that I had to endure.

Education and what was Entailed

Taking stock of my options, I chose to keep the Air Force as a temporary avocation and concentrate more on obtaining an education. I was just past the age of twenty-three; it was high time that I looked ahead at education as a new venue to excite my brain. There was too much to do in the world, and I wanted to check all the possible options. In retrospect it was a wise decision for me, though often painful, frustrating, and confusing. The consequent results at the time have been ultimately beneficial.

I applied to three universities, but I also had received an unsolicited offer from Pan American World Airways. This was just the time when Boeing and Pan Am had devised a plan to produce the USAF KC-135 cargo and fuel tanker as the civilian Boeing 707 transoceanic passenger liner. This aircraft had four jet engines and was about to be launched for passenger service within the next few months, and Pan Am was in dire need of pilots qualified to fly not only jets, but also four-engine jets. I had had time in the KC-135, not much time, but I was qualified to take a position as pilot on the aircraft having flown the type in the Pacific and Greenland. To obtain my civilian Air Transport Pilot rating would be a matter of a few days of training and Pan Am would offer it at minimum cost to them. I did, however, obtain my ATP from the Air Force because I had the required hours and there was an examiner at Elmendorf who not only instructed me but also examined me with a check flight in a training KC-135.

My interview was to be held in Chicago and although I was not enthusiastic about accepting an offer from Pan Am, because it would divert me from obtaining an academic education, the proposed salary was very tempting. Needless to say, I went to the interview and was given a firm offer that came with a high seniority placement, but I did not accept it. As much as flying for Pan Am would be exciting, challenging, and lucrative, my decision to refuse it proved to be wise. Apart from having to put my education on hold, I was not enamored with flying the line from airport to airport on the same route for weeks on end. To me it was one thing to fly for the USAF on missions to different places and another to fly for an airline from New York to London and back five times a month!

In terms of education, in 1955 I was not certain what I wanted to do. I had been immersed in several exciting technical disciplines, many of which were in high technology and on the leading edge of scientific development. In mathematics I found myself to be better than a fair student, not brilliant but able to manage it. My father's talent for linguistics did not attract me as a possible career. Aeronautics and space science were interesting to me, but the path to both was engineering. Olav had studied engineering at MIT and spoke grandly of an engineering career. I had been around engineers and often found what they did to be interesting. When I did have conversations with technical representatives from Western Electric, AT&T, or General Electric in the USAF, they all painted a view of engineering that was splashed with color and splendor.

After all, the late 1950s were the years when engineering was the discipline of preference, especially after the Sputnik event. When the Soviet Union launched the first Sputnik satellite, America and the Western nations were embarrassed that they were behind the eight ball in engineering accomplishments. America immediately began to push engineering as a profession and I heard the predominant call.

This was the time when a personal mentor would have been most helpful, but I had no one who could assume that role. Nevertheless, I knew that it was high time for me to go to college. The USAF was willing and ready to fund my education under several laws initiated by Congress for Korean Veterans, of which I was one. The Air Force allowed me to select any accredited university so long as it was within a 50-mile radius of an active AFB with an operational flight line/runway. The operational runway really referred to my current permanent status assigned at Ent AFB, Colorado Springs, which did not have an operational runway.

Education in a University

I searched for the appropriate university, one that would satisfy not only the Air Force's needs but also my own. I was interested in technical work, but preferred a broad agenda, which would allow me to sample various subjects. I also wanted good weather with a climate less cold than in Alaska, the Midwest, or the Northeast. I applied to the Universities of Oklahoma, Pennsylvania State, Cornell, and the University of Tennessee. I visited each one but selected the University of Tennessee (UT) in Knoxville because it was close to McGhee-Tyson AFB, which had an ADC group, the weather was mild, and the countryside green and blooming, and I loved the Elm trees framing the entrance to the main group of academic buildings. Furthermore, the university offered a broad spectrum of subjects and was attached to the scientific community of Oak Ridge where research in physics and chemistry were at the cutting edge. In addition, UT had good engineering, liberal arts, and science colleges, and it was small with approximately 7,000 students. I would be able to sample many disciplines, and I did.

Jumping into serious academic work in America would be a totally new experience for me. I had attended many training courses in the Air Force but university was different, and the American system and pedagogical approaches were foreign to me. It seemed that the educational attitude was more creative, less strict, more informal, and more open to discussion where student opinions were heard, respected, and dealt with honestly. It was a difficult period for me.

Adapting was only one of the problems that I had to solve. I had to learn something of the social environment that included dating, recreational activities, and language, which was a great deal more polite than that commonly used in the military. My study habits from preparatory school had to be revitalized and employed daily. Studying was difficult and the courses were not particularly exciting.

As a freshman, there were many aspects of university life that were totally foreign to me. That I was a veteran did not help all that much. In 1955 I was 23 years old, much older than most incoming students. Of course there were other veterans enrolled at the university, and although we were a large group, we were still a minority in a sea of incoming students who were 18 or 19 years old and fresh out of high school. The boys dressed in jeans and the girls wore white socks, pleated skirts, and cardigans. My association with the younger generation while in the USAF had not included those in high school. Sophomores and upper class students were still much younger than I.

I remember attending my first football game with my first date, another freshman. Rochelle Anderson (sister of Newell who is often mentioned in later years) was an attractive and striking redhead from Knoxville who had been introduced to me by a fellow student who wanted me to become a Sigma Chi fraternity brother. Not being much interested in football and having gone to the game because of "that's what freshman do" syndrome, I suffered the noise and the boredom of a game I could neither understand nor follow. After the game I invited Rochelle to join me for dinner at the Regas Restaurant, the exclusive dining place in Knoxville. She happily accepted and was quite impressed that her date would take her to a fashionable restaurant. Young college students never took their dates to premium restaurants; they were above their financial capabilities. For me, after enduring the boredom of the football game, Rochelle saved the day by rewarding me with a pleasant evening.

Soon after beginning my courses in mechanical engineering, the major I had chosen, I became unhappy with the choice. I discovered that engineering was a shallow-thinking discipline where problems were often resolved by plugging in a formula that surfaced from other disciplines, especially the hard sciences like physics and chemistry. I found that I had no room to breathe because engineering required a minimum of liberal arts courses; even foreign languages were not part of the curriculum. Engineering did not seem to satisfy my needs and, at the time, I did not know what would. I decided to search for other options.

The GI Bill permitted one, and only one, change of university discipline. My first move was to learn that I could take many of my required engineering courses in the Department of Physics, which was under the purview of the College of Liberal Arts. The second move was to take elective courses in logic offered by the Department of Philosophy, which counted as "technical thinking" in the engineering curriculum. Both ended up being rewarding eye openers for me. I soon learned that I could substitute courses from other departments for those required in the College of Engineering, which proved to be salutary for me.

It was not that academic and military obligations were minimal and that I had a lot of leisure time, but I was searching for an avenue that would lead me to a productive and interesting life. Because I was still under the College of Engineering and required only a few courses in English, I chose to take a public speaking class, which fulfilled the requirement. The professor was Dr. Frederick Field, who was also the lead theater director for the innovative Carousel Theater at the University of Tennessee.

A few weeks after classes started and after I had faced the fire by presenting my first speech on the doldrums instilled in American political life by the Eisenhower administration, I returned to my seat to commendatory approvals. Then followed the normal critique by my fellow students and a summation by Fred Fields. My speech had been very well received and the discussion that followed was heated and positive in content. I was quite satisfied that my presentation had been good, if not excellent. I was proud of my accomplishment and the several presentations I had given in the Air Force served me well. I felt good and more than gratified.

Towards the end of the class Fred Fields said that he was directing *The Silver Whistle*, a play about a girl who had been brought up in a convent. Then Fred said that he needed someone to play the small part of an old man. Was there a volunteer in the class? For some unknown reason I raised my hand. No one else volunteered. I was chosen for the simple part and there began my career as a thespian, and, more to the point, as a "ham."

This first step before the lights and applause prefaced a series of 26 plays, of which I directed seven. I loved the theater and would have headed to a professional career except for the horror stories I heard about life as an actor — until fame arrived, if ever, for many actors life was a struggle and less than satisfying.

During all these academic exigencies, I was still doing my duty with the USAF and fulfilling missions for ADC. I was assigned a North American F-100B, an all-weather interceptor, and flew often with other F-100B pilots on most weekends over Cuba, the Caribbean, and the Gulf of Mexico; because of weather all of them demanded a great amount of attention, and we flew many missions in the area and over the Gulf of Mexico.

I acquired a good knowledge of extreme weather conditions, especially thunderstorms and hurricanes, and became convinced that the former should be avoided at all cost and the latter were obviously dangerous because of the nature of the high wind, the heavy rain, and massive area they affected. A close venture near a hurricane in the summer of 1957 rattled my teeth and frightened me to the nth degree but I managed to come out of it without a scratch. From then on I gave both hurricanes and thunderstorms a wide berth of at least 20 miles.

I enjoyed flying the F-100B. It was a wonderful aircraft that responded softly and rapidly to control inputs. One of the special aspects of being assigned an F-100B was that it was practically mine to use whenever I wanted it for a mission, for training, or for chasing clouds. There were six F-100B rated pilots stationed at McGee-Tyson and only six F-100B aircraft on the base. There were other aircraft such as C-47s, C-54s, a squadron of F-89s and others. The F-100s were an exclusive group. Five of the F-100s pilots were on active duty but I was the only one on special active reserve duty, hence not involved in the daily activities and duties of the base. On one occasion, to maintain my flight proficiency I scheduled a flight to Mitchell AFB, in Long Island, to attend the opening night of the musical *My Fair Lady*. After the play was over, I returned to McGee-Tyson and was in class the next morning!

Crucial Changes in Directions

When engineering became too boring for me, and when I learned that I had taken enough courses in the physics department to warrant almost a major, I switched in 1958 to a double major in theoretical Physics and Philosophy, with a minor in French, for which I had to do very little work. This seemed to make more sense, and I loved being able to approach problems by asking "why" instead of "how," which was the engineering standard method for finding a solution.

December 1958 was a momentous time for me. Not only had I embarked on a new approach for my education but also I was toying with the idea of Holy Orders, something I knew nothing about, and I knew even less about God. At the time, I was attending church services, programs, and social events at Tyson House, the Episcopal Student Center at the University. In fact, in my second year at UT, I moved into Tyson House as a tenant and "houseboy." My duties were to share in the cleaning of the house, act as a host to the visiting students, and perform some minor repairs when necessary.

I shared a spacious room with Bill Teague, a chemical engineering student from Nashville. Living at Tyson House was enjoyable and a great social learning experience in the art of hosting and time management; much as it was fun to talk with and discuss various topics with fellow students for hours on end I still had to manage my time scrupulously.

The Reverend William Therrel Holt, Jr., was the Episcopal chaplain at Tyson House and he and I had many involved personal conversations. I had many questions and he helped me find some answers. Chaplain Holt was patient, responsive, and willing to help me think through many issues that confronted me. He took me seriously. He did not rush me. He understood that I was struggling with a decision that would alter the course of my life. He invited me to participate more in the affairs of Tyson House. I was trained as a lay reader and an acolyte. I read a great deal and discussed many issues with other men who were seeking Holy Orders. Chaplain Holt urged me not to let my thinking about Holy Orders divert me from being a student, flying, and socializing with both men and women.

"Holy Orders does not preclude one from having fun and a full life," he would remind me as a warning. I was not one to put on the mantle of seriousness as a sign that I was thinking about God and the Church.

The university was entering into a major program of foreign student exchanges and was looking for bilingual students to help with the process. Because of a student exchange program instituted by Senator William Fulbright from Arkansas, a graduate student from Paris arrived on campus and I was asked to sponsor and guide her. Jeannine Dupont was from Neuilly-sur-Seine, a suburb of Paris. This was a premier opportunity for me to practice my French and regain the crispness of the language I so loved.

Jeannine was a delight as a companion. She was studying English and hoped to be able to teach the language when she returned to France. She soon discovered that English in America was American in tone, syntax, and pronunciation with the added quality of a southern flavor. I, however, gained much from speaking with a Parisian. Jeannine was a most attractive woman who was, unfortunately for me, engaged to a physician working in Gabon, Africa, as a volunteer with Medecins Sans Frontieres.

Jeannine's tour in Knoxville was for one academic year and in May 1958 I drove her to the Atlanta airport for her return flight to Paris. Before she left she made arrangements for me to instruct beginning students in the French Department, a welcome task that I performed until I went to Chicago in June 1959.

A young student from Memphis arrived to do some post-baccalaureate work in the philosophy department on Paul Tillich, the theologian. Donald McKenzie Williamson was a postulant (one who is accepted by the bishop) for Holy Orders in the Episcopal Diocese of Tennessee. We became good friends and we often engaged in discussions of ethics, theology, philosophy, and life in general with Margaret (Meg) Blackman, a senior student in English.

Meg was engaged to a new deacon assigned to a parish in Virginia. That I had a very serious crush on her need not be emphasized, and I suspect that she also felt deeply for me but she was committed and faithful to Ed, the young deacon. Both Meg and I tried to change the situation, but she would not break off her promise with her fiancé to be. The last time I saw Meg was on the eve of her engagement announcement and reception, which I did not attend because of a flight mission. In 2013 I located Meg and correspondence followed via email; her parents, who lived in Knoxville, died in the early 70s.

Soon after his arrival at UT, Don was accepted as a resident at Tyson House where we continued our several discussions in greater depth. Don never did complete his research work on Tillich but instead proceeded to get married in New Orleans to a wealthy, young, attractive student in social work by the name of Grace. The marriage unfortunately did not survive for long after he was ordained to the priesthood. Nevertheless, Don and I kept in contact somehow, if irregularly. He was quite helpful and a clear guide to me when I was a new deacon assigned to St. Mary's Cathedral, Memphis. Don and I remained friends with many aspects of a shared and confidential history, and for this I am most happy and thankful. I have great regard and respect for Don as a delightful and thoughtful friend. When he died I lost a dear and close friend.

Midway through his parochial ministry, Don decided to sit for law and became a lawyer in the 80s. Don died in 2007 of leukemia and I was fortunate to see him and to meet his wife Connie in 2001 over a couple of days in Andover, MA.

Another most helpful and dear friend, who participated in my life with great camaraderie, loyalty, and devotion, was Newell Anderson. Newell, better known as Do, was a student in the Business College at UT and a regular visitor to Tyson House. He was a prince of a person who was most gracious, loving, and always ready to offer help when it was requested. He often joined in our discussions and brought a calming tone to any heated argument that surfaced. As with Don, Newell and I have kept sporadic contact through the years, and we have recently reinforced the bond of friendship. A devoted Episcopalian, Do was instrumental in giving me a very personal view of how one person's devotion to the Church can affect another.

Do, Don, Chris Clements, Bill Senter, Warren Robertson, Meg Blackman, and Elizabeth Taylor, a lovely girl who was condemned to bear the same name as the actress, were a few of the Tyson group who particularly contributed to my understanding of Christianity, the Church, and interpersonal relations.

Digressing for a moment to bring a few issues into better focus, let's recall that while in Alaska, I had returned to the Anglican (Episcopal) Church after a hiatus of many years. The Air Force person who was most helpful was Elmendorf's Episcopal chaplain, Major Howard Bliss Scholten. By a "hiatus" I mean that not since 1947 had I been involved with the Church, although I had attended services, especially in Mill Valley, California, while assigned to the 666 AC&W Squadron atop Mt. Tamalpais. For all practical purposes I was a novice in the church and most of my religious education was through reading and research. I had never attended formal classes, which probably would have dulled my interest in God, Jesus, the Universe, and the lot of mankind in Creation.

At the age of 10, while in school in England, I had asked the visiting Anglican Archbishop of Jerusalem if he would baptize and confer upon me the laying-on-of-hands without my doing anything more than just asking. The Archbishop assured that he would. I explained to the Archbishop that the priest at St. Joseph's Roman Catholic Church demanded that I recite by rote the Lord's Prayer if I wanted to be baptized. I refused.

My refusal was based on the fact that I did not need to do anything to be accepted by God. Even at my young age I was convinced that God's love for me was not the result of barter. If reciting the Lord's Prayer was necessary in exchange for being baptized, then I would not be baptized or have anything to do with that kind of "church." Thus when the Archbishop assured me that he would act without my doing anything more than coming to Jerusalem, I decided that I would accept.

My future godfather, Ted Beadle, was in the RAF and reassigned to a RAF base near Jerusalem. We had already made arrangements for me to see him when I returned to Cairo for my first visit home after my initial two years in school at Victoria College, Trumpington, England. Jerusalem was just an 18-hour train ride from Cairo. Ted Beadle came to Cairo and returned with me to Palestine for the momentous occasion. We were accompanied by my mother who was more interested in the trip than in seeing me baptized by an Anglican bishop. My father was unable to come with us because of a commitment with teaching and a conference. I was happy to be baptized by the Archbishop of Jerusalem in the Jordan River. While still in the water, I received the laying-on-of-hands and was anointed with oil.

Being immersed in the Jordan River near Bet Ha-Arava is an unforgettable experience. I was in shorts and that was appropriate for the dip in the warm and muddy water. The Archbishop wore a thin alb over his shorts that took on the brown color of the muddy water. After the sacrament, a shower was appropriately prepared for us, after which we donned clean clothes for the reception to be held in Be'er Sheva, located several kilometers south of Jerusalem and Bethlehem, past the town of Hebron.

The reception was on a farm owned and operated by an American Jew who was a friend of Ted Beadle and the Archbishop, and was located not too far from the RAF base in Ofaqim. Ted Beadle, the driver, and my mother rode in the cab of a weapons-carrier truck, and the Archbishop and I rode in the truck bed that was covered with a flapping canvas cover. Ted had given me a box of chocolates for the occasion. The Archbishop and I in short order ate the entire half-kilogram box. Result: we both suffered from stomachaches and could not eat anything at the reception. Nevertheless, we all had a wonderful time, especially in the morning when the Archbishop and I made up for lost time with the food.

Parochialism Negated for Me

Back in Knoxville, many years after the Jerusalem event, conversations with Chaplain Holt continued on a regular basis and I began to learn more and more about what it was that attracted me to God, Holy Orders, and the sacramental world. There was an ordering of my thoughts through conversations, readings, and discussions as I learned more and more about what I believed, what was important to me, what the theology of the Episcopal Church adhered to, what was questionable to me, and what I was going to do about it. The theology that was professed by the Church and what I was beginning to piece together was discussed with Chaplain Holt and he was a very perceptive person. He recognized that I was inquisitive about life in the Church, life in a parish, and how I would handle my interests and needs that lay outside the ecclesiastical parochial mainstream. The Church attracted me but I was wary of the parochial and administrative prospects that accompanied it. Parochialism appeared to limit me as an effective and active person in the world of activities. Not wanting to be isolated from the currents of society or precluded from working in the commercial-industrial world, parochialism was a major concern to me. I had informed Holt of my concern that if the Church kept me away from my lay professional interests I would have problems.

Chaplain Holt suggested that I attend a conference that was to be held at the University of the South, at its St. Luke's Seminary. I was not quite sure why he wanted me to attend but I went anyway, especially because he had already registered and paid the necessary fees. It was a three-day conference planned to discuss the role of the ministry in the future of the world and of the Church. Under the direction of the Rt. Rev. Stephen Baynes, Bishop of Olympia, Washington, the conferees were all men who had one foot in the Church and another in secular work. Bishop Baines was a consultant architect and a member of the American Institute of Architects.

In attendance were A.T. Mollegen, priest, consulting engineer, and professor of systematic theology at Virginia Theological Seminary, VA; W.G. Pollard, priest, physicist on the Manhattan Project, researcher at Oak Ridge National Laboratory, and professor of physics at UT (and my professor); D. Miller, priest, consultant in space mathematics to the National Aeronautics and Space Administration (NASA), and professor of advanced mathematics at UT (and my professor); and J.A.Pike, Priest, newly elected dean of St. John's Cathedral, New York City, and consulting attorney to the US Supreme Court.

I was a student of both Pollard and Miller but I had not known that these two extraordinary professors were also active priests of the Church. I became friends with all of these men of stature and kept an active correspondence for many years until their deaths. In many ways, the conference shaped much of my thinking and fashioned much of my approach towards the priesthood: that ministry is akin to ambassadorship and is firmly planted in the world and is not limited or curtailed by the parochial priesthood.

Indeed, meeting these men and others at the conference was an eye opener. Chaplain Holt's perceptiveness was extraordinary. Although at times he appeared to be rooted in a traditional mode, he was often part of the leading edge of society. He understood that the parochial ministry was limiting to many and recognized that the secular ministry had an august position in the Church.

In many ways Chaplain Holt took steps that were not expected from a man who was one of a third generation of priests, who had never held a secular job, and who was a disciplinarian and a scholar. One instance is worth mentioning:

Racial segregation was the law of the land in Tennessee. There was a small Afro-American college in Knoxville that had no Episcopal chaplain; Chaplain Holt initiated a joint program to bring black students to Tyson House for Sunday events. This action caused some problems with the University, but soon the governors of UT were told that Tyson House was private property and anyone could enter the "house of God." Holt prevailed.

I also learned that Holt had been a mentor for both Pollard and Miller in their decisions to enter Holy Orders. At the time when these two men sought Holy Orders it was not common for candidates in secular work to continue as professionals and still function as priests for the Church. The non-stipendiary priesthood was still in its infancy.

The idea of heading to seminary was both attractive to me and frightening. Indeed, I wanted to explore more facets that made the Church tick, but the thought of spending time doing that rigorously rested heavily with me. Some decisions are not easy to make, especially those that will define one's life. I needed one more course in philosophy, a course in ethics, to complete the graduation requirements. The course would not be offered for three quarters and even though I could have substituted another course for it, I decided to wait it out to give myself time to think.

Entrance into a New Stage

I headed for Chicago in July 1959 to visit my mother. Mother had moved to Chicago to work in the accounting department of Helene Curtis Cosmetics after Olav died in 1957 of a heart problem. Olav's brother, whom I had met only once, had encouraged Mother to relocate from Passaic, New Jersey, to Chicago, where he could help her find employment. I'm not certain how much help Olav's brother gave her but she did find a good position and soon discovered that Chicago suited her very well.

Mother left Chicago in 1981 to relocate to San Mateo, California upon her retirement; she was never as happy in California as she appeared to be in Chicago. Unlike Chicago, the Bay Area is less traditional, less conservative politically, and difficult to manage without an automobile. She never learned to drive a car with confidence. Furthermore, the explicit racial mix present in California was a major problem for her. Apparently, while living in Chicago, on the North side, just off Michigan Avenue, she did not notice the mixture of races but in California the overt racial intermingling, the political liberalism, and the informality between people was difficult for her to accept.

My curiosity about seminary was sharpened during this hiatus away from UT, my move into inactive reserve from the USAF, and the wait for my last course to be offered by UT to complete my studies. In the mean time I accepted a research position with General Electric-Niehoff to explore new methods for extending the life of batteries. I called Father Therrel Holt to discuss the option of applying at the Church Divinity School of the Pacific (CDSP) for the fall term of 1959. He thought my application would probably be accepted even though I had not yet completed my work at UT.

In a later phone conversation Holt informed me that he had resigned as chaplain and had accepted a call as rector of St. Timothy's Parish Church, Signal Mountain, Tennessee. This parish had an active congregation in a town atop one of the mountains surrounding the city of Chattanooga. Transferring my Episcopal membership from Tyson House to St. Timothy's, Holt became my rector and hence no longer a "chaplain" to me. As my rector he was the clerical sponsor and mentor assigned to that task by the Bishop of the Diocese of Tennessee, the Right Reverend John Vander Horst.

The seminary informed me that I could begin my studies immediately in the fall semester of 1959, and when possible I could complete my pending course at UT, either during the summer or as a reading course. Dr. John W. Davis, my professor of philosophy at UT, was willing to work with me and offered me several options. Once the issue of completion of the last course was settled I was free to re-conquer California.

I packed my car and headed west to Berkeley, California and subsequently to experience seminary life. I was well received by the faculty of the CDSP and was introduced to the current intellectual giants of the Church and especially to one professor who would become my second mentor, Massey H. Shepherd Jr., Professor of Early Church History and Liturgics. Dr. Shepherd became not only a mentor, but also a friend, and, with his wife Gaby several years later, godparents to my children.

I also was introduced to Professors James Pritchard, Old Testament; Robert Rodenmayer, Homiletics; and Sherman Johnson, Dean and renowned New Testament scholar. Other faculty members were introduced to me, especially Greer Taylor, professor of Canon Law and Greek New Testament, a renowned authority on St. Paul, the Epistler. In addition I was introduced to Norman Mealy, musician par excellence, creative friend, and charming personality.

A Temporary U-turn

After settling in and attending several orientation meetings, I discovered that I was not comfortable in the environment of the religious community. On the third day I went to speak to both the dean and to Dr. Shepherd. I informed them that I was not quite ready for seminary life; could I obtain a "rain check" for a future date. They both agreed that I could leave, and if I so wished, I could return when I was ready. No disappointment was shown by anyone. Shepherd suggested that I take a few years to let the idea of Holy Orders simmer further. There was no rush, he advised me.

Into my packed car and off across the Sierra, I returned to Chicago. The trip to California had exhausted a good portion of my financial resources. Obtaining an immediate job was paramount.

While looking for employment and taking time to reassess my position, I was invited by friends of my mother to a party to celebrate the baptism of an infant. The child had been baptized at the Roman Catholic Cathedral of Chicago by the Roman Catholic legate of the Curia to America. The Curia is the administrative body at the Vatican by which the Pope governs the Roman Catholic Church.

At the reception, I was personally introduced to the legate, His Excellency Archbishop Julio Morello, who a few months later was elevated to the rank of Cardinal. He was visiting the United States to assess the projected needs of the Roman Catholic Church's complement of priests. After I was introduced to His Excellency as a potential candidate for Holy Orders, he was exceedingly interested and concerned about my interest, especially my connection with the Anglican Communion. Recognizing that I had returned from an abbreviated visit to the seminary where I had applied, he invited me to come to Rome to study for Holy Orders. Of course the Roman Church would pay all my expenses and I would be given several opportunities to use my talents — perhaps even receive a recommendation to be accepted in the Society of Jesus.

On several occasions after this initial overture Morello invited me to lunch and continued many attempts to move me away from the Episcopal Church. He was obviously not successful because I was not in the least interested in the Roman Catholic Church, the Jesuits, its theology, and its ethical posture. I disliked its teachings, its social point of view, its hierarchical approach to the solution of problems, and its assertion that it was uniquely endowed with God's authority on this planet.

I thanked Fr. Morello for his concern but firmly declined his offer. Rome was not for me because it offered a view of God that was limited, controlled, and too much under the audacious rule of the Pope and his minions. God for me was grand, enormous, superlative, extraordinary, all encompassing, and bigger than my conception of life on this planet, and in this solar system. My

God was too big to be limited and imprisoned by the frame of Roman Catholicism or even by Anglicanism. To me the earthly Church was a tool offering me a community for my relations with the divine; it neither defined God or Providence for me nor did it dictate my thinking.

At my last meeting with Fr. Morello, which took place at a dinner in the house of one of Mother's friends, he cautioned me that "only one priesthood was legitimate for the Church, and that one was ordained through the authority of Rome!"

I thanked him for his advice and concern but I was ready to challenge that position by proving that my eventual priesthood through Anglican channels would be as effective and as legitimate as his and the Pope's — if not more so. He refused to shake hands with me when I left that evening.

I continued to search for a job. One of my professors at the University of Tennessee, Dr. David King, a physicist who was quite involved with research, gave me a letter of introduction to the deputy director of a research program jointly funded by General Electric (GE) and BWX Technologies at Fermi laboratory under the management of the University of Chicago.

After phoning for an appointment, I headed 25 miles south of Chicago to DuPage County. When I arrived, the director had already been in conversation twice by phone with my professor and my previous supervisor at GE-Niehoff, and I was consequently offered a research job at the Argonne National Laboratory's Fermi Program (ANL). I accepted the offer and lived with Mother for two weeks.

After the second week with Mother, I moved to Evanston, north of Chicago and further from Argonne but commuted to a new laboratory facility that had been implanted in North Chicago, just off Lawrence Avenue. My responsibility in the laboratory was to monitor a few experiments performed at the Advanced Photon lab and to write narratives about them for public consumption, which explicitly implied that I needed to understand them first, myself.

While in Chicago, a small part-time job came my way through a friend at the laboratory. The job called for someone to help in writing obituaries for the *Chicago Tribune*. I was employed evenings with the Tribune for seven months and wrote more than 500 obituaries. The pay was small but the opportunity to be part of a major newspaper was magnificent. As a reward I was given several press passes to events and a special press pass to attend the 1960 presidential debate between John F. Kennedy and Richard M. Nixon. In total I had been unemployed for less than two weeks.

Odd Jobs and Courting

I worked at ANL until December 1960 and left to return to the University of Tennessee, when the new dean of the department of philosophy, Dr. John Davis, invited me to write the chapter on existentialism for his new book. With the $1,000 payment and the chapter written, which completed all requirements for my degree, I finished in March 1961. I reapplied at CDSP and was reaccepted for the fall semester of 1961. From March to September was a long time for idleness. I needed both money and a leap of faith to continue this educational venture.

I digress a bit to catch up on some history that is more pertinent at this point: with a bachelor degree and a double major in physics and philosophy and enough mechanical engineering under my belt, I searched for a temporary job. Alcoa was a known entity near Knoxville, and so I applied and asked for an interview. The interview went well and the fabrication department was interested in my work in 1957 with Prestolock, Garfield, New Jersey. I had returned to New Jersey when Olav died and had stayed during the summer to make certain that Mother was well cared for and comfortable living alone.

Through UT's summer employment office I had found a job to work at Prestolock Company to help design equipment for the manufacture of luggage, hangers, and their locks. The location was convenient because it put me close to Mother and allowed me to be creative in a totally new area. It was an enjoyable task that I found to be most rewarding and challenging. The head of the design department was Warren Brownstein, a most delightful, patient, creative, and paternal individual. I ended up working two summers at Prestolock, and enjoyed every minute of the time spent there.

After working a month at Prestolock, Warren asked me to look at a garment-hangers-bending machine for aluminum rods. The machine would form the rods but in the process would score the outside edges, which made it rough for hanging fine clothing such as wool, silk, or cotton. To add a sanding wheel to correct that problem was too cumbersome, would slow production, would never quite restore the original polish of the aluminum, and would produce a fair amount of aluminum dust which would have to be vacuumed out for removal.

I worked on that problem for a few days. I slipped rubber hose slices onto the rollers. I went to Warren and suggested that hard rubber wheels be manufactured to replace the current steel rollers to check if the scoring would disappear even if the rubber would have to be replaced after a number of operations. He accepted my idea but we had to test at least 1,000 hangers to see what would happen. Hard nylon rollers were installed to replace the steel and subsequent hangers were no longer scored. After the test of 2,000 hangers, the process became standard operating procedure and the scoring problem was resolved. Of course, the nylon wheels had to be replaced after each 2,200-batch of hangers — not an expensive or time-consuming solution. Warren gave me a raise in salary as a reward and two tickets to *Silk Stockings*, which was the hit of New York, starring Hildegard Neff as the Soviet operative.

After the hanger problem, Warren asked me to look at a new lock for a piece of lightweight luggage that was specifically designed for use by airline passengers. It would be made of leather or tightly woven synthetic material and with a metal structure made of aluminum, not only to reduce weight but also to allow the bags to go through the new airport conveyance belts without snagging. The problem now facing Prestolock concerned the locks. The contract required that the lock be light, strong, and able to withstand the possible abuse inflicted on luggage by baggage handlers. Luggage that opened when tossed caused several problems: articles had to be gathered or the conveying system jammed damaging not only the bag and its contents but also the equipment itself. All locks were traditionally made of steel and had internal steel mechanisms, such as tongues, latches, and springs.

"Why not make a lock of aluminum?" I asked. "Too complex," was the reply from the engineers. Locks, especially sturdy locks, had to be made of steel, the engineers were quick to remind both Prestolock directors and the client. Warren's position was to ask me to search for a solution to the problem. After all, as a summer hire I was not costing the company much and I could delve into areas that could be embarrassing to "professional" engineers when failures were encountered. In other words, I could make stupid mistakes and get away with them. I was merely a summer intern and quite dispensable.

With Warren's help, I learned that Prestolock had recently acquired the equipment to cast aluminum with the accompanying instruction documents but no one had done much with the process. I asked a die designer to design a mold for a two-piece specific aluminum body, but with three internal posts to be placed as supports for the upper piece. The experimental aluminum shell was cast, cleaned, and polished.

Now I had to develop the locking mechanism that would fit inside the two shells. I chose strong, hard, nylon-type material to create the mechanism. The nylon would be malleable, machinable, self-lubricating, and emitted no sound when engaged against another piece. The locking mechanism was anchored, as I envisioned, to an aluminum post protruding from the bottom shell cast.

The mechanism was checked by Warren and he liked it very much, especially the fact that I had chosen hard nylon for the mechanism. Using hard nylon reduced the production cost and was inexpensive. It was now necessary to find a way for both sections to be married permanently for the lock to withstand the wear and tear incurred by passengers, luggage handlers, and conveyor equipment. The cover would have to display the engraved name of Prestolock. It too was made of aluminum. That was the simple part. The difficult part would be to unite the cover with the bottom that held the locking mechanism.

Aluminum welding was in its infancy in the late 50s. Even aircraft manufacturers used rivets and avoided aluminum welding as much as possible. Aluminum was difficult to weld and the welding temperatures were difficult to manage because the temperature margin separating joining from melting was small. I wanted to weld three posts that would fit snugly into three holes with a snap — thus the covers could be separated in the event that repairs of the locking mechanism were necessary. Little did I anticipate that I would need to unsnap the lock so soon in a demonstration before the client.

For more than a week I literally fiddled with aluminum electric arc welding, often working well into the night and more often than not making a mess of the sample aluminum pieces. Finally, one early dawn around five, I phoned Warren at home and asked him to come over to the workshop. Suspecting that I was successful, he came right away to my work area and brought coffee and Kaiser rolls. I welded three different casings and each was perfect. He took pictures and asked me to write the details of the procedure. Within the week he had a drawing made of the parts and after presenting them to the Executive Committee of Prestolock for its approval by way of the legal department he sent the whole package to the Patent Office.

Two days later, Warren presented the final physical lock attached to a piece of luggage to the Executive Committee and to a client and received complete approval, except for a request to make one modification. Because it was a noiseless locking assembly, there wasn't the expected and customary closing "click" sound. That noiselessness disturbed several executive members and also the client. The consensus in the Executive Committee was that a lock had to emit a locking noise to ensure that it was operating well.

I was sitting on the sidelines listening to the discussion, hoping that the request would be resolved without my doing anything to the lock. I was also thinking of a simple way to produce a locking noise. Warren came over to me and said quietly,

"Raymond, I don't think the request will go away. Should we remove the new mechanism and replace it with one of the older ones?"

That would be impossible because the older mechanisms were made of steel, and joining steel to aluminum would cause electrolytic problems. I replied to Warren by clearly whispering, "No, I'll be back in a minute," and left the room.

Out of the conference room, I asked one of the secretaries if she had a plastic paper clip. No she did not. She had instead a plastic hairpin. "Would this do?" she asked. Indeed it would. After unsnapping the top from the bottom of the lock assembly, I inserted a piece of the plastic pin and wedged it firmly between the tongue latch and first aluminum post, making certain that a piece of the pin would rest against the wall of the section with the mechanism. Every time I moved the tongue latch it would snap the hairpin end against the wall. I closed the cover, using the welded retaining posts and receiving holes. Voilà! We had a click sound.

I went back into the conference room and handed the piece of luggage to Warren.

"Here, try it now."

He did several times, and then passed it around the table for each member to test. Every time it was locked, a click was heard. Now Prestolock had an aluminum lock that made a clicking sound!

Soon after that event, I left Prestolock but I stayed in touch with Warren until his death from a heart attack in 1961. Corporate America lost a good man when Warren Brownstein died.

And so ALCOA was impressed with my patent (Warren had put my name as the originator and designer of the aluminum lock for the Patent Office). In March 1961 Alcoa offered me a job in fabrication. Now that I had completed all requirements for graduation and had written a chapter on existentialism for a new book written by my professor, Dr. John W. Davis, it was time to consider a job to keep me solvent until I started seminary in October. I had also applied for a job with Combustion Engineering Co., Chattanooga, Tennessee.

When I returned to my apartment in Knoxville, I had a letter waiting for me from Dr. Ralph Smith, Vice President of the Nuclear Division of Combustion Engineering. His offer was just as good as Alcoa's: $8,500 per annum for 1961. That was an excellent salary. I declined Alcoa's and accepted Combustion's for several reasons: I would live on Signal Mountain, which was where the Reverend Therrel Holt was now rector of St. Timothy's Episcopal Church and I would be able to attend the services and participate in the life of the parish; beyond that, Dr. Massey Shepherd and his wife Gaby lived there for the summer with Gaby's sister who also was a member of the parish; moreover, with Combustion Engineering I would be involved in nuclear research and power generation (my interest in physics had been thermodynamics and particle acceleration). Physics was just entering the age of quantum mechanics and superstring and I was interested in their development, application, and exploration.

The work at Combustion was exciting and interesting, especially because my academic focus in physics had been in thermodynamics and my attention was now directed towards power generating plants. My first task was to work on the cooling piping for the Selni reactor in Italy, which required a short visit to Selni. At Selni my specific task was to ensure that cooling liquid in the pipes were not in anyway hampered; the valves, the bends, the pressure gauges, and temperature thermostats had to be perfect for the job of keeping the reactor operating at its most safe and efficient level to produce the electricity needed. Much as it appeared to be primarily a mechanical engineering project, in reality it required that the reactor's internal system was functioning as its physics specified. I spent approximately two weeks in Selni but did allow myself a few days in Florence and Siena to regale myself once again with the art of the Italian Renaissance.

This was a joint reactor built by Combustion and Westinghouse Electric with the Italian Trino Power Reactor firm. It was elegantly designed and quite state-of-the-art in its approach. In the final analysis, the cooling piping was exquisitely designed to the highest level of engineering. I learned a lot from this first experience, especially to see that good design can produce good and safe results.

My second assignment was to see why the cooling pipes in Hanford, Washington were cracking and leaking, even when new pipes replaced those damaged during operation. The new replacements would develop the same problem: cracking and/or pinholes. I was becoming a so-called expert in cooling piping.

I checked the drawings and rechecked the piping geometric calculations using the monstrous Monromatic calculator. That calculating machine was an impossible tool to use, and I never mastered it. To avoid using the monstrous Monromatic (a calculator designed by the devil), I purchased my own hand-held Texas Instrument advanced calculator. After rechecking all calculations, I asked several colleagues to examine the calculation and each one supported my results.

A Washington firm from the Seattle area and subcontracted to Combustion by government demand had designed the geometry of the cooling pipes. Because it was a government contract, I had to go to Hanford — even though I already knew the cause of the problem. The problem was bad piping geometry. It was not because I was a fantastic engineer or had superb experience. It was simply because I recognized a fault that had been overlooked by better people.

In one of my physics hydro courses, I had come to understand the cause of cavitation produced by the power of striking water when rapidly flowing and subjected to sharp turns. When water travels fast and is forced around tight curves or slung against hard surfaces, the water acts as a cutting tool and subsequently weakens the material that holds it in check, such as metal pipes.

This problem is often experienced by submarine crews when the power propeller (screw) is forced to accelerate rapidly before the submarine can move fast enough to attain the required speed; the screw rotates too rapidly and hence produces small water packets that pit the metal of the rotating blades.

In many mechanical tasks, water at high speed is employed as a cutting tool, especially for fine and intricate cuts. Hanford's piping designers had tightened the curving angle of the cooling pipes to increase their number with the thought that more pipes would increase the cooling effect for the reactor. Best would have been to reduce the number of pipes but increase their carrying capacity by enlarging their radii. At Hanford, the piping curve radii were small; therefore, the water produced severe cavitation that in turn produced cracks and pinholes, which resulted in severe leakage.

My report was submitted to my supervisor long before I visited the Hanford site. In fact, my visit was tantamount to a walk in the park. Upon my return to Chattanooga, Dr. Smith called me into his office and asked me why the report was dated the day "before" I arrived on site. He accepted my explanation and soon I was informed that the cavitation had ceased when new pipes with broader curving radii had been installed, and that cooling had improved. Often the neophyte seems to have all the luck because nothing is taken for granted.

Romance and More

While working at Combustion Engineering I also met Trudy Hale, a junior in English at UT. I used to make repeated trips to Knoxville, either to review galleys for Dr. Davis or to visit Tyson House friends. On a visit to Tyson House during the spring of 1961 I met a young, attractive blond named Trudy Hale who seemed pleasant, jovial, and interesting. I asked her out to dinner but she informed me that a friend was visiting her from Yale University. Trudy, after a pause of a few minutes, added that she would meet me for ice cream after her dinner date. I agreed.

Trudy (Mary Gertrude) was majoring in English and minoring in Spanish. She was also a fine musician, a very beautiful blond, and an Episcopalian. Her shyness was quite attractive and the fact that her life at home was miserable added to the drama of our relationship. It was remarkable that two people like us, with parents that were not too terribly engaged in the nurturing of their children would find common ground for marriage. I realized that we had a similar dislike for broken marriages and hoped that our common history with our parents would give us the means to make ours successful. Far from being a knight rescuing a lady, I was a common traveler with Trudy on the pathway to seek a more durable marriage. I think that, unfortunately, we both chased a rainbow.

We dated in the spring and summer of 1961. She invited me to Memphis where she lived with her paternal grandmother and grandfather.

Her father was in Haiti doing something with the bauxite mines. He had abandoned Trudy in more ways than can be enumerated. He had divorced Trudy's mother, Helen, several years earlier, then he had remarried and soon abandoned, without divorcing, his second wife. Trudy now was older sister to a half-brother and a half-sister.

At any rate, I went to Memphis on the overnight train from Knoxville. I immediately loved Trudy's grandmother. If Trudy would age that way and have the same temperament, then she could become a fine wife. But I was dead wrong to make that assumption. Dead wrong indeed.

The grandmother was a fine piano teacher who had been a teacher and mentor in Trudy's musical education. All the pieces fell nicely into place. I also was introduced to Trudy's maternal family and to Helen, her mother. Helen was a most attractive woman, a bit on the sexy side, charming, with a fine low voice, but also very irresponsible and immensely self-centered. She was a licensed practical nurse and lived with another woman by the name of Edith. I could not fathom the relationship, but that did not matter to me.

Unlike her grandmother, who was forever giving love to Trudy, Trudy duplicated her mother's attitude and was unconscious later of her children's lives, aspirations, and wellbeing. Trudy mimicking her mother was very much what gave her a center: her universe, a universe that was centered on her; totally divorced from reality, from other people, and from the effects of give-and-take relationships.

As a mother Trudy was minimally dutiful and sporadically dependable but expressed her love in a limited way — always placing herself at the forefront, and fulfilling her maternal obligations as if they were performed under duress or as favors to her children and to her husband.

Corrections and reprimands of the children were assigned to me, the father. The pattern was established without my consent but soon I discovered that it was my job to "correct the children" in their behavior. It was a role that I accepted as part of my supposed function as a father but that today I regret very much because it turned me into an avenging monster — the Arabic *babulah*, the devil, the evil enforcer.

Her matriarchal grandmother headed Trudy's maternal family. It was a pleasant family and one with which I could live — but at a great distance. There was a great interest in "metaphysical or spiritual" religion as some Episcopalians of one parish in Memphis adopted it. Helen and many of her siblings supported this mode, this trait of personalized religion sprinkled with punishment for acts performed, exorcism for satanic visitation, and visions of a creation that was neither forgiving nor redeemable. God was a harsh judge who wielded his authority with little mercy and certainly with no mercy for those who did not walk the line of righteousness.

Trudy was prone to view her Christianity in the same light, as did her maternal family. It was only for a short time and under the influence that I brought to bear that Trudy lightened up. Yet I was often convinced that she did not like my Christian orientation, liberal approach, or view of creation.

My Christian liberalism was emerging daily and moving rapidly away from the traditionalism of Southern biblical fundamentalism. The Episcopal Church in Tennessee was inclined towards some theological conservatism but it was becoming more open, more inclusive, and more accepting of new thoughts. With the changes brought about by the global Anglican conference on Mutual Responsibility and Interdependence (MRI) and the effect of Pope John XXIII's Vatican II liberal movement in the Roman Catholic church, Christian theology was beginning to be remolded in new thoughts that reflected a more graceful and loving God. The Episcopal Church was in transformation both theologically and liturgically.

I don't believe that Trudy accepted the change that was being manifested in me. She did not accept the epiphany of liberalism that was beginning to show itself in my common conversations, my homilies, my theological and philosophical expositions, and my attitude to the Church, its canons, its authority, and its rigidity to changes.

I courted Trudy both in Knoxville and in Chattanooga while I worked at Combustion. I introduced Trudy to Therrel Holt and to his family and to a few members of St. Timothy's congregation. It was a lovely spring and a fair summer in East Tennessee, and I had a good time courting, working, and living on Signal Mountain.

One clear moonlit evening while enjoying a picnic on the shore of Chickamauga Lake by the dam of the same name, I proposed marriage to Trudy. She accepted immediately. Except for the mosquitoes, the evening had been a happy one.

Had I rushed into a marriage because of reasons that were not well thought out and to a woman who was not quite in command of her personal worth? Had I missed the opportunity to help Trudy and in so doing to develop a solid, loving, and lasting marriage? I didn't know. Years later I would.

Going West to California

After resigning from Combustion Engineering, I headed for Memphis to say goodbye to Mrs. Hale, Trudy's grandmother, and to see Bishop John Vander Horst, my diocesan bishop. Bishop Vander Horst took me to lunch at the Peabody Hotel and after that we went to his office to be briefed and to be given his blessing. The bishop was concerned that I was going to the west coast where clergy wore grey suits, invented strange ceremonies, and rubbed elbows with the likes of that rebel James A. Pike, bishop of the Diocese of California. Bishop Vander Horst informed me that he would keep close watch on me.

We got along very well throughout the years I served in his cure but he liked a heated discussion with me every so often, especially one touching on politics. Prior to leaving for California the next day, I was invited to spend the night at his house and to be his guest at dinner, where a Republican candidate for the US Senate would join us.

Before dinner, Howard Baker, the senatorial candidate, joined us and we all had bourbon and branch water. Mr. Baker was very interested in my theological and political perspective, as was the bishop. Why was I a Democrat who looked favorably on Senator Barry Goldwater? How could I have voted for John F. Kennedy instead of Richard M. Nixon, the proven Vice President and Khrushchev's debater?

In response, I asked Mr. Baker how a bright person like himself could be a Republican centered only on avoiding responsibility for the less fortunate and unable to comprehend the intricacies and dynamics of economic processes? Moreover, how could he willingly ignore the racial issues facing America? How could he continue as a member of a mean-spirited group?

Our discussion carried us well into the early hours of the morning but no resolution surfaced from it. At any rate, it was a fine evening and morning and I enjoyed sparring with Howard Baker. I believe that on that particular night I rejected permanently any respect for the Republican Party, the Grand Old Party. I recognized that Goldwater's approach was honest, honorable, and not entirely faulty. To me Goldwater was a conservative politician who did not pander to the basest form of political thoughts such as racism, disenfranchisement of the poor, and the isolation of America from the world's arena. Yes, he did threaten to drop nuclear bombs on the North Vietnamese, but no one thought that he was serious or that he would do it if he became President. He was the last and only member of the Republican Party that I supported by a vote.

A few years later, when I visited Washington D.C. and phoned Mr. Baker, he invited me for dinner and gave me a detailed tour of the Senate and an introduction to my favorite Republican senator from Illinois, Baker's father-in law, the man with the golden and throaty voice, Everett Dirksen. Much as I enjoyed that evening with Baker and Dirksen, neither one was successful in convincing me to support the GOP.

Back to now mid-August 1961, when I left Memphis in a small black Volkswagen (I had sold my grey 10-year-old and worn out Ford Six) for Berkeley and life in seminary at the Church Divinity School of the Pacific, Berkeley, California. This time I completed the three-year program and received my master's degree.

I suspect that my attitude had changed and my view of seminary had been altered immensely. Could it be that I had matured in my commitment, belief, and purpose? It could also be that the Church's position had been modified so much that I could feel comfortable with its new stance on its effect on society, its involvement in the management of human affairs, and its open sacramental posture.

Berkeley, California was beginning to emerge as the center of controversies, of new ideas, and new approaches to government. Women were taking a more active role in society and it was no longer assumed that they were lesser human beings. In the Episcopal Church women were moving into holy orders. Racial discrimination was beginning to be seen as a cancer gnawing on the very fabric of American society. Young people in Berkeley were voicing their opinion to liberalize politics, to move against the Vietnam War, against racism, against the foray of Nixon's attempt to become governor, and in support of Caesar Chavez's drive to improve the lot of the farm workers. It was an extraordinarily dynamic time where nothing was considered impossible to accomplish.

It was also the era of the drug explosion where marijuana, LSD, heroin, cocaine, speed, and other intoxicants were rampantly consumed with devastatingly fatal results to many users. Yet in spite of the drug issue there was vitality, a hope, and an expectation that the future was controllable, if not manageable, and that it could produce good results. John F. Kennedy's Camelot administration was youthful, progressive, and enchanting — at least on the surface.

I concentrated completely on my new venture. I resigned from the Air Force, stopped flying, and moved totally into the arena of the Church, its life, its thinking, its attitude, its mission. I was determined to immerse myself fully in the intellectual aspect of the Church.

I must admit that I was unconcerned about the mundane gymnastics of churchiness. Spirituality as a methodology to obtain whatever one obtains left me cold and uninterested. I was eager to improve the approach to prayer, but I understood prayer to be a conversation, nay even a discussion, with God (still undefined).

In the liturgy, I saw the validity of prayer stated quite clearly as a corporate means of communicating with the Creator but the private approach needed something else. In examining several options for defining private prayer, I soon returned to the one I felt more comfortable with and that was a form of discussion with God — and at time an argument, when necessary.

It was also a struggle for me to understand evil and its various ramifications. How did injustice, suffering, cruelty, racism, terminal and incapacitating illnesses, and accidental death fit in the worldview of a benevolent God? Was there a reasonable explanation to my questions? Would I be privy to the answer?

It was not a question of absorbing the dogmatic offering of the ecclesiastical hierarchy, but it was definitely a search for understanding. I was not stupid and neither was God. In my study of physics and of philosophy I had been convinced that the universe is a reasonable entity. If God was the "manager-creator" of the universe, then to quote Einstein, "God does not play dice!" There is a systematic framework for the universe and in that frame one locates God. But what image, if any exists, of God does one muster?

To understand what image I could fashion, I had to draw upon my whole philosophical and physical store of knowledge. I just could not, and still cannot, envisage God as a human being. The concept of God that surfaced more often was more akin to a formula, an event, an harmonious impression, a perception of a simple but powerful source of energy; something more powerful than the human understanding, explanation, and experience of love.

Obviously I reckoned that there was a clear distinction between God and Jesus. Sonship for me was neither paternal nor filial in its exposition but universal for all human beings but with specificity for Jesus. In other words, the uniqueness of Jesus' relationship with God is definite in the Sonship context, but human beings also have access to that Sonship. Now, what about the reality of evil in light of what has just been said? That's a problem that has taken much consideration on my part and that I'll discuss later.

Seminary was a happy and enjoyable experience. My class was made up of mature and bright people, most of who had worked in the "cold, cruel" commercial world, and all were ready to learn. We were a collection of top quality brains searching for answers and evaluating them when we obtained them. Nothing was accepted on face value. For example, we all questioned anything that was dogmatic in theology, preferring systematic or philosophical theology rather than dogmatic or moral.

In fact I categorically refused to take an elective course in moral theology, opting instead to do a reading course in ethics with Jim Pike, now the new Diocesan Bishop of the Diocese of California. The dean and faculty of CDSP approved a program of study I had prepared with Bishop Pike. The course had been designed to last a whole year, or three academic quarters. The study of ethics was not new to me; at UT I had had several courses and read a great many books on the subject. The reading course with Jim Pike was exciting and most rewarding, and the reading bibliography that we developed was most enriching.

On one occasion I met Jim in Sonoma at the Diocesan Bishop's Ranch, a center often used for conferences and retreats. We were not scheduled to have a session on ethics during the retreat at the Ranch. It so happened that after dinner, Bishop Pike took me for a walk on the property to discuss what I had read and some issues that were making news at the time. The Vietnam conflict, the assassination of Kennedy, the weak economy, the Cuban missile issue, abortion, and racism were a few of the "hot" topics open for deliberation.

It was a moonlit night, warm but with a slight ocean breeze. We walked, sat, and talked throughout the night. He smoked cigarette after cigarette, pack after pack, and we still discussed. It was only when the breakfast bell rang at seven a.m. that we realized that the whole night had been spent in conversation. I was exhausted. He was not. The quiet night had been spent exploring many facets of ethics with a person whose mind was perpetually delving, focusing, analyzing, and then reaching out just beyond the very edge of ethical boundaries. Pike was a pioneer, just as much as Joseph Fletcher who coined the term "Situation Ethics" in his seminal book by the same name. Pike, however, was the one who reached beyond the boundaries and stepped onto the uncharted territory ahead — dangerous as that might be, Pike never flinched but invited others to follow him.

The point that was crystallized in both my conversation with Pike and my reading of Fletcher and others of the same ilk indicated that ethics is fundamentally a "social lubricant" to facilitate human interrelations. Codified ethical approaches (such as "moral" codes) are self-defeating because the human being is forced to live by systems that are obviously of human origins but ascribed to be generated by ultimate good sources such as God, the Pope, a civil authority, or a majority vote devising a law.

In other words, the giver of the code is attributed to be an all-knowing creature, a god, when in reality it is a person who assumed that role. Divine revelation is given credit for being the conduit through which the code was received. In such a case who can argue for or against such a given code? How have the Ten Commandments been given to human beings and from what authority?

Moreover, human failings are categorized in workable order, are anticipated in expected form, and are dealt with in standardized manner, which assumes that all failings have a universal commonality. Individuality is precluded and what emerges from individuality is ignored. "Aren't we human beings all the same after all?" goes the saying. Indeed, we are not quite the same.

Of course there are many ethical issues that have a common root and are connected by a common thread. But there are many that do not. Each human being engages a new situation differently and quite often in his or her life. And that's not all. We interact differently with different people, and at different times in our aging lives. On top of that, circumstances, coincidences, and randomness affect all of us at different times and in different ways. One solution just does not resolve all problems. Each situation is in reality quite different from another, just as each human being is quite different from another. That is what the content of situation ethics suggests. Approaches to ethical solutions must be dynamic and suitable for each situation, each human being, each occasion. In ethics issues discretion is the better part for resolving a problem.

Seminary Mentors

When I was a student the faculty at CDSP was first class. In fact it was the envy of all seminaries. Because the faculty of CDSP was superb the Regents of the University of California were willing to have the University of California at Berkeley become associated with CDSP and, eventually, with the Graduate Theological Union, which was in its formative phase.

As for my mentors, because I've already mentioned Bishop James Pike, I will not dwell on him even though he measured greatly in my quest for understanding the Church, its purpose, and ethics as a system for understanding life as it is lived — and without Emmanuel Kant's "ought" that was commonly superimposed on society.

Dr. Massey H. Shepherd Jr. headed the list of mentors. Shep, as he was known, was professor of Liturgics and Church History, and was recognized by most Christian scholars as the leading liturgical authority alive.

Married to a first class artist, a painter and dramatist, Gaby Shepherd, he often entertained a few seminarians in his home in Berkeley. Good food and play readings were the fare of the evening. Shep would often read passages from plays with a German, French, Italian, or Russian accent, and these imitations were crisp and as near to the authentic language as humanly possible.

Shep was also my guiding light during seminary and even after graduation. To a great degree, it was Shep who influenced me to study for a doctorate and use liturgics as a staging subject to understand creativity, aesthetics, art, and process thought.

Shep was also instrumental in helping me formulate a sensible prayer life and an intimacy with God.

"Speak with God and not to God," he would remind me.

"Don't tell God what to do or how to do it, that's insulting and ultimately diminishes your relationship with God — as you say, 'who ever *that* might be?'."

"Remember that God responds to His Creation. He is neither immune to action nor is He unable to participate in the process of Creation."

"Responding to Creation affirms the dynamic being and denies that God is static, unchanging, and unwilling to make a change — if and when it is necessary."

This understanding of God as a dynamic entity was not current parlance in Christian theology. By and large, theologians suggested that God was unmovable and unchanging. In a sense, Christians were afraid to address and confront a dynamic and processive God. A static god is much easier to handle. For Shep, liturgy was an open and corporate (the work of the people) response to God's active participation in the Universe. The response was a confrontation with nothing less than the Holy, in the world, in creation, in us, in me!

Massey Shepherd was introduced to my class as "the personification of the Incarnation." Gaunt and always appearing as a possible model for an El Greco portrait, Shep stood before us as one who was obviously the personification of wisdom, grace, holiness, and knowledge. Yet Shep was always approachable, always ready to sit in a cafe to discuss an issue over espresso or wine. More than that, I shall never forget being invited several years later while I was working in Rancho Cordova, to spend the night in his home during a conference being held in Berkeley.

It was early morning, perhaps 7:00 a.m., when Shep knocked at my door to ask how I wanted my eggs cooked for breakfast. I was going to eat eggs cooked by Shep! Now that was an honor. It was a wonderful breakfast with sunny-side-up eggs, hash brown potatoes, sausage patties, and freshly-made-by-Shep South Carolina cathead biscuits. Shep donned the cook's apron because Gaby and her daughter Nancy were in Tennessee during that period.

Gaby was a delightful person, a southern lady with the corresponding accent and customs. An artist with numerous watercolor paintings to her name, Gaby was also a fine theater actress and director. It was Gaby's custom to invite seminarians to her home once a week to read a play and to be regaled with her cooking. Her daughter Nancy, who was still of high school age, often joined the reading group. Shep also participated by taking a part. I looked forward to the Wednesday evening play-readings at the Shepherds as a rewarding break.

Shep solemnized my marriage with Trudy in 1963 and when it fell apart in the late 70s, he was saddened that it hadn't been lasting or happy. We had several long conversations about marriage and the breaking down of relationships. Fault was never an issue. Human beings were not perfect and therefore relationships were not perfect. He saw no redeeming purpose for maintaining untenable relationships. That was a great help for me but for years I have not quite accepted the fact that the marriage was not sustained.

Professor Norman Mealy was a musical genius, a thinker, a humorist, and a delightful friend.

Being fundamentally a musical ignoramus, I treasured the pointers that Norm gave me to help me manage plainchant and the music of hymns.

Norm also gave me the temerity to handle hard questions on social topics and theological questions with the use of dialogues. I could write a dialogue between two or more speakers to explore an issue. For example I wrote dialogues discussing salvation, grace, holiness, sin, and the thoughts in a monologue that went through the mind of a prisoner a few minutes before being executed. This last was so well received by Norm that he asked me to read it during chapel Evensong while he accompanied me with music that he composed. Many in the congregation made up of faculty, students, and visitors were in tears when we finished the reading and the music.

Norman Mealy and his wife, Margaret, were the musical inspirations for the Episcopal Church's revision of its music during the early 70s. "Sing for Joy," a book of folk songs for the Church written by Norm and Margaret, was so successful that it moved the Church's Standing Hymnal Committee to accelerate the publishing of the new hymnal in the late 70s. Unfortunately, Norm, a member of the Committee, died at a relatively young age before the new Hymnal was published. He was not mentioned in the Preface of the Hymnal for his extraordinary work, obviously a sin of omission!

Sunji Nishi, chaplain at UC Berkeley for many years, professor of Philosophical Theology at CDSP, and a prince of a person was my support when I rebelled against the course in dogmatic theology and its professor.

To me dogmatic theology was another way of saying that certain pronouncements by the church were inviolable. The church, being a microcosm of society, is plagued by human frailties, especially when it describes God or makes pronouncements about what is supposed to be God's teachings, moral laws, and definitions of creation. In truth, dogmatic theology denies deductive reason. As for inductive reason, the pronouncements of dogmatic theology are based on faulty or unsubstantiated premises.

Nishi allowed me to work in theology through the discipline of philosophy. Hegel, Kant, Kierkegaard, Whitehead, Robinson, Tillich, and other giants were my sub-mentors helping me to travel the circuitous paths used when thinking of God and creation.

Samuel Garrett, historian and dedicated teacher who taught European history in the early 60s, had never set foot outside the United States of America.

Father Sam, as he was fondly called, had received his PhD from Harvard, had been a student of Shep, and often was scholar in residence at UC Berkeley.

On the faculty at CDSP since the mid-50s, he taught in detail the history of the Church in Europe (and in the USA). It was amazing to me that he had never visited the places he described so admirably in detail.

Father Sam also helped me expand my learning by including me in a weekly book discussion group at his house with members of UCB's faculty. For my third meeting it was my assignment to present a paper on Hegel's view of the universe. That I was scared hardly describes my inner feelings of ineptitude.

I wrote my paper and asked Father Sam to review it. He did and made just two suggestions: "Read it slowly, and type it in triple space!"

The presentation was a hit. The questions were difficult, and many that were posed produced long discussions, arguments, and controversies. The group decided that another meeting was necessary to explore further what had surfaced at the first attempt.

Several years later, in early 1984, I was asked by then-Bishop Shannon Mallory of the Diocese of El Camino Real to present a paper on "The Need and Purpose of a Cathedral." This was the time when the new diocese of El Camino Real was separated from the jurisdiction of the diocese of California in 1980 and was trying to define itself and its needs.

Two or three papers were read before my turn arrived. My presentation emphasized the role of the bishop, the episcopal presence with his seat in the see, the diocese. At the completion of my address I called for questions. A few were asked. One question asked about the location and the means for building such an expensive facility. I answered by suggesting that the whole diocese accept the responsibility for building the cathedral just as was done in early times, and that perhaps the cathedral could be located on a hill that did not impinge on the agricultural community that was a major part of the constituency of the diocese.

Father Sam was the next speaker and I was both thrilled and embarrassed when he alluded to my presentation several times to support his points. This was quite complimentary to have my past teacher and former mentor refer to my thoughts as authoritative sources.

Father Sam was a wise, humble, and loving person who was not bothered by an ego. He had readily admitted that travel had not come his way because studies and family needs had precluded any opportunity for foreign visits. In later years, long after I finished seminary, he had taken a year's sabbatical from CDSP to travel to Europe, Asia, and South America.

In fact, while I was in Cambridge in 1973, I received a phone call from Father Sam. He was in London and would be coming to Cambridge for a few days. I found him a suite in King's College and devoted two days to showing him Cambridge and Ely, especially the Cathedral. It was my privilege to act as his tour guide and to introduce the good Dr. Samuel Garrett and his wife to members of the faculties of several colleges.

Post-Seminary Time

Trudy and I were married at the end of my second year in seminary in St. Margaret's Chapel. The celebrant was Massey Shepherd, the organist was Norman Mealy, and the harpist was Barbara Payne (wife of Claude Payne, later the Bishop of Texas), the best man was Wallace Sprague, and the attending bridesmaid was Grace Langfeldt.

Mrs. Gaby Shepherd and Mrs. John Williams (wife of the recently deceased rector of St. Mark's Parish Church, Berkeley) hosted a champagne and caviar reception for the wedding party.

Our honeymoon was spent in Carmel, Las Vegas, Flagstaff, and Memphis. We drove our black VW to Tennessee, then on to North Carolina before returning to California. When all the dust settled and after we had visited Trudy's family and some of our friends in Tennessee and North Carolina, she started a teaching job in September 1963, first in Calistoga and then in Napa.

Dominique, our daughter, was born in Napa at the end of my senior year, May 1964. Dominique was a fine, noisy, and hungry baby who entered the world just two weeks before my comprehensive examinations and three weeks before my canonical examinations.

After I graduated from CDSP, Trudy, Dominique, and I headed for Tennessee, again in the black VW, to start life as a clergy family in the Episcopal Church. I was made a deacon by Bishop William Evans Sanders in June 1964 and assigned to St. Mary's Cathedral for the deacon-in-training program. We moved to Memphis to an apartment rented by the Cathedral and began to set up housekeeping. After years of living on the good graces of others, such as funds remaining from the GI Bill, support from St. Timothy's Parish, and gifts from individuals and from the diocese of Tennessee, I was finally earning a paycheck; although it was small, it was an income that I earned.

The 14 months in Memphis were difficult but presented me with many learning opportunities. My relationship with Trudy at times was difficult, but the environment was not easy for her either as a new clergy wife and mother. I knew little of the practical aspects of being a priest, even less about being a husband or father. I was feeling my way in a totally strange setting.

Church was not something that was part of my culture; philosophically, theologically, and liturgically I was on secure ground, but all the other stuff known as "priest craft" made my head swim in a rough sea of confusion. Perhaps because the tasks assigned to me were new and unfamiliar, I gave more time to understanding and carrying out that part of my life than to the husbanding and fathering part. My days were overflowing with demands. I will never forget that during my deaconate of 14 months I buried 75 people, including Trudy's maternal grandmother. Indeed, I felt as if my new profession was that of a mortician.

The good part of this whole experience was that I could draw on good support and practical help from William Dimmick, the dean of St. Mary's Cathedral, Dr. Massey Shepherd, Therrel Holt, my mentors, and many friends such as Robert Watson, George Khunert, the assistant of the Dean at the Cathedral, and Dan Matthews (assistant at Holy Communion in Memphis and a fellow CDSP graduate).

May 1, 1965, on the feast of St. Philip and St. James, I was ordained priest by Bishop John Vander Horst and was sent to St. Mark's Church in Copperhill, Tennessee — a mission church of my choosing, located in the heart of copper mining Appalachia. This location was not exactly what

Trudy, a native of Memphis, considered to be an upscale living environment. We had our differences, but we both hoped to resolve them in due time. Unfortunately, many of those differences were never resolved but were left to become insurmountable problems in later years. From the genesis of our courting Trudy knew that I was headed for the priesthood; she did not know me as an active pilot; she did know me as one who might go into airline work; and she certainly did not know me as one who would one day end up working in industry. Trudy had been forewarned that I probably would never be wealthy and certainly that I did not seek wealth.

Trudy did not like being a clergy wife, and more than that, she did not appear to like the Church, the liberal theology that I ascribed to, and my role in it. I am not quite sure what Trudy wanted or what she would have found to make her happy, if anything. It was impossible for me to identify a few issues that could make her happy. Nothing was sufficient, good enough, or agreeable for her. There was always a "but" in anything offered to her.

Appalachia was fun for me. I enjoyed the work, the people, and the challenge. St. Mark's was a "company" church situated in a "company" town and nurtured by "company" employees, mostly upper management people. I soon determined that the mission needed to become a local church for the whole community.

At the time of my arrival, the Tennessee Copper Company's upper management directed the affairs of the congregation and, I learned, also all past vicars assigned to the church. Indeed, it was a company church in a company town run by an overbearing, elitist, and highly discriminatory company. By the time I left, it was no longer a company mission church but a church for the local residents, many of whom were not affiliated with the company. I was also involved with the Federal government's effort to upgrade the living and economic conditions of the Copper Basin, an area that covered Western North Carolina, Northern Georgia, and Eastern Tennessee — three states, three counties, and three dioceses.

The Copper Basin gave me a group of lifelong friends who communicate with me to this day. Several people have shared their lives with me and we have continued the bond of friendship without interruption throughout the years since 1965. The Finch family, the Postelle (especially Grace) family, the Abernathy (especially Doris) family and the Quintrell (especially Roy) family, have all acknowledged me as their friend. Sandra and Buddy Finch and their youngest daughter Martha have kept up a current correspondence with me peppered with occasional visits to my home, the Goose and Turrets B&B, in California.

Serving Copper Appalachia was a most rewarding experience for me, an experience I cherished. I love the people who live in the mountains of Copper Appalachia; I enjoy their customs, their speech, their food, their history, their independence, their wisdom, and their culture. Perhaps I was accepted by the residents of Copper Appalachia (a notoriously private enclave) because I was a foreigner, neither a Northerner nor a Southerner but French. They had no historically correct position with regard to Frenchmen. Therefore they accepted me as an okay person until proved otherwise. It was, indeed, a tremendously positive position from which to move on.

In 1969, we moved to Rancho Cordova, east of Sacramento, California. The purposes of this move were for me to begin my doctorate program, for Trudy to resume her teaching career, and for Dominique to attend better private schools. Michel was born in Copperhill in 1967 and was still too young for school, but Dominique was of age for school and at the time schools in Appalachia were not quite what we considered to be top institutions.

But the primary reason was that I could not work on a doctorate in an area that particularly interested me in Appalachia, Nashville, or Atlanta. I looked carefully at Vanderbilt University as a possibility, but I could not find a suitable faculty in either the philosophy or art departments to help me develop a program that could please me. Bishop Sanders even proposed I take the position of chaplain at Vanderbilt, but that did not help me with my program problem, which was specific in that it married aesthetics, liturgy, and process philosophy in one package. So, I accepted an offer through my friend Wallace Sprague to take the vicar's position at St. Clement's, Rancho Cordova, California — approximately 100 miles from Berkeley, where the Graduate Theological Union (GTU) and the University of California were located. I knew the difficulty that I would encounter in the Diocese of Northern California with its bishop, but the risk and the challenge were worth it, or so I thought.

St. Clement's Mission, Rancho Cordova, was part of the Diocese of Northern California and was located a few miles east of Sacramento. St. Clement's was a new kind of challenge. As much as in Tennessee Bishop Sanders was enormously supportive of the work I did, the Bishop of Northern California, Clarence Rupert Haden, was not. I was not quite what he had hoped to get when he offered me a position in his diocese.

My liberalism, interest in liturgical changes, and my intellectual focus towards further education came into play and my relationship with the Bishop soon deteriorated rapidly after my arrival at St. Clement's. I was too socially active; the bishop wanted me to live in the cocoon spun by the Diocese. I was a political liberal; he was a political conservative. Liturgy was my passion; it was of no interest to him. Because the vicarage was less than adequate I wanted to purchase my own house but he was opposed to the idea of clergy owning their own houses. My obedience was tempered with reason; he wanted absolute unquestioning obedience. I was the wrong person for what he wanted.

The congregation supported me to the very end. Several have remained my dear friends to this day. Finally, I was fired. Trudy did not approve of either my attitude nor of the fact that I had no job but was merely a student pursuing a doctorate in some "obscure" area of art — a discipline that had no long-term value for lucrative employment in her eyes. I empathized with her difficult and uncomfortable position yet I could not be any more helpful because I could see that my pursuit was a valid quest for the long haul. At least it was for me.

After leaving Rancho Cordova in May 1971, Trudy found a teaching position in Merced and we all moved to that central valley town. Later that summer, I found an apartment in Oakland, and obtained a good research grant to fund much of my studies and to cover all of my household expenses. That the family was split between Merced and Berkeley was not the best situation but it was not the worst either. Trudy and I had some serious marital problems and we felt that the geographical separation would help us see our problems more clearly and hence help us resolve our differences more readily. That was not to be but we did add a few more years to our frayed marriage.

As for Trudy and Raymond's marriage, what was the problem? Why was our marriage frayed? When did indications that problems existed first surface?

It was early in the marriage that several problems materialized to affect our relationship. Many of these problems perhaps were caused by my search for some routine, some practical understanding, and some coherent approach to the profession that I had selected. Moreover, there was much in me that needed support because I was, for all intents and purposes, a new Episcopalian; I was also — and still am — an incurable philosopher. Thinking is my normal pastime. Trudy did not savor a good thought, an idea, a concept. It was on our honeymoon when Trudy entered the swimming pool after we had had a discussion on ethics in politics, a subject that was deemed irrelevant by her, when I thought to myself, "What have I done?" I was as much shocked by my question as by the idea that I had married Trudy.

Trudy saw the world quite differently than I. Her world had no intrinsic value other than it was hers to manipulate as she pleased. For me the world and the universe were special, precious, and holy. Added to that was the fact that for me the world is and has always been sacred. Food, material things, books, and art matter a great deal to me — hence "things" do make a difference to me.

None of what I considered important to me, vital to my life, mattered much to Trudy. Her standard and usual comment to something that was important to me, such as a concept, a political position, an idea, a house, an artistic form, the car, a bottle of fine wine, a well-crafted martini, an excellent dish or meal, was "what difference does it make." I'm sorry to say that this comment ignited my temper. At first I simply ignored the comment but when I discovered that it was coupled with Trudy's implicit and explicit self-centeredness and that she meant it, I could no longer discount it. Over the years this indifference became a chasm between us that grew deeper and wider to the point where it could no longer be bridged.

I was at a loss to make myself understood to her. I ached for some sign that she understood what was affecting me. The search for understanding the mystery of God, church, liturgy, art, universe, love, relationship, and friendship — even that was foreign to Trudy and a good example was how she abandoned Rebecca Moore Bell Jernigan, who was her friend long before I entered the picture — were distant and unimportant issues for Trudy. If these issues and these friendships were important to Trudy it was never apparent to me, and no signs from her offered any indication that she was sharing or even aware of the concerns.

I must admit that understanding Trudy was a problem for me. Perhaps we spoke in different languages.

The night at a clergy meeting when I confronted Bishop Haden because he wanted to move the diocesan office to Cameron Park was what put me irrevocably in his enemies' box. The issue was that currently the diocesan office was a stone's throw from the State Capital, but moving it to Cameron Park, a large piece of property developed by the golfer Arnold Palmer, would mean that the bishop's office would be located 30 miles from the center of Sacramento. It would be in a development where the wealthy could land and taxi their corporate jets into the hangars adjacent to their homes, play golf on a pristine course, drink and have dinner in an exclusive, high-end clubhouse, and be completely removed from the less fortunate working stiffs who had to live in the capital. It made it obvious that the church was supporting the flight from the inner city and was henceforth identifying itself with the suburban wealthy escapees.

I objected to the move from the Capital to the distant suburb. I raised the point vehemently and received support from the clergy. The Bishop accused me of sedition and ordered me to shut up. I did, but it was too late for him because the clergy that evening ultimately voted unanimously against any proposed move.

When I returned home and related the issue to Trudy, her comment was that I should have kept my mouth shut. Perhaps I should have. By confronting Haden I added fuel to my being dismissed as vicar, but I couldn't and wouldn't have kept silent. Should I have been more concerned about the future of my family? Should I have been less concerned about the diocesan move, political involvement in local affairs, taking my congregation to see musicals, indicating that the Vietnam conflict was a mistake for America, making a woman's right to choose abortion an issue for the church, the move for revising the 1928 Prayer Book relevant to Episcopalians, and admitting women to the ranks of acolytes, lay readers, and holy orders? On these issues I could not keep my mouth shut.

I so much wanted Trudy to stand by my side. I wanted to discuss issues that mattered to me with her, my wife. I also wanted to hear her position, to make things better for her, to understand what I could do to bring pleasure to her, make her happy, and to let her live a full life. All that proved to be impossible. My failure was obvious and culminated in the inevitable dissolution of our marriage.

Any attempt on my part to develop a more caring relationship fell on deaf ears. Trudy was living in her own world and any connection to me, to the children, or to reality was limited, at least as far as I could recognize it, which I didn't. She taught school, obtained her credentials in Library Science, eventually received her master's; all these activities were of interest to me and received my sincere support.

As for my own doctoral work, however, she showed no indication of interest and offered no support. For the work I contributed to the new Prayer Book and to the liturgical renewal of the Diocese of California, Trudy appeared to care not at all. When I confronted her with her indifference, her attitude and reply indicated that she was too busy to pay attention to what I was doing. My pursuits for the doctorate were of little value because they would not bring in a sizable income.

When I developed Easter Eve liturgies for Grace Cathedral and also presented Dominique and Michel to Bishop Myers for the Laying-of-Hand (Confirmation), her interest was not even apparent. Trudy lived her life in her own impregnable cocoon. Her role as wife and mother were obvious interferences in her life.

After finishing my residency at the Graduate Theological Union (GTU) and passing my comprehensive exams, the real work on my doctorate began.

Now with the comprehensives completed, I was officially a doctoral candidate. My doctoral advisory committee was composed of faculty members from several universities, all of them under the umbrella of the Inter-University Graduate Program, which allowed candidates to secure faculty members from any accredited university in the world.

My committee included nine members. Of the nine members six came from six different universities — none from the University of California although that institution co-sponsored me. I had faculty members from the universities of Santa Clara, Southern California, University of Texas at Austin, GTU, Chicago, and King's College, Cambridge, England, where I had spent much time in research.

Three non-active university faculty members with doctorates were specialists in particular areas that affected my course of research. One was a Jesuit philosopher-theologian (Jim Mara) on permanent disability leave; another was a practicing musician (John Jeter); and the third was a retired anthropology professor (Earl Count) who was still pursuing research and speaking at international conferences. It was a splendid committee.

Some words are needed to describe a few of the excellent men of my doctoral committee. Dr. Massey H. Shepherd, Jr., has been introduced earlier. Shep's contribution was primarily for liturgy, early Christian history, and music as they affected the content of my work.

Dr. Wayne Rood was the chairman of the committee, and chair of the department of art at GTU and at Pacific School of Religion (PSR).

A playwright and renowned director of several acclaimed plays; Rood was also a keen aesthetic philosopher, a fine teacher, and a glorious mentor who guided me gently, definitely, gracefully, and trustingly.

For example, on the night of my defense, he called me out of the conference room before the session began to give me some last minute advice and to inform me that I would act as the chairman of the committee because each member of the committee knew a great deal about portions of the topic to be discussed but none was an authority on the whole content.

Dr. Bernard Loomer, professor of process philosophy and theology at GTU was the guiding light in my reading and understanding of process thought, especially of Alfred North Whitehead's superb but complex writings.

Bernie was an extraordinary lecturer in a small seminar and was able to mesmerize us for two or three hours with his philosophical explications, as he smoked three thin cigarillos, never more.

Loomer had been dean of the University of Chicago and also dean in his later years of its Divinity School. Completing his undergraduate education at Bowdoin College, Brunswick, Maine, he worked on a master's at the University of Maine, and received his doctorate degree from Harvard University.

Loomer was the foremost authority on process thought, but unfortunately, he never published much. I do have a whole year of his lectures on tapes, which will end up as a gift to the GTU.

Jim Mara, the voice of reason, the instrument of grace, and the beloved scoundrel requires a whole book to describe him.

James Mara PhD, PhD, SJ (this not a typographical error, Mara had earned two PhDs) was an unbelievably complex human being who was caught in a trap that for him had no exit.

Mara had obtained his first doctorate from the Sorbonne in philosophical anthropology. His second doctorate was from the University of Heidelberg in ethics.

James Mara, retired from academics, was a marvelous mentor and beloved friend who kept me on track and often helped me out of inertia when it threatened my progress. Jim was a clone of the incarnation of all that is good and holy. He had a rasping voice that could not be ignored and to this day I can still hear it. He died in the early 90s and I still miss him.

Norman Pittenger was professor of process thought at King's College, Cambridge, and one of my masters when I studied at that august institution.

Dr. Pittenger was a renowned lecturer in process thought in Europe and in America and the author of more than 20 books.

After I had received my doctorate and visited him in Cambridge with Michel and Emily, Dr. Pittenger took Michel through King's to show him the grounds, the seminar rooms, and famous Kings Chapel with the wonderful painting by Rubens.

Norman was a dear advisor and wonderful person with a fatherly personality that exuded graciousness, kindness, the ability to listen intently, and an enormous interest in all the people he met.

Dr. Earl Count was a wonderful man, premier cultural anthropologist, secular priest, researcher, writer, global lecturer, and retired professor from Hamilton College, New York.

Dr. Count was attached to neither GTU nor UC Berkeley, but was often a guest lecturer at both institutions. Bishop Kim Myers, Diocesan of California, visionary, scholar, and liturgist, had introduced Earl to me.

Once a week, Earl and I would meet in UCB's Faculty Club for lunch and a three-to four-hour conversation on topics ranging from God to neutrinos, to gravity, to the art of early human beings, to $E=mc^2$, and literature. Friday was often the day we reserved for our "tutorial," as we called it. On many occasions and depending on the topic, the role of tutor was exchanged without forewarning.

Professor Count was a jewel of a friend with the most perceptive, keen, and inquisitive mind of any person I had ever met. Earl was also a fine cook who produced an enchanting bouillabaisse, even without the required native rascasse fish from the Bay of Lion, France. Earl was the priest in his 90s and sharp as a tack and to whom I turned to for counseling and to solemnize my second marriage.

Apart from the faculty there was a doctoral student, Stuart White, and his lovely wife, Jane, who supported me while my research progressed. Stuart, who joined me on the CLR, was a fine sounding board for my ideas. Jane was always willing to lend me her ear when I had a problem, and play the flute when I needed musical support for a liturgical innovation.

Both are still my dear friends although they are no longer married to each other. I often speak to both Stuart and Jane and when in Michigan visit them, and stay with Jane and her husband Douglas.

Stuart is now married to a wonderful person called Kate. Stuart and Kate have three lovely children, and I'm godfather to William, the middle child.

Stuart, with a sharp mind, an agile sense of reasoning, and an excellent knowledge of aesthetics has been a dear and supporting friend for more than 30 years.

Soon after setting my program and receiving the committee's approval, I set out for England and the Continent to work on research on Whitehead, Archbishop Thomas Cranmer, and the aesthetic school of thought at Cambridge University. I took Trudy with me in an effort to reconcile our marital differences.

I was well funded by grants for the research and for the overseas travel, and had also saved money doing several jobs covering vacant parishes, translating documents from French to English for Dr. Conrad Bonifazi, and teaching at both GTU and PSR. Therefore I was able to purchase a new diesel Mercedes in Germany for use in Europe and then bring it with me to California; to take my wife to Europe; and to pay for the children's care while I was away.

I made two visits to Cambridge, one for four months in the winter of 1973, and another jaunt for three months in the summer of the same year. The second visit was after I had accepted the position as part-time vicar of St. Edmund's Mission, Pacifica. The first visit to the UK was alone, but the second was with Trudy. My dear friend from my time at Rancho Cordova, Ruth Eger, accepted willingly to care for Dominique and Michel in Merced, thus Trudy was not burdened with children while in Europe — only with a husband doing research.

When I accepted the fellowship and grant to study at Cambridge University, Trudy and I discussed what that would entail, what we would visit, where we would live, and what the program of research would demand of us. Nan Youngman, an artist friend, agreed to locate a flat for us, and even offered to shepherd Trudy around the Cambridge area. The horizon for the first time looked less bleak and more hopeful. How long would this hiatus last?

Living in Cambridge with a researcher was not quite what Trudy expected even though we had discussed what that entailed. We did have time to visit Scotland, France, the Netherlands, Italy, and Germany, where we obtained our new Mercedes Benz automobile. I was obligated to attend meetings, to be a speaker for several engagements, and to visit major liturgical institutions and cathedrals in the UK and the Continent. In addition, I had to spend much time in dusty libraries gathering early documents of Alfred North Whitehead and other thinkers.

All this time alone did not please Trudy at all. She had the option of visiting places she wanted to but never did. We had a spacious flat in Cambridge on Maids Causeway, two bicycles, and a spanking new automobile but Trudy insisted that she was a prisoner, that she had nothing to do, and could not make friends. I must add that Nan Youngman, my painter friend who found the flat for us and who introduced us to several people was always ready to help Trudy. Yet Trudy did not particularly like Nan or her friend Anna Crossly, who had traveled with us on the summer visit and who lived in San Francisco.

After a few weeks in Cambridge and facing Trudy's incurable unhappiness, I gave up and spent more time researching and less time with her in the flat. Trudy could not be moved to attend faculty teas or dinners at Kings, services and occasions at Ely Cathedral, or to go to London for one or two plays or concerts — with or without me.

After returning to California in September 1973, Trudy remained in Merced for another year teaching high school. In February 1974, after living in Pacifica for five months in the vicarage, the children and I moved into our new house in Montara. Dominique and Michel had started St. Matthew's Episcopal School in the fall of 1973 and I began to sort out and assemble all the material I had acquired for my dissertation.

Upon returning to California and presiding in the first Eucharist at St. Edmund's, Pacifica (I was to be their part time vicar) I met Emily McCormick Price who, as a technical writer and editor, kindly offered to edit my dissertation and do the final typing. This was a most gracious offer and one that only Providence could have furnished. Editing and typing the text of my dissertation, which I anticipated would be approximately 600 pages long with perhaps 13 chapters, a full index, and a preface had been a worry to me.

After purchasing a new house, catching up on the outstanding bills still coming from the trip to Cambridge, paying for the children's school tuition and supplies, and supporting two households, my savings and my income were stretched to the limit. In fact, a $20 bill was beginning to represent a huge sum of money for me. Therefore, because I had worried about the cost of hiring an editor and also engaging a typist, when Emily offered to do both pro bono I was more certain that grace had been extended to me. I may repeat this note of gratitude a few more times, but Emily performed a superb job with both the editing and the typing, and especially with her contribution of clarifying questions that made the text clear and easy to digest. The faculty commended me on an excellently lucid and coherent dissertation, and Drs. Shepherd and Loomer, sticklers for proper usage of English and clear thinking, were impressed by the work and often in their other committees suggested that dissertation writers scan my text as an example.

It took six months to complete the dissertation. During the same period, my family was increased by an addition, a ward by the name of Nicola Rice Griffis. Her parents, parishioners at St. Edmund's, had died and she had been awarded by the court to the care of a family in Pacifica, also members at St. Edmund's. Nicola was unhappy with the arrangement so she asked the court if she could move in with us — then she asked me if I would be her guardian.

My home situation was tentative at best. Trudy had settled into our new house in Montara and had obtained a teaching and librarian position in the local grammar school; our relationship had remained strained. To add another person, a teenager, to that uneasy family was difficult for me to accept. I informed Nicola that it would not be possible for me to accept her in my family. Nicola, out of desperation, went around me to Trudy. The result was that Trudy came to me and insisted that all would be fine with the addition of this young teenager. I had developed a great deal of affection for Nicola, found her to be pleasant, sweet, helpful, charming, beautiful, and very bright. In a moment of weakness and hope that the strain that existed between Trudy and me would disappear when a teenager entered our fold, I agreed to let Nicola move in with us.

Nicola was most helpful with the children and with the management of household chores. Soon the situation between Nicola and Trudy deteriorated to the point where I became Nicola's main adult mentor. Trudy used or tried to use Nicola as a maid, her lady-in-waiting, and her staff assistant. The children loved Nicola and she loved them but Trudy became more and more unpleasant to Nicola. Nicola became a dear and special person to me, and the more I knew her, the more she gained my affection.

After writing from four to seven a.m. every day; preparing breakfast for the family; and doing the primary editing, new writing, selecting and organizing my notes until two p.m.; I would drive over the hill to Belmont and Pacifica to pick up Ashley (Emily's daughter), Nicola, Dominique, and Michel from school.

In May 1976 my doctorate was awarded. It had been creative, difficult, and intense labor yet it was rewarding and satisfying work.

Receiving my doctorate on the 8th of May 1976 (my 44th birthday) was a most memorable day, mostly because my children were present at the award ceremony and were of an age to understand the meaning of the occasion. With the degree in hand it was time to consider a job and to reduce my enormous debt. Teaching was one option, but not a very appealing one. I was more interested in industry but had been out of the competitive arena for many years. Church parochial work did not appeal to me because in as much as I liked the sacramental responsibilities I did not enjoy tending to the administrative tasks, which included budget, vestry meeting, summer bible school, and the many chores that get in the way of the core sacramental functions.

The Commission of Liturgical Renewal

Bishop Kilmer Myers, an interesting, learned, kind, and saintly man who had the vision and good sense but was not physically strong enough to be diocesan, had received me in the Diocese of California in 1972. A few months after being received and at the recommendation of Massey Shepherd, I was appointed to the Diocesan Commission on Liturgical Renewal; Bishop Myers asked me to chair it.

This diocesan commission was exceptional because of its association with Shep and several other key leaders and scholars of liturgy, music, and

264 · RAYMOND HOCHE-MONG

art and were closely associated with the national church's Standing Liturgical Commission. This body was directly responsible for producing the new and revised Book of Common Prayer (BCP). For me, it was a fine opportunity to learn, to work with some extraordinary minds, and to test many liturgies at Grace Cathedral and in parish churches around the diocese.

These were times of great upheaval in the Episcopal Church: not only was a new BCP in the offing, the celebration of Easter Eve Eucharist (Paschal Mystery) was being reintroduced in the American Episcopal Church, and women were permitted to enter Holy Orders. Because a revised Prayer Book was being introduced, large factions of the Church were unhappy with the product and with the events around the change. The current Prayer Book had been in the pews since 1928, and many people had assumed that such a book was unchangeable and divinely written by some ("bad" I'd add) redactor angel.

By 1976 those in the mainstream had begun to accept the revision but in the process, several congregations, bishops, and priests opted out of the Episcopal Church to go into what became the Orthodox Anglican Church. The corporate communion atmosphere was abandoned by a few who did not care to participate in what the majority and the spirit of the Episcopal Church agreed upon in its liturgical practices. By the end of the century, the BCP issued in 1979 would become, piece-by-piece and section-by-section, replaced with loose leaf revisions for review by members. The 1979 BCP is still in the pews and generally used but there are noises made to offer a new revision in the next decade. I'm happy to admit that I'll not participate in the work of revising the BCP — once was enough.

To fan the fires of discontent, the Church opened its Holy Orders to women. The first woman bishop and the first woman priest arrived on the scene, and even in the liberal Diocese of California, the shock of having women as priests was not without some discomfort. Bishop Myers at first objected to having women in holy orders with the weak argument that Jesus and his original disciples were all men. On second thought and after much discussion the Bishop switched sides and supported the ordination of women.

Adding this issue to that of the prayer book made for very interesting times for the Commission on Liturgical Renewal and its Chair.

Directing the work of this Commission during the transition, debacle, and consequent fury of many over the acceptance of the revised Prayer Book had further cooled my zeal for parish work. It was decision time for me, and time for immediate action.

I had purchased a house in the village of Montara in San Mateo County, in sight of the Pacific Ocean. I had first visited Montara and this particular coast in 1951 and fell in love with the place. So, a little more than 21 years later, here I was living where I wanted to live. This should be an indication of how particular I would be in selecting employment because relocation was out of the question. I was ready to accept any position in the San Francisco Bay area that offered upward mobility and an interesting future. Academic life was not part of my long-term plan. My interest in liturgy (the work of the people) moved me to look more at industry rather than academic institutions or the parish. Emily, my dear friend, offered me a temporary job with Bechtel Corporation as an editor. There were, I could foresee, several interesting possibilities with a firm nearby in San Francisco. A foot in the door of Bechtel was like a passport to new ventures, and that proved to be the case.

The camel pokes its nose inside the tent! Soon after my interview with a couple of people in the publications department, I started work with Bechtel Corporation as an editor. This position was not quite what I wanted to do but it paid well and allowed me entrée to a diverse entity. The position with an engineering and construction firm allowed me to join the ranks of non-stipendiary clergy — clergy who work in parishes but do not receive salaries. This was a wonderful act of freedom after my experience with Bishop Haden of Northern California.

Onward to New Adventures

The climb within Bechtel's corporate ladder was tortuous but interesting. Bechtel could have displayed more graciousness towards its employees, but the company did offer opportunities for exciting projects, provided one could make strategic judgments to maneuver through the maze of internal politics. From the editor's slot I was laid-off as a contract worker and then hired to take a position as assistant support manager for the Jubail Industrial Complex in Saudi Arabia.

The next move found me in aviation, an area that allowed me to make substantial contributions and to develop my own disciplinary specialties. Regional and infrastructure planning was subsequent to aviation and often connected to aviation, especially air space design and the management of the airspace above airports.

The move after that pulled me from the airport to the understanding, creation, and planning of the airport city, then to creation of the concept for the dynamic city, then to the intelligent city, and then to the global regional city with its peculiar economic, financial, educational, technical and "incubator" requirements. Finally I was manager of the technopolis projects, "knowledge-based revenue-producing communities."

A technopolis can emerge in a city, a region, or a whole country and presents options for improved education, better employment offering upward mobility, quality amenities and living surroundings, and ecological systems to support them. The program was exciting, challenging, and called for my creative energy to be applied at every turn.

Several projects required me to travel to many corners of the world but it was common knowledge at Bechtel that I accepted work only in places with good desserts! This simple rule served me well throughout my 18 years at Bechtel.

In 1993 I retired to start my own small consulting firm continuing my interest in aviation and technopolis and to devote time to the bed and breakfast inn Emily and I had created in an old and venerable house in Montara built at the beginning of the 20th century.

Goose & Turrets, a 100-year-old villa

The Goose and Turrets Bed & Breakfast inn was the culmination of an idea that I had nurtured for many years. My goal was to develop a friendly place for readers, eaters, conversationalists, and artists creating in all forms, and also congenial folk who would be my guests more than clients at my bed and breakfast. After more than two decades of operation the B&B seems to be a success and reflects what it was designed to do. Emily, who participates in the operation of the B&B more than I, has been the real key in making it a working entity.

Moreover the B&B was created to be a stable financial platform to allow me, with GT Ideas, to be selective in the kind of projects I might accept, remuneratively or not. I continue to be very interested, as a consequence of work I had initiated at Bechtel, in regional economic development supported by the commercialization of knowledge.

My vision has always been directed by a long view that penetrates the future, in so far as I can evaluate what the present will produce for the emerging subsequent tomorrows. I was often called a futurist, a term that I've never endorsed, which casts me into the prophetic mold as understood in the Old Testament. An Old Testament-type prophet I am not. Prophetic functions include examination, evaluation, performance of due diligence, identification of a magnet issue, and drawing potential conclusions; these were my stepping-stones for any of the projects that I worked on. My work was always cradled in the inherent understanding that creation was providentially active and that I was introspectively part of and responsive to it.

Once that was understood by others, and also by me, then I tended diligently to the process of creating something anew. The task begins by carefully identifying a strategic community, a place and an environment that offers potential, economic growth, and some magnets that make it interesting and attractive to investors. Then one searches for a group of locals who are willing to roll up their sleeves and give time and energy to make it a place where their dreams may be realized. It is at this stage that conversation begins to use the term "knowledge-based revenue city" or "technopolis" to describe the project's goal.

The group selects items, ideas, features, issues, qualities, and necessary steps that I call occasions, which would help achieve the goal. With their contributions I move ahead to give birth to the creative elements that could produce the results anticipated and for which the effort had been directed. Much of the detailed work is done by the group; the creative edge is the product of a single mind, a mind that can take the occasions and place them in a coherent scheme — rejecting some and incorporating others much as a painter uses some pigments, mixes a few, and rejects others, for a tableau. Consequently, I would then envision and push ahead to realize — give life to — the event, the technopolis. The birth of the knowledge-based revenue community emerges.

This is the heart of a process-thought approach to the human condition. Of course there are some ramifications, some adaptations, and some incidental fine-tuning because there is no one-size-fits-all formula.

The goal is, in effect, to improve the condition of the people in a particular region through the availability of better soft and hard infrastructures. To accomplish this goal the schedule cannot be set with an exact completion date any more than maturation of a person is definitive at a certain age.

A final point that needs to be considered is that a knowledge-based community cannot be nurtured without a core group of resourceful people who possess knowledge, who are educated, are creative, and have vision with goals that are attainable. In addition, the will to achieve the goal must be inherent in both the selected group and in the community. No event can emerge *ex nihilo!*

II

PART TWO

My Beginnings with the Church

The moment has come for me to speak about my interest in the Church, especially the Episcopal Church. I want to address and focus attention on the relationship that I developed with the Church, the theological and philosophical perspectives that ensued from (or predated) that relationship, and my active engagement in the proceedings of the Church and my priesthood, as I understood and interpreted the whole package. For obvious reasons, the approach will be sketched in general language because this is not a theological treatise but an autobiography.

This section attempts to understand the cause or causes that influenced me to commit myself to God by way of Holy Orders. This did not preclude committing myself to God in other ways that are just as effective.

Understanding the Causes

Although I have described much about the route that led me into the Episcopal Church, some details need additional exposition to fill in the numerous gaps and to help further the reader's understanding of who I am. The Church connection is one of the principle clues required to understand my personality.

Seminary education was a rich experience for me. My classmates were mature men and women who had learned much from their experiences of life's vicissitudes and shared their experience with the rest of the class. Many of my colleagues were professional people such as physicists, shipmasters, lawyers, economists, college professors, airline and military pilots, architects, pharmacists, interior decorators, musicians, and business entrepreneurs. A variety of other disciplines were also represented.

One seminarian and the exception in my class, was the youngest, a Harvard graduate. He had graduated at the age of 19 with a master's degree in history but had to wait until his 21st birthday before being admitted to the seminary. Not to waste any time, he attended class as an interested student and when he turned 21, he was enrolled as a full-fledged seminarian and included on the roll of postulants awaiting candidacy to Holy Orders.

Indeed, my group was not a naïve collection of wide-eyed religious fanatics whose sole purpose was to be duplicates of Don Quixote on a mission to save the world from perdition. None of us were that pretentious. None of us thought that we were hatched behind the altar. We were all searching for the reason that motivated us to be in seminary and to seek Holy Orders.

That I was not alone in this quest for understanding did help some. The fact that I wasn't quite sure why I was seeking Holy Orders allowed me the freedom to discuss certain issues and to compare some experiences. None of us had a universal answer. I certainly did not have answers to great questions: What was the meaning of life? Who was God, if there was a God? How did the Universe function and how do I fit in it, if at all? I'm still searching for answers. We were all searching for a very elusive answer, if one existed at all. It was not a community that would dispel the questioning by producing canned answers. The community merely added new questions to existing queries. It did, nevertheless, produce a few *outlines* for general answers. I went back to my physics and philosophy education and examined what was emerging from those disciplines. I found that philosophy was still struggling with the meaning of ideas and of life. Physics was searching for understanding, coherence, and seeking a grand unification theory that included gravity

— a theory that brought the standard model and quantum together. Theology was unable to think out of the envelope or so it seemed to me.

A few members of our class had been active in the Church and had parents who were active in it or were still serving in Holy Orders. Several were neophytes to the Church, thus a few were quite new to Christianity having experienced what appeared to be the divine presence through Buddhism, Judaism, Islam, American Indian religions, and secularism.

Why had I taken the road to seminary? There was no history of ecclesiastical ministry in my family, which was a mixture of Roman Catholics, Huguenots, Free Thinkers, Jews, and possibly in the distant past some pre-revolution Russian Orthodox Christians. It had been hinted to me that I had some Russian connections through the paternal branch of the family. I learned also that my paternal grandfather, whom I did not know, had gone to Russia to fight as a volunteer on the side of the Tsar's supporters and had he probably died in Siberia either in a battle or as a prisoner. In later years and in conversations with my father, more of the Russian association surfaced as part of my family's genetic history. If I remember correctly, the root of the family was coming from the St. Petersburg region or thereabout. I suspect that somewhere in that region a few French-Russian "Hoche" names are etched on gravestones.

When the Russian connection first merged with the French family is out of my knowledge store. Mother spoke more about the Modianos and almost nothing of the Hoches. I learned a great deal about the Hoche roots from books, civil archives in Germany and France, and from my father, but always in sotto voce. There were hints that Peter the Great had invited many French families to Russia to encourage greater cultural development among his people. Whether this is apocryphal or real is beyond my knowledge but it does seem plausible because Tsar Peter did invite German, Dutch, and English professionals to teach Russians several European trades and skills.

I believe that what this root connection means to me is that I have come to consider patriotism as a meaningless exercise in futile thinking. What does allegiance to a flag really mean and what does another nationality imply? The US fought hard and lost in Vietnam and now we are its best customer, its best supplier, and its good neighbor on the Asian turf, especially when the tension between Vietnam and China is given light. My own feeling is that it is time to become accommodating to others who have dissimilar points of views, looks, and eating habits. I may not be as accommodating toward a rightwing Republican, but there it is, and I will force myself to be because we are human beings planted on the same planet sharing the same hopes and aspirations. We are brothers and sisters and there is no way to exit from that.

I did find several facts indicating that one of my great-uncles was an important general in Napoleon Bonaparte's military: Lazare Hoche, General of the French-German Army at 25, known as the *pacificateur* (peace maker). Hoche was Napoleon's premier general and the principal military tactician who tried to dissuade the Emperor from the Russian adventure. Hoche as a young man was involved in the western insurgency during the Revolution and was arrested, but escaped the guillotine. He died of a pulmonary illness at age 29 and 3 months on 19 September 1797.

A few years ago my daughter Dominique became very interested in genealogy and did much research on family connections but especially on Lazare Hoche. In 1982 I went to see the fine monument and tomb that was erected by his German supporters in Coblence (Koblenz) near Weissenthurm D-5452. The caretaker was Mr. Daniel Mathieu, a retired officer of the French Army who had volunteered for the task as something to occupy him during retirement. We had a long time to see the monument and for me to learn much about the man Lazare Hoche.

General Lazare Hoche

Lazare was a tactical genius and very much the conscience of France's military. Hoche was the product of the revolutionary period but not a member of the Robespierre group; in fact he was imprisoned by them and released only after the fall of Maximilien Robespierre.

Lazare wanted to stabilize France and Western Europe because the French revolution, the religious discords, and the break up of duchies had put the Continent in turmoil. Hoche was totally against Napoleon's quest to become emperor and his plan to invade Russia. It is suspected that had Hoche not died so young Napoleon would neither have become emperor nor invaded Russia, and would probably have focused his leadership on improving French society and living conditions.

Hoche, who was not particularly fond of the strength of the Roman Catholic Church, wanted Napoleon to limit its grip on society, on wealth, and how it maneuvered the political fabric not only in France but in Europe. For the young general, religion and especially the Church, was causing more problems than he could manage. His concern was that the few groups that had broken away from the Church, groups such as the Huguenot, Waldensians, and the Cathars were denied any standing and in many cases were massacred. Hoche wanted the restoration of the Edict of Nantes that gave non-Catholics the right to exist in France, but that Edict was abolished under Louis XIV, and not restored even under Napoleon although he pursued its restoration. Hence I've inherited a substantial antipathy for religion from both the Hoches and the Modianos.

The Modianos, coming from the Liguria and Aosta regions of Italy, were anti-religion advocates as much as the Hoches. With a mixed history of Catholicism, Protestantism, Free Thinkers, and Judaism the Modianos were not attached to any religious fabric or persuasion. During the reunification of Italy, many of the Modianos worked hard to limit the authority of the Vatican in the new nation. With the help of the Republic of Genoa, Liguria worked to reduce the Church's influence in the government that was emerging in Rome, the new national capital. To this day Ligurians are the least attached to the Vatican and they are mostly Protestants, Free Thinkers, and Jewish; the latter is still a major presence.

Religion and its Effect

As far as religion was concerned my parents appeared to be unbelievers and hence connected to no active religious groups. Mother played with Roman Catholicism, and Father was a free thinker who admired the historical richness of Judaism and Jansenism, but disagreed with the post-Tridentate theological position that affirmed Original Sin and accepted the efficacy of Grace through works, as obtained from the Roman Catholic Church. My Uncle Mathieu, who married my Aunt Camille, a Jewess, had embraced Judaism. His daughter, my cousin Francis, married an Algerian Muslim who was a scientist, and who had little interest in either Islam or religion — I believe that they both turned to Baha'i.

Being away from the family in England, my only connection with religion was through Anglicanism, and principally the Church of England. Of course I had been exposed to Islam, Judaism, Greek Orthodoxy, and Roman Catholicism simply through common contacts in Cairo. My interest, however, led me to read many simple books on religion and especially on Christianity and Judaism.

I mentioned earlier that my mother had sent me to St. Joseph's Catholic Church in Cairo. Her intention was for me to be baptized. I suspect that she wanted to make certain that I would become something acceptable and not be classed with a religious group that was denigrated in Egypt, as many offshoots of Christianity were. Perhaps both parents thought that as a baptized boy I was less likely to fall into the anti-Judaism hatred that was prevalent, especially in Nazi Germany, and by Nazi admirers in Egypt. At least I surmised that was the intent when I declined baptism. Circumstances and my stubborn attitude negated her effort. You see, the priest at the Roman Catholic parish told me that I had to memorize the Lord's Prayer before I could be baptized, and I refused, although I knew the prayer and could have recited it in French and in Italian. My position was, and is to this day, that I can do nothing to earn God's love. God's willingness to adopt me is a gift of love — and not a purchased commodity obtained through something I do.

My refusal to be baptized caused me to receive a stern reprimand from my mother. My father just ignored the whole incident; nevertheless, he did discuss the issue that I had been circumcised as a baby for health and not for religious reasons. This further infuriated my mother because she observed that I was a marked boy with a Jewish signature. Caught in the middle of this situation I stood silently and reminded myself that few would ever know about my being circumcised because my pants were not transparent.

Holy Orders

When I first began to consider Holy Orders, I wanted to explore the reason I had taken this fork in the road when I could have taken another. Why Holy Orders? Why the priesthood? I dug back into my past for some indication but except for my refusal to be baptized in a Roman Catholic parish and for accepting to be baptized under the Anglican liturgy in the Jordan River, I could identify no specific clue to guide me. Never have I felt or demonstrated any deep religious attitude. That which is holy was recognized as a fact present in creation but beyond that I displayed no particular sign by my actions, my behavior, or my speech. I was puzzled and still am.

I need to be clear that Anglicanism attracted me because it did not fence me into a particular mode, limit me from looking elsewhere, and ask me to do anything in return, or require me to sign any agreement. The Book of Common Prayer (BCP) was to be simply the proposed road map, and within it there were many options from which to select. One weakness of Anglicanism is its great dependence on Scripture, even as it knows that it is limited, narrow, and of human making. I would prefer if it considered the writers of the early church known as the Church Fathers; if it would put more emphasis on tradition and history to resolve issues; and if it would reflect more its catholicity and less its biblical Protestantism.

No one had ever asked me why I was choosing the priesthood. Emily believes that I chose the priesthood because I could not accept any boss but God. I am not particularly religious. I give little weight to most explanations of "spirituality." Church attendance is not a paramount requirement for me. Participating in liturgical services has some importance for me, but I am neither addicted to it nor driven to attend. The Eucharist is important to me because of its universal dimension of magnifying the sacred, the holy for me, and for not localizing it. I love the phrase "at all times and in all places" when speaking of the Eucharist because it de-localizes the holy, the sacred, and universalizes it.

I recognize that privacy is an inherent characteristic of my personality. I've cultivated this characteristic to a fault over the years by being independent and by being my own driver on life's bumpy road. Privacy is a cloak that keeps me safe from foreign intrusion and protected from those I do not want trespassing in my space. To open myself to others is terribly difficult and although an autobiography or a memoir is the medium with which one tells about one's self, it is still difficult. My inner feelings and thoughts about my relationship with God, the Other, the Ruah (the wind), the Power on High, the Lord of Creation, Jesus the Christ, Jesus by-any-other-name, or $E=mc^2$ are extraordinarily difficult for me to convey to someone else.

There is a theory to which I ascribe that few human beings open themselves up to others, if they ever open up at all. Some reveal a minuscule degree of themselves in everyday conversation but that is hardly sufficient to warrant much of an understanding of the person. A colleague, a seatmate on an airline, a conversant at a cocktail party, all exchange tidbits of who they are, but insufficient information is exchanged to reveal more than superficial knowledge. Others reveal a little more of themselves in their relationships with some of their loved ones, their lover, their wife, their children, their mentor, or their intimate friend, but that level is just a little deeper than their veneer, at best. Still others reveal more of themselves in their writing, be it prose or poetry; their art, in whatever form it is expressed; and in their behavior, which is mostly the reflection of their body movement, their long term attitude, and their in-depth philosophy of life. Such revelation is even exceedingly superficial when one considers the human being's whole life. Human beings are just caged in their own private world, their own self-constructed cocoons, their own minor universe wherein few others are allowed, and if so, only for a glimpse, a glance, a peek, and no more. I'm certain that it is a position inherent in humans, a chosen attitude, a trait that we should not endeavor to overcome, and a trait to be cherished. Human beings are not the product of an assembly line; each person is unique and that uniqueness is to be protected as much as is possible. An autobiography opens a window to that uniqueness, but only a small window.

I suspect that I fear that any act of disrobing will allow someone else to see my frailties and my inner person which harbors all my thoughts, visions, expectations, loves, and hopes. Therefore throughout the years I have avoided too much openness. Who I am still lies within me, unknown to others. Privacy is protection. Privacy is security. Privacy is also control. By being private I only reveal what I want to reveal and thus I control what others see of me and certainly not what they think of me. Indeed, I am who I am. I must, however, explain a few particles of my thinking if I am to give my memoir validity and integrity. I will do my best.

Yet, there was something inside of me that urged me to select the path that led to the Church's Holy Orders. I have had neither a supernatural encounter nor a deep sense of guilt that needed atoning. In fact I pay little note, if any at all, to guilt. My understanding of God's presence in the Universe was (is) unshakable, firm, graceful, and obvious.

That the Universe was God's creation was common sense for me. My study of physics and philosophy supported much of my understanding that God was in the Universe as an active force, and not as an observer. Deism was not my cup of tea. The idea that God started the dynamics of his creation and then removed or distanced himself from it was not only abhorrent to me but also downright repugnant. I sympathize with Thomas Jefferson's rejection of Deism. I see God participating actively in his universe, not interfering, but participating with care, concern, and especially love. God for me is the epitome of love. I wanted to work for this type of God. This said, I don't see God in human terms or as a being with some shape. The most I can do is have God as a force, a loving and coherent but certainly not "designer" force.

Many have assumed that I am in Holy Orders because God is the only boss I can accept. That assumption is not too far from reality. A God who cared, loved, empathized, and struggled with his creation is one I can work for and with. I want a God who did not need me to bargain for or earn his love, no matter what I did. That I was not perfect was reason enough for me not to assume that I could ever purchase God's love. I never saw God as an examiner, a tester, and a grader of my behavior. My God was love. The only guiding principle that mattered for God and for me was love. It was a love of his creation. For me it was a love for his creation too, at times a "tough" love but nevertheless a love all the same, and always forgiving, redeeming, affectionate, and brimming with grace. Yet I do not paint God in anthropological form. He, It, She, $E=mc^2$ if you will, is the energy of Love, willingly dispensing grace unexpectedly. Love for me is recognizing that "thou" is much more important than "I" in any interaction.

Hence I was seeking a relationship with God, not necessarily a special or selfish relationship, but a connection that told me that he was all-important in my life. No bargain. No trade. No return necessary. Just that somehow in my life God was important. I was ready to serve God in creation. Now that this was settled, I had to concern myself with what is historically acclaimed, by many in the past two millennia, as God's human intervention: Jesus the Christ. I had to struggle with that bit of Christology.

Christic Presence

Revelation and the cultural-historical affirmation of the events surrounding the life and acts of Jesus of Nazareth are not to be considered separately, at least not for me. I always question revelation, however, because I am never certain of its veracity. Every religion, Christianity included, is conditioned by cultural-historical factors. When I read the Gospels (even the non-canonical texts) the cultural-historical influences were present and upon close examination, quite obvious.

Applying the tools of hermeneutical evaluation on primitive Christianity and its subsequent development was useful and necessary for me. What were the times? Who was present and who was listening in proximity to Jesus? Who was Jesus?

I have no doubt that historically he existed, lived in Palestine, and offered a new approach to human beings and their relationship with God. I recognize Jesus' uniqueness as a man and his attributed Sonship to God, the Father. Historical accounts (Philo Judaeus of Alexandria, Josephus Ben Matityahu, Publius Cornelius Tacitus, and others) of the period hint at who Jesus was and what his displayed authority suggested. The available sources do not, however, offer a coherent picture of Jesus. The Jesus of canonical writings is in certain respects quite different from the Jesus of at least some of the non-canonical documents — for example of the Nag Hammadi codices.

The Nag Hammadi library is a collection of thirteen ancient codices containing over fifty texts, which was discovered in Upper Egypt in 1945. This immensely important discovery includes a large number of primary scriptures — texts once thought to have been entirely destroyed during the early Christian struggle to define "orthodoxy" — works such as the Gospels of Thomas, of Philip, of Mary of Magdala, and of Truth were found. These were probably not written by the given names directly, but could have reflected their understanding.

The Jesus of these documents is scarcely recognizable in the veiled picture of Jesus in the later rabbinic material. What does the evidence tell us? Almost all scholars still contend that the earlier the material, the more likely it is to bring us into contact with the historical Jesus.

How is the resource of the earliest material tapped? What is earliest and what is later? But I will not quibble here.

- Paul is our earliest. (There is some question about John that he may have written part of his gospel when Paul was still alive). Paul says little about the historical Jesus; hence he is not a principal source.

- Quelle (Q) is the earliest written layer in the gospels written most likely in the 50s C.E. It contains very little narrative material and both Matthew and Luke used it in writing their accounts.

- Mark is the earliest of the existing canonical gospels, written around 70 C.E. It offers the narrative frame for the other two synoptic gospels of Matthew and Luke.

- Matthew and Luke each had access to Mark's account. They also had a copy of Q and other traditions.

- John's gospel is very different from the synoptic narratives of Mark, Matthew, and Luke and is not a primary source for the historical Jesus. It is, however, a powerful witness to what Jesus had become in the early Christian community in which John was written and it has a connection to the text of Thomas.

- Thomas' gospel, a series of sayings, was discovered in 1939 in Egypt and is very much like Q, a collection of sayings (114 in all). In its present form Thomas dates to the first half of the first century and in sequence to John's text (this dating is questioned by some scholars). Most scholars, and I, see Thomas as being independent of the synoptics. Thomas taken, however, with John in interlinear form adds insight for achieving a more complete picture of Jesus. Much as John's narrative is dualistic in its exposition of Jesus — good versus evil, sin versus salvation — Thomas presents a singular approach: namely, salvation, the making whole of a person.

I look at Mark, Q, and John as the three primary documents for a direct understanding of Jesus. In addition, the text of Thomas gives me substance, depth, and heartfelt love for the man Jesus. But I don't depend entirely on the canonical gospels to substantiate the historical presence of Jesus, the man.

So who was Jesus?

When asking that question I could imagine that authorities in the early Christian community, the architects of the several Councils, especially that of Nicea, the awesome writers, preachers, missionaries, and evangelists all had the capacity to fashion the embryonic Christian cult into a manageable trust whose adherents could be readily governed — and whose critics could be ostracized. I can see Irenaeus, bishop of Lyons; Polycarp, bishop of Smyrna; and Athanasius, bishop of Alexandria, struggling to impart cohesiveness to the Christian community. The question about who Jesus was had to be answered if cohesiveness was to be maintained in the Church. Was Jesus divine? Was Jesus human? Was Jesus part human and part divine?

The New Testament (NT) is the Christian interpretation of what had been people's experience with Jesus; in that effort, the Old Testament (OT) plays an essential role, because Jesus is talked about in the NT as the prophet, the son of God, the exalted one, the Lord, the Messiah — all of these titles reflect a non-Christian Judaism of the post-Old Testament period. This examination of the OT explains somewhat the multiplicity of NT interpretations of Jesus, which may have led to diverse Christologies, a process that was to be continued in patristic, and even modern theological explorations. So again, for me "who is Jesus?" is of paramount importance.

A partial answer to that question was found in the liturgical expression of the Christian community. Here I am not speaking of the attendance of the folks who come because of an obligatory response to their feelings of self-unease. No. I am speaking of the people who participate in the Christian liturgy because it is the ultimate response to the love emerging from the Christus Rex, the Paschal Mystery. Jesus' unique universal significance touches many human beings. Moreover, it is also historically mediated through the eschatological (future thinking) assembly of the committed people, the "believers," the Church of the Christic Presence.

In my search for understanding or for better grasping the importance of Jesus for the Christian, I saw yet another aspect which seemed to become clear in the light of the eschatological Son of God. For me the future is not a still-outstanding hope unless and until I have myself settled accounts of the past. The future is opened to me only as I become reconciled with my past. In this sense I find that Jesus, the Christ, is the means by which I can bridge the past with the future, to make life whole. All of this is the result of what Jesus' life points to: the changing, the turning about (metanoia) as a consequence of the coming reign of God. *Metanoia* encompasses having finished with the past and moving to meet the future in confidence that it is open but does not exclude risk and tentativeness.

Jesus for me is the light at the end of the tunnel. He is the human connection with God, the Universal Creator. Jesus says to me over and over again, "Ok, so you have screwed up badly. What are you going to do about it? Get up and get going anew."

With this advice I can recognize my limitation, my imperfection, yes my stupidity, but I also know that I can move ahead anew and with a clean slate — if only I don't dwell on my mistakes or relish them. I am bound at times to miss the mark as the archer might aim for a target and miss, because I am imperfect, but that is not the end (in Greek the word for sin is *hamartia* — missing the target). There is another arrow left in my quiver!

More will be said about Jesus in subsequent portions of this writing, but for the moment I do admit that for me there is the magnificent divine spark in Jesus (and no imposter has been able to be as convincing) that makes him unique among all other people who have influenced world religions.

In a sense the approach to Holy Orders was more through reason than directly through emotion, though the latter cannot be discounted because it is part and parcel of who I am. Moreover, I admit that there was a great amount of vacillation in my approach. One moment it was all very clear and the next it was not only opaque but obscure. There was no mentor who could guide me through this struggle, and anyway the struggle was too personal to be discussed directly with just anybody. I did pose questions to Therrel Holt, Massey Shepherd, James Pike, Stephen Baynes, and to several professors such as Norman Mealy — and I did obtain some answers. Before entering CDSP I talked with William Pollard, the physicist-priest; Donald Miller, the mathematician-deacon; Leo Sowerby, the organist-composer; and others. The discussions, however, were episodic and not direct. No one could lead my life. No one could decide for me. It was my decision and it involved God.

How could I know God's position? What did being "called" imply? And I felt that it didn't apply to me. Now nearly four decades later, I find that the decision to enter Holy Orders was valid, correct, and satisfying. If that decision can be called a response to God's call, then so be it. There must be something positive in my commitment to the priesthood. Indeed, I have not destroyed the Church. The Church is still alive, though in great need of reform. At times the Church suffers from a nausea produced by the inflated ego of some of its members; the lack of attention to the people in their cure and care by members of the clergy; the laziness of the clergy to inform themselves and to inform those in their cure; the indolence of many members when confronted with difficult and intellectual issues; and of the extreme adherence to traditions that are meaningless, sexist, racist, politically incoherent, and stupid for the 21st century.

That I do not seem to act, in the eyes of those who do not know me, as a priest molded in the role of their ideal form of a "priest," is unfortunate. That my demeanor does not ooze religiosity is true. I do not play the role of priest; I am one. I have also other facets to my persona. Priesthood is the foremost facet but other facets do participate in the composition of who I am.

I see God's creation as being a sacramental creation. I have an abhorrence of dualism that looks at the universe as made of matter and spirit, of good and bad, of this and that as St. Augustine of Hippo conceived it. For me the universe is of a piece and it is not fragmented in sections that are separated from each other or in juxtaposition to each other. From the religious side there is constant pressure to keep the spiritual free and separate from what is felt to be the contamination of the material world, which is considered and viewed as in some way gross and unworthy.

I suppose that some see the life of the spirit as characterized by the good, whereas the physical world of mechanical forces with physico-chemical elements is regarded as merely alien from what is good and holy. Perhaps this caricature is excessive but with such a view, the unity of a human being's life is broken; the material world, with human beings' economic activity, hence becomes a happy platform for unrestrained possession, greed, selfishness, and sham religion. The veneer of Christianity becomes a refined occupation for the leisure of pseudo mystical endeavors, such as "new age" shaded spirituality. The idea of dualism is toxic to any view of the universe I have; it is just as poisonous to good thinking as is alchemism.

Archbishop William Temple put the thought correctly in his famous Gifford lectures of 1932-34 when he said:

"It is in the sacramental view of the universe, both in its material and in its spiritual elements, that there is given hope of making human both politics and economics, and of making effectual both faith and love."

Indeed it is a sacramental universe. Every square millimeter of this universe is sacramental. There is no site that is excluded from this sacramentality. Yes, even toilets are sacramental! Because it is God's universe, therefore it is gracefully sacramental. That should give thought to those who deny the value of ecology or who believe that this planet Earth is here for them to plunder or to reduce to nothing more than a garbage dump.

The Contrasting Issue

My concern for religions, be they Christian or whatever, entailed the great problems that surfaced from their adherents, their disciples, and their protectors.

On the one hand, organized religions are the bane of civilized societies, of governments, and of nations. Organized religions seek power. Power to control. Power to dictate their points of view, their indigestible doctrines, and their prejudices. Organized religions want to take possession of God; to put him in their service; to employ him as their defender for any cause they wish to promote; and ultimately to tell God what he should or should not do — and how to do it.

On the other hand, organized religions want to control their disciples. Organized religions want to manipulate the lives of their adherents in all ways and conditions. Organized religions' aims are to dictate how one lives, how one eats, how one thinks, how one behaves, how one relates with others, and how one views the past and the future. Options on how one thinks are anathema to organized religions.

Thomas Jefferson's abhorrence of organized religions, the State religion, and the established religion is what identifies America as being extraordinary. No religion has a corner on America's behavior, thanks to Jefferson. In America you may believe what you wish — perhaps to your own detriment. No one will tell you what to believe, not even the State. If you wish to dig your own grave, then buy your own shovel, there are no government-furnished shovels for you. Yet we forget that important fact.

In the hands of organized religions, scriptural documents written by human beings are purported to be divinely transmitted pronouncements. For example the Bible, clearly written by human beings, becomes in the hands of Christian fundamentalists and literalists the unequivocally given or inspired dictates of God. For Muslims, the same is true. The Koran is transformed into a document with divine dimensions that is applied to justify any cause, any political score, and any purpose. Judaism uses the Old Testament as a weapon to keep the Jewish masses in check, and to control them with the tools of rabbinical laws. Eastern religions are no better or worse. Confucianism, although a philosopher's declarations, has shaped Chinese society as if it were divinely revealed, in such a way that neither Communism nor other political systems have been able to overcome. Shintoism in Japan has been fuel to the military mentality of the nation several times, has instilled an ethical system that is shamefully corrupt, and has diminished the role of women and of non-Japanese to that of vassals. Neither Buddhism nor Hinduism offers any better perspective for humanity.

That the Founding Fathers of America saw fit to separate the power of organized religion from the authority of the national government is not accidental or without reason. Each of the architects of the Constitution, especially Thomas Jefferson and at his urging witnessed what was being done in Europe and in South America in the name of the Christian religion. Even in "Magna Carta and common law justice" England, the heavy hand first of Marian Roman Catholicism, and then of the Established Church of England (C of E), caused disjunctions in society.

And that was not all. When, under Oliver Cromwell's rule, Puritanism replaced the C of E for a few years, the heavy hand of the sect was still savaging the population. Puritans immigrated to America to escape the C of E's edicts, and soon when the roles were reversed, members of the C of E immigrated to America to escape Puritanism. The Continent fared no better and the exodus to America of Hussites, Baptists and Anabaptists, Huguenots, Quakers, Jews, and even Roman Catholics from France, is sufficient evidence to remind us that organized religions are tools used to restrain human rights and to fashion God to their own needs.

A distinction must be made between religion and organized religion, especially organized religion with the authority of government to do its bidding. Even within a denomination, the authority of the hierarchy can be obnoxious and dictatorial — for whatever reason. The papal enforcement of clerical celibacy (1917 Codex Iuris Canonici), the rejection of birth control, and other restrictions by Rome are groundless but they do control disciples. Rome is not alone and need not be singled out. Other denominations do pretty much the same but use different restrictive tools to exert control over their members.

After all is said and done, I willingly joined a branch of organized religion. The Episcopal Church, an offshoot of Anglicanism but with American characteristics, whose home base was the C of E, became my Christian domicile. Would I know that the Bible, the Book of Common Prayer, and the dogmas are used as tools to control the people? Would I bow down to the bishops and unequivocally obey their edicts? Would my judgment be absolutely controlled by the pronouncements of the Church? Did I not agree to obey my bishop's authority? It was my turn now to examine my behavior, to understand from whence my judgments emanated, and to live with a reasonable set of ethical rules.

I must admit that I have neither been nor intend to be absolutely bound by the edicts of the Episcopal Church. When the Episcopal Church was ignoring racism, I made my voice heard. When the Episcopal Church denied access to Holy Orders to women, I made my voice heard. When the Episcopal Church continued to propose a major role for the Devil, I made my voice heard. When the Episcopal Church in some regions wanted to deny gays their rightful place at the Eucharist, I made my voice heard. When the Book of Common Prayer, which was cast in the archaic theology and misguided language of the 1920s needed to be revised I made my voice heard loudly and clearly.

Some of these issues caused me pain, job loss, and ridicule. Yet no authority can be changed, altered, or cast into a new paradigm unless one of its own forces it to see its misjudgments. One does not always come out a winner in such conflicts, but soon enough the change does come about. Indeed it does. I cannot take all — if any — credit for the Episcopal Church when it ended racism, accepted women in Orders, and looked kindly at gays at the Eucharist and in Orders (but not quite as yet accepting for ordination to any level of Holy Orders, especially the episcopacy). Mention of the Devil, especially in the Baptism service, is still a bone of contention for me, but the day will come when that symbolic crutch will be cast into the cleansing fire of reform.

On the whole I tried to develop a set of ethical rules that allowed me to live with integrity. I am certain that at times, because of expedience, I relied on some ecclesiastical rubric to dismiss an issue, but that was not often. For me God was not to be used as a club to beat people into submission. I did not see the Church's hierarchy as the ultimate source of all solutions, the repository of all answers to all questions, and the fountain of wisdom. Christianity was there to help one project a graceful life, manage to be ethical, live with integrity, and make coherent decisions on matters related or not related directly to everyday issues. I am convinced that love, not principle, is the gauge for making decisions.

John A.T. Robinson reminded me one afternoon as we took a walk, that basing an argument on "matters of principle" was a way to avoid love. If a decision is not structured by love, then there is something amiss. I interpreted divorce and the dissolution of marriage in that light. If two people were finally unable to resolve their difference, most of which probably surfaced from different levels of maturity or revised perspective, then a binding promise made in previous decades needed to be abrogated for the health of the couple, the children, and even of society.

Yet the Church has resisted any effort to deal with divorce creatively or with love. It has been until recently quite authoritative in its pronouncements against divorce, especially the Roman Catholic branch — which hides behind what it calls the "Matthean" privilege and is based on the premise that adultery (without understanding the cause) is the only valid reason for divorce. Even the C of E has a restrictive approach to marital divorce, especially when it pertains to the monarchy (e.g., Prince Charles and Camilla). Such positions are not exactly reflections of love. It seems, unfortunately, that in the eyes of the Church, legalism takes precedence over good judgment and graceful pastoral care. Understanding by the Church is currently replacing dogmatic principles on some issues — not all yet, but some. Paradigmatic changes take time and require much effort to be accomplished. Are we patient? I hope that we are not. We need outrage!

Currently the issue that is avoided by the Church, and not just the Episcopal branch of it, is the meaning of marriage. Soon the civil court will define marriage. It will define marriage between different sex genders — and also between same sex genders. How will the Church respond? Will the Church make a distinction between same sex union and opposite sex marriage? Or will the Church simply swallow and ignore the whole issue because it does not wish to explore the ramification of the distinctions, if there are any? I use the Church as an example, but in reality all religions are in the same mode of avoidance on the issue.

Islam is no better when it allows divorce to be the privileged tool of the husband. That a man who can afford four wives, which is sanctioned by Islam, can also reduce women to the status of vassals, is preposterously unethical and inhumane. And the copycat position of the Church of Latter Day Saints is an indication that anything can be pronounced as possible when a hierarchy wills it — and in the name of a dubiously represented God! It is not that God is dubious but his representation surely is.

There are examples galore but at this juncture it is not useful to identify them, except to say that I tried to walk carefully through the ecclesiastic mine fields. Have I been successful? Time and witnesses will tell.

I see the Good News offered by Jesus in the Gospels and in the several oral traditions as being a process by which human beings can manage their affairs with love. Politics is no different: it is the management of human affairs with empathy or love. Thus an elected politician is responding to a format that is similar to that of the Gospel. He is elected to manage human affairs. Now there is a further similarity between the structure of the Church and the political arena. Both are of a piece in the sense that they are dealing with a microcosm of the entire human fabric. The same types of people are found in both arenas.

Finding myself in this domain, I rapidly adjusted to the requirement placed before me. The Church as a participating entity was alien to me. I was on the outside looking in. Once in Holy Orders, I was no longer a parishioner but a member of the clergy — inside looking out. On 28 June 1964 the Coadjutor Bishop of the Diocese of Tennessee, William Evans Sanders, made me a deacon. The occasion took place at St. Timothy's Parish, Signal Mountain, Tennessee. With me were my wife Trudy; Dominique, our daughter of one month; my mother; and friends. The presenter and preacher was Fr. Holt, the rector. It was a grand day but I remember very little of it because of the pressures placed upon me by the circumstances. This grand event took place on Saturday. I do remember that Holt, at the lunch that followed, informed me that I was the preacher the next day. Not much time to prepare a sermon or to quell my anxieties. Moreover, I had no books to use for research and I was not about to ask Fr. Holt for access to his library. And that's a story by itself.

Off to the Copper Hills

Soon it would be time for me to move to another location, either as an assistant to a rector or as vicar in one of the missions of the diocese. The traditional approach was that the Bishop called you into his office and announced the new assignment — the marching orders. Unknowingly, I had a different approach.

There was a small congregation in East Tennessee that had the reputation of being a clergy killer, a place were no one wanted to go, a place too remote and unpleasant for most new priests. Copperhill was the town "owned" by the Tennessee Copper Company. It was an area that had been polluted by the emission of sulphuric acid and the razing of the hardwood forests to feed the boilers of the company before oil and electricity came into the area.

I was interested in the area and the challenge it offered. After my time in Knoxville at the University and discovering East Tennessee and learning about its people, its history, and its culture transplanted from the western part of England, I thought that it would a good opportunity for me to meet the "hill folk" personally. St. Mark's Mission was without a vicar.

I asked to have an appointment with Bishop Vander Horst the week before my ordination to the priesthood, which was scheduled for Saturday 1 May 1965, the feast of St. Phillip and St. James. On Tuesday before the day of my ordination, I was informed that the bishop would see me. As I entered the office I saw that Bishop Sanders was present too — he was charged with overseeing the missions of the diocese. I was greeted and asked to sit. Then the bishop asked me what it was that I wanted and if it was all right if Bishop Sanders remained for the meeting.

"Of course it is," I replied.

"What was the purpose of this meeting?" Vander Horst asked.

"Bishops, I would like to be assigned to St. Mark's Mission, Copperhill," I asked. One would have been able to cut the silence with a knife. Both bishops looked at each other. Disbelief is not quite the word needed to describe what was on their faces. The silence was almost too long.

"Copperhill," repeated Sanders.

"Copperhill?" asked Vander Horst.

"Yes, Bishops, but with one condition. I want to buy a house with the help of the diocese. A house of my choice." The bishops looked at each other and the silence extended a little while longer.

"Raymond, leave the office so we can discuss this request," Vander Horst instructed me.

"Bishop, any discussion about my request and potential assignment should be done in front of me. I'm the one making the offer."

The bishop looked at me. I wondered if I had been impertinent. Vander Horst stared at me with fixed and penetrating eyes accentuated by his thick white eyebrows. A few moments passed and Bishop Sanders broke the silence by admitting that he had no one selected for St. Mark's and that the last vicar had left six months ago after a tour of 18 months. A priest was tending Copperhill from the parish in Cleveland, sixty miles west.

"Why do you want to buy a house?" Vander Horst asked. Without letting me reply he added, "The diocese will furnish you a vicarage."

I gave him my reply, "Because it will give me some credibility for a long term stay in the area. And I want to build some equity."

They discussed openly more of the details that included salary, automobile allowance, and my reason for wanting a house.

"Why are you choosing Copperhill?" asked Vander Horst.

"Because I like East Tennessee and I cannot understand why it has become the Hellhole of assignments, the brunt of all assignment jokes." They looked at me.

I continued, "It is not so remote as people think. It is equidistant from Chattanooga and Atlanta, close to Asheville, and near some of the best forest land in North Carolina — and I know Bishop George Henry of Western North Carolina and can work with him."

"How do you know Bishop Henry?" Vander Horst asked.

"I worked in Mount Holly through the Valle Cruces summer program," I replied. Then I continued, "This was the first step towards the creation of the Appalachia South Program, which Bishop Sanders now heads."

"Now Raymond, please wait outside the office. I'll call you back in a few minutes." Less than ten minutes had elapsed before I was summoned back into the office.

"Raymond," Bishop Sanders said, "the diocese will pay the down payment and help you find a good house that you'll end up owning. I agree that owning your own house will convince folks that you are interested in them and that you want to belong in the community."

When I was given Copperhill and before my family arrived, I lived at the Blue Goose Hotel, which was owned and operated by the Tennessee Copper Company (TCC). After tending to my new Cure, my next task was to find a house suitable for my family. With the assistance and the good relationship I had with Bishop Sanders and the Diocese, we were able to purchase the Longworth house in Epworth, Georgia.

Mr. Longworth, the late president of TCC, had owned the house that I had selected. Mrs. Longworth was moving into a retirement institution in Atlanta and hence the house was on the market. It was a grand house on an acre and a third of land. It was a lovely house for one starting a family and earning $800 including automobile and housing allowances. We moved to Epworth on 15 September 1965. I had been commuting in my black Volkswagen back and forth between Copperhill and Memphis every other week since 15 May, when the title Vicar of St. Mark's was given to me before my ordination.

Appalachia and Its People

The household movers arrived with the delivery from Memphis on schedule. The house I had purchased was located in Epworth, Georgia; a village situated approximately six miles from McCaysville and the Tennessee-Georgia state line. The house was two stories, white and stately, and had a curved driveway.

The house was empty as I waited for the movers to arrive from Memphis with all the furniture. It was a large house and comfortable too. Heating was radiant from the floor, which we soon found was not very effective and very costly because it consumed a great deal of electricity.

The yard was very adequate for us and a garden could be developed in an open, sunny location. Lots of trees were on the property, mostly poplars, yews, apples, peaches, and oaks, and other trees that challenged my knowledge.

The house had four bedrooms, three of which were on the second floor. I decided that one of these would be for Dominique and the other for any future child. The fourth would become a guest room where I would place the two Longworth rosewood double beds I had purchased from Mrs. Longworth, the widow. Mr. Longworth, late president of TCC, was related to the Roosevelt family, which had given the United States two presidents, each from a different party.

The Afro-American driver and his assistant finally arrived mid-morning. They had driven all night because they knew that the Basin was not friendly towards non-whites. By mid-afternoon, and after they had unloaded and placed everything correctly, I suggested that we go for lunch and obtain something cool to drink. The closest place was the Tastee Freeze in McCaysville, which I had learned was owned by the wife of an employee of the TCC.

As I pulled up in my newly purchased Volkswagen Microbus to place my order, I was promptly accosted by two burly guys who warned me that "niggers" were not welcome and would not be served. I asked if they worked for Tastee Freeze Drive-In.

"No," they said. They then indicated unequivocally that I should leave without causing any trouble. That was unacceptable to me. I ignored them and placed a take-out order. The order arrived and the server suggested I drive a way down the road to eat. Instead I drove to St. Mark's and to the small parish house. We went inside, ate our lunch and the men were able to use the facilities.

After lunch, I returned home and delivered the workers to their truck. They departed immediately. As I was putting stuff into the garage, the two men from Tastee Freeze drove by my house very slowly, but did not stop. They returned and drove by again, this time tooting their horn. A little while later several cars drove by the house with their horns blaring. Trudy made certain that she and Dominique were away from the windows. Fortunately, the house was not close to the road but was set back approximately 80 or 90 feet, and giant poplar trees obstructed the view.

Later that evening several cars passed by the house slowly. Even though the house was set back from the street, we could hear the horns and the shouts of "nigger lover" and other profanities. We became invisible to the outside when we switched all interior lights off. We did not want to excite the folks who drove by the house.

That evening our neighbors, the Joneses, had invited us for dinner. Mr. Jones was a retired metallurgist from the TCC, and his wife had been a schoolteacher in Blue Ridge. We walked next door to the house using a path that had been worn through the years when the Longworths and the Joneses visited each other. Dinner was simple but good, and I received a scolding from Mr. Jones reminding me that the Basin did not tolerate nonwhites and I should not have forced the issue. Blah, blah, blah was my mental response to such an approach. Feeding two hungry black men was not tantamount to a violent challenge to integrate the Copper Basin.

After saying goodnight, we returned back to the house. The car parade had stopped and all seemed quiet for the night. We went to organize our new bedroom, and to get Dominique ready to sleep upstairs.

After putting Dominique to bed, I noticed a shimmering light reflected on her wall coming from the front yard. Dominique's window did not face the road but to the woods located behind our house. I went down the stairs to look out from our bedroom, which did face the front yard and the road. Trudy was in the bathroom. I looked out the window and saw a burning cross that was 10 or 12 feet tall. It was a frighteningly gorgeous sight with the light from the tongues of fire shining in contrast to the shadows cast by the tall poplar trees.

It was placed on a small open area that had neither anything growing nor was close enough to the trees to cause damage. I decided to call Trudy and then took a picture of the setting. Trudy was in the bathtub and could not hear my call. The Jones telephoned to see if we were safe. I telephoned my friend Buddy Finch, the funeral director, and he advised me to just stay indoors and ignore the Klan's visit; he knew who was responsible for the cross and would tend to it the next day. It was not long before the burning cross, constructed of pine, quickly transformed into a pile of ashes. I don't think the burning lasted more than 10 or 15 minutes. Trudy never did see the burning cross.

The message was clear. I had violated the tradition of the Copper Basin. But more to the point I could recognize the men of the Tastee Freeze parking lot. And that was dangerous. The incident slipped from my memory and I continued to learn more about the Basin.

Several days later, the editor of the *McCaysville Times* stopped me in the street and asked about the incident of the burning cross. I discounted it as the actions of deranged men. He wouldn't let the incident die out. He wrote editorials that were published in several issues and openly accused the people of the Copper Basin of being "nigger-hating racists." Much as I agreed with Mr. Kirby, the editor, I did not want to fan the embers and confront the local population quite yet. In an editorial Kirby accused me of being just like the rest of the local ministers, "all pabulum and no guts."

As the new kid on the block my strategy was first to gain the people's acceptance, then trust, and then approach the racial issue. My intention was to have the community hear me rather than shut me off. In the long run that strategy worked well, especially when I began to assume responsibility with the Appalachian Act 202 program. That story will be told later. I must, however, state that Grover Jones and Buddy Finch both gave me support and shared their willingness to be my friends in private and in public.

Even though I was a distinct foreigner to the region of the Copper Appalachia and an Episcopalian who wore a collar, I was well received by the people. There were some objections by a small group of diehard primitive Pentecostals, but on the whole I was made comfortable by the residents of the Copper Basin, which included Copperhill, Ducktown, and Bura Bura, Tennessee; and McCaysville, Epworth, Blue Ridge, Morganton, and Hell's Hollow, Georgia.

My initial contact was with Finch Funeral Home, and Ralph (Buddy) Finch and his lovely wife Sandra. Both of them were charming, helpful, and quite hospitable; in fact three decades later I am still considered their friend. Buddy speaks pure Appalachian and embellishes his unconventional anecdotes with unusual but pithy expressions. Buddy is also a fine storyteller in the best Southern tradition. Today I can say that his daughter Martha has inherited his talent and his style and her two master's degrees have not changed her wonderful Appalachian speech or her storytelling.

Subsequently I went to see the minister at the First Baptist Church, the Rev. Charles Duncan, in McCaysville who was kind enough to introduce me to other ministers and by his effort some of the ice was sufficiently broken to permit me to make friends, especially with the Rev. Grover Jones, minister of the First Baptist Church in Epworth, located not far from my new house.

Once I began to work, it became quite obvious that the executives of the Tennessee Copper Company (TCC), most of whom were members of record, controlled St. Mark's with a tight grip. Few of the local residents were members or even invited to be members. Polly Morgan, the assistant post master of Copperhill; Grace and Oren Postelle, residents of the Basin (Oren was an employee of TCC but was not a corporate executive of the company); Ralph (Buddy) and Sandra Finch; plus two or three women who lived near the Church were active in the congregation of St. Mark's. For a mission church that had 60 families, 50 families were linked to management or executive positions at some level with the Tennessee Copper Company.

With a substantial history of funerals carried over from Memphis, I decided that my first pastoral visit would be to the largest funeral entity in the Copper Basin. In working clergy uniform, I went to meet the directors of Finch's Funeral Home. Ralph (Buddy) Finch and his father Millard were the owners. They received me most graciously. Buddy introduced me to his wife Sandy; they lived in a doublewide mobile home on the property of the Funeral Home. They were a delightful couple and became strong and active members of St. Mark's. Both Buddy and Sandy became our friends, and today we still talk on the phone quite often.

Buddy, as I said earlier, speaks in a pure Appalachian dialect that is peppered with delightful expressions and contains fascinating anecdotes. He quickly took me under his wing to guide me through both the customs and the geography of the Basin. He often drove a bright red Cadillac ambulance, and a ride in it when he was on call was an exhilarating experience. Big Red was the fastest vehicle in the area; even the Sheriff could not catch the big Cadillac when it was speeding to reach an accident.

Sandy tried to be a friend to Trudy but I must admit that the relationship did not mature. Even the charming southern artist Grace, Sandy's older sister, was not able to establish a friendship with Trudy. Both sisters, however, became good supporting friends to me. I also met Doris, the middle of the three sisters, who lived in Atlanta and was married to a fine fellow by the name of Carl Abernathy. Carl had a wonderful voice and played a mean guitar, often accompanying Chet Atkins and other great guitarists in the music trade. Carl was also an insurance broker and lived in an upscale area of Atlanta, near Lenox Square. When I had to be in Atlanta I often stayed with the Abernathys and enjoyed their hospitality immensely.

Work in the Copper Basin never did become routine. St. Mark's congregation was growing slowly and was welcoming families from the region. The grip on the mission by the TCC was diminishing. Several business people were starting to serve on various committees and on the vestry. Local people were being baptized and confirmed as the months went by. After joining the Junior Chamber of Commerce (JCs), whose members were the active, civic minded, and responsible young men of the community, I was able to obtain a better understanding of the people living in the Copper Basin. With Ferris Maloof, Hoot Skelton, John and Ronnie Jabley, and other young men of the community inviting me to share their visions for the Copper Basin, I became a local citizen painlessly.

Because Appalachia was a focal point of President Lyndon B. Johnson's Great Society (a region just as impoverished as East Texas where Johnson was born), the President put great emphasis on helping the people of both coal and copper Appalachia. My knowledge of what ensued with Congress only focuses on the copper portion of Appalachia.

Johnson, in his 1965 State of the Union address, asked Congress to establish the Appalachian Act 202 with funds to bring economic assistance to the southern copper region of Tennessee, Georgia, and North Carolina. By a strange tour de force I became the regional director of the program, all this on top of my normal tasks as vicar. In fact, Bishop Sanders helped establish the Church-sponsored Appalachia South (AS) program, which melded well with the Act 202 program. Moreover, Sanders encouraged me to become more involved in the program. At any rate, I became more than involved: I took on, or rather accepted, the task of becoming Director of 202 for the Copper Basin.

Appalachia South (AS) was a cooperative effort, sponsored by the Churches of the region that included Tennessee, Georgia, Virginia, Kentucky, and North Carolina. In addition it also included the Episcopal Dioceses of Tennessee, Western North Carolina, Southern Virginia, and Atlanta. My cure encompassed the three adjacent corners of Tennessee, Western North Carolina, and Georgia. AS met regularly in the most interesting towns of the region, places such as War and Hungry Mother, VA; Hazard and Harlan, KY; Kilmer, Asheville, Valle Cruces, and Bat Cave, NC; Chattanooga, and Knoxville, TN; and a few other places.

I was called for a meeting in Hazard, KY, to discuss several topics on economics and social improvement that I had highlighted in a paper which had been circulated to several key AS leaders. Hazard is located in the eastern hills of Kentucky, an economically impoverished section that at one time was coal rich but when the coal boom ended because of greater availability of fuel oil, high wage demands, and the requirements for cleaner burning energy, mining ceased and it became too poor to cope with modern day environmental requirements.

The making of illegal whiskey, "moonshine," was just about the only revenue producer emanating from the region because the fundamental religious groups banned the sale of legal alcohol. Of course when liquor is legally banned, the illegal production and sale of it makes it so a tax is no longer paid, hence no revenue is obtained. That this tax-avoidance scheme was a ploy of the fundamental churches seemed obvious to anyone with any sense. Tax avoidance was not limited to liquor because bartering goods was greatly accepted in the hill society. In fact, bartering was so widespread that I soon discovered that there existed an active underground economy producing good revenue.

The folks of Appalachia, although poor when gauged against the people of Nashville, Lexington, or Atlanta, were to some degree better off because they had less overhead expenditures. One who scrapes out some coal could exchange it for chickens, and one who raised pigs could exchange the bacon for the vegetables that someone else raised. A car could receive necessary repairs in exchange for milk, chickens, or whatever was available for barter. It was a simple system that functioned well within the confines of the region. Outside the region barter was not practical, and the Internal Revenue Service (IRS) did not approve of it simply because there was no account reporting and no tax payments made. How could taxes be paid on undocumented revenue? In addition the IRS was famously unable to enforce their tax rules about reporting such.

When I arrived in Hazard several members of the adjoining states and of the federal government joined the meeting. The discussions were longwinded but ultimately fruitful in that they moved Congress a few months later to pass the Appalachian Act 202 for the region. For my part in this meeting I had prepared a paper that I presented. Briefly, I had suggested that Appalachia was not actually economically deprived but that a different economy prevailed, one that was quite alien to that of Nashville, Chicago, Atlanta, or New

York. The convener distributed a few copies of my address, as I mentioned, to several in attendance, however, not everyone was able to obtain such.

On the third day of this high-powered meeting, we were told that President Lyndon Johnson and several representatives and senators were to arrive and join our discussion. The president had received a report from his advance team. Johnson wanted to reply to the meetings by making a few points of his own. He also wished to meet privately with a select few who worked in various capacities in Appalachia. Johnson addressed the meeting and reminded us that he came from East Texas, a region that was not too unlike the hills of the Smokey Mountains. After his address, which lasted about an hour, he departed but left a retinue of administrative people. At a coffee break after the President's address I was met by one of the President's aides who informed me that I was invited to attend a meeting in Washington DC. Somehow I was chosen to meet with President Lyndon Johnson at 6:30 p.m. three days hence in Washington DC. I had never met a president even though I had shaken the hand of then-Senator John F. Kennedy after the debate with Nixon in Chicago in 1960.

Once alerted that I was chosen to meet with LBJ, Bishop Sanders came over to my room at the hotel to discuss what might be on the President's mind for my meeting. The gist of the conversation was that I needed to be myself and to speak candidly when questioned by Johnson. This was good general advice that left me to my own ingenuity but assured me that Sanders trusted my judgment. I telephoned Trudy to inform her that I had been selected to meet with President Lyndon Johnson but she was not impressed at all. That her husband would meet with the President of the United States was no grand news for her, although she was a Democrat.

The next morning after breakfast and a parting conversation with Bishop Sanders I got into my trusty black Volkswagen and, after stopping at home in Epworth for a change of clothes, headed north to Washington DC. There was a light rain that turned to snow but nothing unmanageable. I was accustomed to hill driving but I chose the safer but slower Appalachian Trail highway instead of the secondary roads. My intention was to drive the Trail until I approached the vicinity of the capital, then I would switch to the freeway to enter the city.

Meeting with a Common Man

I arrived in Washington DC late in the evening. I had been told to go to the gatehouse of the White House for further instructions. At the gate, I was given a large envelope that contained all the needed instructions and the identification form. I was led to a small room where my photo was taken, fingerprint recorded, and papers filled out, signed, and stamped. There was also a formal invitation from the President.

A room had been reserved for me at the Hay-Adams hotel, located not far from the White House and some distance from the National Cathedral, which stood on a prominent hill. I was very much awed by the arrangements, the hotel, and my room. A large bowl of fruit was waiting for me in the room and on the desk a note informing me that my suit would be cleaned and pressed and my shoes shined. Next to the note was a set of tickets for meals and a hotel letter asking me to select the wines or other alcohol I wished to have brought up or served at meals.

A note in the large envelope informed me that I had a meeting with the presidential staff at 11:00 a.m. the next morning. A little while later there was a knock at the door. I opened the door and a young man introduced himself as being a secret service agent; his badge indicated the same. He spoke quietly and instructed me on how to enter the White House. He would meet me inside the assigned gate to escort me to my destination. He also gave me a badge to wear the next morning. A car would be sent for me, but I replied that I would walk the short distance to the gate and then to the assigned door. He asked me when I wanted to eat dinner and my reply was, "As soon as possible!"

He picked up the phone and gave instructions to someone. Dinner was grand and the wine was a superb California pinot noir.

The next morning after breakfast I headed for the White House. Here was a naturalized citizen of a little more than a decade heading for the seat of power, the home and operations center of the President of the United States. Inside the door where a guard was posted, I was met by the same secret service agent who had paid me a visit the previous night. He escorted me to the elevator and then down a long corridor lined with statues of past presidents (I think). Where was I headed? I was scheduled to meet with the President at 6:30 p.m. and now the time was just 11:10 a.m. The SSA man opened a door and inside I saw a long table. Many people were sitting around and talking quietly. As I entered, the room was drowned with a frightening silence and all eyes were focused on me. Help! What was I doing in this place?

After the introduction was made, I was briefed and given a folder, which contained a stack of documents on what became known as the Great Society, the President's pet project, and the one that included my sector of Appalachia. I was asked to describe my tri-state area and give my evaluation of the problems I identified. I proceeded to speak in a slow and deliberate manner. Lunch was served around 2:00 p.m. but the business of the meeting did not stop, except for the interruption of the dishes being served and removed. Soft drinks and coffee were offered. At 5:00 p.m. we broke up for a move to a different room where drinks, the harder type, were served, as was food. At 5:45 p.m. a young woman approached me to ask if I wanted to refresh myself before my meeting with the President. I accepted.

After I had refreshed myself the young woman escorted me to the waiting room outside the presidential office. Promptly at 6:30 p.m. I was led into the Oval Office. President Lyndon Baines Johnson greeted me warmly; his six feet plus size overwhelmed me.

"Father, please sit down," he said with a broad smile and a very Johnsonian East Texas accent. "Would you like me to call you 'Father'? You know we attend the Episcopal Church and often priests prefer a different title," the President politely asked.

"Mr. President, Raymond is sufficient."

"Now that we are informal, you may call me LBJ if you wish and would you like a drink?" he reached to the cart then asked, "Bourbon and branch water OK?"

Indeed it was, although I disliked bourbon and still do, but I accepted it. The President poured himself a Scotch and I salivated. There was no way that I would address the President of the United States of America with the acronym LBJ. I kept to "Mr. President." He asked about my family, my education, why I had become a priest, why I had chosen the Episcopal Church, and what it was that I was working on in the Copper Basin. We spoke about politics and my opinions. I did admit that I had voted for Mr. Goldwater but was very happy that he had been elected instead.

"You, Mr. President, had defeated the Republicans — and you had taught me a lesson that would last for my life!"

He laughed, took a long sip of his drink, and then said: "If Goldwater had won you wouldn't be sitting here."

He then added, "We all make mistakes. Goldwater is a good senator, a fine general, but would have made a lousy president. Ideologues cannot govern because they can neither be reasonable nor are they able to listen to the people."

I agreed and expressed my apologies. He forgave me and placed his big hand on my shoulder.

Soon after we settled the introductions, he in an armchair and I on a sofa, LBJ set up his ideas and asked for my opinions. We discussed Appalachia and its problems and the possible solutions. It was an unbelievably candid discussion. LBJ listened to my ideas. He took notes and made audible sounds. He even asked if the salary was acceptable. I admitted that I had not thought that there would be a salary. I had seen a number but had not taken it seriously. Yes, I admitted that the salary was more than adequate; it was fantastic. LBJ reminded me that all expenses were to be covered by another account, and a clerk would guide me through the accounting process.

LBJ was interested in my evaluation that we could not declare that the people of Copper Appalachia were economically disenfranchised when they had a different economic program and way of doing business, which relied mostly on the barter system. True, the people had to rely on the common financial tools when purchasing goods outside the region, goods such as new automobiles or refrigerators, but in the Copper Basin things could be exchanged for other things quite readily — even when used cars had to be re-placed or repaired. Labor was shared and folks would offer their services to build, repair, or modify buildings and whatever structure required the help of more than one person. Now this did imply that taxes for financial exchanges were often not collected but that was not a new issue in the region. How would the IRS collect taxes from a bartering economy? Yet the financial world outside the Copper Basin had to realize that any taxes levied on the barter system would be small, even insignificant, because there was not enough trade to make a dent in the general economic program of the country.

What the Copper Basin needed were health and sanitary facilities, educational options, and job training programs. Because of the remoteness of the region, health facilities were too distant to serve the people well and the local health facilities were operated by the TCC, which was just on the edge of bankruptcy. Attention should be given to both the primary and secondary school systems because the people were keen to have their children obtain a better life than the parents had. Several parents of college-aged young people had saved to send them to Ivy League schools. I pointed out that I knew several young people attending top universities and graduating with high honors, not only with bachelor degrees but also with doctorates. Finally, I suggested that job training was important for those youths who were not cut out for college. I pointed out that the J.C. Campbell School in Brasstown was a good model to replicate because it focused on the regional crafts that were of value for the area but that another focus should be directed at information technology education and training.

LBJ listened and when I stopped he asked if I could point to a specific example where local people had been able to function in industries apart from TCC. I related the most direct example that was still operating.

Several power plants had been built by the Tennessee Valley Authority (TVA) to provide electricity to the remote villages of Appalachia and the South. Monitoring several gauges in control centers was critical not only to the operations of the power plants but also to maintain the high standard of safety required. In conversation with one high level acquaintance at the main TVA office in Knoxville, Dr. John Bachman, I suggested that senior men from the Copper Basin needed to be considered for such sedentary jobs. John Bachman appeared to be incredulous.

"The task requires concentration and some training and most of the men you are suggesting are not able to handle the long hours and the tasks."

I needed to be specific.

"John, a corncob pipe smoker whittling wood and rocking in a chair on the front porch is perfect for the task you suggest." I pointed out that the person could be trained quickly to watch the dials and he would be patient and undistracted by anything because he was accustomed to just sitting quietly and watching flies, birds, and rabbits fill his field of vision.

"A dial is as nonintrusive as is a fly circling in a ray of sunlight before his staring eyes!" I said.

The President smiled and wrote a note in his book.

I left the office of the President elated and quite satisfied that perhaps the project for injecting economic development into Appalachia had merit and longevity. Appalachia Act 202 lasted until 1971 when President Richard Milhous Nixon and Congress killed the funding which subsequently terminated the Act. Fortunately I was gone and living in California by then, but my people stayed in the Copper Basin and continued to live in conditions that were less than excellent. Yet, while I was director of the Appalachian Act 202 Project, the community received a new tertiary waste treatment system, a hospital, a cleaned river and lake, and a "reformed" copper company that was instructed to keep its nose and its environment clean and was monitored closely.

My appreciation and respect, however, for LBJ's work and concern are engraved in my heart. I'm sorry that the Vietnam War, the disgraceful advice given to him by Robert McNamara, the then-Secretary of Defense, by the ill will from leftover staff members from the John F. Kennedy administration, and the shameful and insulting treatment from Robert F. Kennedy, trapped him. After all is said and done, Lyndon Baines Johnson moved more legislation through Congress to help end the legal obstacles to racial integration, to move millions of people out of poverty, and to enforce and augment civil rights as the law of the land than any president before him, including John F.

Kennedy. LBJ may have sounded like a hick, may have been a manipulator of legislators, may have appeared superficially uncouth in comparison to Kennedy's Camelot culture, but LBJ was a "common man" and not a knight wearing soiled armor. I still admire LBJ as a good man and a fine president.

I am grateful that the circumstances dealt me the opportunity to meet LBJ, a great man, and one who recognized that there was more to a nation than war, wealth, oppression of one race towards another, and the greediness of those who have over those who have not. So far LBJ has been called a legislative manipulator, among other names, but he was a strategic operator of the Congress for the benefit of the people.

As I mentioned about Appalachia, the economics of the Copper Basin also included a generous portion of bartering. In terms of cash flow, except for those who worked for the Copper Company or had revenue-producing businesses, much of the economy was barter. Employment outside the TCC largely depended on small businesses. Work was available in cities within commuting distance of the Basin, such as in Chattanooga, Cleveland, Ellijay, and Murphy with Duke Power and the Tennessee Valley Authority. The people of the Copper Basin were the source for blue-collar labor, and employment came from small enterprises that operated tentatively at best.

Meeting on several occasions with managers from Duke Power in Blue Ridge to discuss employment or the lack of it, I suggested that many of the monitoring tasks in power plants (as I had indicated when I spoke with LBJ and Dr. John Bachman of TVA) could be done by local people. At first this suggestion appeared to have no merit, and Duke managers discounted it. I mentioned that mountain folk were able to sit for hours in a rocking chair, smoke a pipe, and while away the time thinking or whittling; they could just as well while away the time by watching monitoring instruments.

Several days later, when I spoke to a supervisor of the TVA Sevierville Power plant (who was a local East Tennessean from birth) about hiring mountain people to monitor instruments, he thought that it was a good idea. A few days later he put the word out for potential hires from the Copper Basin. After several interviews he hired several to cover the three shifts at the power plant. Within six weeks he called me to thank me for suggesting local mountain people to monitor instruments. He was very satisfied and had suggested that resource to other supervisors in other plants.

Duke Power also needed people to monitor instruments. I telephoned my contact at Duke and told him about Sevierville. After checking with Sevierville he too hired a team to test the possibility. He did mention, as did the Sevierville supervisor, that after each shift the cleaning people had to sweep the operation room of wood chips left from the whittling!

After a month, I was called and asked if I could recommend other potential workers for the monitoring tasks. I called Buddy Finch who suggested I contact the preachers and ask them to help with the task of recruitment. After months of having these monitors on the job throughout the power system, Duke Power admitted that local Appalachian men were better at the task than those from the cities because they exhibited patience, concentration, and a certain lackadaisical approach to their performance. After leaving the Basin, I was informed that both Duke and TVA were employing a number of local hill folk for monitoring tasks.

The TCC managed several copper mines and a cracking plant that produced sulfuric acid from copper sulfate. Because TCC supplied the paper pulp mills in East Tennessee and North Georgia with the acid it produced, that product alone accounted for the bulk of TCC's revenue. Bowater Paper Company was one of the major customers for the acid produced by TCC.

The toxicity of the sulfuric acid was such that the escaped vapors affected almost everything in the Copper Basin. Cars had to be washed daily and TCC, after many complaints by the locals, installed free wash racks — wet douches — for driving through. It was a quick wetting system, and the toxic rinse water was drained directly into the Ocoee River, which flowed a few hundred feet away. Incoming drivers could smell the acid 30 miles away, even before the eyes shed tears!

Ecology was not of prime concern to TCC, even though all its executives lived nearby and were subjected to the same toxic emissions produced by the company. Nearby hills had not been excavated but had been denuded by the clear cutting of trees for the furnaces before the advent of oil, and by the acid vapors mixed with rain. These denuded hills owned by the TCC were divided into five-acre lots and sold at very low prices to employees who wished to build houses. The selling price was just a few hundred dollars and loans to purchase these lots were granted without interest. It was a bargain for anyone willing to build a new house and live on denuded land that required tons of expensive imported topsoil for anything to grow.

By working in the Copper Basin I became by hook or by crook involved in the general condition of the region and the primary concern for me was the health of the community. I soon became aware that ecology was such a foreign concept to TCC, which was the primary entity affecting the community, that not only was industrial unit cooling water released into the river five to ten degrees hotter than the normal river water temperature, but it also contained a large percentage of acid and other toxins in the solution.

One day after having driven the river road from Cleveland, Tennessee to Copperhill, I commented to Buddy Finch that the Ocoee Lake was a gorgeous and pristine lake, the likes of which I had never seen. It was blue, clear, and free from weeds and algae.

Buddy in his direct way of speaking informed me that it was clear and clean because, "there ain't nothing growin' in it!"

There were no fish in the lake and not until one fished past Cleveland and beyond, some 75 miles west from Copperhill, were fish to be found in the Ocoee River.

In my new job as Regional Director I had access to the laboratories of the Tennessee Valley Authority (TVA). I asked if the river and lake water could be tested. A few weeks later I was informed that not only had the water been tested, but also that the federal government was taking the Tennessee Copper Company to court for polluting the river. I was subpoenaed by the prosecution as a witness to the trial, which was held in Chattanooga.

Many of the top executives of the Copper Company were members of St. Mark's Episcopal Mission and I was their vicar. Moreover many of the top executives of the Copper Company were also subpoenaed as witnesses, but for the defense. These were interesting times. In a real sense I, as vicar, was testifying against the majority of my congregation! I alerted Bishop Sanders, who in turn notified Bishop Vander Horst, and both gave me the green light (not many bishops would take that risk) to do what needed to be done. I testified.

The trial proceeded with the testimony of many water, fish and game experts, TCC management and their experts, several local residents, and the federal government. Expert was pitted against expert, vicar against senior warden, wives against husbands, and city mayors against city mayors. I was called to the witness stand and repeated my question about the pristine appearance of the lake. Other witnesses related their stories of catching no fish and seeing no waterfowl.

When the issue of water temperature was discussed, the federal water experts mentioned that they had found the water to be clean but warmer than normal. There was a moment of silence in the court. The prosecution directed a question to one water expert representing TCC's position. The reply stunned the courtroom.

"It was nothing more than thermal enrichment — and no toxicity can be found in the water," came the expert's reply.

He continued his testimony by adding that, "heating of the water occurs in the summer and has no effect on river life, and as for the acid, well, dead vegetation produces acid in all rivers."

TCC did not consider that the 15 or 20 degrees temperature above normal was either toxic or deleterious to water life. In addition, what did it matter "if the Ocoee was a little acidic, at least it was neither dirty nor polluted."

Ocoee River "thermal enrichment" — clean, clear, and lifeless!

The Company lost the case, was fined a healthy sum, was required to build adequate cooling ponds to dissipate the heat before it was released into the flow of the river, was required in the next 30 days to stop the leeching of acid into the river, and was compelled to pay the Tennessee Fish and Game Administration for restocking the river and lake water by the next summer, which was six months away. The fallout was soon noticed as TCC opened discussions with a larger firm for its sale.

St. Mark's and I survived this episode. Nevertheless, congregation members from the company were none too happy about the results and about me.

To offset this negative atmosphere, the congregation had already begun to have a majority of local residents as its core. The occasion of the trial made St. Mark's a little more popular although it had been a primary opposing force against the main employer in the region.

The Tennessee Copper Company, soon after the trial, was sold to Tenneco in 1966, a petroleum firm that was more interested in diversifying the mined products. Sulphur, gold, copper, and some rare metals were of great importance and the production of sulphuric acid was reduced immensely, since paper companies were switching from acid to other drying methods. It was also underground knowledge that Tenneco had estimated that its entire operation in Copperhill had longevity of no more than five to six years; it would be closed as a tax loss sooner rather than later.

Apart from the lawsuit, the difficulties that came with being Vicar of a small congregation that historically had been a company church, and other issues, living and working in the Copper Basin was a delight. I was close to Atlanta, able to do some lecturing at Emory University, able to avail myself of excellent shopping, attend several concerts and symphony offerings, and to enjoy the general amenities of southern living.

The house in Epworth was grand and comfortable. The yard was well landscaped and I was able to select a good spot for a vegetable garden where I planted white corn, Mr. George Beefsteak tomatoes, and other delicious veggies. I learned how to become a small time farmer and supply my family with fresh vegetables, fruits, and herbs.

After settling in and finding the old servants' quarters to be adequate space for an office and a library, a routine was soon established. Dominique was two years old and the yard was just the place for her to run around. Friends of ours on Signal Mountain gave me a beautiful black shepherd dog that I quickly named Behmer, after the great German liturgist of the 19th century. Behmer was a frisky dog but was plagued with a bad right hip, the endemic problem with many German Shepherds. He was a fine, lovable, beautiful puppy. Dominique loved the dog and he loved to tug and play with Dominique.

One Sunday afternoon as Dominique was playing with Behmer, I heard her cry and the dog bark. I went out to see what the trouble was and I soon discovered that Dominique had been hurt in a tumble, perhaps while wrestling with Behmer. Her leg seemed somehow to give her pain. I called Trudy after taking Dominique inside the house where we examined her leg. I chose to believe that it wasn't broken but Trudy insisted that it was. I was wrong.

We called Dr. Bill Lea, our physician and left a message for him to call us back. A short while later Dr. Lea called and we explained the problem with Dominique's leg. He instructed us to come to the Copper Basin Hospital where he would meet us. Lea lived in Ducktown, Tennessee and we lived in Epworth, Georgia; the hospital was located mid-point between us and approximately 15 miles for each of us to drive.

Dr. Lea had X-rays taken of the leg and after looking at the negatives announced that Dominique had a hairline fracture. Cast put in place, we took Dominique home but first stopped at Tastee Freeze for some ice cream. Dominique was full of smiles and back to being her old self.

Once at home she said "Behmer see leg. Big leg. Behmer see."

She wanted to show the dog her leg. Behmer came over, sniffed the new plaster, and then immediately licked Dominique's face. With the plaster on her leg, Dominique became a destructive weapon around the house, knocking everything along her path as she crawled through the house dragging her cast. Dominique was a juggernaut on the loose. Fortunately the cast was removed three weeks later; it couldn't have lasted another week because the plaster was barely held by the fabric.

Making friends in the Copper basin was easy. As the outsider I was taken into the local fabric of the community with open arms. The Postelles, Grace, Oren, and their bright daughter Becky were always ready to give me a few hours of enjoyable conversation. Oren was a quiet man who worked at the Company and was always willing to build frames or cut blocks for his wife's art. Grace was a fine artist from whom I learned a great deal, both in technique and in creativity. Becky was a young, loving, genius child who was inquisitive and determined to become a biologist (in later years as a professor at the University of Tennessee she had a marine creature named for her).

Other friends offered us warmth and support but all of them cannot be mentioned here because that would take another several hundred pages. Suffice it to say I had friends from both sides of the fence. From TCC and then from Tenneco we made friends who not only agreed with me but who quietly supported us. Locals saw us as interesting people who were willing to live among them as equals. We were introduced to apple moonshine, ramps, poke "salat," sassafras, and sourwood honey. Mrs. Quintrell, Grace's mother, who lived near her, was the one who in the spring would invite me to enjoy Appalachian cooking. It was wonderful.

The Quintrell clan included John and Roy. I did not know John very well although he was always present when special occasions were celebrated. Roy was a dear person to me, and much younger than John.

Roy was a high school dropout who owned a used car lot in McCaysville. A hardworking man, Roy was too bright to be in a regular high school — he should have been placed in a special educational center for gifted students, but none was close by. Married and the father of fine children, Roy was not satisfied with humdrum living or with being a car dealer. At one point in frustration at his condition and the assumed lack of opportunity, he turned to alcohol. Sandy, his younger sister and adoring fan, called me to see if I would speak to him. I would be happy to speak with him but I was not a counselor I reminded her. I would speak with him as a friend if he approached me first, alone and sober. He did. He called me one cold morning and asked if I would have lunch with him in Ellijay at his favorite boarding house restaurant.

We had a good lunch and he opened up. After lunch he drove to the Blue Ridge Lake area and he showed me a piece of property on a hill overlooking, but not on, the lake. He wanted to live on that hill. He said that he was selling his used car lot but didn't know what he would do next.

What did he want to do if he could? He wanted to build log houses and help young folks prepare for adult life. Roy had done quite a bit of research about log house and building development.

I asked him what was it that stopped him? We discussed the houses he wanted to build and the business that might develop from such a venture. He also had thought of a program for helping young folks obtain a start in business. I found his ideas to be wonderfully well planned.

"Go at it Roy," I said. I was not a businessman but had some knowledge about what a coherent approach entailed. Part of my discussion was to have him make notes so a business plan could be produced. I suggested that he approach the local bank and apply to the Small Business Administration (SBA) for a loan. Once that was done, Roy walked out with a line of credit from the bank.

Roy and I met regularly after that first meeting. He sold his car business and made a small profit on the sale. He also stopped drinking alcohol completely. He then went to contractor's school and after completing the program obtained a building contractor's license. Working with a local attorney he started and incorporated a small company. After some due diligence, he selected a particular log house supplier, hired a real estate broker, and moved ahead and constructed his first demonstration house. It was an immediate success. The house sold an hour after he opened the door.

Roy has become a success. He is an ethical, wealthy businessman and an asset to the community. He did not forget his program for young folks. Roy started an internship program for young people that provides pay, college or skill training, and business education as long as they remain in the program. Roy is quite active with the young, and his program has attracted the attention of other organizations that duplicate what he has done.

The St. Mark's cure in the Copper Basin was not only challenging and interesting but also rewarding. It required much of my energy not only to work with the congregation but also to attend to the community at large, to see what improvements could be made to provide health services, clean water, and adequate solid waste disposal facilities. My time was divided between the Mission, directing the Appalachian 202 Act, and serving on the Fannin County Board of Supervisors as an advisor to the Board, a token Democrat. I relished this latter task beyond anyone's imagination. There was much work to be accomplished.

Young-Harris Liberal Arts College

There were other tasks that excited me and kept my brain actively engaged. Young-Harris Liberal Arts College, in Georgia, 40 miles east of Blue Ridge, was affiliated with the United Methodist Church and had a student body that wanted to hear another aspect of religion or a different approach to what was identified as religion besides the literalist and fundamentalist approach that was spoon-fed to them by the scores of uneducated preachers tending the region, but beyond the campus. I was called by a small but influential group of students who had heard me speak on some civic occasion to come for an informal lunch presentation at the college. Before accepting, I telephoned the Dean of Students to inquire if my presence was acceptable to the college. The reply was welcoming, and he assured me that even the members of the faculty were interested in opening the subject of religion. I was, however, asked not to act as a missionary determined to recruit students into my denomination. I assured the dean that was never my mode of operation.

When I arrived at the college I was escorted to the theatre where I was slated to give my presentation. The dean and the president of the student body formally introduced me. My presentation reflected my position. I said that Christianity was a tool that could be used to manage one's affairs; that it sponsored the free thinking of individuals; that in its early intent it shunned codified rules; that principles did not matter as long as love was in effect; that each individual was responsible for his or her decisions, whatever these might be; that the Bible was the product of human beings interpreting life and history from the perspective of the writers or the redactors, hence, as the divine and unequivocal word of God much of it had to be taken with a grain of salt — perhaps more than a grain; and that integrity and introspection (knowing one's self) were the key to an ethical approach to life. I summed up the presentation by adding that in its pure form as culled from the sayings of Jesus, Christianity was quite simple to follow. Christianity had no prescribed codes, no preclusions, and no systematic requirements; loving God and one's fellow human beings was all that it required of its adherents.

At the termination of my college presentation, I opened the session for questions and comments. One hour had been allocated for the presentation; it lasted two-and-a-half. Most of the questions and comments were not geared to sectarianism but were either theological or philosophical in content.

Many asked, "If the Universe contains all there is, where is God?"

Others questioned the need for denominations and other religions.

"Which religion is the most correct?" many inquired.

Finally the classic question surfaced of why I was an Episcopalian. I replied that I was willing to answer that question only privately after the presentation was over because I was not there to promote or to defend the Episcopal Church.

A final questioner asked: "Does it matter if I do or do not believe in God?"

I replied that belief was not so much the issue, because that would neither change God nor any of one's associates or peers. What was the issue was what one did with one's life. I did add that one had to understand the difference between Enigma and Mystery — but it took some intellectual exploration, especially if one was searching for whatever was called "God."

Soon after I finished, the dean asked me if I would be interested in a return visit. My reply was that I would be if the students requested it, and made their request directly to me. They did and I returned seven times to do seminars or open discussions in the student center with equal success. I'm happy to inform the readers that St. Mark's did not gain new members from my Young-Harris presentations but the students became more selective in their church attendance, especially when they changed to other colleges. Many kept up an active correspondence with me even when I moved to California.

Apart from the Copper Basin Hospital in Copperhill, a hospital that operated under the umbrella of the TCC, the nearest facility was either 60 miles west or 40 miles south. A new hospital facility was proposed for development on the road leading to Blue Ridge and designed to serve the entire Basin and more. The TCC was unhappy with the proposal for reasons that implied that they were losing their grip on the community but TCC's longevity was being reduced every day. TCC did not have any authority to stop the process, because funding was primarily drawn from the Federal Government under the Appalachian Act 202. The hospital was completed a few years after I left the region, but Buddy Finch kept me informed.

The entire Basin was in dire need of a sanitary solid waste disposal plant. Two tertiary solid waste plants were proposed: one that would serve Blue Ridge and one that would serve McCaysville, Copperhill, and the surrounding hamlets. A river separated McCaysville, Georgia and Copperhill, Tennessee. Georgia called the river the Ocoee on its official charts, and Tennessee called it the Toccoa on its official charts. As far as Georgia was concerned, the Toccoa River did not exist; similarly as far as Tennessee was concerned the Ocoee River did not exist either. A sewer disposal plant was imperative for both communities but none could be built until the issue of the river's name could be settled.

It took weeks to accomplish that task and required the help from the Universities of Georgia and Tennessee before the two states agreed that the river that divided them was the same and that both names referred to the same river. The names of the river had come from the different Cherokee subtribes that had occupied the region.

Because we had resolved the issue of the name of the river, and both Georgia and Tennessee recognized the necessity of a waste disposal system, a plan was submitted to the Federal Government for approval and funding. Little did the powers in the Basin know that the Feds had proposed a tertiary system in 1964 (which was shelved because of the disagreement on the river's name), some two years prior to the proposed plans submitted by Fannin County, Georgia and Polk County, Tennessee.

The funding was approved and the engineering plans were prepared by the Army Corp of Engineers with the assistance of the Tennessee Valley Authority which had authority over the fresh water system of the area. A firm in Chattanooga was given the contract to produce the final engineering drawings and to manage the construction of the tertiary solid waste plant. In 1967, the first excavations were made to build the foundations of both the tertiary systems and of the hospital. Unfortunately I was not able to remain in the area to see both facilities completed but a decade later I did see them in full operation.

As I mentioned earlier, Tenneco, a petroleum firm, acquired Tennessee Copper Company. A new upper management cadre was put into place, "company paternalism" was greatly diminished, and St. Mark's Mission began to feel some of the financial strains produced through less pledging and hence less income from the company employees. But the Mission continued to cultivate a more local profile. Soon, the non-Tenneco members presented to the bishop for confirmation were local people such as a pharmacist, a high school shop teacher, a dentist, an attorney, a physician, a nurse, an automobile dealer, an American Baptist minister who became an Episcopal priest after going to seminary, and a US Forestry Ranger from Blue Ridge; the latter two ultimately also became priests in the Episcopal Church. The number of parishioners at St. Mark's had grown to 75 families by 1968, when I resigned as vicar. Much more work was needed but a start had been made. I resigned from my cure because I wanted to work on a doctorate. In addition, I felt that a new person would have the energy to continue the current ongoing work and to expand the vision that had been initiated.

So the family would not feel like captives in the Basin, Trudy and I often put Dominique in the VW Bus and escaped here and there for short vacations and to explore parts of the region that we had not seen. On occasion we visited our friends Raymond and Betty More. I had met them when working in Mount Holly on the Valle Cruces summer intern program. They had taken me in and given me room and board for two months in their large house.

Raymond was a dentist and also mayor of the town. They had two daughters, Mary Ellen and Betty Ann, 15 and 11 years old in the summer of 1962. At first impression, I was convinced that the Mores had the perfect marriage; it was not until years later that the veneer wore off and I discovered that there was a mental problem that especially affected Betty, the wife.

Betty was the typical southern belle who needed to be cared for all the time otherwise she went to pieces and was unable to do anything. Betty could not write a note, a bank check, or a simple grocery list. Raymond was the glue that kept the family together. As long as he was running the family, the enterprise functioned mostly well. The two daughters were a little wild but managed to hold themselves together as long as Raymond was around and able to help them recuperate from their goofy mistakes.

When Raymond died, the structure of the family collapsed and everyone went to pieces. Betty gave herself more completely to alcohol, the girls ended up with very problematic multiple marriages, and the financial security that Raymond had carefully built up for his family was dissipated soon after he died.

The last time I visited the family in 1994 in Myrtle Beach, South Carolina, I was most disappointed with the girls and especially with Betty. Betty Ann owned and operated a sleazy massage parlor catering to motorcyclists, and Mary Ellen owned and operated a bar in a notorious section of Myrtle Beach. Each girl had been married four or five times and the last four for each were to men of questionable character. Having planned to visit them for a week, I never once saw Betty sober for the two days I managed to stay — she was never able to stand up or speak coherently the entire time of my aborted visit. Much as I wanted to be of help, I found that I was overwhelmed by the human disintegration that I witnessed.

On a more joyous note, on 6 March 1967 Trudy gave birth to our second child, Michel. He was born at Copper Basin Hospital. Michel was a quiet baby who made few demands, unlike his sister Dominique who was noisy, demanding, and always into something. On the whole both children are joys to have and each is quite different from the other. In those early years, Trudy was a fine mother who gave much of herself to raising the children so that they could read at an early age and could speak correctly even earlier. Fortunately books, libraries, and storytelling were part of the family's normal operation. It was a happy time and both Trudy and I attempted to make the most of it. We tended our flower garden together, which was beautiful, and our vegetable plot was rich with tomatoes, onions, melons, peppers, and even a few dozen ears of white corn.

We had often discussed how long our stay in the Copper Basin would be. I was interested in pursuing a doctorate. As parents we wanted our two children to attend good schools and none were readily available in the Copper

Basin. Then there was Trudy's need to return to school teaching. I sensed that rural life was not meeting her needs; her interests were elsewhere but certainly not in the family, except out of a sense of duty because of tradition.

Trudy was a Memphis girl and not a rural person. She liked the country but not too much and Appalachia was much too country for her; it was too rural; it was too different from what she had been accustomed to. I am not quite sure where Trudy's interest lay. She was a good pianist and had a fine trained voice but never did much with the talents she had in music. There were several groups playing serious music in the region but Trudy never indicated any interest in them. I began to put feelers out for a position in California and a place that interested Trudy. Making friends in the Basin was difficult for her; although several local families attempted to include Trudy in their klatches she never tried to become a member or to reciprocate.

It had become the custom at St. Mark's to have a house Eucharist on the 4th of July, and in 1966 the Finch's home on Blue Ridge Lake was to be the host location. Millard Finch, Buddy's father, owned the house but had ceded it to his son. Sandy, a frustrated house decorator had worked hard to convert its drab appearance into a magnificent lakefront house. Buddy had kidded Sandy, in front of members of the congregation, by saying that for this occasion the vicar was going to walk on water as part of the liturgy. Buddy had a marvelous way with language in that he spoke the local dialect that was always peppered with rich local expressions. He insisted on calling me the "goat man." He announced again over coffee in the parish house that "the goat man was going to walk on water on the 4th." I never discovered why I was called the goat man, but I suspected that it had to do with the way I dealt with my parishioners or perhaps because I had traveled a great deal. The Eucharist was always celebrated in the afternoon and was followed by a scrumptious potluck dinner — a non-pareil potluck dinner.

An hour before the event Buddy arrived at my house to pick me up. It had been my plan to drive my family and myself in our blue VW bus. Why was he picking me up? He wanted to show me something, and anyway Trudy could drive the VW with Dominque to the lake.

Buddy drove me to John Quintrell's house, his brother-in-law, who also had a house on Blue Ridge Lake. Tied to the dock was one of those open houseboats mostly used for fishing. We climbed aboard and started the small outboard engine. Soon we were putt putting along towards the Finch's estate. Buddy was at the helm and I was standing in front.

As we approached the Finch's dock, Buddy switched off the motor and announced through a bullhorn that "the goat man had walked across on the water!"

It was quite an entrance. The Eucharist had been launched and people, many not from St. Mark's, had been invited to the celebration. I intoned the Sursum Corda to the tune of the "Streets of Laredo," a tune that I had experimented with at a Valle Cruces outdoor celebration.

The potluck was as good as ever. There were no baked beans, rubber-style chicken, or macaroni salad. Mrs. Quintrell, Sandy's mother, had brought poke salat and her superb fried chicken, first soaked in moonshine, then seasoned with local herbs. Corn bread, crisp and buttery, mountain sausage, sourwood honey, fried green tomatoes, cucumber salad, sliced Mr. George beefsteak tomatoes, green beans with ham hocks, and pies, several fresh fruit pies but especially Georgia Peach pies made up most of the dinner. I mustn't forget the pickles, some sweet, some sour, but all delicious and included watermelon rind, small green peppers, okra, string beans, cucumbers, and some that I did not recognize but which were wonderful.

After dinner we told stories, recounted segments of local history, and Buddy told about some of his experiences with the "holler" people, "them that live in the hills and hollers." Buddy was referring to the folks who lived in Hell's Hollow, a remote section of Blue Ridge County. The man who was so tired, Buddy told, of his second wife moving the furniture around, that he poured three inches of concrete mix on the floor of the whole house — thus the furniture was forever embedded in it. "Hiss chair was n'er moved agin!"

After everyone was gone except the few who were Buddy's personal friends, a jar of apple moonshine was brought out. We then all experienced the classic and extraordinary taste of that pure nectar of the gods. It was good whiskey. The moonshine was smooth, transparent, and without a kick. It just flowed into one's inner being without so much as a hitch, a tremor, or a gulp for air. It was like velvet, crisp and delicious. I still receive my yearly ration via private transport, and always in a mason jar.

As I mentioned earlier our house was located in Epworth, a small village between McCaysville and Blue Ridge. Also living nearby was the Baptist minister, Grover Jones, of the congregation of Epworth. We were good friends and we often took time off to have lunch, coffee, or to exchange stories.

Peaches and Sugar

It was my custom to make brandied peaches and I had two large clay jars for them. Glover was a man who never had any alcohol but knew quite well that I consumed some in moderation; he was also puzzled that we used wine in our church service. One warm afternoon, Grover came over as I was replenishing one of my peach jars. I stopped and invited him into the house for a dish of vanilla ice cream. After serving each of us three scoops, I topped mine with two brandied peach halves.

"May I have some too?" Grover asked. I served him a similar portion. He took several spoonfuls of the ice cream and exclaimed that both the vanilla and the peach topping were excellent.

"Where do you buy those peaches?" Grover inquired.

"I get my peaches from the Georgia Peach Growers Association," I told him.

"But what do you do to them?" He took several more spoonfuls. "Are they preserved peaches? The juice is really good and it has a sweet bite on the tongue."

I said to Grover that I was preparing another jar when he came over.

"Show me how you make those peaches," Grover was insisting. I didn't want to explain that what he liked was the brandied juice.

"Raymond, tell me how you make the juice."

"Well, Grover," I explained the process, "Get a large clay or glass jar. Wash the fuzz off some fresh peaches, but don't peel them. Pit them, and then halve them. Place a layer of peaches in the bottom of the jar and add sugar. Place another layer of peaches on top and add sugar. Continue the process until the jar is full. Cover the jar with a loose lid and wait a week or so to see what the good Lord does to them!"

Grover wrote all this down and a few weeks later he invited me to his house for vanilla ice cream and brandied peaches. Had I corrupted Grover?

A few weeks before Easter and the school break in 1968, the principal of the Copperhill High School telephoned me to invite me to address the student body. What was the occasion and the general subject of the school gathering? He informed me that because Easter was in a few weeks, it was the custom to invite a "preacher" to speak to the students about Jesus. In my best diplomatic tone and language I reminded the principal that his was a state and public school and religion was not to be forced on students.

Anyway, after some further discussion I agreed that I would speak about Jesus only as a historical figure. The more I thought about the subject, the more I was opposed. I decided to write a play about how a witness to the execution of Jesus would have reacted and how the news of his resurrection would have been treated by the media of the time. What emerged was my play, *Two Reporters at the Crucifixion.* This short play was recorded several years later when I was at GTU. When I read the play to the students there was at first a silence among them that worried me, but when I finished the reading, the auditorium burst into applause. Many students came to thank me for having treated the subject matter with delicacy and humor, and for bringing the whole issue to our time and with our doubts. In addition to the immediate response of some of the students, I received a few letters thanking me for breathing fresh air on the subject. One letter, written by the son of a prominent minister of the community, especially thanked me for helping him to find the courage to question accepted platitudes. I also received a handful of letters condemning me to a life of hellfire and brimstone because of my "radical and blasphemous" thoughts.

I found the Copper Basin to be a pleasant and exciting place to live. But Trudy and I had determined that when Dominique reached the age of six we would move to an area with better schools. Moreover, as I intimated earlier, I was interested in obtaining my doctorate and a move would be necessary. Bishop Sanders proposed that I move to Nashville and work on a doctorate at Vanderbilt University, but the subjects of my interest were not readily available with the current faculties. I had been in the Copper Basin for four years and Dominique was approaching the magic school age. Although she was enrolled in a preschool program, we felt that we needed something better for her. I was not too upset with the local school system or its quality, but frankly, I wanted to do my doctorate work in California at the Graduate Theological Union and/or the University of California in Berkeley. My area of interest was aesthetics and I wanted to investigate research approaches that would incorporate art and liturgy. In essence I was searching to understand the building blocks of art and also the creative process. Moreover, there was Trudy's need to escape from the rural environment of the Copper Basin. Trudy had experienced California and was maneuvering to return there, where teaching positions were available. I recognized that Trudy was unhappy in the Copper Basin and I agreed to look immediately for options of employment that would help us move to California.

The Road Back to California: Rancho Cordova

Wallace Sprague, a classmate from CDSP, informed me that there was an opening in the Diocese of Northern California and that he had spoken to his bishop, Clarence Rupert Haden. I disliked Haden because I had seen him mistreat his clergy when I lived with Trudy in Calistoga and Napa. I had done well with the bishops of Tennessee, Western North Carolina, and Atlanta and was certain that I would be able to get along with Haden. Soon, I received a letter from Bishop Haden asking me to meet him in Augusta, Georgia, where the House of Bishops was scheduled to have a meeting. After discussing the offer with Trudy and the congregation, I drove to Augusta.

The primary topic discussed by the members of the House of Bishops in Augusta was the writings of the Right Reverend James Pike, retired bishop of the Diocese of California. The House was divided 3:1 in support of Pike, but the antagonists were noisy, vicious, and out for blood. Bishop Haden was supporting the antagonists but because his was the adjoining diocese he kept a low profile. Haden was to meet me in the cocktail lounge at 3:00 p.m. Arriving at two, I went to the lounge, ordered a pot of tea, and took a table. My résumé was prepared and my not-often-worn black suit was freshly pressed. With my book whose author was explaining a new direction in quantum mechanics — no churchy or theological subject — I was prepared to spend the time quietly. In the middle of my reading I was interrupted by Bishop Pike.

"Raymond, are you here to witness the lynching?" he asked. I told him why I was in Augusta and my plans for a move to California. Pike was no longer bishop of the Diocese; he had resigned and the new diocesan bishop was C. Kilmer Myers.

"If I still had the authority, I'd offer you a place," he said. That was kind and I knew that he meant it. We had been friends for several years. "It is, however, certain that you should not be seen by Clarence talking to the likes of me." A few minutes before the appointed time, Pike left. He was scheduled to state his case before the House Committee on Theology and Canons. Pike was an attorney and litigator. It would prove to be no contest.

The meeting with Haden went well. I was offered a cure in Rancho Cordova, near Sacramento, which I could begin before the Christmas season. I was invited to visit St. Clement's as soon as I could. I did that a few weeks later and found the congregation interesting but resembling a passing parade: most of the members were attached to Mather AFB, a training base for Air Force navigators. Once the program was completed, the men were sent on assignment and the wives often returned to their parents' towns. Many wives, however, waited in Rancho Cordova for the return of their husbands if they were assigned to Vietnam.

St. Clement's was a struggling and challenging mission. Soon after arriving I discovered that there were 17 divorce cases awaiting some legal judgment — also a pastoral review. The only thing I disliked about the assignment was the vicarage. The house was small, lacked any air conditioner, and suffered from mistreatment. The bishop did not want to spend any money to repair the house and refused to let me buy my own house. Because of the traditional housing allowance given to clergy (which was for tax purposes part of my salary), he threatened to cut that allowance if I disobeyed him. Nevertheless, I accepted the cure — thinking all along that it was a temporary assignment that would allow me to begin work on my doctorate at GTU.

On 1 December 1969, I left the Copper Basin after resigning from both the Mission and from the position with the 202 Act. Trudy and the children went to stay in Atlanta while my mother rode with me in the VW Bus to California. Trudy did not want to share the driving across country with me. I was towing behind me a VW Squareback that we purchased in 1968. Behmer, my German shepherd dog, was in a portable and comfortable doghouse that Oren Postelle built for him. The trip was long and tiresome. Mother did not drive but complained most of the time. The only mishap was a broken tow bar that was repaired and reinforced by a welder in Oklahoma City.

The drive I made again across the southern portion of the United States was not as difficult as I had anticipated. The storms offered some interesting driving experiences but the scenery was splendid. The second day of driving, I learned to shut out Mother's complaints. That Trudy had not wanted to help with the driving was puzzling. At one time we had discussed the possibility of the children being cared for by Mother while Trudy and I drove the caravan to California. A relief driver would have made the trip less stressful. Trudy's acting as a second driver had been the reason why Mother had come to Georgia prior to our departure. That had all been changed by Trudy a couple of days prior to the start of the journey. Any consequential changes would have complicated the departure, because Mother would have melodramatically accused me of not loving her. Enough of that, I wanted no problem. So I bit the bullet and pushed on.

After two major snowstorms we arrived in Rancho Cordova on 8 December 1969. The movers arrived at the vicarage a few days after we did. Trudy and the children arrived by airline on 15 December. When Trudy arrived she found that several of the boxes had been unpacked, the beds were all made, the kitchen was mostly ready and a stew was simmering on the stove. Francis Xavier Petraglia had helped in the process of unpacking the boxes. Mother had returned to Chicago in a huff because it was too cold in Sacramento. Colder than Chicago in December? But she insisted.

After briefing Trudy and showing Dominique her new room and Behmer his place in the yard, I went to St. Clement's to prepare for the Advent and Christmas seasons. There were many tasks needing my attention. A knock on my office door roused me from my thinking. Ruth Eger entered and asked if I needed any help. My reply must have been stupid because she reached for the telephone and quickly mustered a brigade of helpful parishioners. Work was started in many areas. Bulletins were written, typed, and printed. The head of the altar guild was summoned and a plan for the liturgies was designed. The organist, Gloria Hall, was brought over to tell us what was planned. Gloria was a fine musician and also a fair painter and a most open and delightful person. Would I mind if a brass ensemble was brought over to supplement the organ? Of course I did not mind. Each party took over in good spirit and with enormous energy. By close of day much of the necessary work had been accomplished.

Ruth Eger continued to be my friend and as I affectionately called her, "my hair shirt." She was always able to point me in the right direction, make me attentive to the needs of this or that parishioner, and remind me that Christian education was the principal task at hand: I would look after the adults and she would look after the youth, and she did admirably.

Ruth Eger was five years older than I. A lifelong and devoted Episcopalian, she had a heart of gold and a wise mind. When I buried her on 20 May 1998, I buried part of me with her: she was my friend, my keel, and my confessor. Ruth died after nearly twenty years of illness that emanated from Diabetes II. Chuck, her husband, was a superb nurse to her. Soon after Ruth got sick, he retired from Westinghouse, and dedicated himself to nursing her. He should be given an award for the selfless care he gave to his Ruth. As often is the case for many families, Ruth was the glue that held the Eger family together and gave it a sense of who it was.

I cannot think of a more extraordinary example for sainthood than Ruth. Her love for people was boundless and her devotion to God was supreme. Many years later after my time in Rancho Cordova, I reconnected with Ruth when I served at St. Edward's Parish, San Jose. Again, she was my staff and my guide willing to help me whenever I needed it. For both my second wedding and for Dominique's, she made two delicious four-layer chocolate cakes. Ruth was one of God's lively messengers on this planet earth. I still miss her.

There was also Francis Xavier Petraglia, retired master sergeant in the USAF, who was now a most secure pillar of the Episcopal Church. Pete, as he was called, was another supportive member who finally ended by going to CDSP and becoming an ordained priest. Petraglia was a lovely person to whom I often turned when situations became tense under the rule of Haden. I am one of the few who always used his complete Christian name, Francis Xavier.

A surrogate father to many at St. Clement's and a dear friend to me, Francis Xavier was all heart, all humor, and all service. Up to the week he died, Francis Xavier was a friend and a regular correspondent (Francis Xavier died in February 2003). It was our custom to chat several times a year and to try to visit each other at times. Xavier was a patient man with vision and understanding.

At St. Clement's, Ruth acted as my mentor in guiding me through the difficult process of caring for a congregation that could have used the help of several clergy. As vicar, the task of caring was daunting, especially with a bishop who was not helpful but a thorny hindrance. I immediately went to work to improve the liturgy, organize the church school, train an altar guild, coordinate the music with the seasons, establish a weekly mission letter, visit as many parishioners as possible, and organize the vestry into an informed team that could direct the ongoing management of the mission's affairs.

The congregation was admirably enthusiastic, especially now that dynamism was being injected into the life of the mission. The mission had two non-parochial clergy who were willing to help with liturgy whenever their time permitted; they were both fully employed. Robert Gould was an employee of the State of California's social service system. The other brother in orders was Lee Page, a most creative person who could not quite find his niche in society and especially not in the Diocese of Northern California. Bishop Haden found Lee to be unmanageable. I found Lee to be a fine person who reflected boldly and with integrity the person of Jesus Christ. Bob and

Lee were men who solidly supported the increasing work at St. Clement's. I could not have managed without their help, their kindness, and their care.

Being settled in Rancho Cordova meant that we had to live in a small house, which was neither insulated nor adequately planned. Moreover, Bishop Haden strictly forbade me from purchasing my own house! The backyard was in terrible condition, and the soil was tantamount to solid clay: rock hard in the dry summer heat and oozy in the wet winter months. Dominique was of age to attend Sacramento Country Day School and Michel was ready to spend half days at the nursery school organized by the local American Baptist Church. Because Trudy was unhappy with the house and hated staying home with the children, she began to do substitute teaching in the local high schools. The unpleasant relationship with the bishop did not make for a happy atmosphere. Neither Trudy nor I found respite in Rancho.

Dominique was growing up and becoming a most creatively artistic child and her enrollment at Sacramento Country Day School helped her blossom further as a fascinating person. She learned much and produced several good pieces of sculpture. Dominique was a loving and active child who was constantly on the go, making things, painting, reading, and playing. Learning, for Dominique, was what life was all about. We gave her a bicycle and that offered her freedom to play with children all along our street. Training wheels were beneath her; she quickly conquered riding on two wheels and soon outgrew the bike, which Michel later inherited. Often I say to people who knew Dominique that she did not have an off button: she was always and in all ways active.

One of Dominique's great contributions to Michel and to her parents was that she took it upon herself to teach Michel how to read. Sitting him in a small chair, Dominique would help him learn the alphabet, the words that surfaced from the alphabet, and the sentences that could be made when the words were assembled. By the time he was a little over three, Michel could read, and reading became for him important and necessary. Also emerging was Dominique's ability as a teacher, and an exciting teacher at that, a talent she has honed well to this day and that serves her admirably as a professor at university.

Michel was also a fascinating but quiet child when compared to Dominique. He made few demands. Engrossed in a book, he would remain in one corner for several hours. With trifocal glasses as a requirement to align his slightly crossed eyes, he looked a bit pitiful and unfocussed. That he outgrew his sight problems was not only miraculous but a credit to his ophthalmologists. Too young to ride his own bike, I would let him sit on the frame bar of mine and we would go to church or make several calls in Rancho. He loved scooting along on my bike in Rancho and we both enjoyed chatting and playing "lock, lock, unlock, unlock." This was a game that suggested that either one of us would "lock or unlock" the other person's nose by lightly squeezing the nose between bent index and middle fingers, and thus simulating that it was inoperative. Michel loved to play this game, as did I. It was a silly game but it was fun!

To break the spell of Rancho, Trudy organized a month vacation to Mexico, in the summer of 1970. I had an air conditioning system installed in the VW Squareback, a box built and fiber-glassed to place on top of the roof for our luggage; this configuration allowed the kids to use both the back seat and the hatch area for reading, sitting, or sleeping. Of course this was long before safety belts were mandatory.

The holiday was enjoyable but the weather was quite warm. Many of the lodging establishments had pools or access to the ocean, and this made the visit all the more enjoyable. In one town, Mazatlan, I think, Dominique, a good swimmer herself, saved Michel from drowning; he had jumped into the deep end of the pool after removing his floatation vest. He wanted to see if he could float as well as his sister. Although he could swim, Michel was shocked that his water displacement volume had diminished greatly without the vest and he panicked. His sister came to his rescue.

Long before books on tape were invented, when we drove long distances and found it necessary to entertain the children, Trudy would read a story to them as I drove. While driving I would participate in the process by inventing a fable. The favorite story was *Charlie and the Chocolate Factory* and particularly the problems that the character Violet Beauregard caused. Of the stories I created, they loved "The Black Handed Man." This was the story of a man who had a pet Bengal tiger named Mark. Episode after episode marked mile after mile of covered territory.

Upon returning to Rancho Cordova, I was greeted with an invitation to attend a liturgical conference in Milwaukee, Wisconsin, in October 1970. The invitation had come from the Chair of the Church's Standing Liturgical Commission and all my expenses were to be paid by the Commission. Bishop Haden reluctantly agreed to let me go, but he wanted to reduce my salary during the time I was away, principally a week. Fortunately, the diocesan chancellor, when he heard of this action, immediately told the bishop that I was still on the Church's business and hence would continue on the Church's payroll. I went to Milwaukee to attend the conference. It showed some of the first moves by the Church to test the revisions proposed for the Prayer Book. At the conference I met my old friend and past boss, William Dimmick. Bill was still Dean of St. Mary's Cathedral in Memphis, but was also bishop-elect of the diocese of Upper Michigan.

I was happy to see Dimmick elected bishop because he was both learned and a fine pastor. Bill was a bachelor who was truly married to the Church, not in a sweet sentimental way but with a coherent and reasonable relationship. As a man who read Alfred North Whitehead and William Temple nothing less could be expected. It is unfortunate that Dimmick was not a writer; society would have gained much more from his contribution. His consecration to the episcopacy was scheduled for the Feast of St. Andrew the Apostle, 1 December 1970. Dimmick asked me to be his chaplain for the celebration, but when Haden heard that I been invited to attend he immediately forbade me to go.

The conference was an eye opener for me. It made me realize that good liturgy is a powerful tool — for promoting good or bad responses from the public. Good liturgy is an art and it can encompass all the different forms of art. I also recognized that Anglicanism understands this power, and its liturgy was the tool that empowers its worshippers. Archbishop Thomas Cranmer, because he understood this phenomenon, placed a great deal of importance on his preparation of the Book of Common Prayer (BCP) of 1549 and the BCP of 1552. It was not merely that the putting together was an important task under the umbrella of King Edward VI, but that the BCP during the time of the infancy of England's "Anglicanism" became a tremendous instrument that could help counter Roman Catholicism and also produce sound theology.

Queen Mary recognized the empowering force that Cranmer was releasing and she had to stop it. If she did not, all allegiance to Rome would quickly dissipate, and Protestantism would emerge as the leading form of Christianity in England. Rome's authority would be diminished irrevocably. Mary's death was, in a sense, providential for the BCP and for Anglicanism.

Queen Elizabeth the First recognized the value of the rallying force of the BCP on her subjects and legitimized its use but did not forbid the continued use of the Roman Missal as long as it was used in parallel or as a companion book for those who adhered to Rome's approach to theology. Although Elizabeth I herself was not interested in what people believed in their conscience, she expected outward conformity, thus signing the Act of Uniformity of 1559 which applied to clergy and laity alike. Elizabeth I often told her people that she was not interested in what they believed as long as they used the Book of Common Prayer!

Uniformity of liturgical worship is the unifying issue of Anglicanism; each Anglican can and may have his or her personal interpretation as long as it is framed in the BCP. Alas, many Anglicans and surely Episcopalians forget that inherent freedom, which is at their disposal "at all times and in all places."

Unlike the 1928 liturgy that was dull and disempowering except for its poetic prose reflecting much of the language used in the King James Bible, the proposed new texts for the revised BCP were exciting. The language was easily understood although it lacked the beauty that Episcopalians expected. All who attended the conference accepted that it was a liturgy in draft form. That more work had to be done was obvious to all of us. Yet the liturgy with its rewritten consecration prayer and its hints urging congregational participation was a breath of fresh air.

Upon my return to Rancho Cordova I wrote a detailed report for the bishop and gave a summary of it to my congregation from the pulpit supplemented by several adult class discussions. With the permission of the Vestry we moved the chairs in a semicircle and placed the altar nearer to the worshippers. We celebrated with the 1928 liturgy in the round to introduce a certain flexibility and to announce that the altar with the celebrant's back to the people was soon to be changed. The proposed approach was for the altar to be freestanding and the celebrant to face the congregation. We were as yet not authorized by General Convention to use the proposed liturgy, and I honored that.

The Vestry of St. Clement's was excited by the report on the new proposed work on the liturgy and the BCP. They suggested that we invite other clergy from different denominations to discuss the new direction that the Episcopal Church was engaged in. One evening we convened an open conference and six members of the local clergy attended. We had American Baptist, Roman Catholic, American Lutheran, Methodist, and Southern Baptist clergy at the table. The discussion moved to a point where a proposal was made to have a joint celebration followed by a picnic. This was a splendid idea, especially since St. Clement's had already considered constructing an altar outside for such open celebration. With the help of a few hardy men we purchased a large lava rock, cast a flat concrete rectangle to be the top surface of the altar, and poured a concrete slab for the stone. We did this work in three days and it took three days for the concrete to set. We started on Monday and by the following Sunday we were able to celebrate the Eucharist on it.

Outside Altar at St. Clement's

Two weeks later we had the American Baptist and the Lutheran ministers, plus the Roman Catholic Monsignor present for another outside Eucharist where I asked the Baptist to give the opening prayer, the Lutheran to do the offertory bidding, and the Roman to give the final blessing and all from the BCP! It was a great day and the congregation was delighted with the event.

Four weeks after my return from Milwaukee and a week after this ecumenical event, I was summoned to the Bishop's Office in Sacramento. I was informed that what I had written was not to be publicized. The proposed liturgy was not to be used. I was not to continue responding to communications from the Church's Standing Liturgical Commission (SLC). At the meeting with the bishop I was instructed that I was to listen and not speak. What he had said orally was given to me in a letter as I passed by his secretary's desk, a communicant of St. Clement's. June Galante was as stunned as I was, but she had typed the letter.

"Father Raymond, let that episode be ignored," she said to me.

That was easier said than done. The SLC had noticed my interest at the conference, especially in the seminars. Dr. Massey Shepherd, who was on the

SLC, knew that I was interested, not only in this seminal work on the Canon of the Eucharist, but that I was interested in pursuing further work, perhaps by way of a doctoral program.

Another issue surfaced because St. Clement's had plans underway for a group of people to see a performance in San Francisco of Andrew Lloyd Weber's *Jesus Christ Superstar*. The group was composed of 15 adults and five high school seniors, whose parents were among the adults. With dinner in San Francisco and the excellent performance, we all marked the evening a success. The following Sunday in the regular adult class the topic was centered on the plot of the musical, especially the role of Judas Iscariot. Why was he being blamed for Jesus' death, if the death was a necessary step in the plot of salvation? The passages in the Gospels were reviewed and examined. I brought some of the Greek texts of the Gospels and we all discussed in great depth the Passion narratives. All in all it was a good educational exercise for all of us. As is usually the case, lauding by those who enjoyed the discussion was heard as were also the complaints by those, few really, who felt that the musical, which they had not heard, was blasphemous. Negative comments were small and the few who voiced them were also small.

A few weeks later, the drama department of Sacramento State University sent me an open invitation to see a performance of *Godspell*. I could bring fifteen guests to the mid-week performance. We went to the performance and enjoyed it and the discussion that followed. The drama department had prepared the discussion to encourage conversation between it and the congregations of the several churches that had attended. We all found the evening stimulating and enjoyable.

Again at St. Clement's a group of six members who had not heard *Godspell* complained that it was just as blasphemous as *Superstar*. At the vestry meeting one member suggested that not everyone could be pleased, but that the experience of both musicals had helped open up discussions that he hoped would lead to further learning. Indeed, that was the intent that prompted us to attend both the performances.

It was time to do something about what the Episcopal Church traditionally calls its "Every Member Canvass." In short this is canvassing the congregation for financial support through pledging a certain amount of money towards the budget. The budget includes obligations for mortgage, salaries, and assessment support to the diocese, mission and outreach beyond the operating needs of the mission or parish, and other financial requirements.

Fundraising was never something I liked to do nor had any gift for. One of the members, Robert B. Lynch, an attorney and past employee of Aerojet, was keen to help me. Bob was a tall, forceful fellow who was searching for a cause and a purpose to pursue at St. Clement's. Bob volunteered to chair and run the fundraising program and I must admit that he did a fine job not only meeting our budget but also exceeding the total established by the vestry.

Because the fundraising had produced good results Bishop Haden rewarded us by increasing our assessment by 20%; that was a kick in the gut of the mission. Bob went to see the bishop to complain, but Haden refused to listen to him and even threatened to sue him and me for doctoring the budget of the mission. When that threat did not stop Bob, the bishop switched tactics and asked Bob to represent the Diocese and sue me. Bob told him in no uncertain words that he would not represent Haden, would not sue me, and furthermore, if a suit was instigated he would initiate a countersuit and focus on the bishop and the Diocese and publicize the news. The bishop decided to avoid the whole issue and use other means as will be explained later.

Now I need to say that I did not intentionally try to antagonize Bishop Haden or to cause him any problems. It was my intention to serve him and the mission under my cure, and it was my purpose to educate the congregation in what was being developed in the Episcopal Church in the late 60s and early 70s and prepare them for the coming liturgical changes, theological expansions, and social developments. Soon a new BCP would be given to congregations, women were to be ordained, racism was slowly being addressed and new perspectives established, lay folk were offered new authority and new controls, and in many ways the old staid church was subjected to new currents of fresh air, new thinking, and new directions. I supported the changes.

Robert B. Lynch was an extraordinary and bright person but a Europhobe. Bob disliked the French, but excused me. He was an aerospace engineer who could see that his firm Aerojet was going nowhere, and that in fact under the Nixon Administration, space development was at a standstill. After several discussions with me and projecting some of his concerns on how best to handle his own future, Bob decided that admission to McGeorge School of Law in Sacramento was a good idea. He passed the bar exam after I left Rancho Cordova. Through friends I learned that Bob had developed a sound practice in Sacramento and appeared to be heading towards a good future, even a judgeship.

One Sunday in February 2004, Bob telephoned me after locating me through the Internet. He announced that he had retired from law as Chief Municipal Judge and was presently living in a small rural town near Tucson, Arizona. How he came to call me was a bit touching and humorous. After attending Eucharist at the mission church near his town, a mission that had opted out of the Episcopal Church because of the ordination of women into the priesthood, the so-called priest who had delivered an awful sermon according to Bob, donned his Beretta after the service. Both the poor sermon and the silly Beretta triggered an inclination that he needed "to find Fr. Raymond."

Bob called me to reminisce about our friendship and the dramatic sermons that often were projected with puppets, short plays, and films that were delivered at St. Clement's Mission, Rancho Cordova. Bob admitted that women in holy orders were a little unacceptable to him and that was the reason he attended a renegade mission.

"How does one address a woman priest?" he puzzled. I chose at the time not to fan this issue, assuming that there would be a better time for that.

By the end of my first year as vicar, I had opened the sermon to the congregation for discussion after the service and had often supplemented the address with a short dramatic presentation or puppet display. A member had built a puppet stage for me and often, with the help of eager parishioners manning the puppets, we offered performances to emphasize the current theme of the sermon. Adults and children thoroughly enjoyed these events that helped enlarge the attendance. That was just as well because it indicated, to me at least, that things were going well. In response, the vestry and I had eliminated the dreaded funding canvassing program, so that giving was fundamentally a purely voluntary effort. Giving increased and pledging units increased too. Our financial health was getting stronger, and the vestry even considered applying for parish status. This was not a motion that I endorsed quite yet; I wanted to see a secure increase both in pledging units and congregational participation first.

Dr. J.P. Edwards, an obstetrician-gynecologist, was a kind and devoted man but a difficult one at times. Leaning towards the high churchmanship, he often asked that the liturgy include the ceremonious appendages that were identified with "popishness." J.P. was a good man, but coming from a Baptist Missourian heritage he wanted to go all the way to high ceremony in the liturgy. With teaching he was willing to tone down his demands and accepted simplicity and reasonableness in the liturgy. I was not against high ceremony in liturgy but preferred to use the adornments attributed to it during important feasts. His wife Sara, a fine person in many ways, was unable to cope with her husband. J.P. was a person who had many interests and a keen mind, and who made the most of his talents.

At the end of my first year, J.P. asked me out for lunch to discuss an issue that bothered him. He was interested in holy orders and was willing to attend seminary and carry a full coursework. I suggested he meet with the bishop as soon as possible. I could not see any reason why he could not pursue studies for orders. A few days later we met with the bishop who quickly endorsed J.P.'s request. It is customary for the postulant to be shepherded by his own priest to assist him through the maze of requirements leading to orders. In this case, J.P. was assigned to the dean of the Cathedral in Sacramento, the Very Reverend John Hoffman. J.P. asked why he could not continue to work with me. Bishop Haden replied that his decision was not open to discussion or change. The dean and I were good friends, and he was a learned man, hence I suggested to J.P. that he might gain more from having someone else be his guide.

Soon after this issue was settled, I started my own work at the Graduate Theological Union (GTU) in Berkeley, and J.P. began his work at the Church Divinity School of the Pacific (CDSP). He had to drive from Sacramento three times a week to a class that lasted only a few hours, and was scheduled for the afternoon. My schedule required that I spend a whole day, one day a week at GTU, which was next door to CDSP. On the days when I was at GTU, J.P. often joined me for lunch, and if that was not possible, we made arrangements to have dinner. This gave him the opportunity to discuss ideas with me in spite of the fact that he was quite satisfied with his mentor from the Cathedral.

Soon into the second semester, faculty members told me on several occasions that J.P. was a good and devoted student and that his work was excellent. J.P. continued to apply himself well; he graduated in 1974 and was made a deacon soon after. When he was ordained a priest in 1975 he immediately closed his practice in Sacramento and packed his bags to serve as a priest-physician on an Indian reservation in North Dakota. A few months later, with their four children out of college and working, Sara (his wife) filed for dissolution of their marriage. When Bishop Haden heard of this action, he tried to have J.P. deposed, defrocked as a priest. Fortunately J.P.'s letter of canonical transfer had already been filed with the Bishop of North Dakota, and Haden's appeal was simply ignored. J.P. continued to support Sara until she remarried in 1977 to a widower priest. J.P. died in 1990 after serving the Indians of his diocese both as a priest and as a physician.

To escape from the difficult times I would go to my office at St. Clement's and write articles for several magazines; some texts were on Church affairs and others were on socio-political issues. I managed to be published in the *St. Luke's Journal of the University of the South*, *Liturgia*, *The Atlantic Monthly*, the *Princeton Review*, *Witness*, *Nation*, and several other reputable magazines; even a short article on marriage appeared in the *New Yorker*.

I also tried my hand at writing a play dealing with the social times of the 60s and 70s. I wrote a long poetic play, *Love, Bribes, and Things like That (LB&T)*, wherein I discussed the changing ethical atmosphere in the American culture. Dr. Becky Jernigan, my dear friend, stage and motion picture actress, playwright, and professor of English had moved to Rancho Cordova to regain her life after two very difficult and disappointing marriages. After reading LB&T she suggested that it be turned into a musical and she would write the music for it. I took that with a grain of salt, thinking that perhaps she was flattering me. Soon, however, after she had written the music, she talked the manager of a small theatre in Rancho Cordova into giving her rehearsal time and a firm date for 15 performances, and had recruited a young and able cast of volunteers for the play. While rehearsals were in full bloom, Becky had contacted Channel 10, Sacramento's affiliate station of the Columbia Broadcasting System (CBS), to inquire if they were interested in the play. On 15 May 1970, the play opened to a full house (approximately 2,000 people) and CBS-TV did a nationwide hook-up of the complete play for broadcasting the next day on Richard Boone's Theatre Scene. Becky had turned a simple poem into a major performance; all this was done in less than five months.

Activities at St. Clement's were open for everyone. A large musical group was involved with the selection of both the liturgical and entertainment music. A small brass band played often during the services and supplemented the small organ. Four string players were often added to the music for the liturgy when the brass was not involved. St. Clement's had three cantors who in turn supported the chanting of the liturgy under the leadership of Charles Eger and Gloria Hall. Several tenors and sopranos also offered their voices for liturgy or joined the rest of the music group for concerts that were open to the public. Trudy was often asked to participate and to lend her voice but to my recollection she always refused. At St. Clement's a babysitting service was always available, hence Trudy was not tied to the children or imprisoned in the vicarage.

When I went on business trips, often I would ask Trudy if she wanted to join me. Only on a few occasions would she accept. I'm saying this to dispel the notion that, as the vicar's wife and the mother of two children, she was kept homebound against her will. On several occasions we went to stay together and without the children in Nell McVeigh's Squaw Valley condominium.

I had first met Nell McVeigh when I attended a conference on the Church and Politics hosted by the California Council of Churches. During lunch Nell and I sat at the same table and we struck up a friendship that bonded us for many years. Nell lived on Conn Valley Road, St. Helena, on a working ranch that she owned. Initially from Colorado Springs, where her husband Charles and she had lived as young people before he had been given a position at Harvard as professor of history, the McVeighs were devoted Episcopalians and strong supporters of the Church in many areas. Charles McVeigh owned several hundred acres of land on the outskirts of Colorado Springs that he had purchased with a little inheritance from his grandfather. It so happened that the Defense Department wanted much of that property to build and develop on it the future Air Force Academy. The McVeighs readily sold the land and with the cash bought a ranch in St. Helena, thus avoiding paying any capital gains tax.

Unfortunately, Charles suffered from an aneurism and died soon after he and his wife moved to their new ranch. Nell was left with sufficient resources to operate the ranch and to become a small philanthropist, especially for the Episcopal Church. Nell became a benefactor for many programs that the Church, her bishop, and her friends proposed. Her kindness helped me attend the six-week research fellowship at the College of Preachers located on the property of the Washington National Cathedral, and she often invited my family to spend small holidays in the cabin near her small lake or in her large house. Nell was always ready to entertain groups and to offer her hospitality for any just cause.

At her house, I had several meetings with young groups discussing politics, social issues, the future, and the state of religion. State Senator John Vasconselos, the late Mayor George Mascone, Speaker Willie Brown, Dr. Massey H. Shepherd, and others joined us as leaders, participants, and facilitators of two-or three-day conferences where Nell poured her warm hosting care upon us.

I also had retreats with the Bishop's Committee from St. Edmund's, Pacifica and with the Vestry from All Soul's Church, Berkeley where I was interim for several months. Nell's house on her ranch in St. Helena was always available for me to use. She was also most gracious in allowing me to use her condominium at Squaw Valley whenever she was not using it.

A more gracious woman than Nell I did not know. She was openhearted, benevolent, and always willing to share her gifts with others and with me. Nell died at the turn of the century when I was in Russia and could not be present for her memorial service; she is in my prayers whenever I am serving at Grace Cathedral.

The Hoche-Mongs went camping to Dunsmuir and to other places. We traveled to Mexico for a month and explored places around Sacramento. Leon Combs and his wife Gladys often invited us to dinner at their home or to join them at new and interesting restaurants for a night out and some solid conversation. Leon, a devoted liberal, was from Texas but educated in Arkansas, and Gladys was from North Carolina but a graduate of Southwestern University, Memphis, so there were a few Southern points of commonality between us.

By and large, I never felt that Trudy was too terribly interested in participating or joining activities that moved her away from herself. In later years and after we had dissolved our marriage I came to the conclusion that Trudy was either extremely shy or absolutely uninterested in developing long-term friendships.

Juggling St. Clement's Mission Church, the Graduate Theological Union, Trudy's difficult attitude, and Bishop Haden was almost more than I could bear. Yet there were some light sides during that period. For example I had two wonderful parishioners, Carol and David Camomile, who were socially fun to be with. Carol was in her early fifties and always ready to help out at St. Clement's whenever some need arose. She also possessed a wicked sense of humor that always defused a tense situation. David was a power engineer employed by William (Bill) Lear on a project at Stead Airport in Reno Nevada.

One day in a casual conversation, I asked him what he was working on with Bill Lear. He replied that Lear was developing a steam engine for automobiles that would probably be marketed in a few years.

Now Bill Lear was known as a genius, an inventor, and the creator of the automobile radio, the 8-track cassette tape, and the first turbine (jet engine) powered aircraft for civilian use adapted from a Swiss reconnaissance aircraft. The Lear Jet was a phenomenal airplane that cruised at nearly 400 miles per hour, climbed to 38,000 feet, and seated six passengers, two pilots, and a flight attendant. Bill had adapted a Swiss reconnaissance aircraft and modified it to serve as a corporate high-flying vehicle in the General Aviation category. The Lear Jet could also be configured after much convincing of the FAA and much training, to be flown by a single pilot in good weather. Even the military, often sticklers about aircraft, purchased several "Lears," as they were called. General aviation, especially the corporate side of it, was given a vital boost in its operational agenda when the Lear Jet was marketed. It was fast, demanding, efficient, and a terribly "sexy" aircraft.

David worked in Reno during the week and spent weekends at home in Rancho Cordova. One Sunday morning after the Eucharist when wine and cheese were served as a substitute for coffee and doughnuts, David asked me if I would be interested in seeing the facility at Stead Airport.

"Would I meet Bill Lear?" I inquired.

"Of course," was his response. He gave me directions and asked if I could be at Stead the following Tuesday. I agreed with joy and anticipation. Meeting Bill Lear was a treat that few people would refuse, at least not with a life full of flying devotion.

Reno was less than two hours away by car. I drove my VW up the mountain to Stead Airport, through the guarded gate and on to the Lear compound. David met me and took me inside the large hangar where the research and testing of the steam engine prototype was taking place. I stood at a respectful distance to be out of the way. Several people were working on the engine of about the size of a V-8 automobile engine. Steam was visible and a clanging noise was deafening every time the flywheel rotated. The engine was running but not too smoothly, at least not for use in a passenger or truck vehicle. It was too noisy and too shaky for human comfort. After several hours of watching the steam, hearing the noise, and listening to practically inaudible conversation — and several hours after the lunch hour — Bill Lear shut the engine off and called for a meeting to discuss the problems they had encountered.

I was left standing and was totally ignored for an hour. During the time when I was left alone, I approached the engine that was mounted on its stand and examined it all around. It was a fine looking piece of mechanical engineering and suggested that possibilities existed for it to be refined sufficiently for use in a vehicle. The log attached to the stand indicated that it developed 400 horses at 2,200 rotations per minute (rpm). That was a substantial power plant using crude oil or jet grade fuel for its operation at a rate of two gallons per hour at full rpm. The oil producers would first dynamite such an engine to keep it off the streets, and then they would destroy the factory producing such a devilishly efficient power source.

While I was engrossed in my cursory examination of the engine, David came over and asked me to follow him into Bill's office-laboratory. My chance to meet the genius had arrived. Bill took my hand in his big hand and welcomed me. After the preliminary small talk we discussed flying when I asked about his jet airplane project. The Lear Jet was selling well and he informed me that two aviation manufacturers were interested in acquiring the rights to produce the aircraft.

"I'm not in the production business but in the invention thrill. I'll readily sell the rights if, and only if, the sale contract states clearly that the name 'Lear Jet' is never changed, altered, or given a prefix or a suffix," he stated. "Have you any turbine time?" he inquired.

After giving him my reply and the hours I had spent in turbine-powered aircraft, Bill (we were now on a first name basis) asked me if I wanted a ride in his personal Lear Jet aircraft. Would I? I had not ridden in a small jet, apart from commercial passenger types, in at least ten years.

"Yes," I replied.

"OK, tomorrow morning at nine o'clock meet me at the hangar."

I admit that the night was too long. I counted the hours until morning and even then arrived at the hangar at 7:45 a.m. I waited and considered my good fortune. A ride in a Lear with its inventor was more than I could have hoped. I had come to see a steam engine and, perhaps, to meet Mr. William Lear, if I was lucky. At exactly 8:15 Bill Lear arrived, opened the hangar and did his own preflight inspection. A crew came out of one side of the hanger and towed the Lear onto the apron. The aircraft had received fuel for three hours of flight, and the maintenance crew had checked all systems. The aircraft was ready to fly when Bill Lear was ready to pilot it. Bill came out of an inner office and announced that we were ready and that the flight plan had been filed. He indicated that I was to sit in the right seat.

"Is there a copilot?" I asked.

"You are the copilot," he replied, or rather ordered.

"But I'm not rated for this aircraft," I told him.

"You are legal; this aircraft is especially rated for single pilot operation." After a moment he added, "Pete, the copilot, will ride with us in the jump seat right behind us!"

After giving me a brief review of the instruments, the operating numbers, the radio, and the altitude we were to reach and cruise level, he started the engines, examined the power instruments, released the brakes and we began to roll towards the runway.

Once off the runway and in the air, he set the autopilot and altitude hold to 11,000 feet with a cruise speed of 230 knots. When the aircraft reached that altitude he reset the auto and altitude to 33,000 feet with a cruise of 380 knots. That done he turned to me and we chatted about his work, his creations, his aspirations, and his next project which was a single engine pusher aircraft for the GA market. Once the aircraft reached the set altitude, he checked his instruments and settled back to enjoy the flight and continue his conversation with me.

"Raymond why don't you take the controls?" he never waited for my answer. He disconnected the autopilot and altitude hold, and his hands were off the yoke.

"It's yours," he ordered. I had not flown an aircraft in years and my altitude management was not the best, yet it was within the 100 feet tolerance permitted. A few moments later I settled into a more reasonable flying routine with altitude not oscillating up or down but holding steady. I became more confident and less tense. He called Oakland Traffic Control and informed them that he was operating a familiarization flight and wanted a clearance to deviate left and right from the airways.

"Raymond it is all yours. Try some steep turns to check your own equilibrium. We have clearance by ATC but maintain your altitude," he advised. I did a few 30 degrees turns to the left and then to the right and after discovering that I was holding the altitude well, I pushed the Lear to 45-degree turns at 380 knots. Wow! The thrill was extraordinary and reminded me of my USAF flying in hot interceptors. It was time to return to sane flying. I recaptured the centerline of the airway and positioned the aircraft back on course.

"Bill, thanks for the thrill. It's a fine bird that you've created."

He took over and we continued our cruising. Over the Tehachapi Mountains, I noticed that we were approaching Los Angeles and asked where we would be landing.

"Lindberg, San Diego," he replied as he began the transition to descent. We arrived at Lindberg and were given a straight entry to the runway. Bill taxied to Fixed Base Operator (FBO) serving GA Aviation and shut down. As he removed himself from the aircraft, he ordered fuel and entered the waiting room. In the room a tray of sandwiches was ready for us. Lunch tasted good but I was still in the air. Pete joined us after tending to some business for Bill.

During our lunch Bill informed me that we had been flying the Learjet 23 with a length of 43 feet and a wingspan of 35.5 feet, which weighed 12,750 pounds empty and was powered by a pair of General Electric CJ610-4 turbojet engines. The 23 had a top cruise speed of 564 miles per hour, a range of 1,875 miles and could climb to 39,000 feet in less than 10 minutes!

Our stop lasted just about an hour, and Bill motioned that it was time to head back North. Again he went through a thorough preflight inspection and we boarded the Lear. Door shut, chocks removed he signaled to the ground crew that he was starting the engines, one at a time. After obtaining clearance and local weather he moved the bird to the threshold. We held short until an incoming PSA flight landed, then we were cleared for takeoff. Again, once off the ground and gears retracted, he adjusted his autopilot and altitude hold for 34,000 feet. Our flight path would follow the coastline until Monterey, and then would shift to a more northerly direction heading for the Sierra and Reno. Bill again offered me the yoke after we reached our assigned altitude and after he had disconnected the autopilot. I took command and enjoyed the touch of the aircraft.

Bill and I talked about how he decided to create this jet aircraft, who his supporting engineers were, and how he managed the whole process of FAA certification. I asked him about a few technical issues, such as short takeoff or landing (STOL) characteristics, fuel consumption, Mach speed limitations, and ceiling limitations. He was eager to answer all my questions and to discuss his problems and his successes. Often we returned to his idea of developing a single engine pusher aircraft for small companies that could not afford a high performance turbine plane.

Soon the Sierra section near Reno was in sight and we prepared for our approach to Stead Airport after passing over Truckee. After a midfield crossing over Stead's runway we turned downwind, then on base, and slipped into final for a greased landing. After all was shut down, the maintenance chief asked if the part he'd called for had been delivered and Bill pointed to the aircraft.

"They're inside for you," he said. So Bill had gone shopping in San Diego! I thanked him and shook his hand, then he reminded me to follow him home and that dinner would be at seven o'clock. That evening David joined us for dinner and we all relaxed in Bill's comfortable but not extravagant house.

I left the next morning after breakfast but continued to keep up a correspondence for several years until Bill's death a decade after our meeting. The automobile steam engine did not develop as a commercially applicable power plant for vehicles. Bill abandoned the engine but hoped that a younger generation inventor might make a success of it. Bill did not stop his creativity but developed a composite single engine pusher turbo aircraft that would be fast, economical, and fly at high altitude. Bill Lear died before the aircraft could be fully tested but his wife continued the project. The aircraft was never commercially produced because she died also a few years later. The Swiss aircraft firm Piaggio showed some interest but never took it beyond that level.

Meeting the great inventor William Lear and flying in his personal Lear-jet, which he piloted, can be listed as one of my most cherished encounters and experiences. He was an amazing man, beloved by his employees, and respected by the aviation community. He was unique.

On my day off from St. Clement's in 1970, I attended seminars at GTU. The work on my doctorate was progressing slowly through the Interuniver-sity Doctoral Program (IDP) that had been initiated in 1967 first with recognized American and Canadian universities, and then in 1969 it was en-larged to include universities in the UK. I had entered the doctoral program just in time to benefit from this expanded approach that permitted me to gather faculty members from other institutions. Taking advantage of this pro-gram, I began to look at other institutions for faculty members willing to participate in my course of study.

Bishop Haden and I had numerous altercations that ended in my being fired in January 1972. St. Clement's Mission congregation was growing and was consequently financially strong. In the two years that I had been vicar, the mission budget had grown and had stabilized to the point where we were required by diocesan canon law to begin the process of establishing the mis-sion into a self-sustaining parish. Ted Kaden was treasurer at the time and was repeatedly called by the diocesan treasurer to initiate the process for par-ish status. I wanted to wait another year and wanted to have less of a throughput congregation and more of a local civilian base. I resisted the move to initiate parish status. In response to my resistance, Bishop Haden wrote to me and accused me of "dereliction of duties." I wrote to him and explained that another year was not too much to ask to affirm that financial stability was a fact and not an aberration.

At about the same time that St. Clement's was growing in a place east of the County of Sacramento, the national economy was weakening and was struggling with increased fuel costs, reduced aerospace investments, an enormous financial debt caused by the Vietnam War, and social uprising against the way the government was conducting the business of the nation.

Several members of St. Clement's found themselves either laid-off or terminated and several firms that had major facilities in and near Rancho Cordova were forced to close or just to maintain a skeleton crew. Douglas, Westinghouse, and Aerojet were among the ones to close, and that added 10,000 more to the unemployment rolls. Ted Kaden and Chuck Eger were immediate casualties. The Kadens moved to San Francisco and the Egers transferred to Virginia. In less than four months St. Clement's parochial budget was reduced by 40 percent.

The clergy conference was scheduled that year at the Arnold Palmer Golf Center in Cameron Park; a new development with two golf courses, an airport where pilots could taxi their aircraft to their houses and then to their attached hangars, and a planned community for the aspiring rich and famous. Bishop Haden opened the conference with a stunning announcement that he was proposing to move the diocesan offices from downtown Sacramento, in the heart of the State Capital area, to — guess where — the new suburbs of Cameron Park, a residential area. Out of the thick of things into the wilderness, into an affluent residential community several miles east and not plagued by the realities of Sacramento's social problems, away from the State Capitol, and away from where it could be effective and could affect the affairs of its jurisdiction, Northern California.

I stood up and raised my hand. The bishop allowed me one minute to speak. I explained that the business of the diocese was to remain in the center of events, in the core of the state government, in the inner city, in a place that was accessible to all people. Locating in Cameron Park was telling the people that only the "yuppies," the aspiring rich and famous, mattered to the diocesan leadership. Several other clergy in attendance followed me and all supported my objection and promised to vote against any such proposal and assured all in attendance that they would instruct their delegates to vote against it too. A young courageous priest from Alturas, the remote northeast corner of the state, closed the objection by stating that he'd rather move his parish to Oregon's jurisdiction than to ascribe to this "asinine" move. The bishop's bald head turned crimson in color. At the coffee break, I was called by Haden and given a dressing down and accused of inciting rebellion, discontent, and insubordination.

That night when I returned home and related what had been discussed at the clergy conference, Trudy's comment shocked me:

"You should have kept your mouth shut!" I could not believe it. I could not even rationalize it to make it more acceptable. My wife was asking me to keep quiet. That night I did not sleep, couldn't sleep, and did not want to sleep — least of all with Trudy. It was a terrible night. In the morning I took Dominique and Michel to school and went to the local coffee shop.

My schedule was clear that morning so I could sit and think things out.

A few days after the clergy conference, I received a telephone call from the bishop's secretary summoning me to an audience with Haden in his office. I went and arrived on time. When I entered his office Haden never even acknowledged my presence or asked me to sit. After a few uncomfortable moments as I stood there in front of his desk, he gripped his pipe tightly, and stared at me.

"You have been going to school while neglecting your cure," he accused me. I explained that we had agreed in Augusta that I would be starting my doctoral program and would travel to GTU only on my day off, which I did.

"You will immediately stop this doctoral program," he ordered. I explained that I was in course, had paid my tuition, purchased my books, and was expected to continue my work.

"Either you stop or you are out of a job. It is that simple," he shouted. I was just about to explain again our agreement in Augusta, when he slapped his fist on the desk in a rage.

"Stop now. Immediately. Now," he yelled. "You have been a destructive force in this diocese. You have destroyed a perfectly healthy congregation. You have incited rebellion and discontent among the people and the clergy. You have gathered clergy around that are despicable, men like Lee Page and Bob Gould and who knows who else." His face was red and he kept banging his desk with his fist.

I tried to reply but thought better of that approach. I was certain that if I replied he would have a serious heart attack or stroke. He could not stop banging his fist on the desk. I stood there for a few moments, then turned and left. He continued to rant and rave and bang his fist on the desk. I asked his secretary to look in on him, to check that he was still OK. I was concerned that if he died I would be accused of bringing about his demise.

The secretary looked in and found him still red but a bit calmer. He had broken his pipe stem! Her comment when she returned was that he was totally incoherent and that his face was red. I left the diocesan house a bit shaken. I knew that I was going to be fired, and there was no point in my pleading reinstatement. I had had enough of Clarence Rupert Haden. I drove back towards Rancho Cordova but did not want to face either an empty house or my church office. I drove to Sharon Calvert's house, a dear friend and coffee partner. Sharon prepared lunch that consisted of eggs, sour cream and mayonnaise, and a pinch of Coleman's mustard. It was delicious and to this day often I've offered the same recipe to my guests and called it "Sharon's Eggs."

After a time of decompression over a nicely prepared lunch I tackled my office at St. Clement's. Ruth Eger telephoned from Virginia to inform me that the position Chuck had with Westinghouse had been eliminated and they were returning to California. I told her that my position at St. Clement's was about to be eliminated too and that Chuck and I could sell pencils on the doorsteps of the State Capitol. After tending to the mail I went to Sharon's house to fetch Michel and take him home. When Trudy returned home from her day in school with Dominique, I offered to take everybody to dinner. This was going to be my attempt at celebrating the deliverance from Haden's shackles.

Over dinner I related the high points of my audience with the bishop. Again, Trudy's reply was that I should have kept my mouth shut and that I had a family to consider before I voiced my opinions. I was convinced that I had done nothing untoward in my mind to warrant such a response from both the bishop and from Trudy. Moreover, I was disappointed that Trudy felt unwilling to understand my position as vicar, my sense of integrity, and my responsibility as a teacher. I just could not and would not let pass some idiot idea.

The sum total of my discussion with Trudy was that we had different approaches. Yes I understood my responsibility to my family but I had a responsibility to maintain my self-respect. Who was I? How was I going to sleep if I had simply swallowed my judgment? I admit that I'm not the most passive or tolerant person, that my many warts offend people, and that my attitude grates on many people, but I believe that I'm neither mean nor self-serving. Yes, I am at times intolerant, opinionated, and difficult, but I don't know how to change or hide those characteristics. I attempted to discuss that issue with Trudy but it was to no avail.

Two days later in the mail I received my marching orders. A letter from Bishop Haden stated in no uncertain terms that I was "fired" and had to leave St. Clement's within 30 days. The cause for firing me was not for reasons of morality but for insubordination, inciting other clergy to become insubordinate to their ecclesiastical authority, and abandoning my cure. Although I had prepared myself for this letter it was a shock and I was disappointed. I picked up the phone and telephoned Bishop Sanders who was in Knoxville and told him about the letter and the situation I was in. He offered me a slot in the diocese and would gladly pay all my expenses for the move. There was a position open in Nashville as chaplain to the college students at Vanderbilt University and Fisk University. He further suggested that I could study at Vanderbilt. Indeed I could study in Nashville but the subject would have to be radically changed. I thanked Sanders and told him that I would consider his offer, but first I needed to discuss the matter with Trudy, with the dean of GTU, and eventually with the head of the philosophy department at Vanderbilt.

Because I had been granted a six-week research fellowship to study the effects of the spoken word in liturgy, I called the College of Preachers at the National Cathedral in Washington D.C. The provost assured me that I was still invited and that my transportation costs would be taken care of. I asked for a postponement of 30 days so that I could relocate my family. The postponement was granted. I then phoned the dean of GTU and apprised him of my situation. He would convert my status from part time to full time student in order to help me obtain funds from grants and from what balance I had left from the GI Bill program.

My next move was to write a letter to the congregation explaining the situation. I then wrote letters resigning from all public organizations and boards. I was going to shake the dust of Sacramento from my sandals. In fact if my memory is correct I did not return to Sacramento for 20 years, and if I did it was only to drive through on my way to Tahoe. With all the letters written it was time for me to get my shipping boxes out of the storage room and begin packing my books and office things. After 27 months in Rancho Cordova, it was time for me to exit.

At home when I gave Trudy the news, she replied that there was a teaching position opening in Merced and she had already applied for it. We would be moving to Merced as soon as we were ready. That evening the Suffragan Bishop, Edward McNair, stopped by to tell me that my salary would continue until June. That was five months of salary, from February to June. Since I was to be terminated by the end of January I was entitled only to three months of salary. The Suffragan bishop informed me that the Diocesan Council had voted for that extension in spite of what the bishop had suggested. That move implied that many in the diocesan hierarchy knew a great deal about C.R. Haden's lack of grace. It is difficult to remove a bishop from office in the Episcopal Church.

A few years later, Haden retired and moved to Dallas, Texas to become the mentor of the schismatic Anglican Orthodox Church, a group that refused to accept either the revised BCP or Holy Orders for women. Much as Haden was an advisor to the Anglican Orthodox Church, he never officially left the Episcopal Church. Bishop Haden died in the early 1990s.

J.P. Edwards volunteered to put together a moving crew and a truck for the transfer to Merced, all at no cost to us. Trudy and I and the children took a few days to visit Merced and select a rental house. While in Merced, Trudy was interviewed for her teaching position and obtained a firm offer to start teaching at the end of June for the summer session. After Merced we drove to the Bay Area to find an apartment for me so I could continue to meet the residency requirement for GTU and for the University of California. I found a charming apartment across from the county hospital in Oakland with a garden and an orchard. The apartment we found was a perfect place for me, and also for Trudy when in the following year she swapped with me in June and July to complete her required teaching-upgrading course in library science at the University of California, Berkeley.

Upon our return to Rancho Cordova to start the packing effort, I called Bishop Sanders and declined his offer. He was disappointed but understood that Vanderbilt's program was limited in the area of my interest. Then I wrote to the Church Pension Fund to request an extension of three years on my insurance while I was at GTU preparing a program that would ultimately be beneficial to the Church. I would be studying aesthetics through liturgy as a medium that incorporates all the forms of art. In response to my request the Church Pension accepted my program but asked that my bishop approve my study program by signing a form letter. I forwarded the letter to Haden and added a brief note explaining the procedure. The denouement of this letter is discussed a little later.

With that done, we moved to Merced. The family settled nicely in a pleasant house. With Trudy preparing for her summer class, I advised the College of Preachers that I was ready to start my research as soon as travel arrangements had been made. A round trip ticket from Sacramento to Dulles arrived two days later and I was ready.

The Split Condition

Six weeks of research away from anything that was remotely connected with Haden or Rancho was pure delight. My lead professor at the Graduate Theological Union (GTU), Dr. Wayne Rood, had approved my research program and considered the result as part of my doctoral work. The library at the College of Preachers was excellent, and access to the Library of Congress made for a happy sojourn which included reading, writing, good liturgy, excellent food, fine sherry and wine, luscious desserts, plus a quiet, comfortable, and private room.

Francis Xavier Petraglia, my friend from St. Clement's, had his brother, Walter, who was an executive at National Public Radio (NPR), give me a tour of the facilities plus an interview on the program *Talk of the Nation*, which was just beginning.

I finished the research for my program and had it reviewed by the Fellowship Committee. The final text, which explored the dramatic development of liturgy during the first five centuries of Christianity, was accepted with honorable mention and I prepared myself to leave Washington the next morning. There was a farewell dinner and great joviality among the fellows.

I left for Sacramento. Trudy met me at the airport and announced that I had an evening interview for a job with a social service organization in Stockton. This was an application for employment that I had filed months earlier when I learned that I was to be fired from St. Clement's. I went to the interview, made a very good impression, was short-listed, but did not get the position. We drove to Merced so that I could retrieve one car, some of my books, and the rest of my clothes. I stayed in Merced for several weeks to spend time with Dominique and Michel. They were growing right in front of my eyes and I wanted to enjoy them. With no pressure of work, schedule, or commitment, I could ride bicycles with Dominique (Michel would sit on my cross bar), visit the local public pool for a refreshing swim, and find any occasion for an ice cream cone. It was an enjoyable summer, yet tension with Trudy grew a bit more emphatic as the days passed by.

There were, however, lots of interesting things to do in Merced, especially with the children. The Merced River was nearby and cycling was cool and entertaining near the water. The local park had many attractive games for children including a pool, several jungle gyms, and swings. Because the weather was warm, a picnic by the lake was always a winner for the kids. A ride in small bike paddleboats was invariably something the children enjoyed. Investigating the small coves of the lakes was a challenge to Michel's internal sense of direction. Dominique was reading as well as an adult, and Michel was reading well beyond his age level, thanks to Dominique, who tutored him.

Dominique, the innate teacher, had the patience of Job when she was in the teacher's mode. Her patience also carried through when she was creating, as in art, sketches, paintings, and sculptures. As a phenomenally bright and active child, she was a pleasure to watch, to encourage, and to offer material for her creative urges. As a college student her interests were focused in literature, art, drama, and writing, especially novels. As I write Dominique has earned her doctorate, a proud moment for me, her father. Dominique was a pleasant and complex child who required much attention; as an adult she still requires much attention from me, but she is a pleasure, especially now that she has rediscovered her father, for there was a time that I was practically nonexistent in her mind!

Currently, Dominique is closer to me than she has ever been; we have mostly resolved several problems that surfaced through the years of separation and miscommunication. She has returned to her inborn affectionate self and I find that affection between us can be exchanged readily, easily, and without inhibitions. She is a professor of medieval literature at Northern State University, Aberdeen, SD and has recently receive a promotion to Assistant Professor and has had her first book published.

Michel, a quiet and acutely intelligent sort of person, was also creative in a different manner and with different outward expressiveness. He was artistic in a medium that did not find expression in painting or sculpture but in concepts, mathematics, and technical problems. Michel was adept at sports and activities that required precise body movements because he was instinctively coordinated. As a young person, Michel was quite affectionate and his relationship with me was always warm, intimate, and open. In college, Michel chose physics as a discipline (a most complimentary selection to me) but directed his attention upon completion to the products that emerge from that discipline, especially as they touch computer sciences. I do regret that he has not completed his degree, lacking just three credit hours, because I feel that he has the capability of acquiring a more advanced degree, such as a doctorate. Perhaps, someday, he will. Nevertheless, I am proud of Michel's accomplishment, success, and creativity in computer science.

I am most impressed by his several pursuits in areas that have emerged in his later years. He has started an ice hockey team that has shown some extensive promise in competitions. Moreover, hockey has brought out his leadership and strategic talents. Recently Michel has decided to enter competitive auto racing but I am still not certain where that will lead him, except that he finds it relaxing, strategically demanding, and entertaining. In addition, Michel is an aircraft pilot and will probably take possession of our red Cherokee 6-300 (PA-32-300) N4004R.

Then while still in Merced, there was always an excursion to Wawona in Yosemite Park. The old Wawona hotel was an attractive place to head to when we wanted to spend a few days in the Yosemite Valley. The hotel was not extravagant, the rooms were comfortable and adequate for two children, and the food was exquisite. In the meadow near the hotel we could encounter deer, coyotes, foxes, and brown bears. Keeping our distance for safety, we could watch these animals act naturally, and the children learned to be careful, watchful, and to appreciate the animal visitors. Or were we the visitors?

Summer of 1971 was hot in the Central Valley but air conditioning made the day bearable as long as one did not venture outside. Being in the valley of California had one special reward: produce was fresh and inexpensive. Luscious red tomatoes, cucumbers, several varieties of green leafy vegetables, and fruit were abundant, and the weather was clear with a sky that was infinitely blue and cloudless. In aviation this sky condition is described with the acronym CAVU, which means Clear And Visibility Unlimited.

Soon I would be leaving Merced for graduate school in Berkeley. I knew that most of the burden of caring for the children would fall squarely on Trudy's shoulders. We had discussed the issue of her responsibility and of my moving north to study. We came to an agreement. I would come to Merced every other weekend. My presence at home in Merced would offer Trudy a weekend without the pressures of tending to the house or the children. Domesticity was not what Trudy considered to be her task or even something shared with a husband. Preparing dinner was not her responsibility or part of her daily plan. I was happy to cook but a little help or shared support from Trudy would have been preferable and greatly rewarded. In some sense for

Trudy, the whole world revolved around her. Self-interest was Trudy's passion. She was a concerned mother about the children's education, health, and clothing, but little of her attention was spent on mere domestic chores or attentiveness to the children's discipline and personal needs. When she came home from school the first things were soaking in the bathtub and a self-rub down with lotion. Then followed a period of rest. All this meant that dinner was not considered until early evening such as seven or later, then because of lack of planning the result was either boxed macaroni and cheese, canned soup, or canned stew!

That approach was always anathema to me. Eating for me is a necessary part for making life joyful. A good meal, a fine glass of wine or ale, a small dessert, and good conversation adds zest to life. Food is not merely fuel for the body, but the accent that gives living its tone, its good quality, and its intriguing character. Food is an important element of my passion. Food is also the product of a creative effort and demands forethought, patience, and time for the blending of the flavors, and love; love of God's bounty and of eaters.

In preparation for graduate work, I purchased a new International Business Machine (IBM) red Selectric typewriter, which was the latest model produced. Raiding my piggy bank, I was able to buy the Selectric for $500; it was my preliminary investment to produce good, clearly typed papers. The typewriter has served me well and to this day it still serves me well, although it could use a cleaning and some lubrication. At present, however, I have advanced joyfully to the computer — a wonderful tool.

The summer was ending. It was time for me to move into my apartment in Oakland and prepare myself for the academic year as a full time graduate student. The conditions under which my program was about to proceed would require that the family be split between two domiciles, Merced and Oakland. It was not an ideal arrangement but it did give to both Trudy and me a chance to evaluate our relationship and to assess the state of our marriage. Every other week, I visited Merced and on several occasions, Trudy and the children would come to enjoy the Bay Area. The orchard backyard of my apartment was an ideal play area for Dominique and Michel, and for us it gave us a "pied-à-terre" to see sights in the Bay Area.

The Bay Area and Graduate School

A few days after my arrival in Oakland, Massey Shepherd suggested that I attend the Diocese of California Commission for Liturgical Renewal (CLR) as a visitor. Because I was not canonically resident of the Diocese of California, I could only attend as an inactive observer. I made an appointment with Bishop Kilmer Myers and after a pleasant chat he authorized my participation on the recommendation from Shepherd. Bishop Myers had notified the current chair that I would attend as an observer, and on the first day of their biweekly meetings I was properly introduced to all the members present, and especially to the grand lady of the diocese, Mrs. Anna Crosley.

Anna was English, a close friend of the bishop, and a keen liturgist who also directed a sewing seminar for the making of vestments. This would be my first experience with a working, dedicated, and knowledgeable group of liturgists. The issue that the commission was preparing to tackle was the proposed revisions of the 1928 Book of Common Prayer (BCP). The CLR had been given only a small section of the liturgical calendar, a proposed outline of the content of the BCP, a draft of the proposed Eucharistic canons, and several drafts of Collects. These pieces had been distributed to acquaint and prepare the church for the 1973 General Convention. Canonical law required that any revision be approved by two meetings of the General Convention of the Episcopal Church in the USA. Hence by 1973 much of the content had to be in the hands of the bishops and deputies to examine before the Convention. This was 1971 and as yet little of the revision had surfaced. The church had a long way to go before final approval would be given; in fact the new BCP was not approved until 1979.

Working with the CLR was an education in itself. Roswell Moore, the current chair, was an effective leader who had recruited an excellent team of interested liturgists, clergy and laity to help the congregations of the Diocese of California prepare themselves for the upcoming revisions of the Prayer

Book. It was a phenomenal contrast with what I had experienced in the Diocese of Northern California.

The Church's Standing Liturgical Commission (SLC) sent a great deal of material to the CLR, the group instructed and authorized by Convention to work on the revision. The CLR was well regarded by the SLC because the material exchanged was always well examined, editing was immediate and serious discussions well recorded, comments were cogent, and the CLR was not only supported by the bishop but disseminated the information quickly and thoroughly to all congregations. The SLC regarded the CLR as a responsible and thoughtful supporting group. In effect the SLC began to give us, the CLR, more and more work to do, and sections to produce, revise, or initiate for the forthcoming BCP.

Three months after my arrival on the CLR, Ross Moore announced that he was resigning as chair to accept a membership position as a Deputy of Convention to work on the revisions of the Church's Canon Laws. The California Commission on Liturgical Renewal was now without a chair.

I was working on the core of my dissertation and too busy to give much thought to the CLR, except to attend the meeting and absorb what was percolating from the SLC. In addition, I had another issue to tackle, which for the moment would occupy me. It is important, however, to share the details that led me to the issue that would have terminated my studies. Life is filled with twists and turns and patience is a requirement, even for the reader at this juncture. A full explanation comes soon that explains my association with the CLR.

Dr. Wayne Rood was the chair of my doctoral committee, or as it is called in the first stage, a comprehensive committee. With the inter-university program in place, I had recruited the following committee members:

Dr. Charles Atkinson, an anthropologist from Northwestern University, Evanston, Illinois;

Dr. Frederick Tolleni SJ, a dramatist and theologian from Santa Clara University, Santa Clara, California;

Dr. James Mara SJ, a retired philosopher and paleontologist from the University of Rome, Italy and GTU;

Dr. Bernard Loomer, a process philosopher and retired dean from the University of Chicago and GTU;

Dr. Massey H. Shepherd, Jr., a liturgist and historian from CDSP and GTU;

Dr. Earl Count, a retired anthropologist from Hamilton College, N.Y.;

Dr. Norman Pittenger, a philosopher from Kings College, Cambridge; and The Rt. Rev. Dr. John A. T. Robinson, a linguist and scriptural anthropologist who was also a bishop, from Trinity College, Cambridge, UK.

The committee would remain the same except for one addition, Dr. John Jeter, a musician and composer from Indiana University, Indiana who would be added at a later date to participate in the corpus of the doctoral commentary and my defense.

The course work was planned to satisfy my needs, the requirements of the institutions involved, and the knowledge of my chosen committee. That I would have to amalgamate emerging knowledge not only from the United States but also from Italy, the Netherlands, and England did not frighten me. I had a general idea of the product I wanted to discover, examine, and obtain and I was not put off by any assumed inflexibilities. For example, the chair of the department of philosophy at UC Berkeley was locked into the philosophy of British logical positivism, an intellectual movement that did not speak to me, so I decided merely to use the philosophy department as a resource and not as mentoring or supporting faculty. I was convinced that one obtained a bachelor's degree because of parental or peer pressures, a master's was attained because it was necessary to earn a living, but a doctoral degree was acquired because of a personal, private, and selfish need. In fact one always said, "I have my doctorate," and the emphasis is placed on the possessive.

The doctoral program demands pioneering research in areas that have never been examined by others. The dissertation is a corpus of original labor and that is why the final phase of a doctoral endeavor is called the "defense" and not an examination. Hence, I was determined to fashion my course work in such a way that I would be satisfied with the result, and this is why I selected members of my committee carefully, specifically, and made certain that they understood my goal. To achieve that goal I needed an institution that was not rigid but was willing to give me the space to search other institutions for mentors. The Graduate Theological Union was exactly that type of institution and with the support of UC Berkeley, Kings College, Cambridge, England, and with other academic establishments and their faculties I proceeded to develop my doctoral program.

Funding the work would require several loans and grants but I was mentally prepared for that complex problem. Loans were available, grants were possible, and some employment was in the planning. I set out to be "processively" involved in what would allow me to reach my goal. I accepted the plan to search, seek, and explore all the possible avenues to help me have the necessary funding for my doctorate: this was what I called a processive tactic. Two issues intrigued me. First, I wanted to open, like one peels an onion, and see how art includes several forms. To do this I would be using liturgy as the medium. Why liturgy? Because it is the earliest complex medium that can incorporate all forms that are art. Complex liturgies date back 20 or 22 centuries. Second, I wanted to explore and understand the creative process and when human beings began to create art. Moreover, I was interested in examining how liturgy related to the business and industrial fabric, not merely as a "churchy" element but as a management, creative, and motivating energizer. Industry was made up of a complex of people; hence how did liturgy — the work of the people — affect it?

The path I would be taking would use the disciplines of process thought, anthropology, paleontology, aesthetic, drama, and liturgy. I was prepared to use these disciplines as a carpenter uses tools to build a cabinet. At the beginning I was fretful that liturgy would be the most difficult to examine in the raw. Church liturgies are mostly dull and canned, and rarely produce or permit much in terms of creativity. Priests, ministers, rabbis, mullahs, and other liturgical leaders are so bound by their ecclesiastical or assumed faith practices that the liturgies they command are simplistic, self-aggrandizing, and repetitious. The path to be taken would be filled with complexities but it would be fun, exciting, and challenging to me and to my committee — and it was. With their support I was striving for dramatic aesthetic liturgical creativity, current relativity of expressions, and peer responses backed by ancient truths and practices.

I was working diligently to develop a new approach to art, and to the forms that are the building blocks of art. At the same time I was opening up the Church's liturgy to determine a way for it to recapture its artistic heritage. As I worked on the program for my doctorate I was also managing some aspects of the work being done on the revision of the Episcopal Book of Common Prayer (BCP). The CLR and I were giving particular attention to the Easter Eve Canon for the Celebration of the Paschal Mystery and to the Baptismal service. We were hard at work not only in textual writing and editing, but also in offering liturgical expressions on Easter Eve and at diocesan gatherings. The CLR was also working closely with liturgical committees from other dioceses to assist them in developing a clearer understanding of what the CLR and Standing Liturgical Commission (SLC) were proposing to the Church at large.

Now to return to the issue that would have terminated my studies. It had been a long and arduous day. It was late one evening in the spring of 1972 while living in Oakland, and after a seminar and a CLR meeting, and initial preparation for a short trip to Cambridge to do research at Trinity on Whitehead, I went to check my mail and there I found a letter from the Church Pension Fund informing me that Bishop Haden had refused to sign the form affirming that I was pursuing church-related academic studies. In fact he accused me of not pursuing a subject that was in any way related to the Church. Haden was lying and misinforming the Pension Fund. This was tantamount to freezing my retirement fund and declaring that I was no longer actively involved in the Episcopal Church.

Retirement funds are usually paid for the clergy by the hiring congregation; when one leaves a congregation to pursue academic studies that are church related, the Church Pension Fund contributes for three years what a congregation would have allocated. This way there would be no disruption in the building of the pension fund. The only hiatus for this procedure to take effect was for the bishop not to sign it. Haden had refused to do so simply out of meanness.

The second point surfacing from Haden's refusal was that I could be placed by the national church in abeyance and after three years considered inactive and hence literally deposed, forbidden to function as a priest in the Episcopal Church. I was furious. In fact I still had not yet planned to become non-stipendiary — earning my total salary outside the church although I did receive a small income from consulting. For the moment I considered myself quite active in the church and willing to continue as a salaried priest in that respect. If a bishop, be it Haden or another, was going to treat me in such a shoddy way, I was ready to call it quits. To leave. To abandon the ecclesiastical circus.

When I cooled off a little I telephoned Massey Shepherd (Shep) to tell him what I had received from Bishop Haden. I blurted out that I was ready to renounce my holy orders if Haden was an example of the Holy Spirit's choice of an apostolic bishop! What was it that he suggested? Had he any advice for me?

"Calm down, Raymond. Calm down," he advised. Then he added, "Do nothing for 48 hours and certainly not until we talk again." Shep's voice was comforting and authoritative.

I did nothing except to write a draft letter of resignation for my holy orders to the Presiding Bishop, in case I needed it, indicating that I was renouncing my priestly vows because of the intolerable behavior of Bishop Haden. Then I went out for a fish dinner at Spangler's in Berkeley. The next morning was Tuesday and I had a special liturgical meeting that afternoon at Grace Cathedral to look over a section of the new Paschal liturgy that I had drafted with the assistance of John Oda-Burns, rector of Christ Church, Portola Valley. Massey Shepherd phoned me to announce that the bishop's secretary would be phoning me soon. Just before lunch, Binnie Graham, Bishop Kim Myers's secretary, telephoned me to ask if I could stop by the bishop's office for a moment before the CLR meeting scheduled for that afternoon. I did.

Bishop Myers invited me into his office and asked me to sit down.

"Raymond," I remember his words clearly, "as a member of the Commission on Liturgical Renewal you will need to be canonically resident in the Diocese of California. Do you want to change your residency?"

Of course I did. Indeed I did. My answer was simple and clear.

"Yes I do."

There was a long pause. Then he said, "As of today you are canonically resident in this diocese and I am your new ecclesiastical authority. Here is the signed Church Pension Fund form approving your course of work."

In addition, the envelope was addressed and stamped, ready to be mailed to the Church Pension. I was speechless. I thanked him and rose to leave, but he stopped me. Then Bishop Myers added, "Of course you will become the new chair of the Commission on Liturgical Renewal (CLR) effective today."

I was stunned. He then reached over and hugged me adding, "Welcome to the Diocese of California, brother."

I had tears in my eyes, which Kim noticed and reached to give me a tissue.

"I will also recommend that you and the CLR offer themselves as adjunct to the SLC. Shep is already working on this. Go now and do your duty as chair and inform Ross."

The Battle for the Revised Book

There I was in one day rid of the Rt. Rev. Clarence Haden, a new canonical resident of the Diocese of California, Chair of the Commission on Liturgical Renewal (CLR), adjunct to the Episcopal Standing Liturgical Commission (SLC), and completely petrified by what was expected of me.

As I approached the meeting room Ross Moore met me outside and congratulated me and also offered any assistance I would need. Kim had already informed him that I was to be appointed as Chair.

I entered the meeting room and just stared at the members. Because I knew all of them did not mean that I was not intimidated. The leader of this august group was standing in my shoes. My knees were not buckling, no, not at all.

Dr. Massey Hamilton Shepherd, Jr., stood and announced that standing before the Commission was their new leader and chair. The group rose and applauded. I sat before my knees gave way. After a short silence I informed the group that it had a tough road ahead with much work, and most of the work required study, learning, vision, creativity, common sense, and a good feeling of the dramatic. The year was 1972 and by 1976 we should have a near final version of the BCP and definitely by 1979 a final text of the BCP for General Convention to approve.

I cautioned the members that we would be loved by one group, hated by another, accused of destroying the holy fabric of the Church, reviled for corrupting the language of the precious 1928 BCP, and adored by many who had the good sense to recognize that no BCP is everlasting. Perhaps I added, "A new loose leaf prayer book is given birth so that revisions might be inserted on occasion!"

As chair of the CLR for the Diocese of California, I was leading a fairly prominent team in charge of liturgical developments for the diocese and much support to SLC for the greater Church — the Episcopal Church. As I mentioned earlier, the CLR included both clergy and lay members. Some were appointed directly by the bishop and others were selected by the CLR membership after being approved by the bishop. The Diocesan Convention also gave its approval of the members when the bishop submitted their names and qualifications. Thirteen persons comprised the CLR membership. Disciplines represented on the CLR included liturgists, historians, musicians, poets, educators, theologians, biblical scholars, political scientists, lawyers, and doctoral candidates. It was a superb group.

It was time now to gather the CLR together and focus mainly on the developments of the revisions of the BCP, a difficult task. The CLR was being asked by the SLC not only for editorial comments but also for fresh and creative textual contributions for the BCP. Now that the CLR had been informed that Bishop Myers had appointed me chair, it was time for us to roll up our sleeves and get down to business. After the meeting ended and most of the members had departed, Shep stopped me (he was also on the SLC) and advised me to find a competent secretary immediately, one who could take notes, assist in writing text, and edit draft liturgical texts. A few days later the bishop sent a letter to each member of the SLC confirming that I was the new chair of the CLR and that the CLR was attached as an adjunct support entity to the SLC.

At the suggestion of the bishop — so that I would have practical hands-on experience with a congregation — in 1973, I accepted a position as part-time vicar of St. Edmund's Mission church in Pacifica, California. While in Cambridge I continued to manage the CLR by mail and telephone with the help of John Oda-Burns, rector of Christ Church, Portola. After my two long sojourns in Cambridge, I returned to take over my duties as vicar in September of 1973. One of the parishioners I had met was a professional editor, member of the altar guild, and quite knowledgeable about the Church. I asked Emily McCormick Price if she had time and interest in working with the CLR. Her response was shockingly positive. As a self-employed editor she had some time to give to the CLR. After being introduced to the members of the CLR at the next meeting and receiving a thorough briefing, Emily dove into the work and in a few days straightened the accumulated mess that I had made when I took over the files from Ross Moore.

As the secretary of the CLR, whose contribution was imperative because she also performed the duty of editor and wordsmith, Emily became indispensable to each member. Unfortunately, during the crucial time of 1975, Emily, who had been rehired by Bechtel, was sent to Lebanon. Upon her early return a few months later because of the war in Lebanon, she reclaimed her position and was most helpful in keeping the CLR on the proper track of syntax correctness and clear thinking. That she had missed a few meetings and several important liturgical events was important but not devastating. She soon fell back into the groove and the work proceeded well again.

The commissions of New York, Chicago, Washington D.C., and California exerted a great deal of influence on the Church's Standing Liturgical Commission (SLC). Massey Shepherd was the primary thinker and authority on the SLC; not that the other eight members were insignificant, but Shep was the known authority on liturgy, its history, and its celebration. Hence, since Shep was also canonically resident of the Diocese of California, the

CLR was asked to help produce liturgical material, test portions of new material, and offer editorial comments as new texts surfaced. There were four phases that produced the final BCP for approval in 1976 and issuance as the canonical BCP in 1979.

The first phase included reviews of ancient liturgies with modern applications.

The second phase was the issuing of loose-leaf versions of texts for trial by selected congregations. Written responses were requested from the congregations explaining how the trial text had been celebrated, how it had been received, and any comments — changes or deletions — that emerged from the experience.

The third phase was the publishing of what was called the "Green Books" which contained the separate liturgical texts with their histories and comments prepared by members of the SLC. These Green Books were made available to the whole church for a nominal price and were suggested for usage at regular services. Again, the SLC invited comments, suggestions, and in-depth editorial analyses to be sent to them. The SLC also suggested that study groups be created to acquaint congregations with the new texts. In California, members of the CLR took to the road and visited congregations throughout the diocese. At the time of the revision, the Diocese of California had not yet been divided; the Diocese of El Camino Real was yet to surface.

The fourth phase was to produce any draft liturgies that needed to be included in the final book but did not exist in either the 1892 or 1928 editions. Because both 1892 and 1928 were modifications of the English 1662 book derived from the 1789 book when the American Episcopal Church separated from the Church of England, there were many texts that were not included. These texts had been either removed or simply were not included because of the influence exerted by the Puritans, the Roman Catholics, the Lutherans, and general Protestants who did not accept them. Indeed, in my view these omissions impoverished the BCP and its projection of the liturgical calendar.

In California the CLR was particularly asked to review the historical liturgical documents and test with actual use the reactions of congregations and clergy. The CLR took this assignment seriously. For Easter Eve 1973, the Milanese Liturgy of Bishop Ambrose (3rd Century) was used for the first Easter Eve Paschal Mystery Eucharist ever celebrated at Grace Cathedral, San Francisco. In fact, the Easter Eve Paschal Feast had been rarely celebrated in the Episcopal Church, and if celebrated then only on rare occasions or occasions of demonstrations. There was neither an Easter Eve Paschal text in the current 1928 Prayer Book nor was there one in the previous published books. Thus the first celebration of the Easter Eve Paschal Liturgy in the United States was celebrated at Grace Cathedral, San Francisco, CA in 1973.

The Right Reverend C. Kilmer Myer presided at the service and in attendance were less than 200 people. It was curious that none of the regular Cathedral staff offered to assist with the service. Dean Julian Bartlett did not find the process interesting and continued to focus on the services for Easter day, the next morning. One small concession made by Dean Bartlett was that the Paschal Candle that was lighted at the Saturday evening liturgy could be used for the Sunday Easter service.

The next year, 1974, a draft text of the Paschal Mystery liturgy was prepared by the CLR at the behest of the SLC and with its major contribution. The draft of the 1974 Easter text was written by several members of the CLR, especially John Oda-Burns, John Schively, John Rawlingson, Stuart White, and me, and we asked Professor Norman Mealy and his wife Margaret for their review because both were fine musicians and knowledgeable liturgists. The text for the rite for The Great Vigil of Easter (the title we used) included the following:

- The Lighting of the Paschal Candle
- The Exsultet (the ancient hymn for the occasion)
- The Liturgy of the Word, which included nine scriptural passages, psalms, and collects
- The Renewal of Baptismal Vows (without mention of Satan or the Devil)
- Baptism and the Laying-of-Hands (Confirmation)
- The Eucharist

After the submitted text was reviewed by the SLC, the CLR was asked to use it at the Easter Eve service in 1975. Again, with Bishop Myers presiding, the Great Vigil of Easter was celebrated at Grace Cathedral, but this time it was with the liturgy of the Episcopal Church and not of Milan. Bishop Myers was the perfect president of this noble liturgy. He knew how to handle the ceremony and make it come alive — and better still he enjoyed doing it. His blessing over the font was a classic ceremony that accentuated the inherent value of water for humanity; he touched the water with his long fingers, parted it with a stroke of his extended hand, and finally he blew his breath over the water. It was the ecstatic display needed for giving dramatic meaning to the motion of the blessing of the water.

In 1974 attendance increased to approximately 400 — double what was counted the previous year. It was still curious that again none of the Cathedral staff offered their services (although they were invited) or was interested in viewing the celebration. We had to recruit the choir from St. Mark's Parish, Berkeley, courtesy of the Rev. George Titman, rector. George Titman came and read three of the scriptural passages. The Rev. Edgar Parrott chanted the Exsultet and played the organ, and Brother Paul from Holy Cross was the censer who swung a mean thurible. Stuart White was an extraordinary assistant to me as I managed to have all the leading participants in place and on queue. Because the liturgy had not been rehearsed there was freshness and a spontaneity that was a gift we all recognized.

Just before midnight in 1973, Bishop Myers administered the Laying-of-Hands (confirmation) to Dominique and to Michel, and several others, both young and old. Dominique and Michel, although young and quite sleepy, remember the event vividly and consider it a memorable milestone in their lives.

At a meeting held in Amarillo, TX with the SLC, the CLR was invited to give its report; several diocesan liturgical committees were present to hear how California had responded to the changes in BCP and the new approaches to liturgy. The CLR was asked to respond to questions asked by those present after a description of the Paschal celebration had been given.

There was a great deal of discussion and some objection by the committee from the Diocese of New York about joining baptism and confirmation in one service. The objection principally centered on the possibility that if that became the norm in the Church, bishops would then lose their function as being the exclusive person administering the rite of confirmation. In spite of substantial historical support that the laying-of-hands would be administered in conjunction with baptism, the representatives from New York objected vehemently, and the Rt. Rev. Paul Moore, their bishop, asserted his objection strongly. The SLC decided to postpone the issue for discussion at a later time.

Objections about the removal of mention of the Devil and Satan from the Baptismal liturgy came from the Dioceses of Dallas, Texas, Eau Claire, Wisconsin, and San Joaquin. No amount of explanation could convince those who voiced objections, and so in exasperation we temporarily abandoned the issues questioned.

The meeting ended the next day and no resolution was attained on the issue of confirmation or of Satan. In 2008, the Church was still struggling with these nonsensical issues. As the world is heating with global warming, poverty a drain on human life, and religion dissension prevailing in the Middle East, the Church sets its focus on the hot issues of same-sex gender union, ordination of gay bishops, and the potential schism that is surfacing because conservative bishops are unwilling to look beyond their crosiers.

A few weeks later, the SLC asked the CLR to prepare a draft alternate Eucharistic Canon for discussion. This request was in response to my query that a new approach was needed in the Eucharistic prayer that touched upon space, the stars, the galaxy — all in tune with the walks on the moon by our astronauts, and American and Soviet explorations of the far reaches of our solar system. The CLR, with a team that included John Oda-Burns, Stuart White, Anna Crosley, and me drafted a text that we sent to the SLC with separate copies to Dr. Shepherd and Bishop Myers. After much discussion and final approval by General Convention, out of our draft text emerged Eucharistic Canon C that focuses on the firmament. It became one of the beloved canons of the Church.

For Easter Eve 1974, the new Great Vigil of Easter, which was taken from our draft texts, was used at Grace Cathedral as it was published in the Green Book. Once again we had to recruit a choir from a local parish, this time St. Edward's, San Jose whose rector was John Schively. Attendance for the Paschal service, with baptism and laying-of-hands, increased to approximately 450-500, and included several groups from various local parishes led by their rector or vicar.

For this service we called upon the Suffragan Bishop, Richard Millard, and the Assisting Bishop, C. Edward Crowther, to participate in the celebration with Myers presiding. Again, Edgar Parrott sang the Exsultet and Brother Paul swung mightily the thurible. To assist me in the general preparations and for the fire to be lit at the door for the lighting of the Paschal Candle, Stuart White was again a most dependable assistant master of ceremony.

In conjunction with the Easter Eve services, the CLR took upon itself in 1974 the task of redesigning the structure of diocesan convention. Starting with the liturgy of the word, and at appropriate breaks in the presentations of the issues, with the Bishop's Address replacing the homily, the whole assembly was then couched in the Eucharist with the Communion and Bishop's Blessing coming at the culmination of the Convention. The format was sent to the SLC, and it in turn sent copies to other dioceses. This format of couching the Diocesan Convention in the Eucharist continued until I resigned from the CLR and Bishop Myers resigned as diocesan bishop. At present in 2001, I am not aware of any diocese continuing this format.

The various services in the Green Book were modified, edited, and printed for larger consumption by Episcopalians. Final corrections were made in the services for submission to the 1976 General Convention. With the final submission, the Diocese of New York under Bishop Paul Moore won the fray against California and his friend Kim Myers: Confirmation remained as a free standing service although allowance was made to include it with baptism as the prerogative of the local diocesan bishop. The SLC did take the CLR's advice that baptisms should be administered principally at Easter (preferably on the Eve), Pentecost, All Saints, and Epiphany and at other times only when deemed necessary. This rule for baptism remains to this writing as the correct mode for when to administer the rite of initiation.

Indeed, in 1976 another edited and finalized Great Vigil of Easter liturgy was celebrated at Grace Cathedral with Kim Myers presiding. Seventeen young and old people were baptized and were administered the Laying-on-of-Hands. The number of attendees surpassed the previous year by a couple of hundred. In recent times, namely in the year 2008, the attendees exceeded 2,800 and those baptized and administered the Laying-on-of-Hands numbered 77. It appears definitely that The Great Vigil of Easter celebrated at Grace Cathedral is a service that will endure through the coming years and decades.

For Pentecost 1975, the CLR offered a Eucharist at Grace Cathedral on the eve of that great feast that included music, dancing, and the experience of chaos overtaken by solemnity. Borrowing twelve choirs from local parishes we positioned them at various key locations and directed them to sing pieces that were contrastingly different from pieces sung by the other choirs. The cathedral lights were dimmed and brightened as if they were subjected to electric power shortages. Clergy were directed to wander about individually without a distinct pattern. Bishop Myers was directed to rush in the Cathedral brandishing his crosier simulating anger and impatience.

The bishop entered the cathedral with his crosier poking the air and when he reached the great altar, the choirs fell into one unified coherent piece of music. The clergy, the choirs, the supporting acolytes, and the lectors, as if by a power beyond them, were all of a sudden gathered in a unified procession. In less than 30 seconds what had been a chaotic situation overwhelmed by cacophony became order. After the choirs completed the hymn selected, silence followed for several moments, then the bishop intoned:

"Alleluia. Come Holy Spirit."

The choir and people responded: "Alleluia. Our souls inspired."

"And lighten with celestial fire."

Torches were lit, incense smoke rose to the heights, and drum rolls were heard. Grace Cathedral was made alive. Rite Two of the Holy Eucharist Canon followed with the bishop presiding. After the service was terminated, compliments abounded from those who were present. I did not have a count of attendees but I suspect that there were approximately 1000 or more present.

General Convention approved at its first reading the new prayer book in 1976 and approved it again as the canonical Book of Common Prayer in 1979. For a prayer book to become the book of standard usage in the Episcopal Church, two consecutive General Conventions must approve it. After much struggling, hundreds of disapproving letters from communicants in and outside the Diocese of California, and thousands of supporting letters for the work done by the CLR, it was time for another chair to replace me. I had a dissertation to write, a doctoral degree to earn, and a family to consider. As for chairing the CLR and being the curmudgeon for a better BCP, it was time for a new leader to step into the fray. Charles Mortimer Gilbert, the Custodian of the Standard Book of Common Prayer, replaced me as the new chair of the CLR and in September 1979 the new prayer book became the official and authorized BCP for the Episcopal Church.

With my work completed for the CLR and SLC, and General Convention ratifying for the second time the texts of the revised BCP without additions or corrections, in 1976 after Easter I tendered my resignation from the CLR to Bishop Myers and also resigned as vicar of St. Edmund's. As I said, it was time for me to devote a great portion of my time to writing my doctoral dissertation. I did just that and in May 1976 I was awarded my doctoral degree.

Three Good Friends Lend a Hand

Developing a liturgical service is not the result of one person's work. Liturgy is not only the process of a corporate effort for its response to the Ultimate, to God, but also the product of many minds, many hours of labor, and many cooperative contributions. As I mentioned earlier, Grace Cathedral's hierarchical staff was not able to offer me much support except for the use of the facility. The product of church liturgy requires help from clergy, choirs, writers, editors, musicians, and others. When I needed assistance, a small choir, a congregation upon which to test an idea, a theme, or a choreographical element I often turned to John Schively. In 1978, John was concluding his tenure in Montclair and was moving to St. Edward's in San Jose to become the parish's new rector.

John was most gracious to me; he permitted me to preach to his congregation while at the same time he indulged me when I questioned my listeners or asked them to question what I had said. He trusted me. He tolerated me with much affection. He let me present ideas that often were controversial, probing of orthodoxy, and at times less than traditional.

Once a young conservative called me a heretic when I admitted that the Devil was a figment of the imagination, a religious crutch of no value, and a disgrace to God's creative and benevolent attributes. Another person, a woman and the wife of one of John's assistants, threatened that she would report me to the bishop for denying the value of Satan and wanting to remove the reference in baptism. John supported me and continued to trust me, whereas his successor, Bill Eberly, was threatened by my approach and soon ordered me to not ask questions after the sermons and to not tackle controversial subjects.

I learned a great amount about compassion from John. I also learned how to love people more openly. I learned how to allow a congregation to become an active and participating voice and movement in liturgy. In practice, John Schively taught me to preside at the Eucharist, to be a facilitator, but to let the congregation become the dynamic celebrant of the liturgy. From John, I learned a great many good things and in particular I learned something about humility. John was a dependable sounding board for a supporting friend even to this day in 2015. I've always appreciated his different perspective, his quiet approach to solving problems, and his loyalty to me and to others. John has an innate liturgical sense that is a treasure; he knows what is correct, enhancing, and appropriate. His liturgy is always in the correct key.

I cannot mention anything about the work on the BCP without noting the great help that Stuart White, my friend since GTU days, offered when thinking, research, brute force, dramatic requirement, and general grunt work was demanded. Stuart has the capacity to cut through the chaff to the grain. He is able to address a problem directly and coherently, and explicate the details cogently to any attentive group. On several occasions Stuart was able to discuss fine theological points with bishops and convince them that their position was either ill thought out or just plain faulty. All I can add is that Stuart has a bear trap for a brain! He is also loving, kind, and ready to serve when asked. Stuart White studied for holy orders but decided not to become a member of the clergy; as a layperson he exerts quite a bit of authority whenever his type of analytical thinking is necessary.

Stuart White is a colleague, a dramatist, and a perceptive mind who was a student at the GTU: he had graduated from CDSP and then had crossed over to GTU to work on his doctorate. Stuart became my dearest friend and sounding board. Together we started a non-profit organization called Anthropos Theophoros, or AT for short. The purpose of this organization was giving creativity and creative talents a venue. Stuart was appointed to the CLR in 1973 upon my return from Cambridge. He immediately rolled up his sleeves and went to work. To this day we are friends and often I call on him for his advice and wisdom. I baptized two of his children. We keep in communication regularly and have had him and Kate, his wife and mother of their children, at our home often, but not often enough.

The third person I cannot omit in this triad is Stuart's first wife and my still dear friend, Jane. Jane is a musician, a fine wordsmith, a fine cook, a beautiful woman and person, and is always ready to lend a hand and share her creativity. Jane often has accompanied me when I presided at the altar for the Eucharist. Jane shared my frustrations either as a result of my problems with my first wife Trudy, or when I needed a bit of shoring up because of some philosophical, theological, or general dissonance in my affairs, my thinking, and concern with my offspring. Jane always responded calmly, coherently, lovingly, and openly. At times we changed positions when she was undergoing some difficulties with Stuart. Both Stuart and Jane were my dear and beloved friends, friends who should never have married each other. Fortunately both Jane and Stuart have remarried well to lovely spouses. I'd like to add that it has been a rewarding experience to know Jane Goodrich.

A Few Thoughts on Religion

There is nothing sacrosanct about a religion. There is nothing holy about the content of a religion. Religion is a tool, no more and no less. Religion is the content of what a group has agreed to use as a guide for its life, its behavior, its outlook; it is human made and did not come from on high. As it was made, it can consequently be unmade, discarded, and replaced. God did not give human beings a codified religion. God did not ascribe a particular format for the structure of religion, any religion. Human beings developed the structures of the various religions used today and through the ages. No religion in existence today offers the absolute way to God, to understanding existence, and to the meaning thereof. Neither Rome nor the Pope is the sole arbiter of what religion should be. The Patriarchs of Moscow, Kiev, Athens (Constantinople-Istanbul is out of the fray) or of anywhere else are not the defining voices of what a "true" religion is. Islam does not offer humanity the voice of finality as to what religion should be. Judaism may offer humanity its ancient mythical history but even that is not the absolute guiding code for constructing a religion. Other faithful persuasions such as Buddhism, Shintoism, and Hinduism have enriched human thought about the truths of life and existence but they are nevertheless still not absolute guides for religion. A comment about Buddhism: the Buddhist approach is not incompatible with Christianity because it is a philosophical perspective that can be incorporated into one's life without forsaking another creed. I suspect that the same may be said about Shintoism and Hinduism, even if they practice a monastic confraternity. Other lesser-known faiths or less-practiced beliefs such as shamanism or voodooism, although interesting, offer no special way as to how religion should be constructed, adhered to, or receive our unerring devotion. Hence, where do human beings stand in the search for the true meaning of life?

I suggest that religion is the result of our search for meaning. As we look out on life, our lives, and on ourselves, the very activity involved in this quest for meaning gives rise to religion. The effort exerted is our way of connecting ourselves to the mystery of life. We know that we will not find the solution to the mystery of life because it is a mystery, and mysteries do not afford ways to comprehend them. That is why I propose that atheism is a religious endeavor, because it is an endeavor to understand the ultimate concern, that final question we ask ourselves. The atheist cannot accept the answers given by various religions; hence the denial of God surfaces because it becomes a form of continuous search for the ultimate concern. Others, unlike atheists, ascribe to faith of one sort or another. Faith is a response to that which human beings cannot affirm with certainty. Many human beings look at faith as a salve that will solve all doubts, will offer belief, and will circumvent the practice of serious thinking.

To supplement faith, religions have employed symbols of one kind or another to bridge the gap between belief and unbelief. Because the word symbol (Greek: symbolon) means to "bring together or make a connection" it is generally used as a way to attain a kinship with the ultimate focus. An important quality of a symbol is that it is given a life of its own after it is created. A symbol never retains its simple characteristics. It always becomes more than it was intended to be.

For example, a national flag becomes emotionally potent for expressing patriotism. Designed as a brief statement or identification of the nation, it takes upon itself a quality of sacredness that often, if one burns a flag, one is accused of desecrating the nation, and in some countries this act is considered a capital offense. It is always important to distinguish what identifies from what is: the symbol as is the flag, the Eucharistic elements are not the *thing* but representation of the thing. In Christian communion services, quite often, the bread and wine used attain levels of such sacredness that they become the focus of worship rather than what they point to. I venture to say that God, by the actions of the worshippers, takes a less important place than the elements of the symbol — the bread and wine.

I witnessed in many cities of Spain processions of the bread in elaborate monstrances being given the full attention of worshippers with actual human self-flagellation, even on the afternoon of Easter when liturgies had pronounced that the resurrection of Jesus had taken place. No, the symbol inside the monstrance was more important to those processing than what it bridged, connected, and depicted. Soldiers have given their lives to protect a flag, which is merely in reality a piece of cloth and not the nation to be protected — the nation may be thousands of kilometers away and well secured from destructive forces.

Similar acts of self-flagellation were seen when I was in the Eastern Province of Saudi Arabia where the majority of Arabs are Shiite. On certain feasts it was dangerous to be present in the small towns north or south of Dammam because the religious processions often took a turn for the worse and the self- flagellation excited not only those directly involved in this bloody act but affected the population witnessing it. At the end of the day several people were found seriously cut by the tools they used to flagellate themselves — and all for religious causes.

Religion can make people unreasonable!

In liturgy, which can be a religious dramatic discourse, God is the ultimate symbol. This word of three letters connects us all to the question we ask, to the answer we seek, and to the longings we have. As one of the most ambiguous of human words, the word "God" holds a powerful grasp over us. We cringe when the word is used in an exclamation as in "Oh my god!" We balk when the word is used as an insult, such as "goddamn." Ancient Hebrew people were so conscious of the disconnection between the symbol of God and what it was meant to connect human beings with, that they were afraid of using it. In place of the word God they employed other words like Lord or Yahweh, always avoiding the word itself because they recognized that the letter symbol "YHWH" had powerful connotations. In addition the Hebrews used myth as a way to mediate their most intimate experience of God.

Myth is neither true nor false. Myth is neither history nor an anecdote created around a falsehood. Myth is a narrative way of addressing a complex human experience. As such, a myth is always available for new interpretations, which is what philosophers and theologians attempt to do when they wish to study the deep essence of an anecdote, a story, a portion of history: they call for a process of " demytholization," which is a determined act of thinking about how myths function. When encountering a myth we must ask: What is it conveying? The renowned scholar Joseph Campbell, who spent a lifetime understanding myth and its meaning, affirmed that myths are not lies, anecdotes manufacturing history or foolish stories, but realities, truths, events explained in terms that are palatable to human beings.

Like symbol, myth may take on a life of its own and may become more powerful than what it is supposed to convey. The narrative of Adam and Eve suffers from this problem: Were Mr. Adam and Mrs. Eve actually the first human beings? Is the story a myth? Are Adam and Eve symbolic characters? Was Abraham a man or a composite figure that reflected the proposition or propositions that surface when it is shown that he was really ordered to sacrifice Isaac, his son? A harsh action for mankind to accept. What can be said about the temptation episode of Jesus by Satan? What about the Resurrection narrative (was the body reconstituted and the sub particles reassembled)?

Applied to liturgy, myths are important vehicles for illustrating truths. It is in this arena where myths and symbols are operating that human beings, in this case Christians, fall into deep traps that pull them away from coherence. For example, we find that the symbol of Satan (the Devil, Lucifer), which implies evil, selfishness, bad activities, and movement away from good and charitable acts has been given a life of its own. The myth of the Devil has been accepted as the story of a real personage such as a fallen angel, a conspirator against God, and an opposing power at war with God. The symbol of the Devil has been given life as if it were a living being. By giving the Devil life, s/he is assumed to be competing with God and recruiting human beings for his/her domain.

What happens when the Devil emerges as a living creature, especially in liturgy? Immediately, the primacy of God loses some importance because now creation is divided between God and the character Devil. Human beings can now begin to blame the Devil when evil actions surface: "The Devil made me do it." The Devil becomes a convenient crutch for human beings. And in the liturgy, the Devil, especially in the service of baptism, assumes an important role. Those who are to be baptized have to willfully renounce the character Devil. The rejection becomes a direct act of will by the person to be baptized. God's support is no longer an issue in the willful act of rejection. In baptism one has to take sides by rejecting the character Devil in order to be of God!

In early Christian history we find that the people who were different and who thought differently from the followers of Christ were assumed to be followers of the Devil. In the second century, Irenaeus, bishop of Lyons, called all Christians who were different in their thinking heretics and "secret agents of Satan." Tertullian, a Christian convert from Carthage and a contemporary of Irenaeus, also called Christian "deviants" heretics and disciples of Satan. Justin Martyr, another contemporary of Irenaeus, called Roman persecutors agents of the Devil. He distinguished between Hebrews, ancient followers of God's revelation to Israel, whom he liked, and current Jews of his time, whom he disliked, and called them stewards of Satan. Even Augustine of Hippo, who denounced the mythological language of Satan and declared that Satan and even evil do not exist, in sermons and prayers often blamed Satan when people performed evil acts. The bishop of Hippo was ambivalent in this and other matters.

I'm quite certain that most religious people, especially Christians, do not believe in Satan, but like Augustine, continue to use the symbol to identify those who think differently, who are of foreign religious persuasions, and who appear to be culturally different. Otherness is not Satanic, evil, or demonic. Otherness is a characteristic that enriches human nature, and we need to incorporate in our thinking that reconciling otherness in humanity is what Jesus recommended; it may even be part of our inherent divine quality. We all face otherness in our daily lives, be it ethnic, sexual, racial, or political difference. Otherness frightens us, but that is not necessarily evil.

To continue, when religious liturgical texts support this type of gross misinterpretation of myths and symbols, the messages projected are invariably destructive to people who aspire for the ultimate. In the resurrection narrative, adding pseudo-facts for emphasis detracts from the valuable message. Jesus died. Jesus did not regain his earthly life. Jesus did not breathe, walk, eat, or display his side wounds. These "little" facts are falsehoods. Jesus was resurrected by his presence in the hearts of his disciples, his subsequent followers, and the real fact that he is still known, still effective, and is still a graceful force in his followers' hearts even more than two thousand years after his death. That's the powerful message that emerges from the resurrection narrative. No need to actualize the myth. Keeping the myth of the resurrection as it has been told is drama of the best kind, but rendering it into a historically factual event diminishes its value. Moreover, it diminishes the value of the Eucharist, which is at best a recalling, a remembering, of Jesus' loving mission to humankind. "Do this for the remembrance of me," loses its eternal loving power when the myth is converted by a false fact — contorted into a false supposition. In whatever form the bread and the wine are consumed, they are not, really not, factually, elementally, and physically transformed into flesh and blood, they are vehicles used to transfigure the communicants by God's love into loving human beings. Otherwise, we fall into some aspects of cannibalism, mismanagement of history, or propagandizing because we misrepresent the message of Jesus, and mislead people into believing falsehoods.

The same filtering needs to be applied to the Jewish perspective on the Torah, the Tenakh texts that are assumed to be directly given from on high but are in reality the product of the Babylonian exilic period (ca 600 BCE) and completed during the Persian period (ca 400 BCE).

We are, I hope, in agreement that Jesus' Resurrection was not a flesh, bone, and blood occurrence but a corporate essential affirmation that Jesus was, after his death on the cross, a real presence in the hearts and minds of his followers, such as in Mary Magdalene, his disciples, and others, especially to the redactors of the canonical and non-canonical Gospel and Epistle texts. Now as for the Ascension, indeed, Jesus did not "ascend" to anywhere. He did not rise to a level beyond us on this Earth, on this Planet, or in the Galaxy. What happened to Jesus' physical body is an enigma, which will not be resolved now or ever. Jesus died and was buried just like any poor soul who suffered an execution. The uniqueness of Jesus' death is that his active presence was implicitly — and even explicitly — felt by others after he died. His after-death presence was recognized in a way that was too surprising, too extraordinary, too real for anyone to ignore. This may be the crux of the meaning of the Resurrection for those who are willing to abandon the physical aspects — actualizing the myth — and to move to a position where Jesus is present in our human lives.

Moreover, his ascending is a way to explain that once he was recognized as being resurrected in the hearts of his followers, he was also recognized as displaying the empowerment of one who is superior to mere human beings. His Lordship over human beings and over creation is the gist of the meaning of the Ascension. No upward motion but an elevation of Jesus' authority that allows him to manage aspects of creation. Thus the Ascension is the accent, the emphasizing signal that reminds us that Jesus is authoritatively superior than we are.

Moving to Pentecost, we must remember that Resurrection and Ascension take place in human hearts. As a follow-up, we also recognize that once that has taken place there is a new force energizing his followers, even the followers who are not quite in full agreement in understanding what has happened, such as the Disciple Thomas, or Peter who denied ever knowing Jesus, or Paul who at first was against the followers of Jesus but then changed his stance and became a principal proponent of Jesus' message. It is these changes that the community of Jesus' followers affirms when they recognize that a new force is empowering them, and that that force may be the Spirit of God that Jesus promised his followers before he died: "And I will pray to the Father, and he shall give you another comforter, that he may abide with you for ever" (John 14:16).

Perhaps the empowering force is the Spirit that this Nazarene had alluded to, often in his conversation with his disciples and with his other unnamed followers. This Spirit has dwelt among his followers as a force through the centuries, a force that is often discounted, suppressed, and misinterpreted by human beings to satisfy their own egocentric needs. The result is that we have splinter group after splinter group (denominations and schisms) that assure their followers that each has the "true" empowering spirit. The proof of the pudding is in the eating and a splintered Christianity does not show us much of the "true" empowering spirit. Might we not reexamine our positions and agree that none of us reflect the true Spirit of God because we have submerged it in our own assumed self-importance?

I venture to add that if religious myths and symbols are to retain their power, their purpose, and their validity they must be capable of constant reinterpretation and must be adjusted to changing perceptions of meaning. Unlike signs such as a stop sign, which has a single meaning — such as an explicit reminder to stop, cease motion, and become stationary — a symbol possesses many interpretations, most of which are valid. If symbols and myths are to suffer the same limitations as signs, then they will soon be discarded, superseded, and ineffectual. The unfortunate issue here is that the conservative guardians of myths and symbols of religions appear to misunderstand the dynamic nature of religion and thus place the quest for comprehension, nurture, and enlightenment into great peril. Why? Because they nurture confusion, and confusion is exasperating. The task of the liturgist is to ensure that this does not happen.

A Lovely Artist

I want to say a few words about a first class artist. Anna Crosley introduced me to Nan Youngman when I went to Cambridge. U.K. I recall that prior to my arrival in Cambridge I had had a telephone conversation with Nan and in the course of that telephone call she asked me if I had located a flat near the University. I had not, so Nan offered to find me one near King's College. As I mentioned earlier I lived on Maid's Causeway, which was located within walking distance of King's College. Nan had taken the trouble to decorate my flat by hanging several of her paintings. One of her works was a reversed charcoal of a spider's web; a superb piece of art that I eventually bought from her because I couldn't part with it. Nan was an artist's artist.

Nan was not very tall; in fact she was quite short. Her eyes were piercing and intent. Her walk was goose-like in that she appeared to waddle with each step. Although not an admitted Anglican or a church member, she loved Anglicanism, Ely Cathedral, and its bishop, Peter Walker. Nan was a declared socialist, conscientious objector, liberal, and passionately English. Nan had never married but had kept company with another artist, a woman sculptor of some fame. Keenly interested in politics, she was knowledgeable of local, national, and world affairs. After I joined Bechtel, Nan was always interested in what I was doing, what projects I worked with, and where I was traveling. Our discussions often kept us awake past midnight while sipping single malt scotch — the only hard liquor she drank, although she did have a glass or two of wine with dinner.

Nan lived in Waterbeach, a hamlet not far from Cambridge, on Route A-10. The old part of her cottage dated from the 15th century and the "new" part was constructed in the mid-19th century. The cottage had running water, and the charcoal-fed Aga kitchen stove, which was installed in the late-19th century, heated the hot water and the whole house. It was a comfortable cottage and in later years when I traveled overseas through Cambridge on my way to or from an assignment, I often stayed with her in the second bedroom. It was across from hers, but I was instructed to use the modern bathroom located in the new part.

If I remember correctly, the old section of the house, where Nan lived, was remodeled in the mid-1950s by her nephew, an architect. In the new section Nan had her studio, a "modern bath," and a storage room that could be converted easily into a spare bedroom if all her paintings were to be relocated somewhere else. The original house, really a cottage, had a good-sized sitting room, a kitchen, a large storage room, two bedrooms upstairs, and a private bath, which only Nan used. The sitting room had a coal fireplace, a big bay window, and several recessed shelves where she displayed mechanical wind-up toys. I brought her a wind-up sheep made in East Germany, one of the last available toys from that portion of Germany before reunification. Nan's house, both the new part and the old, was lovely. Nan had a large garden with several fruit-producing trees.

Nan was an extraordinary artist but her eyes were beginning to deteriorate with the years. As a consequence of her cataracts, Nan's paintings were becoming less colorful, less bright, and less vivid. In 1982, Nan underwent two operations on her eyes to remove the cataracts. As a holiday treat, her nephew took Nan to Cornwall. She spent two weeks by the sea and produced several small but bright paintings. Her colors were returning to their vividness and her art was once again sharp, clear, and precise. Because she could see clearly again, she embarked on a spree of paintings for the Fitzwilliam Museum in Cambridge. Her exhibition won her first prize and notice from Queen Elizabeth II, who awarded her the Order of the British Empire (OBE) in 1984, in recognition of her work as an artist and teacher of art.

I saw Nan for the last time in the fall of 1985 when I returned from Italy. I did not stay with Nan, but rather stayed with my friend Bob Hodgson in Sawston, a few miles from Waterbeach. Nan could no longer drive her car. She was getting weak in the legs and her health was deteriorating rapidly. She had selected her burial place, which was to be located at the foot of an apple tree that she had planted when she first settled in the cottage in Waterbeach.

Nan Youngman died in 1986. With her death the world lost a lovely person, the artistic community lost a fine artist, and I lost a dear and beloved friend.

Cambridge, Spring and Summer 1973

Some events are never recognized as being good and gracefully endowed. There are those who, consequently, look at life as a glass that is perpetually half full and no amount of water poured into that glass would fill it to the brim. Such was the way Trudy experienced a wonderful spring and summer in Cambridge, England. Because it offers insights into how we both looked at life, I shall recount a few aspects of the summer of 1973.

It should be told that prior to my trip in the summer of '73 with Trudy, I had made a 17-day visit to Oxford soon after Easter to hear a series of lectures on the Church of England's effort to revise its own 1928 Book of Common Prayer, and a presentation on the contributions made by Archbishop Thomas Cranmer to the First and Second Prayer Books, and those that followed. Two grants had been given to me by the SLC, plus a small allowance from Bishop Kilmer Myers' discretionary account.

In the summer of 1973, however, I needed to do some specific research in England on two sectors of my interest. I wanted to learn more about Archbishop Thomas Cranmer, and I wanted to thumb through some of Alfred

North Whitehead's papers purported to be stored in the library at Trinity College and at the British Library. Dr. Norman Pittenger had kindly made it possible for me to have access to the archival library of Cambridge University, and this access allowed me to conduct research in all the colleges, both at Cambridge and at Oxford University. To do this research I had given myself 70 days.

Because I had funds, an apartment, and an inexpensive loan to purchase a new Mercedes Benz (my own VW was craving the grave), I asked Trudy if she wished to accompany me. My thought was that since she had never been to Europe and because we were attempting once again to reconcile our shaky marriage, a holiday together would be romantic and exciting. I forewarned Trudy at the outset that my primary purpose was to do research and to meet with key scholars, but there would be sufficient time for a trip to Scotland, a jaunt to France and Italy, and of course, a short visit to Germany and Holland when I took possession of the new Mercedes Benz 220D (MB). In addition, Ruth Eger volunteered to care for Dominique and Michel in our house in Merced. Chuck Eger, her husband, was in between jobs and was temporarily living in a studio apartment in San Jose. As soon as he located full time employment, he would search for a house, but for the time being using our house in Merced suited them to a T.

After applying in 1972 for two grants and receiving them, I was ready for the adventure in Cambridge as a scholar in residence. Our travel companion was Anna Crosley, who would be staying with Nan Youngman in Waterbeach. We boarded a TWA B-707 aircraft chartered by the San Francisco Symphony Auxiliary for the trip to London and Frankfurt. Anna was getting off in London, and we would continue to Frankfurt, West Germany to take possession of our new blue MB. I was looking forward to this study holiday and was pleased that Trudy had accepted to accompany me to Europe. Because my research schedule was fairly full during the week, I was certain that with the MB, a loaner bicycle, and the exciting city of Cambridge and the university, Trudy would be able to entertain herself without difficulty. Wrong.

We arrived in Frankfurt late in the evening and after locating a hotel we took the train to Russelsheim, a suburb of Frankfurt where the Opel automobile is manufactured. It was a charming hotel with a roof garden, a large room for us, and a full and enormous bathroom. After a shower and a change of clothes, we went to the roof restaurant for cheeses, sausages, bread, and several beers. Sleep came easily once in bed because we were both tired from the long flight.

In the morning after breakfast I telephoned MB and was told that my car was ready. With good directions from MB and the hotel, we took a train to Frankfurt and then a taxi to the MB agency, but before taking the taxi I stopped at a pharmacy to purchase a bottle of special extract of some vegetable for Trudy; she could not continue the journey without the extract.

The taxi sped (all taxis in Germany drive at great speed) to the MB agency. When we arrived at the office of Daimler Benz we signed the necessary papers. Then we were transported in a shuttle car, a MB 220 D, which carried us to another MB location where our new car was parked. At the new location, we were received cordially and shown our new blue MB. It was lovely. It was my first expensive automobile; at $8,325.00 it was more expensive than any car I'd ever purchased (and compared to the current 2011 model I ordered it was so much cheaper). I was in awe and thrilled by the purchase. What was I, an unemployed graduate student on a study grant doing, buying such an expensive automobile? There is no answer except that I did it and never regretted it, especially after 30 years of owning the same blue MB, now with over 1,000,000 miles on it. It is a wonderful car that serves me well even after three decades of reliable service.

Anyway, after Frankfurt and taking possession of the new MB, we drove to Cologne, where we spent the night, then on to Utrecht where I had a meeting with two members of the philosophy faculty who were specialists on the European Reformation and the influence that German and Dutch thinkers had on the English Reformation. After a pause at a pastry shop for coffee and éclairs in Utrecht, we then proceeded to Amsterdam and to our hotel in the Damrack section, which is the center of the city. After finding a covered garage for the MB, we registered at the Red Lion, which was a fair but not extraordinary hotel. The advantage of the Red Lion was its location near the city's activities, and it was not far from St. Dominic's Roman Catholic church where I was scheduled to speak the following Sunday to a group of drama students from the universities of Amsterdam and Utrecht. Our arrival in Amsterdam was on Thursday May 1973, and my speaking engagement was scheduled for the following Sunday at 1300 hours, following lunch.

We took the time to explore Amsterdam by walking, riding the canal boats, and simply enjoying the sights slowly and deliberately. Friday evening, after dinner, I asked Trudy if she wanted to explore the city for an hour or two but she refused with the claim that she was too tired. Because I was not, and it was still early in the evening, I asked if I could go for an hour's walk before retiring. That was okay with her, so I took my inner city map and proceeded through a major garden where both young and old where either chatting or playing chess. Once through the garden I crossed the canal, and without consulting my map, I entered a busy street where small shops were open and doing good business. At the end of that street I took a right or left turn, I don't remember which it was, but I stumbled into what I discovered was the red light district of Amsterdam.

A fascinating and quite strange street it was. Women were beckoning clients from behind glass windows. The women were scantily attired, mostly quite beautiful, and welcoming. Their voices could be heard in spite of the glass, and many spoke in German, French, English, and Dutch. Men stopped by the stores to window shop, bargain prices, or simply to make appointments for later dates. In a nearby street I saw men standing behind windows beckoning women. I soon learned that sex for sale was not limited to men, but included women clients too. After a while when I had enough and absorbed much of this fascinating learning experience, I resorted to my city map to find the Red Lion. I too was now tired enough to enjoy a good, restful night's sleep.

The next morning we boarded a bus to Haarlem to see the tulip farms. Our eyes were filled with tulips of every color and shape, several shapes that I had never encountered. When I saw the tulips closely in the nursery, I understood why at one time they were considered to be as valuable as currency:

they were exquisitely beautiful. Brought from Turkey by Dutch traders, the tulips were planted in the rich coastal soil of Holland where they soon took root and became abundant with little care. The Dutch tended the tulips and promoted them as flowers of great worth. I was enthralled by the sight of millions of colorful tulips swaying in the gentle sea breeze of coastal Holland.

On Sunday, after reviewing my presentation for St. Dominic's group, Trudy chose not to accompany me; she wanted to sleep longer. I walked over to the church and was warmly received by several members of the attending faculty and the graduate students present. St. Dominic's church was a large edifice attached to the Jesuit University of the same name. Dr. Joseph Powers SJ, professor of philosophy on the faculty of GTU, was my host. Joe was on sabbatical in order to complete a book on the history of various liturgical forms. I had written a paper for another professor at GTU called "Liturgy as Drama" and Powers had read it and asked me to speak on the subject in Amsterdam. Both the presentation and the discussion that followed it were satisfying and very well received.

After my presentation, Dr. Powers invited me to stay for dinner. I informed him that my wife was at the Red Lion and could I bring her over to dinner? Joe walked over to the hotel with me and waited in the lobby while I went to my room to fetch Trudy. The plan was to have a few drinks before dinner; Joe was a most interesting and lovely person and in possession of a fine sense of humor.

Trudy declined the dinner invitation because she did not wish to be "again among religious people." I accepted her decision and returned to see Joe in the lobby. I asked him to join me for a drink in the hotel lobby and informed him that because Trudy was unable to join us for dinner, I would also decline his kind offer. After a beer or two, we said goodbye and Joe returned to St. Dominic's.

My Return to East Anglia

The next day, after fetching our MB from the nearby garage and loading our luggage, we drove the short distance to Hoek van Holland to board a ship that would take us to Harwich on the coast of East Anglia, England. From Harwich, it was only a short drive to Cambridge and our waiting flat on Maid's Causeway. The crossing to the Eastern shore of England was six hours over a very calm North Sea and excellent weather. Often I have the tendency to become seasick but on this crossing I was well enough to go on deck, visit the restaurant and have a meal, which Trudy refused although she was not seasick.

I met several students who were heading to Cambridge University after spending weeks exploring the continent, learning languages, and visiting parents. All of them assured me that I would find the university a welcoming place and good source for the research I was scheduled to do. The reality was that I was focused on Alfred North Whitehead, the great mathematician and philosopher resident of Trinity College; his papers, however, had been transferred, unfortunately for me, to Harvard University, where he had been a resident professor in his later years. Fortunately, there were many of his papers and writings still shelved in both the university's main library and in Trinity College's adjacent library. Because I was a resident of King's College, I was able to have access to these libraries and any others that served my purpose. Thus I found the library at Jesus College to be a well lit, quiet place to write without interruptions. Being in attendance at Cambridge University and living in Cambridge was tantamount to being in heaven. I loved it. The seminars, the teas, the dinners, the formality, and the faculty, especially the graciousness of Dr. Norman Pittenger, added up to a wonderful experience.

After settling in our flat and finding that Nan had stocked it with smoked haddock, ale, bread, cheese, and apples we satisfied our hunger and went for a walk towards Jesus Pieces and the Camb River. It was a lovely evening and the air smelled of fresh mowed grass.

The next morning my routine began promptly at nine after a light breakfast. I located my assigned reading room at King's, visited the libraries of the

University, Trinity College, and the archive at Christ's College. I performed the same routine with some minor changes from Monday to Friday. On the weekend I took Trudy to see parts of East Anglia, including Ely Cathedral, the cathedral of my youth, and other interesting places. Nan often invited us for drinks and dinner, and Anna Crosley was always able to add to the history of the area with tid-bits that were either interesting or merely said to promote a theological discussion. The bait was easy to identify, but it was all so interesting. On several weekends we visited one of the remaining Fen old water pumps, Bury St. Edmund's and its rebuilt small distinctive Cathedral (several years later its head verger visited the cure of St. Edmund's, Pacifica), and other nooks and crannies and churches where I did many brass rubbings on the original tombs.

Scotland

After a month of intense research with some small success in finding what was left of Whitehead's papers, I was able to set aside ten days to drive to Scotland and show Trudy one of the charming bed and breakfasts that I had visited as a young man off Loch Lomond on the western side of Scotland. Stuckgowan B&B located near Tarbet on the western edge of the loch had been built by a sea captain who had sailed round the Horn to America in the 19th century. On one of his voyages, Captain Stuckgowan had brought back a California Redwood tree seedling to plant in his garden. In 1973, the tree had reached the height of 90 to 100 feet and was identified by the Scottish tree society or the like as a treasure to be cared for and preserved.

When we reached the B&B, and were shown our room on the upper floor with windows overlooking the loch, we found a box of chocolate from the dean of the Anglican Cathedral of Glasgow with a note inviting me to deliver the sermon the following Sunday and to have both lunch and dinner with him, his wife and a few guests. Norm Pittenger had notified the dean that I would be in the region. I telephoned the dean that very evening to thank him and to accept his kind invitation. He suggested that I not drive to Glasgow but that instead I take the train and then a taxi to the cathedral.

In the mean time, Trudy and I explored the loch area, had tea and scones in a small tearoom located right on the shore of the loch, and pushed on further north to the end of Loch Lomond and made reservations to have an "authentic" Scottish dinner the following evening of haggis and swedes (turnips) washed down with single malt scotch.

Back at our B&B, we settled in for the night for some reading and note taking. I had a great deal of reading to do so I had brought a few manuscripts to review. Trudy did not mind that I worked because she was able to sleep quite easily if my reading was done with a small light focused on the material. I don't think that I worked for more than an hour because I am usually not a night person, and when the clock indicates nine o'clock it is time for bed. As it is often said, "Raymond loses his vocabulary after nine p.m.!" This comment is not too far from the truth.

On Sunday morning, after an early breakfast, we drove the MB to the station in Tarbet for the train to Glasgow. When we arrived in Glasgow, I hailed a taxi and asked the driver to take us to the Cathedral. He did. When we arrived I paid him, took my vestments, and entered the large edifice. Something inside did not appear to be quite familiar or as I expected. One striking element that puzzled me was that at 10:10 and with an eleven o'clock service, there was no one present inside the cathedral. I proceeded to what I assumed to be the sacristy but the sign on the door said "vestibule" and not sacristy. Inside the room, all I saw hanging were black academic robes, nothing in color. I just assumed that acute low-church Protestantism had taken hold of Glasgow's cathedral. Just as I was about to hang my vestment bag, an elderly gentleman entered and he looked puzzled. After he introduced himself, I introduced myself and announced that I was the speaker for the eleven o'clock Eucharist.

"We nay have a ucha-rist tedai," he said in a thick Scottish brogue. He must be mistaken, I thought to myself.

"But I am the speaker and was invited by the bishop and the dean."

"We nay 'ave a bishop like Anglikhans. We nay have a dean, we have a super' tended," he asserted.

"But isn't this the Anglican Cathedral?" I asked.

"Nay, nay, nay" he repeated shaking his head.

"Church of Scotland, nay England, it is," he noted still shaking his head and putting his hand on my shoulder. "Wruuuung place, wruuuung cathydral!"

He was quite kind to call another taxi and direct the driver to take "the lost Americans," to the Anglican Cathedral, and at "quick haste." I thanked him and off we went, arriving at the right cathedral a mere ten minutes before the service began. A bit frazzled, I recovered sufficiently during the reading of the Propers to share my piece of wisdom with a full congregation.

After the service and the greetings, we went to lunch with the bishop and dean and their wives. After lunch, as I expected, we were taken on a tour of the muscle city of Glasgow with its shipyard, submarine base, museums, and a pleasant walk along the Clyde River to tea. Indeed it was a most pleasant day even after arriving at the wrong place at the beginning. Trudy seemed to have an enjoyable time, especially when she learned several choice elements of Scottish history and the clan that was associated with her family.

After our restful few days at Stuckgowan B&B, we drove north to Inverness, and then on to Culloden where Trudy thought she had a few ancestors who fought and were killed at the great and decisive battle in that location. The Scottish warriors, after fighting bravely, were devastatingly defeated by the English. We found lodging at Balagan Farm B&B within walking distance of the Culloden battleground and not too far from a high Roman bridge still in use by modern automobile traffic.

From Inverness we motored down the eastern coast of Scotland to St. Andrew's and then on to Edinburgh, staying at another charming B&B in Bigger, a suburb of the city on the Firth of the Forth. Bigger is a very small town located approximately 10 miles from the center of Edinburgh. It is a proud town that displays a large sign that says, "London is big, but Bigger is bigger."

We spent a couple of nights in Bigger in a small B&B on West High Street where I was given the opportunity to sample several single malt scotches and partake in the traditional haggis meal of stuffed stomachs, swedes, and peas. The meal was accompanied by conversation on several topics, humor, and suggestions for us to "really" experience Scottish life and culture. Bigger was a good find and a most pleasant location, especially since it was accessible to Edinburgh and easily reached by local public bus.

In Edinburgh we dutifully saw all the tourist sights from the Castle (where in 1566 Mary Queen of Scots gave birth to a son who in later years became James VI of Scotland and James I of England), down the Royal Mile, to Prince Street, the statue of Sir Walter Scott, St. Giles, Holyrood Palace built in the 16th century, and other interesting and exciting places.

The return route to Cambridge was driven quickly because I had several meetings scheduled at King's College, London and in the British Museum's library. Trudy was not interested in exploring London while I did my tasks so she stayed in our apartment in Cambridge where I left the MB for her to use. This in itself was curious because Trudy had complained on several occasions that she was homebound while I explored interesting places; meaning, I presumed, that I spent my time in dusty basements searching for information. I accepted her decision and took the train to London. Trudy would have the bicycle and the MB if she wished to explore the area around Cambridge while I was away for two nights and three days.

London and the British Museum

The train was quite sufficient for me since it would take me to Liverpool Street Station, which is just a few hundred yards from where I had to be. I found a small and affordable B&B in the vicinity of the British Museum that was quite good for my purpose. At the Museum I was given a carrel to use for the summer. I anticipated being in London at the Museum at least once every week or staying over to not interrupt the research. The arrangement at the B&B was such that I could bring Trudy over and she could explore London while I worked. It did not work out because Trudy joined me only a very few times.

After completing the formalities for the carrel and obtaining a pass to search the books and manuscript stacks, I settled in my carrel with three or four books that promised to be interesting for my topic on art and its philosophical aesthetics dimension. Soon I discovered that I needed a certain book that I had seen in the catalogue but had not taken. I rose from my desk and went to the particular stack where the book was kept and on the return trip to my carrel I looked at the desk immediately ahead of me and noticed a plaque with the name Dr. Karl Marx. I examined the desk and noticed that there was his name etched on one corner. An etching probably done with a penknife or other sharp object that read KM! Soon after I went to the librarian in charge of my location and asked if that was really Karl Marx's carrel and if it was could I use it? The librarian said of course I could use it because he suspected that Dr. Karl Marx was not expected to return soon. I moved my belonging to KM's carrel and considered the strange situation that found me in the bosom of history's famous controversial figure. My research on art took a sabbatical so that I could devote some research time to Karl Marx — it was an opportunity that was beneficial in and of itself even if it did not relate to my core subject. My habit was never to miss an opportunity that offered me more knowledge, knowledge of whatever type or subject.

Dr. Karl Marx (1818-1883) filled the last part of the 19th century and most of the 20th with an enormous presence that instilled an economic and social point of view that is still currently considered by many people to be an effective alternative to capitalism, free market, and independent thinking. Indeed, I was, however, intrigued that not far from me a century earlier had sat a poor scholar who by his writing had caused so much pain to the world and to the world's largest nation, mostly because he was misinterpreted or used to support the political philosophy that human beings were unable to act for themselves coherently and to their best purpose. Marx was naïve enough to assume that all people were subject to oppression and that no system was able to liberate the masses. The industrial revolution had placed many in impossible conditions, and the abuse of power was rampant. Labor was mismanaged, management was avaricious, and the market was a pressure cauldron that required more and more production from many more workers at lower wages. A new form of economic system was evolving and it was affecting capitalism drastically. The captains of industry were greedily pushing the market for more and more revenue. The wealthy sought more wealth and the less fortunate had to provide their labor to satisfy the demands of the market. In the process human rights were neglected. It was at this point that Karl Marx and Friederich Engels entered the scene.

My curiosity got the best of me and I proceeded in a tangential search to learn more about Karl Marx. I wanted to share and to relate much of the knowledge I acquired from my research on Marx and Engels because it showed how interesting the pursuit of information can be and where it can lead a person and the value that this information contributes to one's acquired knowledge. Many decades later, I found that my knowledge of Marx and Engels served me well when I met citizens of the Soviet Union, Russians and Ukrainians, who lived and endured great pain under this political system.

It was also amazing to me to discover that it was not so much the writings of Marx and Engels that produced the havoc in Russia and its adjacent republics, which later became the Soviet Union, but the interpretation of these writings by Lenin, Stalin, and others. Marx and Engels were attempting to correct some of the civil inadequacies that were produced by the Industrial Revolution and the emergence of capitalism in Europe. The rapid industrialization in Europe had caused misery among the working class because of the demand for long hours of work in factories. Yet industrialization had also produced a wealthy class of capitalists. Marx and Engels were concerned that such social inequities had to be corrected. Now we know how their writings were misinterpreted and converted to become an abusive tool for establishing a cruel dictatorship.

In 1849, Karl Marx fled to London from Berlin. His wife's financial resources became exhausted, and the couple fell into poverty. Marx also tried to make ends meet by writing as an international correspondent for the New York Tribune and other newspapers.

Karl Marx is considered to be among the most important thinkers of the 1800s. Few writers in all of history rival him for his broad influence on world affairs. His writings helped form a foundation for the political and economic system known as Communism.

Marx had predicted that capitalism would collapse in industrialized countries and that Communism would eventually take its place. He thought capitalism would end with a workers' revolution against the owners of factories and other properties used to produce goods and services. In the revolution, the workers would gain control of economic resources and of the government. Personal property would no longer be permitted; especially property of real estate and value, and every citizen would be an owner of the national wealth. Of course if everyone owns everything, then it comes down to the fact that no one owns anything, and that's exactly what emerged. The Communist Party, in the form of its privileged few, ended up appropriating everything with the general population possessing absolutely nothing.

I remember discussing the issue of property with a citizen of the Soviet Union and the response was emphatic that ownership was not forbidden in the USSR and that he owned the shirt, the pants, and the furniture he possessed. I asked him about estate, land, automobile, etc., and he replied that it was not necessary because he was assigned an apartment and public transportation was readily and cheaply available.

"Why do I need to own land, in this, my country?" he tried to convince me.

A few years later and after the USSR imploded, he was among the first to purchase a piece of land to build his own house.

In the 1900s, Marx's thinking shaped the policies of Socialist and Communist governments in many countries. His ideas also influenced numerous academic fields, especially economics, history, and political science, even in capitalist nations.

Through my research I learned that Karl Heinrich Marx was born on May 5, 1818, in the town of Trier, Germany, a town I visited in 1982. At that time, the region was part of Prussia. Marx's father, Heinrich, and his mother, Henrietta, were born into Jewish families. In fact, both of Marx's grandfathers were rabbis. However, Marx's father had converted to Lutheranism about a year before Karl's birth. The conversion probably resulted from the enforcement of anti-Jewish laws by government authorities. But it also helped Marx's father, a lawyer, advance in his career. The children in the family, including Karl, were baptized in 1824, and Marx's mother converted the next year.

In 1835, Marx began studying law at the University of Bonn. The next year, he transferred to the University of Berlin. There, he switched his focus to philosophy. In Berlin, he became known as a critic of religion and of the Prussian government. He earned a doctorate in philosophy at the University of Jena in 1841. But his criticism of religion and the government ended his hopes for a job as a professor. The Prussians and especially Prussia's royal family, who were deeply religious, controlled the jobs at most universities in the German-speaking world. By his controversial writing, Marx was immediately precluded from any lectureships or teaching posts at universities.

With an academic career closed to him, Marx turned to journalism, becoming an associate editor of a radical newspaper in Cologne called the Rheinische Zeitung. Prussian authorities opposed the paper because it often criticized the Prussian government. Soon the paper was closed and Marx was left without possibility of employment in Germany. He left Germany for England.

In London in 1864, Marx founded the International Workingmen's Association (later called the First International), an organization dedicated to improving the life of the working class. About this time, Marx also wrote his most ambitious work, *Das Kapital* (*Capital*). He planned a four-volume work but completed only three volumes. Only the first was published during his lifetime, in 1867. The others were published in 1885 and 1894.

Marx's closest associate and benefactor was Friedrich Engels, a German social scientist, journalist, and professional revolutionary. Engels made important contributions to Marxist theory, of which the most important was his introduction of Marx to the study of economics. Marx's knowledge of military and political affairs also came largely from Engels.

Engels and Marx wrote several books together. The most famous is the *Communist Manifesto* (1848), of which Engels wrote the first draft. He edited the second and third volumes of Marx's influential book *Das Kapital* and wrote several articles published under Marx's name.

Engels outlived Marx by 12 years and developed some of their joint ideas in directions of his own. He was largely responsible for the Marxist preoccupation with the scientific method and the application of Marxist views to all areas of knowledge. Some scholars believe that in his philosophic writings, Engels showed a misunderstanding of his friend's ideas. Engels also made assumptions about human nature that proved to be devastatingly wrong. He forgot about the individual's needs and focused more on the community, an entity that is fundamentally nonexistent unless one considers the unit that makes the whole possible.

Engels was born in Barmen, Prussia, and the son of a textile manufacturer. Hunted by the police because of his revolutionary activities, he fled from Prussia in 1844. He returned during the revolution of 1848 but fled again after the revolution collapsed. He then settled in England, where he managed one of his father's factories. He earned enough to support Marx and his family. Engels was well read in many languages and on a wide variety of topics. He was a keen observer with a creative mind that often went in directions that led to wrong conclusions.

I admit that it was a thrill to read about Marx and Engels but the whole study bore little weight for my research. The next day I returned to the carrel assigned to me and resumed the research for my topics. I needed no more distractions.

I've always believed that knowledge is cumulative and hence these side ventures into Marx and Engels were not only worth the time but were a refreshing interlude from the subject matter that had occupied me for several years. Much as I had been interested in politics most of my adult life, it was unknown to me at the time that by reading Marx I would be lured into learning more in later years about economics.

In retrospect and as I mentioned earlier, I believe that the little intellectual side trip into the history of Marx and Engels proved to be useful when I began in later years to work closely with members of the USSR. When I witnessed the beginning of the USSR's rejection of the political thinking of both Marx and Engels, it was not difficult for me to share their pain, a pain that surfaced when many members of the Soviet Union discovered that their whole political system was falling apart like a house of cards. Indeed, learning is a cumulative endeavor and one never knows when knowledge acquired will prove to be useful, effective, and applicable to a particular situation. No acquired knowledge is ever wasted.

In subsequent weeks I returned several times to the British Museum and its august library to pursue my research. Trudy did accompany me on a few occasions and I took time out to show her around the Egyptian section; she later bravely wandered by herself to a few other sectors. Collecting information in the British Library is almost the closest thing to being in a temple. I could feel knowledge enter my brain by an osmotic force that was way beyond my understanding. Just being in the surroundings of books, immersed in the scent left by people who have spent time within the library's walls, and knowing that great minds had produced extraordinary thoughts while walking around the stacks or writing on the old desks is enough to give me goose bumps and a rapid heart rate. I loved it. I believe that Trudy found great joy in being in the library and perhaps that experience reinforced her wish to become a librarian, for which she sought California accreditation in later years. I was pleased that Trudy had found joy in London and especially in the British Library.

St. Paul's Cathedral

My day trips to London also gave me opportunities to visit places that were not exactly on my itinerary. One of these places that left an indelible impression on me was St. Paul's Cathedral. St. Paul's was built after the Great Fire of London in 1666; Christopher Wren redesigned part or all of 55 of the 87 churches that the fire destroyed. Fascinated by his architecture, I added a little research about Wren to my store of tangential knowledge. Moreover, studying St. Paul's offered insights into how Wren understood liturgy and the dynamics within liturgy. Many important liturgical services are achieved in Westminster Abbey (Royal Peculiar, not a cathedral or abbey but directly responsible to the Crown) in the elongated nave under its high ceiling and between its impressive columns, but it seems that a preferable location would be in St. Paul's Cathedral, which truth be admitted has less of a history than the Abbey. Yet Wren's structure has an extraordinary space for extraordinary liturgies, and sound in that arena is enhanced by the fact that its bell shape accentuates the various qualities of liturgical music, spoken words, and visual movements. Frankly I would prefer that great liturgies were implemented in that great St. Paul's Cathedral.

Sir Christopher Wren (1632-1723) was an architect, scientist, and mathematician. The most famous of his edifices was St. Paul's Cathedral built between 1675-1710. The grace and variety of many of Wren's church spires is still a feature of the London skyline, and his free arches are extraordinary structural elements. His other major buildings include the churches of St. Bride (about 1678) and St. James (about 1684); Royal Hospital, Chelsea (1682-1689); and Greenwich Hospital (about 1715) where he introduced the double ceiling to allow piping to be connected to any room requiring water or other liquids — today such ceilings can also accommodate electrical conduits and gas piping when required in any room.

Wren was born in the county of Wiltshire. His early interests and training were in science and mathematics. From 1641 to 1646, he attended Westminster School in London, where the poet John Dryden and the philosopher John Locke were fellow students. Wren got his B.A. degree from Oxford University in 1651 in mathematics, and received his M.A. degree there in 1653 in astronomy. In 1657, he was appointed professor of astronomy at Gresham College, London.

In 1661, King Charles II appointed Wren to the important architectural position of assistant surveyor general. Unlike other English architects of his day, Wren neither went to Italy to study classical architecture nor worked as an apprentice under other architects. However, he did visit France in 1665, and the architecture he saw there can be discovered in his work. Wren was to a large degree a self-taught architect who applied his mathematical knowledge and his common sense to create architectural wonders. He once admitted that had he studied architecture he would have rejected the discipline with great disgust. Wren received many honors and was recognized as a founding member of the Royal Society in 1660.

I became interested in Wren because, like so many professionals today, people seldom do what they are expected to do when they graduate from university. He was a graduate in astronomy with a special bent on mathematics and both are a long way from architecture. He became a self-taught architect who made quite a name for himself. Wren was not part of the architectural club, the fraternity so to speak. Wren was a creative person with talent and a keen mind that supported his quest for design. We must all be grateful that he never attended architectural school! To me he was a fascinating example of what a creative mind can do if allowed to move beyond the boundaries of codified academia. Don't we encounter the same maverick talent in IT and computer science in people like Bill Gates, Steve Jobs, and others?

St. Paul's Cathedral, also known as the London Cathedral, is also the first Cathedral designed and built to accommodate specifically Anglican liturgies. It is unlike other cathedrals of its time that were taken over from the Roman Catholic communion during the reign of

Elizabeth I. St. Paul's is a vast open structure that is acoustically nearly perfect. Built with many bold arches holding the high ceiling, it thus allows the nave area to be uncluttered by columns that are typically encountered in Gothic structures. Though less of a cruciform shape and more of an arena in style, St. Paul's congregation never has the feeling of being remote from the activities performed in the sanctuary. Unlike Westminster's Abbey with its long nave encased in column after column, St. Paul's is open and its altar is visible from many sides, especially now that the Church has returned to the ancient freestanding altar style. One's presence in St. Paul's and one's listening to the music from Vaughan Williams is tantamount to sitting in the lap of God.

Outside St. Paul's, one finds an open place where people come to sit on benches to read or mull around street vendors hawking food, trinkets, and clothes. Painters find spots here and there to catch a side of St. Paul's and its surroundings for a watercolor or oil rendering. On the steps of St. Paul's I never missed seeing an old woman feeding the birds, and following the lore, I gave her my two-pence (English money had not been decimalized yet) for the birdseed. Once off the grounds of St. Paul's, London's financial and newspaper businesses take over. This is the heart of London. A few hundred yards off to one side stand the Bank of England and the British Stock Exchange, edifices that celebrate the power of money, industry, investment, and capitalism. If New York is the heart of Western capitalism, London is the liver that supplies the wherewithal to convert it all into manageable assets. London has remained important for finance because it is the oldest stock exchange and it is the most accessible by air transportation in the global economy. Perhaps now that electronic communication is readily available London will diminish in importance but that is yet hardly the case.

Part of my autobiographical musing is to share with the reader the learning approach that has always guided my life. In many ways I'm a linear thinker but at times I diverge because there are interesting bits of information that attract me. Perhaps it was curiosity and perhaps it was to rest from the intense research that I was engaged in. Anyway, there I was enthralled by Wren's masterpiece and so I paused to enjoy it and learn a bit about the work and the person who created it.

Returning to Cambridge after taking the train from Liverpool Street station always gave me a sense of comfort that I was returning home. In Cambridge I no longer had to resort to street maps, read street signs, or stop momentarily to reconnoiter the place. From Cambridge station, I would walk this way and that and soon I was in Maid's Causeway and my apartment. Trudy would either be reading or dozing. Grabbing a shopping bag we'd go to the market for the evening dinner, something that could have been done by Trudy while I was away. But I was having fun in the big town, while Trudy was left alone in "rural" Cambridge. Dinner completed and various subjects explored, I returned to my notes or my books to prepare for my needs the next day. After several more weeks of research, we decided to take two weeks for a driving trip to the Continent and a visit to some of my old haunts. On this trip, Anna Crosley asked if she could join us, and we gladly accepted since she offered to share the expenses.

Le Continent, La France et L'Italie

"Maman, voilà la France. Je pense que je verrai Calais tout de suite!" the little English schoolboy shouted as he pressed his nose against the front window of the Channel ferry. We had crossed the English Channel and were heading in our MB to Paimpol and a little hotel, Hotel le Phare, on the Golfe of Saint Malo. This was a place that I had visited many years earlier and always wanted to return to for a few days, mainly to enjoy the English Channel (La Manche) and to "manger des fruits de mer."

On the way to Paimpol we stopped in Caen for lunch and a few moments of rest. Lunch was in a bistro that offered local food. I ordered for us bowls of fish soup, sautéed fresh seafood, and pommes frites; our host added the obligatory VIN rouge de table. After Caen, we continued to Paimpol, which was approximately two hours further west on a smooth road that followed the coastline. We avoided Cherbourg because I wanted to have a longer visit there and would make it an outing while in Paimpol. We drove through Saint Malo and on to Saint Brieuc, and then a turn to the north took us directly to Paimpol.

After settling in and enjoying a short nap, I asked Trudy if she wanted to sit in the lounge and enjoy a drink before dinner. The lounge had a veranda overlooking the Bay of St. Malo, the evening was clear and the water was the bluest blue with bursts of white froth punctuating its surface here and there. Anna joined us and we discussed our aperitifs and the choice was agreed to be Campari and soda. Trudy admitted that she had never tasted Campari and was asked to join us; we did suggest that she have a sip from mine first, but she was willing to be adventurous.

When the aperitifs arrived we offered a toast to La belle France, and sipped happily the wonderful Italian contribution. Trudy took one sip and made an awful grimace. She found Campari to be unpleasant and bitter. I took it away from her and ordered her a sherry and certainly not a dry one. With the sherry her smile returned and all was well again, except that I discerned a bit of tension between her and Anna. I could neither identify the cause nor the reason. I sensed, however, the scent of a feud. I was sitting next to Trudy and I reached for her hand, but that did not seem to dissipate the tension between the two women. At dinner, I again took my place next to Trudy and translated the menu. Trudy chose salad and stuffed pork cutlets. My choice was fresh seafood, principally a tray of oysters, winkles, cracked crabs, clams, and oursins (urchins) plus bread and regional red wine. I do not remember what Anna ordered because I was paying more attention to Trudy, being more interested in making her happy, a task that I failed to accomplish.

The next day we drove to Cherbourg to look at the famous windmills and to walk on the Corniche, as I had done in my youth. In the distance we could see the Islands of Jersey and Guernsey; both of these Channel Islands are British. After doing much of what tourists are known to do we returned to Paimpol for a light dinner and some reading. The next morning, I indulged myself with a swim in the not too warm La Manche and a hearty breakfast. After breakfast we toured the town of Morlaix and the coastal village of Saint Pol-de-Léon.

The following day, after leaving Paimpol, we drove to Chartres to visit its grand cathedral and for Trudy and Anna to pace its historic labyrinth. I wasn't interested so I walked around the giant nave. Chartres was the stopping place for Archbishop Thomas à Becket in 1164 when he was alienated from his king, Henry II. After Chartres we pushed on to Paris to spend a few days in the City of Light. Because this trip was Trudy's first visit to the great city we did all the tourist places on both sides of the Seine River. From Paris we drove to Lyons, then on to Chamonix / les Houches (village of my paternal side of the family), and the Mont Blanc Tunnel to Aosta, in Italy where I wanted to show her the Franco-Italian community from whence part of my family emerged. Curiously, Trudy indicated no interest in that section of Haute Savoie.

Aosta is a delightful place surrounded by the ancient walls from a castle of the same name. Our hotel was in the center of the small city and most sights were accessible without driving the MB. I had, however, to have the oil of the MB changed. The MB maintenance garage was on the northern side of the great castle wall and to reach it one had to drive over the drawbridge and then through the ancient wall. Anna accompanied me because Trudy wanted to rest and have time for herself. After depositing the MB at the maintenance garage and arguing as to what type of oil should be put in the car (Italians shout at the drop of a hat) because I had not specified the brand, we went to a café located within the wall to wait for the car. After a few hours sitting in the café reading my book and discussing various topics with Anna, we retrieved the MB and drove back to the hotel. The next day we drove to several villages in the Alps to explore the atmosphere and to speak with the people, most of whom spoke French rather than Italian, although we were still in Italy.

The return trip to France took us by way first of Geneva, Switzerland, then on to Autun near the Saône River to the great cathedral. The cathedral of Autun is famous for its humorous gargoyles, friezes, and fine sculptures. We proceeded north along the autoroute directly to Amiens, bypassing Paris. We wanted to look at the great cathedral of Amiens with architecture that rivals Chartres and Notre Dames de Paris.

Amiens is one of the least adorned Norman cathedrals left in France. Unlike Chartres and Notre Dame de Paris, which have had structures added to them, Amiens remains as it was centuries ago. It has a purity that excites the eyes of artists and structural lines that fascinate architects, engineers, and builders. Inside the cathedral the nave, sanctuary, and choir are well lit by the natural light from outside. Open, well lit, and well proportioned, Amiens is a cathedral worth seeing for its artistic splendor.

Leaving Amiens we drove to Boulogne-sur-Mer to board the ship that would take us to Folkstone, England. We spent the night in Canterbury and the next day toured the Cathedral and the town until early afternoon, after which we pushed on to Cambridge. We arrived in Waterbeach in time for a drink of Scotch and dinner at Nan's. It was a marvelous two weeks except for the little elements of friction between Anna and Trudy, which I soon decided to ignore and subsequently discounted. That Nan had prepared dinner for us was a genuine act of kindness. Nan Youngman was a dear person, a saintly person indeed.

On the way to our apartment in Cambridge, Trudy vented her annoyance of Anna. Trudy felt that Anna had monopolized the conversation and forced us to visit too many cathedrals, too many religious structures. I accepted her complaints but kept silent. Any comment that I made would be grist for further attacks on Anna by Trudy. Frankly, I was not interested because nothing that we did, alone, with Anna or with anyone else was pleasing to Trudy.

Even lunch with Dr. Pittenger or tea at King's was an unpleasant experience for Trudy. Driving to the Continent in a new MB and staying in fairly good hotels were not satisfying ways to respond to her needs. I discovered that summer that it was practically impossible to please Trudy. So much for our anticipated romantic visit to Europe!

Wings near Ely Cathedral

It was a restless night for me after our return from the Continent. All night I had tried to understand where I had gone wrong with Trudy. It seemed that nothing was pleasing her and that I was unable to make her happy or to have her return some aspects of joy in my direction. She wanted much more than I could provide. I knew that I was difficult, demanding, and an over-achiever, but I was not impossible to live with. It was a most difficult night for me. At five in the morning I dressed and slipped the MB out of its carport to drive to Ely and to catch the seven o'clock Eucharist. Few clouds were in the sky, and East Anglia was barely awake at this time of the morning. The sun's rays were piercing the horizon ever so lightly. It was beautiful, quiet, and peaceful. The drive to Ely was exceptionally quick because there was no traffic on the A-10.

I parked the MB in the Cathedral car park at 5:45 and chose to wait for the service by taking a walk to the embankment, which separated the wet Fens from the city. Few houses were in that area and I could look at the Cathedral and the Fens by directing my eyes either to the north or to the south. It was quiet and the sky was turning a golden color. My thoughts were sliding through my head at nearly the speed of light, many of them, too many. My doctoral work, the children whom I missed greatly, the ongoing work on the revision of the Prayer Book, Trudy and our marriage, and future employment; each thought flashed though my head and produced no resolution. It was problem after problem with no end in sight. I was almost at the end of my wits. The Eucharist would be a tool that might calm me, but that was improbable and too much to expect. Tension was building in me, my heart was racing way too rapidly, and my breath was becoming shorter and shorter.

What was happening to me? I even considered the possibility that a heart attack was on the way.

A flight of white-winged pigeons against the background of the golden sky interrupted my thoughts. They were not a hundred feet away from me. I was transported in a flash to my childhood in Cairo. The pigeons flew here and there in a solid flight of nearly one hundred or more pairs. Up, around, left, then right they flew as if controlled by some magnetic force that directed their actions. I turned towards the Cathedral and saw who controlled this flight of pigeons. A young boy holding a white silk flag was directing the flight. The boy was probably no older than eight or nine, yet he was the master of his squadron of pigeons. The birds followed his every signal, obediently and without distraction. I walked over to the young man. We said hello. I asked him how old he was. He was eight and a half years old and attended King's School, which was attached to the Cathedral. His schedule was that every morning before school he would release his pigeons and exercise them. Sometimes after school, when homework was quickly accomplished, he would exercise the birds again.

"How many pigeons have you?" I asked.

"A hundred and fifty pairs, here I fly only eighty pairs," he informed me. We chatted for a while as he controlled his flight of birds, keeping his eyes on their every movement.

"Do you like pigeons?" he asked me.

"Yes, I used to have pigeons when I was a boy." I told him that as a young boy I too had raised pigeons but because of the war I had to give them away. He told me that his uncle had given him several pairs the year before and before long they had multiplied. "My uncle Thaddeus," he paused to move the flight from the left to the right, "He taught me how to control them." I looked at the obedient flight of birds and wished that I had the courage to ask if I could have the flag for a few moments. I just could not ask him because he would never submit his controlling authority to a stranger.

How I ached to swish around the flag for a few strokes. Could I still manage the touch? It had been years, nay, decades, since I had maneuvered flights of pigeons. If I asked for the flag and misdirected the flight to a dangerous area, lost some of the birds, or led them into a power line and killed a few, that would be devastating to me and to the boy. I just watched him and envied him. He gave the squadron of birds a few moments of rest on the roof of his house. I could hear their murmuring and their cooing. He swished his flag once again and they returned into synchronized flight. "Here, take the flag and you try it," he pushed the flag handle into my right hand. I was frozen stiff.

"Go ahead man, they need directions or they'll be confused," he chastised me. "Go on, they need directing," he ordered me. "Go on," and he pushed the hand with the flag to the left.

I followed the motion he had me start and waved the flag first to the left and then to the right. The squadron of pigeons also moved to the left over his house, and then to the right, and then when I felt that my control was still as good as it had been in my early years, I swished the flag up briskly, and then deliberately around in one determined motion. The flight of pigeons climbed straight up in the sky, turned over sharply, then performed a well synchronized and beautifully performed Roll. "Wow!" the young boy yelled. I repeated the same maneuver signal. The flight of pigeons duplicated the previous Roll. When they completed that maneuver I brought them over to the roof of his house for a moment of rest. They landed and cooed and murmured telling each other that the maneuver had been perfect but difficult to perform. The steep climb was tiring but fun and the subsequent turn was dizzying but enjoyable.

"How do you get them to do that?" the boy asked. I turned myself around to give my back to the pigeons so they wouldn't see the flag.

"Take the flag and raise it, smartly rotate it in a clean circle, snap it down level, and then bring it up horizontally," I instructed the boy. He practiced a couple of times with his back turned so the birds would not see the flag in his hand. He then turned and signaled the birds to flight. They flew overhead and across to the Fens side. We had exchanged names during the instructional period; he was Jack Roberts. Jack swished the flag as I had instructed him and the flight flew straight up and performed another, then another, then another perfect Roll. The maneuvers were perfect but then Jack was a master at controlling his flight. After they performed yet another Roll he brought them over to his roof for rest. This was also the end of the exercise because it was school time, and I had missed the Eucharist. We shook hands and I thanked him for letting me play with his pigeons. That experience was the catharsis that brought me to a peaceful state of being. I saw Jack one more time and had the good fortune to meet his father and mother at a service in the Cathedral. The flight of wings near Ely Cathedral was the precise antidote to my distressed person. It had been a sacramental experience for me.

New House on the Pacific Coast

I continued to tend to my research and kept at it until it was time to return to California. The day before we took the flight back to San Francisco, I drove the MB to London to leave it with the shipper who would make all arrangements to have it transported to Oakland, California. Again Trudy did not want to accompany me to London because it was too tiring for her. Indeed it was also for me because London is not an easy city to maneuver, even with a good map.

After we finished packing our belongings, on the day of our departure, Anna came by the apartment with a taxi we had hired and we rode to Gatwick Airport for the flight home and to Dominique and Michel. I missed them and was ready to see and hug them again. Ruth Eger met us beyond the customs gate of San Francisco's International Airport and we drove down to Merced after depositing Anna at her apartment on Dolores Street. Ruth was most kind to lend me her own car until our MB arrived in San Francisco, which took almost a month.

A few days later I took Ruth and the children, first depositing her in a temporary apartment in San Jose, where Chuck had found a new position with Westinghouse, and then proceeded to Pacifica to the vicarage on Malavere Street. Trudy stayed in Merced to prepare herself for the fall beginning of school. The children were to spend the year with me and attend St. Mathew's Preparatory Episcopal School in San Mateo.

Several chores awaited me in Pacifica and in Berkeley. I had to enroll the children in school, search for a house to purchase, finalize a report outlining my research to my doctoral committee, move some of my books from Anna Crosley's apartment where I had stored them, and call a meeting of the governing body of St. Edmund's to plan for the following season's activities.

The children, as I said, were placed at St. Matthew's Episcopal School, San Mateo. Soon I found a nearly completed new house in Montara and finalized the purchasing arrangement with a temporary loan from Eureka Savings and Loans, which I repaid a month later when my funds arrived from the sale of stocks. I asked members of St. Edmund's if they knew a babysitter, several were suggested, and I selected one, Pat Turner, who was wonderful and whom the children loved.

Trudy visited every two or three weekends and on one of them I had her look at the house in Montara that I had selected to have her give her approval before I signed the final papers. With the help of Tom Edminster and others, I moved into our new house. I am not sure that I could have handled the move without Tom and several other folks from St. Edmund's, especially Emily, Dolores (a fine Afro-American actress, a parishioner, and a delightful person whose last name I've forgotten), and Jane White, now Goodrich.

In the search for a house, I was able to locate just what I needed in Montara, a village on the other side of Mount Montara and eight to nine miles south of Pacifica, past what is known as Devil's Slide on Highway 1. The house was not quite completed so I had ample opportunity to make changes that would suit our lifestyle. I asked for gas to supply both the heater and the kitchen range. Insulating the attic was another item on my request list. The German builder was quite accommodating in making these and other less significant changes for me. As mentioned earlier, we moved into the new house in February 1974.

Our new house was located at 1650 East Street, Montara. It was a most suitable house for the location and for us. The house was located on an unpaved road and across the road was a huge field for the children to have adventures. The house also offered a good view of the Pacific Ocean and sufficient land for landscaping, growing vegetables, and raising rabbits. We lived in that house approximately ten years where many changes in our lives took place. Some of the changes were good and some questionable.

After moving to a larger and older house in Montara to create a bed and breakfast, the Goose and Turrets, we rented the house and it has been a good profit producer for the past twenty years. Purchasing that house was a wise investment. The house on 1650 East Street was sold in 2007 just before the housing market became soft.

It was at 1650, as we came to call the house, that I finished writing my dissertation and started working at Bechtel. It was at 1650 that the dissolution of my marriage took place. It was at 1650 that Nicola became our ward. It was at 1650 that Dominique learned that she was an artist among other talents she possessed, such as writing. It was at 1650 that I entertained Jacques Marsal, the discoverer of Lascaux. It was at 1650 that I raised rabbits. It was at 1650 that the plans for the bed and breakfast first took shape, and that Emily and I drew up the first list of what we would and would absolutely not do in our bed and breakfast. It was at 1650 that Michel first operated a motorized vehicle. It was at 1650 that I learned that sheetrock was not to be cut with a saber saw. It was at 1650 that I learned about dead-man holders for walls. It was at 1650 that I learned about erecting concrete blocks and making stucco walls. I am certain that there are other events that occurred at 1650 but my recollection is not precise at the moment. I learned many things and lived through many events at 1650, but 835 George Street, the place where the Goose and Turrets stands, has been the greater arena for instruction.

As I mentioned earlier, I came to the San Mateo Coast in August 1952 and fell in love with the environment, the people, the violent storms, and the cool fog during the summer months. It is a magical place all year, with the hills, the ocean, the flowers, the birds, and the clean air. No matter where I travel to in the world I'm always happy to return to the coast and to my village of Montara. I have lived in Montara longer than I have lived anywhere else in the world. My roots are deep in Montara and it is my domain, my place on this globe, and my piece of my Earth on this planet.

St. Edmund's, Pacifica

Earlier in the narration I mentioned that at Bishop Myers' suggestion I had applied and then been hired as part-time vicar of St. Edmund's Mission, Pacifica. The timing of this hiring was interesting because it happened just before my departure for Cambridge to do research. The Mission Committee and the congregation accepted my departure to a major extent because the interim priest, Millard Streeter, was a fine, able, and gracious person and was willing to stay on for another three months.

St. Edmund's was a small mission near the Pacific coast in the expanding city of Pacifica. A devout congregation comprised of 50 to 55 families, the people were great supporters of the church but ever since the departure of their vicar, Jack Fredericks, four or five years earlier, they had had no guidance. Jack had retired to devote much of his talents to his marionettes and to developing a small school for gifted children. Since Jack's departure, St. Edmund's had suffered under a parade of mediocre supply priests, until Millard Streeter's arrival on the scene.

Millard, as the assistant chaplain at St. Luke's Hospital in San Francisco, proved to be a gem in many ways. Millard, working as associate chaplain under the able direction of the chaplain of St. Luke's, Fordyce Eastburn, a person of extraordinary compassion, creativity, and love, was quite naturally able to implement the same qualities. Millard worked all week at the hospital but he was able to make time to participate in the life of St. Edmund's during mid-week evening gatherings and on Sundays. When I arrived on the scene as the new hire, I asked Millard if he would continue to guide the congregation of St. Edmund's until my return. He agreed willingly and did a superb job as interim vicar.

While in England I was able to maintain very close watch over the activities of the Mission with the help of Katherine Henwood, directress of the Altar Guild and matriarch of the congregation. Katherine was and is a full-blown Type-A person. As a nurse practitioner, Katherine had the energy to work at her profession and to step in as "mother superior" for the congregation. In addition, Katherine was a gardener of some reputation who not only supervised the facility of the Mission with her husband John, a retired ship maintenance specialist (John was a supporter but he never attended services), but also of managing her own plant nursery — and even made a profit selling plants to other nurseries.

Other great supporters were Ted and Mary-Margaret (Mar) Kaden who had been members of St. Clement's, Rancho Cordova, when I was vicar of that Mission. Both the Kadens and Katherine kept me informed by mail or by telephone about what was happening at St. Edmund's. The arrangement worked well and produced no negative situations. With Katherine's management, the Mission really did not need a vicar, except perhaps for presiding at the sacraments. Katherine offered good support and was a devoted layperson!

When I returned to the coast and resumed my duties as vicar of St. Edmund's, Chair of the CLR, doctoral student, single parent, and Jack-of-all-trades searching for a house and then furnishing it and converting it into a home for my family, my energy level was reduced to near zero. Katherine (as a nurse practitioner) grabbed me by the arm and led me to her physician for an overall examination. The result was that I was on the edge of anemia and courting exhaustion. With the help of a few parishioners under Katherine's direction, I was forced to stay home for a few days for rest and recuperation. All our food was furnished and a few parishioners did all the cleaning. My duty was to study, read, and accept the kindnesses bestowed on the children and me. The physician prescribed pharmaceutical products including vitamin B 12 to overcome the deficiency in my body. Apparently I was not eating enough meat and fish products, which give the body its requirement of B 12, a necessary vitamin for the nervous system. When Katherine took a sample of my blood two weeks later the indications showed great improvement. I would survive and I did, thanks to Katherine Henwood.

St. Edmund's was quite willing to participate in activities that demanded my time at Grace Cathedral. For instance, the congregation of St. Edmund's attended every Easter Eve Eucharist I organized at the Cathedral after I became their vicar. They even attended my last two Pentecost celebrations at Grace Cathedral, and loved it. All in all we had a good time together. Parishioners volunteered to make banners to depict the messages of Teilhard de

Chardin after we had a series of adult classes on his book *The Phenomenon of Man*. When new editions of the revised Prayer Book were issued, St. Edmund's acted as my testing base before I submitted the liturgical texts to the rest of the Diocese of California.

St. Edmund's was located near a cul-de-sac by St. Pedro Creek. It was a beautiful location but the creek bank was eroding sufficiently that it was affecting the foundation of the church. With the help of a professional heavy equipment parishioner, Hugh, who brought in a backhoe, several of the members volunteered to work on the restoration project. One Saturday the team gathered by the creek and work was started with little time wasted. Several families provided lunch and work continued soon after we all refreshed ourselves. By five o'clock the restoration of the bank was complete. Dinner was set up in the patio, and the entire congregation had a party. It was an accomplishment that was not at all painful, except for stressed ligaments, aching shoulders, several black-and-blue marks, and the usual cuts from the bushes. No one, unbelievably, was attacked by poison oak. The next day Grace McCarthy, the mayor of Pacifica and a member of the congregation, offered to have the City of Pacifica landscape and replant the bank with native species.

On a Wednesday morning in 1975 when I picked up the church's mail, I noticed a letter from Bury St. Edmund's Cathedral, England — a place I had visited when I was in Cambridge. The letter was from the dean of the Cathedral asking me if we were interested in exchanging a token stone to bind both congregations in a bond of family affection. I immediately contacted Ted Kaden, the senior warden, for his response to the request I had received from the dean. Ted was receptive and suggested that we frame a stone from our creek and send it to Bury St. Edmund's Cathedral. I consequently wrote back to the dean and conveyed to him that we were delighted to participate in the exchange and would be compiling a brief history of St. Edmund's Mission for him. A week later I received another letter informing me that the head verger from Bury St. Edmund's Cathedral was coming to visit us; he was retired and had been awarded a month-long holiday to visit America. The verger would be bringing a stone from the ruins of Bury St. Edmund's and a document attesting to its history. I was also informed that the verger was licensed to preach by the Church of England, having read for a degree, which he earned, in history and theology at Jesus College, Cambridge.

Ted had gotten the dimension and the general shape of the stone. He had prepared a spot in the cardinal west wall of the nave for the stone, with a brass placard inscribed with the appropriate information. On the Sunday that the verger, Mr. J.A.H. Waddington arrived, and after he gave the sermon address, at the Eucharistic offering he delivered the stone from his cathedral to me, and Ted delivered the stone from our small mission to him. Documents were exchanged, lunch was served and I showed a few slides of Bury St. Edmund's Cathedral that I had taken a few years earlier. So it happened, that a few years later, in 1979, Emily and I paid a visit to Mr. and Mrs. Waddington in Bury St. Edmund's and we all had a wonderful time recalling their time with us in Pacifica. By 1979, however, I had resigned as vicar of the Mission in Pacifica after three years, whereas Mr. Waddington had fully retired as verger of the Cathedral after 40 years of service.

One of the most colorful, interesting, charming, astute, compassionate, and delightful persons in Pacifica was none other than Howard Edminster, teacher, sculptor, poet, and raconteur par excellence. Whenever I craved some intellectual recharging, I would head to see Howard and listen to his golden voice recount stories, discuss political philosophy, listen to him read his poetry, or watch him in his basement create sculptures from bits and pieces of items he found and encase them in epoxy first and then in cement. I have two of his wonderful pieces and feel fortunate to have them and grateful to have known this great man.

Howard Edminster was a Renaissance man. He was a fine teacher of young and old. He was a man who did not find that religious denominational identities counted for very much, for him or for anyone else. A Roman Catholic by birth, Howard was just as comfortable in the Episcopal Church as he was in the American Lutheran Church. He took Rome's attitude as a sign that the See of St. Peter was not learned enough to understand the message of Christ, its founder. He was not charmed by the Lutheran Church of the Missouri Synod because it cared little for theological clarity and sacramental unity; it was ossified and gasping its last breath. As for the Episcopal Church, he saw it as trying to understand the message of Christ and its meaning. Howard approved the attempt by the Episcopal Church to revise its Prayer Book, especially because the PB contained the gist of its sacramental theology and "what one said, one believed."

I invited Howard to deliver an address one Sunday at St. Edmund's. He accepted with great delight. I knew that if Howard simply read the Prayer Book or even the telephone directory, his mesmerizing voice would charm the congregation. As it was, Howard delivered a poignant address that surpassed all my expectations. His topic was "human self-debasement in the light of Christ's love." Howard spoke for less than ten minutes, but in those few minutes he shared with us volumes. He was magnificent. I am sorry that he was not taped, especially because he had not written his address. All that I have is the memory of his message. I can still hear the sound of his voice, his lightly raspy, melodic, baritone, but golden-sounding voice. Howard died a few years after I resigned from St. Edmund's. He left behind three offspring: Victoria, from a previous marriage, whom I did not know very well; Ann, an architect; and Tom, a natural teacher; and his wife Dorothy, mother of Tom and Ann, who fulfilled a civic career on the Pacifica Council, and as mayor for a few terms.

Claude and Diane Turner were a couple of pleasant and hard working people. Claude's first wife had died of cancer soon after he had retired from the Navy and left him with three children; the oldest, Pat, became my regular baby-sitter during the year when I was acting as a single parent. Diane (I cannot remember her last name), one of the more active members of St. Edmund's, had terminated a miserable marriage just about the time that Claude had become a widow. For a few months Diane was Nicola's court appointed caretaker, but soon that was changed at Nicola's insistence and I was awarded that privileged position. Claude was always willing to help me or anyone else with tasks. He was a lead worker on the repairing job on the creek bank, he and Tom Edminster helped me move from the Malavere Street vicarage to my new house in Montara, and Claude was ready to work with me when we landscaped the yard at 1650. A more helpful person was rare to find. When he and Diane married, they decided to move to Virginia where his folks lived; I lost a good friend. We communicated by mail for a few years, then with my travels and Claude's own travels in his recreational vehicle, we soon lost track of each other as time marched on.

In every cure, there is the possibility of failure and defeat. I experienced that down side in Pacifica with Byron Cook. Byron, a young man who was bright and always very willing to help me on small construction tasks was plagued by severe psychological problems. His mother, a delightful woman who was for many years the senior secretary to the principal of one of the local high schools, hoped that Byron would be her first offspring to graduate from college and establish a non-blue collar career. Byron's father, a pastry cook who worked nights, was an avid golfer and a stern disciplinarian. Byron's siblings were able to cope with their father without showing any signs that they were negatively affected. Byron was introduced to golf by his father and came to love the game and was quite good at it. At one period in his life, Byron said that he might turn professional and work for a club. Byron attended the California State University at San Francisco, and majored in mathematics, graduating with a bachelor's degree and commendation four years after he started.

Byron was often found at my house, helping me with chores for which I required assistance. We built a retaining wall together, landscaped the yard at the 1650 house, and completed many, many other tasks. For a time, Byron tutored Dominique in math when she found herself in difficulty at St. Matthew's Episcopal School. He was a good and patient tutor and I was grateful for his time and help. Byron would not accept any remuneration for the work he did; he even would rarely accept lunch but brought his own sack of food with him. He would sit in his car and eat his lunch. An uncle, as a graduating present, had given the little car to him and Byron cared for it meticulously. He would send samples of engine oil regularly to a laboratory to monitor its condition.

I asked him one day why he would not join us in our lunch? His reply was succinct and to the point, although not quite coherent, "I want to be certain that the food I eat is pure!" We were having a bowl of chicken soup, cheese, homemade bread, and strawberries; each item was properly prepared, washed, and served and none of my children indicated that they suffered any ill from the food I was serving. Byron was beginning to isolate himself from the people he knew and those who had cared for him since he was a little boy.

After purchasing the building for the Goose and Turrets B&B, I asked Byron if he would like to housesit for a few weeks while Emily and I went on a cross-country flight in our airplane. He readily agreed to stay at the Goose and Turrets. On another occasion he was also asked, assuming that he had enjoyed staying in the big house, and he accepted willingly but upon our return we found that he was unhappy and a bit cross with us. He left the house as soon as we arrived and refused categorically any remuneration for his house sitting. Byron acted strangely in the weeks ahead but he was always willing to help me with tasks, yet he continued to eat his lunch in his car and would not allow us to feed him.

I had introduced Byron to Meeg Ross, my hairdresser, and he became a regular client for a few years, then one day he announced to her that he was never returning and did not want her ever to cut his hair. Meeg telephoned me to relate the incident but I had no means to explain his behavior except to assure her that Byron was suffering from some psychological problems and, perhaps, when he regained his composure he would return to her. He never did.

In the meantime Byron, as a college student, was hired by a local department store as a clerk. The store soon found out that he was an excellent storeroom clerk but that he could not handle customers at all. As long as Byron worked in the back of the store with inventory he was fine, but when placed in the front with customers he was unable to handle the pressure of face-to-face communication. Because I am not a counselor and have never claimed to be one, I did ask Byron if he was under the care of an analyst. I posed the same question to his mother and to his father. They both assured me that he was, and his father informed me that Byron hated him. The family also told me that he no longer drove his car because people were driving too fast on the highway and it was his duty to drive not as fast as the speed limit suggested. When he was stopped by an officer for driving at 35 miles per hour on a highway with a posted speed limit of 65 miles an hour, he instructed the officer that 65 miles per hour was the maximum speed and not the minimum. His mother related to me that Byron felt it his duty to remind drivers that they should not drive at excessive speeds on public roads.

Both his mother and father have died in recent years and Byron has terminated all contact with me. I saw him once when he was on duty in the department store, but he would not speak with me for very long. What is unfortunate and sad is that Byron is a bright young man who needs intense psychiatric treatment that he is not receiving as extensively as he requires. Such treatment is too expensive today in America for a person of average income. Moreover, contemporary American society is not very much interested in a national health system, let alone a national mental health care system. So the Byrons of our society are left to their own devices, their own faulty thinking, and their own inner hell. I hope that someday Byron can obtain good mental health treatment and achieve a life of self-satisfaction and joy.

It was at St. Edmund's that I first met Emily Morrow McCormick Price when I returned from Cambridge. Katherine had advised me that a new member had recently arrived to St. Edmund's and that Emily immediately volunteered to work on the Altar Guild and to assist with any function where she might be needed. Indeed, Emily was most helpful, even to the point of volunteering to serve on the CLR and to help with the many tasks required for the revision of the Prayer Book, and finally to give her time and talents to editing and typing my dissertation. Indeed, Emily is an extraordinary person and a rare joy to work with.

Then there was John Adams and Elizabeth Sargent, two musicians who gave much of themselves in service at St. Edmund's. John was a fine organist who helped restore the liturgical music program at the Mission. He was also the editor of the monthly Mission newspaper, a paper that he made readable and interesting. John was a chain smoker but that vice ruined his health and after he retired, he was diagnosed with lung cancer and died within a few months. Because we no longer had an organist, Elizabeth volunteered to play the Mission's instrument. Elizabeth normally played the ukulele and sometimes the piano when called upon; the organ was not her preferred musical instrument, but she helped sustain the Mission's liturgical program. As vicar I was pleased to have both John and Elizabeth help the congregation musically and in other capacities.

Mar and Ted Kaden, parishioners first encountered at St. Clement's, Rancho Cordova, moved to the San Francisco Bay Area after Ted lost his job with Douglas Corporation. As an engineer, Ted had worked on several vehicles sent into space but with the economic recession of the mid-70s compounded by the Nixon and Watergate affair, funding was reduced for space and consequently Ted lost his job. Those were hard times for the Kaden family, especially with four children, a mortgage, and an unemployed Mar. Ted found a position with the City of San Francisco Planning Department. He recently retired from that job after at least twenty years of service. At St. Edmund's, Ted and Mar were always in the forefront of the doers. Each served repeated tours on the Bishop's Committee and on other functional groups. When Ted began to consider his pending retirement, Mar took classes and passed her real estate requirements for a license. She worked as a real estate agent for several years until her own retirement in 2002. With four children, April, Carol, Douglas, and Andrew — April , Carol, and Andy are married and have children — the Kaden family continues to be a mainstay of the Church, and especially of St. Edmund's Mission. It is my privilege to have them still as friends and supporters.

In 1976, when it was time for me to begin serious writing on my dissertation, I resigned as vicar of St. Edmund's Mission Church. It was for me a difficult decision because I liked working actively with a congregation but time was of the essence and I had to use it carefully and frugally. I am happy to say that, since my departure, St. Edmund's has moved ahead with a new crop of vicars to become a retreat center and a more influential congregation in Pacifica.

I terminated my time as vicar of a mission congregation when I resigned from St. Edmund's, Pacifica. I still remained active in parish work but thereafter became an assistant priest in a larger parish, St. Edward's in San Jose, a duty that allowed me the freedom to do liturgical tasks and avoid the administrative chores that are inevitable when one is in charge. I was no longer in charge of any congregation, but my parochial responsibility was limited to sermons, extra-liturgical occasions, and some teaching. Thus after St. Edmund's I served at St. Edward's; Christ Church, Portola Valley; St. Elizabeth's, South San Francisco; and then Grace Cathedral, San Francisco, where I remain to this day.

The ecclesiastical phase of my life has always been rewarding in more ways than I can articulate. I learned to become more humane, more attentive to people's needs, and more liberal in my politics. I no longer tolerated the approach voiced by the Republican Party, which governed with the mantra of "cutting taxes" and ignoring the necessary costs required for maintaining the infrastructure, the education, the health, and the possibilities for a better life for the citizens of a nation. National security is much greater than defending the nation with the military; it requires maintaining the domestic infrastructure, the health of citizens, the fitness of the economy, and the nurturing of new jobs to maximize employment and good earnings for the stability of citizens and their families. Slowly I moved towards a progressive and liberal political philosophy, a liberal theology, and a more dramatic liturgy that spoke directly to the management of human affairs, to the people present, and to the future of society and of the ecological dimension of the planet.

My time in Appalachia was the threshold of the expansion of my understanding of society, economics, the relationship between the races and cultures. Many people were added to my roster of friends, life-long friends, and each person enriched me.

Indeed, I am a happy sojourner for the Church and for churchers.

III

PART THREE

The Search for Suitable Employment

Several decades have passed since people looked for employment by searching for announcements in newspapers. A new approach for employment was emerging in the latter part of the 20th century. A prospective employee soon learned two ploys.

The first approach was to create his or her position with a firm, but initially the person had to get a foot in the door and then had to accept any position as a starting point. Once inside the company, then the strategy was to see where the firm needed help and where the person seeking employment could provide that help.

The second approach required that the person obtain knowledge of the firm, a good understanding of one's capabilities, a strategy to maneuver within the hierarchy, and a modicum of courage, self-reliance, and "balls." Most of all what is imperatively required is the ability to be supple, flexible, adaptable, and visionary. A good source to obtain that type of information is from the firm of Dun and Bradstreet, but it requires a small membership fee. Information from Dun and Bradstreet will not help one develop "abilities;" it will help to find a course to follow.

These two approaches produced jobs and options for upward mobility within one firm or with other firms. Unfortunately, the new fabric of employment and productivity reduced the level of loyalty to a firm by an employee or loyalty to an employee by a firm. Of course there were still some diehards who continued to search for employment in the old way, but soon these either learned the new approaches or fell by the wayside and joined the group of unemployed or under-employed.

In the latter part of the 20th century the rule for obtaining employment was changed radically. One had to be creative about what it was that would occupy him or her for several years and what the benefits, remunerations, and perks offered by this or that firm were. In special cases it was suggested that rather than seek employment, it was better to launch one's own firm or become a consultant. But whatever the choice, the rule for seeking employment was changing, and changing radically and rapidly.

Reaching the Academic Goal

It was time for me to look for employment that would give me a reasonable income but I was not quite ready to launch my own firm. I had finally purchased a house in the coastal village of Montara, on the San Mateo coast, just half a mile from the Pacific Ocean and adjacent to 25 acres of open undeveloped land. This was an ideal location for children to explore, play, and follow their curiosity in a safe environment. The house was modern with three upstairs bedrooms, a large ground floor room that made a fine study, two-and-a-half baths, a kitchen with a dining area, and two fireplaces.

I moved with the children from Pacifica with the help of Tom Edminster. I had lived in the vicarage for almost five months with the children while Trudy resided and worked in Merced. As a single parent I cared for Dominique and Michel, cooked meals, tended to homework assignments, braided my daughter's long hair, and fulfilled the required tasks of housefather. The transfer to our new house was quite welcomed. Trudy's move to Montara was greatly appreciated.

Trudy had left Merced and took a teaching position at Farallon elementary school in Montara. We were attempting to save our marriage from demolition, or at least I was.

I still had not begun the task of writing my dissertation but it was imperative that I identify gainful employment outside the Church because I had decided to become a non-stipendiary member of the clergy. Finances were tight and I needed to cover the expanding expenses. Trudy was teaching but our marital situation was worsening from day to day and I did not want to depend on her small income.

Emily, who was freelancing before she returned to Bechtel, had given me some small graphic jobs that paid a little but not enough to be considered as income. One day I was really down to my last penny and asked Emily if I could borrow $20 to hold me until a check arrived from Pacific School of Religion, a GTU affiliate, where I had been teaching a class in Art in the Liturgical Context. I remember the exact location where I asked Emily for the loan: Market and 3rd Streets, San Francisco. Those were not happy days for me. Incidentally, I did repay Emily for the loan!

In spite of the tight financial situation, and with Trudy's teaching salary, we were able to enroll both Dominique and Michel at St. Matthew's Episcopal School. The tuition for the children was covered by a scholarship grant from the school because I was a priest in the Episcopal Diocese of California. Both Dominique and Michel were happy with the school even though the discipline was strict but fair. In the long term, St. Matthew's proved to be a fine investment for their education in that it taught both Dominique and Michel the proper way to study and encouraged them to learn.

The main drawback of living on the coast and attending school 40 minutes away, over-the-hill as we said, was that class friends were not living in the neighborhood. Montara was a small village with not too many children of Dominique's and Michel's ages, so finding companionship during the weekends was difficult. Fortunately, they survived this isolation sufficiently well because as sister and brother they got along and were able to construct games and projects together. Yet I wish that it had been a bit different, especially because the home front was difficult and stressful. I regret the hardship that surfaced at home and the effect that it had on the children.

Happily, few scars from the turbulent home life remain to afflict Dominique and Michel. When the dissolution of the marriage took place, Dominique went to live with Trudy in San Mateo, and Michel stayed with me in Montara. It is my suspicion that Dominique married early, and entered into an unhealthy relationship that ultimately failed, to escape from the maternal environment and the parental breakup. As for Michel, I suspect that he is most careful in his selection of a mate because he has seen how the parental marriage crashed and how his sister's failed. I truly regret not having given Dominique and Michel the nurturing environment that they deserved; they are wonderful and loving offspring.

An agreement was reached with Emily McCormick Price who had to drive her daughter to Notre Dame School in Belmont, which allowed us to share the transportation for carrying Dominique and Michel to St. Matthew's Episcopal School in San Mateo. Emily would drive the morning run and I would do the afternoon. Soon the drive to transport the children included Nicola when she joined my family, and whom we registered at Notre Dames also for her last two years of high school.

In the meantime, I was searching for a teaching or an industrial position near the San Francisco Bay area but these were rare. I admit that my search in academics was not too active because I preferred a position in industry. Several offers arrived from universities located far from San Francisco but I was determined to remain on the coast. Here are some of the offers that I rejected, rightly or wrongly:

I had a good offer from Duke University to fill a slot as assistant professor in the philosophy department. The University of Missouri had a similar position open for me as did the University of Idaho but none of these locations were acceptable to me. The University of California at Santa Barbara offered me a lectureship position with a two-year contract that might be converted into a full-time position if it could be included in their budget, but the latter job was not guaranteed; at least it was not something that I could bank on. A good offer for an assistant professorship in the department of humanities came from Boston University but again the location and a move to the East Coast would have been difficult. Perhaps I should have accepted the position offered me at Boston University because it would have given me access to Harvard University, and at least a lectureship there could have come my way. Unfortunately I thought of that possibility after I had declined the offer from Boston. Was I a fool intent on setting my roots in the San Francisco Bay Area at all cost? Perhaps.

The idea of returning to industry was attractive to me. I recall searching for a position with Combustion Engineering Company, where I had worked before entering seminary. I wrote a letter to Dr. Smith, my old boss, but he had retired a few years earlier. Nevertheless, Dr. Smith attached a personal note to my letter and sent it to the current Director of Nuclear Research and Development whose office was in New York City. I received a reply from Dr. John Drummond a few days later informing me that a position in nuclear project development and sales was opening up in Chattanooga. Of course that position required a relocation move and I was not too keen to return to Tennessee. Combustion had closed its Western Division office in Hanford, Washington; hence any chance of staying on the West Coast was gone.

Again after I thought about it, a move to Chattanooga would have been fine because I knew the city well, it had a certain historical geographic beauty, and it was nestled between Signal and Lookout Mountains and touched the shores of Lake Chickamauga and the Tennessee River. Chattanooga was becoming a dynamic city; its small university had been transformed into a large campus of the University of Tennessee, my undergraduate Alma Mater. I could have been re-admitted in the Diocese of Tennessee and would have been more than welcome to serve in that portion of God's vineyard. I might even have considered courses in physics to raise my level of knowledge. Nevertheless, the thought of moving away from Montara and California was not attractive to me. After speaking with Dr. John Drummond by telephone I declined the offer.

That night, a sleepless night, caused me to reexamine my strategy, the purpose of my education, the life I had managed to make for myself, the mistakes I had made and probably was still making, and the stupid attitude I had assumed. I was poor, my marriage was in pieces, my children were paying a mighty price for what I considered to be my selfishness, and I was going nowhere rapidly. Like a space rocket at the Cape I was flaming out right on the pad of potential accomplishment and purpose. A good education and a good mind were being deliberately wasted.

At the first light of morning, I decided to contact Kaiser Engineering Future Planning Department. That department had published, in the past two or three years, a superb book on ideas that were to be considered as valuable for the future. I had written to the head of that department and his replies had been co-gent, exciting, and promising, although employment options for me had never been discussed.

Midmorning after the sleepless night, I telephoned Kaiser Engineering for an appointment. The interview with Kaiser indicated that there was a position that might be open if funding was available in their Future Planning Department, but the small department was located in Napa at their aluminum fabricating lo-cation. Napa was too far a commute for me, particularly because I was practically a single parent at the time. Don Fabun, the editor of the fine book, *The Dynamic of Change*, was the man with whom I had corresponded but he was no longer with Kaiser. The new head of the department was amiable and promising; if he could manage an increase in the budget it would be possible for me to have a position. Kaiser was very interested in my multi-disciplined educa-tion and experience. If and when I accepted the position offered, if it were offered, it would require either a six-hour daily commute by car or an apartment in Napa, neither of which was to my satisfaction. Was I picky? Was I making my family uncomfortable because I refused to relocate? At any rate I suspect that providence intruded as the position at Kaiser could not be funded. Moreo-ver, the Future Planning Department was being eliminated (the same occurred at Bechtel in the 90s).

A few days later when I was having lunch with Bishop Myers, he suggested that I put my name in the hat for a position in one of the parishes. His advice was that since my dissertation still had to be written and my defense had to be faced, I needed a task that would allow me to do both without interference. A small dormant mission parish would fit the bill by giving me time to do what I needed to do, to tend to the CLR, and to put my priesthood into practice. I wasn't too keen about climbing on the merry-go-round as a vicar or rector of a parish. I loved teaching and sacramental work but I disliked the bureaucratic tasks that accompanied them.

In time, at Kim's recommendation, I interviewed for the position of vicar for St. Edmund's, Pacifica, and served there, as I indicated in the previous section, for three years. The cure at St. Edmund's was enjoyable and satisfying.

While serving at St. Edmund's and enjoying the community, one of my parishioners, Darryl Cowan, invited me for lunch in San Francisco because he wanted to show me what he was doing at Bechtel Corporation, where he was in charge of the microfilm section. Darryl was also a reserve deputy sheriff for the San Mateo County Sheriff's Department. When I went to meet him, he offered to take me around Bechtel and show me some of the projects that he had been microfilming. I was impressed more by the scope of the various and interesting projects than by the firm itself. I thought to myself that I needed to look into Bechtel for a position. I saw in Bechtel a firm that offered a variety of projects, a world view with travel assignments, and a location in the heart of San Francisco. I had worked with engineers and had a technical background, which, although it was a bit dated, could have negotiable and valuable significance, especially since I could think clearly. Bechtel was an attractive possibility. I never did, however, pursue that avenue; I didn't have to!

One day Emily asked me if I would be interested in editing a study that was in progress at Bechtel and the salary would be good. The study was called the "White River Project." Bechtel had been engaged to study the potential for oil extraction from shale deposits in Utah and Colorado. That it was to be a temporary job was quite acceptable to me because my main purpose was to accumulate a cash reserve that would allow me to take a few months off for writing my dissertation. Plus any position with Bechtel would give me a toe in the door and that would prove valuable when I applied for a full-time position. I would also be able to learn a few things about the internal politics of the firm. Not only had I abandoned all options for employment away from San Francisco, but also I was now determined to make Bechtel somehow work for me. Bechtel could become the cash ticket that would let me stay in the San Francisco Bay Area — and it did.

That I knew very little about editing gave me an opportunity to learn the trade under two very able editors, John T. Parker, my immediate supervisor, and Emily. The tools of editing that I received served me well in writing my dissertation and in writing other documents. I learned that when one's thinking is not clear, one's writing is also not clear. I also learned the value of being economical in the use of language. Beyond that, I acquired a capability for understanding what the author intended to say and did or did not say. The operative question to the author often was, "Is this what you really intended to say?" I did not see the task of the editor as being primarily focused on chasing commas or rewriting the text my own way. Editing was fun for a few months, but I much preferred writing original material to correcting other people's prose. My job lasted five months.

After being released from my contract with Bechtel and with a little cash in my bank account, I dove directly into the final coalescing of the research I had done into a full-blown dissertation of 14 chapters. The writing thereof was started immediately. My schedule was rigorously kept hour-by-hour and minute-by-minute. I was determined to complete the dissertation in less than six months. The work would be a revealing affirmation that liturgy was the package wherein all the forms of art could cohabit. I was also determined to compose a work that would earn at least honorable mention.

My comprehensive work on the final days of Archbishop Thomas Cranmer had received laudable mention. I had written an ideational play, *The Crowning Winter*, for my comprehensive thesis that looked at the work that Cranmer had accomplished from the point of view of Process Thought. My thinking followed the manner employed by the mathematician-philosopher Alfred North Whitehead. I took art, the root of the Christian Eucharist, and liturgy, and applied to them the methodology of Process Thought. Pushing the limit and walking the tightrope (as Jim Pike often accused me of but nevertheless encouraged me) was what I did best.

Awakening at four in the morning, I would slip to my desk and write creatively until 5:45; then I would rouse the children, prepare their breakfasts and lunches, and get them ready for pick-up by Emily at 7:15. After cleaning the kitchen I would head back to my desk to reread what had been written, to edit, and to continue writing. At noon, I would do whatever housework was required, prepare the ingredients for dinner, check or do the laundry, and take a power nap for 30 to 45 minutes. I was on the road at two to fetch the children for a 3:30 release from school. But before picking them up, I would stop at Swenson's Ice Cream parlor in San Mateo, for a dish of "sticky, gooey, bitter chocolate." While enjoying the ice cream, I would also continue some of my research and make bibliographical notes on 3x5 cards. Time was not a-wasting!

When the children and I arrived home, they were particularly energized by a snack, and then attacked their homework followed by playtime until I called them for dinner at 6:30 in the evening. Arriving from school at 4:30, Trudy would take a long soaking bath, put on a comfortable housedress, read or take a walk outside, but seldom contribute to any household chores. Even on weekends, Trudy managed to do what she wanted to do and offered little help with the laundry. Dominique and Michel helped with the laundry, the cleaning, and the odd chores that surfaced in a household.

Time at the dinner table was always open for discussion on any topic. Eating time was not to be used for reprimands but as the situation with Trudy became more tense and stressed, dinner conversation took on a more somber tone. Trudy always deferred reprimanding Dominique and Michel to me and the operative command to the children was, "Go see your father." To me it was, "So or so has done this." Yet, after dessert was served (there was always a dessert) Michel would climb on my lap for a few minutes. Dominique was already a bit too big for lap sitting.

After dinner either I would read to the children (sometimes Trudy would read to them too when she wasn't too tired, which was often) or each one of us would read our own book, at eight it was bathing time and bedtime with lights out by nine p.m. I would continue to read for a while, and then I too gave up for the day. In the morning, it was doing a special job, a job I enjoyed, to comb and braid Dominique's long auburn hair. On weekends, I tried to prepare special meals, and meals that could be stored and then eaten during the week. Trudy willingly assumed the role of favored star boarder.

Nicola Rice Griffis

In 1974, an additional soul was added to the household at Trudy's insistence. Nicola Rice Griffis was seventeen, energetic, talkative, helpful, and lovely. We had known each other for at least two years at St. Edmund's, especially since I had presented her for confirmation at Grace Cathedral. Nicola was one of three children of parents who had died. She had been assigned as a ward to a childless couple that had no experience with children and consequently their attitude made her very unhappy. Since I was then still vicar at St. Edmund's and had developed a good rapport with her, Nicola asked if becoming my ward would be an imposition for our family. Much as I liked Nicola, I was not certain that becoming her "keeper" would be a good idea, because my marriage was quite unsteady. Trudy, however, felt otherwise; she thought that it would not only be a good deed but that Nicola could help around the house in return for living with us. My response was that she either joined our family as another equal member and not as a maid or I would not have the arrangement at all.

I did not want Nicola to assume the role of "cheap" help for Trudy. Trudy had elevated the attribute of manipulation to a high degree and I did not want Nicola to fall into her scheme of operation. Nicola had a small income from her parent's social security that would be enough to cover some of her cost and still allow for some money to be reserved as savings for college or future days. Nevertheless, at Trudy's insistence we agreed that Nicola would contribute $70 per month for her room and board. I agreed to that payment because I thought that it would ultimately protect Nicola from Trudy's accusation that she was on the dole and hence had to "work" for her room and board. As it turned out Nicola willingly helped around the house.

After many discussions with Trudy, I finally agreed to have Nicola stay with us on three conditions: that she attend Notre Dame de Namur to complete her high school education; that she follow the rules of the house (she was past 17 and quite mature for her age); and that she not be treated as a maid or surrogate helper to Trudy who had the tendency to use other people for her benefit. That was agreed by both Trudy and Nicola, and by the children who were now 12 and 9 years old.

We went to court and Nicola was granted permission to be my ward until her 21st birthday. We prepared a bed and general accommodations for her on the ground floor in what was my library and study, and she arranged it all to suit her needs and her comfort. The rapport between Trudy and Nicola went sour about a month after her introduction to our family. Trudy insisted that Nicola be responsible for doing everyone's laundry and for housecleaning. I insisted that we share all the chores. Tension developed between Trudy and Nicola. I became more and more Nicola's protector. Both Dominique and Michel loved her and were very happy to have gained a "big sister."

Because Nicola was settled and slept in the room where my study desk and library were located and where I worked starting at 4:00 in the morning, it was fortunate that she was a moderately heavy sleeper. My early arrival and writing neither disturbed Nicola nor did she complain about my presence. I was able turn my desk light on, use the typewriter, rustle papers, and do all my research and writing tasks without Nicola's awakening, and I did all that quietly. I made it a policy that on Saturday morning I would not use my study to allow Nicola some additional time for sleep. I would read in the living room while the family had an extended time for sleep, but by eight o'clock everybody was quite awake. Breakfast was then prepared, served, laundry gathered, rooms cleaned, cartoons watched by Dominique and Michel, and I would return to my study for a few hours. Nicola would monitor the chores, tend to the children's wishes, and then take care of her personal needs. For these tasks, Nicola volunteered and insisted that she was happy to participate as an older sister.

As far as I was concerned she was a lovely addition to our lives. Nicola was especially attentive to the details for making the household more congenial and bright. I was very happy to have her and loved her dearly, as did the children. Nicola was of enormous help in the kitchen, especially with cooking and pre-cooking preparations. Never was she a burden or an obstruction to anything that went on in the family. Quite often there were occasions when Trudy either disparaged her or attempted to use her as cheap household help. Whenever that attitude prevailed, I would send Nicola on an errand or give her a task that could not be interrupted, and then I would speak to Trudy. Trudy, however, continued to dislike her immensely and proceeded to treat her as a maid or as one who did not contribute to the cost of her upkeep — which was totally untrue. On occasion the children would stand up for Nicola and make the case that she was their big sister and not a maid.

Completion of Dissertation

While I was writing chapter after chapter for my dissertation, Emily was editing and typing the final document. Emily had gracefully offered to help me with the typing and editing, and I am certain that without her help the final corpus of writing would have taken me three times as long and would have required the added expenditure of paying for an editor and a typist. I am most grateful for Emily's kindness, support, and expert attention to the text. Emily was able to smooth out the rough spots of my syntax and to produce a text that was concise, clear, and pleasant to read. Her contribution to my dissertation was invaluable.

I resigned after Easter 1976 from the Commission on Liturgical Renewal and from St. Edmund's mission, which freed me to complete the work at hand. It was a good time to leave the CLR and the SLC because the remaining tasks were to edit the texts and manage the publication of the corpus for final presentation to General Convention. As for St. Edmund's, it was time for it to have a full time vicar.

After six months of creative writing on a subject that was difficult because it approached art and the definition of art from a totally non-traditional perspective and included a distillation of traditional historical, theological, philosophical, and liturgical concepts, the dissertation was completed and submitted to the faculty and to each institution involved (it had been read by the full panel as each chapter was written, hence no surprise existed).

It was time for me to assemble my faculty and proceed with the defense, the final step of the doctoral program. At the defense I would face the committee, respond to questions posed, defend points and arguments, and affirm implicitly that what I was offering was the product of a unique approach to an idea, that it was coherent, and that it could be defended before my peers, the faculty, visiting students, and other guests.

Dr. Wayne Rood, my advisor and the chair of my committee, on the night of my defense stopped me before I entered the interrogation room to inform me that I was to chair the discussion because, he reminded me, that I knew "more about the subject than any of the faculty members present." Each member of the faculty, he pointed out, knew a great deal about a fragment of the subject at hand, but I had an understanding of the whole. In spite of the fact that I was taken aback by his announcement the defense went smoothly. Each member of the committee was specific in the questions and kind. The telephone connection to Cambridge, UK, where two members were listening, was clear and free of static. At exactly five minutes to the second hour the long distance operator announced that the clock was approaching the final minutes. The required subsequent two-hour defense went admirably well and in May 1976 I was awarded my doctorate degree with honor.

I received news in 2002 from Anne Rood, Wayne's wife that Dr. Rood had died at the turn of the 21st century. Wayne was a crystal of a man, and one could not find a finer human being. His areas of interest were art (theater) and theology. Through his work in theater and his keen understanding of liturgy, he was recognized as one of the principal authorities on the biblical Book of Revelation. A lifelong member of the Sabbath Day Baptist denomination, he was yet a Christian who was quite comfortable worshiping in the Episcopal setting and understood the intrinsic value, character, intent, and need for liturgy. I would venture to admit that Wayne personified all that a saint is. His influence on my education and my life were phenomenal.

Wayne Rood was that rare human being who was able to find and then have displayed the hidden gifts in an individual, a student. Wayne helped me broaden my understanding of art and identify the harmony and coherence that emerges from it. Drama for Wayne was the key for appreciating any form of art, be the form in the plastic or the performing arenas. A painting had to exhibit drama for it to be appreciated, as it also had to exhibit coherence, harmony, and the dynamism that made you see it anew every time you viewed it. Wayne was an extraordinary teacher. He was also patient, kind, and comforting. He made you feel at ease and you immediately recognized that he was your most keen supporter. Because of my travels with Bechtel I was not able maintain close contact with Dr. Rood but I often thought about him, and always kindly and affectionately. He was a good man, a fine teacher, and a deep thinker.

Montara on the Pacific Ocean

I want to say a few words about living in the village of Montara. Although I have mentioned it in the previous chapter, here the details offer a better understanding of the times and circumstances affecting the family and me.

Montara is a small village with a population of approximately 2,000 souls, situated on the Pacific Ocean and only about 35 minutes from San Francisco's financial district.

When I purchased the house in 1974, I was not employed, except for a part-time position as vicar of St. Edmund's, Pacifica. Because my credit was good, the senior vice president of Eureka Savings and Loan at Eureka Square, Pacifica, Mrs. Marcia Crawford, took the risk of granting me a loan for a 30-year mortgage on the $49,250.00 house. I asked the builder, an immigrant from East Germany, to install both the furnace and the kitchen range to propane gas (in 1982 it was converted to natural gas). In March 1974, Dominique, Michel, and I settled in our new house on the coast. Trudy was still teaching in Merced and would not move to Montara until early summer. As I narrated earlier, the children were registered at St. Matthew's Episcopal School in San Mateo. Commuting to school was first a joint program with Jane Edsel, who had two girls. The commute with Jane Edsel was accomplished when we lived for six months in Pacifica on Malavere Street, in St. Edmund's vicarage. Later when we moved to Montara, the commute was shared with Emily McCormick Price, who drove her high school age daughter Ashley to attend Notre Dame de Namur, in Belmont. The commute was inconvenient but necessary because the schools were excellent.

Life with Trudy was becoming more than I could tolerate. By and large, Trudy behaved like a star boarder. Trudy's comportment was tantamount to verbal violence to me. I might as well have had a lodger instead of a wife; at least the boarder could be evicted. My own state of mental health was torn apart and my anger increased and at times was even directed towards the children through my shouting and my accusatory speech. I regret my behavior and especially the way I inadvertently mistreated Dominique and Michel — innocent bystanders of a relationship that was nearing the point of destruction. I found some comfort in the help that Nicola gave me and her joyfulness added pleasure to the sad and miserable home condition. Emily was also a great help because we were good friends and she would pour oil on my troubled waters. Her help in opening the door to Bechtel, which gave me the beginning of financial independence, was an act of kindness and generosity.

During the tense period with Trudy, on one occasion, Michel packed a small bag and started leaving the property; the intent was to run away from home. Now Michel was the child who was always sitting on my lap and wanted lots of hugs and overt signs of affection from me. Here Michel was escaping an environment that was chaotic and filled with anger. Dominique went to fetch him when she discovered that he had left. I followed after her and found that she had stopped his escape but he was all in tears. After I spoke to him midway between home and the bus station, about a mile away, and calmed him to the point that his crying ceased, I thought that the time to improve my attitude and alter the situation with Trudy was at hand. Dominique's position was that the less control exercised over her actions, the better she liked the environment. Dominique was completing the eighth grade in June, just three months hence.

That night I spoke with Trudy in as calm a voice as I could muster. I told her that we had to separate again but this time the distance would only be reduced if and when we decided to live quiet, normal, and non-abusive lives. Her quiet voice of accusations, self-defense, and assertions of innocence — verbal abuse of sorts — was without effect on me. I was not immune to her manipulative tone but I was determined to remain in control of my situation. My calm demeanor surprised me. I had reached the point where I'd had enough and would accept no more of her abusive behavior couched in sweetness. Pushed to the brink now, I was ending the marriage and this proposed separation was the beginning of the final act. My margin of tolerance had been reached, if not surpassed.

We agreed that I would give her funds for a down payment to purchase a house anywhere she wanted. For the funds, I sold a piece of property that I owned on the Eel River and added money I had earned from Bechtel on the Jubail Project, Saudi Arabia. These funds were sufficient for Trudy to buy a condominium outright. At the time she was teaching at the Cunha Intermediary

School in Half Moon Bay and continued her teaching commitment even after we separated. Trudy also received the VW Bus that she often used and which had a rebuilt engine and transmission. Thus the day after Dominique graduated from the eighth grade in June 1979, Trudy was out of the Montara house. She was given an opportunity to take whatever she wanted from the house but she had to sign a Quit Claim document to give up her ownership of the Montara house. Dominique, who was enrolled as a boarding student in Sacred Heart Girls School, chose to live with Trudy in San Mateo. Michel, who was still attending St. Matthew's, chose to live with me. Because Trudy and I had joint custody of the children, it was simple on our finances if I paid for Michel while she paid for Dominique, but we both shared the full cost of schools. The only requirement I insisted was that the children's legal address remain in Montara and she agreed.

It wasn't long after the separation that I discovered that my temper was less inflamed and certainly less explosive. Nicola, who was attending the State University at Sonoma, noticed that I was calmer and less prone to explosions. Life proceeded after the separation on a much quieter and more even keel. I was unhappy that my marriage was failing, had failed, but at least the solution was not as devastating as I had expected it to be. Outwardly the children appeared to be taking the separation calmly and without obvious pain, but I knew that in the long run, scars would appear — with many that would never heal. I have discovered that as the years have passed Michel is more removed from his mother, and Dominique, who had always insisted "daughters have a special relationship with their mothers" is beginning to distance herself from Trudy. Indeed, I am happy to say that Dominique has found her father, and has realized that he is not such a bad sort after all! I know that Michel is still quite fond of his father as his father is fond of him.

Once I found myself away from Trudy and no longer was in need of my armor, I discovered that my protective reserved composure was drastically reduced. I was again able to be responsive and to welcome affection from my friends and especially from my children — and I was able to be affectionate in return. What was often considered to be my crisp reserved character may have been a façade to protect myself and to hide the anger that resided within me. I don't know. What I do know is that I needed space for myself to resume my good-natured personality of past years. My perception of life was always that it was a bowl of cherries and that the pits, well, needed to be discarded. But for several years with Trudy, the pits were the focus of my attention, which diverted my focus away from the luscious sweet cherry flesh. It was sad and I regret my attitude for those years.

Life, however, is exciting but not always filled with peace and tranquility. It was quite a while before the restoration of my inner person began to be both implicit and explicit. It was not an overnight transformation but more of a slow movement toward transfiguration. My person began to be altered internally, whereas the external outline never changed, except as a cause of age and weight gain; but inside I was feeling better. Many people helped me initiate the process towards transfiguration, to whom I am profoundly indebted. The people who helped me were engaged in my life as friends such that they allowed me to lean on them for strength, stability, and affection. I count Ruth, Jane, Earl Count, Emily, Schively, Nicola, Stuart, and particularly Jim Mara SJ. By far the most influential person in the restorative process was Jim Mara because his approach was to use my intellect, my power of reasoning, my understanding of who I was as an effective force in Creation.

Jim did not hold my hand, he did not serve me "religious pabulum," he simply engaged my reason and my passion, and then put me to work transfiguring myself with the hope that I would recognize that Providence and Grace were assisting the healing task. Unfortunately, Jim was not able to help himself. As a Jesuit he was caught in the trap of severe discipline, commitment, and the inability to negate the oath to the Society he took as an unwise young man. Jim was a scholar, one of a very few I knew who possessed two doctorates. He was a fine educator and a wonderful mentor. Jim, however, had no one to mentor him, and I was not quite the one to step into those shoes.

Indeed, every one of the good people I mentioned was of enormous help, each in his or her own way and with his or her own measure of love, affection, and support. Each was key to my transfiguration and I am grateful for their attention, time, and willingness to refashion me into a better person. To declare that the process is complete would be a gross exaggeration; it is still ongoing and will continue as such probably until my culminating days. I can, however, admit that I am able to be affectionate. I am able to express my love. I neither avoid affection nor do I share it in calculated quantities.

Understanding Creativity

As far back as I can remember the dynamics of creativity have fascinated me. For hours in Cairo I would observe artists carve intricate designs on brass or copper. Carpet weavers in Cairo would produce fine rugs without following a pattern; the design emerged from their inner selves. In East Anglia, I would watch artists sit on a stool with an easel and paint the landscape of the Fens, Ely Cathedral, the old pump buildings, or birds. I remember observing craft people in Appalachia, especially at the John C. Campbell School in Brasstown, North Carolina; express their creativity in all sorts of ways, in textiles, in silver, in leather, in paint, in blacksmithing, in pottery, and in music. I remember speaking with Bill Lear, one of the foremost creative persons of the 20th century about his ideas and concepts. I witnessed creative people in all walks of life express themselves as no other could. Creative people are incapable of not creating. No one sets out to be creative; creative people just are or so they seem. Are there people who are creative? Are there people who are not? Is it a matter of talent, of time or concentration, of willingness, of vision, of self-confidence, and/or of something special inside them — something yet to be identified?

After all my research I tend to lean towards the option that a few human beings have the capability to be creative and many do not have that option available. Perhaps some, who do not know they are creative due to lack of opportunity to engage in creative expression, can be nurtured, taught, or assisted in the discovery of their hidden talents. Creative expression may emerge in any discipline, including mathematics, language, science, and a gamut of other deliveries. Some contend that creativity can be taught, I say that creativity can be discovered by a person in himself or herself. The medium for creativity may be elusive but that does not mean that the act cannot emerge down the road. Nevertheless, the issue of the medium selected for creativity to emerge may rest and may even be in abeyance. How does one channel one's creativity and through what medium?

The purpose of writing my dissertation was to search for an explanation, and then to concretize my understanding of creativity. To do that I took art as being the highest form reflecting the creative effort and liturgy — the work of the people — as the premier means for showing the result of that effort. I was convinced as much as the artist and critic of art Eugène Delacroix who spoke of integrity, harmony, unity and articulated that "La première condition nécessaire pour faire un art sain est la croyance a l'unité intégrale." In other words, Delacroix asserts that for art to emerge from a "wholesome" creative effort it must be integrating, it must bring about the unity of the many. For the artist, aesthetic composition means a harmonious bringing together of all the parts into a coherent arrangement.

For the artist nature is a composition that offers the right tone to life, for the non-artist it is a dictionary, a catalogue of unrelated ideas.

The creation of art is an activity of the artist's consciousness as he/she perceives and relates to the universe. From painter to performer, from poet to sculptor, from physicist to biochemist, from architect to engineer, the artistic expression is incarnated; it is indubitably never the consummation of isolated experiences. When the artist is immersed in the process of creating, he/she recognizes that isolation is nonexistent in art, he/she comes to acknowledge, and even passionately expects, the ensuing resonance that is available from relationship and interdependence. The most obvious medium for this interdependence is found in good liturgy. The simplest explanation of liturgy is: it is the expression of human beings' corporateness in response to something of ultimate worth. As a lens capturing the sight of a single life, life in its fullness, liturgy assumes the task of unifying through public corporate effort the community's collective memory and its myths — the hope for the future as every moment of a human's free existence implies is in its past and in its present.

But what is art? Interestingly enough, what we moderns call art the Greeks and Romans regarded as craft or "technique." The aesthetic meaning of the word "art" is of quite recent origin. As I alluded, the Greeks had no word for art apart from the meaning of craft; craft suited their needs quite well because it encompassed the technique for producing almost repetitive forms. For the Roman or Latin culture, the story is much the same although the definition is different.

Medieval Latin used the word "ars" in the same sense that early English used "art." It meant simply a particular form of education through book learning. This is the reason we hear about curricula of liberal arts or of fine arts and then find that neither is particularly focused on creative efforts.

Unlike the craft person who produces for the sake of developing and perfecting repetitive forms, the artist produces because he/she does not wish to be repetitive and avoids repetition emphatically. In addition the artist must create, because not to create is debilitating to his/her wellbeing. For the artist, art:

- is simultaneously rational and sensuous
- is simultaneously unified and diversified
- is many as well as one
- possesses tension and disequilibrium but also has
  - order
  - proportion
  - resolution
  - synthesis (in the Whiteheadian, i.e., harmonious and not in the Hegelian, i.e., fused sense)
- is characteristically dynamic and specifically implies
  - movement
  - motion
  - mutation
  - evolution
  - transfiguration
  - change
- possesses symbolic qualities because it is enigmatic
- even mysterious in its array of
  - interpretations
  - explications
  - essences
  - exegesis
- is coherently configured, planned; yet it is self-determining in that it

- proposes direction
- provides systematic cohesion
- insists on having termination
- is emphatically abhorrent in its creative composition of repetition: because it offers only one life, it has no duplicate, it is unique

Thus be cognizant that the primary condition is to instill unity and coherence in the work.

In the preparation of food there can be good food and bad food depending on the cook, the recipe, and the ingredients. In art that is not the case. There is only art: no good or bad art. To attain synthesis, art requires selection and elimination, choice and rejection. The product of art that is known as beauty (not generally identified with appeal or attractiveness) is neither easily nor painlessly achieved. Beauty requires an intimate confrontation with several elements under consideration so that through selectivity, concentration, and intent there emerges a creative advance in form. Ugliness or "aesthetic destruction" comes about through the experience of irreconcilable characteristics, disharmony, disjunction, and even malevolence or horror. Art for the artist is neither a means to an end nor the end in itself; it is the undeniable language through which his intimate self, with judgment, passion, love, and creativity, is phenomenally expressed.

This initial attempt to understand creativity and hence art is merely the beginning of a long, life-consuming endeavor. More will be added to this thesis as I proceed further into my life.

Some Thoughts on Anglicanism

Once again it was time to search for employment, to earn a living, and to receive a paycheck. I had a doctorate but what would it provide for me? Teaching was the most obvious option but I wondered if I could find a position with industry? The ivory tower was not alluring to me. Faculty meetings, publishing to maintain one's position in the social educational context, inadequate pay for long hours of work, nevertheless the satisfaction enjoyed when a fertile mind was educated was attractive, yet all these and more were not sufficiently forceful to lure me to join the profession.

It was now early spring 1978. My marriage to Trudy was definitely terminated, perhaps not in the eyes of the state, but as a practical union it was asunder. I was very concerned with the theological implication of a broken marriage and I was working to resolve the issue in my head, perhaps never to be satisfactorily resolved. Trudy approached life from one direction and I from another. I readily admit that I am not the easiest person to live with. I do have my idiosyncrasies, some of which I like, and others I wish not to discuss while I attempt to rid myself of them. Philosophically I see creation as a dynamic, exciting, and ever expanding process, which may offer progress, and yet, which may not. I do not believe that life is a waste of energy but rather that it is energy in its most exciting form.

Theologically, I understand the Universe as being absolutely sacramental. There is no place in the Universe where God's (or whatever you wish to call the Source) influence is not present, where the Holy is not affective, influential, and altering, and where the Source's passion for good is not present, in spite of the malevolent deeds produced regularly by human beings in the exercise of their perverted sense of will. God for me is love in all its dimensions, and iniquity (read evil) is the product of human self-centeredness. I have touched on this topic earlier and I still am convinced that the concept of the Devil, Satan, and the mythological retinue attached is a purely human invention to excuse human responsibility for doing evil, for practicing megalomania, and as a crutch on which to lean to excuse human failings. The whole issue of the devil, Satan, demons and the like is also a product of human malicious self-centeredness and not the doing of the creation of God, in spite of the stories that surface from misguided literature, poorly thought out theological treatises, ignorant pronouncements, and misreading of scripture. It is an inexcusable rationale for human malice. Evil is human nature's contribution to the world and not God's. I wanted a way of thinking that allowed me to reject a lot of the idiocies that encumbered sound thinking of the several mainline forms of religious thought.

In a way that is why I chose Anglicanism (the Episcopal Church in USA) to help me make sense of the experience of God. Anglicanism is not a perfect fit for my point of view but it is open to my thinking, allows me to discuss issues that are important, and does not clobber me with hierarchical edicts telling me what is right, what is wrong, and how to think, how to decide, and how to behave. To me Anglicanism offers a clear approach to reality and to my perspective and comprehension of the workings of the world, the universe, and creation. Again, I am careful to add that Anglicanism is neither perfect nor the answer to all my questions.

How do I (we) understand the world? As a hypothetical example, let's suppose that we have three people who are planning to develop a business. The first person wants to receive thorough training before he embarks. The second person, having experienced near bankruptcy in a previous business venture, wants to examine all the risks before he begins any work for building the business. The third person wants to start the business immediately and feels confident that his previous experience, his knowledge, and his business acumen will supply the needed support.

Each person has a different approach. What then is the real question to ask? The business is fundamentally the raw material for each person. Each person has a valid way of approaching the subject of business building. Training, risk analysis, and experience are all necessary to any successful business venture. Each person, however, has a different worldview. It is the worldview that determines how each person conducts him/herself. Anglicanism (and science, especially physics) gives me the acceptable parameter for my worldview. It is one way to view God, the world, the universe, and creation. Anglicanism offers a perspective that allows me to encounter God as he is revealed in the person of Jesus the Christ. But it goes beyond that too; it offers me the means to embark on intellectual voyages that include new and complex scientific discoveries, new philosophical and intricate explorations, and new definitions, explanations, and theories that affect reality.

One does not need to maintain an ossified view of tradition. Anglicanism opens the doors for conflicting ideas to be exposed, analyzed, and discussed. Consensus is reached in open deliberations on various topics but these can be just as well changed when new facts are discovered.

Copernicus's theory of the solar system, while questioned at first, was fully incorporated in the logic of the Anglican Church not too many years later.

Newton's theories of gravity, thermodynamics, and light have puzzled many at first, but Anglicanism was broad enough to accept these and to live with their effect on theology.

Be it women and homosexuals in holy orders, the Vietnam conflict, the meaning of the symbols in the Eucharist, or a relationship with the American Lutherans, and other points of potential conflict, these all lie within the broad base of Anglicanism. Debate is allowed and encouraged in Anglicanism. Yes, at times decisions are incorrectly reached but the debate does not stop, is not arrested, and continues until corrections are made and implemented. One does not have to wait for a pronouncement from an archbishop or a bishop to accept a position, a theory, or a new development. No one has that authority in Anglicanism: decisions emerge from debate and consensus. As in science, coherency is the final arbiter for an issue.

When the birth control pill was placed before the public, Anglicans did not have to consult their priests to obtain permission for its use. Anglicans do not condone divorce but they are willing to face reality by recognizing that any marriage can fail irreparably. Much as society and the Church like to consider that marriages are or should be fashioned in heaven, the reality of it is that they are lived on the hard soil of earth. Anglicanism in general looks at the disjunction of marriages as a reality, which needs to be accepted and overcome and not ignored. Unlike Roman Catholicism or the current English monarchy's judgment, however, it is not necessary to hide or call upon a Matthean or a Pauline clause or even a monarch's delimiting restriction (usually taken out of context) to justify the sundering of the bond. For Anglicans divorce is perhaps a sign of failure, an unwillingness to adjust, the product of selfishness, but it is an earthly issue and can only be resolved on Earth. It is a separation of two human beings who at one time possessed good intentions but circumstances have injected the makings for a parting of the ways.

There was a lot of work going into the thinking effort about my relationship with the Church, God, and my own ethical position in the scheme of life. This is not the time, however, for such exploration to take place. I merely want to offer a thumbnail apologia for my choosing Anglicanism.

Anglicanism is a mode, a way, of making sense of how we experience God in Creation, in our lives, in the relationships we have with other sojourners on this planet Earth. Anglicanism is a special approach for understanding and confronting reality. Anglicanism helps me understand how justice is expressed and is meted out in the world. To use the words of Urban T. Holmes III:

"There is an inevitable course to our religious profession, which can be aborted only by denying its Lord. That course leads to living in the world as God sees the world. We can debate the trivial points, but the vision is largely clear. To love God is to relieve the burden of all who suffer. The rest is a question of tactics."

Of course, we cannot know how "God sees the world," but we can assume that it is based more on love than on selfishness. Yet we know that nature and the forces of creation are brutal and destructive, but constructive on occasion. None of this frightening violence is cruel for cruelty's sake or for egotistical reasons.

Much thinking has gone into what Holmes has said, especially today when Anglicanism is deliberating the issue of sexuality in holy orders and elsewhere. We can either be exclusivists or be all-inclusive. Which one is the way of love? I move wholeheartedly in the first decade of the 21st century with inclusiveness.

It was time for me to find a real, well-paying job because it was imperative that I maintain my financial head above water.

The Cold but not so Cruel World

To return to the year 1976, before the separation from Trudy, I was once again seeking employment. My résumé was out to several universities and I was waiting for a call, but in the meantime I had to have an income.

Just about the time I completed writing my dissertation, Bechtel called me to manage the translation and production of data for an Algerian liquid natural gas (LNG) project, whose report was to be written in French. This Sonatrach Project, as it was called, was to last a few months but was of sufficient duration to give me a financial breather. I finished the project and managed the material given to me by the petroleum and chemical teams. I also supervised the team of translators who worked on converting the English text into French. I avoided being transferred to Algeria and was quite pleased that I did not need to leave Montara to satisfy the requirements of this temporary assignment. When the job ended I had time to respond to some inquiries by universities and colleges offering me teaching positions. Several more potential teaching offers came, which required my being relocated to such places as Arizona, Kansas, Missouri, North Dakota, Texas, and Ohio. Two offers came to me from Southern California, but both were too tentative to be encouraging or dependable. It was unreasonable for me to move my whole family just for any job offer that came my way, as long as it had merit. Any position that came my way would have to be promising in the long run. Lectureships with tentative promises that they might turn into professorships were not alluring enough to attract me.

In November 1978 I received a telephone call from a colleague at Bechtel, Monika Fischer, asking if I was interested in taking her place to manage a small part of a project for the Jubail Industrial Complex. This was a project to build an industrial city in the desert several kilometers north of the metropolises of Dammam and Al Khobar on the Arabian Gulf. I would work out of San Francisco in the Jubail Support Office, and the task was to respond to the needs of the Jubail client and Bechtel personnel. This would also be a temporary assignment. Again I was in need of money so I accepted the job. I telephoned the project manager for the Jubail support office, Harry Bloom, a prince of a person who discussed with me the virtues of academic education and informed me that his son was majoring in philosophy at Stanford University.

"What will he do with philosophy?" he asked then continued, "I am an engineer but I cannot understand what philosophy will offer my son." I reminded Mr. Bloom that I had a degree in philosophy and that it seemed to be serving me quite well.

"I suppose that philosophy can serve one for a profession," he sighed. He did not dismiss me but sent me to the person who eventually hired me. "You'll have to speak to Waffeya El Dib to complete the interview," he added.

I then remembered that my colleague had forewarned me that I would be working under a most difficult and demanding person, an American-Egyptian woman, by the name of Waffeya El Dib. Miss El Dib was known to be a terror and a slave driver who had a reputation for being impossible to work with, or for. With the warning justly noted I started working with Miss El Dib. Soon I discovered that she was not at all the difficult person who had been described to me. To me Waffeya El Dib was a kind, pleasant, understanding person, and a pleasure to work with. That she was demanding was acceptable to me — I could handle that characteristic. The client in Jubail, however, was difficult and demanded that all work be correct and done promptly; this requirement had been almost impossible to accomplish by my several predecessors. I understood that requirement and made certain that all the work was produced correctly, precisely, and immediately. Once that proviso became the norm, Waffeya and I developed a good working relationship. As for Waffeya, we became good friends and even equals in the performance of the tasks for the project. My relationship with Harry Bloom also flourished in later years when we worked on other projects together, and he remained a gentleman. Harry's son did obtain a degree in philosophy and proceeded to work on a doctorate degree in cultural anthropology.

In early December 1977, Waffeya asked me if I was willing to go to Jubail, Saudi Arabia to work on the Flue Gas Rate Study. This was a task to study the emission of gas that was released into the atmosphere from the cracking process of petroleum and which was traditionally ignited at the top of the chimney vent. In my reading of reports from Jubail, I had questioned the waste of this flue gas that was merely ignited at the stack. It was correctly assumed that much of that "waste gas" could be used to supply a lot of the energy needed for the developing industries in what was to become the new industrial city of Jubail. The job was to calculate the energy available in the exhausted gas, and to determine if that energy would be sufficient to supply the developing industries. Two primary fabricating industries, aluminum and steel, were planned for construction in Jubail. For that assignment I would be working with the deputy project manager (DPM), John Robb; the senior economist Richard Stauffer; and the chief engineer, Frank Comprelli. My job was to compile the data and put them in a clear and presentable book for the client to review. The task would last approximately three weeks. Before I could go to Jubail, I would have to be hired as a full-time employee, which amounted to a better salary with much needed benefits. My response was that I would think about it and consider the offer with my wife over the weekend. Once at home I discussed the offer with Trudy who immediately accused me, if I accepted the assignment in Saudi, of willful "neglect of my parental responsibilities." The fact that I had been operating prior to that time as a single parent for two years while she taught in Merced was neither recognized nor considered by Trudy.

Because the children were still being ferried to private school in the morning by Emily McCormick Price, Trudy would have to be responsible for the afternoon pick-up. This task would not be difficult since she finished her school duties at 2:15 and the children were let out of class at 3:15 from Notre Dame and at 3:30 from St. Matthew's, the latter being fifteen minutes away from the former. After much discussion and convincing, Trudy accepted the arrangement and I, in turn, accepted the assignment to go to Saudi Arabia.

When the opportunity knocked at my door to become fully employed at Bechtel I did not hesitate to accept it. I imagined that with a foot in the door at Bechtel and with all the contacts I had already established, the future would offer unimaginable prospects and travels. Financially I was in debt and almost penniless. On 24 January 1978 I was hired as a full-time employee. Waffeya made all the arrangements for my departure to Jubail scheduled for 1 March, and also offered to grant me a few days to visit Cairo, Egypt, on the return trip. Such was my beginning with Bechtel Corporation: three days in London, three weeks in Jubail, Saudi Arabia, and then five days in Cairo, Egypt. Because Waffeya also had Egyptian roots and was from Cairo, she understood that I wished to reconnect with my youth and the place of my birth. Opportunity knocked twice on this occasion, because another Egyptian acquaintance, Nabil Jacob, living in Berkeley offered to contact his father who lived in Cairo. Soon Nabil informed me that his father and mother would be my hosts in Cairo and that I would be met at the Cairo International Airport, the old Payne Field where I had been held under house arrest in the mid-50s.

The project in Jubail was completed satisfactorily and I arrived in Cairo on 1 April 1978 and visited all the special places of my youth and then produced an essay entitled, "From Whence I Came," a short historical account of my youth in that old city on the Nile River. I arrived in Cairo a few days after President Sadat had addressed the Knesset of Israel and signed the peace treaty between the two nations. The citizens of Cairo were jubilant and whereas I could not take photographs of people or anything else in Saudi Arabia, people in Cairo asked me to photograph them at every opportunity. Upon my return from Egypt I brought back the sweet foods that make Cairo a renowned dessert capital of the Middle East.

I will return to the moment I arrived in Saudi Arabia. At midnight my plane touched down at Dhahran, the location of the international airport for the Eastern Province of Saudi Arabia. I was taken to Al Khobar and the Bechtel compound to spend the night before being driven to Jubail the next day. The next morning, a driver stopped by after I had eaten my breakfast to take me to the Jubail Industrial Complex, located approximately 80 kilometers north of Al Khobar. When I arrived in the old town of Jubail, I could see an old Turkish fort and a village that could have used some cash from the oil prosperity. In essence, old Jubail was a village in need of economic revitalization. Apart from the International Hotel structure, no building showed any aspect of having been cared for. The streets were partially paved and partially made of gravel and compacted sand. As we passed by the old Turkish Fort, we turned right towards the soon-to-be Jubail Industrial Complex.

Entering the Complex was a surprise. Apart from a dozen doublewide mobile homes, four steel warehouses, and a Quonset-like structure that I was informed was the mess hall, there was nothing else to see. Yes, many earthmoving machines were being used on either side of the road, and the noise was deafening. Sand was being moved from one place and dumped in another, or so it seemed. Off the beach I saw a huge dredging boat removing tons of sedimentation and placing it on a barge. I asked the driver if this was in preparation for the future harbor. His answer was that perhaps later it would be, but for now it was a swimming hole for the workers. Because the Gulf is shallow near Jubail, only approximately two meters deep for a distance of one or one and a half kilometers out, it was necessary to dig a hole for people to swim. Well, I thought, that was a generous effort by Bechtel. The driver immediately reminded me that the Jubail Royal Commission, the entity in charge of the development of the Complex, had requested this hole for recreation by the Saudi families who were attached to the Complex.

"Single men can only use the beach after work. During the day, especially in the afternoon, only families can come to the beach. No single men," the driver informed me. I took several dips in the excavated hole and found the water to be too hot for prolonged swims. Even in the evening, after the sun shining all day, the water was too hot for a good swim.

Soon we arrived at the personnel office, which was located in a doublewide. After registering, receiving instructions, and being given a key I was walked over by a young Saudi to my doublewide, which was only a short distance away. I was to share the doublewide in Camp 8 with another person who was to arrive the next day. After I selected a bedroom and dropped my bag, the young Saudi, Ahmed, took me to the doublewide where I would be working. In the office I met the project manager (PM), Red McQuilken, his deputy, John Robb, the chief engineer, Frank Comprelli, and the petroleum engineer, Ken Anderson. Red soon left the group to tend to some last minute tasks before he turned over the management to the new PM, Joseph (Joe) Anderson, who had not arrived yet.

After the greetings were completed, I was given a section of the large table everyone was sharing as a desk and given data to review and organize. Conversation was minimal, except for questions by one or the other in the room to clarify a fact. At noon, we all put down our pencils and headed to the Camp 6 mess hall, which was a short walk away. The residential compound was Camp 8, and the office and construction office compound was Camp 7, but no sign distinguished them from each other, except for Camp 6, which was situated across the main road. The main road, if taken all the way north, would lead one to Kuwait; a slight turn to the left on a fork off the main road would lead one to Iraq. Both Iraq and Kuwait were approximately 300 kilometers north of our location.

The work progressed until six in the evening, when we stopped and headed once again to the mess hall. During the day, tea, coffee and cookies were always available on a side table. The working hours were from seven to six, Saturday through Thursday. On Thursday the work stopped at noon to allow the married personnel to be driven to Al Khobar to visit their families. The PM and Deputy PM's family lived in the complex, as did those of the senior Saudi families. Thursday afternoon and Friday were days for exploring the surrounding area. A bus was available to take anyone to old Jubail village or to Dammam, the largest city in the Eastern Province.

On the second day, my new doublewide mate arrived and shared my quarters. Richard Stauffer was an economist and I knew him in San Francisco and had worked with him on parts of the Algerian project. I liked Dick and he has remained a dear friend over the years, even after both of us retired (Dick died in 2010). The doublewide had two large bedrooms with two bathrooms, a small kitchen, a laundry room, an enclosed porch, and a large living room.

Next to our doublewide was the family of the senior Saudi civil engineer, Mohamed Khoraise. Khoraise, although a lesser prince of the royal family, was a first class engineer who had also attended Victoria College in England, just about the same time I had. We recognized each other after being introduced by John Robb and recalled our common histories in Trumpington, UK.

The work progressed on schedule and my task was minimized by the addition of Andy, Robb's secretary who was a superb typist. He could type 100 words/minute, maintain an active and coherent conversation, eat cookies, and not let a misspelled word or incomplete sentence get by him. He was both a typist and an editor all wrapped up in a pleasant and assuring personality. The other good support worker was Ed Willkie, a graphic designer whom I knew from San Francisco also. Ed took the sketches we produced and turned them into superb graphics; out of our chicken scratches he produced gallery pieces. Both Andy and Ed assured me that I would be able to leave on 1 April for Egypt, and that all work would be completed by that time. All work was completed on March 31 and I took my scheduled flight to Cairo on 1 April.

One of the lessons I learned in Jubail from both John Robb and from the team assigned to the project, was that Bechtel suffered from a lack of overall program management for the project. The project manager and his DPM were totally involved with costing representative, managing the schedule, cost, personnel, and contracts for the development of the Jubail Industrial City, but no one took notice of how the various parts of the overall program came together or questioned the client's demands, even when they were counterproductive. In fact, no one asked if the project was coherently put together. This facet was not their immediate consideration. Bechtel followed the contract to the letter and always had in sight the turnkey day when all would be turned over to the client at the project's termination. I thought that was short-changing both the client and Bechtel. Because project managers focus primarily on schedule, cost, personnel accountability, and contract fulfillment there is not much effort spent on coherency issues touching proposed design to practical or applied design.

For example, I noticed in Jubail that where houses were to be erected, earthmoving equipment leveled several hundred acres before foundations were constructed, then after erection of the houses, the earthmovers returned to add contours and berms, add a few meters of elevation here and there, and restyle the land to give it shape so that it would not be flat and aesthetically boring. My thought was that had the land been treated differently at the beginning by keeping the elevations and the contours, the task would have skipped the wasteful initial pass to level the land, thus saving the cost of the earthmovers. Such duplication of effort wasted a great deal of money and man-hours. Because there was no coherent scheme I also discovered that shopping centers were initially to be constructed miles away from residential areas but had to be relocated when it was discovered that Saudi women, and women in general, were not allowed to drive automobiles to shopping centers or anywhere. Husbands worked all day and had the added task of driving their wives to shopping centers after work. The immediate solution was to have a bus service to transport the women but that required the women to shop unescorted in the shopping center; not a happy event for the Saudi men. The same problem applied to hospitals, clinics, post offices, and childcare facilities. No overall program had been examined with an eye for coherency.

When I returned to San Francisco, I continued to manage the requests that came from Jubail until Waffeya announced that she had accepted a transfer to London and that I was appointed to take her place as assistant manager of the Jubail Support Office. That position continued for 18 months. A new manager was appointed to replace Harry Bloom; consequently I had many problems with the replacement, some of which affected not only the Saudi client but also my own situation. The conditions in the Jubail Support Office became too unpleasant for me. Because I was a full-time employee it was possible for me to search for another department to land a position. Thus I began looking for another assignment in another department, one that was more in my field of interest.

Recognizing that Bechtel claimed to have an open door employee policy, I wrote a letter to Mr. Steven Bechtel Jr., president and chair of the company. I asked if Bechtel was interested in having an aesthetician (a "program" manager) responsible for overseeing the overall programs of projects, to check for coherency in design, and to initiate long term operation and maintenance, and hence replace the "turn-key" approaches that in reality cut off further work for Bechtel on completed projects.

"If Bechtel had a senior economist on its payroll," I said, "then it should also employ a senior aesthetician as program manager."

This letter prompted much discussion. Jim Roach, the personnel director for Bechtel's Petroleum Company, my home, was unhappy that I went above his head to Mr. Bechtel. The senior architect, Robert Reynolds, was furious that I did not consult him because he presumed, as all architects do, that he was the judge of all aesthetic issues. Mr. Bechtel, as an engineer, was puzzled by the letter and did not quite know how to treat it. Mr. Alden Yates, president of Bechtel Petroleum where I was employed, a good and bright man, who became president of Bechtel and who understood my point, called me for a meeting. At the meeting he recognized the point I had made and even agreed with me. Indeed Bechtel could use someone who would examine the coherency of projects. He was unable to act immediately because he was being considered to become president of Bechtel Corporation. He convinced me that he would tend to my request and the issue I had raised when he became president and when he was well established in his position. I considered that to be a fair approach.

Eventually a spot in the developing aviation department came my way via Emily McCormick, my rescuer. Soon after I was settled and happy in the aviation group Alden Yates died of cancer. For the short time Yates was president, Bechtel moved forward extensively but his tenure was much too short to be lastingly effective. The issue of program evaluation was never raised again because Mr. George Schultz, who became president of Bechtel, was too busy advising Ronald Reagan as he was maneuvering his way to the presidency of the United States of America. Schultz proved to be a mediocre president for Bechtel, but he was a good friend of Steve Bechtel and would position the firm well when the Reagan administration took over the White House. I waited for the denouement patiently, but it never materialized in that attempt. If one tool does not do the job, I said to myself, then use another. I did just that.

Aviation and the Sand Box Mentality

In the meantime Bechtel was engaged in establishing a Management, Operation, and Maintenance (MOM) group for the new International Airports of Jeddah and Riyadh. The MOM group was an adjunct to the airport construction group and was an idea generated by Vice President Ivan Nealon but much opposed by the construction folks. MOM was allowed to exist for a few years and Glenn Plymate, ex-director of Oakland Metropolitan Airport, was appointed as manager. It should be told that when Nealon, a pilot, was killed in an aircraft accident, the horizon ended for MOM and the group was slowly starved, neglected, and eventually disbanded five years after Glenn was forced to take early retirement. The reason MOM did not survive was because the construction mentality prevailed. The then thinking was that Bechtel was an engineering and construction firm and MOM was outside its scope. When that occurred I was able to land on all fours in the Planning Department, which became, with my insistence, the Infrastructure Department.

The new Jeddah airport had been designed and engineered by Parsons-Daniels Engineering and Construction Company but the German firm Hochtief, a leading construction firm, did the actual construction. The airport needed a great deal of additional operational fine-tuning work before it could be pronounced completed. Pan American Airways had been called to assist as a subcontractor with the operational phase of Jeddah, but Pan Am was undergoing some financial and management difficulties of its own and was unable to staff-up fully for the task.

To complete the tasks that neither Parsons-Daniels nor Pan Am was able to complete, the Saudi International Airports Project (IAP) contracted with Bechtel to do what needed to be done. What needed to be done were not tasks of construction but of operational programs. In response to the client's International Airport Project's (IAP) request, MOM was given the task, and I must add, reluctantly, by Bechtel. This was a daring assignment that required operational fine-tuning, a detailed security plan, and a complete document listing the spare parts requirement for five years, and production of the International Civil Aviation Organization (ICAO) Annex 14 and the Federal Administration (FAA) Part 139 combined Operation Manual. This was a daunting assignment and for the last part (ICAO and FAA) MOM had no experienced personnel for the task.

Glenn Plymate called on Emily McCormick to take the position of senior editor for MOM, which meant that she read and examined most of what was produced. In that capacity she encountered many problems with statements covering aviation management, aircraft operation, and general large aircraft maneuvering capabilities vis-à-vis the architectural scheme of the airport. Emily often came over to the Jubail offices to ask me questions about aviation and the solution to some operational problem caused when the limitations of large aircraft were not considered. For instance, taxiing distances from the runway to the terminals — aircraft cannot taxi for long distances without possibly causing severe damage to their undercarriages. Large aircraft when in takeoff climbs and fully loaded cannot make sharp turns; in fact they should not make turns that exceed 15 degrees from the vertical.

Finding that I was of help and could give her correct answers to the questions she posed because I had experience with large aircraft from my USAF days, Emily approached the manager of MOM, Glenn Plymate, who was a general aviation pilot, and who had been an airport director. No one in the MOM department or in the airport construction group, except Plymate, had any experience with large aircraft and the largest aircraft Glenn had flown was the Douglas DC3 (C47) which, by comparison to today's planes, was a small aircraft; none had any knowledge of large turbine aircraft such as the Boeing 707 (KC 135), 737, 747, and Lockheed L1011 ground or air maneuvering limitations. My experience included the Lockheed RC-121 and Boeing 707 (C 135) although I did not have recent flight activities; my flying was in abeyance and had been for 13 years.

I did not know Glenn Plymate, the manager of the MOM group that included Emily. By his appearance, Glenn Plymate looked as if he was full of himself and generally unpleasant to deal with. On two occasions, I spoke with him and both left me annoyed. While on the Jubail project one of my responsibilities was to read all the telexes before they were sent to the project. Sometimes sensitive comments were made in the telexes that either upset Bechtel or the client. My task was to act as a censor on all outgoing telexes. One telex from Plymate addressed to Bob Dennison, manager of the developing Jubail airport, inquired if there were any possibility of additional work coming his way. Plymate was trying to expand the work and importance of his department. That was not a question to be sent to Jubail because the Saudi administration was also copied on all telexes; anyway there were other channels, such as the telephone, for that sort of "business development" inquiry. I returned his telex explaining that the message was inappropriate. Plymate was unhappy with my actions and said so over a phone call.

The Jubail project had commissioned a video to show the development of the industrial complex and how it was surfacing out of the desert as a new city. The opening scene showed two Arabian falcons (falco, falconidae) flying over sand dunes in the bright early morning light, then all of a sudden one of the birds performed a wingover, returned to level, and continued to fly in formation. This was an extraordinary aerobatic maneuver. Knowing that Plymate was a pilot, I invited him to see the video. He was pleased and thanked me. In this meeting Plymate still gave the impression that he was full of himself, but the edges were more rounded and the bristles combed. Before leaving the Jubail project I obtained a clipping of the video and presented it to Glenn — he was mainly interested in the flight of the falcons, which was understandable. Several months later the issue with falcons led me into a most interesting project, but that's for a later telling.

Emily was also searching for good editors to work in her department at MOM. I had encountered good work from a young editor who was attached to the publication department of Bechtel's Power Division. Marilyn Smith, a flaming redhead with a master's degree, was an excellent editor, and a wonderful person who had become my dear friend, so I suggested her to Emily. I had worked with Marilyn when I was a contract employee helping the publication group located in the Metropolitan Building, right across from the Bechtel complex on Fremont Street. Often Marilyn and I shared the lunch or coffee time and some interesting conversation. I believe that I had a crush on her but because she was attached to a man and even lived with him in Oakland it never amounted to anything more than friendship.

Marilyn was to be furloughed soon because the publications department in the Power Division of Bechtel was being terminated. Emily interviewed her and promptly put her to work on the MOM books, known generally as the Yellow Books. Marilyn worked for Emily for several years. Marilyn, as I said, was a fine editor and a good writer who took on the task, after much convincing from Emily and me to prepare an editorial style book, not only for MOM but also for other Bechtel publications departments (it was still used when I retired).

Being task-oriented, Marilyn allowed nothing to interrupt her when she was working. One day before Christmas, when the late Mr. Steve Bechtel Sr. took time to visit departments to wish his employees a Merry Christmas, Marilyn was on the floor assembling a book that was due to be pouched that very afternoon. Mr. Bechtel came into her work area and saw her on the floor totally unaware of his presence. He stood before her for a long time, then introduced himself, and then helped her with a few inserts for the book. Marilyn continued to assemble the book, which was pouched on time to Jubail. A few days later, Marilyn received a note of commendation from Mr. Bechtel; I hope there was a bonus attached too.

Anyway, we maintained a solid friendship and celebrated our two birthdays for years with lunches. Over the years, even when she moved to Oregon, we continued to maintain contact. In later years Marilyn visited Montara and brought her new baby son, Scott, with her. On one occasion I took her and her son on an airplane ride but her then-husband, who rode with us, was petrified of flight.

In later years Marilyn married the young man, Ron, with whom she had been living and had a second son, Marc. Marc turned out to be a fine young man. Ron and Marilyn divorced several years later and Scott left home and disappeared. Marilyn never learned what happened to Scott and to this day he is listed as a "missing person." Giving Marilyn comfort is difficult because to assuage a mother's pain is quite impossible. Marc has given his mother much joy and satisfaction and currently graduated in engineering from both California Technical University and Occidental University. I've maintained regular contact with Marilyn. She remained a fine friend and dear person until her death of cancer in 2013.

It was the conviction of the engineering and construction folks that an airport was just another civil engineering project or a mere construction job. After all, Saudi Arabia was just another sand box wherein Tonka Toys-like equipment could be used to move sand and erect buildings, not unlike building sand castles on the beach. Moreover, the Saudis had lots of money and a little construction and subsequent reconstruction here and there was nothing for which we should be too concerned about. Money flowed from oil reserves, and Saudi Arabia floated atop an enormous reserve of sweet, light, crude oil, as it was known. Thus sand that penetrated inside and damaged delicate security equipment such as navigation aids or weather gear could be dealt with by constant replacement. Aircraft maneuvering on the airport operational area (AOA) was an operational issue and not a construction responsibility. Thus taxiway design never considered the long taxi requirement prior to reaching aprons, runway thresholds, terminals, and cargo areas. MOM, however, was attempting to make a point that the operational issue was important and that dealing with management, operation, and maintenance would produce as much, if not more, revenue than construction. Why? Because operational requirements were ongoing while construction ended at some point.

One day when Emily came over to my Jubail office to ask a question on the subject of aviation, I asked her how long this information quest was going to last. As I intimated earlier, I needed to leave the Jubail Support Office because of a personality conflict with the new manager and the eventual termination of the offshore support office. It was time for me to look at Bechtel's personnel matrix for another department and/or another project, one that was more attuned to my purpose, interest, and talent. Emily replied that she was authorized to bring another person into the department to replace her for several weeks while she tended to some personal obligations. Would I be interested? It seemed to me that again a door was opening, this time into aviation, and a topic I knew well enough to make a contribution to. This temporary assignment would remove me from my present position and give me time to search for another project — even investigate possibilities in aviation with other firms.

"With whom would I be working?" I asked.

"You would be working for me until Mr. Glenn Plymate can introduce you to the upper level people on the project — something he would be starting only after you proved yourself."

"So in the mean time I would be working for you?" Emily replied that that's how it would be handled.

I thought about that for a moment then blurted out that, "If I were in your shoes, I would not hire me because I am often difficult to deal with." Emily smiled. I added, "Remember that I am a curmudgeon." She knew that. As for me, I believe when a door is opened, you should at least look inside and check out the environment. I accepted the offer and Emily did not suffer much from my presence.

I left the Jubail Industrial City Project in the summer of 1979 for MOM but not before I took my first vacation in years. With Emily as a travel partner, I took Michel, who was just under 12 years old, to the UK and France. The vacation lasted three weeks and during that time I was able to do a couple of days work at Bechtel's London Hammersmith Office for the Jubail project. At Bechtel, because Waffeya was on a business trip, she kindly invited me to use her office and the services of her secretary.

While working at Bechtel, Michel took a trip all by himself on the Red Robin bus tour and the Central-Green Line Underground to explore the sights of London. Michel left two croissants in a bag on the Underground given to him by Waffeya's cook; he was worried that the police might arrest him for leaving what might appear to be an Irish Republican Army terrorist bomb. He was not arrested!

A few days later, when Waffeya returned from her business trip, we were invited to spend a few nights in the house and were treated to several wonderful dinners prepared by her mother's Egyptian cook who always traveled with her. Waffeya's mother was also visiting London. Emily was staying in Ray Kingsley's house in the East End of London; Ray was working on a novel that was never completed.

After our London stay we rented a Mini Cooper and sped north to Scotland for a few days. Michel was given the opportunity to drive the car across the border separating England and Scotland by sitting on my lap and steering. This was a memorable event for Michel. In the UK we often took Michel for real high tea because he could not stay awake past eight o'clock, unless the opportunity promised some excitement.

After Scotland we scooted south to Folkstone to ride the Hovercraft to Boulogne-sur-Mer, France, and then on by train to Paris and the Hotel Lindbergh located on the Left Bank. After giving Michel dinner early in the evening, Emily and I decided to enjoy a Parisian dinner in one of the wonderful restaurants in the Latin Quarter of the Left Bank. Upon our return around 11 o'clock, we found Michel wide-awake and leafing through a couple of *Playboy* magazines that he had found hidden behind the mirror of the armoire.

Because he was still awake, I asked him if he wanted to go for a walk to the Place de la Concorde to experience Paris, the City of Lights, at night. He was game and quickly got dressed and was ready to explore the sights of Paris glistening on a clear cold night. We walked along the Seine, crossed the Pont Neuf to the Right Bank and meandered to the Place de la Concorde after stopping to buy warm chocolate crepes. Michel was fascinated by the fast circling traffic around the Place de la Concorde. Midnight and Michel was wide-awake and mesmerized by the whizzing cars. He would have watched all night but we all needed a restful sleep because we had a full agenda for the next day. Yes, indeed it was a wonderful vacation for all three of us but I had to return to San Francisco to locate a more enjoyable position and to learn more about how Bechtel's inner politics worked.

I had decided that there were two features about Bechtel that I liked:

1. The firm made it possible for employees to find and to work on interesting projects that tested many of their creative talents, and it also offered a good deal of foreign travel.

2. The firm was located in San Francisco and this factor made many negative political conditions tolerable.

Upon my return to Bechtel, San Francisco, I left the Jubail Support Office as Assistant Manager, and became an active lower echelon member of MOM and in due course became a good friend of Glenn Plymate, its manager. He turned out to be nothing like my first two impressions but was a pleasant, kind, and gracious manager. Plymate was pushing the mythical Rock of Sisyphus uphill everyday. And when it would appear that he was achieving his goal and showing that MOM was a valuable asset to Bechtel, the rock would roll downhill. He tried and tried, but in the end he was defeated by his own shortcomings and these were:

- Poor choice of deputies as part of his team. He was reluctant to dismiss people who were not suited for the task once he had hired them.
- Because his deputies were weak, he was forced to micromanage many tasks and this diverted him from other duties of greater importance.
- Poor political techniques when dealing with his superiors; he was superb with the client but that often antagonized his superiors.

I do give him credit for downward loyalty and fairness. Glenn had rough edges and very basic likes and dislikes, especially in foods; he avoided onions and green peppers with a passion, loved French's mustard — the yellow disgusting condiment that any cultivated tongue would find too embarrassing to taste, and preferred unseasoned dishes, especially if they were Mexican, which were almost impossible to obtain—and yet he found a restaurant near his house in Independence, Oregon, that would serve him bland burritos and tamales. On another level, I've seen Glenn give a good salary boost to a person he truly disliked but who did a good job. He was generous with praise, and unlike many managers, gave credit to those under him instead of claiming all the credit for himself when reporting to his superiors.

I learned much about Glenn Plymate after we developed a strong and productive relationship, especially as two people who considered aviation to be important in our lives. As I shall repeat often, we became good friends as the years passed by. Glenn trusted Emily's judgment and gave me his support when she left for five weeks. The major work was to produce the Yellow Books, which were detailed guides for managing an airport; I believe there were 21 or 23 books for the series. They were delivered on time and within budget and the client was ecstatic.

Now it is time to continue with the story.

Once again, after a long hiatus from aviation, I was working with aircraft, with people who work with them, and the people who build airports, and that was particularly enjoyable and exciting. MOM was my home department until 1984 when it ceased to exist as a result of Bechtel's shortsightedness. I didn't work for Emily all that long because soon after her return from her leave of absence I became involved with airport certification and the requirements of the US Federal Aviation Administration (FAA) and the International Civil Aviation Organization (ICAO), the latter being an arm of the United Nations.

At any rate I covered for her in the editorial group while she was away for almost five weeks and in the meantime Mr. Plymate discovered that he could put my aviation knowledge to good use for the new Jeddah (King Abdul Aziz) airport, the still newer Riyadh (King Khaled) airport, and the small Jubail (King Faisal) airport. Ultimately, Glenn, in consultation with Jerry Rigsbee, the deputy airport project manager who was working on his pilot license, proposed that I join the group and I quickly accepted.

Many of the difficulties that had to be dealt with on airports surfaced from the fact that Bechtel, as I mentioned earlier, was primarily a civil engineering and construction firm and had little sense or knowledge of the ongoing life of aviation and airports. Nevertheless, Bechtel had excellent relations with the key people of the Saudi International Aviation Project (IAP) and many of the leadership in the Royal Family. Yet for Bechtel an airport was simply a construction project, and was considered to be no different than any other turnkey project. In

Bechtel's scheme of things to be built, a terminal was simply a building, a runway was tantamount to a road, and overhead flight patterns for arriving or departing flights were not of much interest to its teams of design engineers, construction engineers, and civil architects.

Ivan Nealon, who was a pilot, a vice president of Bechtel, and someone who knew a great deal about airports, had hired Plymate; unfortunately Nealon died in an aviation accident soon after Plymate had been brought on board. Without Nealon, Bechtel was left adrift in an area that was unfamiliar to its makeup. Even with consultants available off the street, Bechtel did not know enough to ask the right questions. As for Plymate, he was looked upon as a different sort of person. Although Plymate was an architect by education he had also been the director of Oakland Metropolitan Airport, a past member of the Oregon Aviation Department, and was an active pilot with some impressive experience, yet Bechtel's hierarchy did not really trust him. Might it have been a personality clash or was it that Glenn's deputy was not the sharpest tool in the shop, and because of that, he was an albatross around his neck? At any rate, the client liked Plymate.

That a million pounds of flying equipment needed special landing surfaces and consequently appropriate treatment was past Bechtel's understanding. A wheel-load (a gear foot-print) of 45,000 pounds per square inch requires a surface appropriately designed to withstand the otherwise destructive weight. It became MOM's exceedingly difficult task to convince Bechtel that an airport was quite different from "any other" construction project.

Moreover, I soon found that the client also needed to be educated. I must admit that educating the Saudi client was an easier task, especially as they were forced to sharpen their learning curve when it came to the FAA, ICAO, the major airline pilots' professional unions and associations, and the interested airport and airline insurance companies. In the past either the Turkish or British military had constructed the airports in Saudi Arabia. Now as a sovereign nation flush with money because of crude oil, it had the responsibility to develop airports suitably designed for the current century. The Saudis soon recognized that many forces, many organizations, and many international codes were in play when a major new international airport was proposed for development and construction.

The most critical requirements, and ones that needed to be satisfied at the outset, were those of the international airline pilots' professional unions and associations. No FAA or ICAO or insurance approval mattered if the pilots' organizations did not grant their imprimatur. To obtain the approval of the pilots' organization and of the FAA and ICAO, certain requirements had to be fulfilled, and these requirements, which ultimately led to certification, were to be noted in an Airport Operational Manual (OpsM) of some enormous size, which contained details of most of the equipment, navigation aids (NAVAID), rules, weather averages, general security, chain of command, and other pertinent information as required by ICAO Annex 14 (in the United States it was FAR Part 139). It must be noted that the IAP demanded that their airports also comply with the FAA's requirements.

The first obvious concerns for the operational safety of the Jeddah airport were surfaced, although quietly, by the national airline of the Kingdom. Saudi Arabian Airline (Saudia) voiced apprehension about security protection and operational safety at Jeddah, especially from terrorism. What was the level of security at the airport, and that level of security had to consider passengers during the Hajj period, when nearly two million Muslims from abroad came for the pilgrimage to Mecca? During the Hajj, Jeddah's population was quadrupled with Muslims from the four corners of the world. Many pilgrims brought with them items for sale to pay for their pilgrimage. The Hajj is the once-in-a-life time pilgrimage to Mecca that must be made by all devoted Muslims as one of the Five Requirements. Mecca is a city forbidden to non-Muslims. The pilgrimage is to be made between the 8th and 12th day of Dhu-al-Hijjah, the 12th and last month of the Islamic calendar. The Islamic calendar is based on the 28-day month; hence it is not a fixed date like the Gregorian calendar of the West.

Several times foreign terrorists or local dissidents opposed to the Saudi monarchy or to the strictness of the Wahabi Muslim tradition had attacked worshippers and the authorities in Mecca. At the time of the Hajj, appropriate security precautions were paramount. Much as the Hajj is a holy time for worship, and the place where it happens in Mecca is very special, nevertheless there were many instances when antagonistic groups (especially in 1979) found the means to explode bombs, spray worshippers with machine gun bullets thus killing scores, or disrupt the religious proceedings by causing violent disorder. A majority of the Hajj pilgrims came by air and passed through the New Jeddah International Airport, which now was officially called the King Abdul Aziz International Airport (KKIA).

Operational safety was a key issue to Saudia, to its pilots, and to the foreign airlines that were scheduled to serve the airport. Fuel and oil deliveries from the hydrants had to be made without allowing contaminants to disrupt operations or affect flying aircraft. Navigation Aids (NAVAIDs) had to be protected at all times, especially during those times that were indispensable for safe and critical approaches to landings. The airspace over the airport, particularly the routes that controlled approaches and departures, were to be designed to preclude collisions but allow for smooth transition into and out of airways.

A set of runways that are long, wide, and designed to accommodate wide-bodied aircraft cannot just be constructed without consideration for safety, traffic, load factor, egress and access. The runway sections designed by Parsons-Daniels and constructed by the German firm Hochtief were dowelled together, but because the sea water table was merely 10 meters below the sabkah (chalk-clay which was hard when dry, gooey when wet) surface, it promised to shift after years of landing by the heavy wide-bodied aircraft. The Jeddah runways were constructed in large sections connected by dowels: a good method in stable, dry and well drained land but not adequate for Jeddah that was near the Red Sea and floated on the near-the-surface water table. This concern was brought to the attention of the IAP and Presidency of Civil Aviation (PCA) by a memorandum that I wrote as a cover sheet to the developing Operation Manual, but because of Parson-Daniel's denial and Bechtel's lack of knowledge it fell on deaf ears. Yet, in 1991, twelve years after they had been constructed, they had to be reconstructed without the dowels and placed on deep foundation piles that were sunk to depths of 30 meters for stability. A task and an expense that could have been avoided had both Parsons-Daniel and Bechtel executed their due-diligence research.

Plymate and his team were constantly in conflict with the civil engineering mentality of Bechtel. Even the architectural group was designing "monuments" that were accidents waiting to happen. Roof extensions protruded out towards jet-bridges and could act as a pilot's decapitating tool when an aircraft was brought to its assigned gate. Because it was too late to redesign the terminal buildings, which sported roof extensions in the shape of nuns' hats, the dangerous jet-bridges were abandoned and replaced by large buses that met aircraft parked away on the aprons adjoining the terminal. A decade later, the terminal building was torn down and rebuilt with a more practical design that allowed the aircraft to park adjacent to the gate's jet-bridges, thus simplifying the embarkation and debarkation process. When that change was made, the buses were promptly dispensed with.

Another issue was whether the airport's fire and rescue department was adequately outfitted if an incident with a wide body aircraft, like a Boeing 747, occurred. These were inquiries that had not been considered in Bechtel's plan. MOM had been advising Bechtel through the Yellow Books that contained nearly everything required by an airport to operate efficiently and safely.

Saudia's concerns needed to be addressed by Bechtel and by the client. Both security and operational aviation issues had to be examined by Bechtel; this was not simply a turnkey construction project where management, operational, and maintenance matters could be ignored or left for the client to consider when he took over. The client was as much a novice as Bechtel, unprepared to render advice in the arena of MOM for an airport. Topics such as operations, security, and airspace management were critical to the safe operation of these new airports in Saudi Arabia. MOM was able to respond to several questions that surfaced but in the area of security we required an aviation professional team. MOM did not have a security person on its team and had to hire one, if Bechtel could obtain the green light from the client. IAP gave Bechtel authority to recruit a leading security person and a team to work on the airport.

James Harageones, retired Air Force colonel and security expert, was brought onto the scene to handle the issues. He rapidly developed a team to prepare the security program and perform the task for Jeddah. At the same time I also went to Jeddah to prepare the Airport Operations Manual (OpsM), which would be the guide for addressing the concerns raised by Saudia, FAA, ICAO, security requirements, and the airline pilot's professional associations and unions.

It was fortunate that Harageones and I cooperated admirably in this venture; in fact we became close friends. Harageones was a delightful, bright, able, and personable man who knew his security business inside out. In fact, Harageones should have been given a gold medal for resolving many of the security issues without fanfare or drastic redesign of buildings such as the terminals, the gates, and all the locking systems. The builder prior to Bechtel's arrival had placed barcode-activated locking devices, which were unfortunately soon destroyed by sand from the regular storms that have always plagued Saudi Arabia most of the year. Moreover, each building had different locking systems from different manufacturers installed. Jim Harageones was able to work with the various locking devices and produce a uniform system that was not a headache to the IAP.

Harageones also proved to be a splendid ambassador for Bechtel and for Plymate; he not only obtained a security contract valued at several million dollars for Jeddah's airport, but he obtained an added contract for Riyadh's new airport which was yet to be constructed. The dollar value of these two security contracts enriched Bechtel's coffers by a great deal in pure profit. In deep gratitude for Harageones' work, Bechtel soon furloughed him without so much as a note of thanks, after IAP approved the program and plans for Riyadh. Jim, who had gotten the contract, designed the program, and hired and trained his security team, was left out in the cold because Bechtel thought that it could operate without his services. Fortunately, McDonnell-Douglas picked him up immediately for their security needs and gave him a position in Riyadh at the Saudi military base. Because Harageones was no longer a Bechtel employee, he was not even allowed to see what was being constructed at the Riyadh airport — he couldn't even be shown what was being installed as security devices.

At that time, in 1982, I was working on the Riyadh airport and was allowed by the Saudis to bring guests onto the airport construction site. I gave Harageones and his wife Helen a tour on a Friday afternoon of the Riyadh airport. While in Riyadh I was often invited to their home for dinner, especially the wonderful Greek fare that Helen superbly prepared in the style of cooking found on her home island of Lesbos.

Helen was a beautiful woman and a lovely person who was a warm and attentive hostess. She would tell me stories of her family in Lesbos, spelled

Lesvos in classical Greek. The island of Lesbos is a mountainous Greek island in the Aegean Sea. Mitilini (also spelled Mytilene) is its largest city. The entire island is sometimes called Mitilini. The economy of Lesbos is centered on agriculture and fishing. The island produces olives, olive oil, grapes, and fresh and salted fish. Other economic activities include tourism, soap making, and the quarrying of marble. Helen often told me of the local legend that says that Lesbos' people descend from the mythical Greek warrior Agamemnon. The legend suggests that Agamemnon conquered Lesbos in the Trojan War, which probably took place in the 1200s B.C. From the late 1100s through the 900s B.C., many Aeolians from mainland Greece moved to Lesbos. Lesbos was a cultural center from about 600 B.C. to the end of the Golden Age of Greece in 431 B.C. From the poet Sappho of Lesbos the only surviving verse consists of one probably complete poem and fragments of many others. These lines show intense but controlled emotion expressed in direct language. Sappho was born into an aristocratic family at either Eresos or Mytilene on the island of Lesbos. At Mytilene, she led a circle of young women who were her disciples. These women worshiped Aphrodite and other goddesses, and learned music and other arts as well as social graces. Although some of Sappho's lyrics celebrate friendship among women, her circle was for the young, who often left the group to marry. Sappho herself valued the company of both men and women. She was married, and had a daughter named Cleis. I delighted in the wonderful tales that Helen told after dinner, and even Jim who must have heard these stories enjoyed listening to them again and again. Jim's family was from Corinth, a city that also possesses a rich history of myths but he was not a storyteller; he was a good listener. Helen often invited me to visit Lesbos but time and circumstances have yet to offer me that opportunity; someday I'll be able to schedule a visit to modern and ancient Mytilene, and I hope it is soon.

The tour of the Riyadh airport I gave Jim and Helen included the new mosque, the royal terminal, the domestic and international terminals, and other buildings on site. I felt a bit strange to escort Harageones around a venue that had his imprint all over the design plans. Gratitude has never been one of Bechtel's strong points with regards to employees, especially retired employees.

Once off the active payroll, a retiree was no longer considered part of the Bechtel community, no matter what contributions he/she had made.

Jeddah: The Ancient City on the Red Sea

It was my turn to be heading to Saudi Arabia. Many tasks can be accomplished from afar, but there comes a time when the actual item needs to be examined. The airport was about 60 percent completed or so it was thought. Before it could be completed it had to be certified by several authorities and to fulfill this step an operational manual (OpsM) was required. Because Bechtel was new at this game there was no one currently available to manage this task. The tail was pinned on me because I had some experience with large aircraft and I could assemble the necessary documents and ask the right questions. So for the second time I was booked for a flight to Saudi Arabia.

To prepare the OpsM for Jeddah, which was located on the western side of the Arabian Peninsula on the coast of the Red Sea, I arrived at Jeddah's old airport at 2:00 p.m. from London. After a tedious hour-and-a-half clearing passport control and customs, I discovered that the driver who was to meet me did not appear. After several attempts to locate the Bechtel office, I decided to head for the Sheraton Hotel and enjoy a good night's sleep. I would play detective to locate Bechtel later that morning.

Waking at 11:00 a.m. I called Bechtel's office at the new airport but received no answer. I then placed a call to Colonel Amin, the director of IAP; surely he would be able to connect me with someone from Bechtel. Indeed Amin's secretary was helpful and located Jim Ellingsworth, my contact and soon-to-be colleague on the project.

I had met James Ellingsworth in San Francisco when he was first hired to work with MOM in Jeddah. Jim was a knowledgeable person with substantial airport experience, a pleasant personality, and was cool as a cucumber in difficult situations. Working under the less than brilliant George Hext hired by Plymate, and another reason why Glenn's light was dimmed quickly, Ellingsworth was able to surmount the unpleasant situations that Hext caused.

Jim and I worked very well together. I was the aviation person and he was the engineer — his background was electrical engineering. We both set about immediately to gather the necessary data for the OpsM, which was required by both the FAA's Part 139 and ICAO's Annex 14. After the first draft was completed and my three-month visa was about to expire, I telephoned Plymate to ask if he could send me his administrative assistant to complete the assembly of the OpsM because I had to return to San Francisco for a few weeks. Glenn sent me Danilo Simich, a young fellow with a spanking new degree in airport management. Danilo set to work immediately and was supervised by Jim, as I grabbed a flight back to California to tend to some personal issues of school selection and registration for Dominique. I was scheduled to return in four weeks to Jeddah to complete the task of the OpsM. While at the home office, the draft of the OpsM arrived for review, editing, and publication formatting. There were still some data holes that needed to be dealt with when I returned to Jeddah.

Back in Jeddah, we completed the final copy of the OpsM, and IAP, George Hext, and Bob Polvi, Bechtel's project manager, reviewed it. None of these reviews were of value but protocol required that they be performed. The important reviews came from the FAA, ICAO, and the various pilot professional associations such as the International Air Line Pilots Association (IALPA); none of these had yet been asked to review the OpsM. In fact Bechtel had not considered having the relevant entities review the draft because they considered the book unnecessary. Little did they know that the airport they were building would have become a monument, without a single flight landing there, had the aviation authorities mentioned not granted their seal of approval. I had insisted that draft copies be sent for the genuine review, and Glenn backed me all the way, as did Jerry Rigsbee.

Acting immediately, I telexed the various entities that were legally bound to review the OpsM and pouched copies to their principal offices. The chair of ICAO happened to be the respected Saudi aviation executive who had created, for the King, The Presidency of Civil Aviation (PCA) for Saudi Arabia. Dr. Mohammed Hamzala immediately telephoned George Hext to announce that he and the FAA representative would be arriving in Jeddah the following Monday, and this was Wednesday. A few hours later a telex was sent to John Moreno, the IAP airport operations manager, informing him that the IALPA representative was arriving in Jeddah with Dr. Hamzala. John Moreno had been the airport director of San Juan's International Airport, Puerto Rico. Monday was expected to be a major day for Jeddah's new airport.

In the meantime, Danilo was ready to return to San Francisco after he took care of a few minor tasks for Harageones' team. Because Thursday is a half-day of work and Friday is the normal day off, we all headed for the airport swimming pool on these days. The pool was a gathering place for all foreigners working on the airport project. There were Swedes, French, Germans, British, Italians, and Americans. In Saudi it is necessary to carry one's passport at all times because one never knows when the police will stop one for an identification check. Danilo had been told to carry his passport, and like a docile young man had slipped it into his swimming trunk's rear pocket — with good intentions to remove it before dipping into the pool. He forgot. The passport was soaked and all the visa stamps became unglued. A frightening mess. Applying for a new passport took weeks. The Saudi visa alone could only be issued outside the country. He was scheduled to depart in two days and needed to show passport control both his passport and his exit visa — both of which were sopping wet.

Borrowing an iron from an expatriate family, he proceeded with Ellingsworth's help to press his passport and re-glue the stamps. The final product was acceptable enough that Saudi passport control let him exit the country, and American passport control let him enter the United States, but not before the officer laughed at him, and chided him that he could hardly call that messy document a passport. Danilo was the brunt of jokes for months but took the ribbing with good humor.

Jim was married to a lovely German woman, Ellen, who had moved to the United States years earlier. While I was in Saudi, Jim and Ellen had decided to get married in Gibraltar. Ellen was a wonderful lady who made my stay in Jeddah most comfortable and pleasant. Ellen cooked good meals; I was often invited to share whatever the product of her kitchen was. One day we went to the fish market by the old quarter of Jeddah on the Red Sea. There we saw fishmongers clean and prepare the catch that had been brought over from the fishermen. We wanted a local fish from the Red Sea. We were informed that the hammura fish was as local as it could get because it is only found in the Red Sea near the coast of Arabia. We bought the fish and Ellen decided that she would prepare it for the night's dinner. Ellen had never cooked a whole fresh fish before. She, however, never informed either Jim or me. The fish had to be cleaned, scaled, seasoned, and broiled and Ellen was unable to figure out what needed to be done. Looking into a cookbook she discovered that a fresh whole fish is much different from one filleted and packaged.

After a while, Ellen appeared in the living room with tears in her eyes and an obvious look of frustration and despair. Here was a lovely fish that she would have mangled. How would she cook it? Seeing her I went to the rescue. Jim couldn't help laughing. I took the fish, removed the scales, gutted it, cut both head and tail off, buttered the outside, added cut onion inside with salt and pepper and slipped it under the broiler. Ellen just watched me with her large eyes absorbing the whole process. Jim was still laughing and joking. We had a good dinner that night, although it was later than we had planned. Some weeks later, a few days before I was to return to San Francisco, the Ellingsworths invited me to dinner. For dinner, Ellen had purchased another hammura fish and had prepared it herself and it was wonderful. Indeed, it was a fine dinner and one never to be forgotten.

Jim Ellingsworth served with Bechtel in Jeddah, for a short time in Riyadh, then Jubail, and Dammam, and I dined with them at all four locations. In Jubail I used their apartment and car while they were away on R&R and by Jim's instruction left their car at the International Hotel located near the Dhahran airport on the evening of my departure. Jim and Ellen were returning the next day. Upon their return, Jim had forgotten where he had asked me to leave their car in the hotel parking lot and for a few long moments searched for it. Fortunately, they finally found their car and my name was exonerated.

Were I ever to build my dream villa in Saudi, it would be in Jeddah. It is unequivocally my favorite city in the Kingdom of Saudi Arabia. Riyadh has better weather and is less humid, but Jeddah, or the Queen City on the Red Sea, has charm and is a little more attractive because of its heritage, its native art, its ancient souk (market), and its historic architecture. It is a city that has evolved through the ages, and was a vibrant metropolis long before petroleum was discovered in eastern Saudi Arabia. It has a domestic commercial economy that is neither overly dependent on oil nor the result of the influx of the nouveaux riches. It is a "real" city in my estimation, whereas Riyadh is a new city created over a few recent decades for the purpose of having a capital safely situated in the near center of the country.

Jeddah is historically the oldest city and the ancient center of Arab civilization on the Saudi Peninsula. It was and is a trading port city, connected to Africa by trading vessels crossing the Red Sea, and protected from sand storms because of the sea but still quite humid and more lush in vegetation. It is at the foot of the Al-Sarawat Mountains and near Mecca and Medina. Jeddah is the most cosmopolitan and more liberal city in Saudi Arabia. It is home to King Abdul Aziz International Airport where the Hajj Terminal is located, which is constructed of white fiberglass tent-like material for the roof that maintains a comfortable temperature by carefully channeling the breeze under it.

I worked in Jeddah's airport and helped the certification process that finally entered it as a world-class international airport. In fact I worked on six airports in Saudi of which three were rated as international.

Riyadh is located just a few miles from Dhureia, the old fort from which Ibn El Saud, the founder of Saudi Arabia, declared his new kingdom after he unified all the tribes by an extraordinary strategy of multiple marriages to women of the several principal tribes. Riyadh may be the capital, but it has a long way before it can become as interesting as Jeddah or even Dammam, in the Eastern Province.

Developing the OpsM was fascinating in many ways but foremost because it allowed me to meet many people, several of who were members of the Saudi hierarchy. Colonel Amin, the CEO of Saudi International Airport Projects (IAP), was tasked by the monarchy to build three airports, monuments to the nation and its kings. IAP was charged to build airports in Jeddah, Riyadh, and Dammam — King Fahd International Airport. Because of my interest in art I was also able to meet several Saudi artists, and to see their works, especially Miss Waffa Benzager's superb oil paintings. In a local gallery I had viewed the paintings produced by Waffa, and other artists.

Art for Jeddah's International Airport

On a bright morning when I was obtaining information from the IAP's senior architect Ron Thompson, an American employed directly by the Saudis, I learned that there would be a meeting that afternoon where photographs of the proposed art for the terminals would be shown. The art impresario was a Dr. Alexander on the faculty of the Massachusetts Institute of Technology (MIT). Ron asked if I was interested in viewing this presentation and "you can give us your evaluation," he added. Ron and I had discussed art extensively over tea on several occasions. I liked Ron and found him knowledgeable whenever I called on him for answers to airport questions.

After the traditional tea or coffee and the small talk, Dr. Alexander made his presentation. In attendance were Col. Amin and his deputy, Dr. Waddah Alem, a brilliant systems analyst who was Syrian but educated in the United States; George Hext, Bechtel's MOM manager in Jeddah; John; and several other notables, some Saudi and some non-Saudi.

Dr. Alexander's presentation consisted of a collection from artists from the Middle East, but he omitted from the list the artists from Saudi Arabia. After the presentation was made and the applause subsided, Col. Amin opened the meeting to questions and comments. A few questions were posed asking where some of the art would be placed in the terminals, some asked if art would be placed in office buildings, and one asked if a sculpture would grace the large grassy circle at the entrance of the domestic terminal area.

Col. Amin turned to me and said, "Dr. Double-Name," (as he fondly called me) "wasn't your doctorate in art and aesthetics?" I smiled and acknowledged that it was. The colonel continued, "You have been uncharacteristically silent. Have you any comments or questions?" One should never ask for my comments, because they will be given. Usually, I avoid public pronouncements unless directly put on the spot. "Dr. Raymond you must have a reaction to what has been presented," the colonel persisted.

"Yes Colonel, I have a few questions, if I may?" The colonel motioned with his hand and said in Arabic, "Itfahd-dal," (be my guest). "Dr. Alexander," I posed the question, "You have showed some excellent photographs of art from some extraordinary and reputable artists from the Middle East, especially from Lebanon, Syria, Egypt, and Morocco. These pieces reflect the rich culture of some of the Arab world's most prominent people." Dr. Alexander smiled in agreement. "Why, Dr. Alexander, have we not seen any art from Saudi artists?" I asked.

There was a moment of silence and Colonel Amin followed with, "Is there a reason for that Dr. Alexander?"

Dr. Alexander stood silently for an instant then added, "Appropriate art could not be located in Saudi Arabia."

Turning my attention to the colonel I asked, looking directly at him, "Col. Amin is there a culture in Saudi Arabia?" The question could be interpreted in two ways: as an insult or as a genuine cultural inquiry.

"Of course there is a culture in Saudi Arabia, and one that predates many others in the Middle East."

I looked towards Dr. Alexander and waited for his comment. None came. "If there is a cultured civilization in Saudi Arabia, Colonel, then surely, Dr. Alexander, there is art?" I stopped to inhale a deep breath; "I have seen art from Saudi artists." I paused to make certain that was heard. "I have seen art pieces that are superb, and many that have received awards when exhibited in Rome, Milan, London, New York, Paris, and even in Moscow. In fact, I have seen such works in Jeddah. I have seen Miss Waffa Benzager's superb oil paintings, exhibited here in Jeddah at the Queen's Gallery. I have seen Mansur Ashram's oils in the University Gallery. I have seen many more. There is a fine artist, Ahmed Sabram, whose works are on display in Mecca — of which I have seen only one currently hanging in the home of the mayor of Jeddah, Prince Jamal El Jahbbi. Others of Sabram I have viewed only as photographs because, being non-Muslim, I cannot go to his studio in Mecca."

There was a rumble of conversation in the room and the noise covered Thompson's approach to me. Thompson came over to me and shook his head, and said, "I brought Alexander on the job."

I looked at him. "Sorry, John, but I am puzzled by his comments and by his choices."

"He may resign and then we'll have no one to select art for the airport." He stared at me with a look of disgust and added, "you are causing trouble and I'm sorry that I invited you."

He walked away leaving me standing to face George Hext. George looked at me then shook his head, "You didn't have to meddle in this presentation."

I responded, "But George, I was asked a direct question by the client."

Hext was livid and his eyes showed it, "So you could have replied that you had no questions." He turned and left me.

Colonel Amin was speaking with Dr. Alexander and I could hear him thanking him for his presentation but said that he wanted to review the pictures with his staff, and devote a little more time thinking about the selection and where to place art in the airport, since it was a memorial to the beloved King Abdul Aziz. He concluded the meeting then said something to Dr. Waddah Alem who then walked over to me and asked me to come to the colonel's office immediately. George Hext came to me again and said that I had opened a can of worms that did not bode well for me or for MOM. Then he added, "After your meeting with the colonel come see me." I thought of Jim Pike at the moment because I felt that like him, I too had stepped on a forbidden and imaginary boundary line.

I went to Colonel Amin's spacious and well-appointed office. "Raymond. May I call you Raymond? It is easier for me if it is OK with you." Of course it was and I assured him of it.

"Raymond, I know Miss Benzager but I had forgotten that she is an artist. How do you know her?"

"I don't," I replied. "I know her work from what I have seen exhibited at the Queen's Gallery."

"Hmmm, are there many artists in Saudi? You know Wahhabism Islam frowns upon some forms of art?"

"I'm aware of that Colonel, and I suspect that Miss Benzager and the other artists are also as aware as you are, since they are all followers of Abd al-Wahhab's form of Islam." I continued, "Islam in general and especially Wahhabism Sunnis prefer geometrical drawings but that does not mean that other forms cannot be accepted as long as they do not denigrate the fundamental theological premises of the religion." I wasn't here to lecture.

"So you approve of the Saudi art that you have seen so far," he asked me.

"Colonel, I approve of some and disapprove of others. Art to me is neither good nor bad — bad art is not art. Yet, there is some art that I prefer more than others. There are some colors that I prefer more than others, yet I don't shut out of my life those that I consider less appealing."

"Why did you particularly ask if there was culture in Arabia?" Amin asked.

"Colonel Amin, art is a form through which one can critique civilization. Without civilization there would be no critique of the cultural quality of a people, in this case the Arabs of Saudi Arabia. In fact there would be no art."

I paused long enough for Amin to digest my comment then added, "The artist is the critic of his culture, of his society, of his civilization, of his times. That's why the first act of a dictatorship is to restrain artists, artists who produce all forms of art."

He got up from his chair and approached me. "I would like to see Miss Benzager's works. Can you show them to me...say tonight?" the colonel asked me, but it sounded more like an order.

"Of course, sir," I replied.

"Good, then I will fetch you at Bechtel House after evening prayer, which will be approximately seven o'clock." He ended the conversation by patting me on the shoulder.

Arriving in my office after my meeting with Amin, there was a note from George Hext telling me that he would try to quash any difficulty I might have with the colonel and with Bob Polvi, Bechtel's project manager. No problem had or would develop I was certain. Instead of going to his office, I called Hext and assured him that all was well and that I was going out with the colonel in the evening.

"I believe that I should go with you," Hext said.

There was a pause before I added, "Best you check with the colonel if you think that's necessary."

That evening the Colonel arrived and there was no Hext. I accompanied the colonel to the Queen's Gallery. He liked what he saw. When he dropped me at the Bechtel House (known as the Somali Hilton) he asked me to have lunch with him the next day in his office dining room.

The next day at noon, as I was walking to the colonel's office, Hext accosted me and said, "Let's go have a bite to eat and chat about yesterday's event."

"I can't, George, because I'm having lunch with Colonel Amin and I'm on my way there."

Hext looked at me and quietly uttered, "You are, are you?"

I had lunch with Colonel Amin and we discussed Saudi art and Saudi artists. I suggested that we call on Keith Hutchinson, a Parson's employee who knew a lot about the artist scene in Jeddah. After lunch was over, Colonel Amin asked me if I could continue to work with him to find and select Saudi art. He made arrangements for us to meet with Waffa Benzager, Mansur Ashram, Ahmed Sabram, and others.

A few days later a package was brought to my office with a typed note asking me to wear this garment and be ready to be picked up at Bechtel House Saturday morning at nine o'clock. The package contained a white thobe and the traditional head scarf, the red and white ghutra.

When the colonel arrived he checked me over and instructed me not to speak at security checkpoints. "You are deaf and mute," he instructed me.

He took me to Mecca for which I wore the white thobe and the accompanying headscarf. For the checkpoint located at the entrance of Mecca, Colonel Amin reminded me to act like a deaf and dumb Saudi in the event that I was questioned, which was unlikely since the Cadillac we rode in had royal flags on each fender, and we had an escort car in front of and behind our car. I wish that I had been able to take a few photographs but that surely would have landed me in prison.

Mecca, as a city, was not that impressive. But that it had history of paramount interest to Islam made it fascinating and captivating. I shall remember the feeling I had when I entered this community, forbidden to non-Muslims. It was truly a forbidden city for the likes of me, and if caught in it, I would have been immediately thrown out of the country if not beheaded. That Colonel Amin was with me gave me some protection but my inner sense of security was quite thin. I mentioned my anxiety to Colonel Amin but he assured me that I would become a martyr for Bechtel or better, seek conversion to Islam, which was not too bad of a choice after all. We drove by the execution post and it was very near the mosque, so my choice was quite clear. Amin smiled as only he could, showing bright eyes and reflecting a look of naughtiness. He patted my hand and said, "Don't worry, I'm the one in trouble because I can be accused of a great infraction against my religion." He smiled and looked like a Cheshire cat swallowing a parakeet. "Take a good look at the Kaaba, the stone of Abraham." I did with my non-Muslim eyes. "You'll have good fortune from Allah, the Beneficent!"

When we arrived at the artist's house, I was immediately introduced with my genuine identity. Colonel Amin looked at me and assured me that Sheik Ahmed Sabram had already been informed by telephone and he would not betray me. Sabram offered us lunch and sweet tea, and that he spoke English made it all the more pleasant to meet with him and to see the oils of his wild horses caught in whirlwinds. His colors were deep and rich, and his brush strokes were definite and clearly executed. Colonel Amin bought six paintings on the spot and commissioned two more. Those assigned to the international terminal for display would represent the artist's personal choice. I discovered on another occasion and several months later that one of the paintings chosen had been for Colonel Amin's personal house. Had I known that this would be permissible, I would have loved to purchase the one with the horses. Maybe I'll have the opportunity sometime to do just that.

We left Mecca and returned to Jeddah. We stopped at Bechtel House. "Raymond go change your clothes and come, we can go to dinner at my favorite Egyptian restaurant."

During the course of several days and weeks, Colonel Amin also purchased many paintings from both Waffa Benzager and from Mansur Ashram. He bought other paintings from other Saudi artists and some complementary paintings through Dr. Alexander's collection of Middle Eastern works. Several sculptures were purchased with the help of the mayor of Jeddah, Jamal El Jahbbi, who was an architect by training but a sculptor by avocation, and a good one at that. The mayor had acquired several large sculptures for the traffic roundabouts of Jeddah. El Jahbbi, a member of the royal family, donated two marble sculptures, which he himself had done, to be placed at the international terminal and at the Hajj terminal.

From Mohamed Sayire, a Dammam artist, two steel sculptures were acquired and one was commissioned for the grassy knoll in front of the domestic terminal. The selection of art for Jeddah moved rapidly under the direct leadership of the colonel. Dr. Alexander soon dropped out of the picture. I suspected that several local Saudi artists who volunteered their services, and the mayor of Jeddah, who was quite knowledgeable about art and who was, as I said, an artist, replaced him. The mayor was a close friend of the renowned English sculptor Henry Moore, from whom he had commissioned two wonderful pieces that were placed on very tall pedestals in the center of traffic circles in Jeddah.

Jeddah was in many ways the most cosmopolitan city of Saudi Arabia; it was the coastal city with the greatest appeal, beauty, and panorama. Situated on the Red Sea, it lay at the foot of the coastal chain of mountains that included the summer capital of Taif, and stretched south to Yemen passing through the old historical and Biblical site of the town of Abhor with an elevation of 3,100 feet. Abhor still possesses the remnant of an old Hebrew settlement that is fairly well maintained by the Saudi government, a feat that is understood only if one understands that for the Saudis, Jews are people of the Book, whereas Israelis are considered Zionists and hence, intruders.

But back to Jeddah and the good mayor of this, my favorite city of Saudi. Because the mayor had collected a good number of large sculptures for his city that reflected the creative talents of local artists, I was especially interested in photographing them for posterity. Taking photographs of anything in Saudi was tantamount to spying and immediately alerted the police. It was always a sneaking game to avoid the wrath of the police or irate and zealous citizens. I asked the mayor if I would be permitted to photograph the sculptures and would a letter from him keep me out of the grasp of the police. A letter would help, but better would be an escort of police to "protect" me. So, a few days later, with an escort of four policemen and an official police automobile, I went from sculpture to sculpture taking photographs.

Two sculptures in traffic circle

No one interfered. No one questioned me. No one approached me. Many on-lookers looked at me with some sense of interest. I guess that most of the people looking at me thought that I was on a special assignment for the government. It was fun being treated as a VIP. Today copies of the photographs are hanging on my living room wall.

Certification Process

I want to pick up the story of the certification process and how I became in-volved in it and my own specific assignment in Jeddah. I was not assigned by Bechtel to select art for the airport; my assignment was the preparation of the required Airport Operations Manual (OpsM), and walking the Saudis through the airport certification process to final approval by the relevant authorities. First of all the expected Monday arrival of the review team from ICAO, FAA, and IALPA was postponed for two weeks. During the postponement, work contin-ued as was indicated by the various events that took place. I was busy but I was also able to play and do things that interested me.

Two days before the review meeting both Hext and Moreno came into my office accompanied by Dr. Alem, Colonel Amin's right-hand man. The purpose of their visit was to inform me that I was to chair the review meeting with ICAO, FAA, and IALPA. Because I had prepared the OpsM, it was my task to defend it.

"Defend it?" I shouted. "It occurs to me that you guys have reviewed the OpsM, and you also have given me all compiled data used in the document. So, you guys defend it. It is your job and that's what you're paid for."

"Raymond," Dr. Alem said in a quiet voice, "These guys know very little about the process and you've been close to the data. You know more about the OpsM, and the regulations that apply to it, than any one of us."

I thought that this was a trap that I could not avoid. "I must consult with Plymate and Polvi before I accept that task," I stated.

"They have been consulted and they have agreed that you have do it," Alem assured me.

"Yes, Raymond," added Hext, "I telephoned Glenn and he agrees that you have to do it."

"But George, you're the AAAE (American Association of Airport Executives) professional and airport director, you should be the one and certainly you are more knowledgeable and qualified than I?" That didn't go anywhere. That's how I became involved in OpsM reviews and certifications. When I called Plymate that night, he said to me, "Do you want Barry Craig to chair the meeting?" That would have been a disaster for all concerned.

The reviewers met on Monday at the appointed time. My first act as chair was to place my small tape recorder on the conference table. I've always found that a tape recorder reduces and even eliminates unnecessary talking and forces people to be succinct. The meeting with IACO, FAA, and IALPA turned out to be a piece of cake because all the data were correct and relevant to the regulations established by the entities. After going through the OpsM section by section, at lunchtime the reviewers were satisfied. The representative from PCA produced the signature documents and each reviewer signed the multiple documents. That was that. King Abdul Aziz International Airport was certificated. In fact, I was also involved in the certification of the new airport for Riyadh and

Jubail, and participated in the certification of the new airport in Dammam, and Al Jawf, in the Northern Province for Arabian American Company (ARAMCO).

When I left Jeddah after completing my work and delivering copies of the OpsM with the signed certification documents to Col. Amin who had been promoted to General, I was given a limited edition picture book of the royal family. General Amin had signed it and written gracious and complimentary words about my services to the airport.

My particular relationship with General Amin, IAP, ARAMCO, or the Saudi Government did not end with Jeddah. After thirteen trips to Saudi Arabia, all of which dealt with airport and aviation issues, I developed a friendly bond with the Saudis.

Archeology and Early Human Creativity

There is a non-airport side to my several visits to Jeddah, apart from giving my assistance for the selection of art. It was my custom to mix work and play whenever I traveled on assignment. Moreover, I defined work not as drudgery, but as a way for further enjoyment, learning, and exploration. Thus between the assignments to produce the Jeddah Operations Manual, I had received authorization from the President of France, Valéry Giscard d'Estaing, to visit the Grotto of Lascaux, in Montignac — a small town in the Dordogne region of France.

My interest in the paintings depicted in the grottos of France was mostly because I was doubtful that what was called "cave art" was in reality art at all. I had seen photographs of the paintings, read the adulations given by many archeologists, art historians, and cultural anthropologists, but I was not convinced that what was on the walls was art; graffiti perhaps, but certainly not art. I could not rely on their artistic authenticity just by viewing photographs and reading commentaries by scholars; even scholars have their prejudices. In fairness to the issue and to satisfy my curiosity, I had applied for authorization to see Lascaux, the principal and most important of all the grottos, and the one not open to the general public.

In December 1981 I traveled to France with Emily McCormick, who was recognized by the French authorities as "ma adjointe," my adjunct for the visit and subsequent study of the grotto. Only Lascaux required special permission, but I had selected four other grottos for comparison. Lascaux was the second on my list, Rouffignac was first and Niaux, near the Pyrenees mountains, the last. There was also the little grotto of La Mouth owned and operated by a private individual who kept onions and potatoes in its dark entryway. After a few days spent in Solignac, near Limousin, to shake off the jetlag from the flight, we proceeded to the Dordogne Department for our first stop to see the grotto of Rouffignac.

We were taken inside the grotto by way of a homemade electric train that had bench seats for six. There was another couple visiting the grotto with us and the host who owned the property had built the little train, and was a professor of history at Bordeaux University. We rode the train and were informed that we were going to travel approximately one kilometer inside the grotto before encountering any significant paintings. On and on we went.

After viewing several scratches on the grotto's walls, looking at bear lairs, and a collection of head etchings of individual animals I was becoming impatient. After a while, a long while, we turned a corner and there before us was a drawing in black lines of two herds of mammoths moving through each other. It was a phenomenal drawing. It took my breath. It was dynamic, simply executed with light and shadow correctly added, and with a clear understanding of perspective, relationship, and depth. I was struck dumb by the splendor. What I was seeing was unquestionably a work of art simply drawn. I saw a few other memorable drawings but the mammoths were unique in their splendor, quality, and coherency.

Returning to the sun outside and into the cold December wind, I was silent, amazed, and impressed. My brain was racing and reflecting on ideas, theories, and searching for a variety of answers. Here, right in front of my eyes, I saw well-executed art, art of early human beings dating from thousands of years ago. At this moment I was fully engaged inside my mind, until interrupted. Emily handed me a piece of chocolate to revive me. "Are you OK?" she asked. I was indeed very surprised that my previous doubts about the art inside the grottos had been voided in one fell swoop by the image of the two herds of mammoths.

I spent the remainder of the day ruminating on what I had viewed. It was shockingly fantastic.

The next day we went to see the grotto of Lascaux. Our special appointment was for eleven o'clock on the morning of 8 December. We were to arrive no later than 10:45 for an appropriate briefing by the guide. When we arrived, the guide met us with his dog, Loof, a handsome Alsatian, holding a cluster of keys in its mouth. After identifying ourselves, we learned that another couple was to join us. We were instructed that the visit inside the grotto would last 35 minutes and no more!

The guide paced back and forth in the waiting area and it was obvious that his temper was reaching a dangerous level. The second couple arrived at 11:15; hence they were thirty minutes late. The guide was furious and even chastised them in a loud voice. We proceeded to the door leading to the grotto. At the door the guide instructed us to step into a small metal receptacle to disinfect the soles of our shoes. Once the disinfecting of the shoes was accomplished, the guide opened the steel door to steps that led down into the pitch-black grotto. I switched my flashlight on. The guide reached and took it away from me saying, "C'est moi the guide." (I am the guide.) It was dark. He kept us just inside for a few minutes to allow our eyes to get accustomed to the blackness, then he switched on a pencil-type flashlight and showed us the way down the steps.

Once inside the first level of the grotto, the guide switched on a stronger flashlight and turned on the small internal lights of the grotto. The internal lights were emitting a very weak glow that was sufficient to allow us to see where we placed our feet. In the yellowish glow what I perceived was unbelievably beautiful and way beyond anything I had anticipated. No photographs could match the beauty, the splendor, the grandeur, resplendence, or the magnificence in front of me.

It was absolutely brilliant. The colors seized me. I was so moved that tears filled my eyes and I nearly lost my breath. The guide noticed my reaction and the look on my face. I was stunned. The guide approached me and expressed his thought to me, "Comme une cathédrale qui vous pique vos émotions."(Like a cathedral that touches your emotions.) Indeed my emotions were touched to the quick. The guide then took us step-by-step, painting-by-painting, and mural-by-mural and explained what we were seeing. When the 35 minutes were spent we headed towards the exit where Loof again met us and escorted us to the gate of the property. Once we were off the property, the iron gate was closed and locked. Very few words were exchanged. I headed towards a small restaurant perched on a nearby hill, overlooking the domain of the grotto, and ahead there was a valley where Charolais white cattle were feeding on rich green grass.

I was ready for lunch and a glass or two of Dordogne wine. I cannot remember what we ordered but it was good. My brain was engaged in reviewing what had been imprinted on it, first with what I had seen in Rouffignac and then what had enveloped me in Lascaux. The amazing colors, the perspective, the harmony of how each painting offered support to the one next to it; I had been in a gallery where fine art had been displayed. After a while the conversation began to surface and both Emily and I asked each other questions. Why? When? To whom? Neither one of us could offer answers. It had been an amazing morning and an amazing two days. Our next stop was further south to the Pyrenees.

Lascaux has art dating back to the Magdalenian period of France during the Upper Paleolithic culture characterized by flint, bone, and ivory implements, carvings, and paintings. Lascaux incorporates the 25th to 20th centuries BCE; in some still not fully examined areas art has been identified as even older. Unequivocally, Lascaux is very much a collection of many paintings that can be gathered as one extraordinary work of art. Because it was a non-habitation grotto, not much carbon residue can be found in it, except for the soot left by tallow lamps of artists. The painters who worked on the walls and ceilings of the Lascaux grotto employed only four pigments, and none of the pigments contained any carbon — which made it difficult to learn anything from Carbon 14 tests for dating.

The art was created at the quite early age of the Cro-Magnon period — 40 to 15 thousand years ago. Most of the art of Lascaux has been painted within a five or six century period, and the intriguing factor is that no succeeding painter impinged on the art done by the preceding painter; a line or two may be borrowed or incorporated, but the original is never defaced. With four colors, mixed exquisitely to produce the polychromatic tableau before our eyes, we realized that the painter's creativity was technically advanced and that s/he used the four-

color separation process that printers have employed for years for modern printing, before the advent of the computer changed that process. We also realize that
long before the techniques of the painters of the North Italian School during the
Renaissance surfaced, the painters of Lascaux employed the technical trick of
applying some white to show depth in a light and shadow scene. Moreover,
again long before the Renaissance, we find that the painters of Lascaux were
able to blow through bent straws and developed the style of the contemporary
airbrush.

These are but a few examples of the quality and originality inherent in the
art of Lascaux, and I have yet to come across anything that offered a more superb sense of perspective, proportions, and harmony. The painters of Lascaux
indicated that they knew much about composition, contrast, and effect. The
paintings I have seen were impressively laid out for a viewer to appreciate. S/he
who painted knew that it took three units to make a work of art: the creator, the
artifact (tableau), and the viewer. Each unit is carefully played against the other
to offer an amazing and breathtaking result.

Lascaux is situated on a hillside near the village of Montignac, in the De-
partement de la Dordogne, southwest France. On 12 September 1940 Jacques
Marsal, age 15, and three other teenage boys discovered the grotto as they were
playing in the woods. The area is full of caves and the boys suspected, because
of the common depressions in the terrain, that a cave existed in the area where
they were playing. Soon a visible crevice in the soil suggested that the entrance
of a cave might exist. Jacques, after he and the boys removed much of the topsoil, slipped through what looked like an opening to the subsurface. Because it
was dark and the boys were prepared for a cave discovery, they had brought
with them a "stillo torche," a pencil flashlight. Jacques slid into the cave (later
called grotto because wine is kept in caves and grottos are large subsurface
openings) and with one sweep of his flashlight was mesmerized by the beauty.
The other boys soon followed to look at their discovery. They were all impressed but none more than Jacques Marsal.

In the years that unfolded, Jacques devoted his entire life to the grotto of
Lascaux, and was rewarded by three French presidents with three orders of
Knighthood (Chevalier). Through years of research and beyond archeologists,

paleontologists, art historians, and anthropologists, Jacques Marsal was the undisputed authority on Lascaux and on the art of early homo sapiens, even the art found in other grottos. Not only was he the keeper of Lascaux and its unquestionable authority because he was a disciplined student of its art, its history, and its phenomenon, but he was also a consultant to other grottos, grottos as far south as Niaux, in the French Pyrenees, and Alta Mira, Spain.

French Pyrenees Mountains

We then drove south towards Niaux and to our lodging at the Hotel du Lac in Foix. Arriving in the early evening, we found the hotel owner and his staff to be charming, warm, and hospitable. Our room was on the third floor and was quite comfortable. The bed and mattress, however, were sagging, but acceptable if one did not mind sliding to the middle. The restaurant in the hotel had a fine chef; the food was quite good, and the service attentive. The owner was a friendly host who shared with us some of the history of the region and aspects of this southern portion of France, which is still influenced by its Spanish neighbor across the Pyrenees.

The next morning we went to the gate of the grotto of Niaux to meet our guide, Mr. Jean-Luc Archambeaux. Arriving promptly at eleven o'clock, he gave us a brief talk and we followed him inside. After walking without encountering any paintings for nearly a kilometer, we finally encountered our first painting. It was a beautiful piece that was unequivocally art. Yet much as it was superb in every detail, it did not approach the splendor of Lascaux.

After our viewing, which lasted nearly three hours, the guide shared some of the history of this particular grotto, and of the grotto located three kilometers to the north. During WWII, the Germans had used the adjacent grotto to assemble fighter aircraft because it was safely protected from allied bombings. Fortunately, the grotto of Niaux had not been discovered by the Germans, hence it survived unscathed.

Just before we said adieu to our guide Jean-Luc, we mentioned in the course of our conversation that we had seen Lascaux the day before. "Oh, vous avez rencontré le Chevalier Jacques Marsal, le découvreur de la grotte de Lascaux?"

(Oh, you have met the Knight Jacques Marsal, the discoverer of the grotto of Lascaux?)

I was taken back, surprised, and embarrassed that I had not recognized the discoverer. That was impossible I thought; nothing in his behavior or introduction had indicated that he was "the" Jacques Marsal who had discovered the grotto in 1940. Indeed, our guide at Niaux affirmed that Marsal does not permit anyone else to act as a guide for "his" grotto. Marsal was the person who had been Jean-Luc's mentor and he was also the most respected person among the grotto guide fraternity.

Back at the hotel, we searched all the literature we had brought with us and sure enough we discovered that indeed, Jacques Marsal had been our guide at Lascaux. In one of the historical articles, Jacques Marsal's photograph was shown as he pointed to the entrance of the grotto; at his side was faithful Loof, the Alsatian dog.

Emily and I were stunned by this discovery. We had met the great man without knowing it. I suggested that we invite Jacques Marsal to America for several presentations under the sponsorship of Anthropos Theophoros (AT), our educational and artistic non-profit corporation.

The hotel owner, when told what we wanted to do and whom it was that we wanted to contact helped us locate a Mme. Jacqueline Marsal's telephone number in Sarlat, Dordogne. I immediately telephoned her and learned that she was Jacques's sister-in-law and was happy to give me his telephone numbers, at the office and at his home. I telephoned him immediately and reached him. After explaining who I was and informing him that I wanted to discuss an offer for him to travel to San Francisco, we made an appointment to meet two days hence at the grotto of Lascaux. Marsal was friendly and engaging over the telephone. I didn't quite believe that Marsal thought that I was offering him a serious invitation.

We met Jacques Marsal at the appointed hour. Loof, the Alsatian dog, was there to greet us, and Emily, who does not speak French, found that she could enjoy this magnificent Alsatian while Marsal and I talked. Loof was well trained and there was no question as to whose dog he was. He carried the key to the office in his mouth as he usually did. Jacques took us to his private office where

I made my offer for a lecture tour in the San Francisco Bay area. Jacques told me that he could only come in February because the climate control for the grotto did not need much attention during that month, and also that his nephew Jean-Claude Pinheiro, a train engineer, could cover for him, if necessary, during his absence. It was agreed. He was delighted because he always had hoped to see America. This would be an opportunity that he would not want to miss. Yes, he would do it gladly.

After some additional small talk and an invitation to revisit the grotto, this time for a longer period, we returned to his office. I assured Emily that Jacques had accepted our offer. I conveyed to her that we would be his hosts in California and he would be staying at my house in Montara. I was hoping that Emily Oppegard, who was fluent in French, would be willing to be his guide when I was at Bechtel. I was also hoping that Emily O, as she was called, could find two or three weeks to come to California as she lived in Massachusetts.

As we chatted in the narthex to the grotto and because we were on our way to Paris, I casually mentioned our travel plans to Jacques Marsal and that we had read in the papers that there would be an exhibition of a facsimile of Lascaux at the Grand Palais. His temper flared. He began to wave his hands to punctuate his angry explosive speech. "It was a miserable, awful, and treacherous move by the government," he accused. "Lascaux could not be duplicated, especially by a modern painter who did not understand the ancient processes and the critical techniques employed by the artists of twenty thousand years ago!" He continued to speak in a heated voice. He was red in the face, his breathing was rapid, and his voice was beyond the level of shouting.

I tried to interrupt his anger by saying as clearly as I could that I would not go to see the facsimile in Paris. After several moments and after hearing me, he stopped and his anger subsided. I had said nothing untoward during this explosion and had uttered not a word except to assure him that I would not visit the Grand Palais. Finally he became calmer and quieter. We shook hands and added a hug to punctuate departure with a commitment of friendliness. He affirmed that he would love to go to America and make as many presentations as I could schedule. He would show slides that the public had never seen. As I turned to leave, Marsal asked that I not see the facsimile. I promised that I would not and never would. He hugged me again and kissed me three times in the traditional French custom.

We walked out of the office and out of the gate. Emily and I were both silent. Then Emily broke the silence by asking me why M. Marsal had been so angry with me. What was it that I had said? I explained to Emily that he was merely reacting to the proposed exhibition of the facsimile at the Grand Palais and that Jacques was very angry by what had been done. What was being displayed in Paris was to be placed in a dug-out simulated "grotto" some 500 meters below the current real grotto. No, M. Marsal was not angry with me. We were still on friendly terms. Emily was relieved. Now the issue was how we would raise the funds and make the arrangements for his visit to California. I would tackle those issues when I returned to San Francisco, which would not be until sometime in March 1981. I was on my way to Jeddah, Saudi Arabia, two days after Christmas Day.

A Few Miscellaneous Thoughts

"Comme une cathédrale qui vous pique vos émotions."(Like a cathedral that touches your emotions.) That was what Marsal has said to me and the comment just rattled in my brain. Entering the grotto and seeing the art that early human beings had given us was exciting and troubling.

The exciting part was easy to consider because it was art and merely required that I absorb it as any aspect of creativity. As for any painting I usually examined the technique used by the artist. I then considered the colors, the perspective, the idea, the general layout of the subject, etc. Was the work dynamic or static; in other words, would one continue to see things revealed or would it be exhausted immediately — after one has seen one stop sign one has seen them all. The paintings in the grotto of Lascaux were dynamic, and since my first visit I've always found that I could discern more and more and more details revealed in them. No. They were not like stop signs.

After an interruption by the flight attendant serving me a sherry refill I thought about how the art in the grotto affected me. I was troubled because I didn't know how to manage the issue of the spiritual effect that being in the grotto had on me. The place, the grotto, linked me to my ancestors. These were ancestors that were not really related specifically to me but were part of the long link that connected me to them. They had lived and walked on this planet, breathed the same air, eaten comparable food, and even had had similar thoughts about who they were, how they related to the environment, to the planet, to the forces around them, to their friends, enemies, loves, children, pets, and to the larger concepts that affected them. Did they also "worry" about birth, life, and death? Did they think about pain, happiness, and failure? I wonder if they gave a moment's thought to what would happen to them when they died, when their friends died, and when their beloved died. What of the great questions about who they were and how they managed with the great questions they may have been afraid to ask: What was the point of life and how could they learn about it? How did they relate to each other, to their male and female companions, to those who were jealous or interested in them? Were they couples or teams because the clan or tribe saw to it to preclude trouble? When, if ever, did the attitude of life-long union between males and females emerge?

These were questions that surfaced, not once, but many times in the course of my understanding of what I had seen in the grottos.

I was pretty certain that the kernel of religion was planted in their culture or tribe just about the time some of the great questions were asked. I was also certain that nothing dogmatic was implanted in the conscience. There was no authority that guided them to "correct" thinking. That came later and I knew how valueless that turned out to be. Religion, I was convinced, was just a cloak for in-depth thinking. It was a bypass forcing a person to avoid serious thinking about the ideas that mattered.

Here I was, a churchman, a priest in the Church, and an active scholar who had worked to improve the Episcopal Book of Common Prayer (BCP), and I was dispensing with religion without a backward look. The BCP was a guiding element in how I expressed myself, it was not the sum total of what I considered vital in my relationship with the forces beyond me; ergo, God, Creation, Universe, Life, Death, Love, and the grains of thoughts that make me who I am and connect me to what I consider to be "reality." It was not doctrine, authority, religion, ecclesiastic supervision or fear that I would be an outsider if I did not participate in the affairs of the team, the tribe, the sect, the denomination, and the Church. For me these religious parts were mere tools that I used to build the scaffold that allowed me to think about the larger ideas, ideas that I was constantly defining, refining, and fine-tuning.

There is no conclusion available quite yet. I have courted Christianity, Judaism, Islam, Buddhism, Humanism, Scientism, and some that need not be mentioned because of their futile effect. None of these religious approaches were useful. I am still searching for a conclusion but I suspect that like many aspects of contemporary physics, empiricism through lab experimentation is not possible and will not be.

No, the conclusion will remain elusive for a while longer — if not forever!

Jeddah: The City on the Red Sea

Because my work on the airport, the OpsM, and certification was practically completed, my time was spent putting together an operational plan with Jim Ellingsworth. We checked the runway lights, the taxiway lights and signage, and the routes that the passenger buses to and from the aircraft would follow. Enjoying a bit of fun, we tested the public address system, the aircraft control radios, and the internal telephone connections. In addition, we devised at my insistence a plan for having the runway and taxiways inspected four times a day to check the pavements, remove fallen objects from aircraft (you'd be surprised how junk falls off aircraft; remember the Continental Airlines decorative metal strip that punctured the fuel tank of the departing Air France Concorde at Charles De Gaulle Airport?), and ensure that the surface conditions had the correct friction coefficient so that aircraft could stop safely. Moreover, we established a training program for the operational staff that would eventually be responsible for the tasks we had laid out.

Working on the Saudi airports was like working in a class with elementary children who were asked to act like teachers and principals for a day. The expatriates who came from several airports in the west performed most of the work. There were none or very few experienced Saudi airport operators. For westerners, Saudi airports were tantamount to sand boxes used for playing a game with miniature equipment like Tonka Toys or as a challenge to see who could create an aviation aerodrome that could be considered a national monument for this or that monarch. Initially terminals had prominent overhangs, towers with balconies, or internal gardens that, as one did in Riyadh, produced unexpected rain. The terminal enclosed garden in Riyadh became a self-contained biosphere that produced its own weather. Saudi airports were monuments for the monarchy that incidentally serviced aircraft, passengers, and cargo. Every king had to have an airport named for him and the larger the airport the more historical fame he accrued.

All of the equipment employed on these airports was of high quality and very expensive. The Saudis wanted the latest technical leading-edge stuff. But leading technical equipment often was not suited for the wind-blown sand that penetrated the tightest crack in window frames, locking devices, lighting controls, and a myriad of other necessary fixtures. Installed locking devices with card readers soon had to be replaced with locks and chains! In addition, installation of these devices required skilled crews, but most of the imported workers were from countries that could only offer unskilled laborers.

Working in other countries and with other cultures may reveal that what is standard may not be recognized as such. Of course the beauty of working in foreign lands is that one's education is expanded in areas that were never anticipated. I was confronted with this unexpected issue several times, especially in Saudi and in China. The following is one example where directions from one culture to another failed with an expensive but amusing loss to the Saudi client.

Runway center light bulbs are of high intensity and must be handled with care and with white silk or cotton gloves. These high intensity light bulbs must not be touched with bare fingers when they are installed because the skin oil emitted by human fingers will cause the glass of the bulbs to explode due to the intense heat generated when full electrical power is passed through them. We had instructed all involved — the maintenance chiefs and the installing crew of Pakistani workers, their supervisors, and the control tower operators who were still in training — that the lights should not be touched with bare fingers when they were installed, in the hope that the lights would be ready and working brightly when the airport was made operational and received its first aircraft in a few days, which was expected to be the King's personal Boeing 747.

One evening, a few days before the airport was to have a full operational readiness inspection (ORI), Ellingsworth joined me in the control tower for several tests, some of which included the standby generators supplying the electrical power to the navigational aids (NAVAIDs). Because it was imperative that NAVAIDs never remained without power for more than five seconds, it was the custom to operate all NAVAIDs on batteries, and to have commercial electrical power or standby power constantly charge the batteries. With this procedure, NAVAIDs were never without power.

Every piece of equipment was testing well as switches were turned on or off to examine the systems. It was now dark outside and I decided that the runway lights needed to be tested. Ellingsworth stood at my side. I flipped on the light control switch and then turned the rheostat slowly to 75% power. Flash! Wham! It was a sight to behold. As the power reached the runway lights, one by one they exploded! In less than 10 seconds, $40,000 worth of new light bulbs had been destroyed. I was stunned, as was Ellingsworth and the IAP representatives. Ellingsworth immediately knew the cause and in a low voice said, "No gloves." The installation of the light bulbs had obviously been done without the use of white cotton gloves. This was unbelievably ludicrous. Even though we had instructed the supervisors and the workers, showed them the correct procedure for inserting a bulb with a gloved hand, and had given them several boxes of white gloves, they had, nevertheless, omitted the gloves — because it was, we learned later, unbecoming for working men to wear white gloves! The supervisors had instructed their men but none of the men had taken the instruction seriously. Would they the next time? Yes, they would because Ellingsworth and I stood by the workers the next day as each man inserted new bulbs with gloved hands into the light receptacle.

With the general operations plan in place, the airport systems tested, the air operational surfaces confirmed to be in good order, and the maintenance crews trained, all that remained was an emergency fire drill. I posed the following question: Suppose a Boeing 747 performed a hard landing, the gear collapsed and a fire started in the undercarriage? Such an occurrence would be identified as a definite Category 9 incident. Then my subsequent question was: Where was the nearest gear equipment warehoused to raise and subsequently move a B-747?

Strategically the special equipment used for the lifting gear equipment (LGE) to raise a wide-bodied aircraft is stored in various locations of the world; this gear is usually no further than six flying hours away. After a few telephone calls to the FAA, I learned that the closest LGE was stored in Tel Aviv, one hour from Jeddah, but that particular gear could not be used by the Saudis because it was located in Israel. The next nearest warehoused LGE was located in Frankfurt, which was six hours from Jeddah. To overcome the diplomatic issue, I suggested that ICAO propose a reasonable solution that would permit the Saudi government to use the Tel Aviv gear, but that proved to be impossible. Another solution was that the Saudis purchase their own LGE at a cost of 30 million dollars. The Saudi government rejected the ICAO solution and instead purchased its own LGE. I came to find this to be not a bad solution because it meant then that all the neighboring Islamic nations that opposed the existence of Israel could have access to the gear.

The next issue to be resolved was the fire emergency. Remember that the B-747 that was supposed to have crashed had caught fire. The IAP had purchased six large fire trucks for the airport, three of which were designed to contain enough fire-foam for one B-747. I called for the fire trucks to respond to the simulated emergency and Ellingsworth was clocking their arrival and set up time. When they arrived, Ellingsworth chastised them for being way too slow in the response. We tried it again and again until the time was acceptable to extinguish a Category 9 aircraft fire. After congratulating the drivers and the crews for an exercise successfully completed and calling off the emergency, Ellingsworth climbed into his car and invited me to follow him to his house for dinner.

As I was about to depart the airport apron, two fire trucks were racing past us towards the exit gate. We assumed that they were blowing off some steam but they were driving the vehicles way too fast. When the trucks reached the exit gate it was necessary for them to make a left turn. In the turn, one of the trucks skidded and soon tipped over, landing on its side. The other truck managed to brake to a stop and avoided turning over. We drove to the location to see if the driver and the crew of the overturned truck needed assistance in extricating themselves from the vehicle and if they needed medical help. All members of the crew were safely off the truck, but the vehicle was a total mess, a huge piece of junk. "There goes 250,000 dollars," murmured Ellingsworth to me.

We went over to the driver who was being hit over and over again by his crew chief. We stopped the punishment by commanding in a loud voice that we do not hit people who have accidents. After speaking with the driver and bringing some calm to the situation, we learned that when the driver steered the truck to the left, he felt that something was pulling the truck to the right. "How fast were you driving?" I asked him. The driver was Jordanian but had the required knowledge of English.

"About 80 kilometers, sir," he replied. Jim and I looked at each other because we both knew that the internal baffles built inside the truck's tanks to prevent the liquid from sloshing around were only effective for a maximum speed of 50 kilometers per hour. What had occurred was that the driver had steered the truck to the left but the momentum of the liquid had continued straight ahead, or to right from the axis of travel. The weight of the liquid had propelled the vehicle straight. We learned later that the driver had never driven a liquid tank truck and knew nothing of the baffles. His application for the job had indicated that he was a trained fireman, that he had received special training at the Saudi Fire Academy, and that he could drive a truck, even a long ladder truck; he was never asked if he knew anything about tanker trucks or baffling systems. "Money, so what is money?" I said to Jim. "They'll just pump more oil, and Americans will buy it at $30 a barrel, and soon more trucks will be purchased." We went off to dinner and had some of Ellingsworth's three-week-old vintage homemade wine.

Two of Bechtel's local administrative staff men who were responsible for helping us were Mohammed, a Yemeni, and Ahmed, a Somali teacher, appropriately known as Stretch because he was very tall. Stretch was kindhearted and always ready to help us find information, obtain an appointment with a government functionary, change money or cash Travelers Checks for those who used them (I never used them because they were more trouble than they were worth), and do odd administrative tasks for each of us, such as register our presence with the local police. I liked Stretch and always worried that he was treated poorly and was sorely underpaid by Bechtel. When the Jeddah phase of the project was completed, Stretch was transferred to Riyadh to help out in the same administrative capacity on the new airport. I have a story about Stretch when he was in Riyadh, but it'll have to wait until I cover my assignment there. Both men spoke good English but Stretch's was quite good since in Mogadishu, Somali he had been a secondary school English teacher. My story about Mohammed indicates how friendly and warm hearted some of the "Arabs" were to us who treated them with dignity.

Yemen and the Birthplace of Coffee

I had some free time left from my tasks to explore Jeddah and the coastal towns south of the city. From Jeddah to Taif and on further south there were many historic villages that had sparked my interest. Taif was much cooler than Jeddah and had a certain resort atmosphere and also wild baboons. I went to Taif several times but often wished that I could go south towards Yemen.

I had read that in one or two abandoned desolate valleys there were villages where ruins of Jewish settlements could still be seen, but these were located pretty much on the old narrow road to Yemen. I had spoken to Mohammed about these historical sites and had indicated that I would have liked to visit them. Mohammed, a citizen of Yemen, told me that he was just about to go on a few days' vacation so he invited me to visit his parents.

"I am very interested," I said after giving it a minute or two of thought, "but don't I need a visa to enter Yemen?" I only had one exit visa for Saudi Arabia and would need another entry visa if I left the country.

"Not a problem," Mohammed assured me, shaking his head and grinning and making a gesture with his hand that intimated that we would slip under something. We would not pass through any monitored border guard posts. The border surrounding Saudi Arabia was porous and only a few unknowing travelers took the check-point accesses. Trails and back roads would be our highway to Yemen, Mohammed assured me. My Bechtel colleagues warned me that this trip was dangerous and possibly contrary to "logical security procedures." The danger was not so much the border crossing issue but brigands on the highway. Well, I thought, life was one risk after another. I went anyway, and it was fun and turned out to be a wonderful experience.

The drive to Yemen took nearly eight hours and passed over some extraordinary terrain. We drove on the road that had been built on the ridge of the Jubal al Hejaz, the coastal mountains of Western Saudi which rise above the Red Sea to almost 4,000 feet. We drove through the summer capital of Al Taif and past the splendid royal palace built for King Faisal, and then after several hours to the small historic community of Abha, which had been a bustling Jewish town until the mid-seventh century. On the way we did stop to visit a few ruins, and one especially had remnants of what appeared to be walls with the Star of David on them. Not much else could be recognized because these abandoned places had not been protected from vandalism or from the wear and tear caused by shepherds and their sheep, goats, and cattle. In my reading I had learned that several Jewish families had escaped the Roman occupations of Judea in the 2nd and 3rd centuries to settle in the hills of the Arabian Peninsula. Of course in the 6th and 7th centuries, with the emergence of Islam, many of the Jewish settlers had left although they were never forced to, but those who did not leave were, in the following centuries, assimilated into Arab Islam.

We crossed the border into Yemen by way of a dirt road and descended into Al Luhayyah, the coastal town where Mohammed's parents lived. Before leaving Jeddah, Mohammed had lent me a thobe so that I would not draw attention. "Do you like to look like an Arab?" he asked me several times. I found the white thobe comfortable and quite attractive, especially when worn in the climate of the Arabian Peninsula.

When we reached Al Luhayyah, I found Mohammed's parents to be great hosts and my accommodations were excellent. I had my own room overlooking the Red Sea, my own private shower and toilet, and the food was excellent, especially the festive dinner on the second day. A whole lamb was roasted on a spit. It was marvelous. I was glad to have accepted the invitation and Mohammed was proud to have invited me to his family home, the first American to visit his family. His father was a farmer and an entrepreneur who had several small businesses manufacturing household items. Mohammed's mother and sisters were seamstresses who operated a small dress shop. His brother was a fisherman who saved his earnings to pay for a college education. Mohammed was employed by Bechtel in Jeddah as a driver and gofer but was also enrolled at the university to study chemistry.

The venture in Yemen gave me an additional understanding of the Arab mentality. My experience in the Arab world included Egypt, Morocco, old Palestine, Lebanon and Syria, Saudi Arabia, Dubai, and now Yemen. Yemen, with the internal conflicts that exploded every so often between the northern and southern enclaves, sparked an in-depth understanding of how the underdeveloped societies looked at the developed and rich nations. Saudi Arabia, awash in oil money and mimicking the Western nations, was as much hated as envied, as were the Americans and the Europeans. Internally, the Yemeni people fought for a form of self-dignity to be obtained either through better national government or through communism — any means was acceptable if the goal of a better life was accomplished. For the poor nations of the Peninsula a better life included jobs, education, and the few amenities that made daily life less of drudgery. Possessing neither oil nor gas deposits, and with the Port of Aden bringing little revenue, the Yemenis searched for a better life. The small coffee plantations produced some of the world's finest Arabica beans. Forces not sensitive to Yemen's needs, however, controlled the price of the coffee and the land upon which coffee was grown. Because good soil was limited to a few acres in the cooler upper elevation, land for growing coffee was at a premium.

Ethiopian coffee, the original Arabica bean kin to the coffee from Yemen, and of superior quality to other non-Arabica coffees, the Robusta, originating the sub-Sahara region and grown in other countries around the world, was the only real competitor to Yemeni coffee, the primary choice of coffee aficionados. The coffee market was awash on the world market with Central and South American bitter and inferior Robusta coffee that was commercially cheaper to produce and was exempted from the rigors of fair price because of the cartel that controlled the market. Today Robusta coffee is grown in South East Asia, especially in Vietnam and Laos that are major competitors to the Yemeni and Ethiopian product and of far less quality. In Sumatra, however, the Arabica is grown. Once, however, a coffee aficionado has tasted and smelled the aroma of Ethiopian or Yemeni Arabica, nothing else can compare.

Work for the few Yemenis who could leave the country was available in Saudi or in the Emirates. In Yemen, because of the conflicts that erupted often between the northern and southern tribes, little investment was available, either from foreign or national sources, to develop new commercial ventures. Consequently, hardcore Islamic schools incubated dedicated religious fighters who became terrorists in the hope, misguided at best, of improving their lot by destroying the western-style economic fabric. Many of these Islamic fundamentalists assumed that a theocratic government guided by the dictates of Allah through the Koran would give them a better life; if not, then death by martyrdom would let them enter paradise. Mohammed reminded me several times that his people looked upon Saudi Arabia as a satanic nation that had stolen, and hence appropriated, from the Arabian Peninsula, the gifts that rightfully belonged to the entire Peninsula Arab people.

As the poor nation located on the southwest corner of the Arabian peninsula, Yemen emphasized the need for social economic improvement in a portion of the world that had few natural resources, had been bypassed by the economic evolution of the 20th century, and was under the shadow of a wealthy neighbor that had obtained its wealth, not by hard work, but through luck. Saudi Arabia was the recipient of enormous unearned wealth and was catered to by the United States of America and by several European nations because of its oil reserves. Yemen was bypassed. Yemen was a piece of barren land with little economic value. Yemen had a good port in Aden but little freight currently passed through it because security was at best tentative. It was a port for refueling and for the shipping of coffee and a few other products, but it was not a vibrant commercial harbor, not even useful for an active ship chandlers business. Aden, located at the entrance of the Red Sea, had little leverage to charge an appreciable toll to ships going to or coming from the Suez Canal because the channel was wide enough for ships not to have to stop or come close to the port. Many vessels, however, did stop to obtain water and other necessities, but Aden could not compete with Jeddah as a port of call, although it was strategically located and it was essential that it be protected and secured. Because Aden was at the narrow entrance to the Red Sea, terrorists, sinking a few ships, could block the straits, and Somali pirates could inhibit the shipping lanes, thus reducing maritime traffic to zero.

A short walk through the streets of Al Luhayyah towards the souk showed me that the stalls of vendors were not as richly stocked as those of Jeddah. There were practically no gold, silver, or precious stones in the jewelry stores. The women did not wear much gold and the dresses in the clothing stores were shabby and of poor quality. In the gun shops, the traditionally decorated daggers that most men wore hanging on their belt were not as richly adorned as those worn by the Saudis. Even the food and produce shops were not well stocked and the goat and sheep carcasses hanging were thinner and smaller and suggested that they were of inferior quality. The streets were mostly unpaved and when paved, they were full of potholes.

The people, however, were friendly, even friendlier than the Saudis and sporting much less dour looks. Although I was not permitted to take photographs, I was able to walk into mosques without incurring the wrath of the people, as long as I removed my shoes. When I stopped for a cup of coffee with Mohammed in an open-air café, the patrons were curious about my presence, yet they were cordial to me. Even though I wore a thobe it was apparently obvious that I did not look like them. One patron asked Mohammed if I was a Russian. When Mohammed replied that I was an American visiting his family, I became the center of attention and three cups of coffee were ordered for me. I was told that they liked Americans but why couldn't America help the Yemenis become more prosperous? "Why is all the attention focused on the Saudis and their oil?" they asked.

An elderly man smoking his water pipe took my hand and said, "Yemen has the best coffee and is more religiously liberal than our northern neighbors." He continued, this time in fair English, "Yemen needs help, not money, but help to show us how we can improve our economy, expand our coffee business, and educate our people." He continued in a very sad voice, "Exasperation is fertile soil for terrorism. My people are exasperated!" The old gentleman had been a schoolteacher who had taught English. He had studied English in Cairo and had returned to Yemen to teach young people.

The question about helping the Yemenis to improve their economy took many forms but was encountered several times in the course of my stay in Yemen. Even Mohammed's parents asked the same question. "Yemen needs better education, industry, commerce, and hope for the future." The country was too poor to manage its own evolution, and as long as it remained economically deprived, criminal factions and tribalism would find ways to coerce the people into civil unrest.

The few days I spent in Yemen and the conversations I heard through the translation given to me by Mohammed made me realize that much of the antagonism that existed in their hearts was the product of envy, frustration, and poverty. There was little opportunity for people to move higher up the scale of the world's social strata. Upward mobility was practically impossible in Yemen. There was no higher economic ground. Good education was a luxury that was not available to many people and if it were, the university system was pitiable. The religious schools, however, taught the wrong subjects and produced a graduate corps that was bitter, economically incapable of producing revenues, and focused on terrorizing the wealthier nations of the region. Moreover, the religious schools were more focused on training fanatics than on teaching the religion of Islam. Many Yemenis had looked at Nasser, and more recently at Saddam Hussein, and at the Soviet Union for support. The young Yemenis felt that they were trapped, and the older generation had given up any hope of improvement. Many young men, convinced that life was better after death, saw suicide for a religion that was immersed in a fanatic struggle as the outlet for glory. The few Yemenis who had wealth were seen as thieves who stole from and took advantage of the poor. University and secondary school graduates were ready to kill and be killed for any cause that bore the banner of a fanatically misinterpreted religion. Fanaticism is devoid of reason. Right-wing religious commitment is deadly, unthinking, and breeds devastation, be it in Christianity, Hinduism, Sikhism, Buddhism, or Islam. Yemen reflected the latter fanatic attitude.

On the return drive I discussed what I had seen and heard in Yemen. Mohammed reinforced the attitude of despair that permeated the "soul of his people." He was working for Bechtel in Saudi Arabia, but I was the first westerner to give him the right time, to treat him as an equal, and to show some interest in his people, his family, and his country. He was touched deeply, he informed me, that I accepted his invitation to visit Yemen and stay with his family. When in the dining room of the Somali Hilton I was the first American to have gotten a cup of coffee soon after my arrival in Jeddah and sit at his table. He was surprised that I wanted to know about his family and that I did not treat him as a driver, a low-level employee, and as "negess," the Arabic word for filth. Westerners were too busy making money and too blind to the plight of the poor Arabs who were also oppressed by their robber governments. "Someday," he warned, "Arabs and others will cause trouble because they have not been allowed to seek their dignity!" In addition, dictators, Mohamed asserted, rule all Arab nations and the Western powers support that system of government.

To a large extent I saw myself in Mohammed's plight. What would have been my lot had I remained in Cairo? By some enigmatic turn of politics I was sent to England and then to the New World where several opportunities emerged for me to accept. Mohammed's opportunity was to find employment in Saudi Arabia with an American firm. Rubbing elbows with other educated and professional people helped Mohammed to recognize that the world was not all made up of rocks, sand, and impossible poverty. He was exposed to education. I was exposed to education by my parents and by the geography that I visited. Several catalysts to seek a better life had energized me to rise above the miseries that WWII sowed on the world. Mohammed needed a catalyst to spur him further ahead in his personal development and to give him material for dreams — dreams that he could realize.

Limitations of the Saudi Coastal Navy

Because I was working on the Operation manual (OpsM) my hand was in many things and my presence was often in sections that were off limits to most of the staff. My responsibility was to "know" every aspect of the airport, and to know what most of the section managers were doing. On one occasion a manager was scheduled for a 10-day rest and recuperation (R&R). This particular manager asked me if I would cover his section while he was away to Italy to visit with his son. Walker was in charge of the port where the Saudi Coastal Navy was assigned. There were about 2000 men, cruiser ships, helicopters, and fast boats of various sizes responsible for patrolling a large section of the Red Sea off Jeddah. After I was introduced to the commanding officer, it was determined that I would visit the Navy Base at least three times a day for the duration of Walker's absence. This arrangement was not a burden on me because it was part of my general assignment.

A few days after I had gotten acquainted with the operation I visited the base in the late afternoon just before prayer and dinner and met the commander. He was in his office and greeted me warmly and in English. After I learned a few details about the operation of the Navy at the airport it was time for me to leave. The call for prayer sounded and the commander asked me if I would stay for dinner. I was left in his office and he went into a small cubicle to pray. When he returned approximately 10 minutes later he escorted me into a large dining room and invited me to sit on a carpet. Across from me there was a huge, and I mean huge, pot with rice in it. Next to the pot there was another pot with a mountain of meat, possibly a foot high if not more. Several large dishes contained lettuce, sliced tomatoes and onions, and loaves of square Saudi bread.

"Itfad'dal!" he said to me and invited me to eat. "The meat is roasted goat and the rice is Basmati, from the high mountains of India." Placing my left hand under my hip, I attacked the food with my right hand just as I had been taught as a young boy in Egypt when I ate "haghty" or grilled meat, usually lamb. The Navy troops sat all around us and reached, as I did, into the food. There was no silence. There was laughter followed by joking and some attempts to speak to me in English. When I tried my Arabic it made them all at ease and the conversation became lively, especially as the good commander helped me with the translation.

I was amazed how fast the large pot of meat and rice disappeared. I suppose that in total there must have been 40 eaters in this one chamber. "Are the rest of the troops eating at sea?"

The commander answered that there were six refectories large enough to accommodate the entire contingency of Navy personnel. "These men are my officers," he said.

"Don't some of your troops eat on board ship while patrolling the sea?"

He looked at me and said, "No, they come ashore for the evening meal. We do not patrol at night because our men are not able to work in the dark or around the clock like Americans." I was puzzled. "We are a small peaceful nation and we don't need to be out at sea at night. It is too dangerous for our men." So the mighty Saudi Navy comes home to bed at night. Indeed, it is certainly less dangerous but not much of a protecting force. When you have the American, British, and French Navies, who needs to be on patrol and losing sleep at night?

Several years later and not many months after the end of the war to liberate Kuwait, known as Desert Storm, I was driving north of Dammam where the major airport of the Eastern Province is and where the US Air Force had established its Air Base. The road on which I was driving led to Kuwait and Iraq, and also went past the major ARAMCO helicopter base in Ras Tannurah. A few miles north I saw a large open area with paved runways and aprons where several dozen F-16s with Saudi tail colors where parked. This Saudi Air Force was neither on my map nor within the perimeter of King Fahd International Airport (KFIA), which housed the US Air Force's fighter wing employed for the liberation of Kuwait from the encroaching Iraqi military. I was puzzled as to why these Saudi F-16s were just sitting in the desert away from an air base that had been especially built for them. I continued north to see the border crossing into Kuwait and to also see the "no man's land" section separating Saudi Arabia from Iraq. I was merely looking and not intending to cross the borders. When I arrived at the two locations there was nothing to see beyond Saudi security shacks and more desert sand. I turned back towards Ras Tannurah and ARAMCO.

When I arrived at ARAMCO I asked the director of operations if he knew anything about those F-16s. Were they used in Desert Storm? I knew that Saudi Arabia was part of the liberating coalition. The director of operations was himself a Saudi. He just laughed. "No." Then he added, "Saudi Arabia does not fight wars. The F-16s were for defensive purposes and no Iraqi aircraft penetrated Saudi air space."

"Oh," I replied, "But why were they parked outside KFIA?" He smiled and explained to me that Saudi was afraid that the Iraqi Air Force would retaliate and bomb or send Scuds to KFIA. Thus to protect the Saudi Air Force they moved the F-16s out of harm's way.

"And left the harm to be done to the US Air Force?" I said. He was a bit embarrassed and was ready to turn away when it occurred to him perhaps there was a good reason other than the lack of courage.

"The Saudi Air Force was kept ready in the event that the coalition forces needed back up support. Right?"

Then he added with an apologetic look and raised eyebrows, "The Saudi Air Force is neither very good at night nor in actual combat!"

Archeological Neophyte

On Fridays, our official day off, I would drive to the Akhabah Slough north of Jeddah. At Akhabah there was an equestrian club, and I could sit in the breeze, sip a cup of good Turkish coffee or a large glass of hot tea, read a book, or discuss a good topic with the colleagues I brought with me. Often I would take a coworker or two to my hideout at the equestrian club. Larry McGranahan and on occasion Michel Thomet would accompany me. We would also drive a few miles north of the slough on the beach where a failed monument to Saudi architecture and engineering overlooked the Red Sea. The remnant of a badly constructed palace stood in ruins. The old palace constructed for King Faisal rose as a wreck, wrecked not by an attacker but by shoddy construction.

To save money and labor the Saudi builders had used seawater to mix the concrete for the palace. In no time, the salt in the water had completely rusted and eroded the reinforcing iron bars (rebar) in the concrete. Every concrete section was falling apart. The location had become a favorite picnic site for Saudi families and an interesting place for expatriates wanting to learn something of poor construction. The sea in front of the palace was also a favorite diving and swimming spot. We often went to the palace because it was a good location to see Saudi families enjoy themselves without the inhibitions that often characterized their behavior in public.

On my first occasion when I was alone I was invited to partake in a meal of roasted lamb with all the trimmings that was traditional for Saudis. I was well received and we all struggled with a bit of English mixed with Arabic to express our thoughts, our likes, and our feelings. It was for me an enriching occasion and one I wish I could have recorded on film.

Families would bring a lamb or a kid that was often slaughtered on the beach, and then it was skewered, grilled over a fire of driftwood, and carved. Rice and beans were added to the menu, as was flatbread baked in a portable clay oven. The bread dough was prepared as soon as the fire was lit and because it had no leaven, rising was not necessary. The meal was always eaten with the right hand and foreigners were instructed about this before the meal was served. Women and children joined in the meal when it was a family affair; otherwise they ate later and in a separate location. Eating was done while sitting on a rug, and no table was ever used. It was always amusing to me to see several large boxes of Kleenex adorning a meal setting because the tissues were used as disposable napkins. Pepsi Cola and several fruit juices were the drinks par excellence accompanying the meal. It was an occasion that I relished, and even looked for other invitations whenever possible. I was invited three times by different families and there were always one or two members in the group who spoke some English.

Once there was a woman who spoke very good English. Although dressed all in black and looking like every other woman around, in American English she told me that she was an OB/GYN and had received her medical education in Texas. We conversed quite freely of the local culture, education, politics, and the work we did. But what I remember best was watching her eat while she wore the traditional face cover. With every bite, she would lift the bottom part of the face cover with her left hand and feed herself with the right hand. It certainly was an exercise in precision and neatness that she managed to do quite well. She noticed that I was following her actions and smiled telling me that the inconvenience was not too important as long as she could practice her healing art on women who had less of an opportunity to be served by a physician — most physicians were males and not allowed to tend to women.

One Friday afternoon my colleague Larry McGranahan accompanied me to the Akhabah. We skipped the visit to the palace and headed further north on the road to the community of Yanbu, the embryonic construction of a future industrial city. Yanbu was too far for us but the road was interesting because it sliced through an escarpment that was known to date from the time when the Saudi peninsula was a lush land, about seven or eight thousand years earlier. Larry and I stopped at a spot where several large black boulders surfaced from the desert sand. After parking my car, we walked to the boulders on our way heading over the ridge to the sea. We never got that far.

I sat on one of the boulders to remove sand from my boot and with my finger felt an indentation. I focused on what my finger had felt. Spotting a faint design on the flat bolder I focused more intently to examine what graffiti had been inscribed on them. It was my habit to carry a small leather shoulder pouch that contained my wallet, a hand broom, a hard black crayon, and two meter-sized pieces of white muslin in case I needed to make a rubbing of some thing I saw. Grabbing my small hand broom I brushed away the sand and perceived that something significant was on the surface of the boulders.

On the boulders were etchings of female human beings, a longhorn bull, a sheep or possibly a goat but more likely a sheep, and a donkey. Three of the boulders that we could readily see were decorated with drawings also. I was amazed to see the etching of human beings, especially women with prominent posteriors. The figures of human beings were banned from being drawn by existing Islamic law, hence these petroglyphs must predate the birth of the prophet Mohammed's inspired religion. While I made rubbings with the crayon on my muslin, Larry McGranahan took close-up pictures of the drawings and of me examining them. He also took panoramic photographs of the general area so we could find the location again. This was an amazing discovery. But there was a concern that arose in my mind immediately because I had seen a sign on the road specifying that soon a villa was to be constructed on or near the site and I had noticed a bulldozer parked where we had left the car.

Returning to the Jeddah airport, we sought out the official photographer who was a Parsons-Daniel employee. Because it was Friday, not a working day, he was in the photo lab developing his own private shots. I asked him if he would develop and print the roll of film I had as a favor. He accepted on condition that I buy him dinner at a particular Mongolian restaurant in town. It was a deal. He developed the film and made several large print copies for me. The photographs taken by Larry were excellent and clearly showed the details that were invisible when direct Saudi sunlight flooded the drawings.

The next morning, Saturday, I made an appointment to see General Amin. When I showed him the photographs and explained to him that what he was looking at were obvious Saudi treasures of historical value, he immediately reminded me that Islamic tradition was hard pressed to consider anything as relevant before the birth of the prophet Mohammed. After a short discussion he reassured me that educated Saudis did not ascribe to this tradition but understood that history did not begin with Islam. He would telephone the Minister of Antiquities in Riyadh and speak to him. He picked up the phone and spoke rapidly in Arabic, much too rapidly for me to understand. When he cradled the telephone he instructed me to go to the old Jeddah Airport, which functioned until the new one was operational, and fly to Riyadh on the IAP's corporate Gulfstream jet. I was to be back that night and to telephone him as soon as I arrived back in Jeddah.

By one p.m. I was at Riyadh's old airport and was met by Minister Ahmed Al Badrawi, who had been waiting for me. He took the pictures immediately and we headed for the Sheraton Hotel where we had lunch and a detailed conversation on the discovery made north of Jeddah. He knew from his conversation with General Amin that I was not a novice in art or the art of antiquities and that I had experience with the petroglyphs of the grottos of France. My immediate concern, I informed him, was the possibility that a villa would be constructed at the site and that these boulders would be destroyed or defaced. Minister Al Badrawi, an Egyptian citizen fluent in English and French, was very knowledgeable and just as concerned as I. The minister asked the waiter for a telephone, which was quickly brought to us and plugged into a connection under the table. He telephoned General Amin and they spoke for several minutes in Arabic. After the phone call he told me that he was going to Jeddah with me after he picked up an overnight bag. The general would meet us at the airport. By six p.m. we were back in Jeddah and whisked to the Jeddah Sheraton Hotel where dinner was waiting for us. During the dinner, the general told me that I was to take the minister to the site the next day and that the official IAP photographer would accompany us.

The next morning at eight o'clock we drove to the site. A cortege of three cars contained the minister, the general, Prince Sultan's (Minister of Defense) deputy, Prince Al Harridi, the photographer, and me. Photographs were taken, the minister took measurements, and I received a lecture on how important this find was and that the Kingdom would do everything necessary to protect this "national historical monument." We returned to the new airport and I was deposited at my office and the rest of the group sped away.

In my office was a note from Larry McGranahan asking me to phone him in his office at the warehouse. Larry was excited when I recounted the story of my meetings. He would wait for me at the Somali Hilton and we could have dinner together because he wanted to know all the details. That evening I met Larry and showed him copies of the official pictures plus enlarged copies of the ones he had taken. I also told him in detail what had evolved that day.

A few days later I was called into the office of General Amin where the minister was sitting at a conference table with several legal size looking documents in front of him. He asked me numerous questions about my education, what I knew about the grottos in France, my work with Bechtel and with IAP, and how I happened to find the site. When that phase was completed he asked me to sign a document stating that I was asking the Kingdom to protect the site. I reminded him that I had little authority in the matter but was certainly interested in urging the Kingdom to protect this site and that I was interested in asking American and French archeologists to analyze the boulders to determine the approximate age of the etchings. That would be done, I was assured. Nevertheless, my signature was required on the document. I explained to him that as a Bechtel employee I probably had no right to sign the document requesting protection of the site. General Amin motioned me to sign and he would co-sign the document too. The document was written in Arabic and that caused me some concern. What was I really signing? The general assured me that it was all right for me to sign the document. I signed it. General Amin signed it too. Later I learned from the general that what I had signed simply affirmed that I had discovered the petroglyphs and was asking the Kingdom of Saudi Arabia to protect these treasures for the betterment of Arabic knowledge of the Peninsula — or some such words.

Again a week later the general called me to his office to suggest that I drive to the site. He handed me a letter of authorization, which he intimated I would need when I approached the site. I drove to the site with Larry. A cyclone fence eight feet in height encircled the site and guards were posted around it. A kiosk had been erected at the gate stating in English as well as in Arabic that the site was a "National Historical Treasure and special permission was required to visit it." The letter from the general allowed me to enter the restricted site and to visit the petroglyphs. I did have a twinge of inner satisfaction, even of pride, for having found the petroglyphs, and for knowing that they would be protected for posterity. When I returned to the airport site, I went to the general and thanked him for his good work and influence and I also gave him Larry McGranahan's name as my co-discoverer. Larry McGranahan's name was promptly added to the official documents.

Two years after the archeological site was discovered I was informed that the date had been established for the etchings to be between six to seven thousand years before 1981. The Ministry of Antiquities had contracted with the Department of Antiquities of the University of Pennsylvania to date these etchings. Minister Al Badrawi was kind enough to send me a telex in San Francisco giving me the information and the gist of the report from the university. The assumption was that people of African descent had settled on the Arabian Peninsula near the eastern shore of the Red Sea. Several other etched boulders had been unearthed, and researchers from the University of Pennsylvania were continuing their work in conjunction with graduate students from King Khaled University. In 1990, while on assignment with ARAMCO, I was able to visit the site, which is much improved, protected, lit, and covered by a Corning-fabric type white dome similar to that used for the Hajj airport terminal.

Upon my return to San Francisco I soon learned that the discovery had been forwarded to Bechtel's Public Relations office, but the firm took little notice of it except for a paragraph in the company's magazine. Such was the level of interest that Bechtel extended for its employees. Plymate, however, was pleased by the news, especially since General Amin had participated in the event, and any points made with the general were points in favor of MOM, or so he thought.

Focus on Art and Falcons for Dubai

One morning as I was researching the correct filters for fuel hydrants to be installed in Riyadh at the new airport, Glenn Plymate approached me to ask if I was still interested in falcons, art, and aesthetics. He was referring to the video that had had been made for the Jubail project where one of two wild falcons had just flipped over and performed a perfect roll and never broke formation. I had invited Plymate to watch this video because he was a pilot. To his inquiry my reply was yes. "Come to my office now," he told me.

In his office stood a bulky man by the name of Eberhardt Lemke, the project manager for the Dubai International Airport. Glenn introduced me to him and suggested that we discuss the issue at hand. Eberhardt Lemke and Glenn were good friends from the time when they worked on a proposed airport in Jordan.

Eberhardt, or Ebbe, as he was called, was a most interesting and bright fellow. In his late teens he had been recruited into the Luftwaffe to fly the new jet fighter, the Me-262, developed by the German firm of Messerschmitt with engines made by BMW. Ebbe was still a currently licensed pilot who preferred to fly gliders instead of engine-driven aircraft. In the course of the conversation, Glenn asked him questions about the technical details of the Me-262, and one of them was how accurate its machine guns were. With a smile on his round face, Ebbe replied, "We tested them on B-17s and found them to be quite accurate!"

"So how come you lost the war?" Glenn asked.

"We ran out of bullets, airplanes, fuel, pilots, and most of my colleagues, like me, wanted to live beyond the stupid war, so we crashed the planes in Allied territory," was his candid reply.

Ebbe and I remained friends for many years and often exchanged flying yarns. On one occasion, when he was placed on holding status, Ebbe went to Australia and joined a glider club that allowed him to rent a craft. In the two weeks he was in Australia, Ebbe claimed to have flown 64 hours; a phenomenal number of hours accrued in such a short time.

Ebbe was looking for someone who could construct the whole show-and-tell display for the terminal of the new Dubai International Airport.

Let me regress for a moment to bring this whole issue into perspective. Because of what I had accomplished in Jeddah concerning art for the airport, weeks earlier I had been asked to review the text for the proposed art exhibits at the new Riyadh airport. I had read the text then sent a memorandum to its manager, Carol Glass, an architect responsible for the selection and placement of fixtures, furniture, and art (FF&A) in the terminals. My reaction to her scheme was negative. Carol was putting too much attention on the arrival terminal, when passengers normally are rushing to leave the airport, to meet friends or business acquaintances, or to reach their homes or hotels. Moreover, the art she had selected was too intricate, mostly non-Arab of origin, and did not display, suggest, or remind the passengers of anything about the local culture they encountered.

This memorandum had annoyed the senior architect, Bob Reynolds, a man that Glenn, also an architect and who had studied under R. Buckminster Fuller, disliked immensely. Reynolds, a Southerner, was a pompous and visionless graduate from Harvard who survived mainly by doing little, proposing nothing, and catering to a small club made up of "his favorites."

As I indicated earlier, Ebbe was a friend of Glenn's, a pilot, and a superb engineer and a fine and talented project manager. Ebbe had come across my name when he had heard what was being done with art for the airport in Jeddah. This morning, Ebbe and Glenn had discussed a possible role for me on the Dubai airport project. Would Glenn Plymate lend me to the Dubai art project? Both Glenn and I had agreed that I could work with Ebbe and his team to develop an applicable art program for Dubai in the new terminal. When I met with Ebbe I made it quite clear that any show-and-tell display should be placed in the departure terminal, and that the arrival terminal should have merely hints of what Dubai's culture offered. Ebbe agreed with me. It was settled. I was lent to the Dubai Airport Project.

The initial step was to learn all I could about Dubai, then a small Bedouin state, which had been one of the old British colonial Trucial States. In the 1950s the Trucial States became the Emirate States when Britain granted them independence. Dubai is one of the more active and business-oriented of the federated states of the Emirate. My research unearthed three major activities that brought international fame to Dubai: commerce, maritime shipping, and falconry. Today

Dubai is an outstanding example of entrepreneurship talent in action producing success and razzmatazz.

Dubai was renowned for its commerce because in the late 19th century it possessed incredibly fast sailing ships. Dubai employed dhows, sailing wooden cargo vessels with lateen sails, for trade with India, Iran, and many of the eastern African states. The lateen sail, a triangular cloth sail attached to a mast by its perpendicular edge replicating the geometry of a flying wing, allowed the wind, even when blowing head on, to slip over the sail and increase the forward speed of the vessel to a velocity that was higher than the wind's. It was this revolutionary maritime sail design that contributed to making Dubai a leading commercial state because its dhows could sail the seas at high speed and thus enjoyed the advantage this brought to their commercial ventures, which were mostly contraband gold. In the 19th and early 20th centuries India forbade the importation of gold, but the Indians loved it; hence the dhows from Dubai continued to conduct a thriving trade in gold. The gold was mined in Africa but fashioned by Egyptian or Italian craftsmen, then sold to the Dubai contrabands merchants who then would sail to the Indian coast. The dhows of Dubai, because of their speed, could easily outrun and escape coastal controls. Hence both the dhow and commerce were signature issues identifying Dubai.

Even now in 2011, Dubai is a major trading, transshipment, and commerce center attracting investors from all over the world. Several trade shows are held every year and exhibitors and buyers come from as far as China, Japan, Europe, and the United States. Because of its active trading business, Dubai has become a leading financial center.

The third item of great interest was hunting. This type of hunting, however, was not performed with a gun, a bow and arrow, or a slingshot, but with a bird. The bird employed was, and still is, the falcon (falco, falconidae). The Emir of Dubai, Sheikh Mohamed bin Rashid Al Maktoum, was a world-class master hunter and trainer of hunting falcons. The falconers of Dubai were superior to any others in the world and were looked upon as the standard to be emulated. Falconers from other countries would travel to Dubai to sharpen their skill, to meet with the Emir, and to purchase local falcon offspring to enrich their stock.

To develop the art program for the terminal I chose to spend many hours of research, have several meetings with American falconers, and learn what the differences are that distinguish a falcon from a hawk. Part of the learning and research was my choice to travel to Dubai to see for myself the manner in which local falconers trained their birds and what they hunted. A three-day outing in the dessert with the Emir and his retinue was a memorable experience.

As a Bedouin, the Emir was earthy, not ostentatious, and very approachable. The food served was primarily lamb grilled over an open fire. For the final night's banquet, wild birds caught by falcons were served over a bed of carda-mom-seasoned rice and eaten with bread that had been baked in what looked like a primitive clay oven. A cardamom hot drink was served, often misnamed "cardamom coffee" and that was followed with almond-stuffed local dates. The meal was truly a princely banquet, and the Emir and his sons were kind, hospi-table, and ready to help me whenever I needed assistance. I was given a tent (more a portable fabric house) for myself that had a bed, a washbasin, a mirror, and a small potty, which was always emptied and cleaned when I was not look-ing. I was provided with towels, soap, shampoo, and a large container of water that had a spigot. I could go outside and use an enclosed gravity shower when-ever I needed a body rinse. Because the weather was warm, the shower water was likewise warm.

Obviously, the hunt and what the falcons could do was the main attraction of the trip. The Emir and his associates, including his two sons, would hike into the desert, find a good hill, say a word to their falcons (gyrfalcons), and at an appro-priate moment release the birds, but only one bird at a time and never in a flock. This majestic bird, the largest of all falcons, would soar into the blue sky, float here and there, circle and circle again, catch the wind and remain stationary with wings extended as a glider, then all of a sudden wings would be pulled in and a dive would be executed at a phenomenal speed. Gyrfalcons can stoop for prey at a speed of over 200 miles (320 kilometers) per hour. Dashing towards the earth the bird's dive was noiseless, extremely fast, and focused on a target — an aero-dynamic stiletto. Swoosh! The prey, a bustard, a bird the size of a large pigeon with a round body, long legs, and an erratic flight pattern, would be caught in flight in the talons of the falcon. The falcon then would gain altitude, circle once or twice to regain its bearing, and then fly to its master and alight on its owner's gloved hand but not before it released the prey from its talon, a mere instant before alighting, to its master. The releasing of the falcon, the soaring, the attack, the circling, and the returning was an extraordinary performance of a graceful maneuver. The falcon was immediately rewarded with a sliver of raw lamb or goat meat. A head-bonnet was thereafter placed over the falcon's head to curtail its vision lest it seek another prey and take to flight. The prey often was not dead but immobilized by the speed, the wind, and the change of altitude. I'm certain that the bird was as dazed as I after my first aerobatic airplane ride as a passenger. A few moments after the bustard regained its composure, it was released to freedom.

Often falcons made at least a dozen flights and the same bustard was seldom a repeat prey that day. Falconers would compare notes, say quiet words to their falcons, shift places, check their bird's feathers, and make many small gestures that meant something to the falcons but nothing to me, and perhaps to others. These gestures, I was informed later, were secret coaching messages that only the falconer and his falcon could decipher. Falconers are patient with their birds; they have a strong and well-developed left arm to support their falcons. Falconry is a sport limited to a few special bird lovers, and the falconers of Dubai are known as the best in the world.

When visiting Dubai, I also learned about wind-tower houses, an architectural design that I had not encountered at all when I did the preliminary research in San Francisco. Indeed, as it is known, the answer to a question is implicit in the question, but one needs to pose the question first. Often research is directed by what one can anticipate, what one can imagine is available, or what one theorizes. What I discovered in Dubai was totally new to me. I discovered that Dubai possessed the famous, historical, and extraordinary wind-tower houses. These houses are constructed with tall towers as part of their structure, called wind towers, which have a rectangular aperture constructed at the top of the tower facing the seasonal winds. These openings in the towers receive the wind and funnel it down through a narrow neck; a venturi, a constriction in the tower that produces a pressure increase as the air flows downward, this pressure increases when it is decreased by expansion and allowed to expand, cools the air appreciably by dissipating the heat, and subsequently cools the whole house in the warm months of the summer. In the winter months when cooler weather is the norm, the opening in the towers is restricted or shut. In some well-designed wind-tower houses, the venturi is so effective that the temperature drop and consequent expansion of the air as it is made to pass over a large tub of water causes it to freeze.

Neither refrigeration nor air conditioning is necessary for the occupants of these fabulous houses. Wind-tower houses were constructed at one time in the Emirates, Oman, Qatar, and Iran. Today in the 21st century, a few of the wind-tower houses remain in Dubai, Oman, and Iran, but the best of these are protected in Dubai. The architecture of these houses sadly reminds me that a lost technology, such as this one, needs to be regained. I suggested to the Emir that Dubai should preserve them and also promote them as energy efficient dwellings and buildings for a world that finds energy to be at a premium. The Emir agreed and assured me that they are protected as part of the national heritage. Would that they were incorporated in the architecture of buildings in other warm places around the world! Wind-towers are extraordinary examples of energy efficient structures for warm localities used years before electrical air conditioning.

When I returned from Dubai to San Francisco, the team that was compiling the information I had gathered began to design the glass cabinets for some of the displays. In Dubai, I had purchased an old dhow dating from the mid 19th century to be displayed in the departures terminal of the airport. Local craftsmen in Dubai were restoring the dhow to its original condition, sewing a new sail made of cotton and hemp fabric. Two months later our team produced a book that contained what was being proposed for the departures terminal. The book was entitled and dedicated to: His Excellency Sheikh Mohamed bin Rashid Al Maktoum.

His Excellency cheerfully and immediately accepted the program, and construction of the supports and placement of the items followed soon after the departures terminal was completed.

The art program for Dubai was a project that pleased Ebbe and me because once our ideas had been presented to His Excellency, the process to make the idea a reality moved as if it was on greased skids. Even Bechtel was surprised at how rapidly we had moved the project from concept to reality; it took just a few weeks.

The Dubai art program gave me the opportunity to move the San Francisco Art Commission and the San Francisco Airport Commission to initiate art exhibits in the departure terminal then used by United Airlines and American Airlines, in what is usually called Terminal 3 or the North Terminal. In 2004, art was exhibited in all the terminals of San Francisco Airport. The program book for Dubai, which contained all that had been placed in the departure facility for its airport, convinced the authorities in San Francisco that such a program would enhance their airport, would help departing passengers see what the region had offered them, and would be a good marketing tool to remind tourists and others that the Bay Area was a place that offered a good and thoughtful experience.

I need to add a short addendum to this story. While sitting in the business class section of a British Airways flight to London ready to depart the first time for Dubai from the San Francisco airport, which was the day after Labor Day September 1980, I was called by the flight attendant. Identifying myself, the flight attendant informed me that I needed to leave the aircraft and take my carry-on luggage with me. In the terminal Emily, who had come from Bechtel, informed me that my trip had been cancelled. Returning to Bechtel I learned that the trip had been cancelled because the treasurer of Dubai had failed to deposit $25,000 in the company's bank account! Disappointed, annoyed, and furious, after speaking with Ebbe and telling him that the delay might corrupt the whole program, to which he agreed, I left for home.

The next day, Friday, when I arrived at the office, there was a note on my desk to see Ebbe. I went to his office and Ebbe, as apologetic as one could be, informed me that the money had been deposited and that I could leave that afternoon for Dubai. "How much money has Dubai already paid Bechtel?" I inquired.

"About 7.5 million dollars," he replied.

I whistled. "And how much money do we have on deposit from Dubai?" I asked. He lit a cigarette, looked at me with an obviously embarrassed gaze; he stood up and looked out of the window. "Well, how much?" I asked again.

He turned to face me and said in his German accent, "Goddamn it, we have three million dollars in the bank earning interest for Bechtel and for a fucking $25,000 my project is held up by our own people!" His face was cherry red. We looked at each other, and then he lit another cigarette. With two cigarettes in hand he said, "Let's go for schnapps; no, no, for coffee," and he placed his big ham-hand on my shoulder and led me out of the office.

I left for Dubai on Monday morning after an enjoyable weekend in Montara. You already know the rest.

The Jubail Airport

The MOM group had established the standard ICAO and FAA formats for the OpsM for all Saudi airports. This particular task, which also included certification of airports, became my responsibility, but how it came to be mine is an enigma. After working on the Jeddah OpsM and the Riyadh OpsM, I was asked to prepare the OpsM for the new, smaller airport serving Jubail's Industrial Complex, located about 80 kilometers north of Dammam, Eastern Province. This was 1982 and I was prepared for another visit to Saudi Arabia, but Jubail was not my favorite place, especially when it involved working for the Royal Commission (RC).

The RC was as bureaucratic and dictatorial an outfit as one could find. Since my tour was to be short, less than three months, I could manage, however, the assignment. In addition, I would see several of my friends who were serving in Jubail. Jim Ellingsworth had just been reassigned to Jubail and was slated to become the airport manager, thus replacing Robert Dennison who was terminating his assignment to return to Michigan and become operations manager for the Detroit International Airport.

I would also see my dear friend Jeff Holland, senior planner, past officer in the French Foreign Legion (FFL), and author of an interesting book on the Nazi occupation of Greece during WWII. In that conflict, he was taken prisoner by the German army.

Jeff Holland was a stout, erect, jovial person, a very English Englishman, and the black sheep of the famous Holland munitions and gun manufacturing family of Britain. An Eton graduate who refused to go to university but instead volunteered in the FFL to march in the footsteps of the characters in the story of *Beau Geste*, the novel and subsequent film starring Gary Cooper and Douglas Fairbanks Jr., Jeff entered the FFL as a lowly foot soldier and rose to the rank of officer in less than three years. Jeff saw combat in North Africa against the Nazi Afrika Corps, in Malta with the liberation of Valletta (he gave me his commemorative Maltese tie), in Yugoslavia on the coast of Navaronne near Dubrovnik against first the Italian army, and then the as-yet-unbeaten German Mountain Corps, and in Greece where he was taken prisoner first by Greek sympathizers of the Nazi forces, and then by the German Occupation Corps. When he was released from prison at the end of WWII, he worked his passage to New York on a merchant ship and enrolled at Harvard University after passing his Graduate Entrance Examinations with an extraordinarily high score. Obtaining a master's degree (without having a bachelor's) in city planning, he found a position in Irvine, California, as city manager. Irvine was a paper city that had not yet been constructed but was slated to become the home of the University of California's Irvine campus. In 1979, restless and with a broken marriage behind him, he decided to accept an offer to work for Bechtel on the Jubail Industrial Complex project. Interviewing Jeff was one of my last tasks when I was assistant manager on the Jubail project.

The first part of the interview with Jeff Holland was mostly story telling on his part. He was a fascinating individual and a fine raconteur. The second part of the interview included questions from another interviewer, who was the chief planner for Bechtel, Michael Wakelin. A team of two Bechtel planners and two members of the RC conducted the third and final part of the interview. Jeff was hired soon after the interviews were completed and was assigned to head the Jubail planning team whose task was to plan the new city north of the old town of Jubail. Before going to Saudi Arabia, Jeff married Aileen, the delightful young lady who had been his secretary in Irvine. When Jeff was in Jubail, he and I corresponded regularly because we had discovered that we liked each other, had common links, and thus became close friends too. In 1982, when I arrived in Jubail to work on the OpsM and certification of the airport, Jeff greeted me with open arms.

Once in Jubail to develop the OpsM, I was given an office in the Public Works and Traffic Department building. I was assigned a small apartment at the Razziate Motel, which was located several kilometers from the Jubail Complex. I had requested and was authorized a rental car, but the police in charge of the Eastern Province required a copy of my academic degrees before they would issue me a temporary Saudi driver's license (in Jeddah and Riyadh my California driver's license was accepted, but not in the Shiite Eastern Province). At any rate, I was issued a driver's license two days before my departure from Saudi Arabia — a license that served me not at all.

Gathering material for the OpsM in Jubail was like obtaining blood from a turnip. Dennison, the departing airport manager, was not able to give me any details because he either did not possess them or he was too busy preparing for his departure to assemble them. The engineers who had worked on the airport had all left the project and remaining data left behind were not available because no one knew where they had been stored. I was getting frustrated, annoyed, and ready to chuck the whole assignment as a waste of time. Jubail was not an exciting place for me, the assignment was nearly impossible to complete under the current information vacuum, and I felt imprisoned without my own mode of transportation.

Just when I was on the verge of packing my bag, one morning a bright looking and smiling Brit walked into my office to greet me with "Hello Sunshine, I understand that you're up to your eyes in muck." The man came waltzing into my office and continued his greetings by adding, "Bloody Bechtel types are unable to find their butts were they not attached to their rear!" He had a big smile on his face, and then he parked himself in a chair across from my desk. Who was he? Shaking his head from right to left he announced, "I'm Barry Pugh and can give you all the data on the airport that you'll ever need." He handed me a stack of papers, drawings, PCA documents, utilities diagrams, terminal charts and approach charts, and schematics of various sections of the airport and its facilities. I looked at him in amazement because he gave me most of what I needed in that bundle of paper. I leafed through the material in amazement. Here were all the necessary data, and in one stack brought in by one man. After my cursory examination, I looked up at him.

"Do you like Indian Tandoori?" he inquired.

"Why?" I asked.

"Hey, Sunshine, just answer the good man's question." I replied that I did but was living at the Razziate Motel and had no transportation.

"No problem, no problem Yank," he replied as he shook his head again from left to right imitating the Pakistani workers who move their heads for yes or no in the opposite way than Europeans. "Seventeen hours or five o'clock, American time, I'll fetch you here tonight." Off he went whistling an unknown tune. That was my introduction to the great Welshman, Barry Pugh, electrical engineer and airport builder par excellence!

That evening I was taken to his doublewide mobile home and offered a glass of homemade beer. A couple of minutes after the refreshing beer was served Margaret, his wife, arrived. "Raymond, meet Maggie, senior management of this household, and nurse." He turned toward his wife and said, "Margaret meet Raymond, a Yank of sorts who was educated in England, so he is not all that bad."

And thus began my long friendship with Margaret and Barry Pugh, a friendship that is still strong and active. It was Barry, the brew master of Jubail, who started me making my own ale in liter bottles. He directed me to the bottles with ceramic stoppers that come from Austria filled with apple juice — not jack, but juice — for Saudi consumption. I brought back several cases of empty bottles from my trips to Saudi and they have served me well in my ale making.

Barry and I correspond weekly via the Internet and often visit each other's homes. Barry and Margaret are great fans of American square dancing; hence they come to the United States often for dancing events. On most European trips we make a point to allow a few days to visit them in Chichester at their home or they visit us on the Continent.

Yes, indeed, Barry did provide me with all the data needed to finish the OpsM and to complete the certification process. Barry was not a Bechtel employee but was contracted by the British firm, Sir Alexander Gibbs, to work with Bechtel. Margaret was a senior nurse working at the new Jubail Industrial Complex hospital.

With Jeff Holland, Barry and Margaret Pugh, and a few weeks later Jim and Ellen Ellingsworth as friends in Jubail, and each inviting me often for dinners, trips out of the Complex, and weekends away from the motel, my assignment was converted more into a holiday than a chore. I am most grateful to my dear friends and wish that I could convey my gratitude especially to Jeff, but he celebrated "his birthday into eternity" in 1991 and I miss him.

The End of a Company: It Was Time

Thus when I returned to the MOM department after my two-and-a-half months in Saudi Arabia and my month long holiday in Europe, I found the conditions at Bechtel topsy-turvy. The Management, Operation, and Maintenance group had been disbanded. Glenn Plymate was no longer the manager but was shifted to a minor role in the Engineering, Procurement, and Construction (EPC) group. My position had been abolished and I had been reassigned to the new Bechtel Operation and Service Company (BOSC), to work under Michael L.R. Bishop, Deputy Manager, a man I disliked and whom I found to be unethical in his management practices. Emily's editorial department had been wiped out but she landed, fortunately, in another publication department as lead editorial manager.

The rest of MOM's personnel were either asked to seek new positions in other departments or were laid-off. Plymate was given two people recycled from seconded positions with Al Akiel in Riyadh. Al Akiel was a company created by the Saudi Airport Commission to manage the new Riyadh airport. Several Bechtel employees had been seconded to Al Akiel for assignment on the airport. The purpose of this company was to bypass Bechtel in the management and operations of the airports; it was a good attempt but the outcome was a failure because Al Akiel could not handle the task. Both men had been given their walking orders as operation advisors by Al Akiel, and had been reassigned to Plymate because they were under contract and Bechtel wanted to avoid any lawsuits caused by notices of termination without cause. I had interviewed Ronald Chandler, one of the men reassigned to Glenn, and had reported as I indicated that he was a good person to keep, especially because he had been director of the

Santa Ana (John Wayne) Airport, California and had amassed an excellent record there, which was definitely not appreciated by Al Akiel.

My assignment in BOSC was practically to do nothing except some minor research on proposals, then bid for potential jobs — mostly in areas of operations that neither Bechtel Corporation nor BOSC knew anything about! I was researching options to build and operate prisons, to operate hospitals, to operate motor pools for the Air Force, to operate supply bases for the Navy, or to operate the municipality for the New Industrial City of Jubail, Saudi Arabia. Now, Bechtel had no experience in any of these areas, but that did not make any difference, they would hire the experts when they obtained the job.

The president of BOSC, Dr. Leon Ring, was an aeronautical engineer who probably was a good drawing board engineer for designing mechanical subparts, but had no sense of how aviation functioned, how the overall system operated, and how an airport served the airline industry. Once, to my surprise, Leon asked me how runways were oriented and what a wind rose was. He had not encountered in his education that wind roses were used to find the optimal direction of prevailing winds so that the landing end of runways could be placed in the direction that faced the wind to allow for good and safe landings by aircraft. Ring proved to me that anyone can obtain a doctorate if the topic can be narrow enough. His doctorate dissertation at the University of Idaho had focused on screw thread directions and sizes for replacing fasteners on aircraft sheet aluminum. Unfortunately, today neither rivets nor screws are employed; sheets are butt-lapped and bonded, and more composite material is being used that eliminates the whole issue.

Michael Bishop (MLRB), Leon's deputy, was also an engineer of some sort who had functioned primarily in administrative positions most of his working years, with a recent three-year stint as manager in the administrative department in Bechtel's emerging Jubail "City Hall" office. MLRB was, frankly, a despicable being who could neither be trusted nor had any sense of ethics. I cannot add more to that description without sounding awful myself.

I worked on one proposal with Sterling Harwell, another casualty of the reorganization. Sterling was a chemical engineer with a doctorate in metallurgy. He was writing a section for one of the proposals on how Bechtel would efficiently operate all motor pools for the Air Force. I was writing a section on the same proposal on what was needed to reorganize the administrative offices for the military hospitals. Neither one of us was an expert in any of these tasks nor was anyone else in BOSC remotely familiar with the subjects. One morning MLRB asked us to go visit Travis Air Force Base located nearby in Fairfield to discuss what was normally required of motor pools and hospitals. Sterling decided to drive and I was his passenger for the hour's drive to the Base. I found Sterling to be interesting and good company and he was also tired of the brainless approaches that BOSC was using. After we met the military staff and more or less embarrassed ourselves with how little we knew about the process, on the return we stopped for lunch.

We soon discovered that both of us were either ready to escape BOSC within the week or resign even sooner from BOSC and even from Bechtel. For me there was a lesson to be learned in this situation. After almost five years with Bechtel I had to develop a more up-to-date strategy to survive and to make my work with the firm more enjoyable. Up to this moment, I had simply enjoyed toying with aviation with no sense of direction for myself. Because of MOM, I had revitalized my pilot's rating and was flying again. It was a lot of fun playing with aircraft, airports, the rules of aviation and working with aviation types. But that was not enough to feed the soul, at least not my soul. I had to do some serious thinking and devise a new strategy. I did not wish to be subjected to the whims of Bechtel and to the ingratitude that pervaded its personnel policies. Either I would relinquish my own sense of control for my life or I would stand up, redesign my employee strategy with Bechtel or any other firm, and shape my own destiny.

Working for M.L.R. Bishop was an impossible situation but it forced me, fortunately, to take inventory and see what I could plan for the future. When Sterling and I returned to the office Michael Bishop immediately informed us that all proposals assignments had been cancelled and that we were to vacate our desks by the end of the week. In other words we were jobless. I was ready to quit Bechtel. Sterling soon found another slot as manager of the business office for a water group working on a project in South America. I had not looked for a new project. In fact I was not interested in spite of the fact that I needed an income to maintain my household, which included supporting my two children while they attended secondary private schools.

The next morning as I was gathering my personal possessions, MLRB called me into his office. I was convinced that there was nothing Bishop could say to me that mattered. He asked me to sit down but I refused. I had decided to tower over him and standing was the best way of doing it. "Ray," (I never accepted that nickname), "do you want an assignment in Jubail?" I looked at him a bit puzzled. He continued, "I can get you an administrative assignment in Jubail."

I looked at him. Was he serious? I didn't want a permanent, long-term assignment to Jubail or to anywhere else. My place was San Francisco and nowhere else. I stood silent just staring at this poor man who was killing himself smoking cigarettes right before me. "Well, Ray," he asked in an impatient voice, "do you want a job?"

I replied as clearly and as audibly as I could, "NO."

"Well as of Friday then you are without a job, and today is Wednesday."

"I still do not want to go to Jubail," I replied quietly.

"You don't seem to understand," MLRB sucked on his cigarette. "There is no MOM. And I can get you a higher grade if you accept a position in Jubail," he exhaled the grey smoke. "I can give you an upgrade and a bit more money," he took another smoke. "It is within my power to make such an offer to you because I hate to have your dismissal on my conscience."

I held my breath for a moment, and then said, "Bishop, are you bribing me with a higher grade and want me to accept a position in Jubail to sooth your conscience?"

Bishop recognized his error immediately but added, "No, you deserve a higher grade for the work you have done for MOM, and I can put the request through," he fixed his eyes on me.

"Then go ahead and do it but I will not go to Jubail," I emphasized my rejection by preparing to leave his office.

"Ray, you don't seem to understand the situation. I am ordering you to go to Jubail and am willing to sweeten the offer," he stood.

"Michael Bishop, my name is Raymond." I continued, "I will not be bribed to go anywhere and you of all idiots cannot make me go to Jubail." I stopped for a moment and then added, "You have no authority to order me — not even to the urinal!"

MLRB lit another cigarette and I took a deliberate step toward his office door. He shouted, "You are dismissed. You are to be off this floor by noon. You are out of Bechtel. Out of Bechtel."

Turning around I faced him and stared at him, "Bishop, I will outlast you at Bechtel. Remember that. And be very clear on that promise." I repeated my statement, "I will outlast you at Bechtel," and walked out of his smoke-filled office. I stopped outside his office and said loud enough for him to hear, "... And will outrank you."

After lunch that consisted of twelve oysters and a pint of ale on Polk Street, I phoned Plymate, who had an office in China Basin, a leased and large office building not far from Bechtel. Glenn was still manager of a small implementation team of two people working on the new Eastern Province Airport near Dammam. Glenn assured me that he needed me to resolve a keying problem for the terminals. The next morning I went to see Plymate. I no sooner entered Glenn's office than he asked me if I would go with him on a secret assignment to Saudi. The assignment would require a two-month stay in Riyadh and had nothing to do with keys or locks. We would depart in three weeks for Riyadh, but until then, would I work and try to resolve the problem of keys and appropriate locks for the terminals? I asked if I would be able to continue working with his small team after our return. He thought that it would be possible but not guaranteed. I accepted on the spot. He warned me not to mention any of this secret assignment to anyone at BOSC.

Back at my temporary office in BOSC, I found a note from MLRB on my desk asking me to see him immediately. I looked over to Sterling's desk and registered that it was clean and empty. Sterling Harwell was gone from BOSC; mine would be as clean by the end of day.

When I went to see Bishop he said, "Well Raymond I was only trying to help you and to sweeten the pot a bit. I meant it not as a bribe," he replied.

"No I will not accept your offer."

"Well then, Raymond, here is a letter informing you that you will be laid off at the end of this week." I left his office without taking the letter, and started packing my few things for the move to Glenn's section at China Basin.

As I finished packing, Bishop approached me and asked where I was going since I still had a few more days left with him and a charge number. "I have another position elsewhere," I informed him.

"Where?" he asked.

"Sorry, it is a secret assignment."

"You can't accept an assignment, you've been given a letter that you are laid off," he screamed.

"Shut up, Bishop," I replied and left the floor with my possessions. I was still part of BOSC, although I was now assigned to the new airport in the Eastern Province but would be working out of Riyadh until the Dammam facilities were ready for the project team assigned to it. Soon, in less than four months, I would abandon BOSC and I would see M. L. R. Bishop given his permanent walking papers before the year was ended.

That afternoon, after depositing my personal belongings in my new but temporary office in China Basin, I went to an Austrian coffee shop and ordered coffee and a piece of Linzer torte. It was time for me to think, plan, and develop a strategy that would serve me well at Bechtel. I decided that I would see what it was that I had in my bag of tricks. I could manage a project and I could do program and project management well and was recognized as being valuable in that discipline; also I found it enjoyable and satisfying. Aviation was a hobby that still served me well and there wasn't anyone else at Bechtel who had my depth of aviation knowledge and experience. My perspective on how projects were defined was grander than most other employees. I had vision. I could do excellent research. I could see well beyond the limits of projects and Bechtel upper management had noticed that quality. Hence I concluded that the best way of working at and with Bechtel was to become *indispensable*. I would begin to create that aura immediately. I did just that and Riyadh was the launching place for the first step.

By 1989 I was promoted to a higher position as manager of Technopolis, which is fundamentally a knowledge-driven, revenue-producing community. I had created this approach in preparation for the way that regions would adapt or be transformed economically to the financial requirements of the 21st century. After her return from Australia, a trip that was a mix of a conference for me, and for Emily a vacation, Emily decided to retire to operate the B&B. Hence, upon her return to Bechtel she was invited to her retirement luncheon. At the luncheon, I saw Michael Bishop who also was invited because he had accepted early retirement instead of being laid-off from Bechtel. In the meantime my rank matched his and I was involved internationally in technopolis, regional economic development, and an assignment as consultant to the European Union, which required that I travel often to Europe; at times every two weeks.

"What company are you with now, Ray?" he asked thinking that another firm had hired me.

My reply was a delight for me to utter, "I'm still with Bechtel and have been, and will be, for several more years." MLRB was struck silent. He said nothing. He turned away from me. I had outlasted this miserable, nasty, and incompetent man.

The experience with MLRB had taught me that Bechtel was mainly a job shop, in other words, an employee created his or her own project under the umbrella of the firm and its matrix organization. Of course if one could not land a new project then one was laid-off, usually within 30 to 60 days. The key to beating this type of Russian roulette was to become indispensable, creative, and agile enough to manage a series of projects, plus become needed by other departments. I was able to do that after my fifth year, several encounters with job depletions, and managers who were sadly limited. I could always manage a slot on a project in aviation, be it in flight management or airport operation and certification. Then I opened the door to city and city-state development, which eventually focused on knowledge and the revenue rewards emerging from knowledge. The technopolis idea that aimed at assisting a city or region emerge fundamentally as a knowledge-driven, revenue-producing community, was the key that helped me manage Bechtel and firmly secure my position with the firm and launch me into new ventures after I left the firm. There were four departments and companies that sought my services: I was requested by the Airport department, especially William Small; the Infrastructure department, by my immediate manager, Robert Jackson; the Research and Development Company, by its president and my associate in research, Dr. Harold Forsen; and Bechtel's Soviet Science City venture, supported by Denis Slavich, Senior Bechtel Director in cooperation with Bechtel's new President, Riley Bechtel.

The Secret Mission that Was Not

A few weeks after my move to China Basin and the completion of the key and lock task, I was on my way for an overnight stop in Paris, then on to Riyadh with Glenn. Dominique and Michel were to stay with Emily while I was in Saudi. My stop in Paris was to mail an airline ticket to Jacques Marsal and to have dinner with Elena Robinson who had been visiting her father. Elena was Nicola's college friend.

Elena and I had a wonderful dinner in the Latin Quarter on the Left Bank then walked along the Seine looking at the bookstalls and enjoying the Parisian evening. It was a beautiful evening and I wanted to absorb as much as possible of its cool air before I departed for Saudi Arabia and the secret mission.

The next morning I boarded a Saudia Airlines flight for Riyadh. From this venture to Riyadh a new approach to work at Bechtel would emerge. It would seem that our roles had been changed: Bechtel would now virtually work for me. My new tactic helped me until I scheduled my retirement in 1993.

Arriving at 2:00 a.m. or so at the old Riyadh airport, after passport and customs control (which were always tedious and unwelcoming experiences), we were met by Jim Harrington who drove us to our apartments, Glenn to his and I to mine. Jim was on a permanent assignment in Saudi and was presently working in Riyadh on an administrative project. He would become part of our team as soon as we mobilized it.

The next morning, after breakfast, we met in a room in the unoccupied elementary school to decide what approach we would take to complete this still "secret" project. Once the strategy for doing the task was scoped out we decided to go to the supply warehouse to obtain the necessary office material. Our task was twofold: to develop a program for counteracting the work done by Al Akiel and to diminish its authority; and to evaluate the recently selected person who was going to be airport director.

Al Akiel was causing a great deal of problems for Bechtel and even for IAP but because it had been installed in Riyadh by an organization owned and operated by one of the competing princes, it was difficult for IAP to remove its influence from the airport project. We were assigned to the task to prove that Al Akiel was trouble — and it was because it knew nothing of airports and still less how to manage personnel seconded from Bechtel to help it bring the airport to the operational level required. It stood to reason that our assignment was to be done in secret because if Al Akiel got word of it Bechtel would be in difficulty, as would IAP. Mark Stayle, the supply manager, greeted us with the shocking news: "You are here for the secret task to evaluate Al Akiel and the proposed new airport director Saad Tassan!"

What he said sounded like a bomb to our ears. We looked at each other in shock and said nothing. Evaluating Al Akiel was one part of the task and a delicate part too, but the fact that Mark knew about the proposed airport director was critical and a political time-bomb for Bechtel's long term relationship with the government of Saudi Arabia.

On our way out we stopped in the project manager's office to obtain our definite marching orders and learn more about the information leak. Dr. Ronald Brooks was busy with a Saudi delegation but his deputy asked us what we wanted. What we wanted? Fortunately, an instant later, Ron Brooks saw us as he escorted his visitors out of his office and invited us in to see him. After the greeting, he announced that our "secret" mission had been cancelled.

Why? Well, Prince Sultan Bin Aziz, the defense minister, had already appointed Saad Tassan, a 27-year-old graduate from the University of North Dakota's aviation college, as director of the King Abdul Aziz International Airport, the new giant airport in the Capital City of Riyadh. Moreover, the King had decreed that Al Akiel remain on the airport as the operating entity. In sum, these developments meant that we were out of a job!

Glenn decided to return to San Francisco by way of Singapore to look at the Changi International Airport, the new fast track monument that was touted as innovative and extraordinary. The Changi airport was scheduled to open in a few weeks, so Glenn hoped to see the final construction phase. As for me, I was also out of a job. Would I return to San Francisco and search for something to keep me employed? But because I had met Ron Brooks several times while on assignment in Jeddah and we had developed a friendship, he took me aside and invited me to dinner at his house.

Outside the building, Glenn waited for me and asked why Ron wanted me to have dinner with me. Moreover, why I had been invited to dinner and he hadn't. At the time I did not know the answer but assumed that because Ron and I had become friends, he was extending a bit of courtesy my way. Beyond the friendship I saw nothing that implied anything more. So I was as puzzled as Glenn was by this solo invitation. Glenn was quite unhappy and I sympathized with him but there was nothing I could do to change the situation; I couldn't ask Ron if Glenn could be invited too.

At any rate, Glenn was unhappy but thought that if he could visit Changi airport in Singapore he could take a step to lift his falling star in BOSC. He proceeded to obtain permission from Bechtel. Ron was more than willing to authorize his trip to San Francisco via Singapore, but BOSC was unwilling to do so. After some difficult maneuvering and pressure from Polvi, the trip to see Changi was authorized but it could only be paid from Glenn's overhead account, which was quite small. Glenn did go via Changi and did see the final stages of the construction but he did not witness the transfer from the old to the new airport because it had been delayed by four weeks. In the end, however, this visit to Changi did not help him evade the final days of his time with BOSC and ultimately with Bechtel; he was forced to retire.

By some providential quirk I found myself, with Bechtel's insistence, at Changi International Airport the night that the old airport was closed and the transfer executed. I was also fortunate to witness the arrival of the first flight at Changi. That, however, is another tale.

That evening after dinner and affirming that I was free and willing to take on another task, Dr. Ronald Brooks asked me to work on another secret project with him. Ron could not give me any details when we were in his office, hence the dinner invitation. Ron specified that the task was quite confidential and should remain as such to protect other members of Bechtel's team in Riyadh. Not another secret project, I thought to myself.

When dessert was completed and coffee was served Ron explained the assignment. He wanted me to head a team to itemize and order the spare parts that had not been delivered to Bechtel for the airport by the contractors. The contractors had already been signed off and terminated by Robert Polvi, the previous project manager and his team. This signing off legally showed that the contractors were no longer liable for not fulfilling the contracts that required spare parts for at least one year. The point of my assignment was to save Robert Polvi's credibility now that he had been promoted to the position of President of Bechtel Civil Company (BCiv).

This was a project that he wanted to keep hushed but which needed to be attacked as soon as possible. Ronald B. Brooks informed me that the various firms engaged to do the jobs had completed several of the construction contracts. They had, however, departed the kingdom without fulfilling the requirement of supplying the needed spare part to satisfy the warrantees. When Ron took over as project manager, he soon discovered the problem. This meant that in the event of a breakdown of machinery, such as pumps, electric motors, or other critical items, there were no spare parts readily available as replacements. It was then that I began to understand his predicament.

"Ron," I said, "I am not a warehouse specialist."

He looked at me, "Raymond, none of these guys here can keep quiet and none of them are smart enough to find a way to resolve this problem. If it gets around that Bob Polvi has signed off on the contracts without securing the spare parts, his career will be ended. Bob has been appointed President of Bechtel Civil Company and the spare part issue will make him look bad."

My silly response was, "But Ron, I don't know the first thing about spare parts."

"I don't either," he replied, "But we must resolve that problem and have all the parts in the warehouse before the airport becomes operational in fifteen weeks."

I was silent and thought that I really wanted to help Ron, especially since we were good friends, but I did not have the knowledge required for this task. "You can recruit as many people as you need. You have a blank check to do what is necessary but it must be kept hushed."

My feeble reply was "OK." Here was my opportunity to prove that I could tackle any assignment, do it well, and instill in Bechtel that truly I was indispensable! That type of thinking was the stuff for a Hollywood movie.

That night was taken by very little sleep and much thinking about how I would tackle the issue of spare parts. Again in the morning after thinking this assignment over for an hour, I decided to go to my dear friend Larry McGranahan who was a warehouse specialist; in fact he was deputy manager of the warehouse, and was currently working in Riyadh. "Larry, I need a quick course in warehousing, spare parts, tracking systems, and the personnel I will need."

He smiled. "I know your problem and I'll help indirectly." He had already suspected that a problem existed when he reviewed the contract material. Because he was not of sufficient rank he could not make any noise and his supervisor was totally uninterested in challenging his own managers.

"But Larry, you cannot let anyone know that we have a problem," and I explained the details to him.

Larry came to my rescue, and indirectly to both Ron Brooks' and Bob Polvi's. He showed me how to track the parts, helped me develop a personnel requisition and task program, suggested a possible supervisor for the task, and walked me through the entire process several times when I needed more help or was faced with problems. Without Larry, no resolution would have been devised, at least not by me. I ended up by bringing together from various disciplines and from several other projects around the world a team of 95 men to work on the project, which was completed in twelve weeks.

The personnel placed on the spare parts project were categorized as working for the preparation of the future Dammam airport, which would be the King Fahd International Airport. When 4,500 employees are working on a developing project that requires more and more workers, and more are needed on a weekly basis, adding 95 souls goes totally unnoticed. The spare parts task was invisible and the personnel required for it were unaccounted for on the tally books. Moreover, the cost for purchasing the spares was absorbed by the large procurement tally for the new airport to be constructed in the Eastern Province. Ron

Brooks was informed three weeks before the airport became operational that all the required parts were in the warehouse. Inadvertently I had become an important cog of Ron Brooks' team. My star was shining a little brighter when I completed the spare parts task because Al Akiel asked me, upon Ron's recommendation, to review the Operations Manual (OpsM) that was being prepared. IAP asked me also to assist in the certification procedures as I had done for Jeddah and neither job required that I become seconded to the Saudis.

Before accepting these other assignments, I asked Ron Brooks if I could have a month in San Francisco in February 1982 between my tasks in Riyadh. The reason was that the discoverer of the Grotto of Lascaux was to be my guest in the Bay Area and he was scheduled for several presentations. Ron authorized the break in my tour and I left Riyadh for San Francisco but via Changi, Singapore, on 3 February 1982. On this date Changi was to experience its dry run testing with the first aircraft arriving for the inauguration of the airport. Full operational function was slated for May 1982. Ron Brooks had asked me to take a close look at the new fast-track construction for the Changi International Airport and to be present during the transition period. This added assignment allowed for the break in my tour in Riyadh to return to San Francisco. Interestingly I had been assigned to review the Changi Airport but Glenn had had to request permission to stop in Singapore. That didn't make him very happy. However, upon my return to Riyadh I was to head my own team for the transition to a fully operational airport plus review the Ops manual, and was to report directly to Ron Brooks and to no one else.

I arrived in Singapore approximately 72 hours after Glenn had left Changi. Because I was authorized by Ron to fly on Singapore Airlines my flight was a delicious experience in comfort, food, and service. I went straight to the hotel upon arriving and after a short nap had a light meal consisting of oysters, shrimps, and fresh tuna washed down with a glass of fine ale. Then I headed to the new Changi International Airport in a car that had been sent for me by the Airport Authority. I arrived at 1700 hours, just before the transfer was started.

It was a fascinating experience to see how regimented the change from the old airport to the new airport for Singapore was. One main avenue was dedicated for the vehicles hauling material from the old airport to the new. Another parallel avenue was dedicated for the returning empty vehicles. The next morning, by 0500 hours, the move was completed and all was in place. Changi was awaiting the arrival of the Singapore Airlines Boeing 747 flight from Tokyo, the inaugural flight of the flag carrier scheduled to arrive at 0730 hours. Everyone was excited to see the inaugural flight arriving at Changi. Coffee and a light breakfast was offered to all present in the viewing lounge located in the Control Tower.

As the time of 0700 hours arrived we were informed that a British Airways (BA) Boeing 747 from London was circling above the airport. It had been scheduled to land after the Singapore Airlines B-747. The BA flight had been placed on hold but its fuel was critically low. The Singapore Airlines flight had encountered strong head winds from Tokyo, and was expected to be 30 minutes delayed.

The authorities could not delay the landing of the BA flight too much longer. The BA flight had had the advantage of substantial tail winds most of the way. The delay was cancelled and the BA flight was allowed to land.

The BA flight, when it landed, received all the accolades that had been prepared for the Singapore Airlines flight; Singapore Airlines from Tokyo arrived at 0815 hours. Such was the opening of Changi International airport.

When the BA captain met the awaiting greeting group, which included the President of Singapore, he delivered a letter bearing congratulations from the Queen of England. That letter had not been expected.

The fact that the airport was built on a fast-track schedule did make it available for air traffic to begin on schedule and within budget, but it had a few problems. One supporting column was built too close to a down escalator; this prevented passengers from using it when they had carry-on luggage. A lavatory was finished but without connecting the toilets to the sewer system — it could have been a bit messy had a visiting guest not discovered it. The center lights for the right runway were inoperative because the power had neither been connected nor checked but since it was not a landing runway that day no one noticed. There were other minor items but on the whole Changi was a splendid airport and I said as much in my report. Glenn's report was more critical especially because he did not like the color of the paint on the walls, the design on the carpets, and the fact that the building was too cold and the transition to the warm and humid outside air was startling.

The following day I boarded a Singapore Flight for Los Angeles and an American Airlines feeder to San Francisco. I was arriving in time to make final preparations for Jacques Marsal and Emily Oppegard, our lovely translator for the presentations.

Jacques Marsal in the Bay Area

Measures for Jacques Marsal's arrival in the Bay Area had been taken long before my return home. Emily Oppegard ("Little Emily" or "Emily O" as she was known), fluent in French, had been recruited to be Jacques's interpreter, escort, and driver. Little Emily was Emily's second cousin and also her godchild. An extraordinary, bright person possessing a fine sense of humor, Little Emily was one of my favorites of Emily's family. She was her own person with a streak of stubbornness that was miles long, immediately recognizable, and for me, appreciated. I preferred to call her Emily O or EO instead of Little Emily, finding that more appropriate for an adult, an adult who was a most creative individual. EO could sew, paint, work with glass, use professionally and meticulously a large printing press, and cook like a fine chef. Shyness, her stamp for being a quiet person, was for me a refreshing quality. For me she was worn like a warm sweater. I was certain that EO was the right person to accompany Jacques during his days in the San Francisco Bay Area while I tended to my project at Bechtel.

Jacques arrived in mid-February 1982 and was to stay in my house in Montara during his two weeks in America. I wanted people to know more about the creative efforts of early human beings and to see some of the photographs that Jacques had personally taken of the Grotto and its art. Because Lascaux is closed to the general public, this would be an opportunity for people to see firsthand the beauty that was being protected.

Jacques Marsal's presentations were an absolute success, although because it rained most of the time he saw little of the beauty of the San Francisco Bay area. Emily Oppegard was a wonderful translator and a superb escort for Jacques. Jacques was introduced to several artists, scholars, and anthropologists who were intimately acquainted with the art of homosapiens and what was painted on the walls of the grotto of Lascaux.

At one point we were invited to dinner to meet with Dr. Donald Johansson, the archeologist who discovered the three-million-year-old skeleton of Lucy, the young woman found near Odolvai, in Africa. Johansson had visited Lascaux and was familiar with several of the controversies that plagued the theories that abounded around the reasons why the paintings were made. Some of the theories suggested a religious causation for the paintings; others suggested that it was a form of primitive language. In between these reasons floated many other theories, many of which were crudely farfetched. He leaned in support of the quasi-religious justification for the paintings. Marsal did not and neither did I. My aesthetic position was that the painting reflected the sense that art was produced for the sake of art and perhaps as a commentary of the current situation that identified the culture Cro-Magnon. I was quite certain that the whole subject of "religious experience" was not applicable because modern human beings did not understand how early human beings negotiated the factors of transcendence and what we ascribe to religious expressions.

Our discussions were intense and I believe that in the end we were able to move Johansson away from the quasi-religious position towards the phenomenon that artists are symbolically editorializing their times, circumstances, and emotive conditions. We explained to Johansson that using religion as a reason was tantamount to saying that we, of the modern age, knew what and how primitive beings worshipped. I suggested that even today we don't know how human beings worship other than the outer and visible ceremonious activities that pass for signs of worship — in mosques, temples, synagogues, churches, and elsewhere.

A much better reason might be that the art was an expression of what the artist felt inside his person — an affirmation of her/his passionate desire. That approach precluded the theological and psychological traps that surfaced from any theory that involved religion and psychoanalysis of Cro-Magnon artists.

In the short two weeks that Jacques Marsal spent in the San Francisco Bay Area, he conquered the hearts of all who had an opportunity to speak with him. In his presentations he was lucid, informative, direct, and passionate. It was obvious that for Jacques, Lascaux had become the very meaning of his life and of his professional interest. As a young boy, he was one of the four boys who discovered the grotto. As an adult, he remained dedicated to its protection and to the task of learning more about its phenomenon. He managed to learn a great deal about the grotto and its paintings, and in the general scheme of history, Jacques was the renowned authority on the art of the period. Scholars from several universities referred to Jacques on various occasions when it came to questions about the art of Lascaux. Even when I examined other grottos, his name was always used with great reverence and affection. Jacques was the quintessential master of the art grottos of France.

In California, he charmed his audience and impressed the scholars who attended his presentations. I am particularly indebted to Jacques for his willingness to let me learn more about the art of the grotto; his affectionate treatment of Dominique and Michel when they visited Lascaux; and for the wonderful hospitality, including a superb dinner, that he hosted for me and for my family. Mostly I am grateful for letting me spend very long periods on several occasions in the grotto, for his willingness to share with me a wealth of artistic, historical, and personal information, and for enriching my view of the creative aspects of early human beings. Jacques Marsal died of leukemia in July 1989. I have missed his charm, intellect, wisdom, and friendship. His friendship warmed me deeply.

As I intimated earlier, Jacques Marsal was a delightful guest and proved to be a success in the San Francisco Bay. When the time came for him to return to France he admitted to me that his dream had been to visit America and especially to see California. He was in tears when I took him to the departure gate to board a flight on Trans World Airways and he confided that he was "tres ému," deeply moved by my invitation to America and by being a guest in my home. We exchanged solid and extended hugs. Indeed, I was profoundly moved too by his presence, his affectionate friendship, and his graciousness. Several years later Jacques invited Emily, Dominique, Michel, and me to see the grotto and to have dinner with him, his wife, and his nephew. It was a superb dinner and one none of us have forgotten. On other occasions, Jacques allowed me to spend several hours alone in the grotto and after to have long discussions with him.

Being alone in the grotto always elicited an acute sense of awe. Once we became friends at every opportunity when I was in France I allowed time to visit Montignac and to spend time with Marsal and his wife. We often had dinners at special restaurants that were important to Marsal.

I am grateful to providence for having given me the occasion to know him and to enjoy his friendship.

Riyadh: A New Capital

When I returned to Riyadh for the second phase of my assignment in March 1982, after Jacques Marsal's short but exciting visit to the San Francisco Bay area, Ron Brooks left me a note in my apartment for me to see him soon. The next morning I walked into his office, and after being greeted Ron reminded me again that the problem he faced needed to be resolved as soon as possible. Again the issue was that Bechtel had released several firms from their contract when their work had appeared to be finished, but spare parts for each subproject had not been received, as required by the contracts. To do the job Ron Brooks gave me great authority, more than my grade merited.

As I said earlier, because I was neither a warehouse professional nor a contract attorney I had to find a team of specialists for the task. With the help of Larry McGranahan, the assistant warehouse manager, and James Harrington, a contract and administration professional, we began the difficult task of identifying the areas where further examination of the problem was required. By the time we had identified each contract and then inventoried the spare parts needed a team of 95 men had been recruited. The men recruited for the team were engineers in electrical, hydraulic, pneumatic, security, and combustion disciplines. It was discovered that electrical generators, diesel engines, pumps and valves, and security devices were all lacking spare parts. Had the client taken over the operations of the airport, Bechtel would have been sued for improperly managing the contracts, since it was specifically hired as the Project Management firm to monitor each and every contract. There it was. Brooks had been left with a costly problem that Bechtel had to resolve. As I intimated above, we decided to place the whole spare parts cost for Riyadh that included labor and parts onto the new Dammam airport project. In a private meeting with members of IAP (International Airports Projects) chaired by General Amin, it was agreed, after a few hints from me, that the cost, which was less than 7 million dollars, could be absorbed without noticeable effect if the team working on the spare parts would also do some work on the preparation of documents and control systems that would also ensure that this problem did not get repeated in Dammam.

The initial team that I gathered to help me solve the problem was essentially Larry McGranahan, my advisor and mentor for this task, and James Harrington, who devised a system to keep the administrative tasks in proper order and made possible weekly reports for Brooks' review. Laurence, or Larry as he was fondly called, was of immense value to me and to the project. Larry was an expert in warehousing, in procurement, in supply facilities, and knew the correct way to identify and store parts as they were related to construction projects. A happy fellow, Larry was a delight to work with and ultimately we became close friends. His wife Doris was a fine artist and a delightful hostess. Often I was invited to their quarters for dinner, conversation, and a bootlegged drink of homemade wine or purchased siddiki, the illegal Saudi corn booze made by the Bedouins. In spite of its peculiar name and pungent smell, it was not bad with the addition of orange juice and crushed ice!

My other great supporter was James Harrington. Jim had a master's degree in business administration and when in San Francisco, was professor of management at Golden Gate University. Jim had volunteered for an assignment with Bechtel to Saudi Arabia with the express task of developing technical training programs for the Saudis. Unfortunately (but fortunately for me), the training program project never was realized because the Saudis would never let it come to life. Because Jim was free to work on other tasks, I recruited him and applied his brain to develop the management program for tracking the spare parts. The Harringtons were also hospitable to me and often after work I would be invited for a dinner that his wife Betty had prepared. Much as I occupied a large house all by myself, the equipment for cooking was non-existent except for preparing tea and coffee. Jim and Betty, realizing that I was condemned to eating the food in the refectory, invited me often to break bread with them. One evening when I learned that the fare at the refectory was prime beef, a dish that I can easily avoid, and knowing that Jim liked the cut, I gave him my pass so that he could go in my place. That evening I shared with Betty a quiche that I prepared in her kitchen.

In the meantime while managing the spare parts contingent, I was simultaneously reviewing the development of the OpsM by another team working under the jurisdiction of the Saudi firm Al Akiel. A few of the Bechtel O&M team in Riyadh at the King Khaled International Airport had been seconded to Al Akiel for the duration of the airport project. The seconded employees did not like the conditions of employment under Al Akiel. The non-Bechtel employees working for Al Akiel were not knowledgeable about what was required for the OpsM and the ultimate certification of airports, and the work they produced was unsatisfactory. Therefore, what was produced as an OpsM was absolutely a mess, and this is a polite way of expressing my judgment. Nevertheless, after several revisions and with help from editors in San Francisco, the final Operation Manual was completed, approved by the FAA, ICAO, and Saudi's Presidency of Civil Aviation (PCA), which was an emerging Saudi clone of the FAA.

Wearing both hats, spare parts leader and OpsM and certification manager, would have been unachievable for me had I not had the implicit support of Ron Brooks. At every turn and for every request Ron gave me a hand without question. He gave me space to pace myself. When zealous Al Akiel personnel superimposed impossible schedules, Ron Brooks supported me when I defied or adjusted those schedules. Finally when it came time to have the certification conference with the relevant authorities, Brooks made certain that I chaired the meeting.

One morning Glenn Plymate phoned to ask me to interview, without being obvious, Ronald Chandler, the senior Bechtel employee seconded to Al Akiel. Chandler had an impressive résumé and had been the airport director at Santa Ana Airport (now John Wayne International Airport), California. Ron had never, however, worked in Bechtel's San Francisco office having been hired specifically for the Riyadh project. In terms of rank, Chandler was senior to me; hence it was a diplomatic tour-de-force to obtain an invitation for dinner to his house for an informal interview. For the sake of privacy, I could not risk an interview in his office or in mine. I managed to wrangle a dinner invitation on the pretext that I needed some answers to delicate questions about the operation of the new Riyadh International Airport, which soon would be named King Khaled International Airport. I found Chandler to be a delight and a worthy addition to the MOM department under Glenn Plymate. I reported my impressions to Glenn and soon Ron Chandler was on board to fill an opening in San Francisco; but he did not discover the ruse until much later when we both worked on emerging problems for the Eastern Province airport, the future King Fahd International Airport to be located in Dammam. Back in San Francisco, Ron and I shared an office in the China Basin complex that Bechtel had leased for the team working on the King Fahd International Airport.

While juggling two major subprojects in Riyadh, I was still able to see some of the historical sites that made this new capital the premier city in Saudi Arabia. From the village of Dhureia from which Riyadh emerged, Abdul Aziz Ibn Saud (1880-1953) conquered and unified the Arabian Peninsula by finally defeating the Hashemite tribe, the last tribe of consequence in Arabia. Soon after the unification was completed (he married or gave in marriage to his sons or relatives the daughters of the defeated tribes) he declared himself King of the new Kingdom of Saudi Arabia. A very conservative religious group, the Wahabi sect, guided the politics of the Saudi monarchy.

Much of the political control that the monarchy has in Saudi is anchored on the religious controls imposed on the society by Wahabi religious codes, and coupled with the Shari'ah Islamic law, which is vehemently enforced. For example, thievery is controlled by hand severing. Adultery, treason, or murder is punishable by beheading or stoning until death occurs. It was my experience until 1992 when I was in Saudi Arabia, that the country was safe enough that I could leave a roll of $5,000 on the seat of my car while I had dinner in a restaurant without worrying that it might be stolen. I could walk late at night through the city's darkest alleys, go anywhere into the desert, and make my presence known in any large crowd without fear or concern of harm being done to me. I am informed that in 2011 the situation has changed drastically for the worse. Burglaries, assassinations, and terrorist attacks have altered the social fabric of Saudi Arabia. Causes for this change are legion but the most obvious one is that the Saudi monarchy has willfully supported violence and schools that promoted

Islamic fundamentalism in neighboring countries and on its own turf. With the provenance of reward for violence in the name of El Jihad (religious war of revenge against the infidels, who are not Muslims), even the Shari'ah loses its effect because it is overridden by the perceived reward that comes from martyrdom, even when martyrdom is repugnant to traditional Islam.

I was also able to see the development of new architecture in Riyadh. Banks, hotels, villas, department stores, shopping centers, and other structures had the mark of expensive but gaudy architecture. The Sheraton Hotel on Chicken Street was particularly gaudy, but on a street named for a fowl, it should have been expected. Pepsi Cola Street was home for many company offices and giant apartment houses. The sand of the desert still found ways to encroach and penetrate the built-up sections of the city. It was not uncommon to find small mounds of sand against interior walls after a sand storm had overwhelmed the city; Riyadh rose out of the desert but the desert still remained in Riyadh.

Much as Riyadh was to be constructed as the new capital of Saudi Arabia, it never was able to possess the historic dignity that made Jeddah a real city. Jeddah was historically a location that people chose because the geography suited them. Riyadh is the old village of Dhureia writ large! The souk of Riyadh was as rustic as ever in appearance but was never as exciting as the one in Jeddah because it was not a real souk but a mall made to look like a souk. It had no depth but was merely a façade with vendors in front of it. Riyadh was a capital by name and a city by command; it did not have the historical polish and the tradition of Jeddah or even Dammam. But unlike Brasília, Riyadh had the potential for becoming a real city in time because it allowed room for human deficiencies, idiosyncrasies, and the weather was less humid than Jeddah's or Dammam's. Unlike Jeddah, which is not ravaged by sand storms because it is on the coast of the Red Sea, Riyadh and Dammam receive the sand from the desert with the slightest breeze. Culturally, the cities are quite different. Riyadh is peopled by a collection of newcomers from Saudi Arabia's hinterland, from members of the foreign diplomatic services and industries, and from the royal transplants; that is to say, members of the monarchy relocated to the capital. Riyadh is also the center of the Wahabi sectarian power; hence it is more Sunni in practice than either

Dammam or Jeddah. Dammam is an old city on the Gulf with a major population of Shiite adherents. The Sunni population in Dammam is a visible minority and a more liberal minority. Dhahran is home to ARAMCO, the Saudi Oil Company, and Al Khobar is an old commercial city that now is the gateway to King Fahd Causeway that links the island of Bahrain to the mainland of the Eastern Province. All three cities are often called the "Triplet cities."

My old friends James Harageones and his lovely wife Helen, long gone from Bechtel and mentioned when I worked on the King Abdul Aziz Airport in Jeddah, were located in Riyadh. The Military Division of McDonnell-Douglas in Riyadh was Jim's new employer and his position was that of Senior Security Manager. Jim (Big Jim) and Helen lived in a spacious apartment near McDonnell-Douglas, on Chicken Street. Quite often I would visit them. One time he introduced me to the general manager of McDonnell in the hope that I would accept an offer of a position with the firm. I did not because my plans for the future never included a permanent assignment in Saudi or anywhere else. In addition, McDonnell's home office was in St. Louis, Missouri, and that was not where I planned to settle.

The reader will recall that Big Jim had managed the security program for both Jeddah and Riyadh while working for Bechtel. Now that he was with McDonnell-Douglas he was no longer allowed to visit the new airport being constructed by Bechtel. One Friday I invited him as my guest to see the new construction and get a glimpse of how his security plan was being incorporated in the design of the new airport in Riyadh, and to see what he thought about it. The day came, a Friday when all was quiet and I was able to give Jim and Helen a good tour of the airport, including the Royal Terminal and the mosque; both facilities were beautiful and well appointed. Jim did make some observations, all of them cogent and appropriate about security fixtures. He could not make any reasonable comments about security operations because this was not possible when activities were dormant during the construction phase, and especially on a day when nothing was moving. With his consent I did make a list of suggestions that he made and shared them with Ron Brooks, who followed through with their implementation, and then wrote a kind note to Jim.

As the person responsible for the OpsM and the spare parts program I had the freedom to travel in Saudi Arabia whenever I needed to. Often I would fly to Jeddah for a few days to consult with PCA. On one occasion I took the Harringtons with me because I needed a few documents researched and because neither Jim nor Betty had ever been to Jeddah. On another occasion, I needed to consult with both Barry Pugh and Jim Ellingsworth in Jubail, so invited the Harringtons to go with me. As it turned out, I flew as a passenger in the Royal Commission's Hawker-Siddley 125 corporate aircraft while the Harringtons chose to drive to Jubail to visit friends.

On the return, I chose to ride back with the Harringtons to see the countryside from the road. The city of Riyadh is situated atop a plateau in full view of the escarpment that divides the western portion of the Saudi Peninsula from the eastern. Jubail is on the shore of the Persian Gulf (also known as the Arabian Gulf). The drive back was quite interesting and beautiful. Leaving Jubail and Dammam the road climbs rapidly towards the eastern side of the escarpment; a gash in the plateau offers a great amount of archeological and paleontological value for researchers. The western ridge of the escarpment may be reached from Riyadh. Several small towns and villages pepper the road to Riyadh and in one we witnessed a camel auction and in another a horse auction. Still further up the road we witnessed another camel market, not an auction; this one was for camel meat. Camel meat is quite popular and outsells beef in Saudi, as it does in Egypt. Camel meat is tasty and not fat at all. What I've had of camel meat was to my liking, very well prepared, and resembled veal in texture and taste.

Arriving on the plateau, the lights of Riyadh can be seen from far away because the countryside is really flat. Out of the darkness and after driving 14 hours, Riyadh looked good and even beautiful (the flight east took all of 90 minutes). Riyadh is a capital, as I intimated earlier, one that has potential for becoming a great city. I might also add that in time, after the monarchy adopts a more democratic and constitutional posture, the Wahabi religious fundamentalism is reduced or even eradicated, and oil is no longer the primary revenue producer, Saudi Arabia may begin to be a more pleasant environment and a more economically viable nation. Oil production is still the revenue producer and also the obstacle to the real development of Saudi Arabia.

With the spare parts issue solved and tended to, the OpsM finalized, and the process for certification in the pipeline with the FAA, ICAO, and the airline associations it was time for me to leave. I looked forward to a month's vacation and although it was July in Europe, warm, humid, and overrun with tourists, I was looking forward to a view with trees, pork on my dinner plate, beer, and a different venue than the desert nation. I like Saudi Arabia but enough was enough. It was time for me to leave and head west. I also had to redefine the direction my employment at Bechtel would take. I always like to have an agenda, a goal, and a purpose when I go on vacation. What was it that I wanted to learn, experience, and absorb?

On July 2nd 1982, I left Riyadh for Frankfurt, Germany and a four-week holiday. Emily had arranged to meet me at one of the restaurants located in the Frankfurt airport. The purpose of the trip was to investigate small "chocolatiers," see a performance of the Vienna Spanish Riding School, attend a concert of the Vienna Boys' Choir, and spend some time in the Principality of Liechtenstein, a place I have since visited several times and one that I have discussed earlier in another context.

Bits of Theological Thinking

Because I was working on a Saudi project I was required to fly on the national airline for the first leg of any trip; in this case it was to Frankfurt International airport. As usual, flights to foreign destinations began at night or very early in the morning to take advantage of the cooler weather. My flight was scheduled for a one a.m. departure and would last seven hours block to block. Sleep was out of the question for me on such flights, and really on any flight. I settled myself in my seat and thought about the takeoff and the good holiday waiting for me upon arrival in Germany. I had completed the spare parts project, had approved the OpsM, chaired the certification review, and closed my apartment after packing the carpet I had purchased.

As soon as we leveled off my thoughts wandered to more lofty matters and particularly my understanding of and my relationship with God. This deliberation on God surfaced because several of my colleagues with Bechtel in Riyadh had puzzled over my priesthood in as much as I was still active in secular daily work. Why was I a Christian, a believer, and how did I manage to continue as a priest in the Church? Good questions. Questions that I had addressed over time but the quiet of the flight was as good as any place to delve into this issue again.

I must admit that the image of God as a bearded patriarch overseeing his creation has been quite unsatisfactory for me. The theistic definition of God — God the Father — as a personal being with extraordinary supernatural, human, and parental characteristics has bothered me because I could not find any support but suspected that it surfaced when human beings discovered that they needed a crutch, a mentor, a father persona to help them overcome the vicissitudes of life. The Gospel narrative intimates that Jesus called God "Father," but I am not at all certain that it was not the writer's personal comment. When we look at the universe today, the paternalistic persona of God as described by theism is no longer necessary. Is the God of theism unemployed now? The enormous power once ascribed to the God of theism is currently explained in numerous other ways. Human beings have evolved to a level where the concept of a theistic God can be thrown out or replaced.

The same clearing process may be applied to the deistic concept of God, which was quite popular during the Enlightenment. The watchmaker God who started the mechanism ticking could then be removed or relegated to a role of timekeeper. Keep the ticking going, God, but do not interfere in the movement. Remember John Cameron Swayze's advertisement for Timex Watches: It takes a licking but keeps on ticking! That's not too remote from how deists view God-the-watchmaker's role in the universe.

Once upon a time primitive people were prone to worship the Wind or as the Hebrews called it, the Ruah, which for sedentary people had great effect on their lives, their crops, and hence their community. Non-Hebrews identified the Wind as the "Other," the force that caused chaos through changes in the weather and the subsequent impact it had on crops, cattle, and people. They worshipped the wind because of its power and because they could not understand how it originated although they knew from which direction it came. Enigmas are good candidates for worship.

Today we have a better understanding of the wind. We have learned much about weather patterns, atmospheric depressions, highs and lows in pressure, and the jet wind's effect on the climate. Today we do not know all there is to know about the wind, but we do recognize that the Ruah is not mysterious; it is the product of atmospheric consequences that may appear to be chaotic, but are chaotic with rational patterns.

Two major scholars who contributed greatly to our understanding of the origin of religion and sacrifice — meaning the making of sacred not necessarily that which is wrongly associated with bloody killing — are Royden Yerkes and Giambattista Vico. The hypothesis concludes that the nascent start of human community and the emergence of thinking about the supernatural developed when human beings moved from forest roaming to cave dwelling. This change brought about an altered point of view from the uncertainty of the forest to the consequent controllable environment of the cave. This also brought about the condition wherein the family element with a patriarchal or matriarchal direction surfaced.

Both Yerkes and Vico agree that the genesis of what is called religion today occurred when human beings lived in the shelter of caves and this emergence was a reaction to the sound of thunder and the bursts of lighting. Some of these effects are recognized in cave drawings, especially in the communitarian characteristics necessary for painting in the caves, the grottos. A single person alone could not execute such paintings because the need for light, support, food, and supplementary consequent demands required the presence of at least one other person in the cave, and also the benevolent support of a family, a community, to feed and clothe the painter and his or her assistant. Huddling together in dark caves with maybe only a flickering flame, which source of fire was magical and enigmatic, may have produced in a group ideas about their own vulnerability when the forces of nature, especially stormy nature, confronted them.

One wonders how such a group of primitive human beings learned about fire, the making of it, and what it contained. It wasn't too long ago that people thought of fire as a living element because it produced intense heat, it fed itself on whatever it engulfed, and it was able to multiply and become many other small fires or several large unquenchable infernos. Primitive people protected their source of fire, their small flame, to give them the ability to produce other fires for night protection from wild animals, to grill their meats, and to fashion their crude weapons of bone, stone, and wood.

Nature was unmanageable for the early human beings, and it may still be unmanageable for us. What can contemporary human beings do to calm a hurricane, to prevent the Mississippi River from flooding and changing its course by more than 20 miles, as it did not long ago because of the New Madrid earthquake of 1811-12, and to produce rain in reasonable quantity for irrigating, and not drowning, crops? Nature is still a puzzle in its awesome power.

For primitive human beings, the elemental forces of nature were readily identified as the anger of mysterious and unpredictable powers. Perhaps too they gave rise to the primitive (or not so primitive as we recognize some of the issues in modern practices and interpretations) religion of augury, appeasement, ransom, and consequently "atonement." Because human beings believed that these mysterious or, in reality, enigmatic powers had to be placated, many intricate systems of divination, appeasement, bartering, and contracts were developed. Consequently the priestly art form of augury, haruspication, and magic surfaced, and their influence never quite vacated human consciousness. Even when we come to Jesus, the contrary and rebellious religious revolutionary who attempted to redefine the human relations with the God of Hebrew tradition, we find that not only while alive, but soon after his death (a death because he attempted to rid religion of its inherent fallacies), his so-called followers through the centuries revived augury, appeasement, ransom, and atonement characteristics. Consequently, the Eucharist — the Thanksgiving ceremony for God's goodness — is transformed from a banquet, a celebration, a "thank you God" meal, to an act of contrition, appeasement, and placated payment. I will return to this shameful confusion of what the Eucharist is at a later date.

As the airliner droned on towards dawn and the Mediterranean Sea I thought, indeed, we witness today that the so-called advanced and sophisticated religions have developed theologies that avow that their faith is based on a final and true knowledge of God, no matter how misunderstood (and consequently impoverished) the understanding of God may have been in the past and is today. In the sight of mysterious creation, religions tend to assume dogmatic postures. Dogmatism is the human screen that hides the ignorance of those who practice religion. All religions suffer from the disease of dogmatism, and when the cure is knowledge, it is often repudiated and replaced by the formation of additional dogmas. God and creation are construed with explanations that propose absolutely no reasonable image, concept, or meaning. A God surfaces as an imperious being and creation is for human beings to use, as they desire.

Of course not every person is fascinated by this idiotic depiction of God and creation. There are scores of good folks for whom the issue of God is permanently resolved. They either accept the theology given to them or they reject it. A few have not given up but continue to pursue the issue of God in creation. Because there is no absolute definition of God, the task of understanding God requires a devotion to incessant learning through many disciplines, and even then answers are not guaranteed.

I did not wish to recount for myself the details of the history of science and religion but some of its high points were buzzing through my head. I could not avoid remembering the time when western thought insisted that the Earth was the center of the known universe and that the Sun circled around it. Western thought was shocked when Nikolas Copernicus in the 16th century concluded by using rough astronomical tools that the sky was not simply the upper level and God's domain but that it contained millions and billions of stars similar to our Sun, and possibly planets also similar to our Earth. His commentary on the astronomical state of affairs went unnoticed for several decades until the Italian scientist Galileo Galilei (1564-1642), adding cumulative knowledge to Copernicus's insights, revised the way people perceived the universe, our planet Earth, and our Sun. By experimentation, Galileo concluded that the Sun did not rotate around the Earth but that the obverse occurred: the Earth rotated around the Sun every day, and around the circumference of the Sun once a year. Tilted on its axis and affected by its satellite the Moon, the Earth became an acceptable host for life. Moreover, it was this movement in the solar environment that affected Earth's seasons and Earth's daily condition such as night and day. Of course this meant that the Earth could no longer be the center of the universe and that God might not be quite as involved in the day-to-day and moment-to-moment business of Earth's passengers.

The Church, especially the Roman Catholic (RC) branch of it, did not like this proposal. It did not like it at all! In fact, the Church of Rome demanded that Galileo Galilei retract this "foolish" theory. Galileo, to save his life from the burning stake, retracted it openly. His statement of retraction, however, changed nothing. No dogmatic pronouncement can bring to a halt the denouement of knowledge. (Let that also be a lesson for those who want to arrest stem cell research, stop string theory, and inhibit sub-particle explorations). Science was moving ahead with a strong momentum and could not be arrested by Galileo's retraction. The Vatican did not accept Galileo's insights and refused to admit that its understanding of astronomy was faulty. It was not until 28 December 1991 that the Vatican caved in and finally admitted that Galileo Galilei was correct. It took nearly 300 years to change the Roman Catholic position. The Papacy's recent recantation against Galileo's advancements in astronomy came a bit too late because satellites, journeys to the moon by astronauts, and deep space explorations had made the Roman Catholic Church's position laughable. I suspect that soon enough the Vatican's position will change in its opposition against birth control medication, women in holy orders, and a gamut of myopic theological pronouncements such as the invalidity of non-RC Eucharistic celebrations, non-RC holy orders, marriage of their clergy, and its attitude towards homosexuals.

Rome is not the only culprit in its ignorance of scientific development and rational comportment in ethics. Anglicanism and other denominations have also contributed their energies to dogmatic prestidigitations. It is startling to me that the origin of religion is cradled in our search for meaning about God, nature, creation, and us. We look out on life and in on ourselves, and that act gives rise to religion, which is a way of connecting ourselves to the mystery of what is beyond ourselves — however we choose to define it. Yet one of the very tools we use to help us understand, tools such as the religious communities (Christian church, Jewish assembly, Islamic brotherhood or whatever), misguide us by dogmatic false pronouncements.

Soon the renowned physicist Isaac Newton (1643-1727) added more fuel to the scientific revolution that had been started by Copernicus, and advanced by Galileo. Newton's insights in science were always couched in acceptable ecclesiastical language and he was dealing primarily with 17th century Anglicanism, which had become more tolerant than the RC; hence he did not get into trouble. His scientific search was directed at understanding how God worked in the Universe. He showed that there were explanations for many of the enigmas that were ignorantly relegated to God's power. He asserted that his task was to comprehend God's actions in the world, in scriptures, and everyday life. Nevertheless, Newton's work seriously undermined the power of God and increasingly elevated the role of human beings in the actions of the world. Human beings were pressed to learn that the Universe operated according to fixed laws, which were not subject to interference from divine or external sources. Miracles were not to happen by bending the laws of nature; and if they seemed to happen they were simply surfacing within the context of the fixed and universal laws of nature. Many of Newton's ideas were based on good science, mathematics and physics, and the interrogation from philosophy, but were also couched in Descartes' mechanistic model of how the Universe functioned. Descartes proposed that the Universe functioned like a machine with each part working in concert with the next in a cooperative fashion and following the laws of physics.

For example, droughts were not to be explained as the product of divine retributions but by understanding weather patterns and climatic changes. Newton's contributions altered the substance of how human beings understood the dynamics of nature and it promoted further research into physics, mathematics, chemistry, medicine, astronomy and astrophysics. God the manipulator lost his job and became a casualty of progressive thinking. God the source of all that was, is, and is to be became better understood through science. God as the amalgamation of all the processive forces in the Universe received more attention. Newton opened the door to a coherent understanding of God and of the Universe. Other great minds followed Newton's lead, in particular the writings of A. Einstein, H. Bergson, F. Nietzsche, A.N. Whitehead, R.P. Feynman, N. Bohr, M. Planck, E. Hubble, W. Heisenberg, P. Tillich, W.G. Pollard, S. Hawking; all followed Newton's thoughts, refined them, and in some few cases changed them as was warranted by quantum mechanics.

I have always been concerned that there was no clash between coherent theological thinking and either classical or quantum mechanics. In my mind I never saw much that prevented the adherents of science from accepting the proposition of a divine presence in the Universe. It seems to me that much of the conflict lies in how that divine presence is defined. If it is defined as a designing being who is controlling, manipulating, and creating in the narrow sense each miniscule item present in the Universe which subsequently is the direct product of this designer's action then not only is the problem of God magnified but it is also left unexplained and hence relegated to silliness. If the divine presence, however, is recognized as an ideational source of what the Universe is all about, then we are in a more creative arena.

It seems to me that one needs to recognize that in Creation there are the "given" and also the "constructed." Hence as human beings we must distinguish between the two or else we are in a big mess. Our ideas must be in concert with what is the actual. Moreover, we must distinguish between the metaphors and the facts. For instance "heaven" is not a physical place but a metaphor used to convey a theological concept. And of course, an atom is not shaped like a ball, but the ball shape was used as a metaphor to help young students understand some aspects of the subatomic particles. No one really believes that the first human beings ate an apple or had a discussion with a talking snake as it is offered in the Book of Genesis. In physics no one really believes that the Universe is like a large sheet upon which rest the stars, planets, and galaxies — and their masses contribute to how gravity affects everything. Perhaps scholars in theology need to acquaint themselves with physics, especially the recent thinking about space/time, gravity/weak force, and multiple dimensions as it is discussed with the string theory. I think of that as a threshold of expanded appreciation for understanding the universe, faith, God and human beings.

Moreover, the recognition that we exist in a multiple dimensional universe, yes more than four and perhaps as many as 11 or 23, maybe more, does affect our understanding of many key elements making up creation. Perhaps we even exist in the context of a multi-verse! For one: is God explainable in Trinitarian terms, if at all, or should we begin to understand that theological concept in more dimensions? I would venture to say that God is not merely defined by three personas but by many, many personas or dimensions. Why not? Hence the Trinitarian perspective is enhanced to "multi-tarian" — and I don't have a word for it but that which is given is sufficient for the moment. Incidentally, what does it say about Unitarianism (should it be

Multi-tarianism), the current creeds, Islam's approach, Judaism (which may have a larger point of view if not restricted by orthodoxy), and traditional Christian dogmatics? So, when do I get burned at the stake? The same distinction must be applied when we are confronted with the given and the constructed in the Universe. More will be discussed about that approach in later sections.

Except for a few diehards, most educated people accept the biblical story of creation as a mythological drama. The masterpiece known as *On the Origin of Species*, which was published in 1859 by Charles Darwin, offered a new approach for understanding creation. Human beings began to learn about evolutionary creation. That took a lot of wind from the sails of those who insisted that the story of Adam and Eve in Genesis was factually historical. For me Darwin's greatest contribution was that he removed human beings from center stage: we were no longer the focus of God's gaze; we were only one of many species that inhabited planet Earth. Darwin forced humility upon mankind. The scriptural myth of creation was no longer to be taken literally. Moreover, human beings may have a divine spark as part of the essence of our lives, but so does every other living creature. God could no longer be described by using human features: if Bonobos (our nearest primates) could speak as well as human beings, they probably would ascertain that God looked like them, with long black hair covering their bodies, and with two pairs of hands instead of one pair of feet; if he walked at all, he would often walk on all fours much like a chimpanzee, the near kin of the Bonobos, but lower on the evolutionary ladder.

Fortunately ecclesiastical authoritarianism had been weakened by the Reformation, otherwise resistance to Darwin's work would have been much more vigorous, if not violent. After Darwin, as if the windows were opened to allow more fresh air to enter in, the study of science was further giving homosapiens the likes of Albert Einstein, Marie Curie, Max Planck, Edwin Hubble, and several scores of other reputable scientists. Each reached out more and more to open further the windows of our intellectual prisons — some opened, or better, removed the doors and windows altogether. Einstein redefined both time and space by placing them as significant dimensions of the Universe. He went further and with his equation ($E=mc^2$) he introduced us to Relativity as a factor present in all aspects of creation, including the Church's insistence on "unchanging truths." Mass and energy were interchangeable when the constant of the speed of light was included in the process.

As science began to open the universe more to human understanding, and enigmatic issues were being solved, Rudolf Bultmann of the 19th century suggested that the mythology of the Scriptures needed to be clarified (demythologized) to allow the insights of recovering truths to emerge. Of course the theistic understanding of God was part of the mythology that needed to be made clear, because human beings no longer depended principally on myths to understand the world around them — at least not as much. Myths were not discounted as useless, but they were not the basis for scientific understanding; they could be employed to explain ideas, difficult scientific issues, and to popularize concepts for the common person. Myths continue to participate in our thinking because they carry some degree of truth, otherwise they would have been discarded. Myths, dramatic presentations, science fiction novels, and especially metaphors were genres to be used as interpreting tools; they reflected reality but were not reality in themselves.

For my purpose I saw creation and God as part of a process, an ongoing process. Sunji Nishi, my professor of philosophical theology, once drew a large free shape on the blackboard and asked the class, "If all of reality were found in that enclosed shape, where would you place God?" My initial response, and the correct one at that, was that God would be within the enclosure of reality because he was part of the process of reality.

Some time later I was introduced to Alfred North Whitehead's works by William Dimmick, the august dean of St. Mary's Cathedral, Memphis, Tennessee. Whitehead, who was a mathematician and a philosopher, saw God not just as an external being, but also as a process with divine qualities that merged and emerged into being within the life of the world, the universe. I accept that option. He conceived of God as existing with all of reality, not before it, and as processing, incorporating, and transfiguring what is accomplished in the world. God, for Whitehead, was the inherent source of all possibilities. Moreover, God, for Whitehead, was always processing — yes changing, but within the boundaries defined by the controlling laws of the universe. For Whitehead, God was not static, unchanging, and hence unaffected by his universe. I accept that understanding and remain comfortable with it. For me God is always processing; that is, he and we gather and select occasions and subsequently, because of ideas, transform them into emergent events. This is not unlike an artist who gathers then selects color pigments and because of an idea, subsequently produces a painting, a tableau, and a work of art. The same applies to musicians, physicists, writers, and others who are in the creative mode.

Edwin Hubble introduced human beings to the reality of the expanding universe in 1920. He coined the term "big bang" in 1940 to describe the "theory" that this expansion meant that the Universe could be traced back to a minuscule beginning. Marie Curie in the mid-1920s showed us that radiation was being emitted from radioactive substances. In fact she died of an accumulated exposure to low doses of radiation. Max Planck in 1900 worked with a sector of physics that can handle subatomic particles. Planck proposed quantum physics to traditional physicists and Werner Heisenberg added a touch of weirdness to quantum by introducing the now famous "Heisenberg uncertainty principle" which states that it is impossible to be certain, at the same time, where a subatomic particle is located and how fast it is traveling. Nevertheless quantum provides an accurate description of the way subatomic particles behave at the level of the diminutive world.

And this is not the whole story; there is more, and still more to come. I remember quite well Neil Armstrong's walk on the moon and the photograph of this beautiful blue planet Earth taken from there. I also understand enough about the superstring theory to know that it tries to bridge the gap between quantum mechanics and traditional physics. It might bridge the gap someday to help produce a complete and unified theory of everything in the Universe, something that Dr. Stephen Hawking bets will emerge soon. Yet there is a great deal of research still ahead before a unified theory can emerge. There are problems with antimatter to be resolved. Superstring needs to be explored further because it intimates that a number of solutions and extraordinary possibilities exist, such that the Universe itself is not unique, but is simply one example of an infinite number of independent universes. This is probably the definitive lowering of mankind's central status. Yet there isn't much enthusiasm at the moment for the multiple universe theory because neither the current mathematics nor the current physics readily support such a reality — and even the philosophical thinking tends to stay away from it. But once an idea emerges, one pointing to a multiple universe, it is bound to possess in its core some truth. We might know more some day. Perhaps.

The flight attendant nudged me out of my deep thought to announce that soon we would be in Frankfurt. I thanked her.

Now how was I to consider God in my thinking? He/It/She was obviously not the God of traditional and historical Christianity, Judaism, or Islam. How was I to understand "God the Father, God the Son, and God the Holy Spirit" in this context — only as a metaphor? How was I also to consider what science offers as possible explanations for the Universe? I did not want to become a science fanatic who is moved to worship physical knowledge. It can become as intense as those who are religious fanatics. No fear of that happening. Yet modern physics has certainly extended the understanding of the world, the universe, the laws of nature, and of God. The modern creation myth, unlike its mythological predecessors, has real explanatory power. Yet it is definitely not the tool to explain everything or answer every question. Perhaps the universe is truly a mystery and God is the nucleus of that mystery.

In as much as the flight attendant interrupted this deliberation on God, I do not at all imply that I had resolved the complex issue. More is still to emerge. Of course there is the person of Jesus that needs great deliberation. That will come at a later date too. But I must admit that this sort of thinking has never been linear for me. I've always thought that the "things" in the Universe are linked and not independent of each other. Never do I see a single item or focus on a single issue, rather I see the whole as it is interconnected and when I tackle one thing ultimately I recognize that it is connected to several other things, that it influences other things, and that other things are subsequently affected by what was done to the first thing. For me Creation is of a piece!

I should like to quote one of my favorite astrophysicists, Trinh Xuan Thuan from his book, *The Secret Melody*. He speaks of Léon Foucault's pendulum, which many have seen in museums or science buildings. The pendulum swings to and fro and little brushes on its tip marks its travel around the circumference of a sand platform marked in 10-degree intervals for 360 degrees. Dr. Thuan states:

"Foucault's pendulum swings in blissful ignorance of its local surroundings: It does not pay attention either to the Earth, the Sun, the Local Group or even the Local Super cluster. The pendulum's actual movement behavior is influenced by the most distant galaxies, by the Universe as a whole. In other words, what happens here is determined in the vast expanse of space, and the whole hierarchy of structures in the universe dictates what takes place on our minuscule planet. Every part contains the whole, and depends on everything else. The Universe is interconnected."

Both John Donne, the Jacobean poet, and Ernst Mach, the 20th century physicist, discovered that little gem about interconnectedness. As for me that concept led me into the study of physics, philosophy-theology, and the making of the knowledge city.

Now it was time for my holiday in Germany, other exciting places, and the search for the superb morsel of chocolate.

End Note

At the completion of the first draft of this autobiography I realized that the volume was made up of more than a thousand pages, certainly too large and heavy for a reader to handle. The choice was either to delete several portions or to split the autobiography into two volumes. My choice was to produce a second volume. A second volume would also contain more photographs and would do justice to the period of my life from 1938 to 2000. Readers may ask what about the years after 2000? Who knows what will emerge from my hand? Time will tell.

So now that you read the first volume of *The Adventures of Nimon* and have been exposed to the concept of interconnectedness, to Foucault, to John Donne, and Ernst Mach be courageous and go for the second volume and enjoy sharing my adventures, and all that has given me pleasure and the will to live a full life.

ABOUT THE AUTHOR

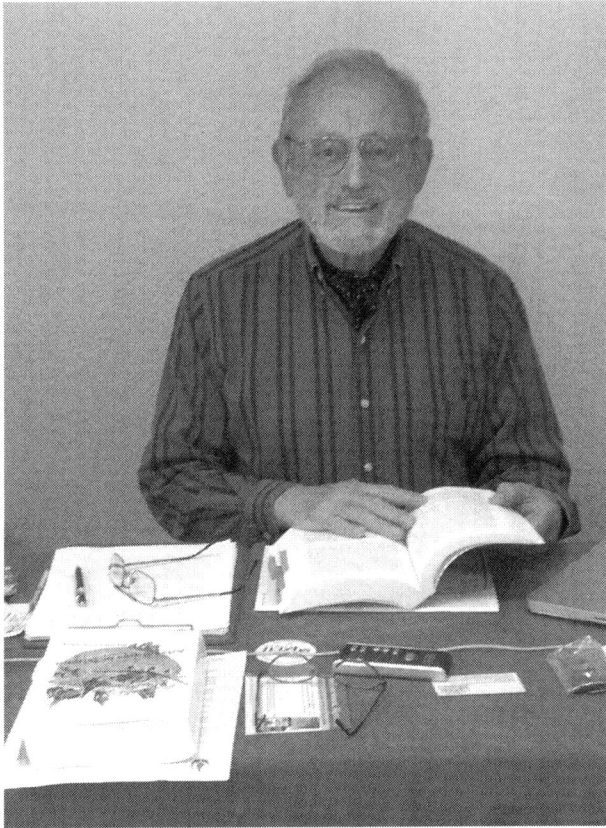

Author in July 2016

Comments and questions for the author are welcomed at
nimon.adventures@gmail.com

Please visit www.adventuresofnimon.info for more photos and information.

Made in the USA
San Bernardino, CA
30 July 2016